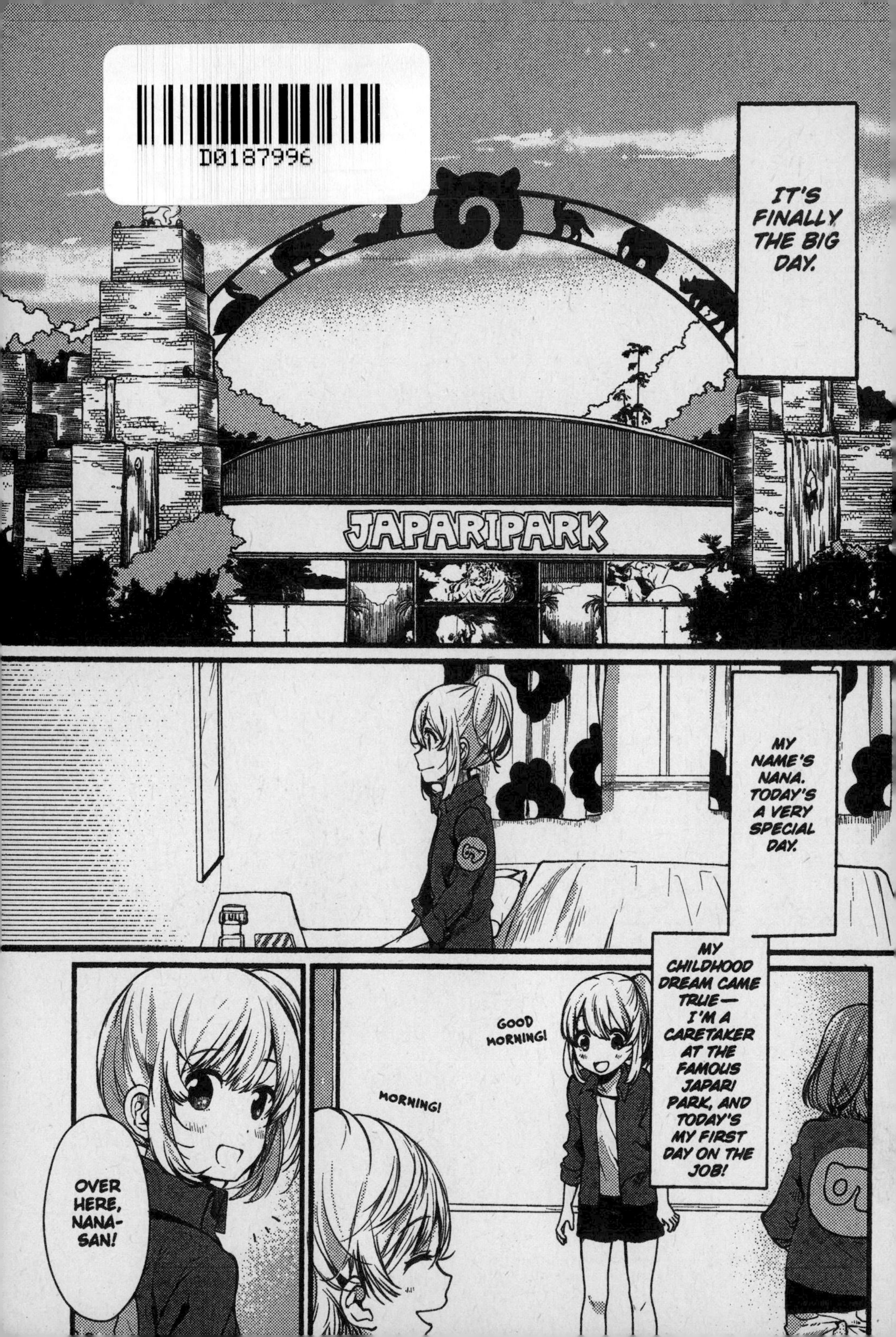
IT'S FINALLY THE BIG DAY.
JAPARIPARK
MY NAME'S NANA. TODAY'S A VERY SPECIAL DAY.
MY CHILDHOOD DREAM CAME TRUE— I'M A CARETAKER AT THE FAMOUS JAPARI PARK, AND TODAY'S MY FIRST DAY ON THE JOB!
GOOD MORNING!
MORNING!
OVER HERE, NANA-SAN!

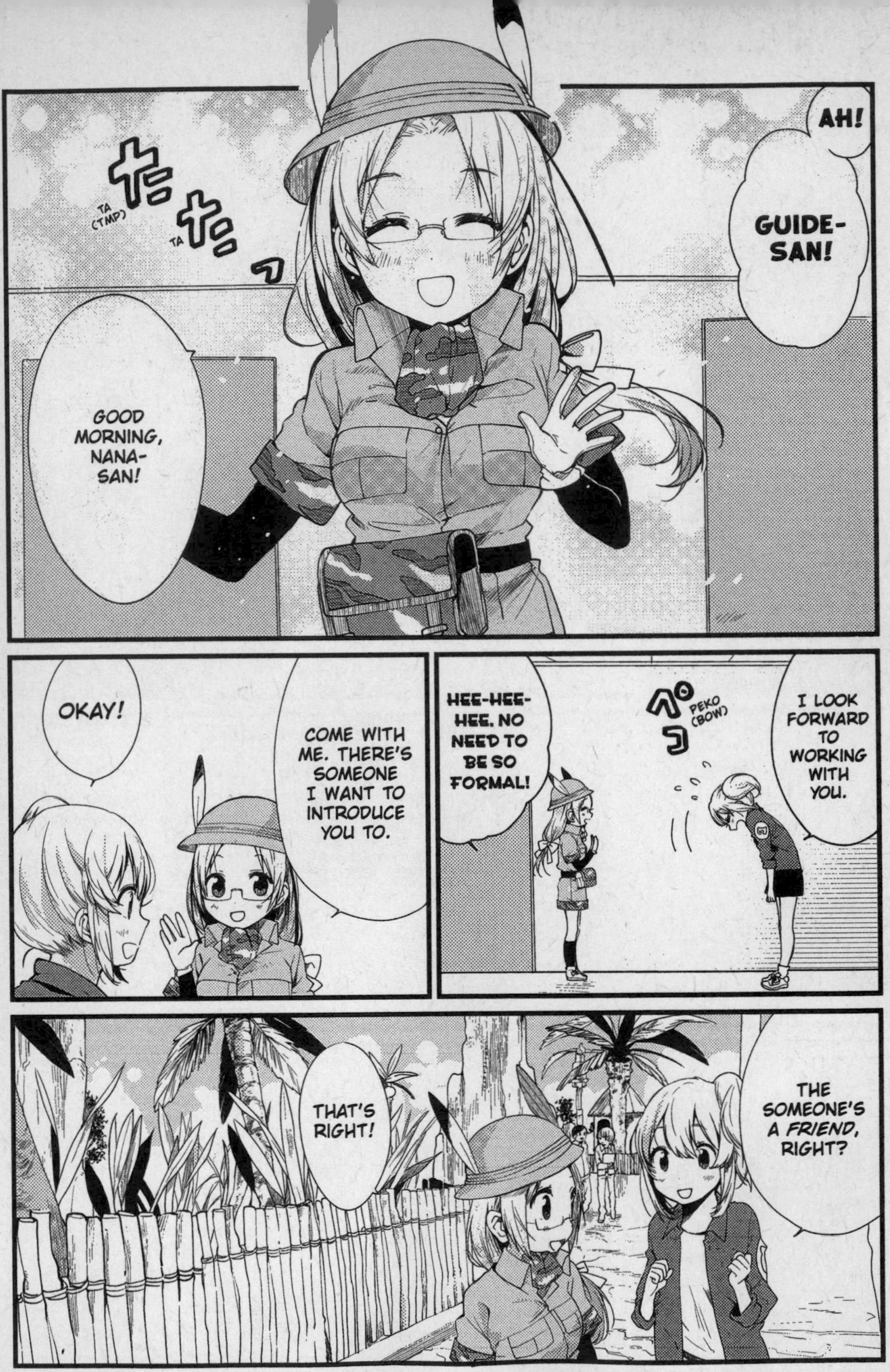
AH!
GUIDE-SAN!
TA (TMP)
TA
GOOD MORNING, NANA-SAN!
I LOOK FORWARD TO WORKING WITH YOU.
PEKO (BOW)
HEE-HEE-HEE. NO NEED TO BE SO FORMAL!
COME WITH ME. THERE'S SOMEONE I WANT TO INTRODUCE YOU TO.
OKAY!
THE SOMEONE'S A *FRIEND*, RIGHT?
THAT'S RIGHT!

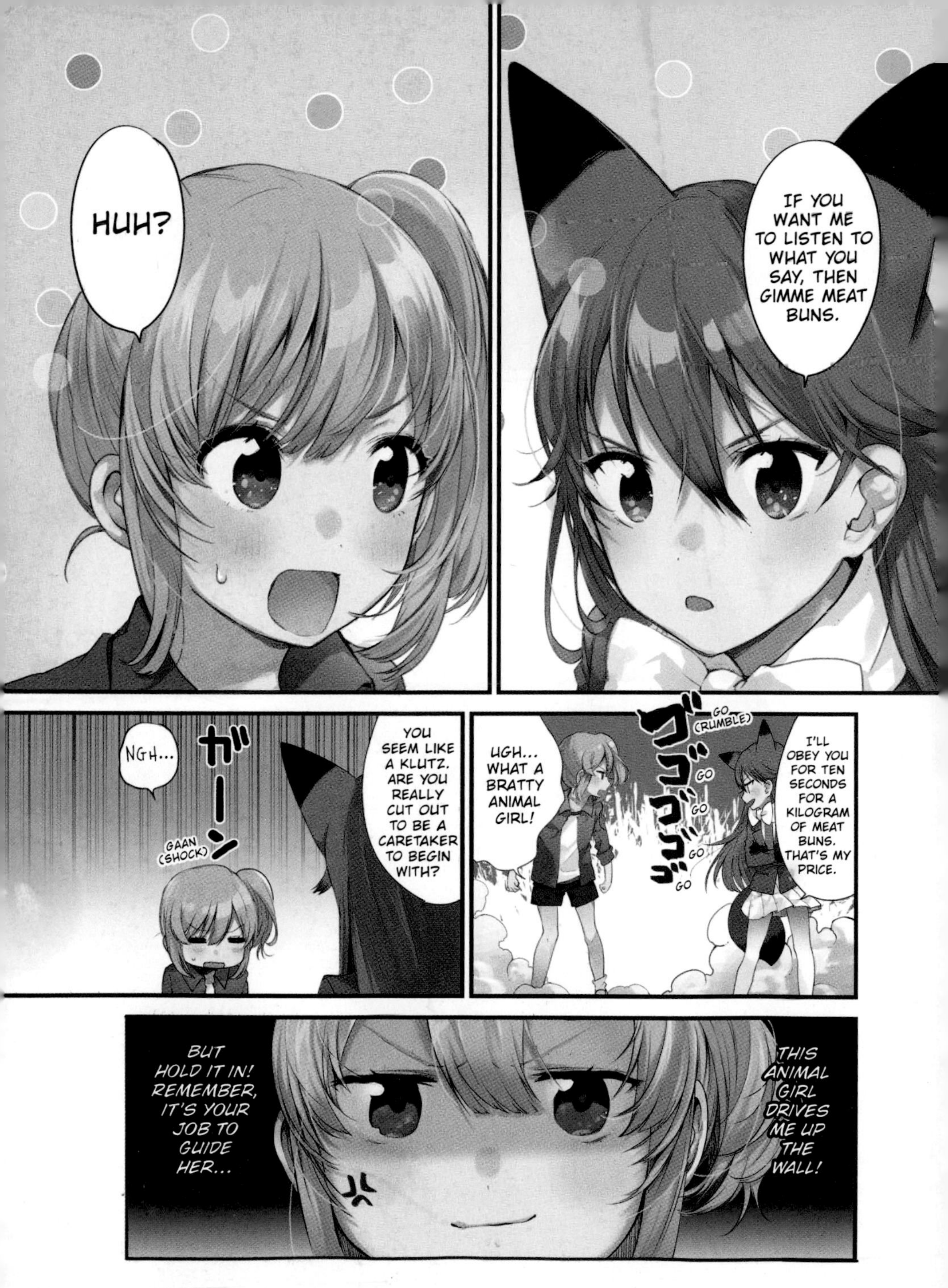
IF YOU WANT ME TO LISTEN TO WHAT YOU SAY, THEN GIMME MEAT BUNS.
HUH?
I'LL OBEY YOU FOR TEN SECONDS FOR A KILOGRAM OF MEAT BUNS. THAT'S MY PRICE.
GO (RUMBLE) GO GO GO GO
UGH... WHAT A BRATTY ANIMAL GIRL!
YOU SEEM LIKE A KLUTZ. ARE YOU REALLY CUT OUT TO BE A CARETAKER TO BEGIN WITH?
NGH...
GAAN (SHOCK)
THIS ANIMAL GIRL DRIVES ME UP THE WALL!
BUT HOLD IT IN! REMEMBER, IT'S YOUR JOB TO GUIDE HER...

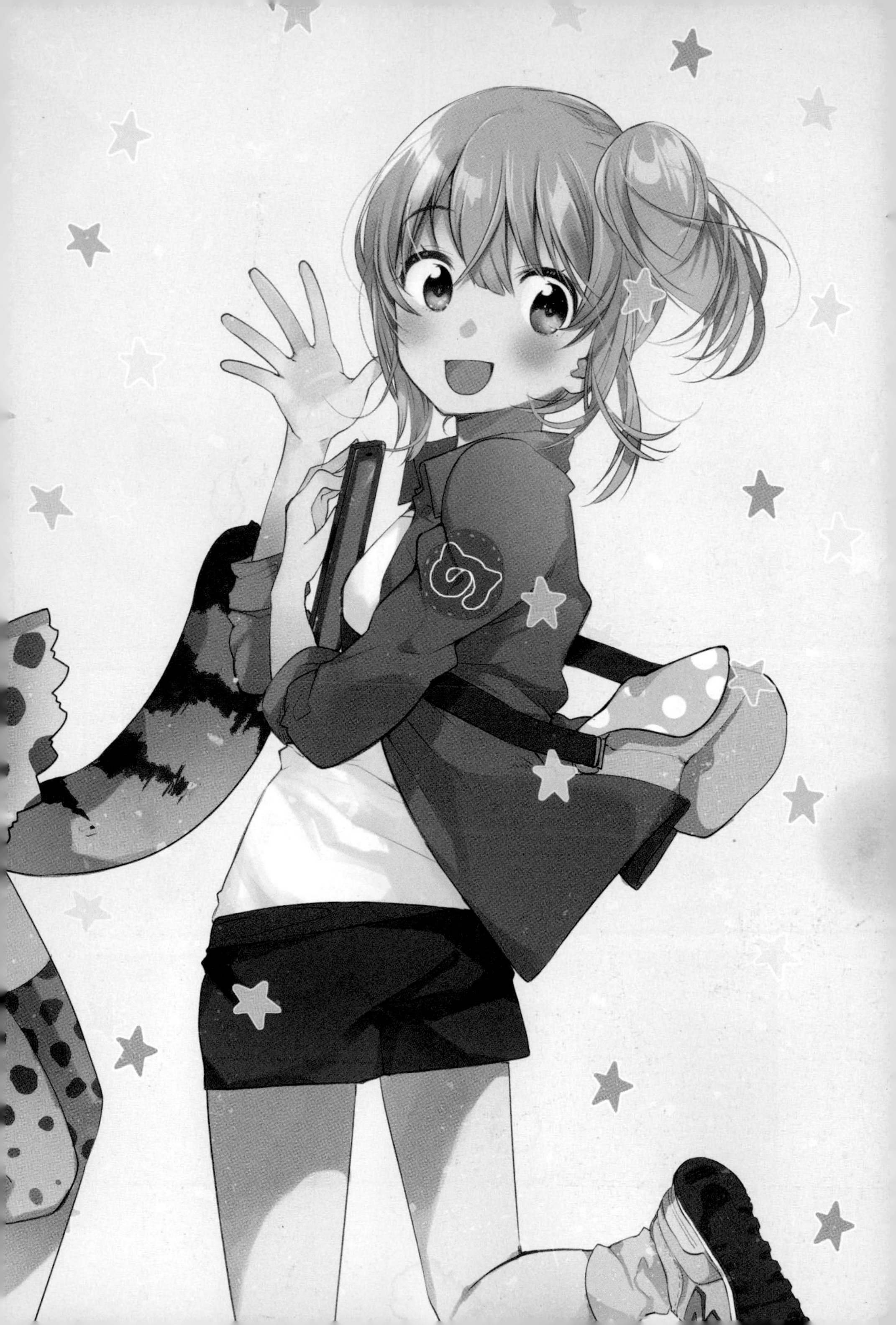

KEMONO FRIENDS
WELCOME TO JAPARI PARK!

Chapter 1

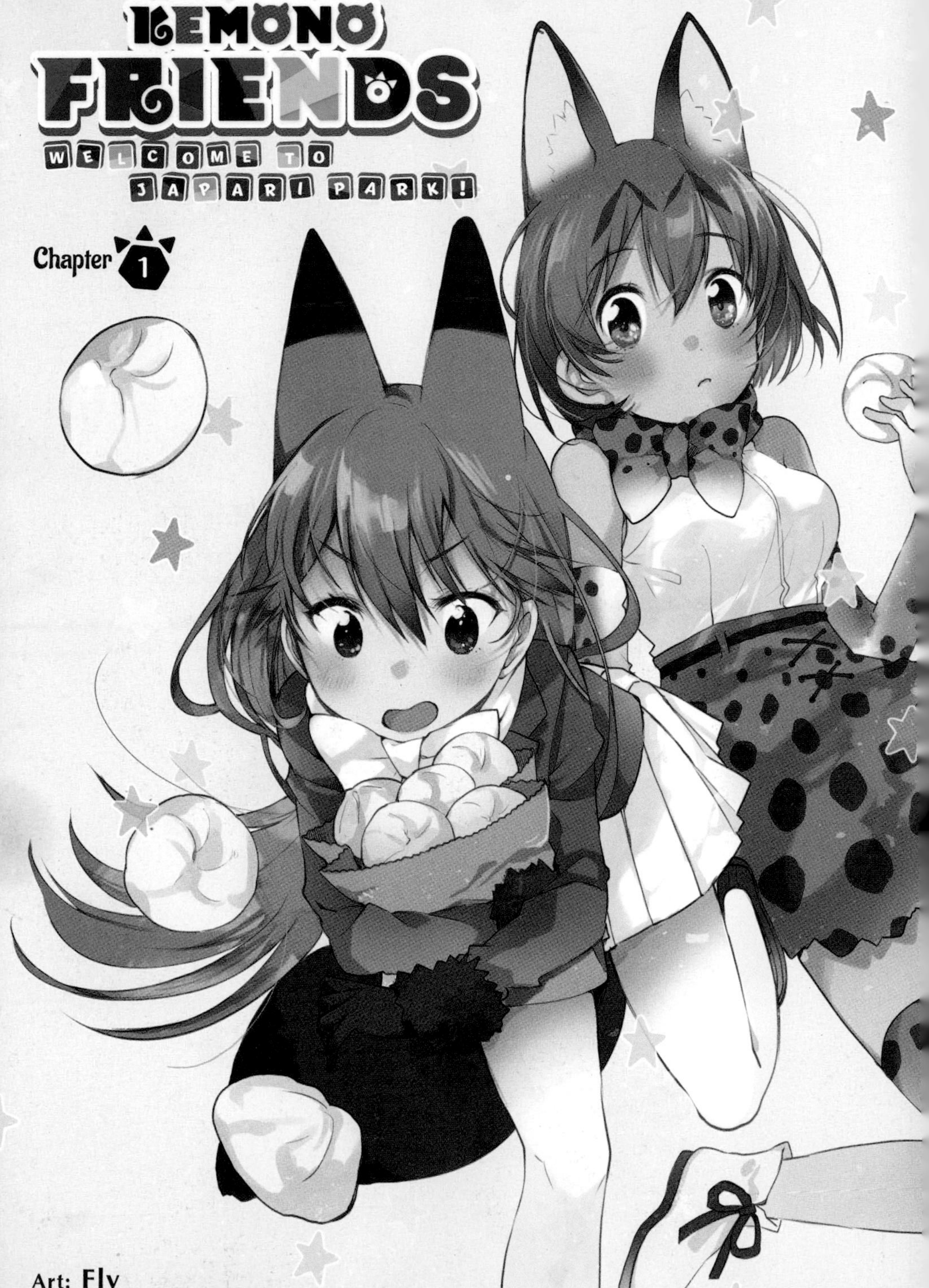

Art: Fly

Created by: Kemono Friends Project

CONTENTS

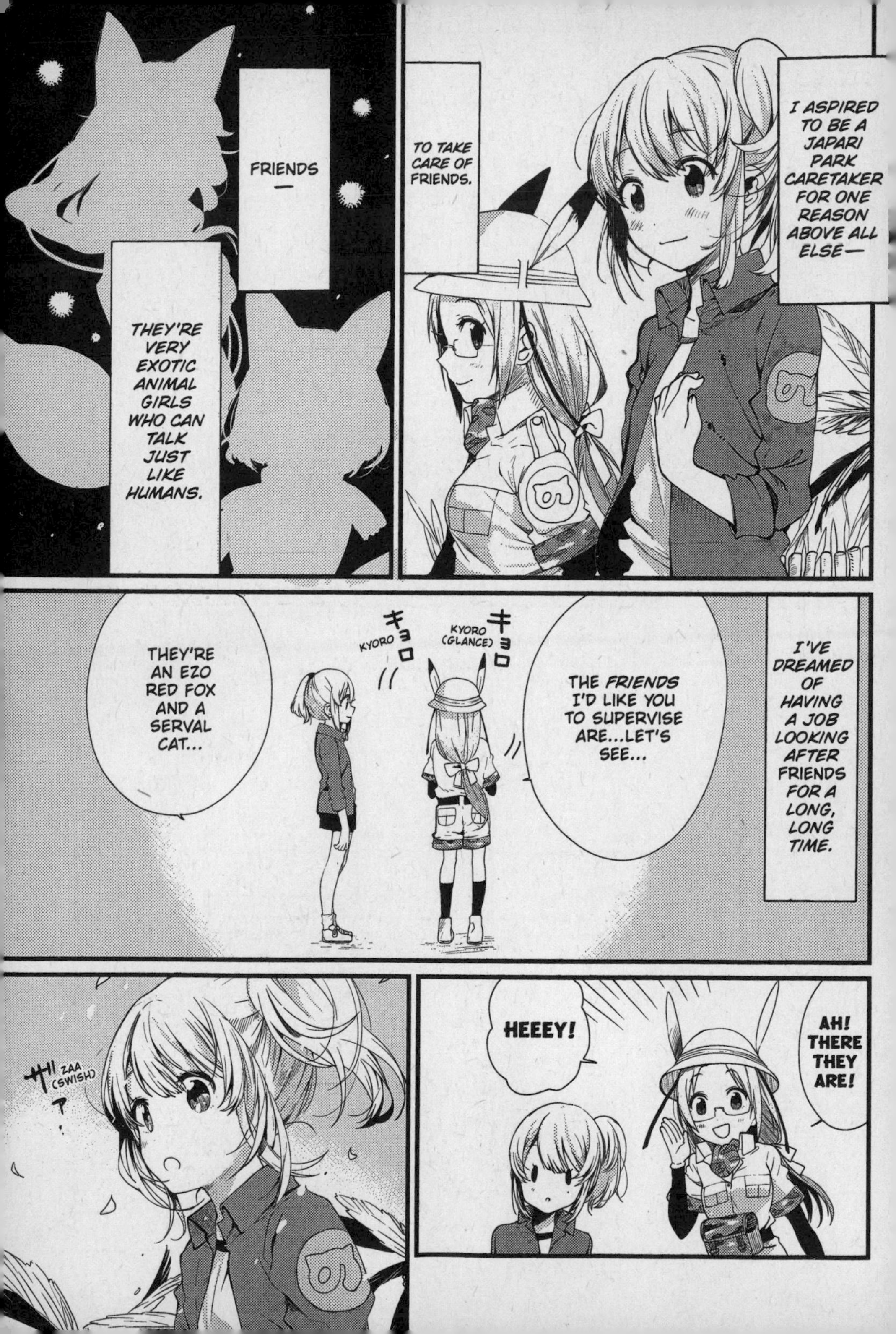
I ASPIRED TO BE A JAPARI PARK CARETAKER FOR ONE REASON ABOVE ALL ELSE—
TO TAKE CARE OF FRIENDS.
FRIENDS —
THEY'RE VERY EXOTIC ANIMAL GIRLS WHO CAN TALK JUST LIKE HUMANS.
I'VE DREAMED OF HAVING A JOB LOOKING AFTER FRIENDS FOR A LONG, LONG TIME.
THE FRIENDS I'D LIKE YOU TO SUPERVISE ARE...LET'S SEE...
キョロ KYORO (GLANCE)
キョロ KYORO
THEY'RE AN EZO RED FOX AND A SERVAL CAT...
AH! THERE THEY ARE!
HEEEY!
ザー ZAA (SWISH)
?

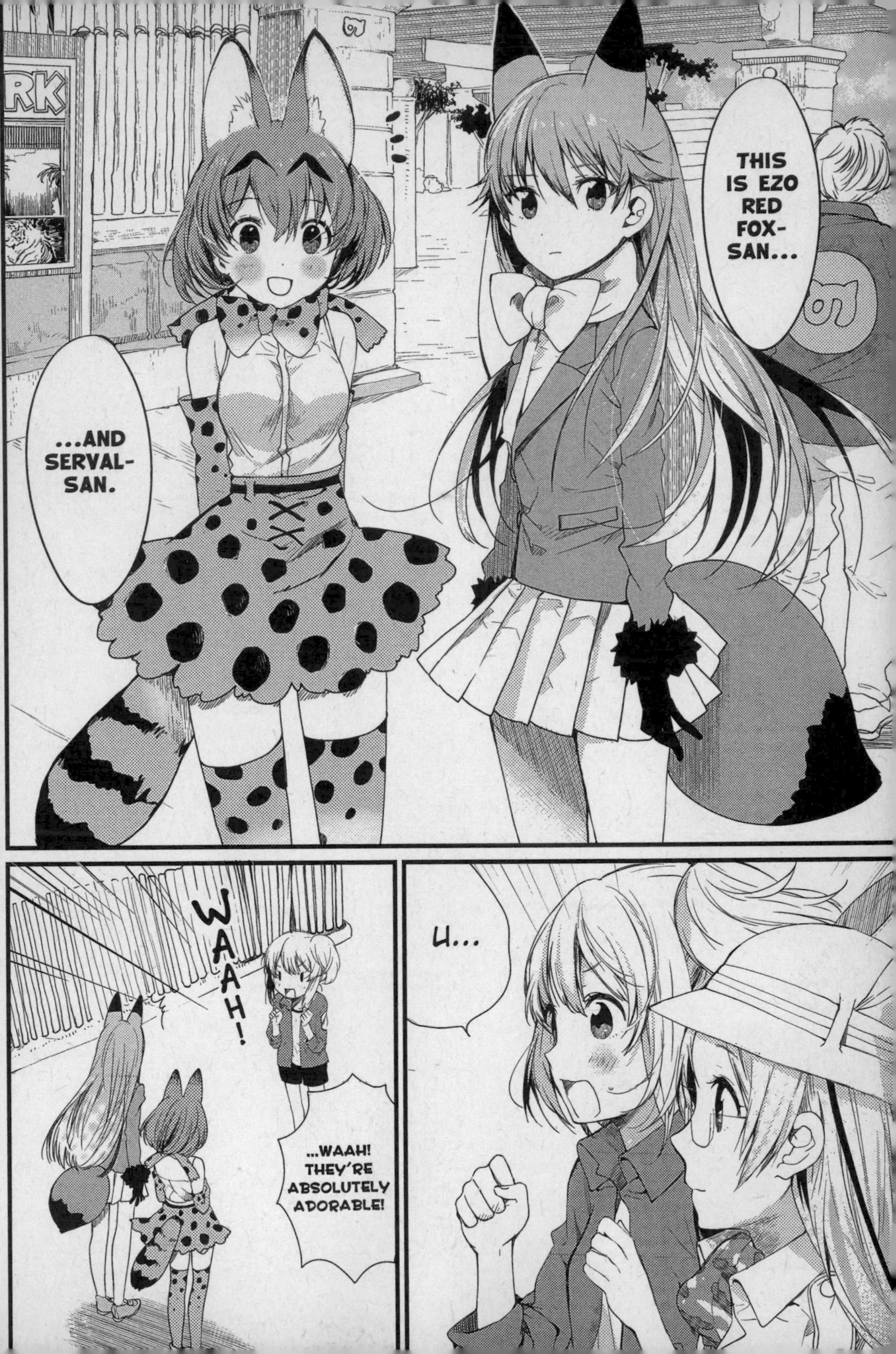
THIS IS EZO RED FOX-SAN...
...AND SERVAL-SAN.
U...
WAAH!
...WAAH! THEY'RE ABSOLUTELY ADORABLE!

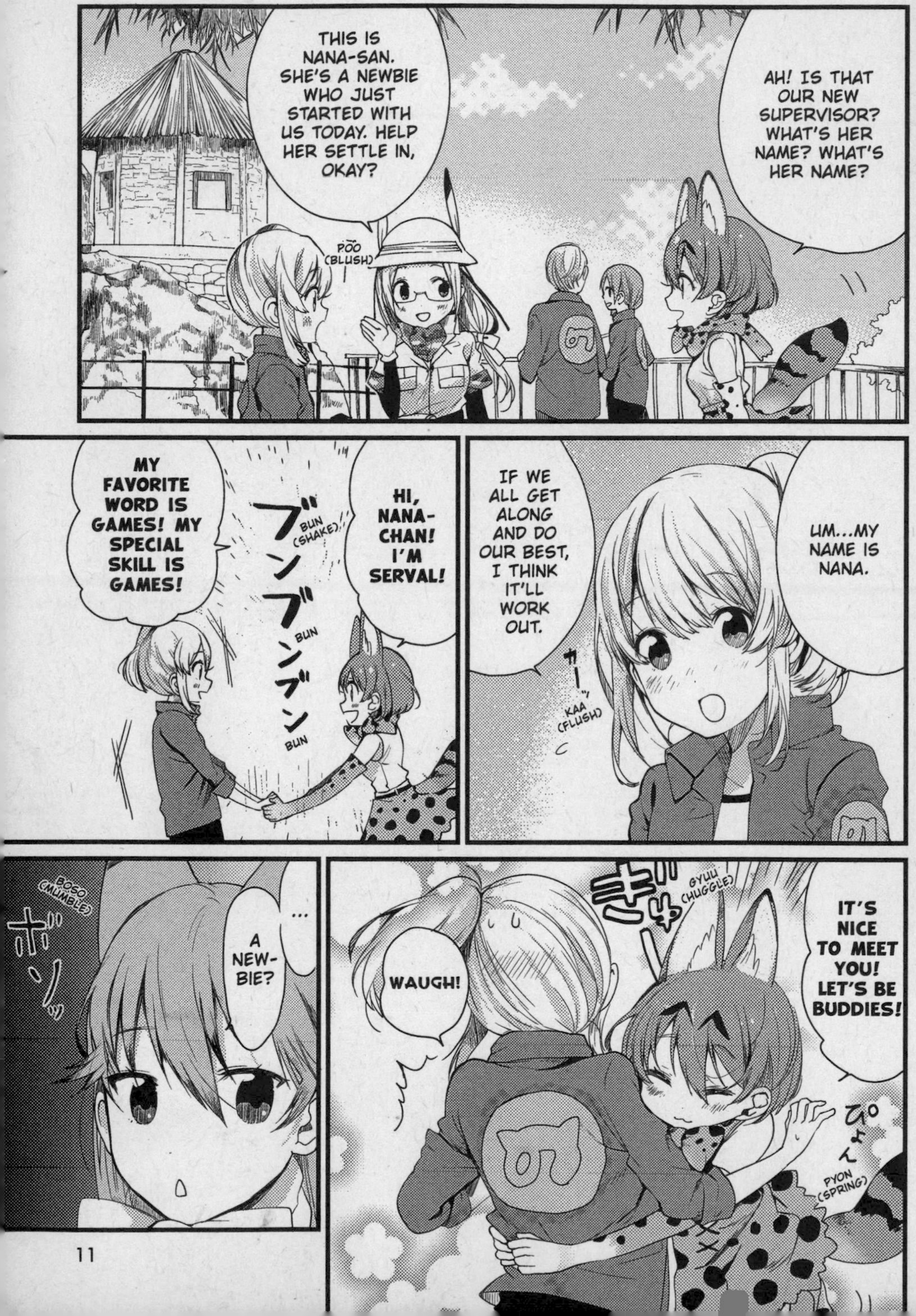
AH! IS THAT OUR NEW SUPERVISOR? WHAT'S HER NAME? WHAT'S HER NAME?
THIS IS NANA-SAN. SHE'S A NEWBIE WHO JUST STARTED WITH US TODAY. HELP HER SETTLE IN, OKAY?
POO (BLUSH)
UM...MY NAME IS NANA.
IF WE ALL GET ALONG AND DO OUR BEST, I THINK IT'LL WORK OUT.
KAA (FLUSH)
HI, NANA-CHAN! I'M SERVAL!
BUN (SHAKE)
BUN
BUN
MY FAVORITE WORD IS GAMES! MY SPECIAL SKILL IS GAMES!
IT'S NICE TO MEET YOU! LET'S BE BUDDIES!
GYUU (HUGGLE)
PYON (SPRING)
WAUGH!
... A NEW-BIE?
BOSO (MUMBLE)

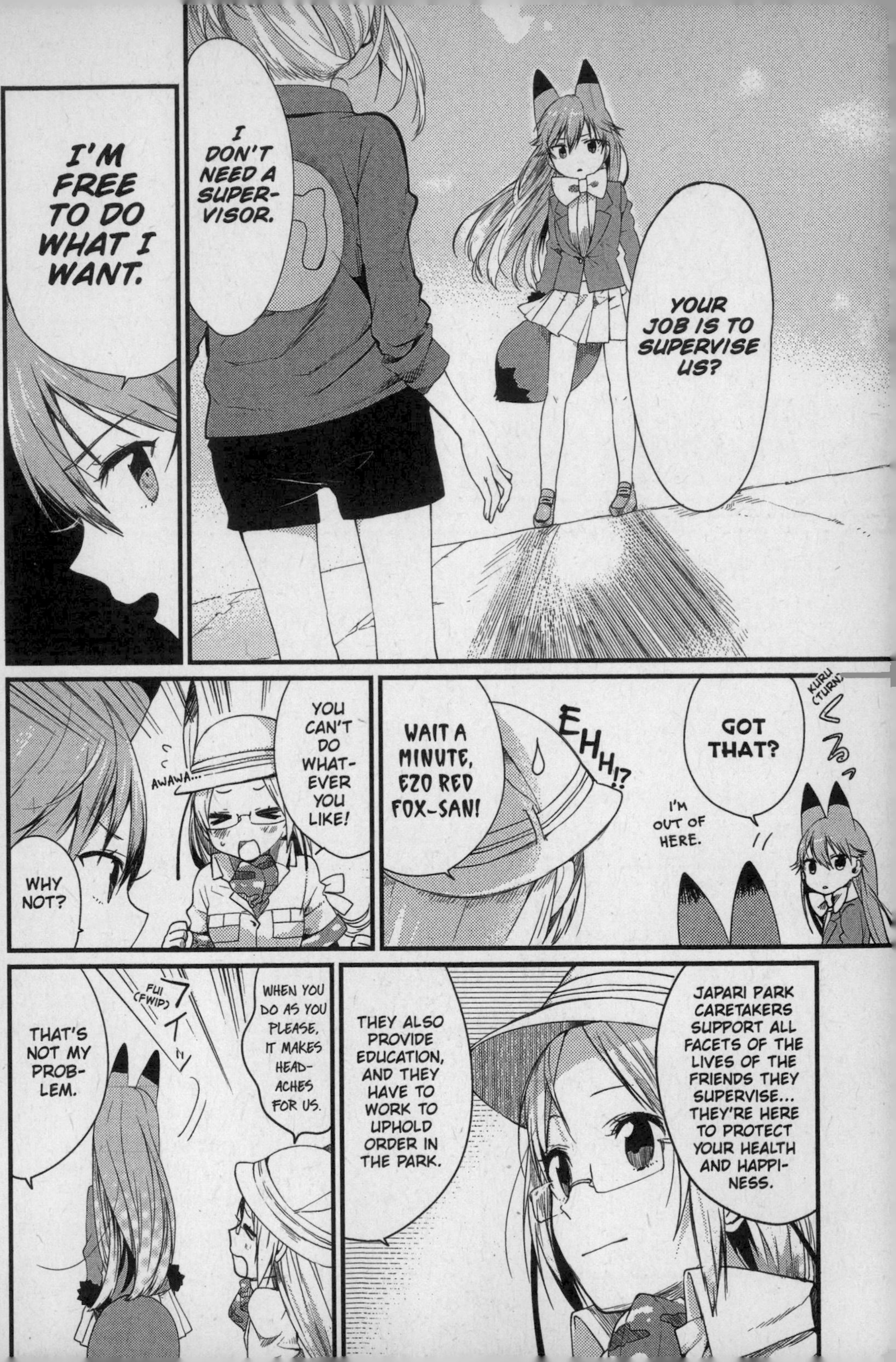
YOUR JOB IS TO SUPERVISE US?
I DON'T NEED A SUPER-VISOR.
I'M FREE TO DO WHAT I WANT.
KURU (TURN)
GOT THAT?
I'M OUT OF HERE.
EHH!?
WAIT A MINUTE, EZO RED FOX-SAN!
YOU CAN'T DO WHAT-EVER YOU LIKE!
AWAWA...
WHY NOT?
JAPARI PARK CARETAKERS SUPPORT ALL FACETS OF THE LIVES OF THE FRIENDS THEY SUPERVISE... THEY'RE HERE TO PROTECT YOUR HEALTH AND HAPPI-NESS.
THEY ALSO PROVIDE EDUCATION, AND THEY HAVE TO WORK TO UPHOLD ORDER IN THE PARK.
WHEN YOU DO AS YOU PLEASE, IT MAKES HEAD-ACHES FOR US.
FUI (FWIP)
THAT'S NOT MY PROB-LEM.

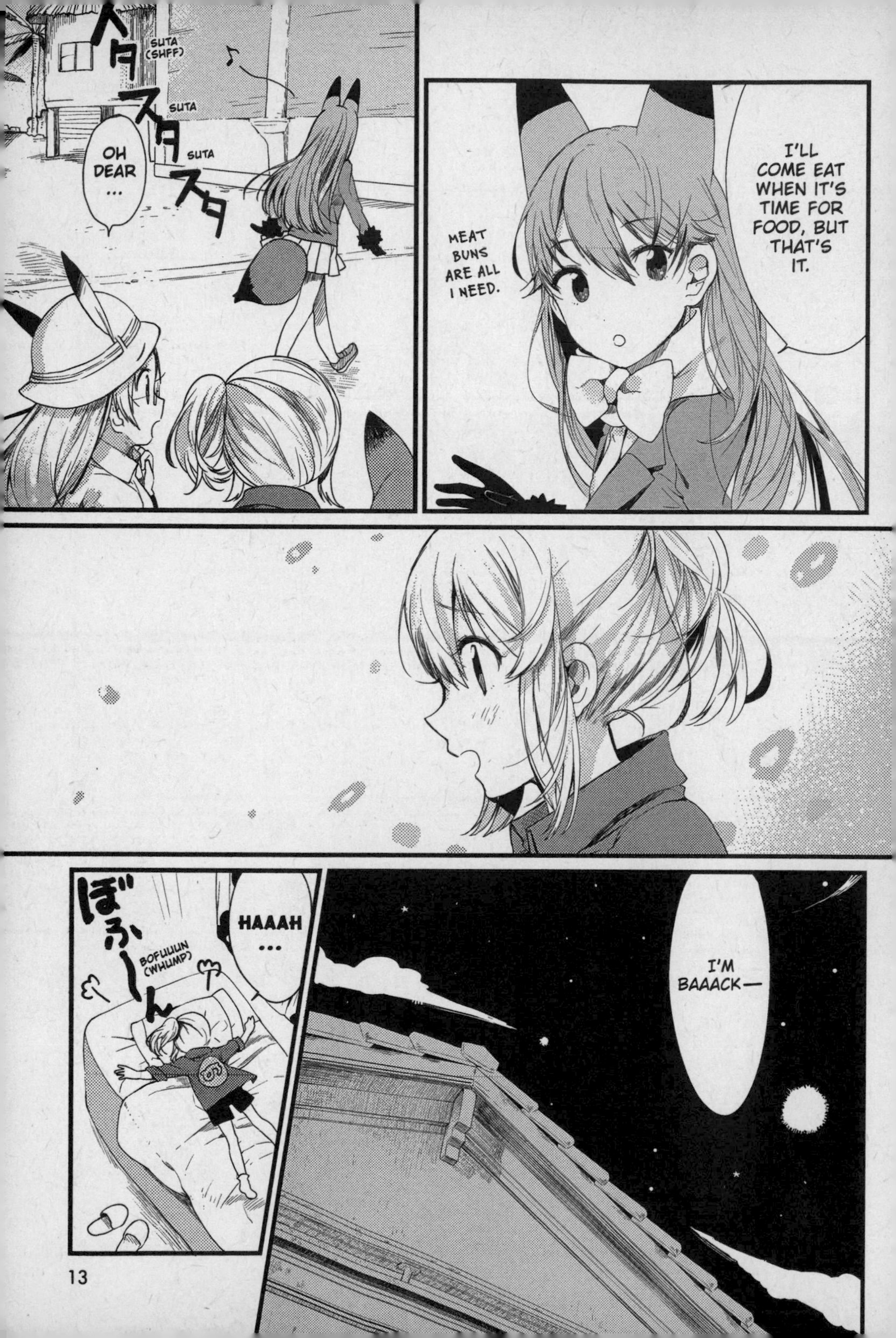

I'LL COME EAT WHEN IT'S TIME FOR FOOD, BUT THAT'S IT.
MEAT BUNS ARE ALL I NEED.
スタ
SUTA (SHFF)
スタ
SUTA
スタ
SUTA
OH DEAR ...
I'M BAAACK—
HAAAH ...
ぼふーん
BOFUUUN (WHUMP)

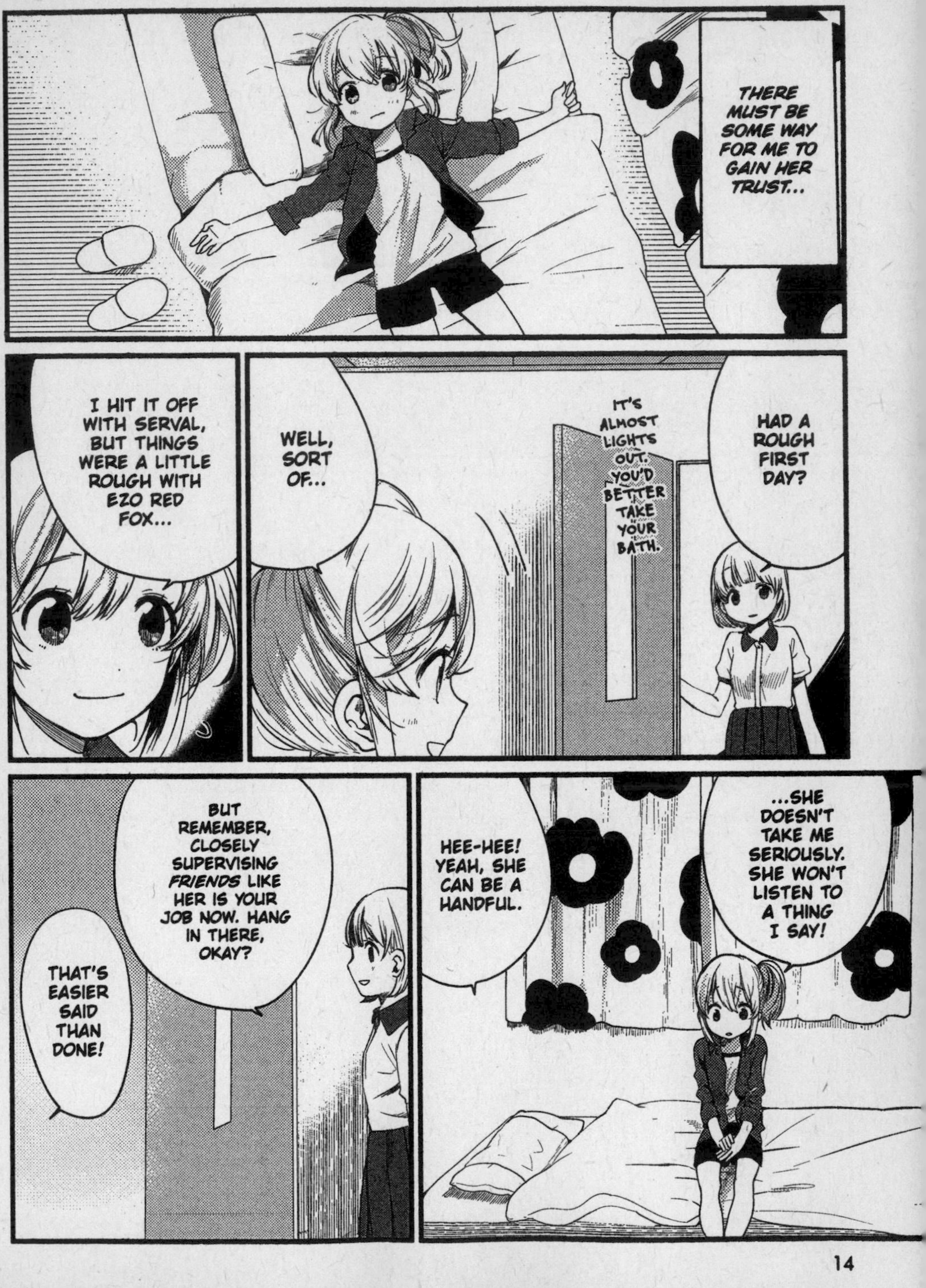
THERE MUST BE SOME WAY FOR ME TO GAIN HER TRUST...
HAD A ROUGH FIRST DAY?
IT'S ALMOST LIGHTS OUT. YOU'D BETTER TAKE YOUR BATH.
WELL, SORT OF...
I HIT IT OFF WITH SERVAL, BUT THINGS WERE A LITTLE ROUGH WITH EZO RED FOX...
...SHE DOESN'T TAKE ME SERIOUSLY. SHE WON'T LISTEN TO A THING I SAY!
HEE-HEE! YEAH, SHE CAN BE A HANDFUL.
BUT REMEMBER, CLOSELY SUPERVISING *FRIENDS* LIKE HER IS YOUR JOB NOW. HANG IN THERE, OKAY?
THAT'S EASIER SAID THAN DONE!

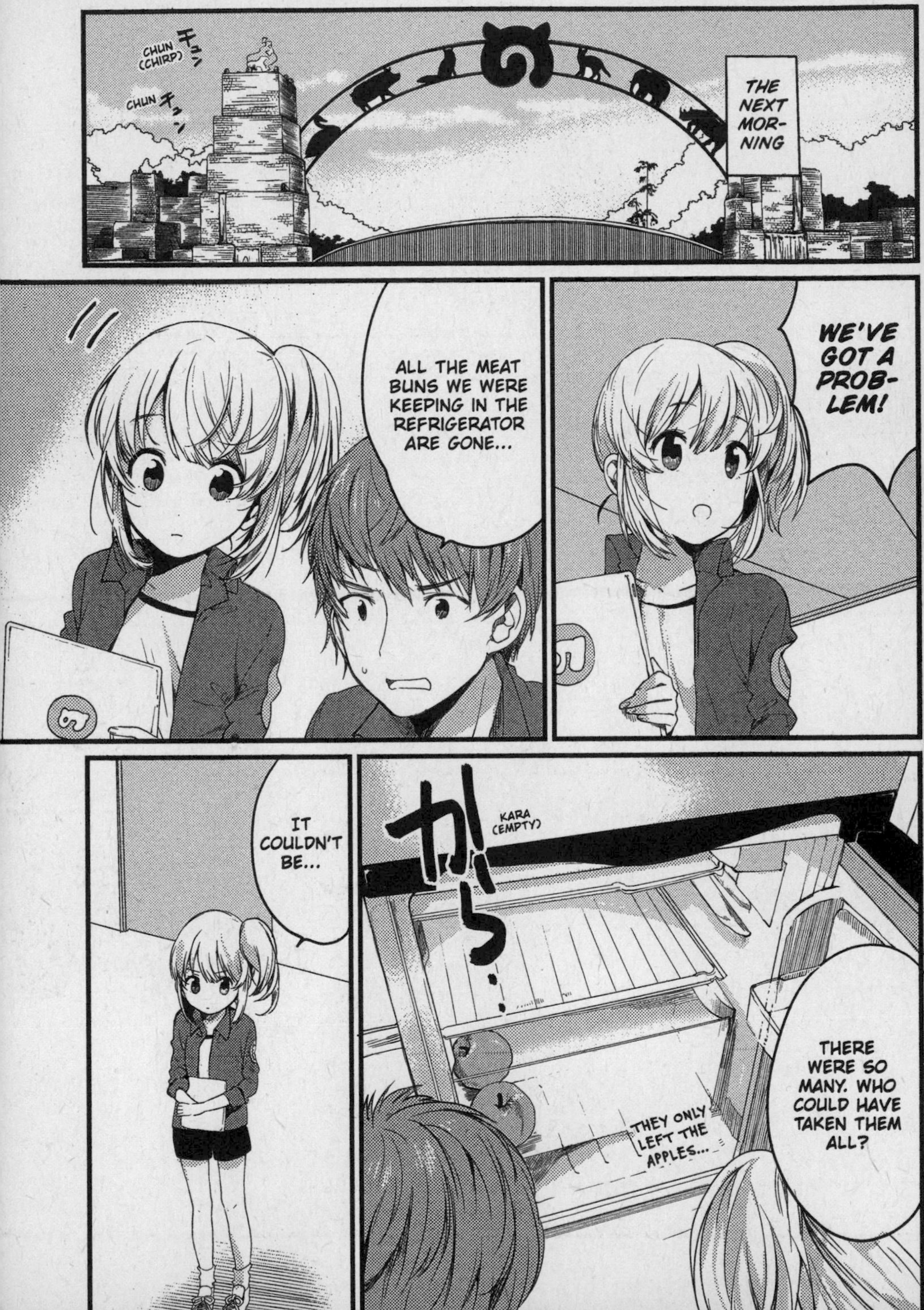
THE NEXT MORNING
チュン
CHUN (CHIRP)
チュン
CHUN
WE'VE GOT A PROBLEM!
ALL THE MEAT BUNS WE WERE KEEPING IN THE REFRIGERATOR ARE GONE...
から
KARA (EMPTY)
THERE WERE SO MANY. WHO COULD HAVE TAKEN THEM ALL?
THEY ONLY LEFT THE APPLES...
IT COULDN'T BE...

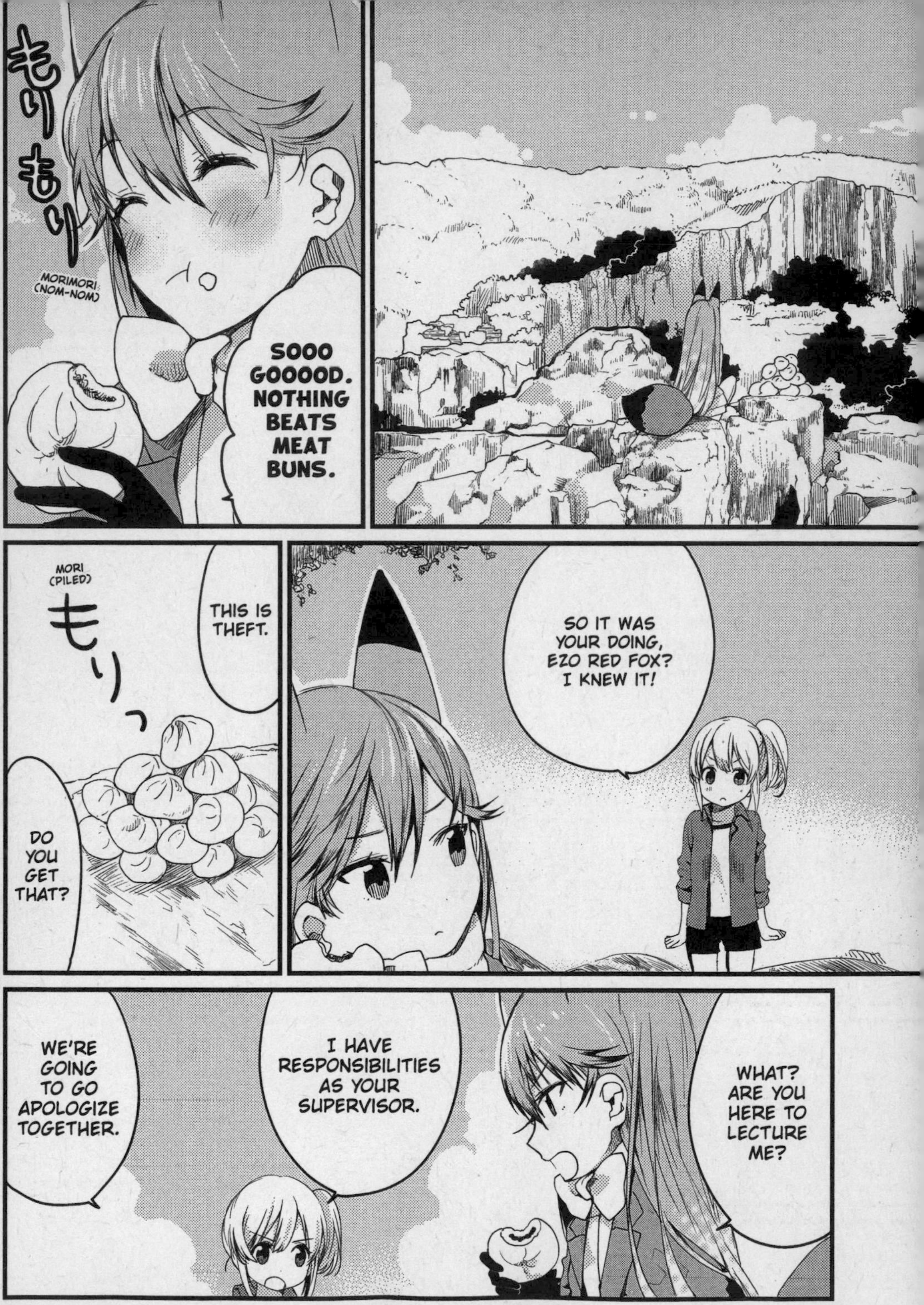
もりもりっ
MORIMORI (NOM-NOM)
SOOO GOOOOD. NOTHING BEATS MEAT BUNS.
SO IT WAS YOUR DOING, EZO RED FOX? I KNEW IT!
THIS IS THEFT.
MORI (PILED)
もりっ
DO YOU GET THAT?
WHAT? ARE YOU HERE TO LECTURE ME?
I HAVE RESPONSIBILITIES AS YOUR SUPERVISOR.
WE'RE GOING TO GO APOLOGIZE TOGETHER.

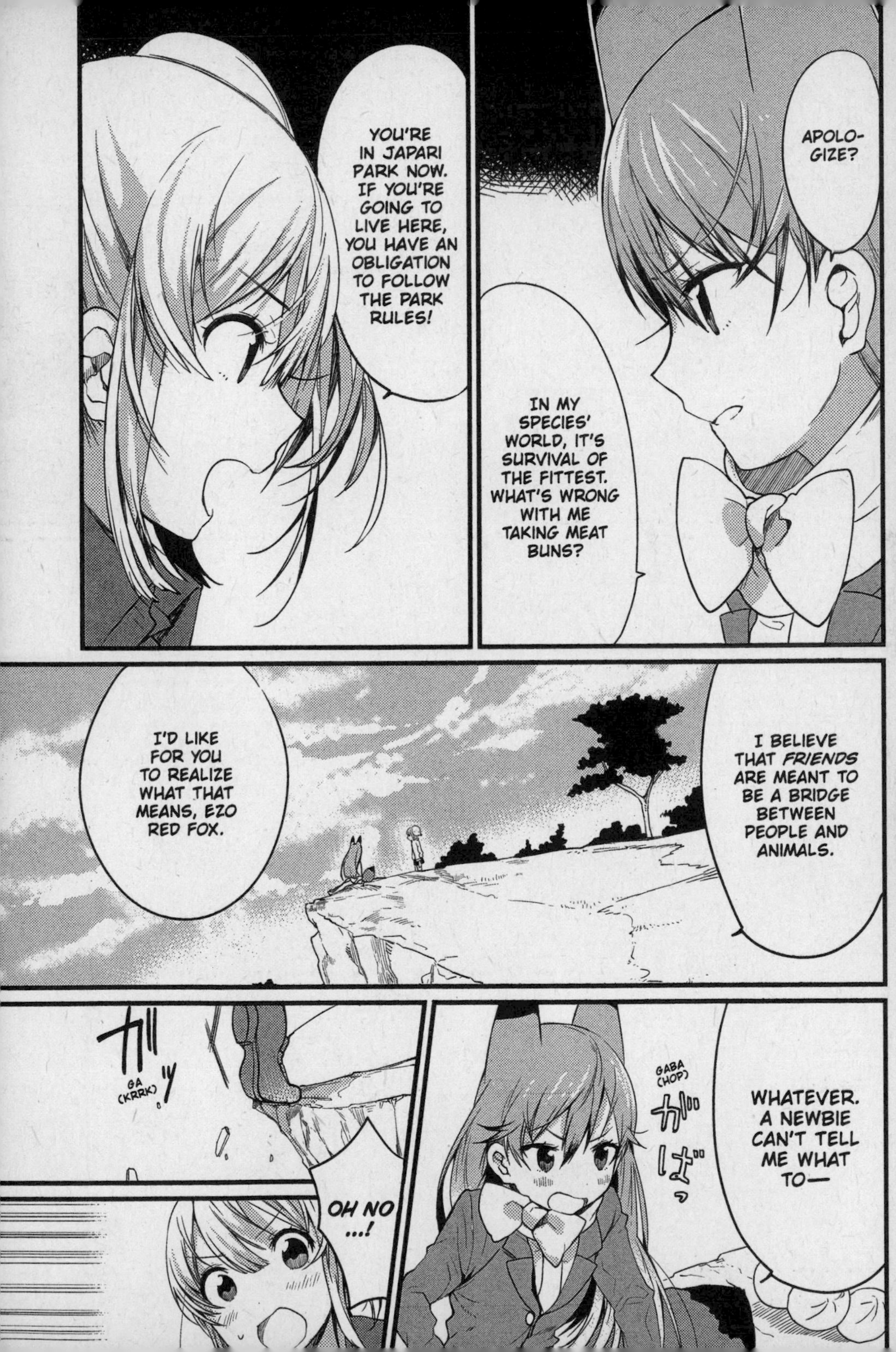
APOLO-GIZE?
IN MY SPECIES' WORLD, IT'S SURVIVAL OF THE FITTEST. WHAT'S WRONG WITH ME TAKING MEAT BUNS?
YOU'RE IN JAPARI PARK NOW. IF YOU'RE GOING TO LIVE HERE, YOU HAVE AN OBLIGATION TO FOLLOW THE PARK RULES!
I BELIEVE THAT *FRIENDS* ARE MEANT TO BE A BRIDGE BETWEEN PEOPLE AND ANIMALS.
I'D LIKE FOR YOU TO REALIZE WHAT THAT MEANS, EZO RED FOX.
がばっ
GABA (HOP)
WHATEVER. A NEWBIE CAN'T TELL ME WHAT TO—
ガッ
GA (KRRK)
OH NO ...!

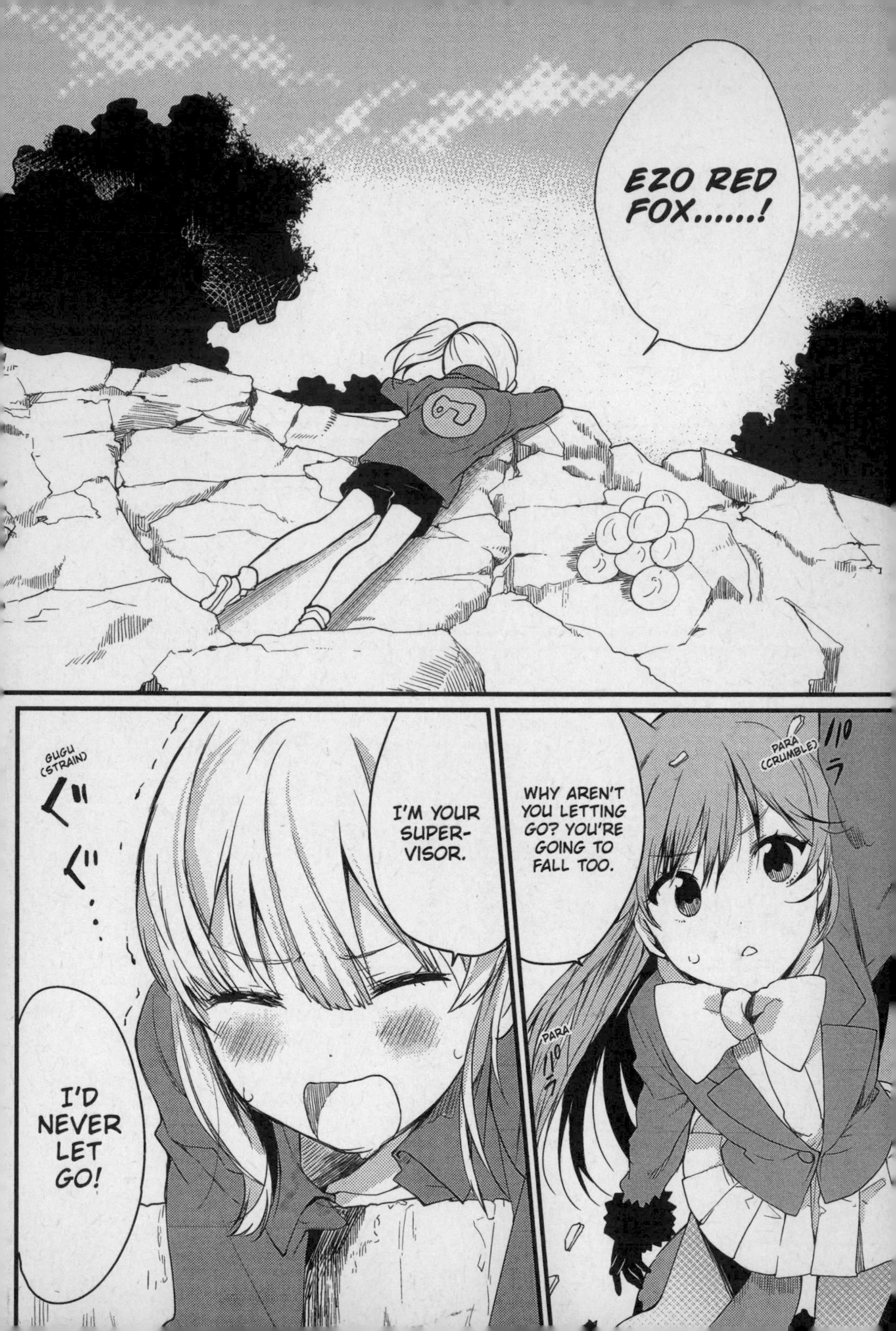
EZO RED FOX......!
PARA (CRUMBLE)
WHY AREN'T YOU LETTING GO? YOU'RE GOING TO FALL TOO.
PARA
I'M YOUR SUPER-VISOR.
GUGU (STRAIN)
I'D NEVER LET GO!

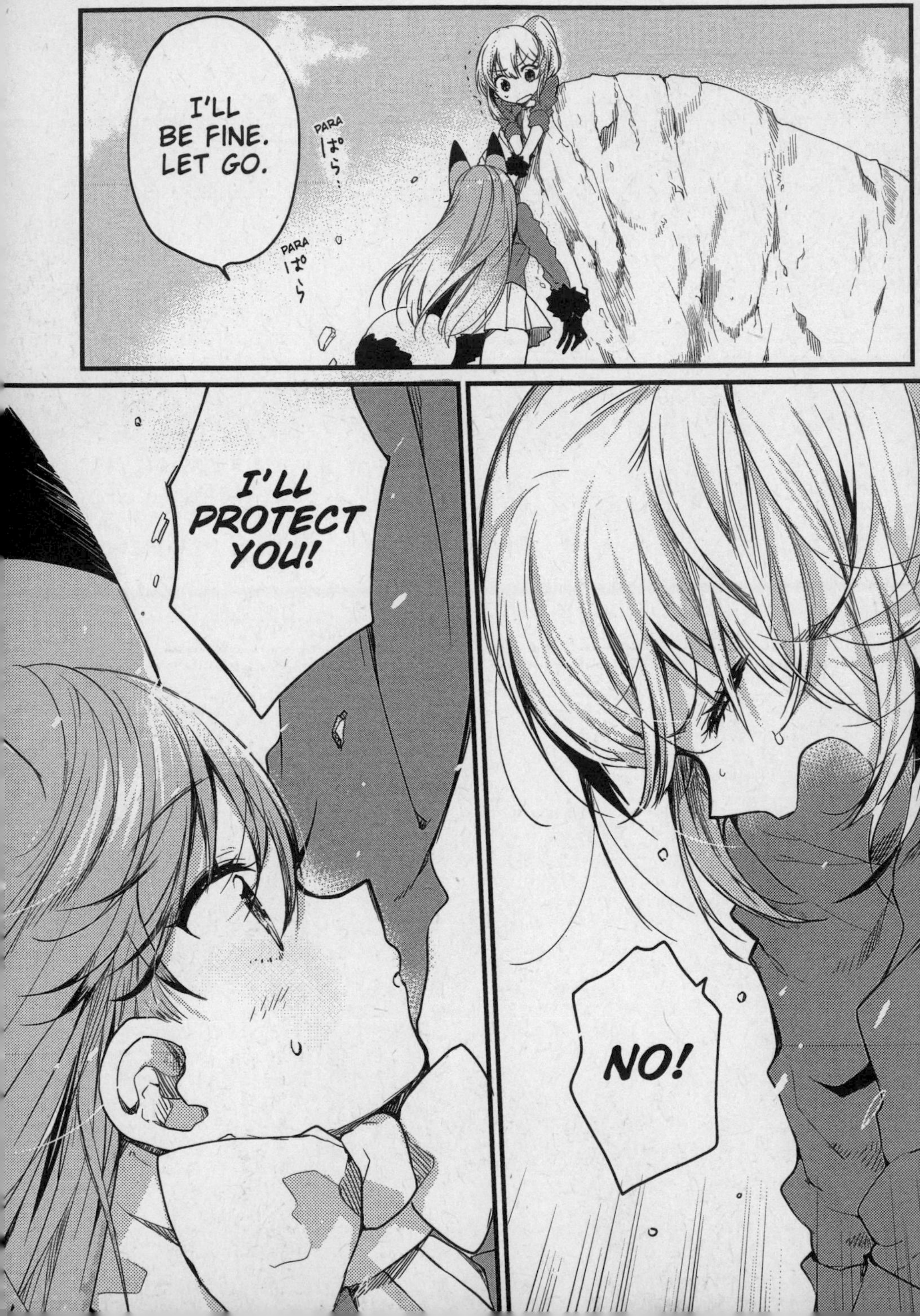
PARA ぱら
PARA ぱら
I'LL BE FINE. LET GO.
NO!
I'LL PROTECT YOU!

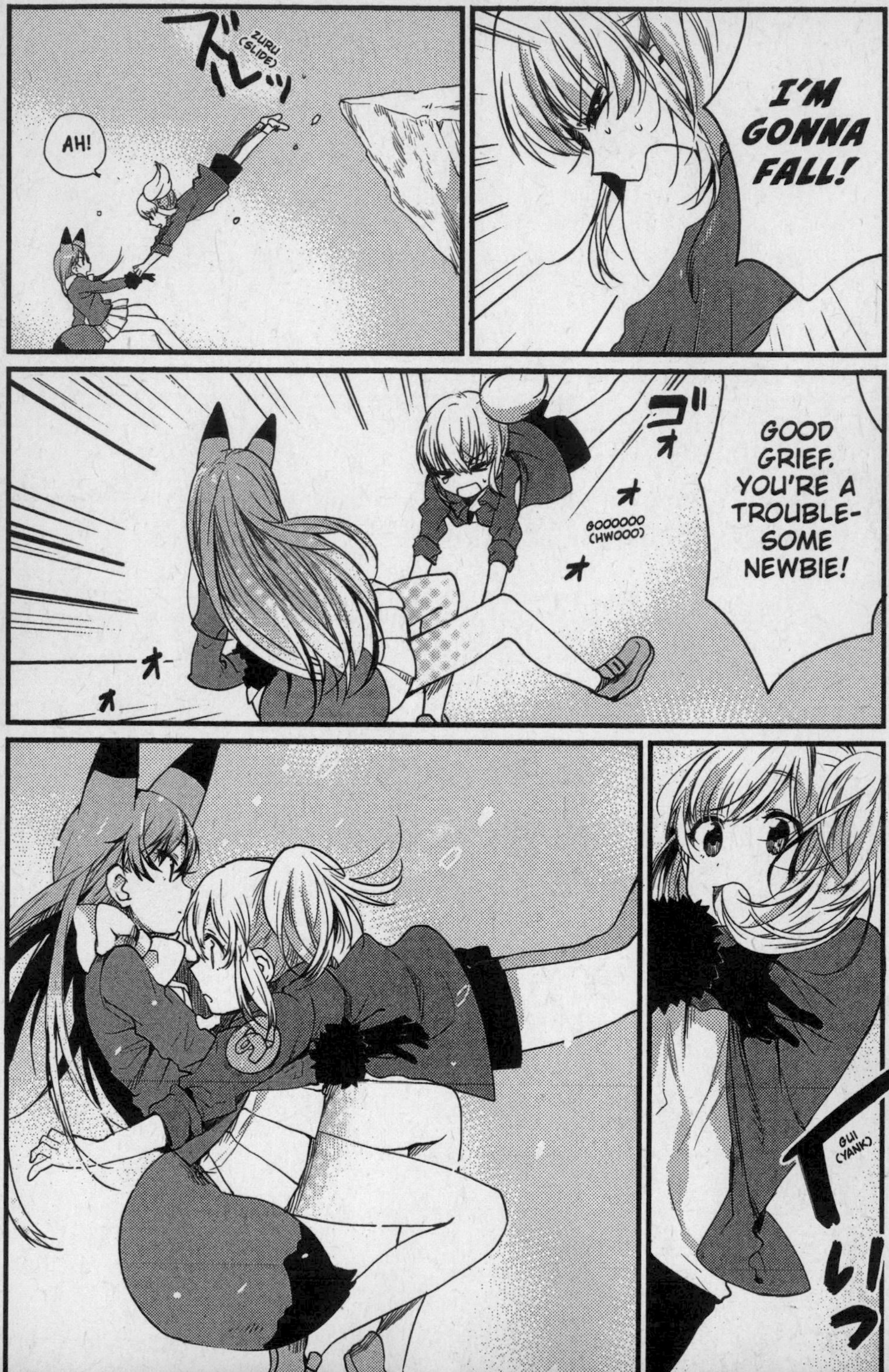
I'M GONNA FALL!
ZURU (SLIDE)
AH!
GOOD GRIEF. YOU'RE A TROUBLE-SOME NEWBIE!
GOOOOOO (HWOOO)
GUI (YANK)

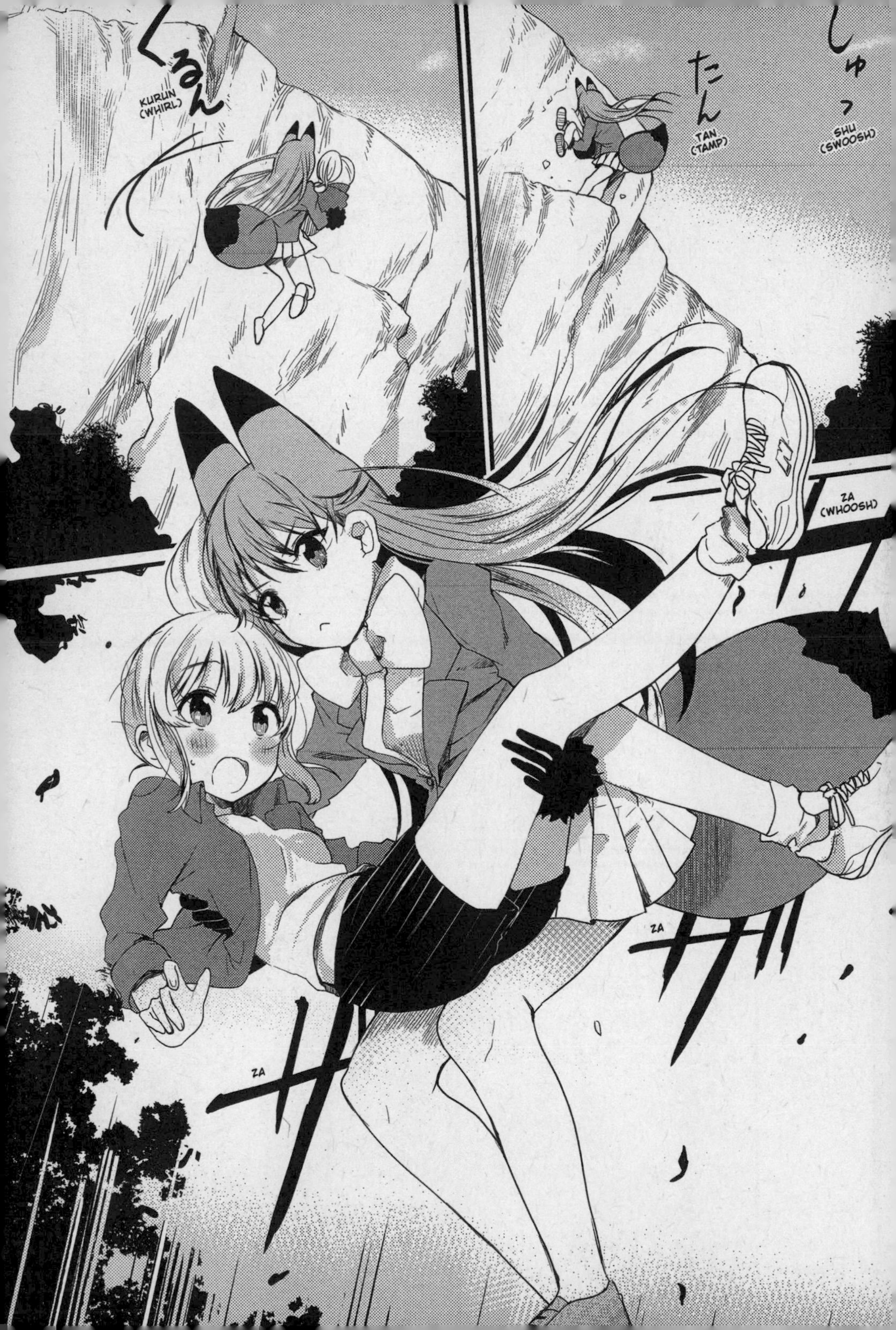
しゅっ
SHU (SWOOSH)
たん
TAN (TAMP)
くるん
KURUN (WHIRL)
ZA (WHOOSH)
ZA
ZA

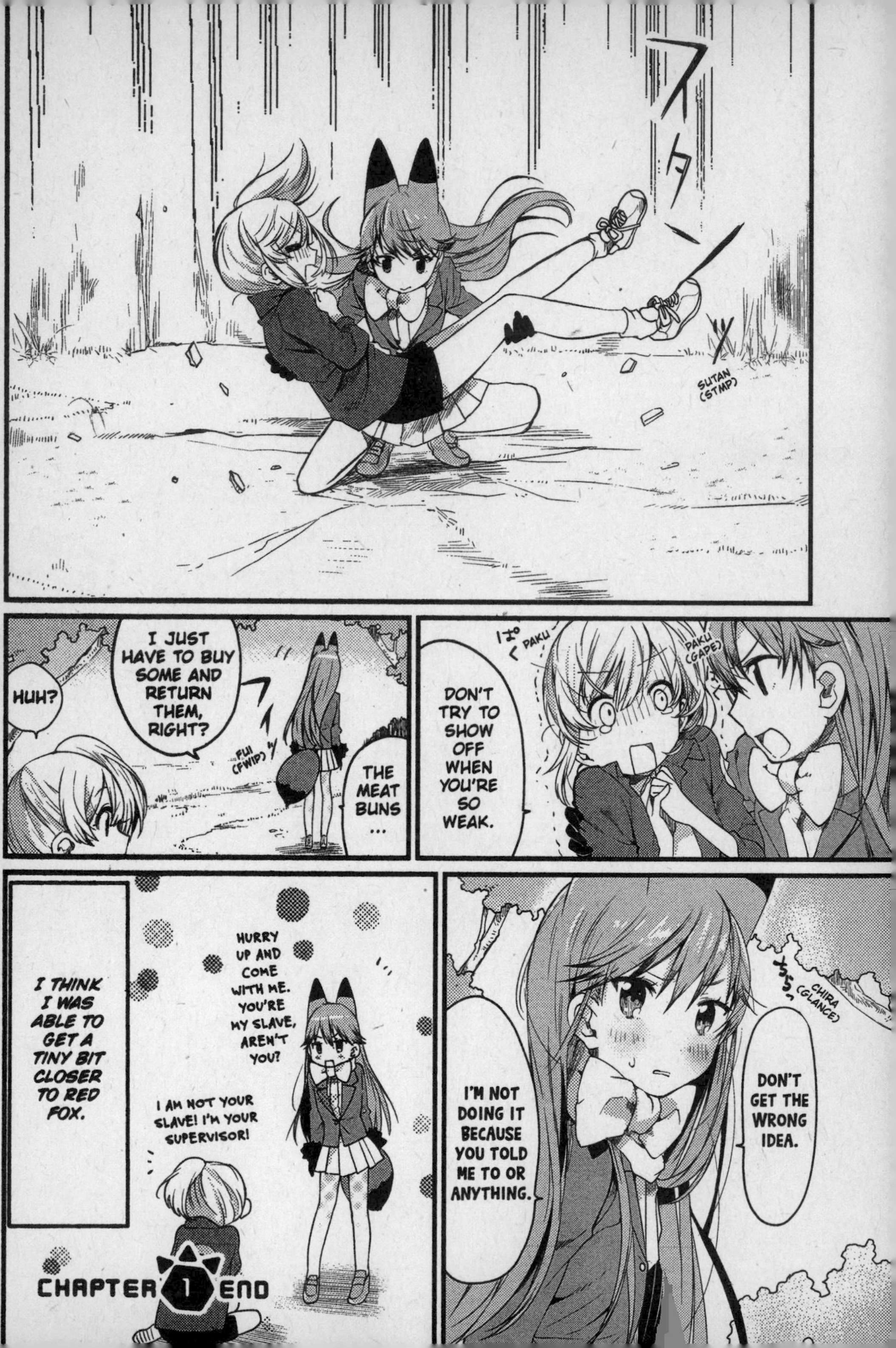
スタッ
SUTAN (STMP)
PAKU
PAKU (GAPE)
DON'T TRY TO SHOW OFF WHEN YOU'RE SO WEAK.
THE MEAT BUNS ...
FUI (FWIP)
I JUST HAVE TO BUY SOME AND RETURN THEM, RIGHT?
HUH?
CHIRA (GLANCE)
DON'T GET THE WRONG IDEA.
I'M NOT DOING IT BECAUSE YOU TOLD ME TO OR ANYTHING.
HURRY UP AND COME WITH ME. YOU'RE MY SLAVE, AREN'T YOU?
I AM NOT YOUR SLAVE! I'M YOUR SUPERVISOR!
I THINK I WAS ABLE TO GET A TINY BIT CLOSER TO RED FOX.
CHAPTER 1 END

CHAPTER 2

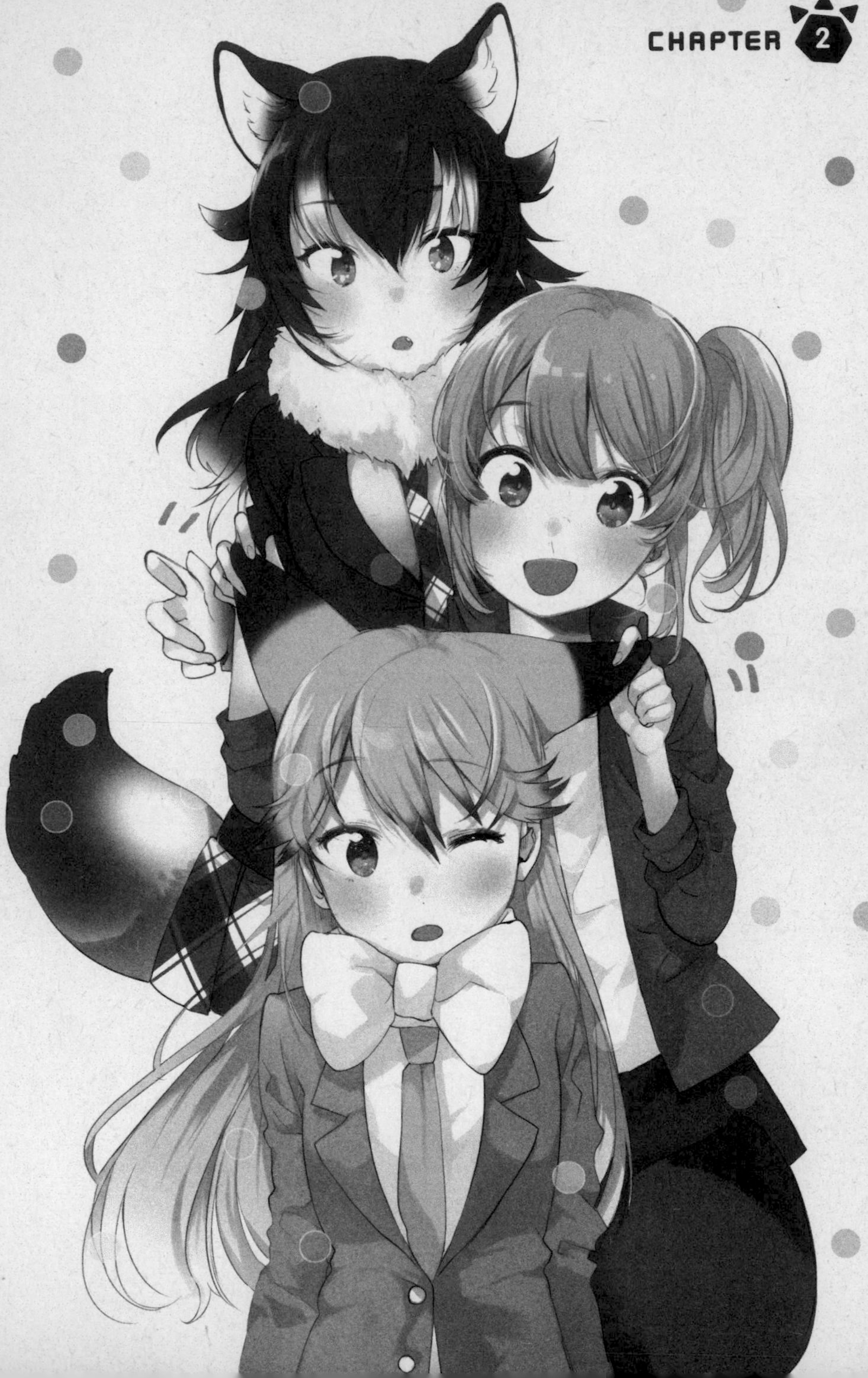

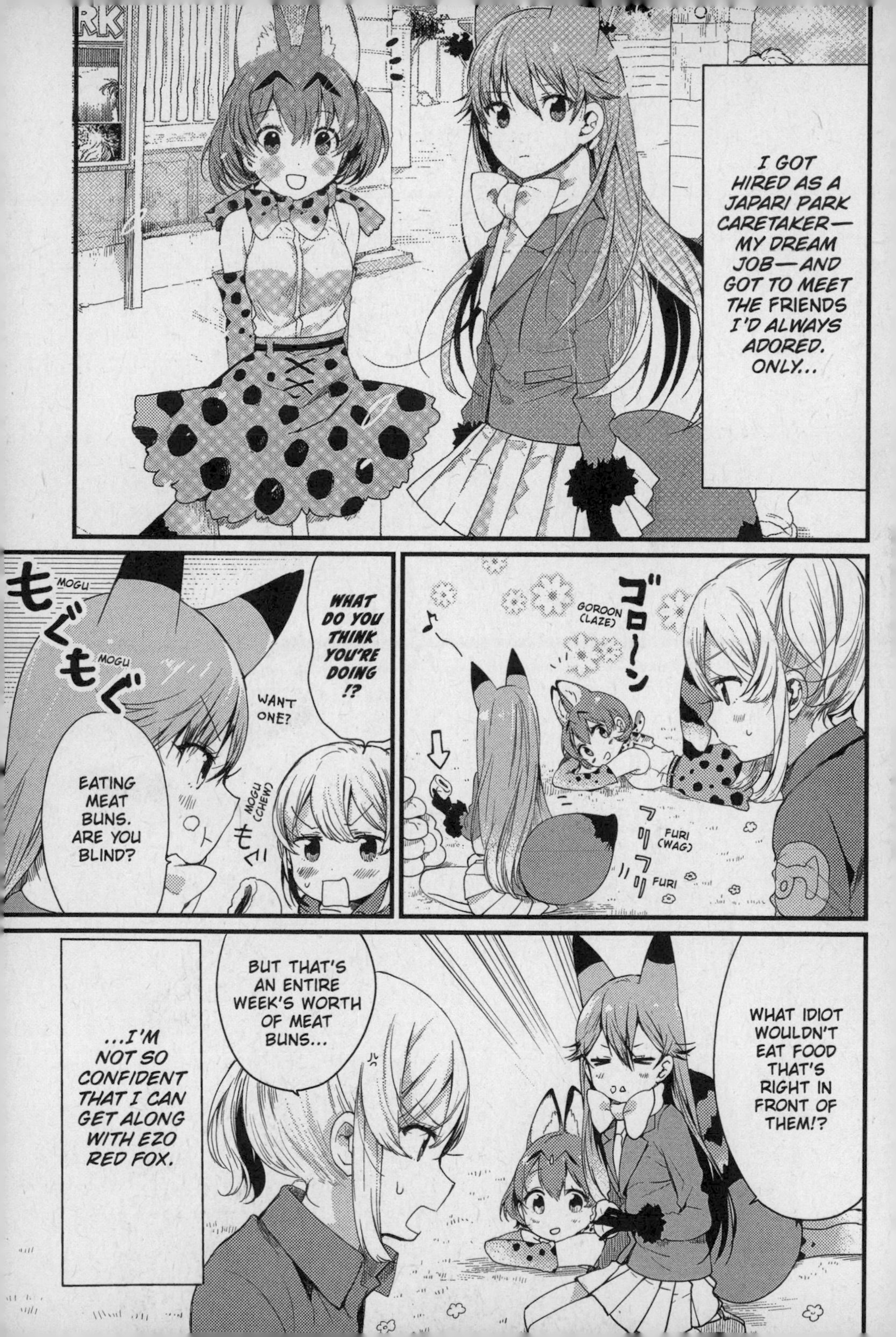
I GOT HIRED AS A JAPARI PARK CARETAKER—MY DREAM JOB—AND GOT TO MEET THE FRIENDS I'D ALWAYS ADORED. ONLY...
ゴロ～ン
GOROON (LAZE)
フリフリ
FURI (WAG)
FURI
WHAT DO YOU THINK YOU'RE DOING!?
もぐもぐ
MOGU
MOGU
WANT ONE?
EATING MEAT BUNS. ARE YOU BLIND?
もぐ
MOGU (CHEW)
WHAT IDIOT WOULDN'T EAT FOOD THAT'S RIGHT IN FRONT OF THEM!?
BUT THAT'S AN ENTIRE WEEK'S WORTH OF MEAT BUNS...
...I'M NOT SO CONFIDENT THAT I CAN GET ALONG WITH EZO RED FOX.

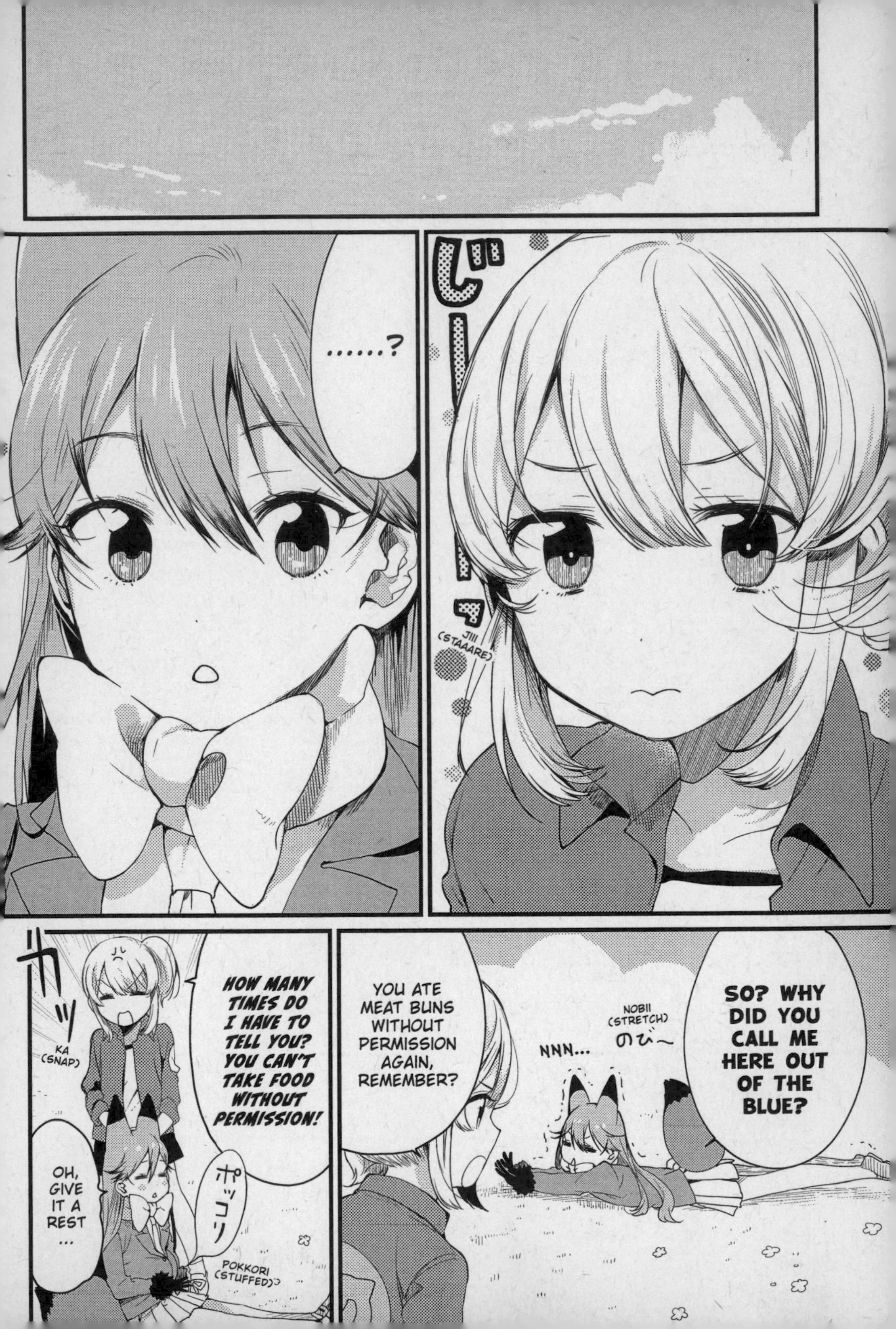

じー
JIII (STAARE)
......?
SO? WHY DID YOU CALL ME HERE OUT OF THE BLUE?
NOBII (STRETCH)
のび～
NNN...
YOU ATE MEAT BUNS WITHOUT PERMISSION AGAIN, REMEMBER?
ガッ
KA (SNAP)
HOW MANY TIMES DO I HAVE TO TELL YOU? YOU CAN'T TAKE FOOD WITHOUT PERMISSION!
ポッコリ
POKKORI (STUFFED)
OH, GIVE IT A REST ...

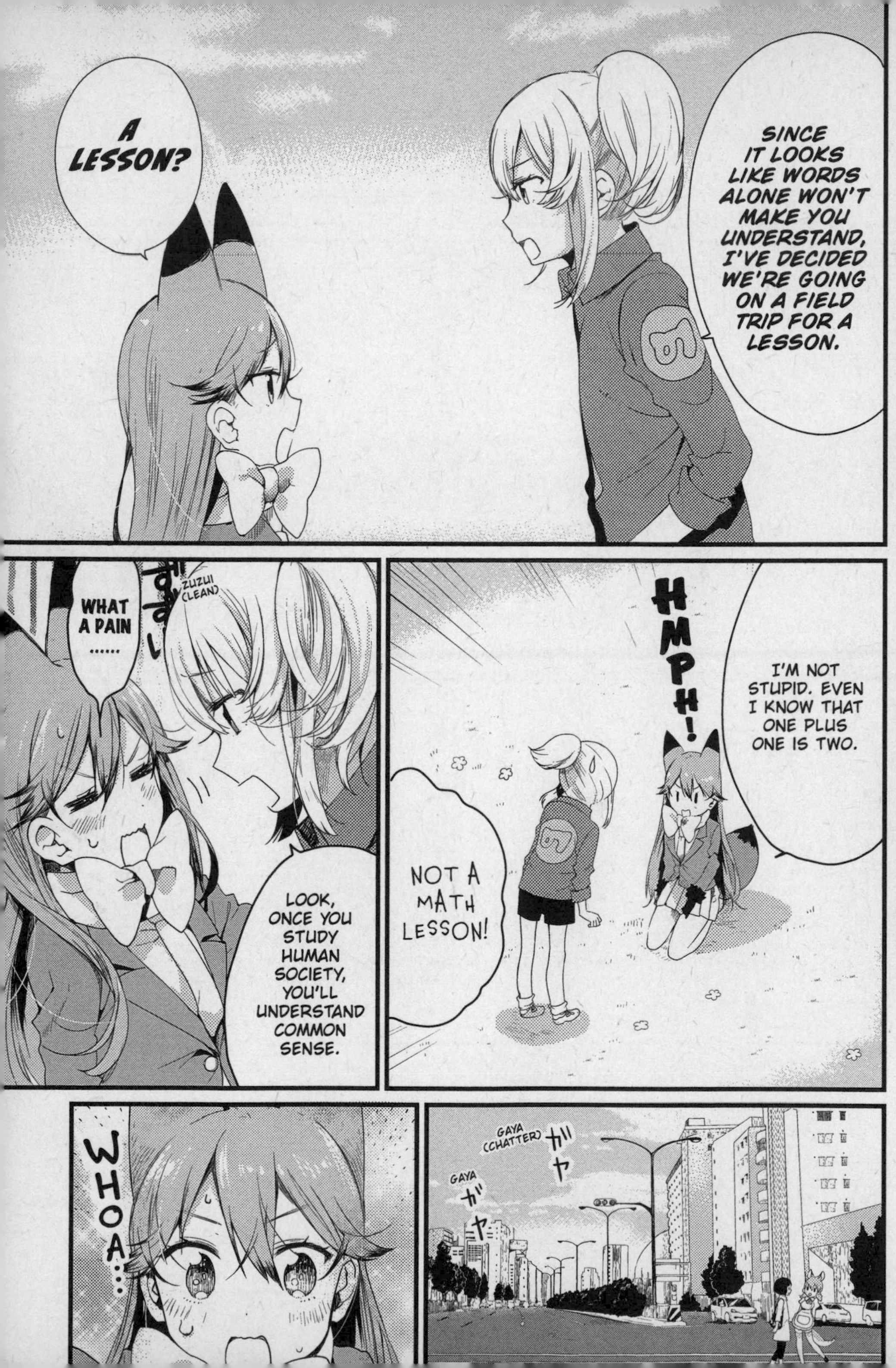

SINCE IT LOOKS LIKE WORDS ALONE WON'T MAKE YOU UNDERSTAND, I'VE DECIDED WE'RE GOING ON A FIELD TRIP FOR A LESSON.
A LESSON?
HMPH!
I'M NOT STUPID. EVEN I KNOW THAT ONE PLUS ONE IS TWO.
NOT A MATH LESSON!
ZUZUI (CLEAN)
WHAT A PAIN......
LOOK, ONCE YOU STUDY HUMAN SOCIETY, YOU'LL UNDERSTAND COMMON SENSE.
GAYA (CHATTER)
ガヤ
GAYA
ガヤ
WHOA...

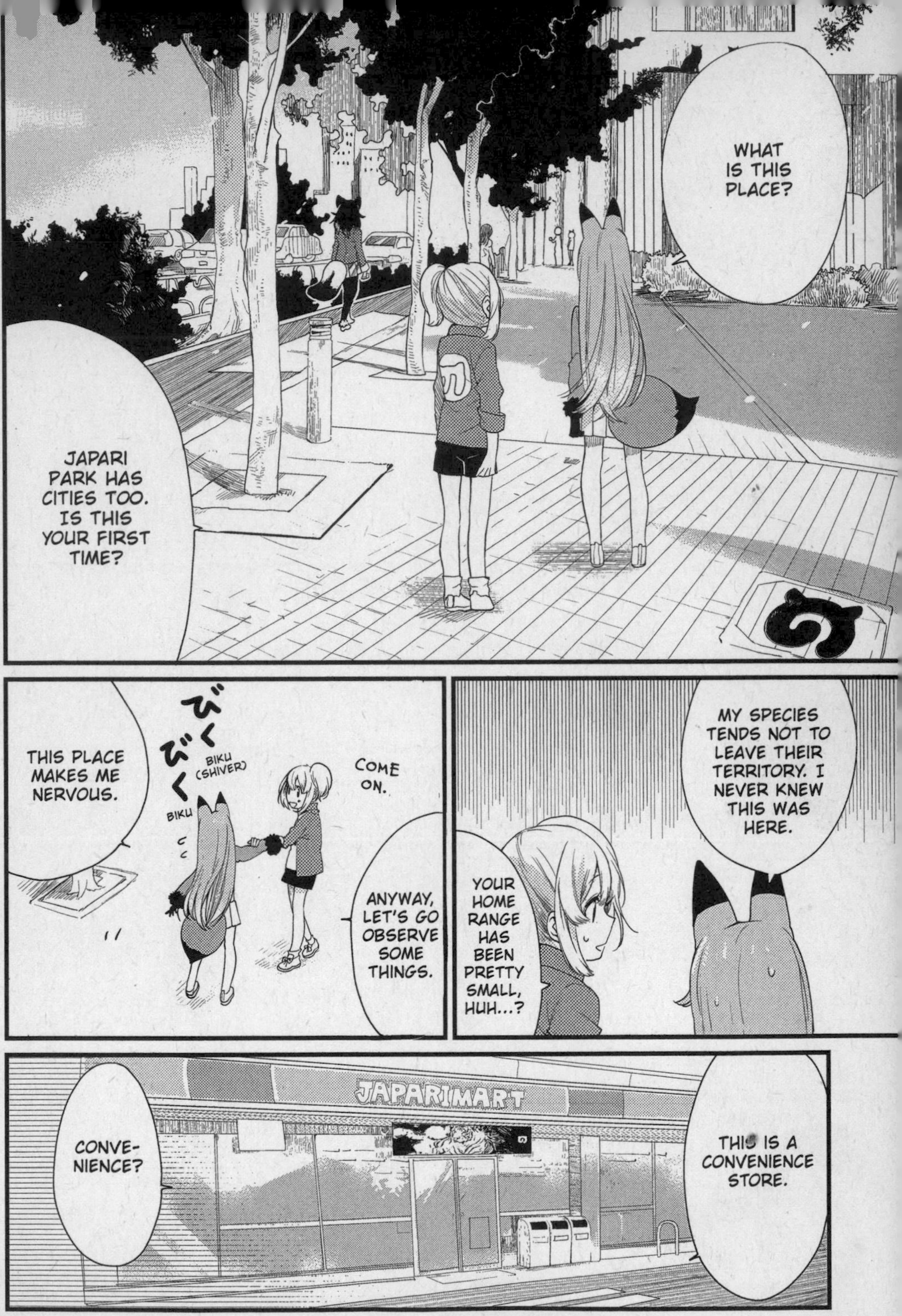
WHAT IS THIS PLACE?
JAPARI PARK HAS CITIES TOO. IS THIS YOUR FIRST TIME?
MY SPECIES TENDS NOT TO LEAVE THEIR TERRITORY. I NEVER KNEW THIS WAS HERE.
YOUR HOME RANGE HAS BEEN PRETTY SMALL, HUH...?
ANYWAY, LET'S GO OBSERVE SOME THINGS.
COME ON.
びくびく
BIKU (SHIVER) BIKU
THIS PLACE MAKES ME NERVOUS.
JAPARIMART
THIS IS A CONVENIENCE STORE.
CONVE-NIENCE?

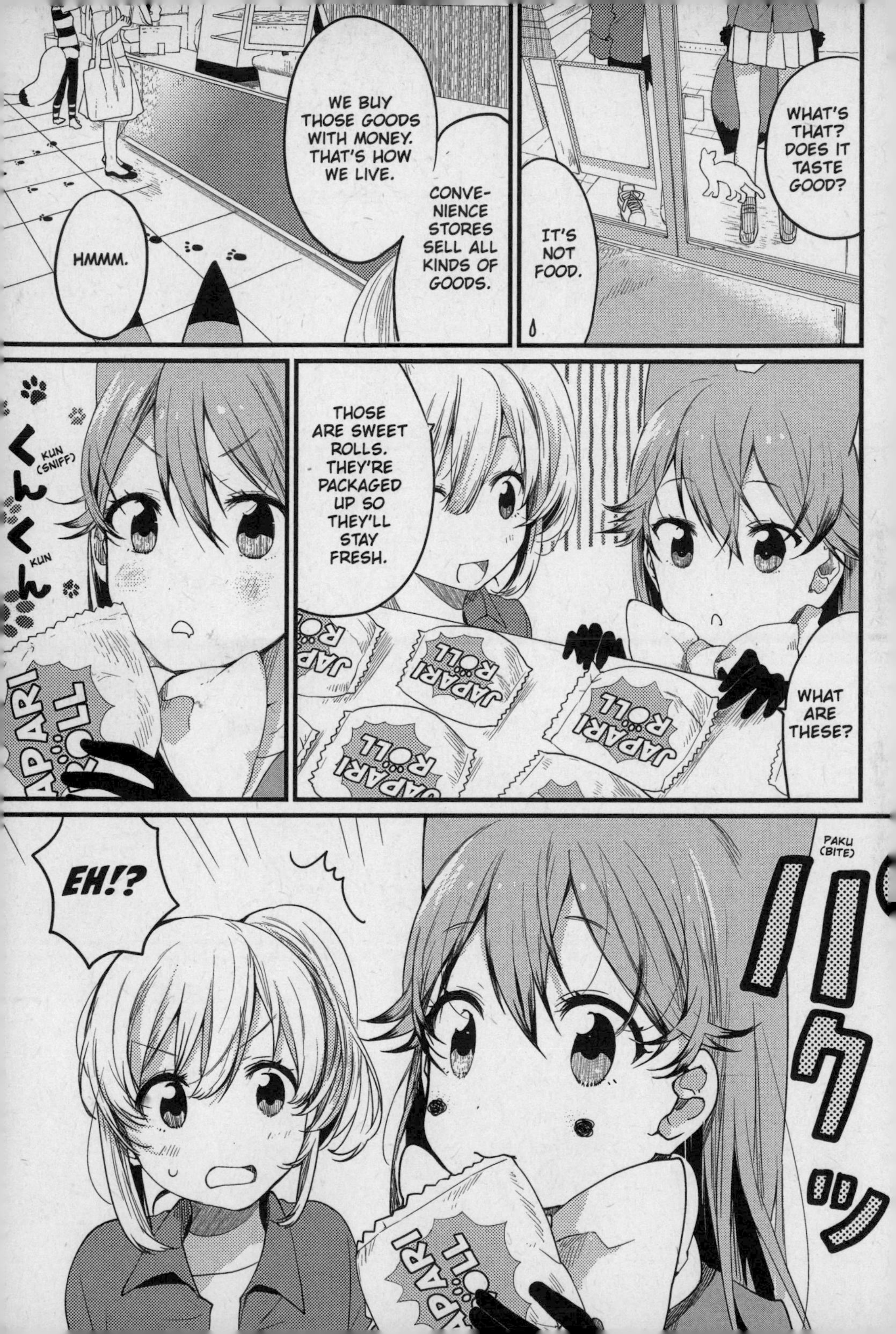
WHAT'S THAT? DOES IT TASTE GOOD?
IT'S NOT FOOD.
CONVE-NIENCE STORES SELL ALL KINDS OF GOODS.
WE BUY THOSE GOODS WITH MONEY. THAT'S HOW WE LIVE.
HMMM.
WHAT ARE THESE?
THOSE ARE SWEET ROLLS. THEY'RE PACKAGED UP SO THEY'LL STAY FRESH.
JAPARI ROLL
KUN (SNIFF)
KUN
JAPARI ROLL
PAKU (BITE)
EH!?
JAPARI ROLL

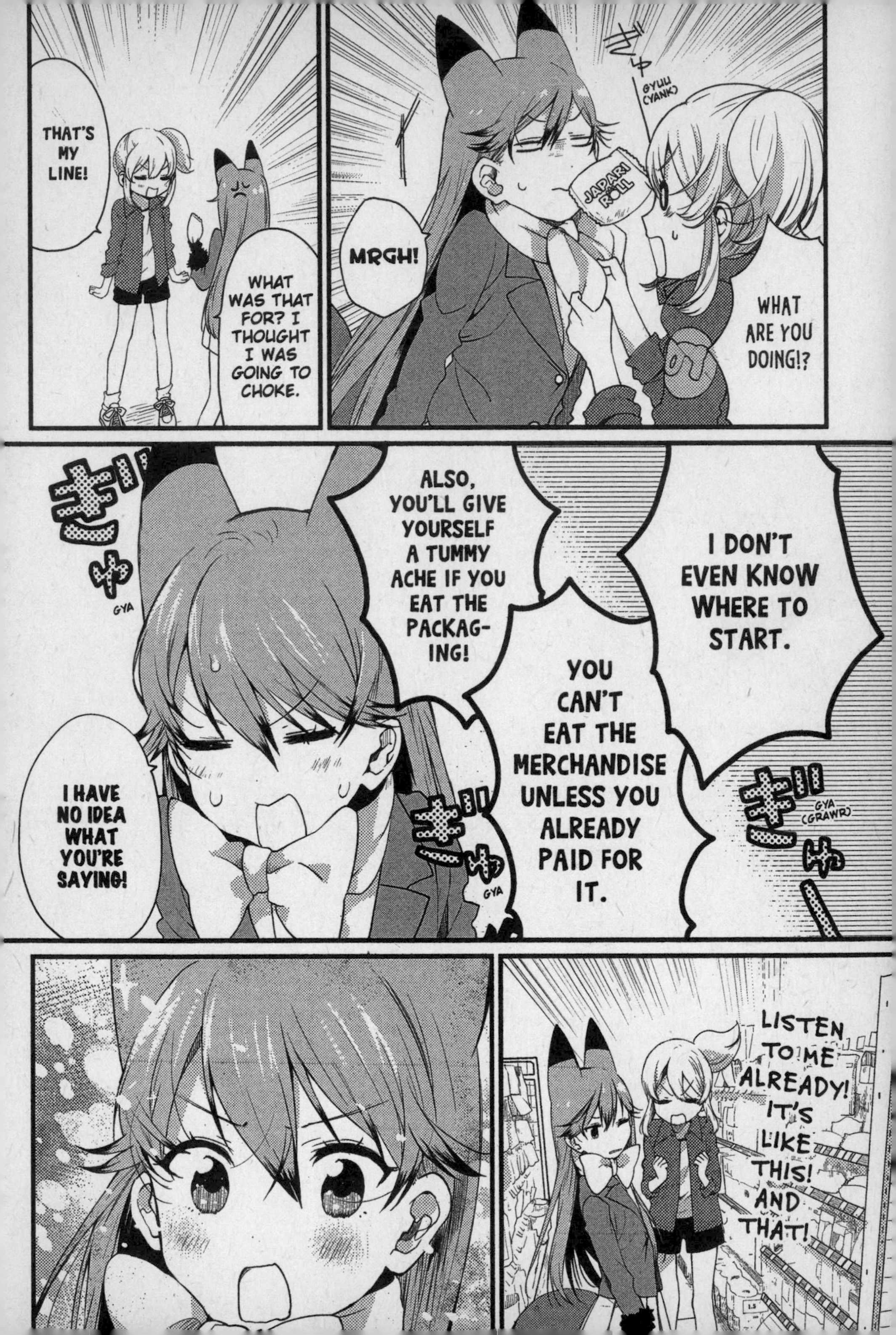
GYUU (YANK)
JAPARI ROLL
WHAT ARE YOU DOING!?
MRGH!
WHAT WAS THAT FOR? I THOUGHT I WAS GOING TO CHOKE.
THAT'S MY LINE!
GYA (GRAWR)
I DON'T EVEN KNOW WHERE TO START.
YOU CAN'T EAT THE MERCHANDISE UNLESS YOU ALREADY PAID FOR IT.
ALSO, YOU'LL GIVE YOURSELF A TUMMY ACHE IF YOU EAT THE PACKAGING!
GYA
GYA
I HAVE NO IDEA WHAT YOU'RE SAYING!
LISTEN TO ME ALREADY! IT'S LIKE THIS! AND THAT!

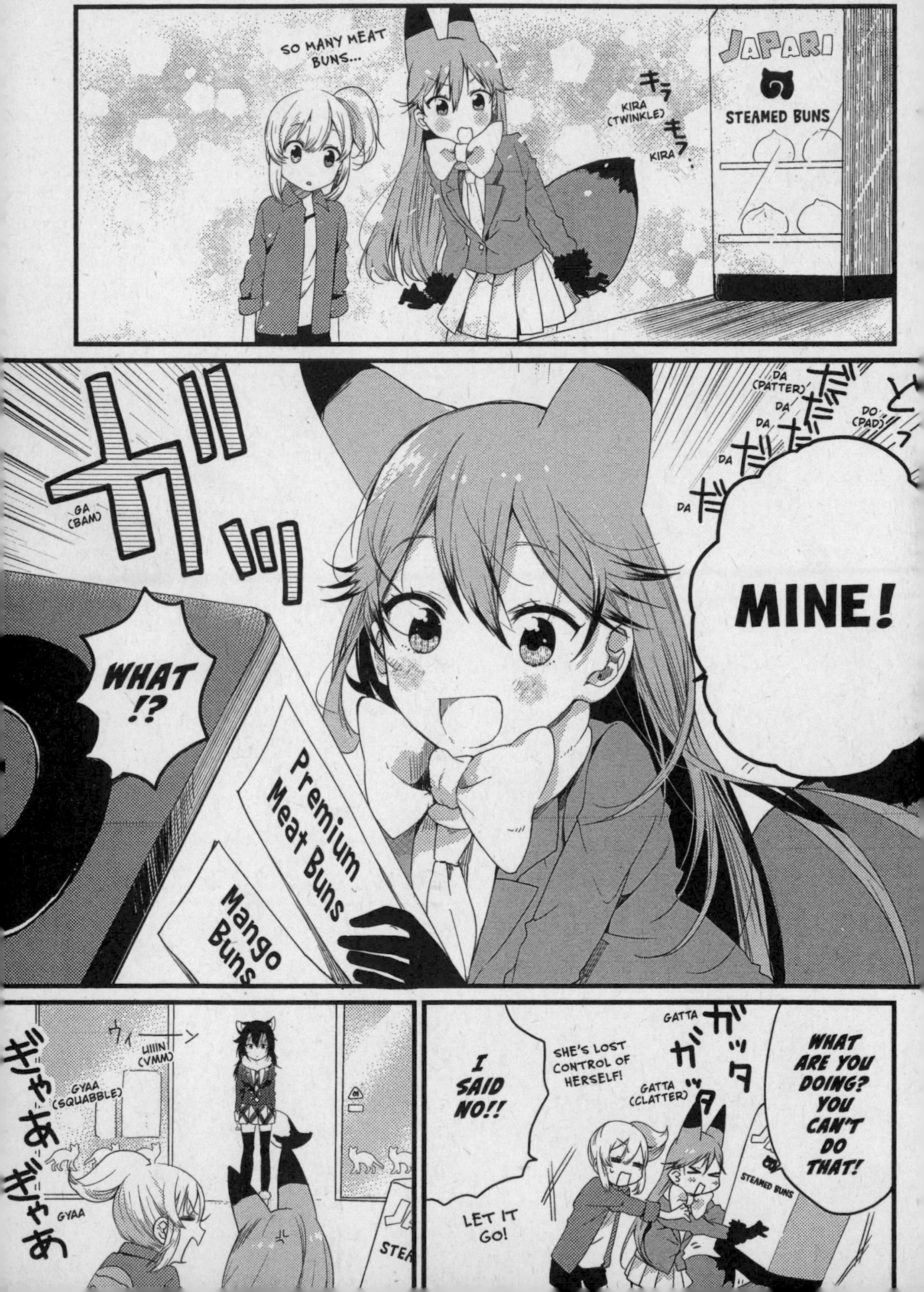

SO MANY MEAT BUNS...
キラ KIRA (TWINKLE)
キラ KIRA
JAPARI
の
STEAMED BUNS
だだだだ DA (PATTER) DA DA DA DA
とっ DO (PAD)
MINE!
ガッ GA (BAM)
WHAT!?
Premium Meat Buns
Mango Buns
WHAT ARE YOU DOING? YOU CAN'T DO THAT!
ガッタ GATTA
ガッタ GATTA (CLATTER)
SHE'S LOST CONTROL OF HERSELF!
I SAID NO!!
LET IT GO!
STEAMED BUNS
ウィーン UIIIN (VMM)
ぎゃあ GYAA (SQUABBLE)
ぎゃあ GYAA
STE

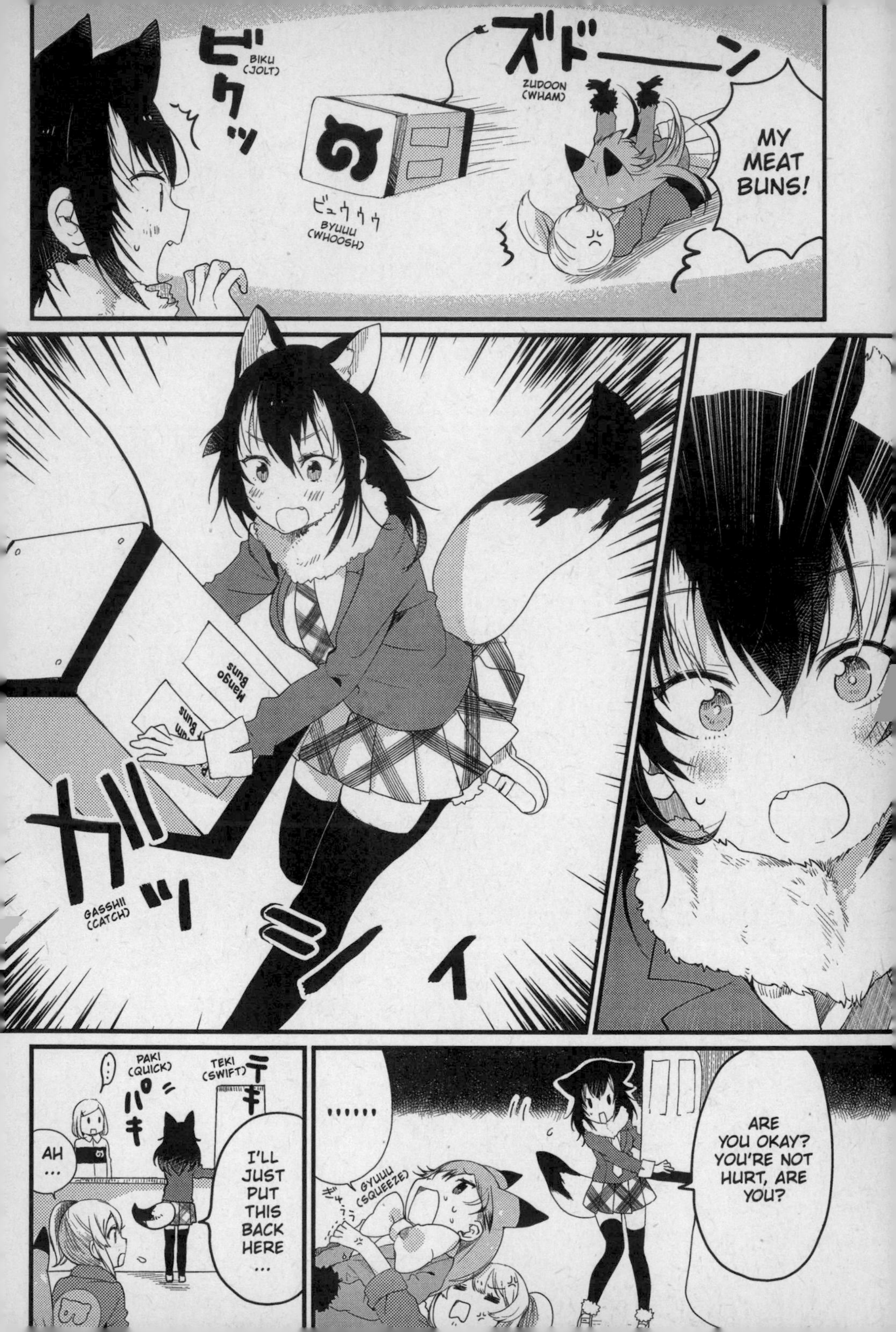
MY MEAT BUNS!
ズドーーン
ZUDOON (WHAM)
ビュウウウ
BYUUU (WHOOSH)
ビクッ
BIKU (JOLT)
Mango Buns
ガッシーイ
GASSHII (CATCH)
ARE YOU OKAY? YOU'RE NOT HURT, ARE YOU?
....
ぎゅうう
GYUUU (SQUEEZE)
テキ
TEKI (SWIFT)
パキ
PAKI (QUICK)
I'LL JUST PUT THIS BACK HERE ...
AH ...

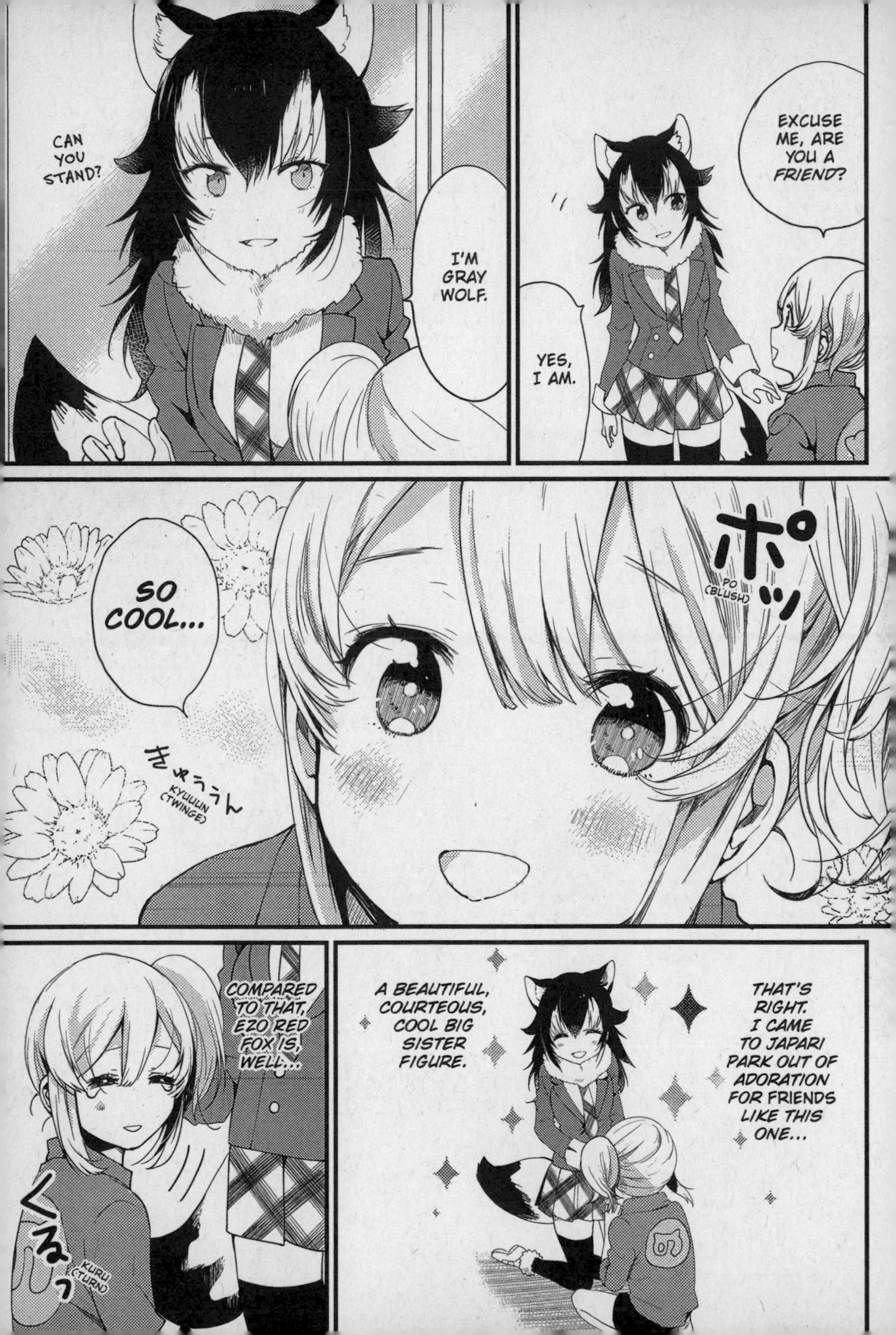
EXCUSE ME, ARE YOU A FRIEND?
YES, I AM.
I'M GRAY WOLF.
CAN YOU STAND?
ポッ
PO (BLUSH)
SO COOL...
きゅううん
KYUUUN (TWINGE)
THAT'S RIGHT. I CAME TO JAPARI PARK OUT OF ADORATION FOR FRIENDS LIKE THIS ONE...
A BEAUTIFUL, COURTEOUS, COOL BIG SISTER FIGURE.
COMPARED TO THAT, EZO RED FOX IS, WELL...
くるっ
KURU (TURN)

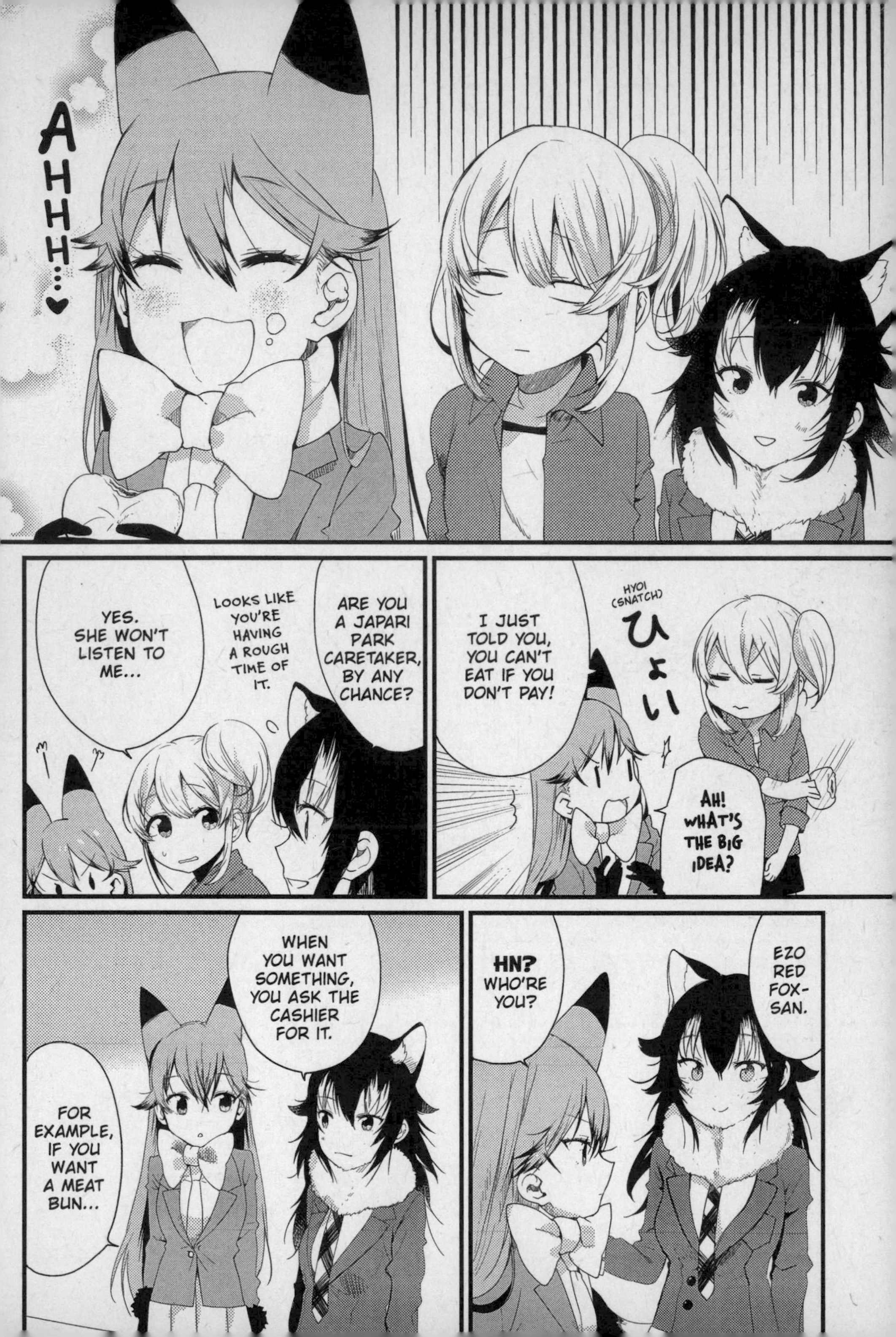
AHHH...♥
HYOI (SNATCH)
ひょい
I JUST TOLD YOU, YOU CAN'T EAT IF YOU DON'T PAY!
AH! WHAT'S THE BIG IDEA?
ARE YOU A JAPARI PARK CARETAKER, BY ANY CHANCE?
LOOKS LIKE YOU'RE HAVING A ROUGH TIME OF IT.
YES. SHE WON'T LISTEN TO ME...
EZO RED FOX-SAN.
HN? WHO'RE YOU?
WHEN YOU WANT SOMETHING, YOU ASK THE CASHIER FOR IT.
FOR EXAMPLE, IF YOU WANT A MEAT BUN...

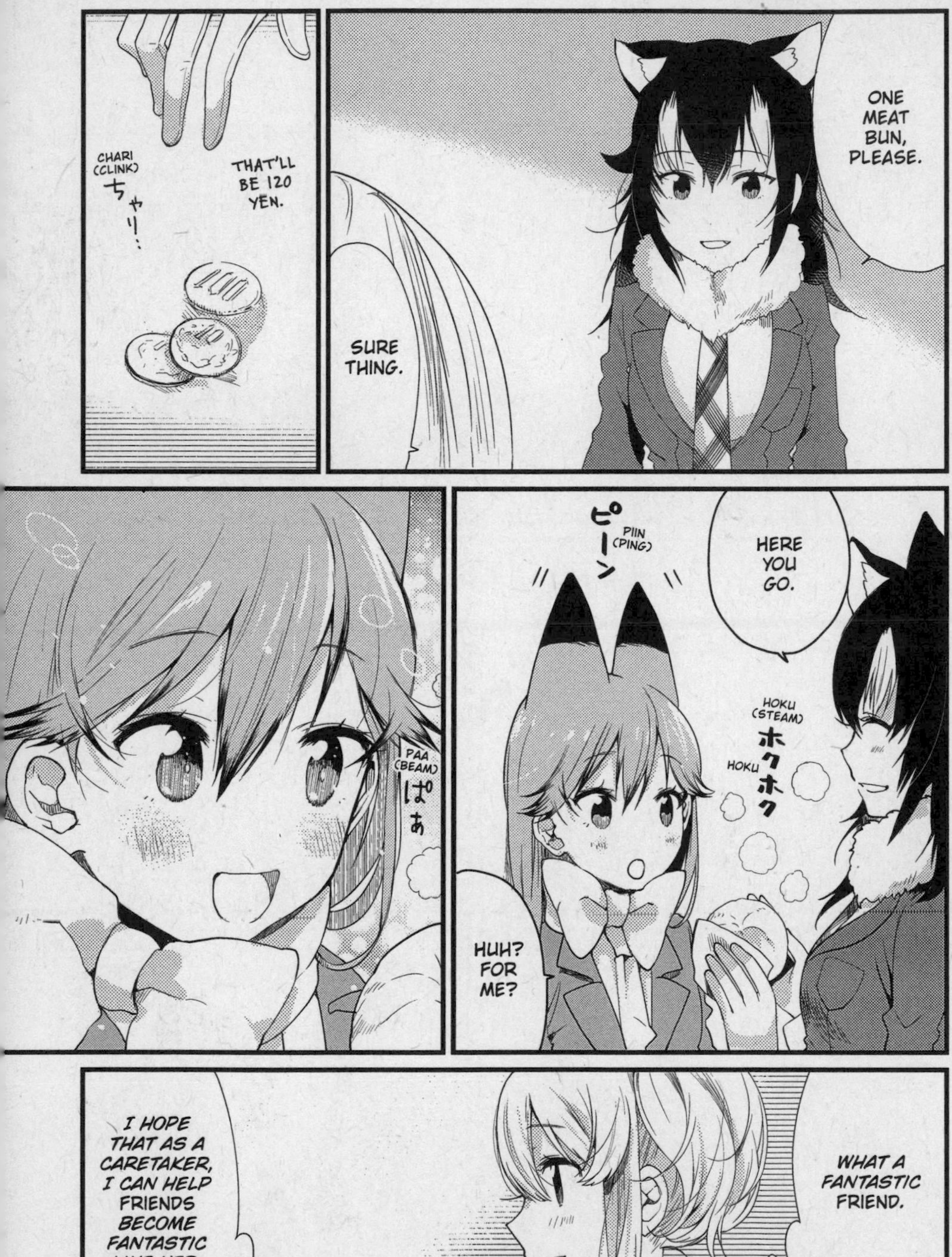

ONE MEAT BUN, PLEASE.
SURE THING.
THAT'LL BE 120 YEN.
CHARI (CLINK)
ちゃり…
PIIN (PING)
ピーン
HERE YOU GO.
HOKU (STEAM)
ホクホク
HOKU
HUH? FOR ME?
PAA (BEAM)
ぱぁ
WHAT A FANTASTIC FRIEND.
I HOPE THAT AS A CARETAKER, I CAN HELP FRIENDS BECOME FANTASTIC LIKE HER.

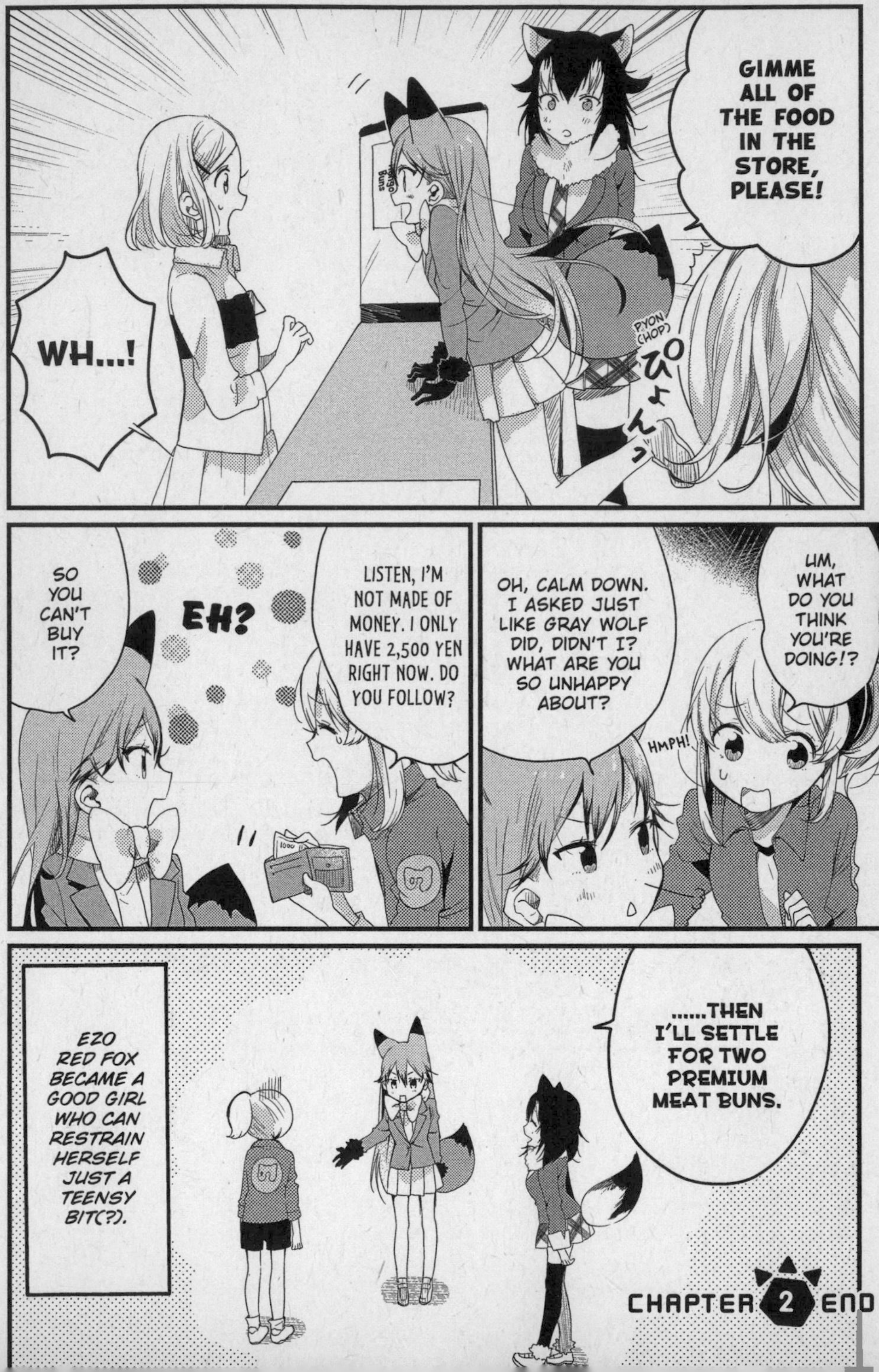
GIMME ALL OF THE FOOD IN THE STORE, PLEASE!
PYON (HOP)
ぴょんっ
WH...!
UM, WHAT DO YOU THINK YOU'RE DOING!?
HMPH!
OH, CALM DOWN. I ASKED JUST LIKE GRAY WOLF DID, DIDN'T I? WHAT ARE YOU SO UNHAPPY ABOUT?
LISTEN, I'M NOT MADE OF MONEY. I ONLY HAVE 2,500 YEN RIGHT NOW. DO YOU FOLLOW?
EH?
SO YOU CAN'T BUY IT?
......THEN I'LL SETTLE FOR TWO PREMIUM MEAT BUNS.
EZO RED FOX BECAME A GOOD GIRL WHO CAN RESTRAIN HERSELF JUST A TEENSY BIT(?).
CHAPTER 2 END

KEMONO FRIENDS
WELCOME TO JAPARI PARK!

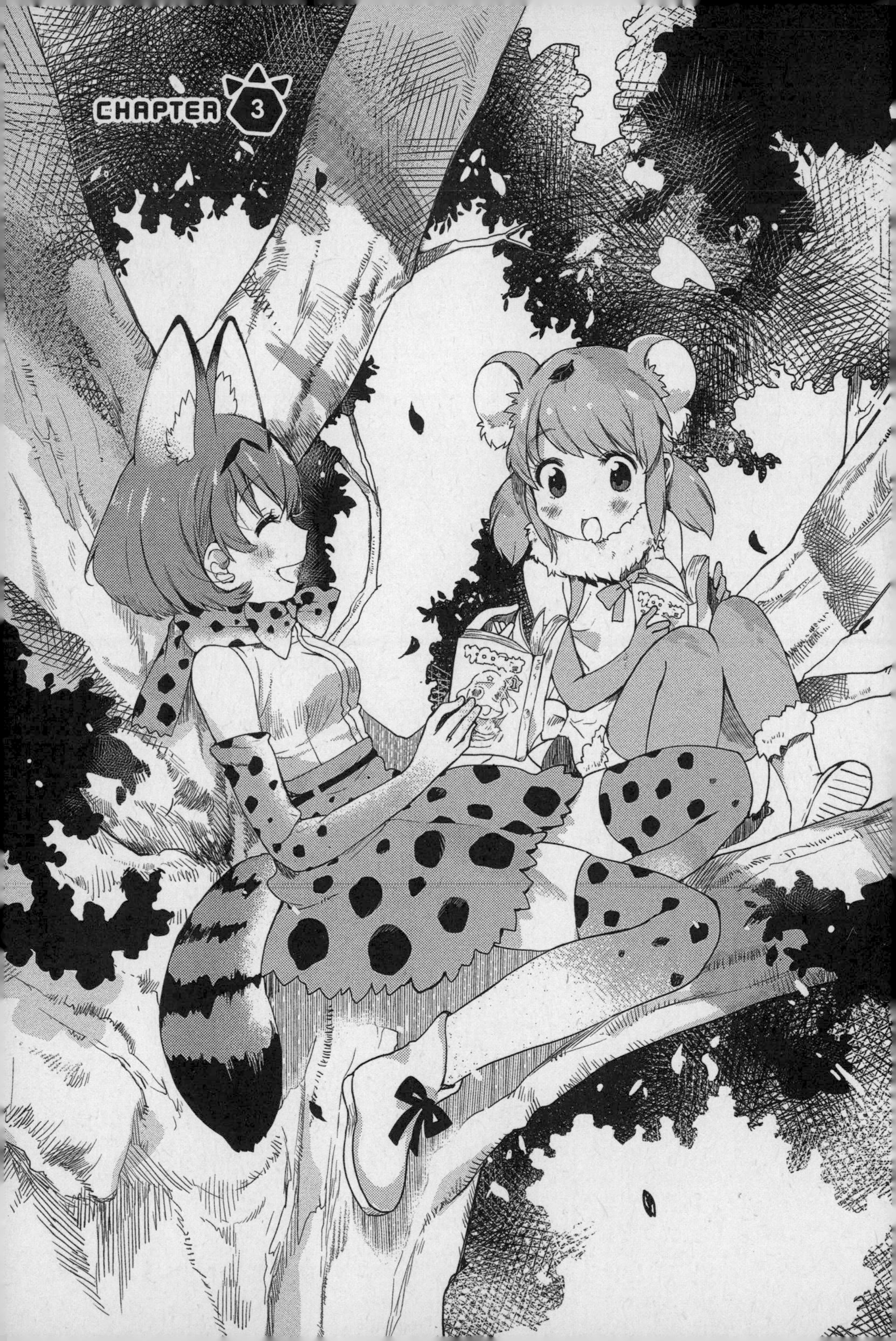
CHAPTER 3

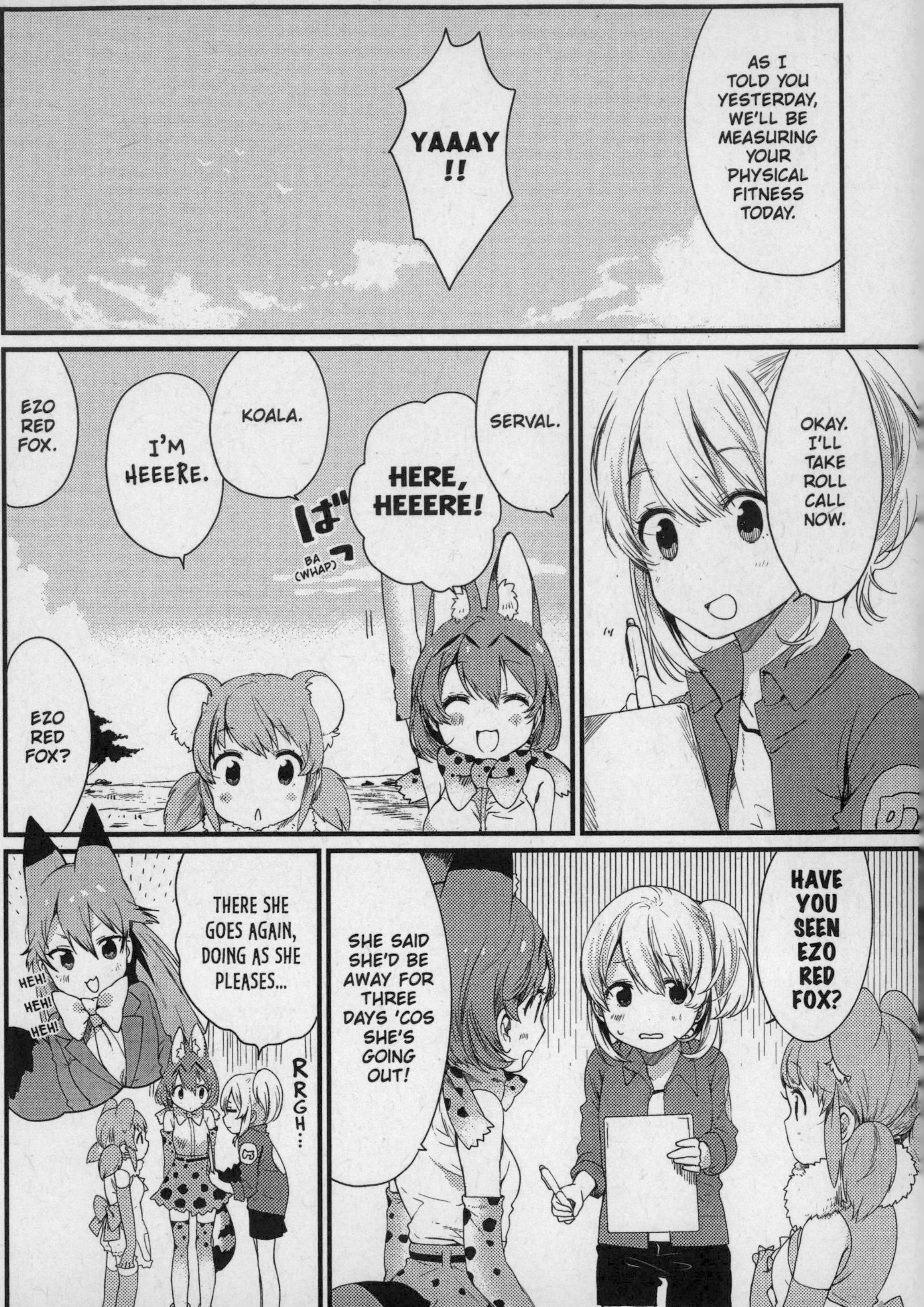
AS I TOLD YOU YESTERDAY, WE'LL BE MEASURING YOUR PHYSICAL FITNESS TODAY.
YAAAY!!
OKAY. I'LL TAKE ROLL CALL NOW.
SERVAL.
HERE, HEEERE!
ばっ
BA (WHAP)
KOALA.
I'M HEEERE.
EZO RED FOX.
EZO RED FOX?
HAVE YOU SEEN EZO RED FOX?
SHE SAID SHE'D BE AWAY FOR THREE DAYS 'COS SHE'S GOING OUT!
RRGH...
THERE SHE GOES AGAIN, DOING AS SHE PLEASES...
HEH! HEH! HEH!

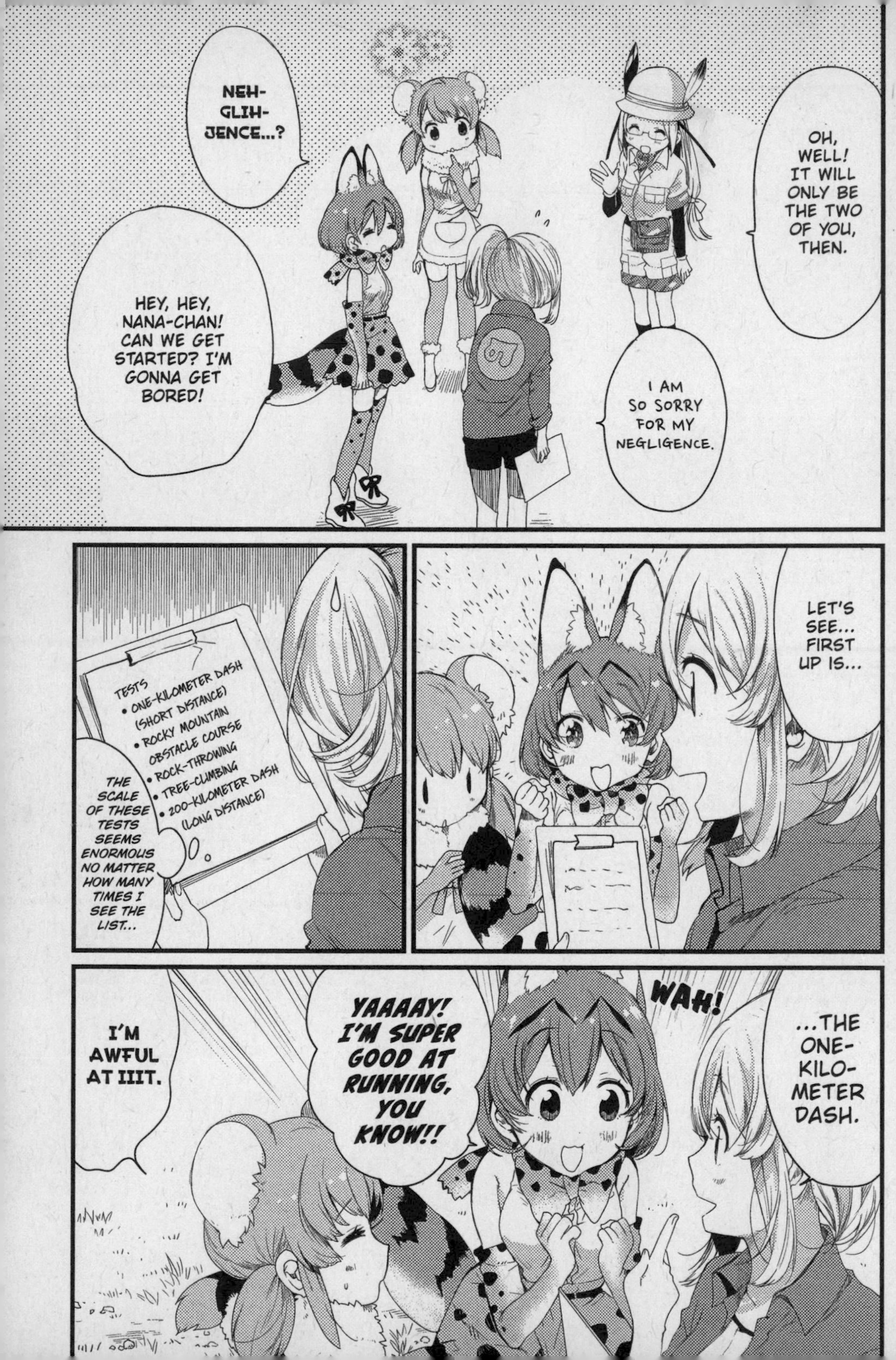
OH, WELL! IT WILL ONLY BE THE TWO OF YOU, THEN.
I AM SO SORRY FOR MY NEGLIGENCE.
NEH-GLIH-JENCE...?
HEY, HEY, NANA-CHAN! CAN WE GET STARTED? I'M GONNA GET BORED!
LET'S SEE... FIRST UP IS...
TESTS
• ONE-KILOMETER DASH (SHORT DISTANCE)
• ROCKY MOUNTAIN OBSTACLE COURSE
• ROCK-THROWING
• TREE-CLIMBING
• 200-KILOMETER DASH (LONG DISTANCE)
THE SCALE OF THESE TESTS SEEMS ENORMOUS NO MATTER HOW MANY TIMES I SEE THE LIST...
...THE ONE-KILO-METER DASH.
WAH!
YAAAAY! I'M SUPER GOOD AT RUNNING, YOU KNOW!!
I'M AWFUL AT IIIT.

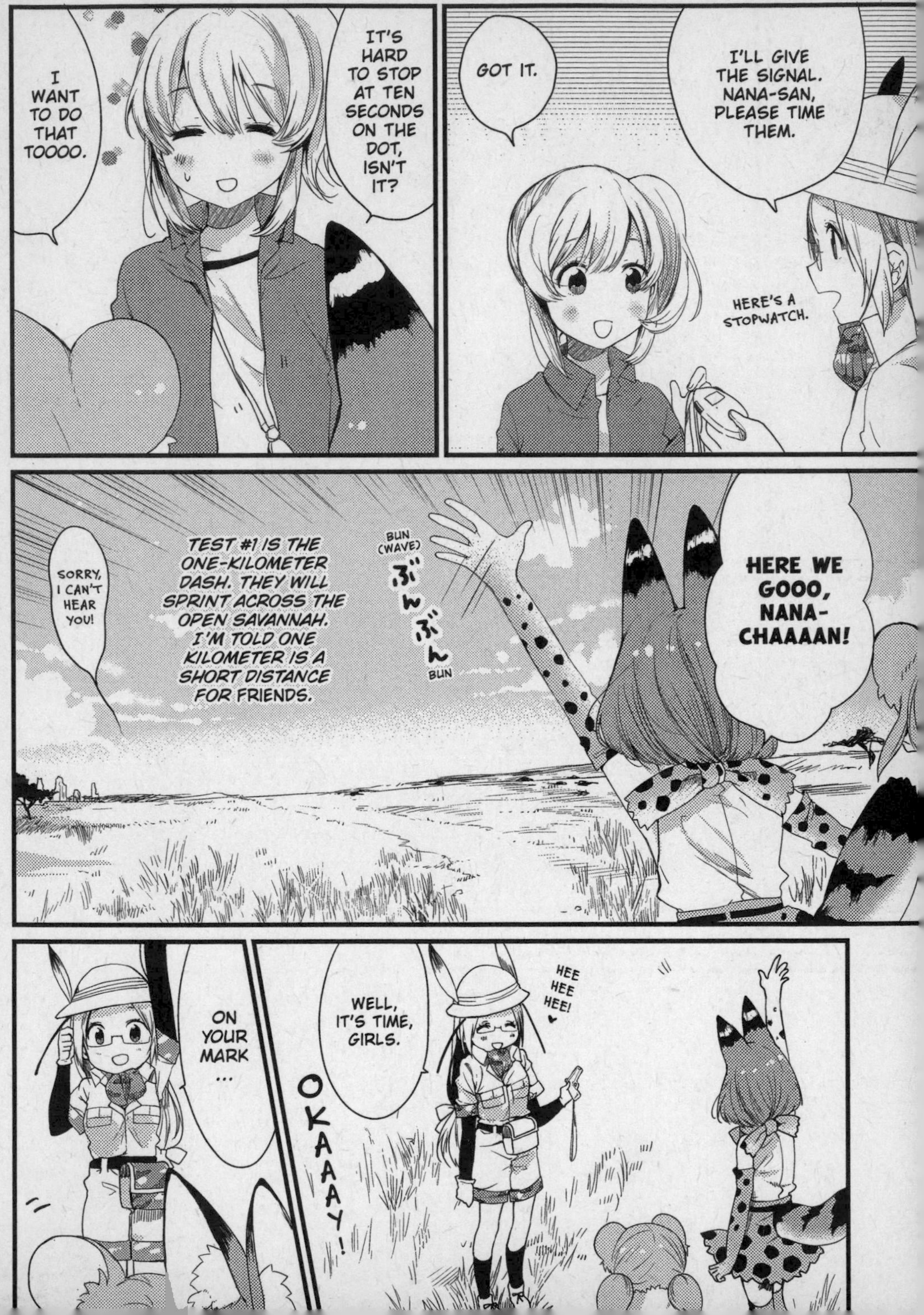
I'LL GIVE THE SIGNAL. NANA-SAN, PLEASE TIME THEM.
GOT IT.
HERE'S A STOPWATCH.
IT'S HARD TO STOP AT TEN SECONDS ON THE DOT, ISN'T IT?
I WANT TO DO THAT TOOOO.
HERE WE GOOO, NANA-CHAAAAN!
BUN (WAVE) ぶんぶん BUN
TEST #1 IS THE ONE-KILOMETER DASH. THEY WILL SPRINT ACROSS THE OPEN SAVANNAH. I'M TOLD ONE KILOMETER IS A SHORT DISTANCE FOR FRIENDS.
SORRY, I CAN'T HEAR YOU!
HEE HEE HEE!
WELL, IT'S TIME, GIRLS.
OKAAAY!
ON YOUR MARK ...

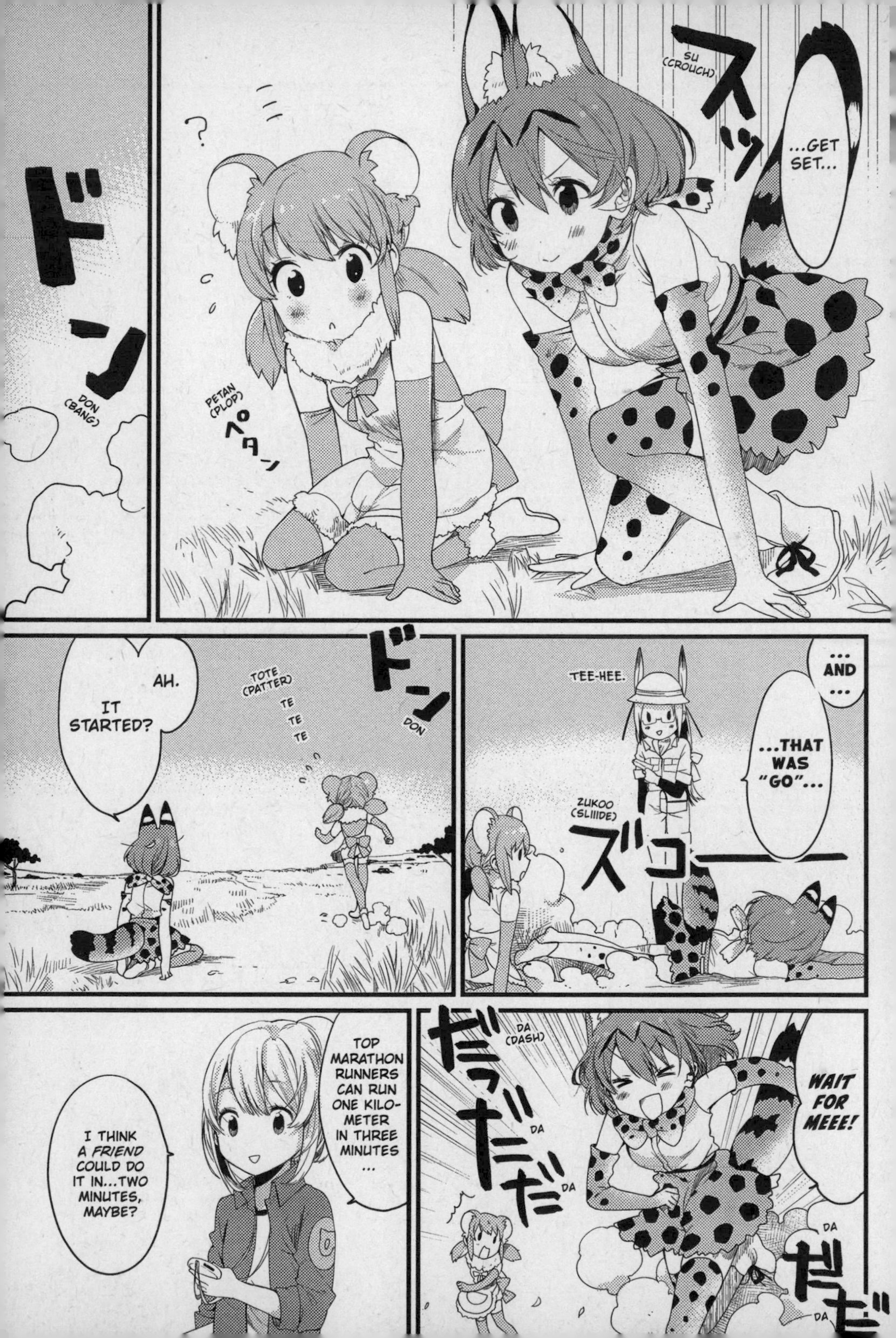
SU (CROUCH)
...GET SET...
PETAN (PLOP)
?
DON (BANG)
... AND ...
...THAT WAS "GO"...
TEE-HEE.
ZUKOO (SLIIIDE)
DON
TOTE (PATTER)
TE TE TE
AH. IT STARTED?
DA (DASH)
WAIT FOR MEEE!
DA
DA
DA
DA
TOP MARATHON RUNNERS CAN RUN ONE KILOMETER IN THREE MINUTES ...
I THINK A *FRIEND* COULD DO IT IN...TWO MINUTES, MAYBE?

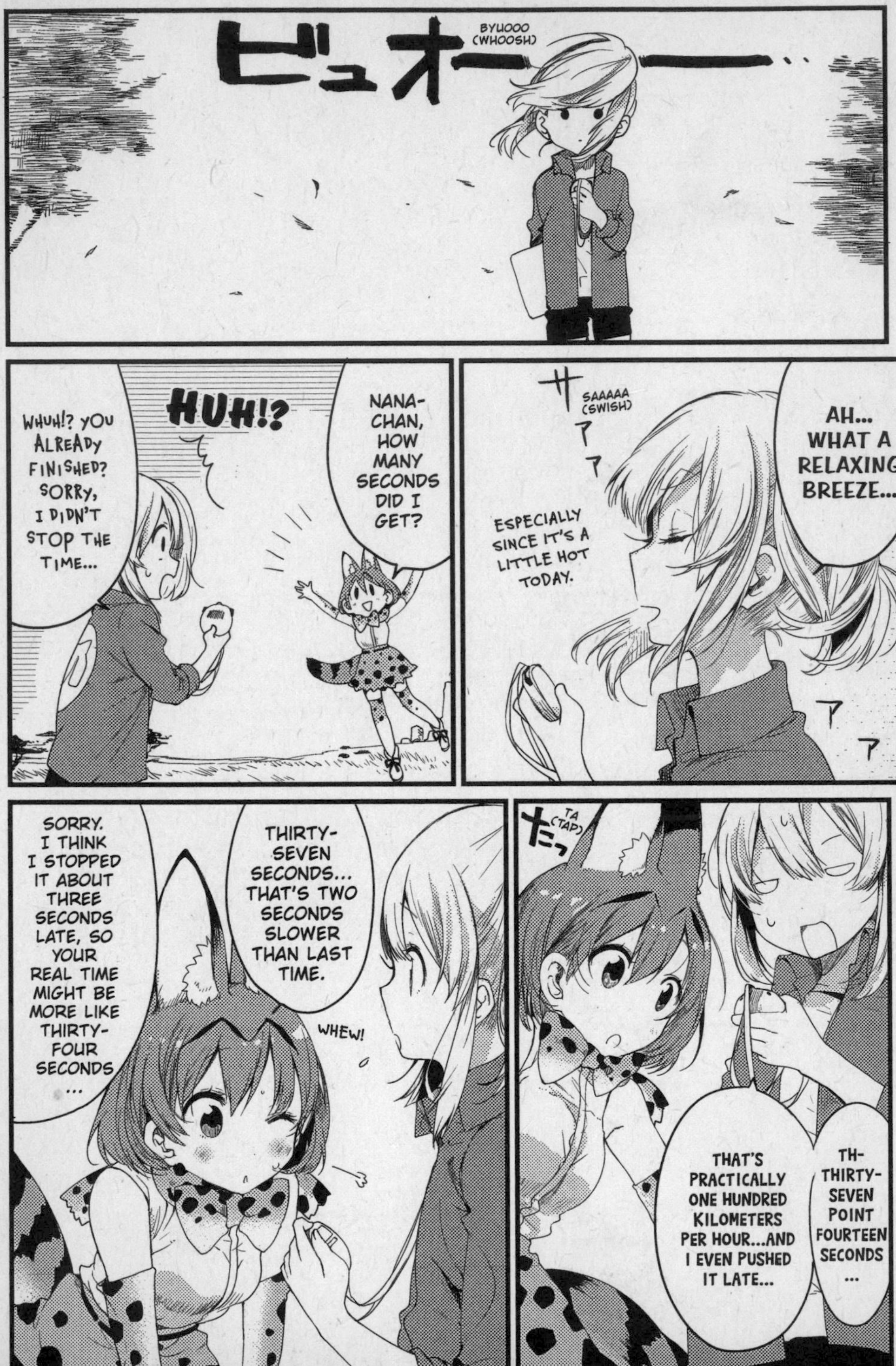
ビュオー
BYUOOO (WHOOSH)
サアアア
SAAAAA (SWISH)
AH... WHAT A RELAXING BREEZE...
ESPECIALLY SINCE IT'S A LITTLE HOT TODAY.
NANA-CHAN, HOW MANY SECONDS DID I GET?
HUH!?
WHUH!? YOU ALREADY FINISHED? SORRY, I DIDN'T STOP THE TIME...
たっ
TA (TAP)
TH-THIRTY-SEVEN POINT FOURTEEN SECONDS...
THAT'S PRACTICALLY ONE HUNDRED KILOMETERS PER HOUR...AND I EVEN PUSHED IT LATE...
THIRTY-SEVEN SECONDS... THAT'S TWO SECONDS SLOWER THAN LAST TIME.
WHEW!
SORRY. I THINK I STOPPED IT ABOUT THREE SECONDS LATE, SO YOUR REAL TIME MIGHT BE MORE LIKE THIRTY-FOUR SECONDS...

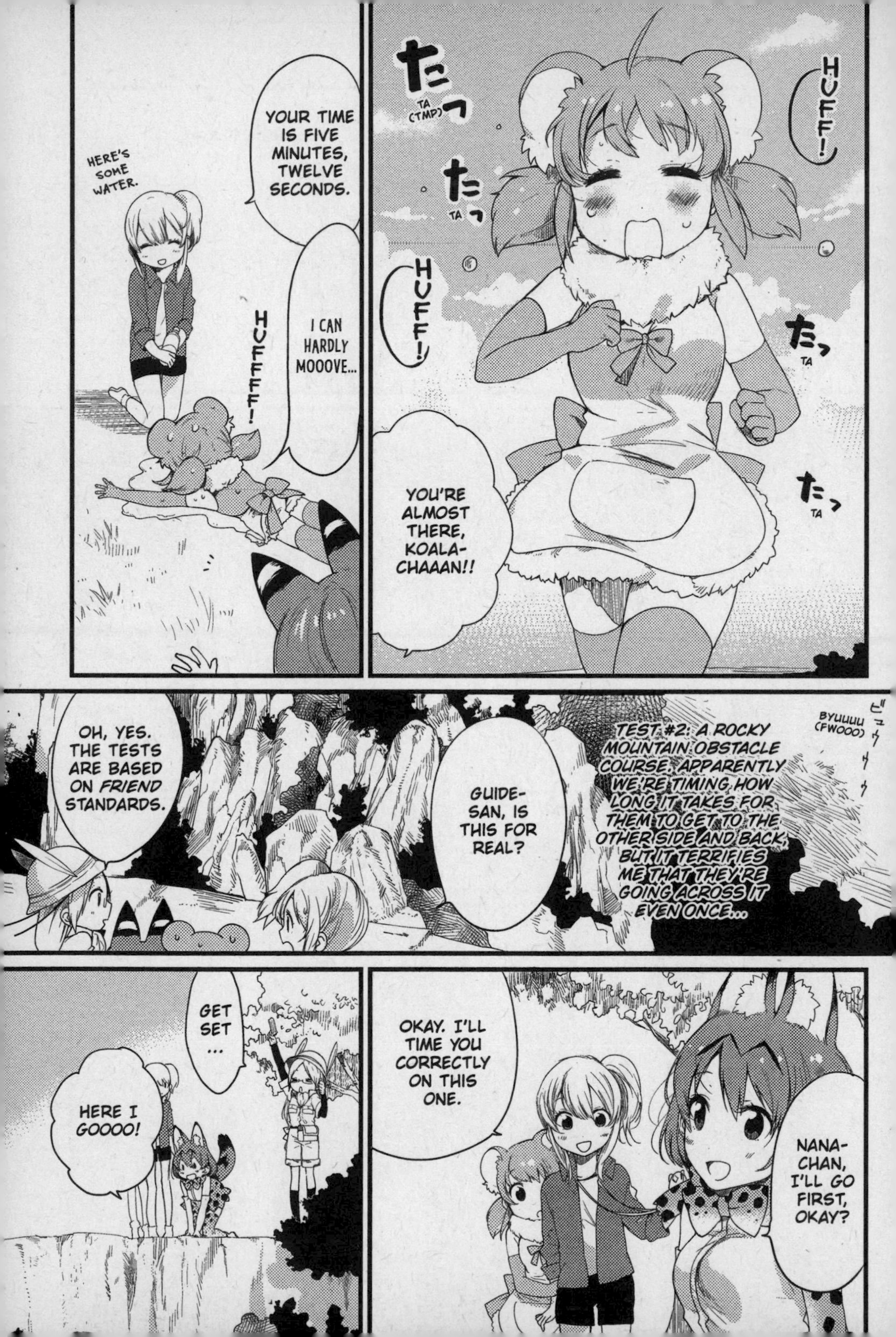
HUFF!
たっ
TA (TMP)
たっ
TA
HUFF!
たっ
TA
たっ
TA
YOU'RE ALMOST THERE, KOALA-CHAAAN!!
YOUR TIME IS FIVE MINUTES, TWELVE SECONDS.
HERE'S SOME WATER.
I CAN HARDLY MOOOVE...
HUFFFF!
ビュウウウ
BYUUUU (FWOOO)
TEST #2: A ROCKY MOUNTAIN OBSTACLE COURSE. APPARENTLY WE'RE TIMING HOW LONG IT TAKES FOR THEM TO GET TO THE OTHER SIDE AND BACK, BUT IT TERRIFIES ME THAT THEY'RE GOING ACROSS IT EVEN ONCE...
GUIDE-SAN, IS THIS FOR REAL?
OH, YES. THE TESTS ARE BASED ON *FRIEND* STANDARDS.
NANA-CHAN, I'LL GO FIRST, OKAY?
OKAY. I'LL TIME YOU CORRECTLY ON THIS ONE.
GET SET ...
HERE I GOOOO!

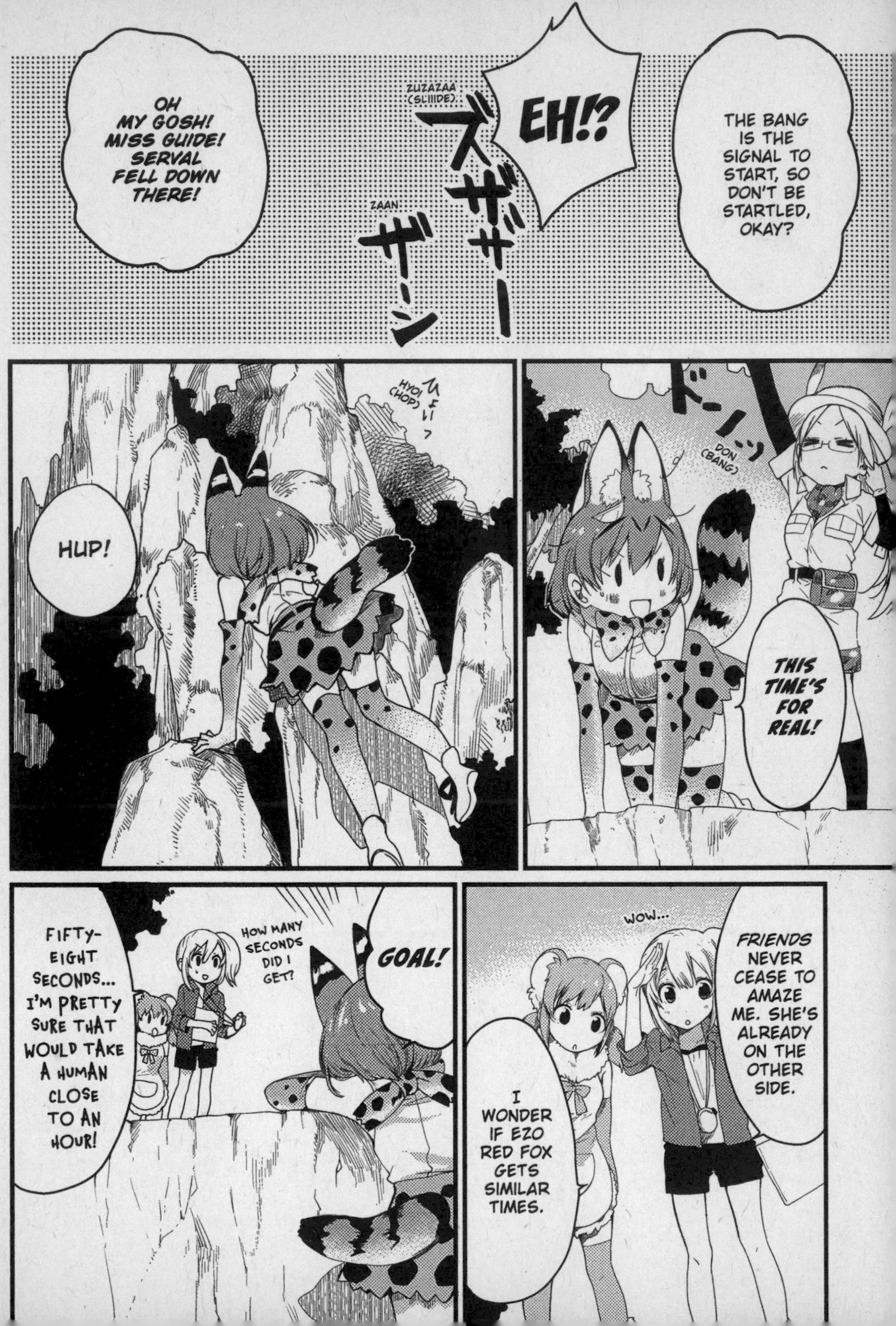
THE BANG IS THE SIGNAL TO START, SO DON'T BE STARTLED, OKAY?
EH!?
ZUZAZAA (SLIIIDE)
ズザザー
ZAAN
ザーン
OH MY GOSH! MISS GUIDE! SERVAL FELL DOWN THERE!
ドーンッ
DON (BANG)
THIS TIME'S FOR REAL!
ひょいっ
HYOI (HOP)
HUP!
FRIENDS NEVER CEASE TO AMAZE ME. SHE'S ALREADY ON THE OTHER SIDE.
WOW...
I WONDER IF EZO RED FOX GETS SIMILAR TIMES.
GOAL!
HOW MANY SECONDS DID I GET?
FIFTY-EIGHT SECONDS... I'M PRETTY SURE THAT WOULD TAKE A HUMAN CLOSE TO AN HOUR!

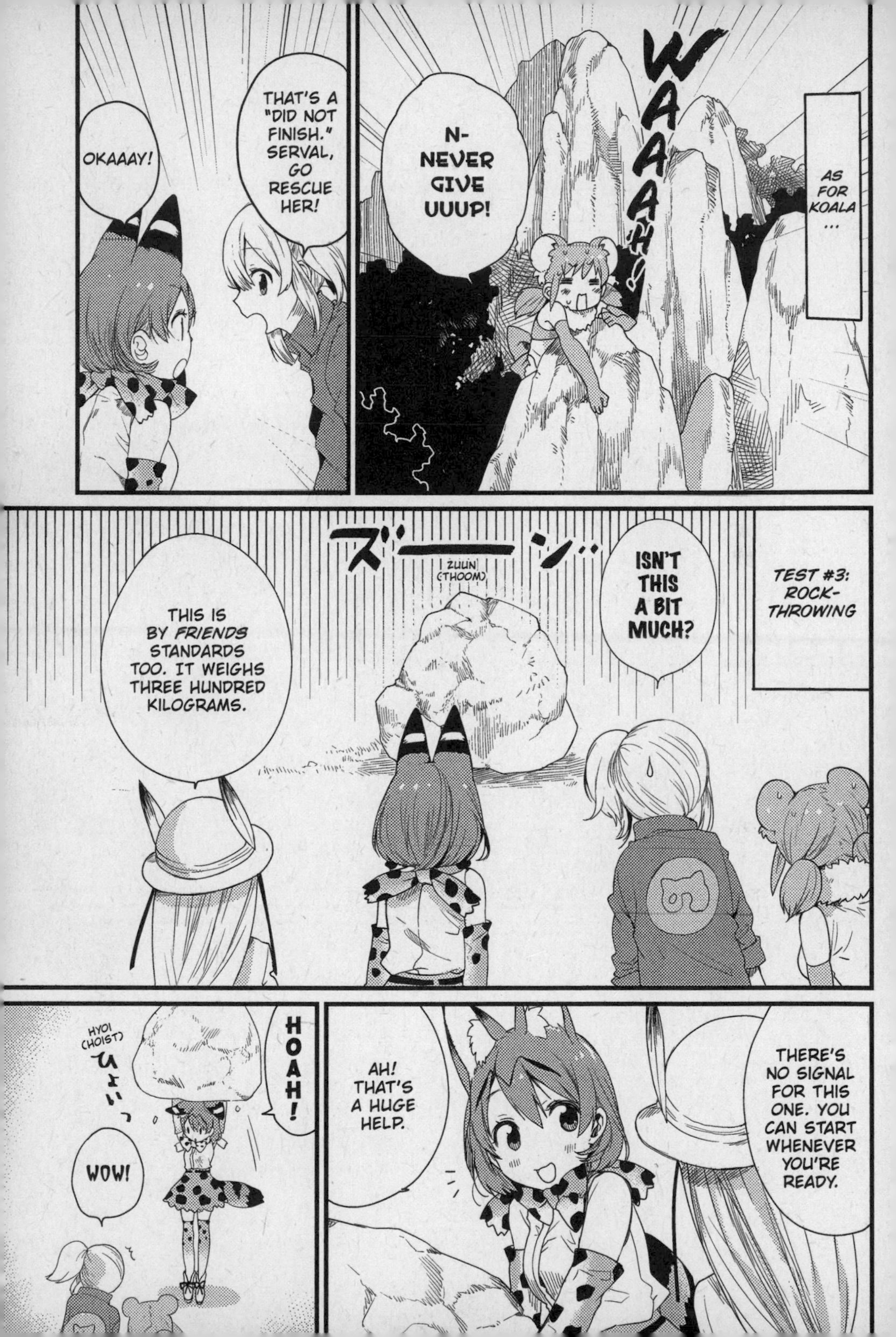
AS FOR KOALA ...
WAAAAH!
N-NEVER GIVE UUUP!
THAT'S A "DID NOT FINISH." SERVAL, GO RESCUE HER!
OKAAAY!
TEST #3: ROCK-THROWING
ISN'T THIS A BIT MUCH?
ズーン
ZUUN (THOOM)
THIS IS BY FRIENDS STANDARDS TOO. IT WEIGHS THREE HUNDRED KILOGRAMS.
THERE'S NO SIGNAL FOR THIS ONE. YOU CAN START WHENEVER YOU'RE READY.
AH! THAT'S A HUGE HELP.
HOAH!
ひょいっ
HYOI (HOIST)
WOW!

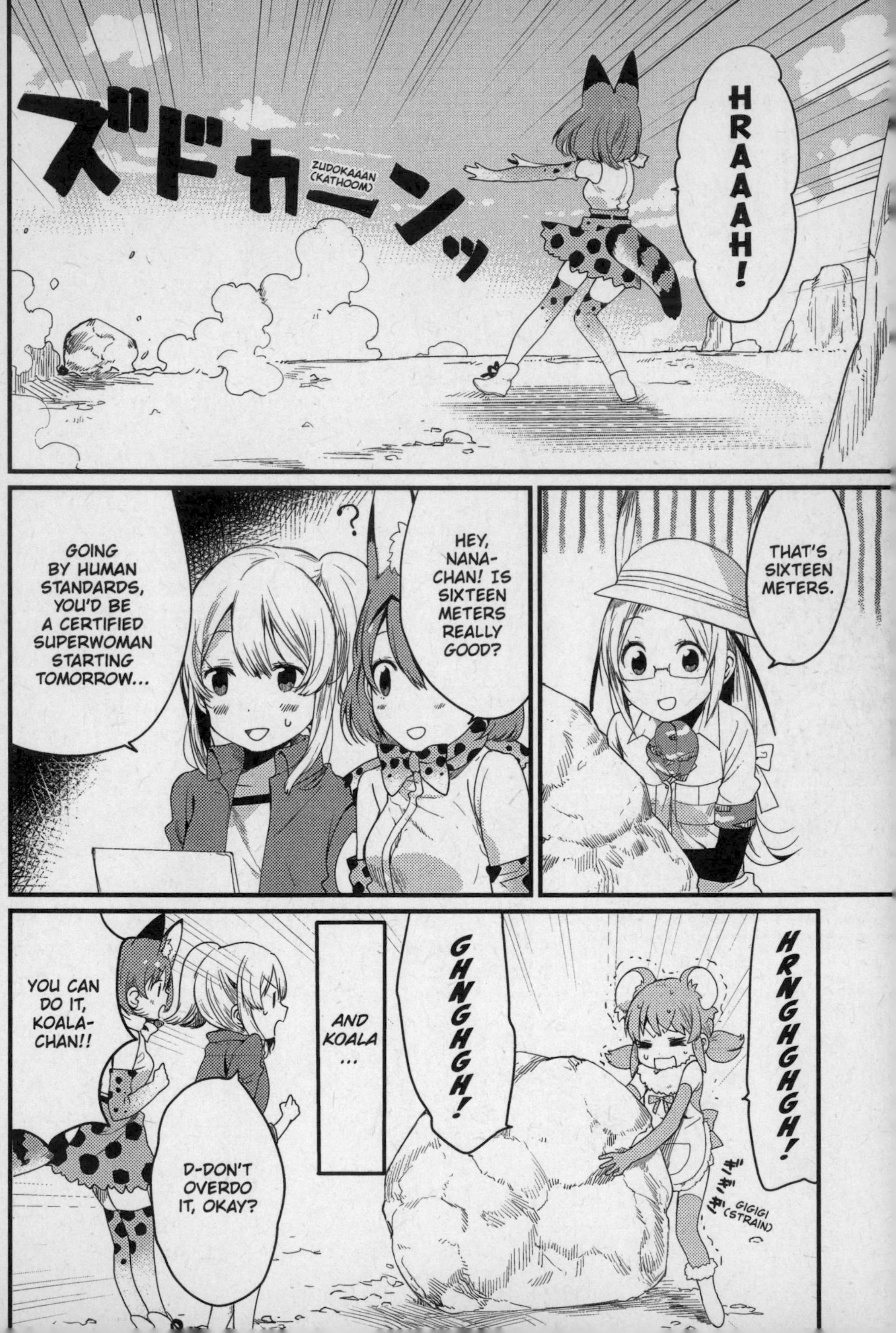
HRAAAH!
ズドカーンッ
ZUDOKAAAN (KATHOOM)
THAT'S SIXTEEN METERS.
?
HEY, NANA-CHAN! IS SIXTEEN METERS REALLY GOOD?
GOING BY HUMAN STANDARDS, YOU'D BE A CERTIFIED SUPERWOMAN STARTING TOMORROW...
HRNGHGHGH!
ギギギ
GIGIGI (STRAIN)
GHNGHGH!
AND KOALA...
YOU CAN DO IT, KOALA-CHAN!!
D-DON'T OVERDO IT, OKAY?

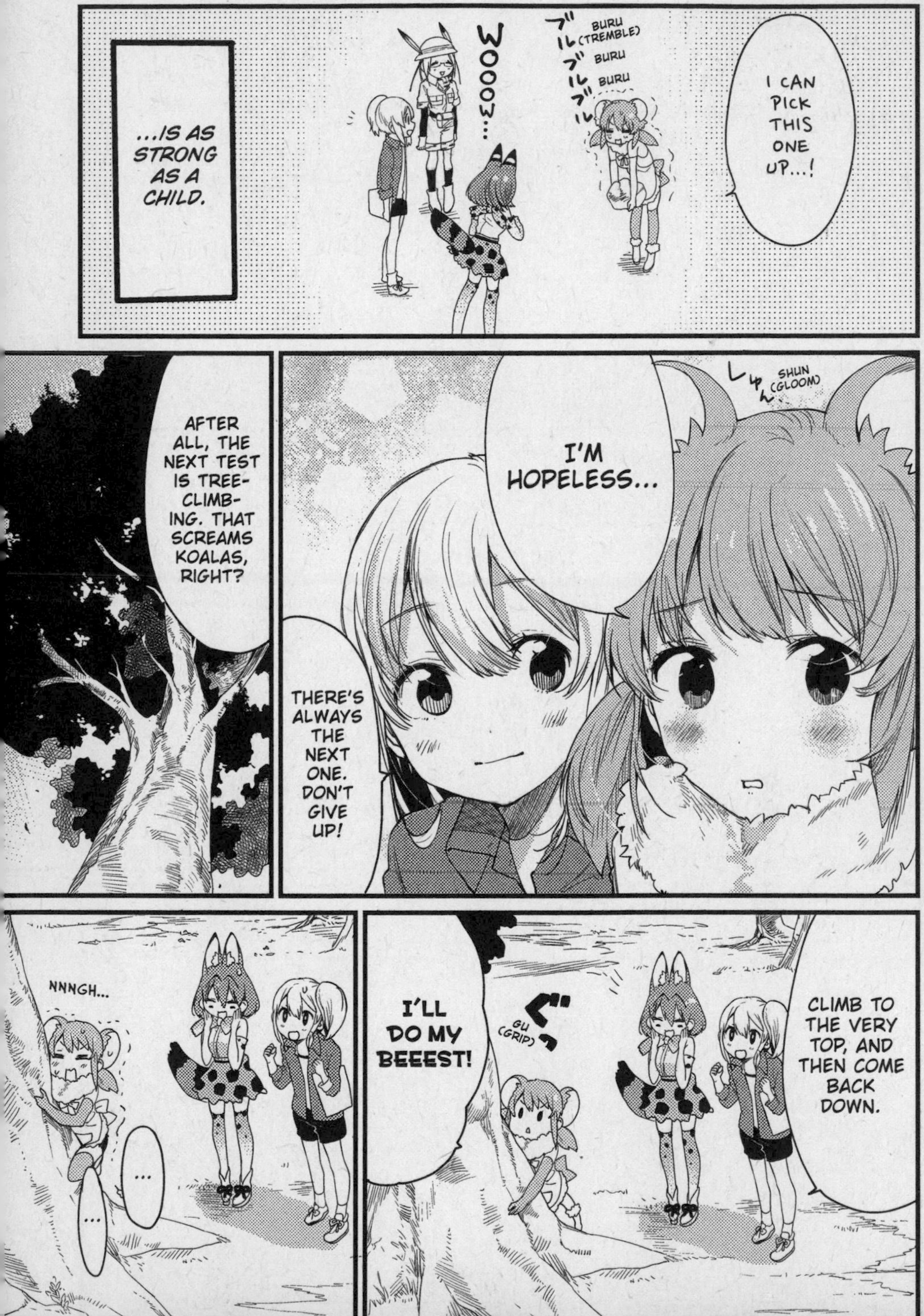
I CAN PICK THIS ONE UP...!
ブル BURU (TREMBLE)
ブル BURU
ブル BURU
WOOOW...
...IS AS STRONG AS A CHILD.
しゅん SHUN (GLOOM)
I'M HOPELESS...
THERE'S ALWAYS THE NEXT ONE. DON'T GIVE UP!
AFTER ALL, THE NEXT TEST IS TREE-CLIMBING. THAT SCREAMS KOALAS, RIGHT?
CLIMB TO THE VERY TOP, AND THEN COME BACK DOWN.
ぐ GU (GRIP)
I'LL DO MY BEEEST!
NNNGH...
...
...

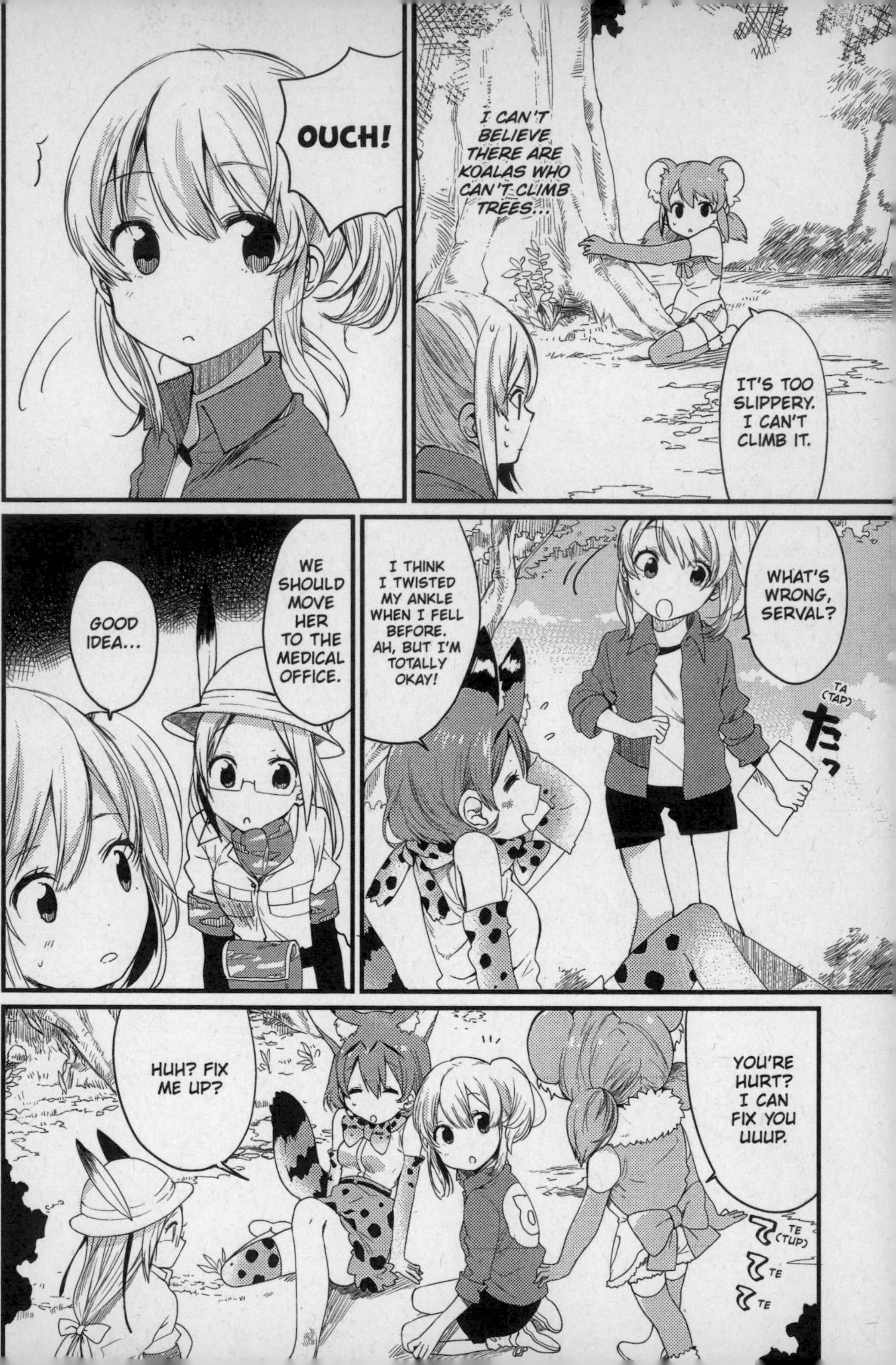
I CAN'T BELIEVE THERE ARE KOALAS WHO CAN'T CLIMB TREES...
IT'S TOO SLIPPERY. I CAN'T CLIMB IT.
OUCH!
WHAT'S WRONG, SERVAL?
TA (TAP)
たっ
I THINK I TWISTED MY ANKLE WHEN I FELL BEFORE. AH, BUT I'M TOTALLY OKAY!
WE SHOULD MOVE HER TO THE MEDICAL OFFICE.
GOOD IDEA...
YOU'RE HURT? I CAN FIX YOU UUUP.
TE (TUP)
TE
TE
HUH? FIX ME UP?

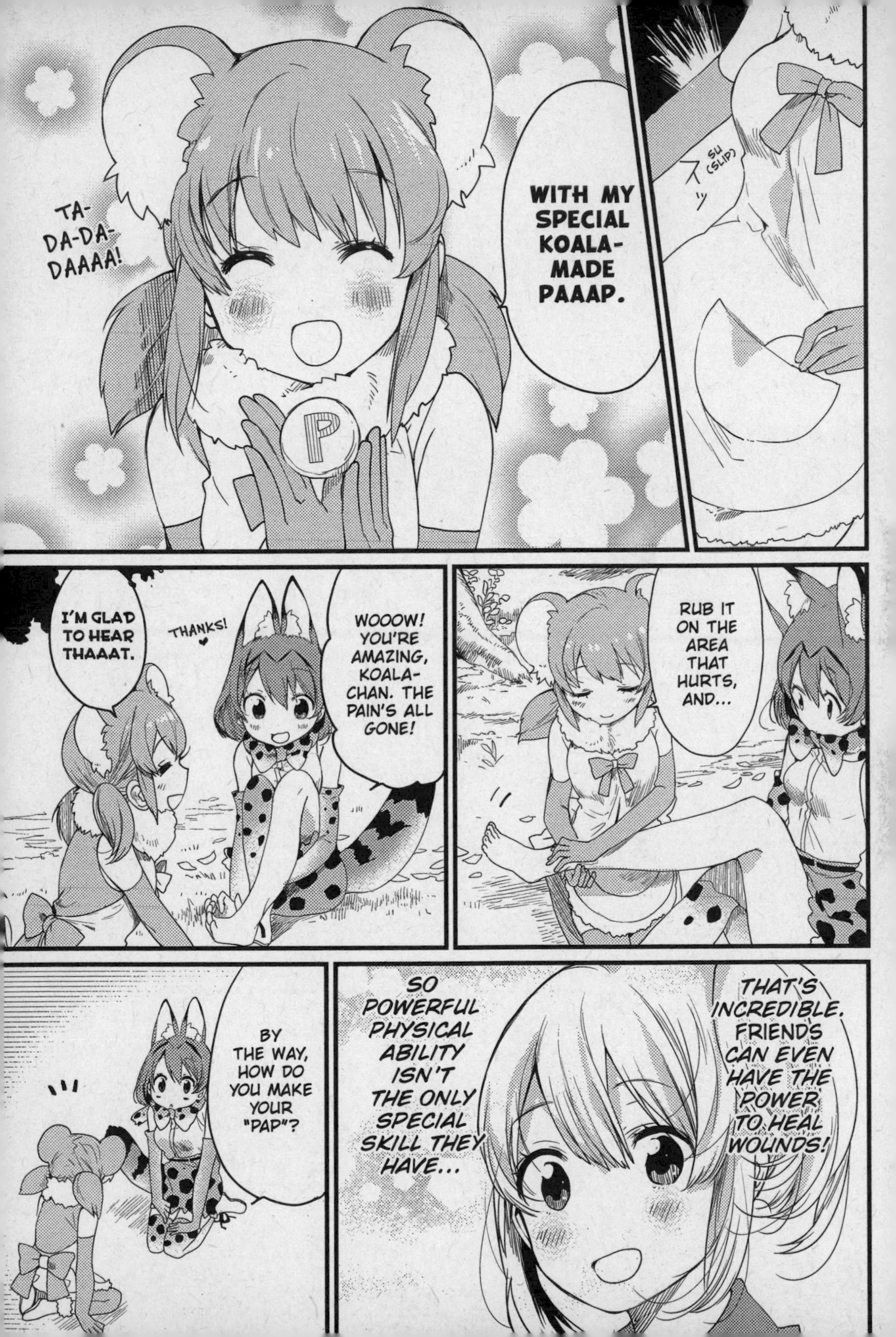
SU (SLIP)
スッ
WITH MY SPECIAL KOALA-MADE PAAAP.
TA-DA-DA-DAAAA!
RUB IT ON THE AREA THAT HURTS, AND...
WOOOW! YOU'RE AMAZING, KOALA-CHAN. THE PAIN'S ALL GONE!
THANKS!
I'M GLAD TO HEAR THAAAT.
THAT'S INCREDIBLE. FRIENDS CAN EVEN HAVE THE POWER TO HEAL WOUNDS!
SO POWERFUL PHYSICAL ABILITY ISN'T THE ONLY SPECIAL SKILL THEY HAVE...
BY THE WAY, HOW DO YOU MAKE YOUR "PAP"?

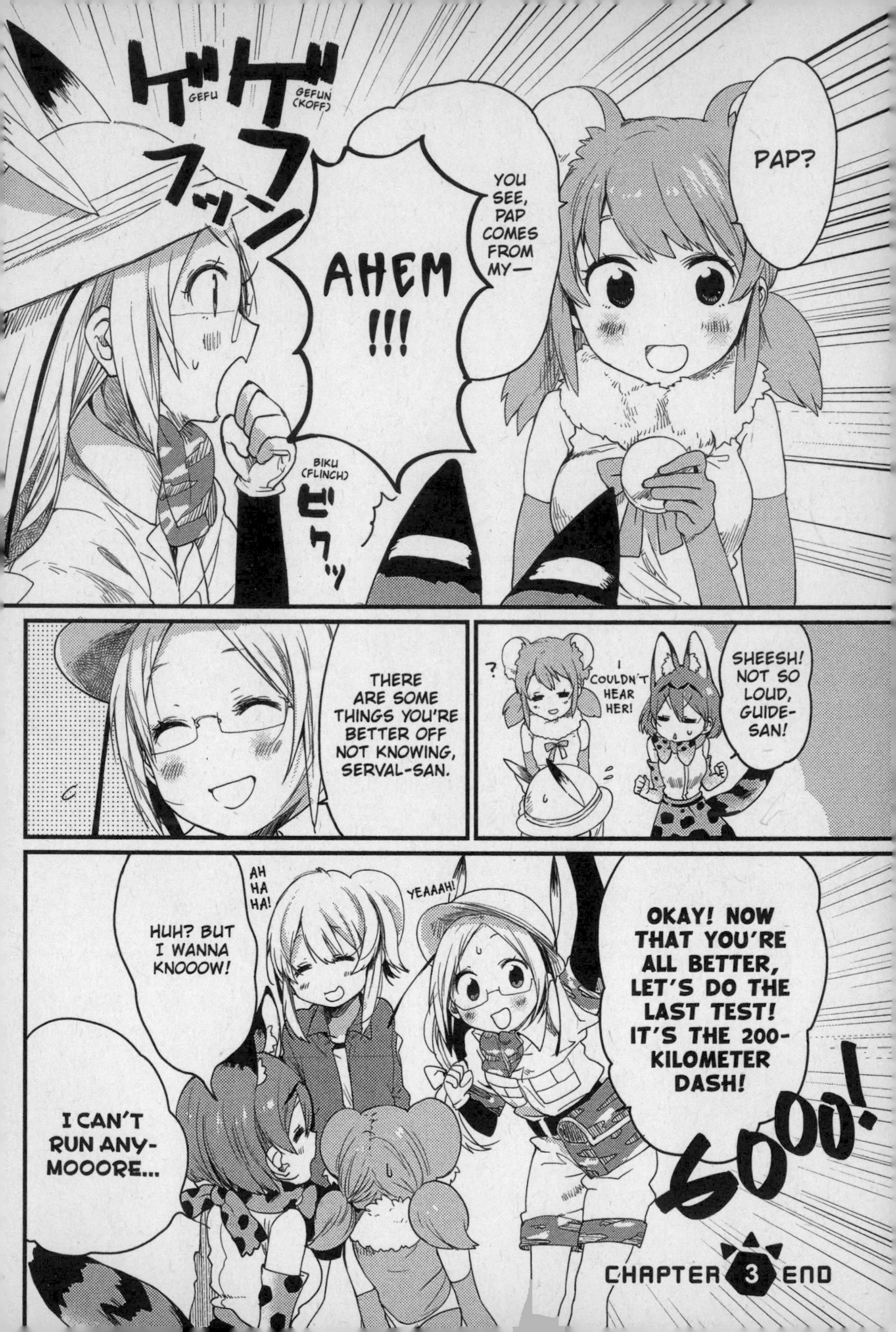
PAP?
YOU SEE, PAP COMES FROM MY—
GEFU GEFUN (KOFF)
AHEM !!!
BIKU (FLINCH)
ビクッ
SHEESH! NOT SO LOUD, GUIDE-SAN!
I COULDN'T HEAR HER!
?
THERE ARE SOME THINGS YOU'RE BETTER OFF NOT KNOWING, SERVAL-SAN.
OKAY! NOW THAT YOU'RE ALL BETTER, LET'S DO THE LAST TEST! IT'S THE 200-KILOMETER DASH!
GOOO!
YEAAAH!
AH HA HA!
HUH? BUT I WANNA KNOOOW!
I CAN'T RUN ANY-MOOORE...
CHAPTER 3 END

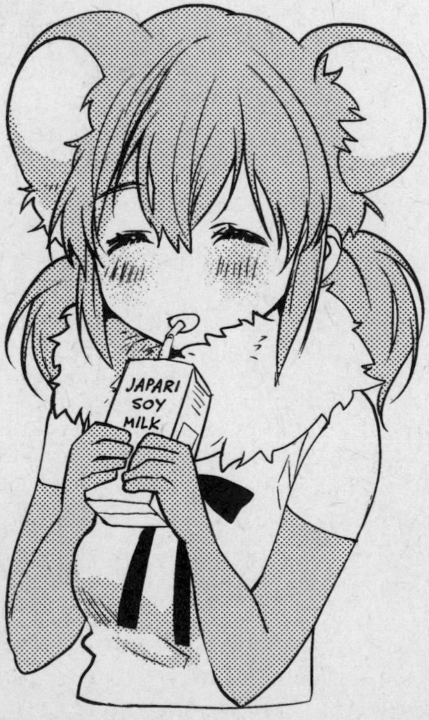
JAPARI
SOY
MILK

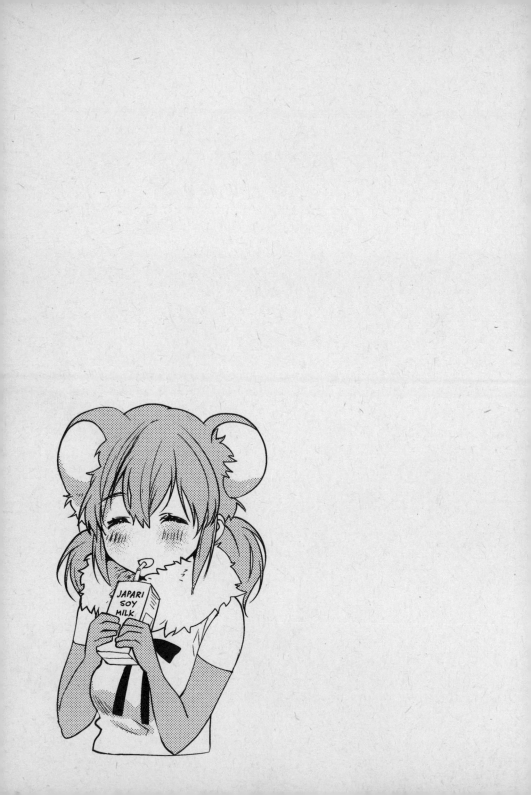

KEMONO
FRIENDS
WELCOME TO
JAPARI PARK!

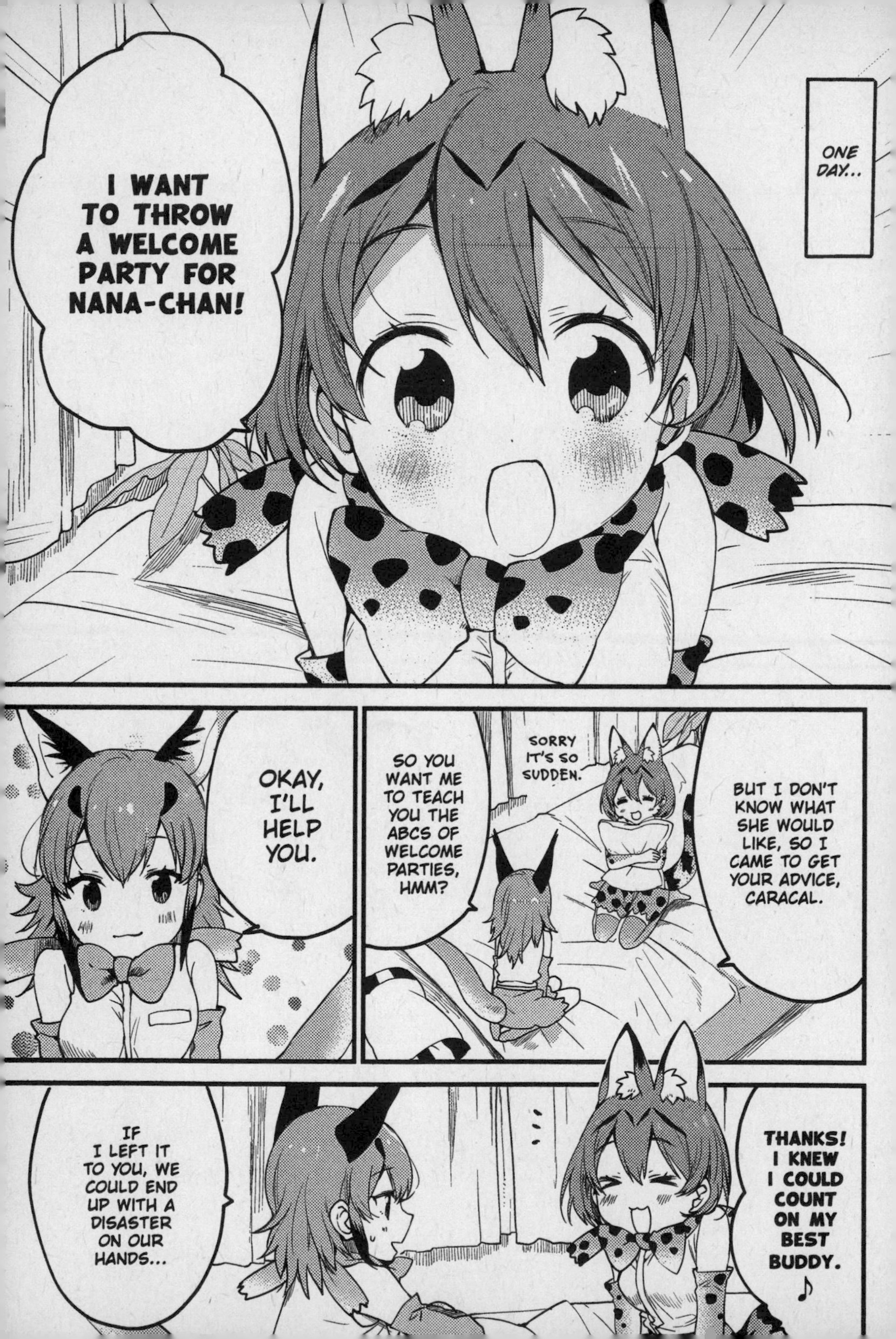
ONE DAY...
I WANT TO THROW A WELCOME PARTY FOR NANA-CHAN!
SORRY IT'S SO SUDDEN.
BUT I DON'T KNOW WHAT SHE WOULD LIKE, SO I CAME TO GET YOUR ADVICE, CARACAL.
SO YOU WANT ME TO TEACH YOU THE ABCS OF WELCOME PARTIES, HMM?
OKAY, I'LL HELP YOU.
THANKS! I KNEW I COULD COUNT ON MY BEST BUDDY. ♪
...
IF I LEFT IT TO YOU, WE COULD END UP WITH A DISASTER ON OUR HANDS...

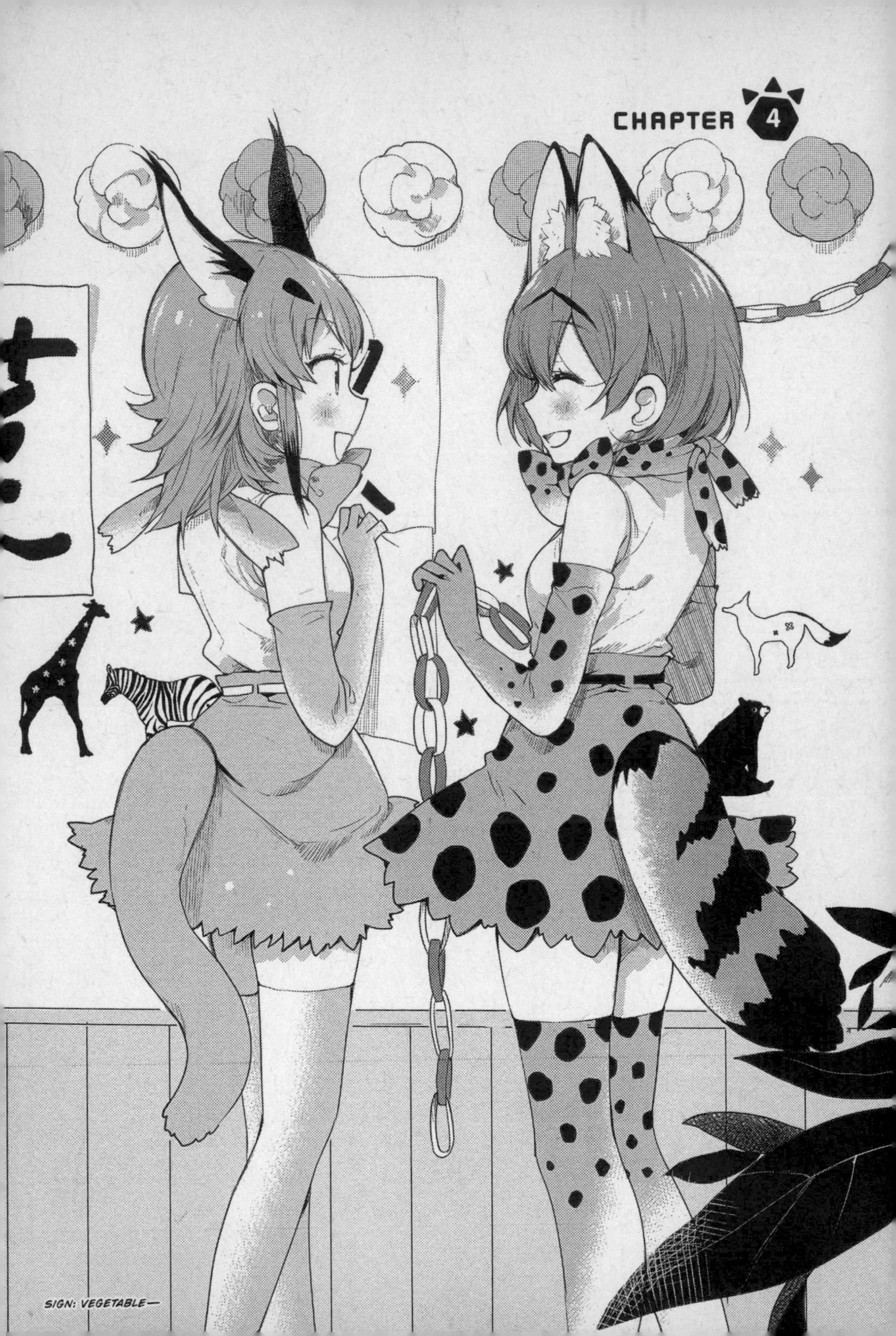
CHAPTER 4
SIGN: VEGETABLE—

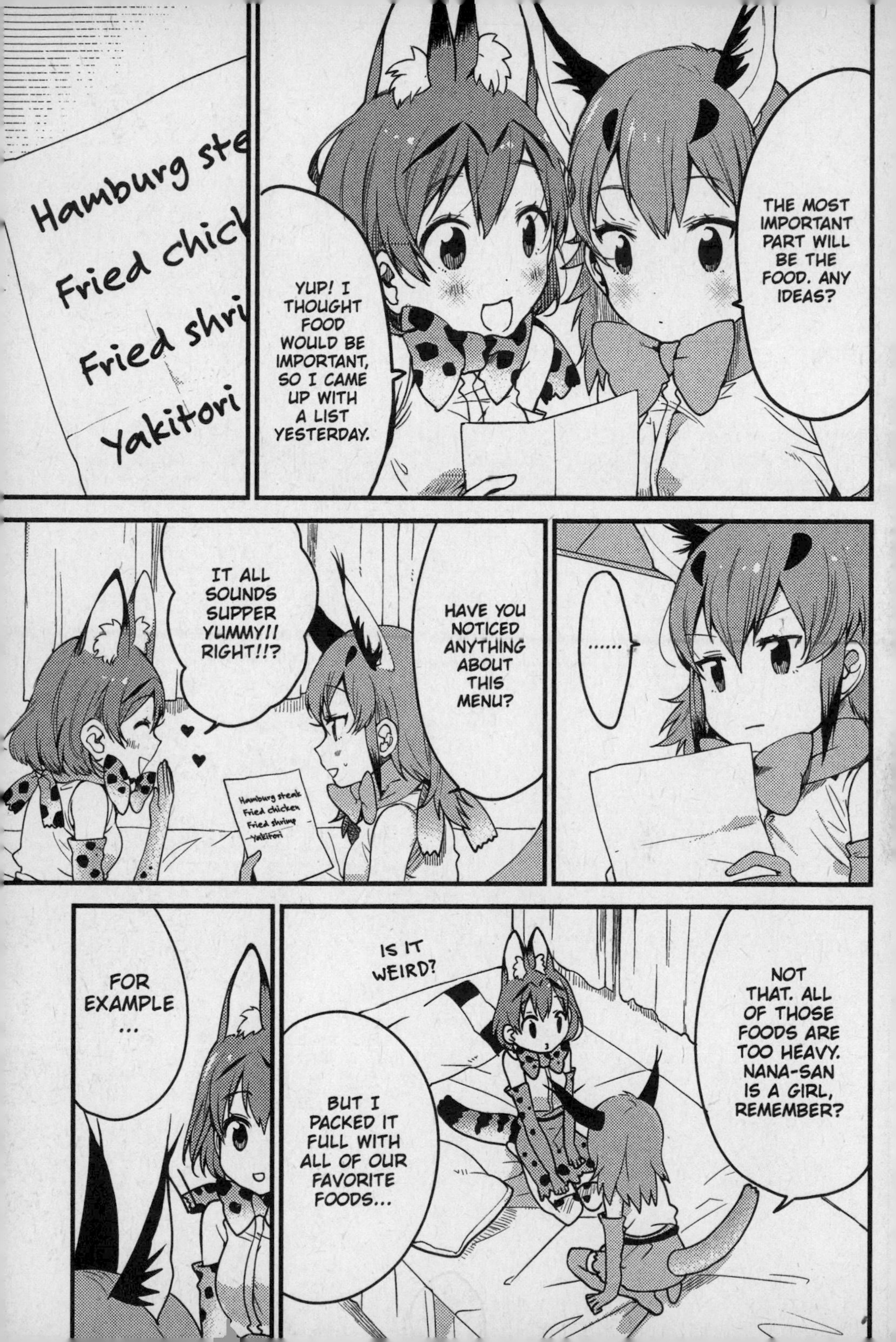
THE MOST IMPORTANT PART WILL BE THE FOOD. ANY IDEAS?
YUP! I THOUGHT FOOD WOULD BE IMPORTANT, SO I CAME UP WITH A LIST YESTERDAY.
Hamburg ste
Fried chick
Fried shri
Yakitori
......
HAVE YOU NOTICED ANYTHING ABOUT THIS MENU?
IT ALL SOUNDS SUPPER YUMMY!! RIGHT!!?
Hamburg steak
Fried chicken
Fried shrimp
Yakitori
IS IT WEIRD?
NOT THAT. ALL OF THOSE FOODS ARE TOO HEAVY. NANA-SAN IS A GIRL, REMEMBER?
BUT I PACKED IT FULL WITH ALL OF OUR FAVORITE FOODS...
FOR EXAMPLE ...

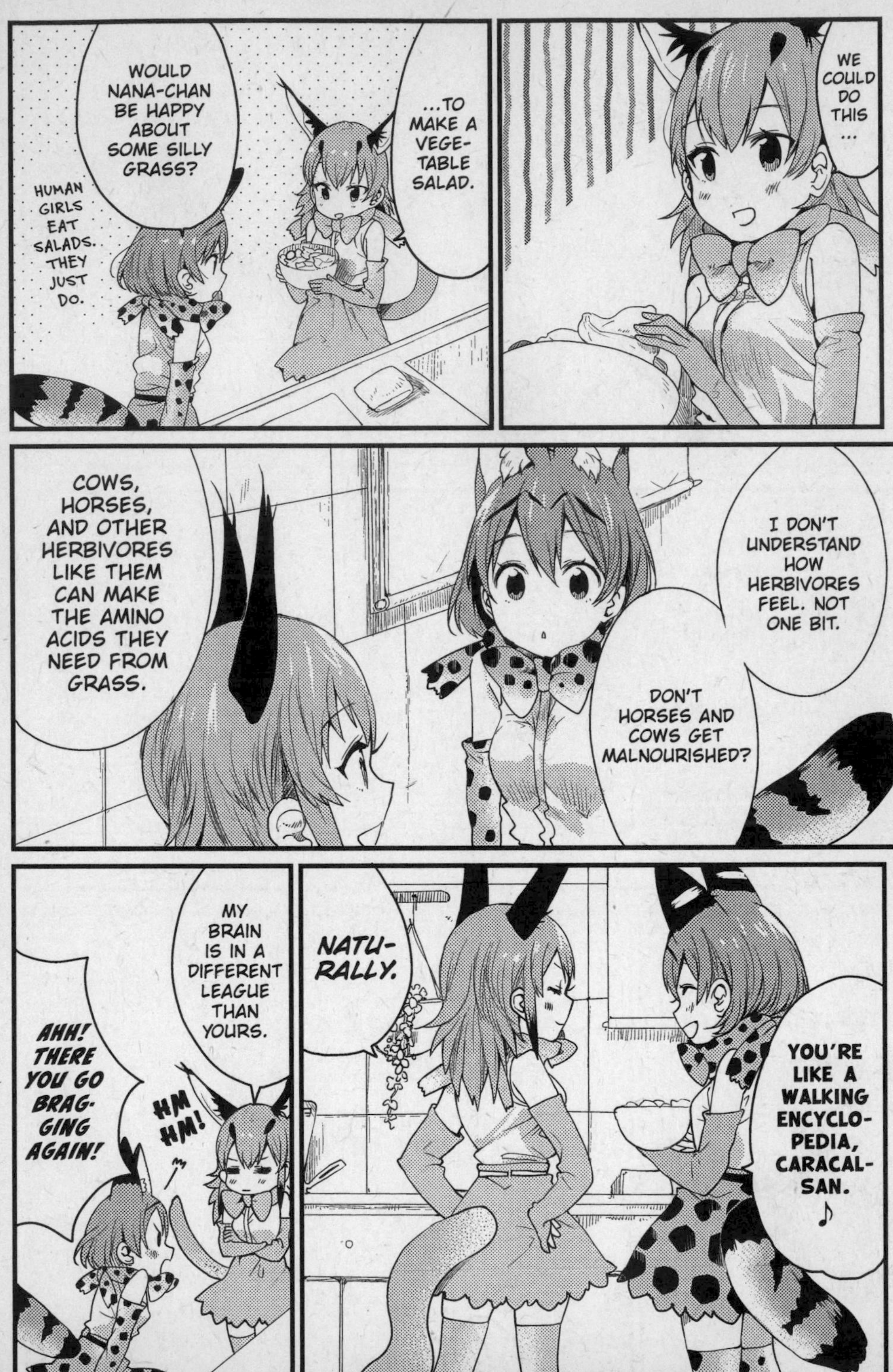
WE COULD DO THIS...
...TO MAKE A VEGETABLE SALAD.
WOULD NANA-CHAN BE HAPPY ABOUT SOME SILLY GRASS?
HUMAN GIRLS EAT SALADS. THEY JUST DO.
I DON'T UNDERSTAND HOW HERBIVORES FEEL. NOT ONE BIT.
DON'T HORSES AND COWS GET MALNOURISHED?
COWS, HORSES, AND OTHER HERBIVORES LIKE THEM CAN MAKE THE AMINO ACIDS THEY NEED FROM GRASS.
YOU'RE LIKE A WALKING ENCYCLOPEDIA, CARACAL-SAN. ♪
NATURALLY.
MY BRAIN IS IN A DIFFERENT LEAGUE THAN YOURS.
HM HM!
AHH! THERE YOU GO BRAGGING AGAIN!

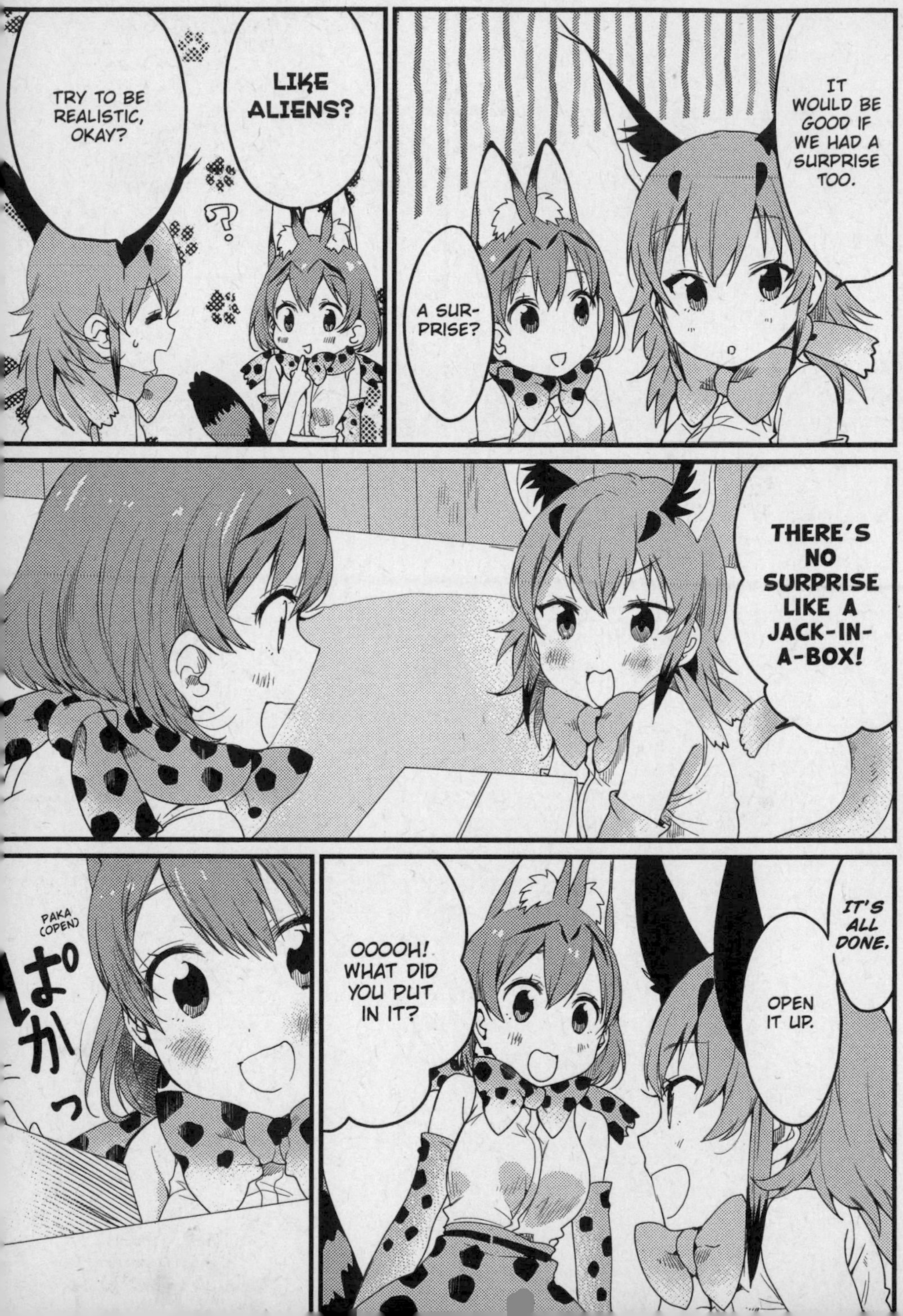
IT WOULD BE GOOD IF WE HAD A SURPRISE TOO.
A SUR-PRISE?
LIKE ALIENS?
TRY TO BE REALISTIC, OKAY?
THERE'S NO SURPRISE LIKE A JACK-IN-A-BOX!
IT'S ALL DONE.
OPEN IT UP.
OOOOH! WHAT DID YOU PUT IN IT?
ぱかっ
PAKA (OPEN)

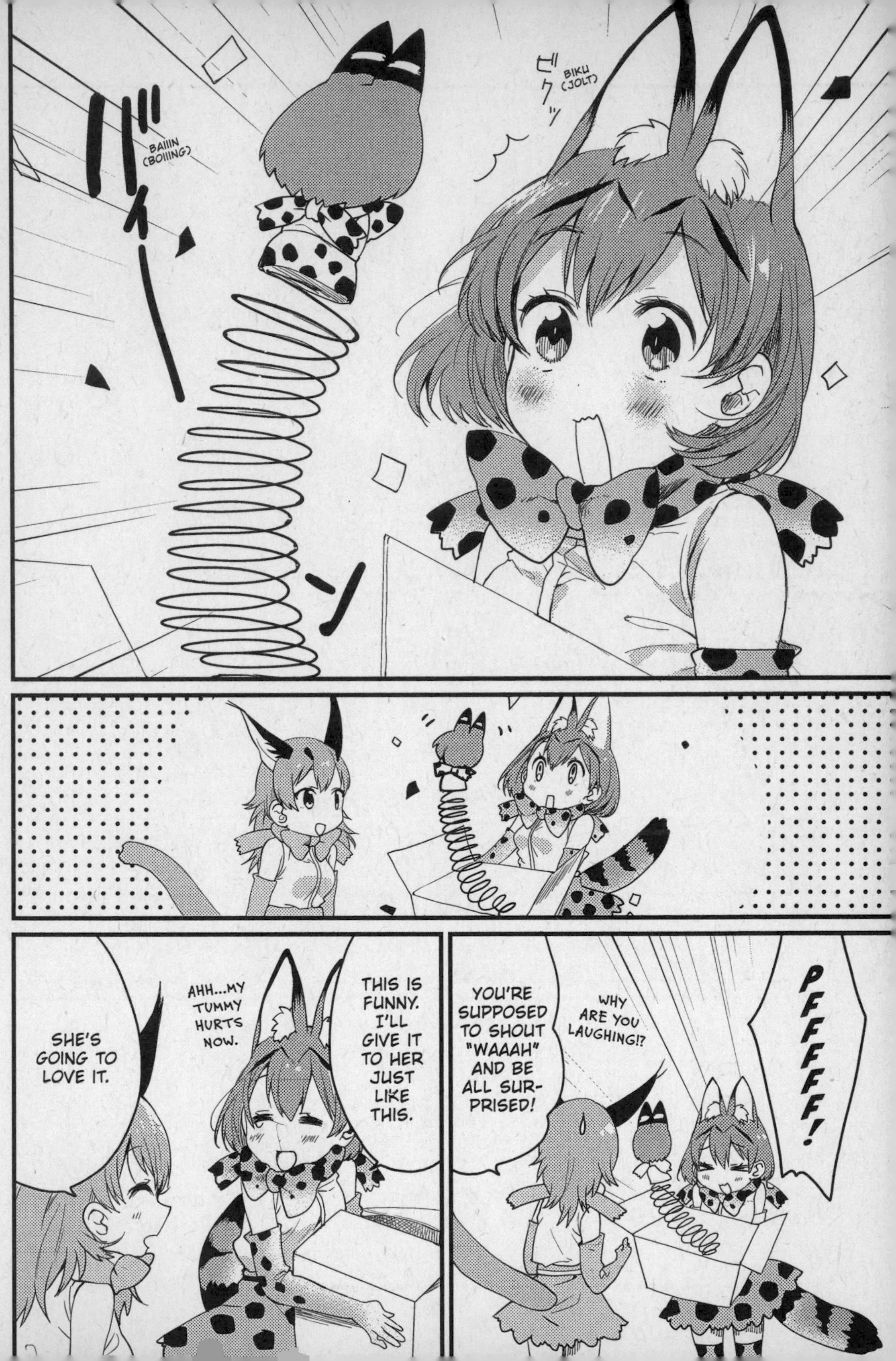
ビクッ
BIKU (JOLT)
バイーン
BAIIIN (BOIIING)
PFFFFF!
WHY ARE YOU LAUGHING!?
YOU'RE SUPPOSED TO SHOUT "WAAAH" AND BE ALL SUR-PRISED!
THIS IS FUNNY. I'LL GIVE IT TO HER JUST LIKE THIS.
AHH...MY TUMMY HURTS NOW.
SHE'S GOING TO LOVE IT.

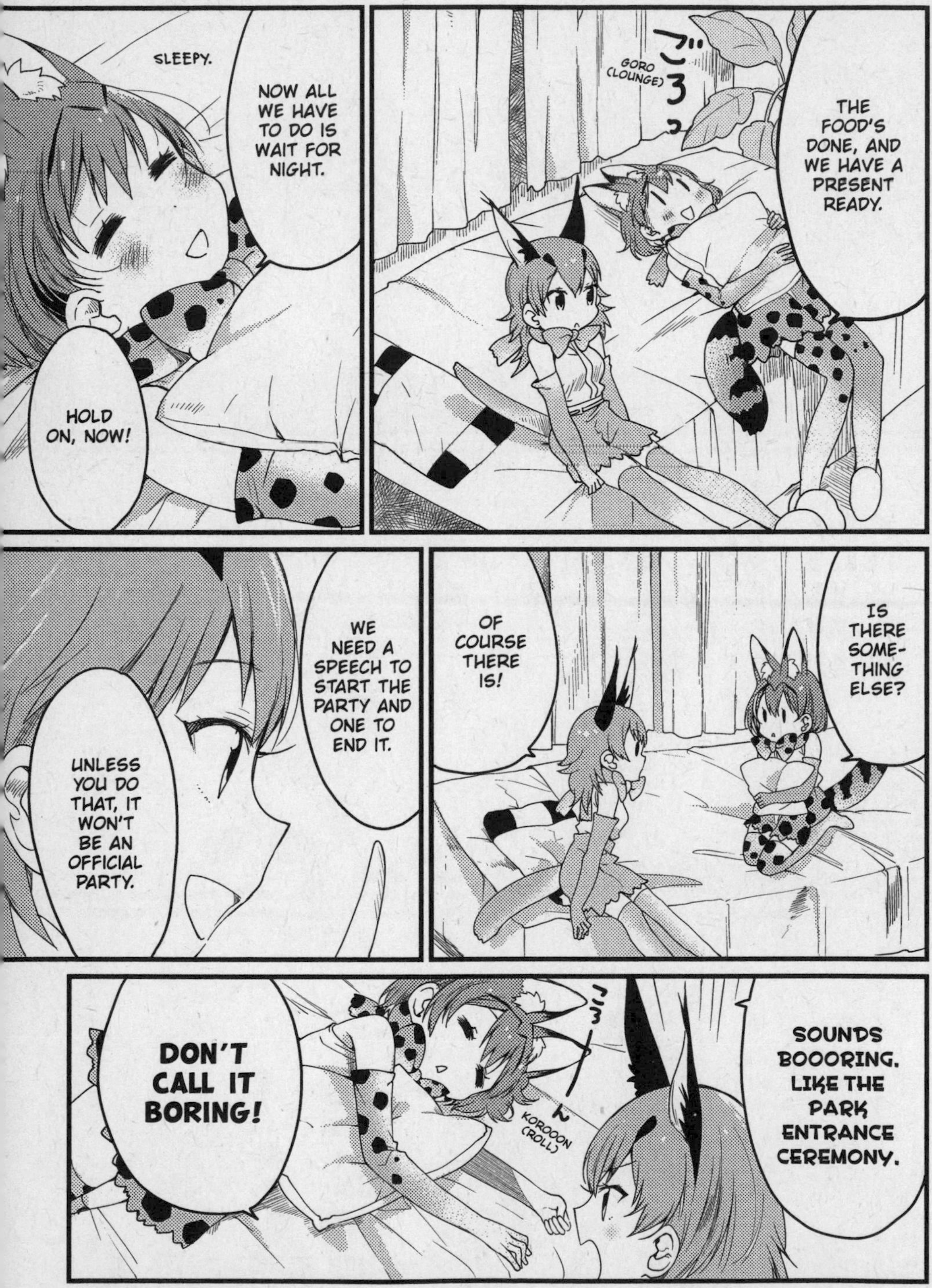
ごろっ
GORO (LOUNGE)
THE FOOD'S DONE, AND WE HAVE A PRESENT READY.
NOW ALL WE HAVE TO DO IS WAIT FOR NIGHT.
SLEEPY.
HOLD ON, NOW!
IS THERE SOME-THING ELSE?
OF COURSE THERE IS!
WE NEED A SPEECH TO START THE PARTY AND ONE TO END IT.
UNLESS YOU DO THAT, IT WON'T BE AN OFFICIAL PARTY.
SOUNDS BOOORING. LIKE THE PARK ENTRANCE CEREMONY.
KOROOON (ROLL)
DON'T CALL IT BORING!

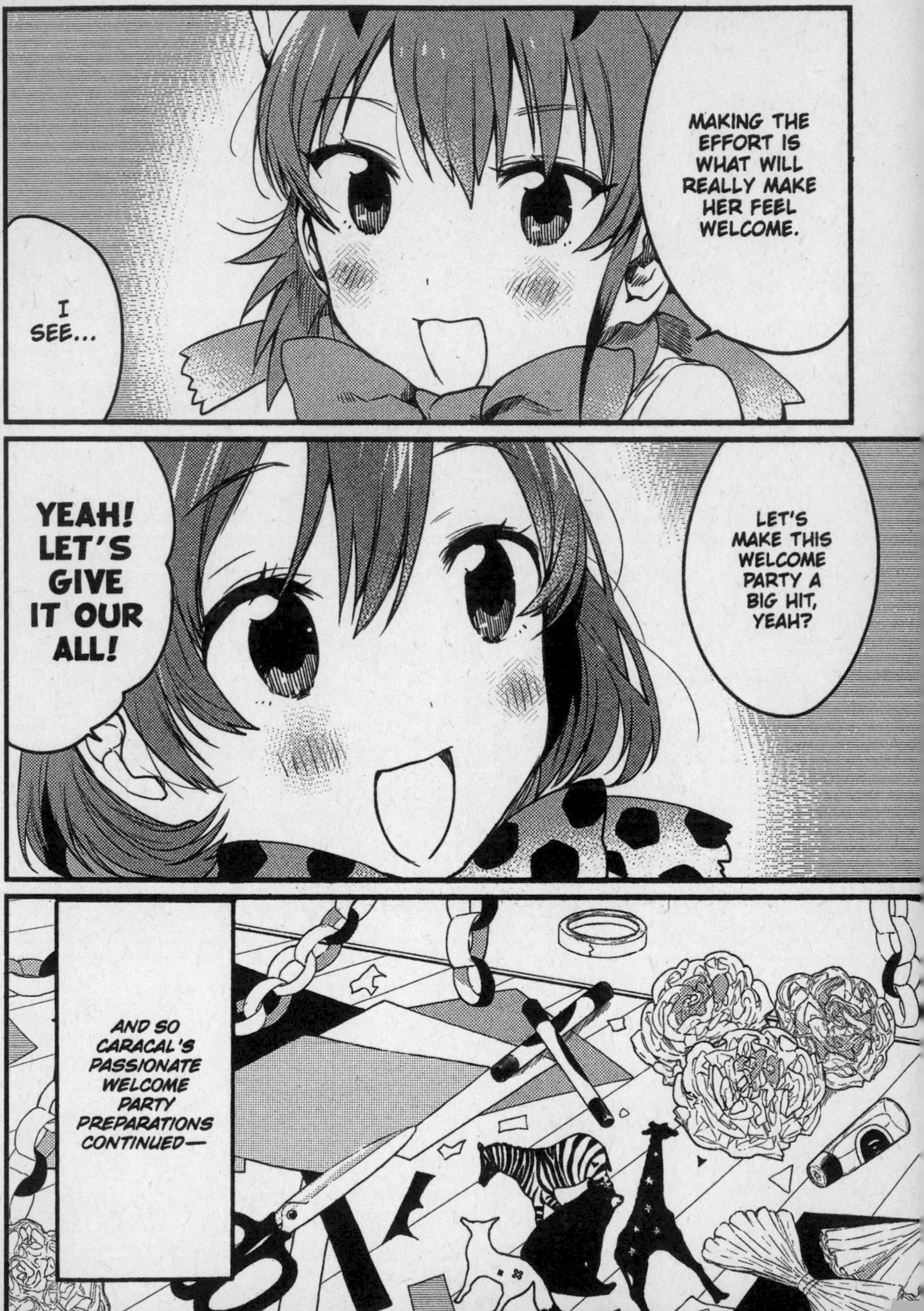
MAKING THE EFFORT IS WHAT WILL REALLY MAKE HER FEEL WELCOME.
I SEE...
LET'S MAKE THIS WELCOME PARTY A BIG HIT, YEAH?
YEAH! LET'S GIVE IT OUR ALL!
AND SO CARACAL'S PASSIONATE WELCOME PARTY PREPARATIONS CONTINUED—

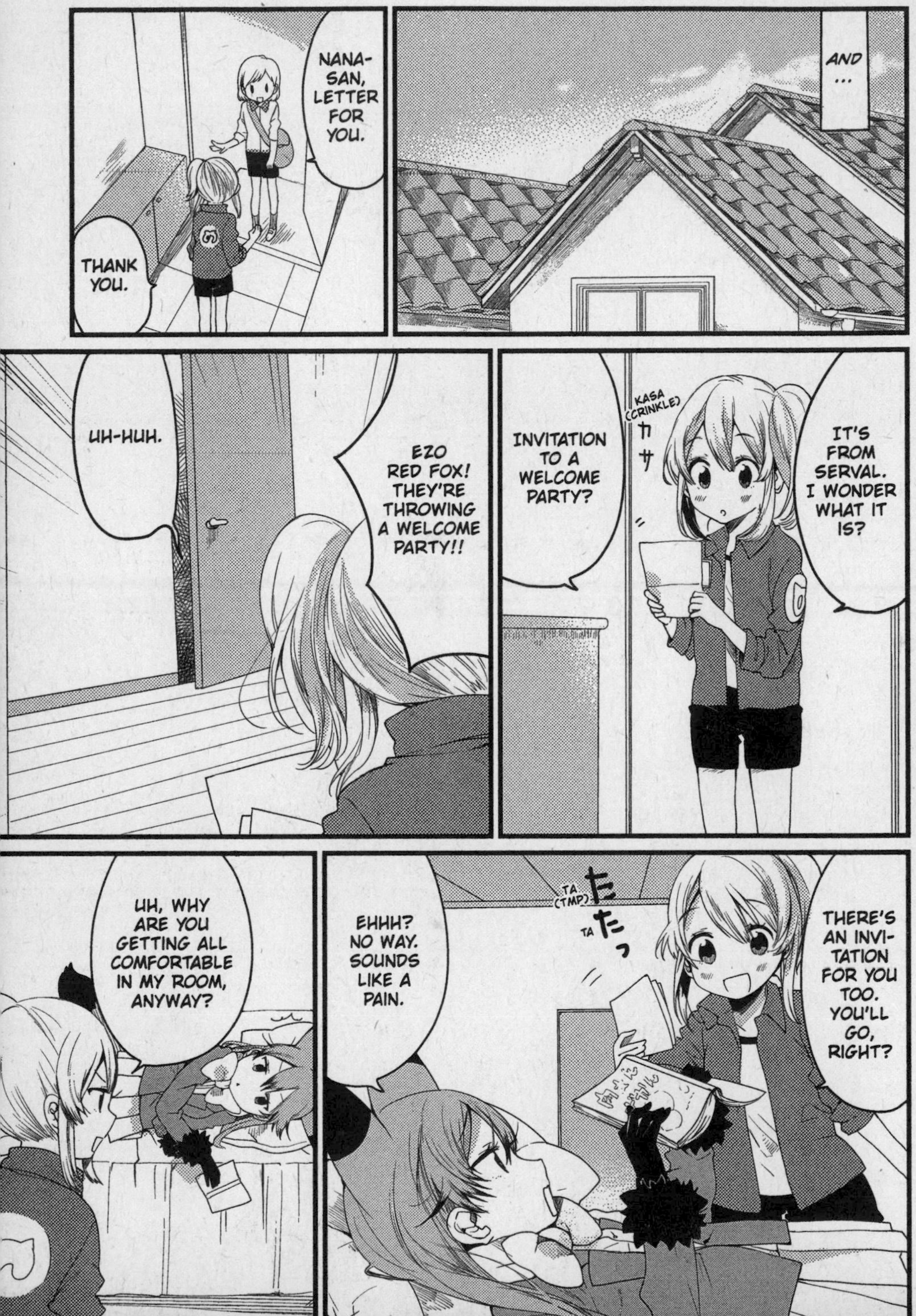
AND ...
NANA-SAN, LETTER FOR YOU.
THANK YOU.
IT'S FROM SERVAL. I WONDER WHAT IT IS?
KASA (CRINKLE) カサ
INVITATION TO A WELCOME PARTY?
EZO RED FOX! THEY'RE THROWING A WELCOME PARTY!!
UH-HUH.
THERE'S AN INVITATION FOR YOU TOO. YOU'LL GO, RIGHT?
TA (TMP) た TA たっ
EHHH? NO WAY. SOUNDS LIKE A PAIN.
UH, WHY ARE YOU GETTING ALL COMFORTABLE IN MY ROOM, ANYWAY?

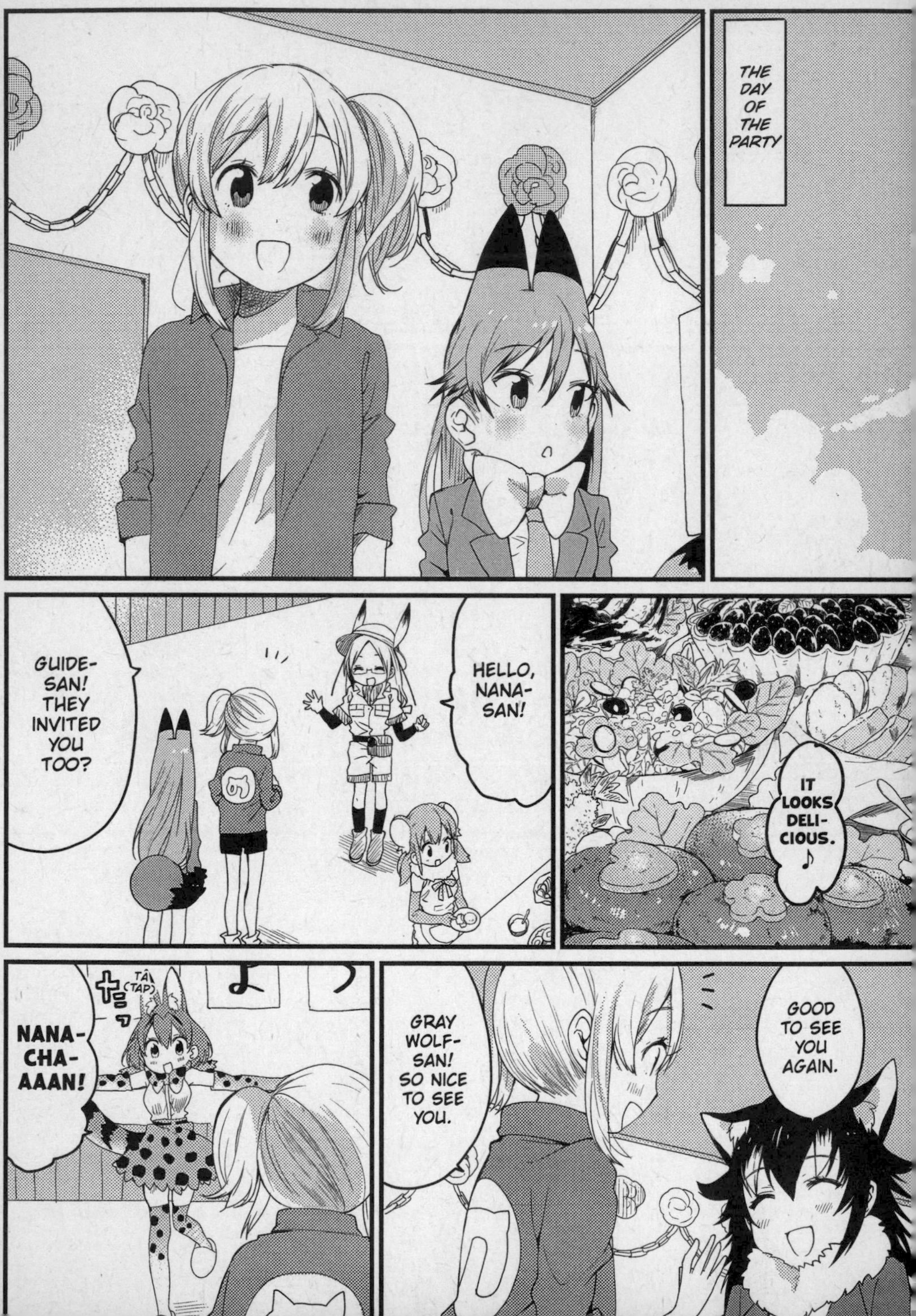
THE DAY OF THE PARTY
IT LOOKS DELICIOUS. ♪
HELLO, NANA-SAN!
GUIDE-SAN! THEY INVITED YOU TOO?
GOOD TO SEE YOU AGAIN.
GRAY WOLF-SAN! SO NICE TO SEE YOU.
TAP (TAP)
NANA-CHA-AAAN!

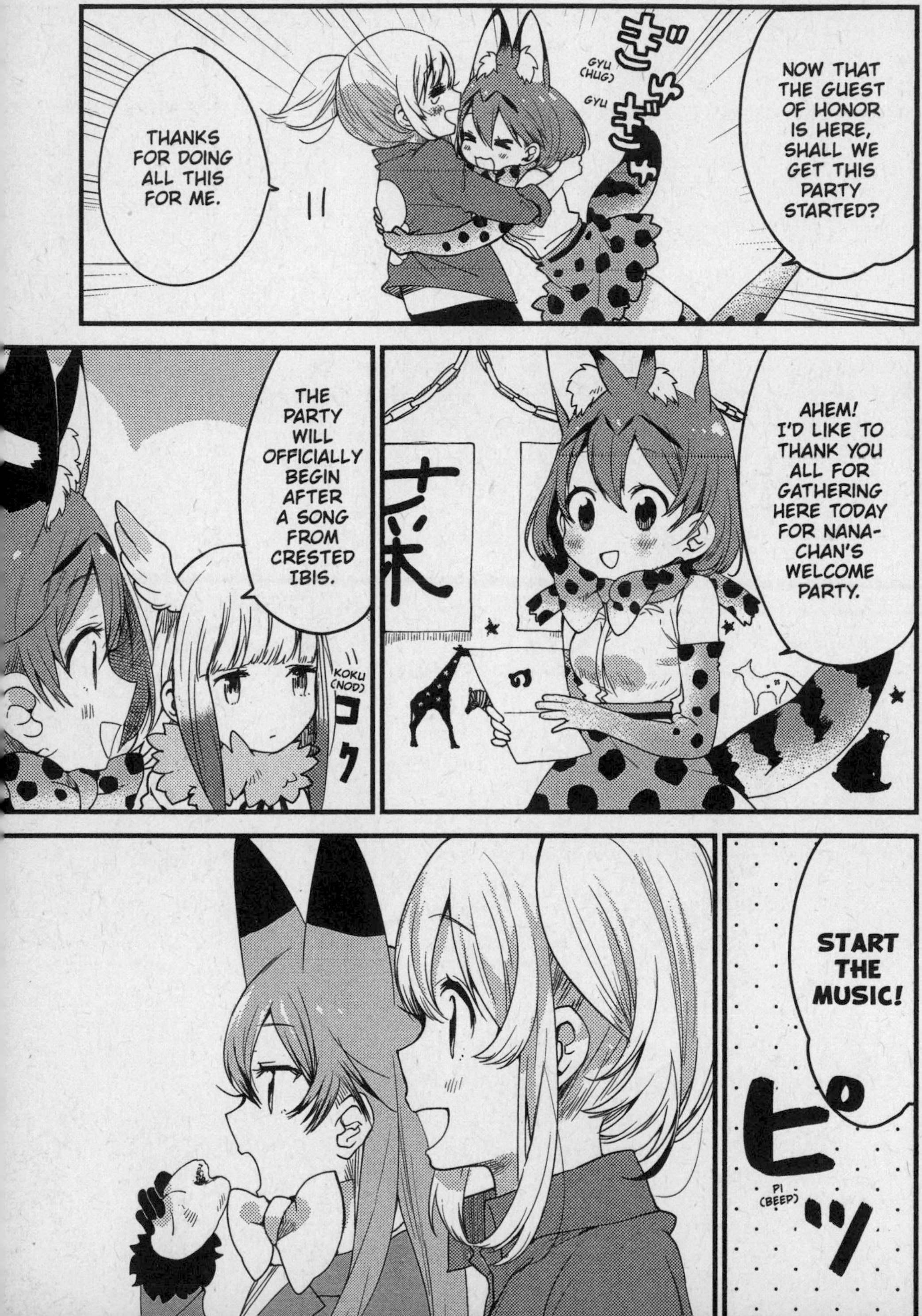
NOW THAT THE GUEST OF HONOR IS HERE, SHALL WE GET THIS PARTY STARTED?
ぎゅ ぎゅ
GYU (HUG) GYU
THANKS FOR DOING ALL THIS FOR ME.
AHEM! I'D LIKE TO THANK YOU ALL FOR GATHERING HERE TODAY FOR NANA-CHAN'S WELCOME PARTY.
THE PARTY WILL OFFICIALLY BEGIN AFTER A SONG FROM CRESTED IBIS.
コク
KOKU (NOD)
START THE MUSIC!
ピッ
PI (BEEP)

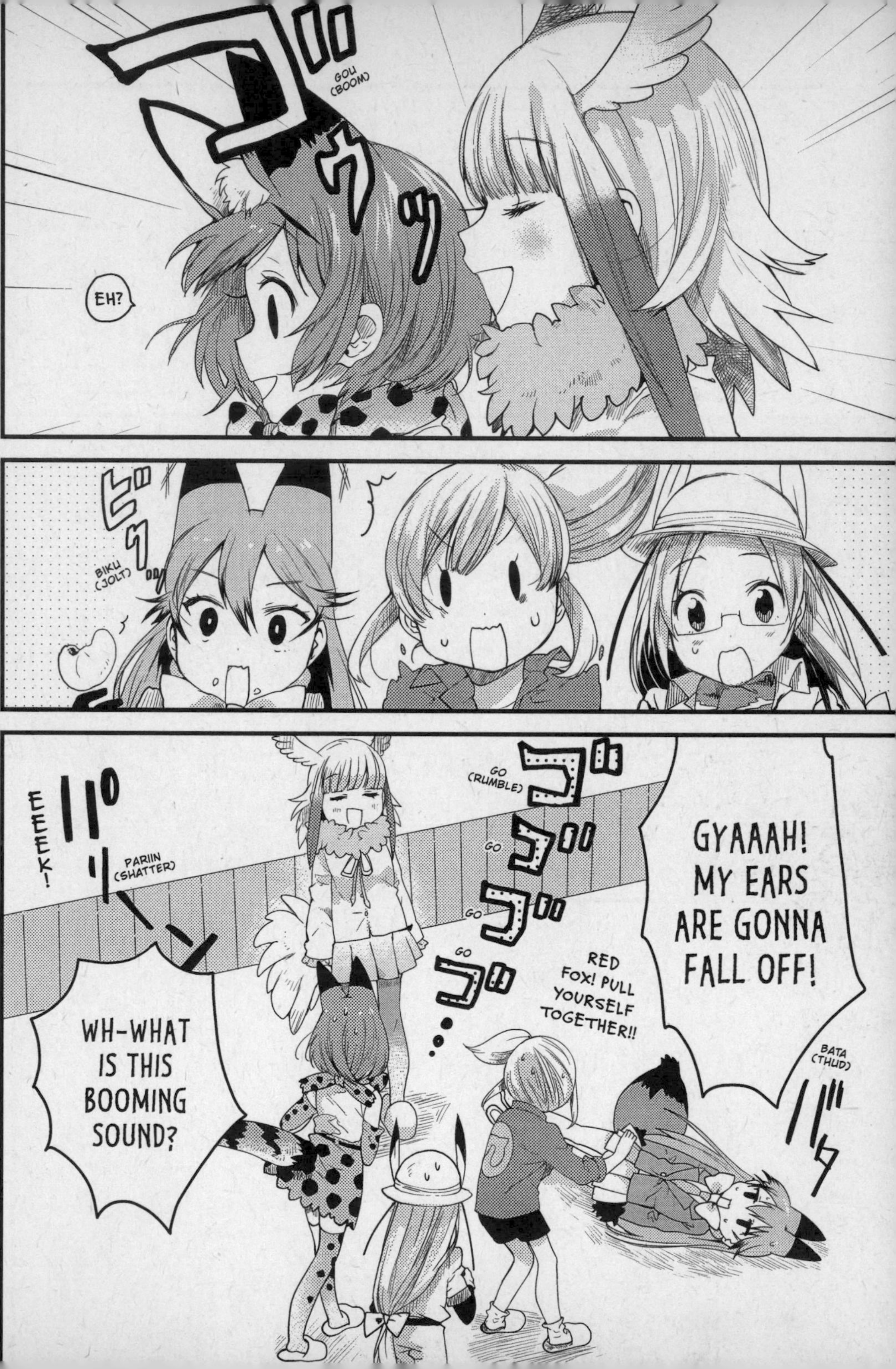
GOU (BOOM)
EH?
BIKU (JOLT)
GYAAAH! MY EARS ARE GONNA FALL OFF!
BATA (THUD)
RED FOX! PULL YOURSELF TOGETHER!!
GO (RUMBLE)
GO
GO
GO
PARIIN (SHATTER)
EEEK!
WH-WHAT IS THIS BOOMING SOUND?

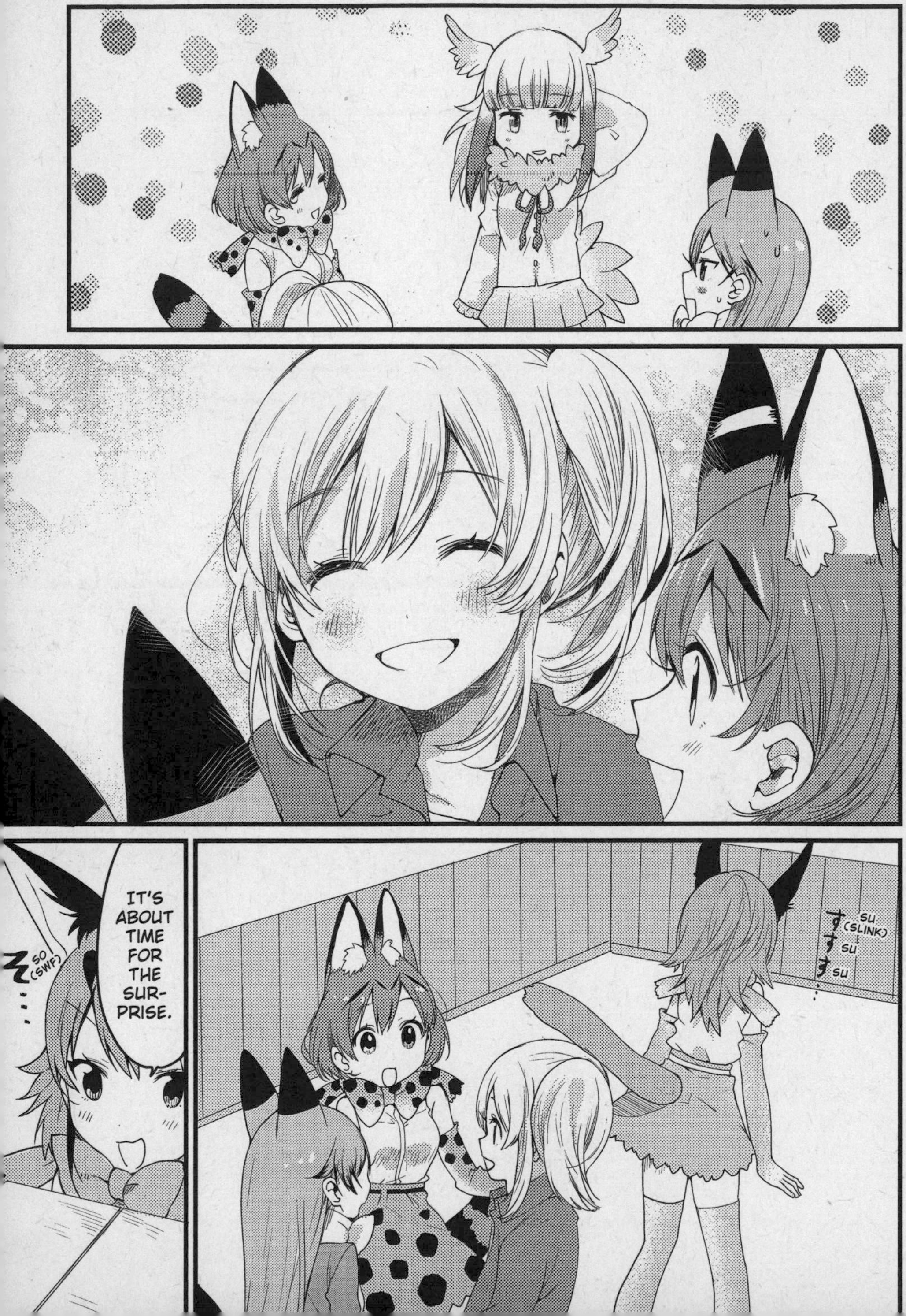
すすす
SU (SLINK)
SU
SU
IT'S ABOUT TIME FOR THE SUR-PRISE.
ス SO (SWF)

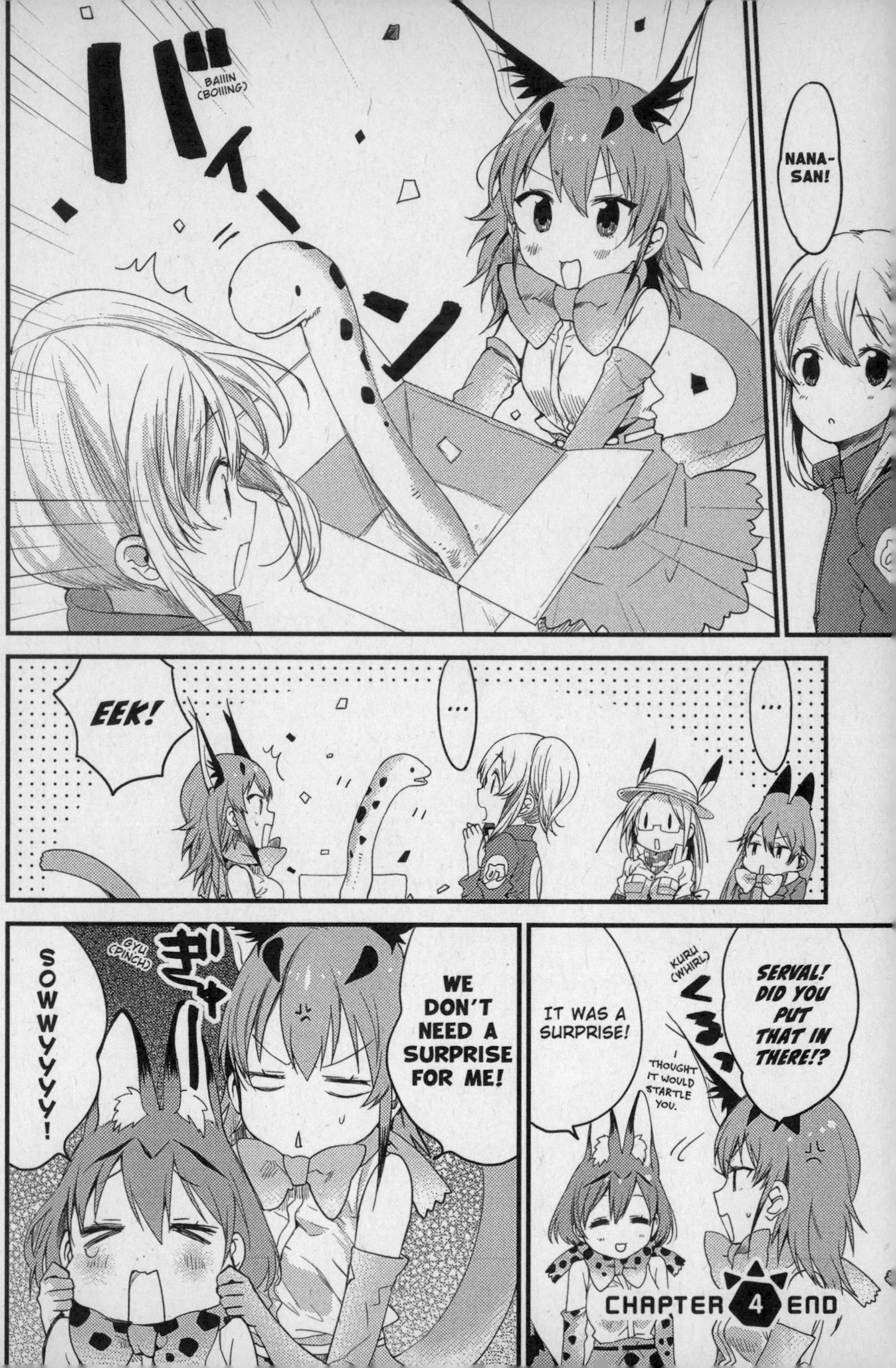
NANA-SAN!
バイーン
BAIIIN (BOIIING)
...
...
EEK!
SERVAL! DID YOU PUT THAT IN THERE!?
くる
KURU (WHIRL)
IT WAS A SURPRISE!
I THOUGHT IT WOULD STARTLE YOU.
CHAPTER 4 END
WE DON'T NEED A SURPRISE FOR ME!
ぎゅー
GYU (PINCH)
SOWWYYYYY!

KEMONO FRIENDS

WELCOME TO JAPARI PARK!

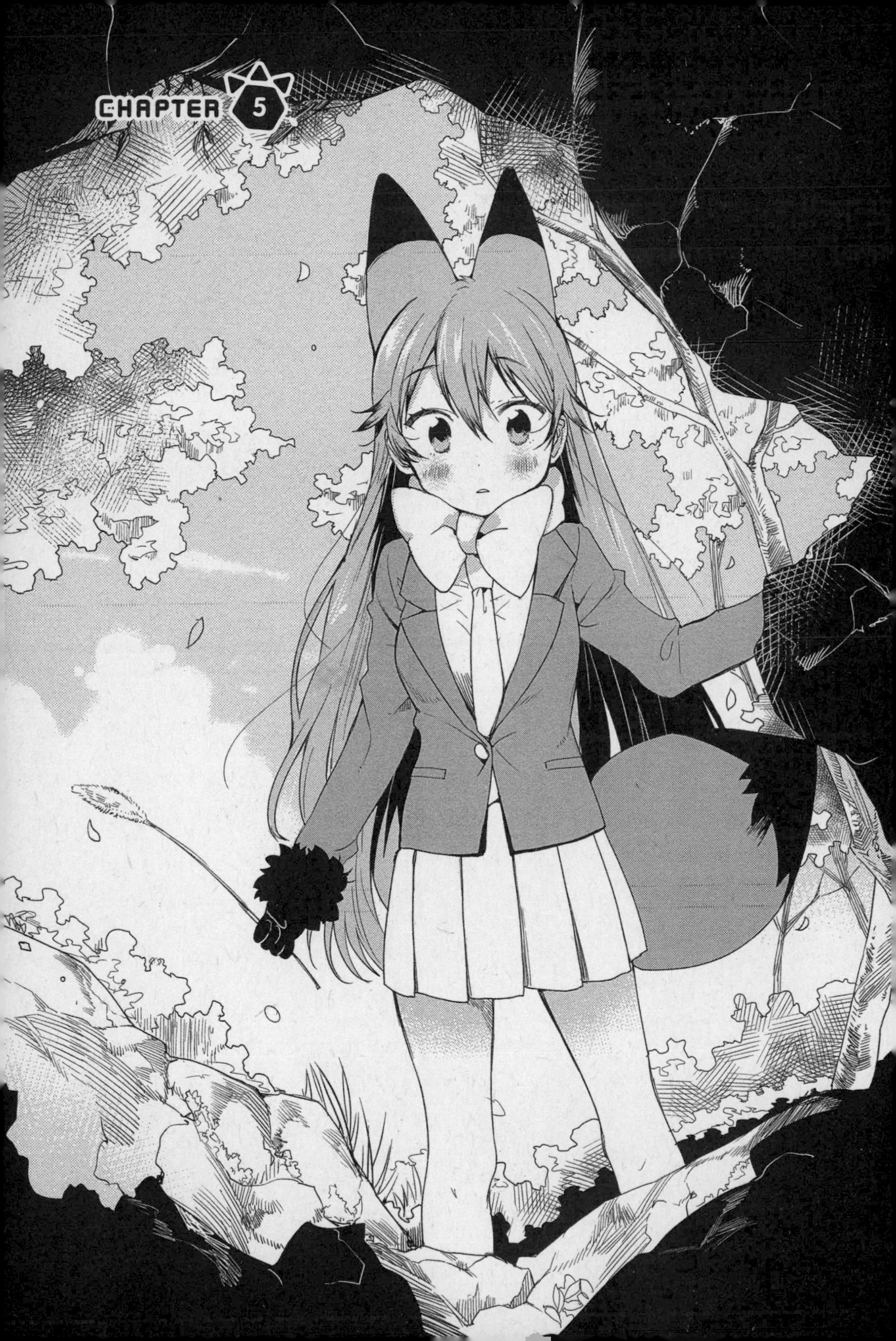
CHAPTER 5

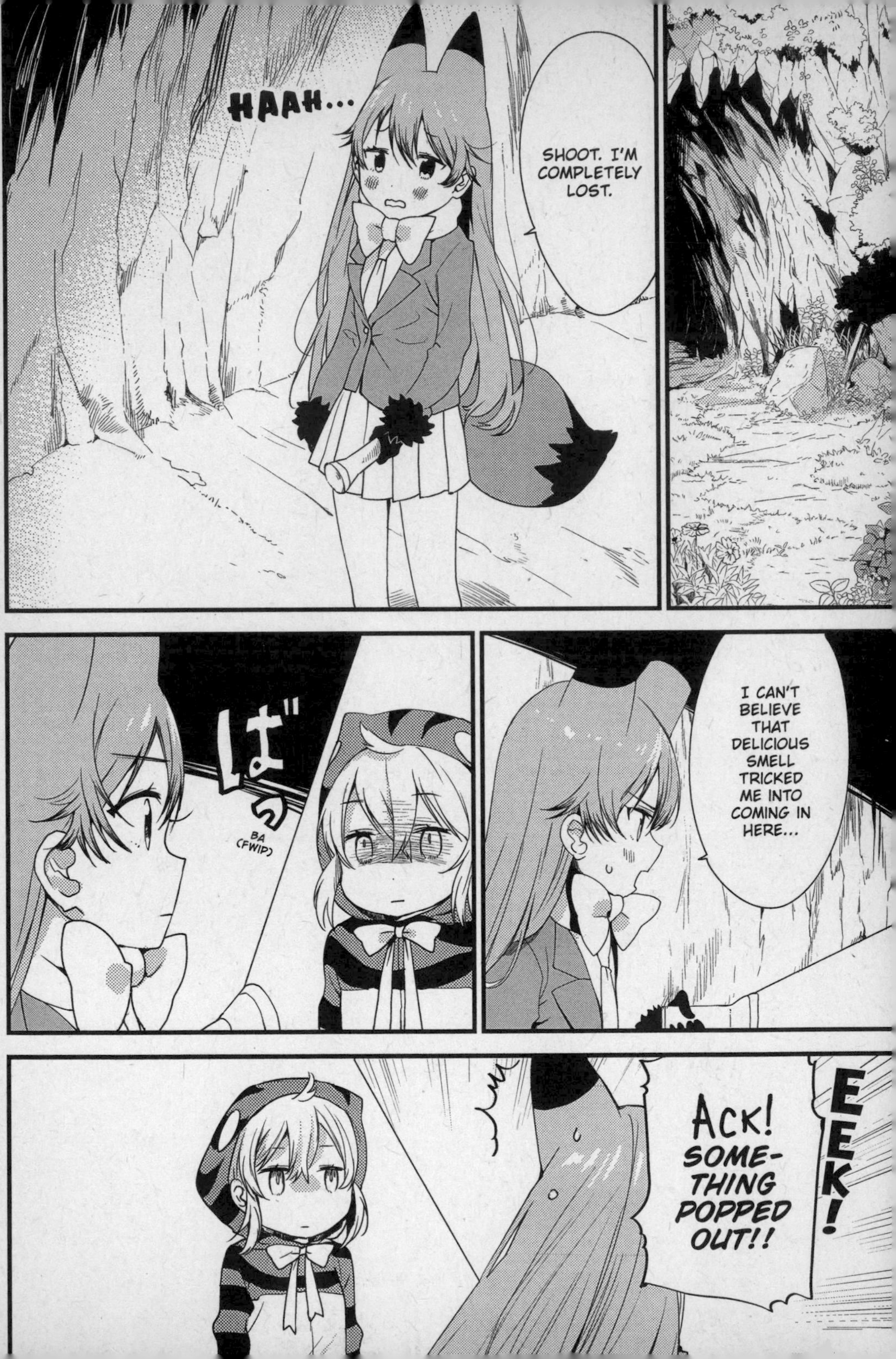
SHOOT. I'M COMPLETELY LOST.
HAAH...
I CAN'T BELIEVE THAT DELICIOUS SMELL TRICKED ME INTO COMING IN HERE...
ばっ
BA (FWIP)
EEK!
ACK! SOMETHING POPPED OUT!!

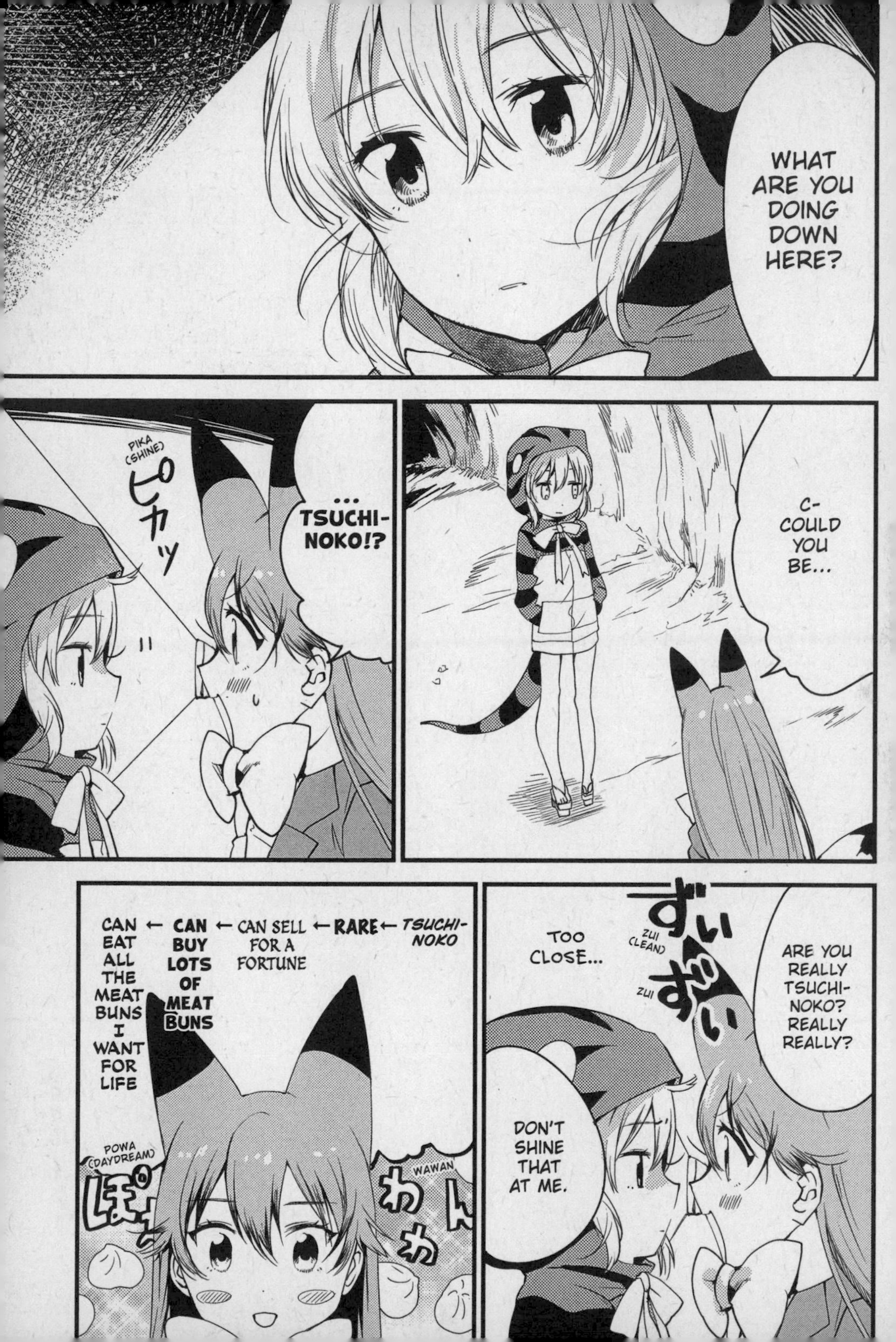
WHAT ARE YOU DOING DOWN HERE?
C-COULD YOU BE...
... TSUCHI-NOKO!?
PIKA (SHINE)
ピカッ
ARE YOU REALLY TSUCHI-NOKO? REALLY REALLY?
ずい
ZUI (LEAN)
ずい
ZUI
TOO CLOSE...
DON'T SHINE THAT AT ME.
CAN EAT ALL THE MEAT BUNS I WANT FOR LIFE ← CAN BUY LOTS OF MEAT BUNS ← CAN SELL FOR A FORTUNE ← RARE ← TSUCHI-NOKO
わんわ
WAWAN
ぽわ
POWA (DAYDREAM)

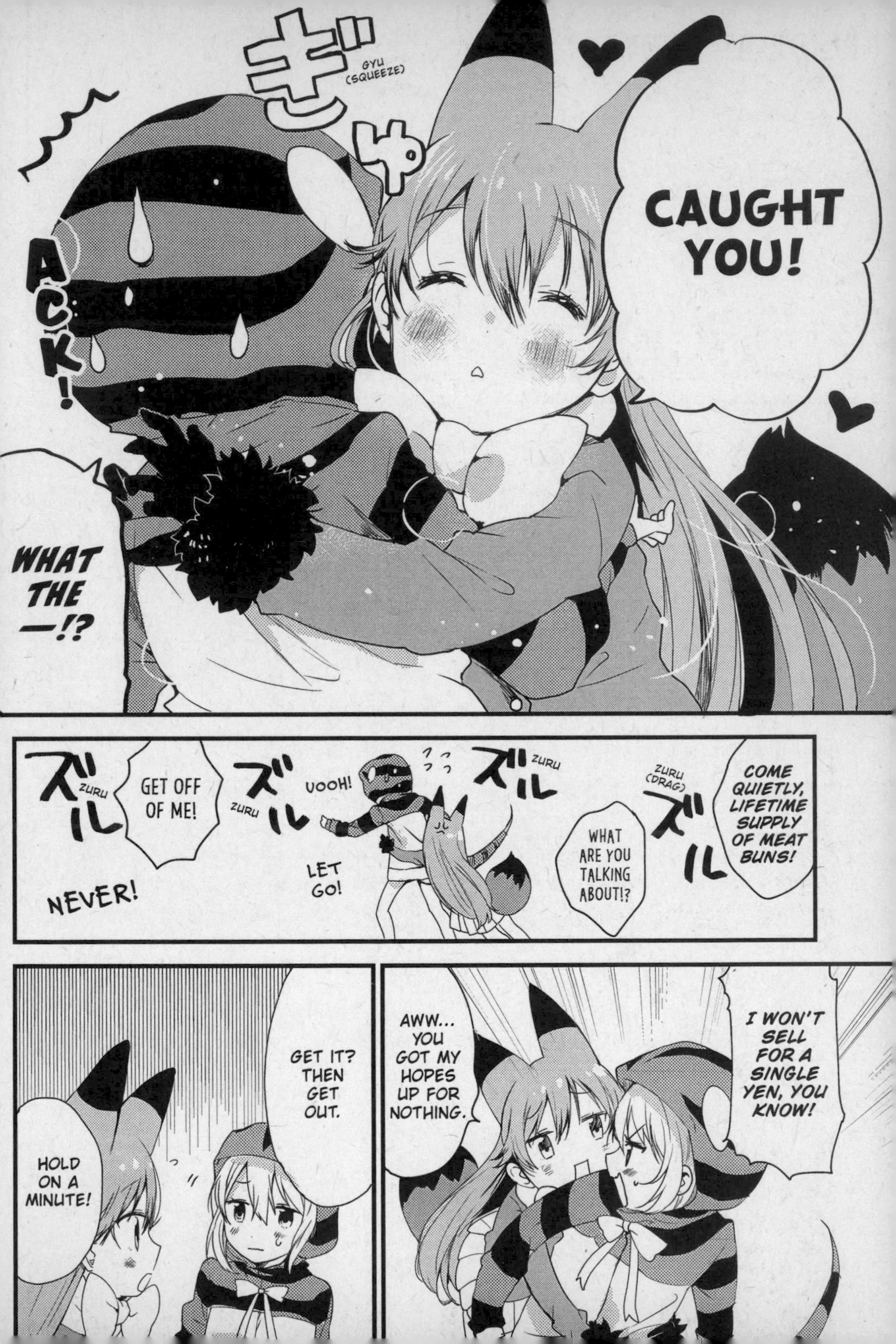
CAUGHT YOU!
ぎゅ
GYU (SQUEEZE)
ACK!
WHAT THE—!?
COME QUIETLY, LIFETIME SUPPLY OF MEAT BUNS!
ズル
ZURU (DRAG)
WHAT ARE YOU TALKING ABOUT!?
ズル
ZURU
UOOH!
LET GO!
ズル
ZURU
GET OFF OF ME!
ズル
ZURU
NEVER!
I WON'T SELL FOR A SINGLE YEN, YOU KNOW!
AWW... YOU GOT MY HOPES UP FOR NOTHING.
GET IT? THEN GET OUT.
HOLD ON A MINUTE!

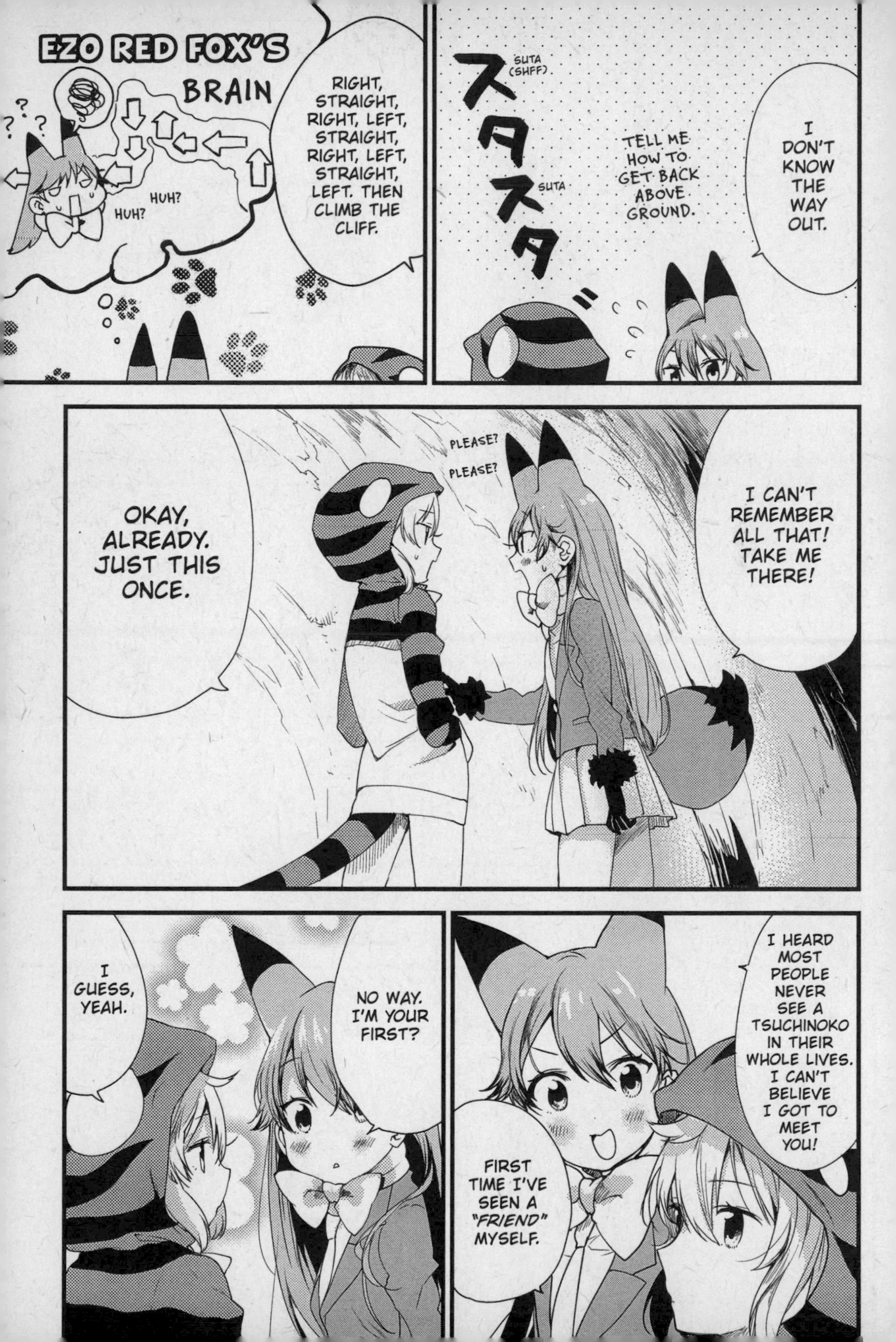
I DON'T KNOW THE WAY OUT.
TELL ME HOW TO GET BACK ABOVE GROUND.
SUTA (SHFF)
SUTA
スタスタ
RIGHT, STRAIGHT, RIGHT, LEFT, STRAIGHT, RIGHT, LEFT, STRAIGHT, LEFT. THEN CLIMB THE CLIFF.
EZO RED FOX'S BRAIN
HUH?
HUH?
I CAN'T REMEMBER ALL THAT! TAKE ME THERE!
PLEASE?
PLEASE?
OKAY, ALREADY. JUST THIS ONCE.
I HEARD MOST PEOPLE NEVER SEE A TSUCHINOKO IN THEIR WHOLE LIVES. I CAN'T BELIEVE I GOT TO MEET YOU!
FIRST TIME I'VE SEEN A "FRIEND" MYSELF.
NO WAY. I'M YOUR FIRST?
I GUESS, YEAH.

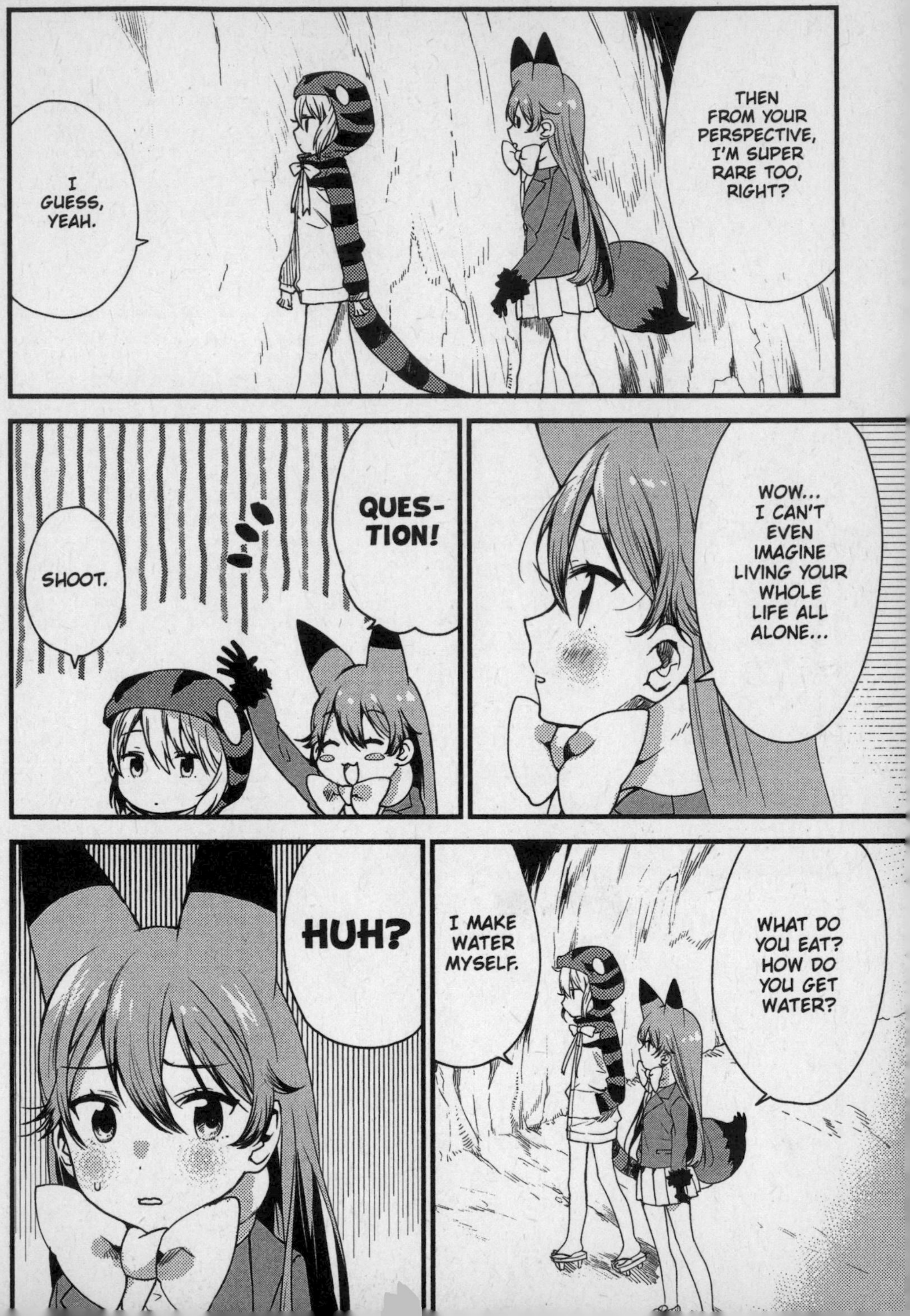
THEN FROM YOUR PERSPECTIVE, I'M SUPER RARE TOO, RIGHT?
I GUESS, YEAH.
WOW... I CAN'T EVEN IMAGINE LIVING YOUR WHOLE LIFE ALL ALONE...
QUES-TION!
SHOOT.
WHAT DO YOU EAT? HOW DO YOU GET WATER?
I MAKE WATER MYSELF.
HUH?

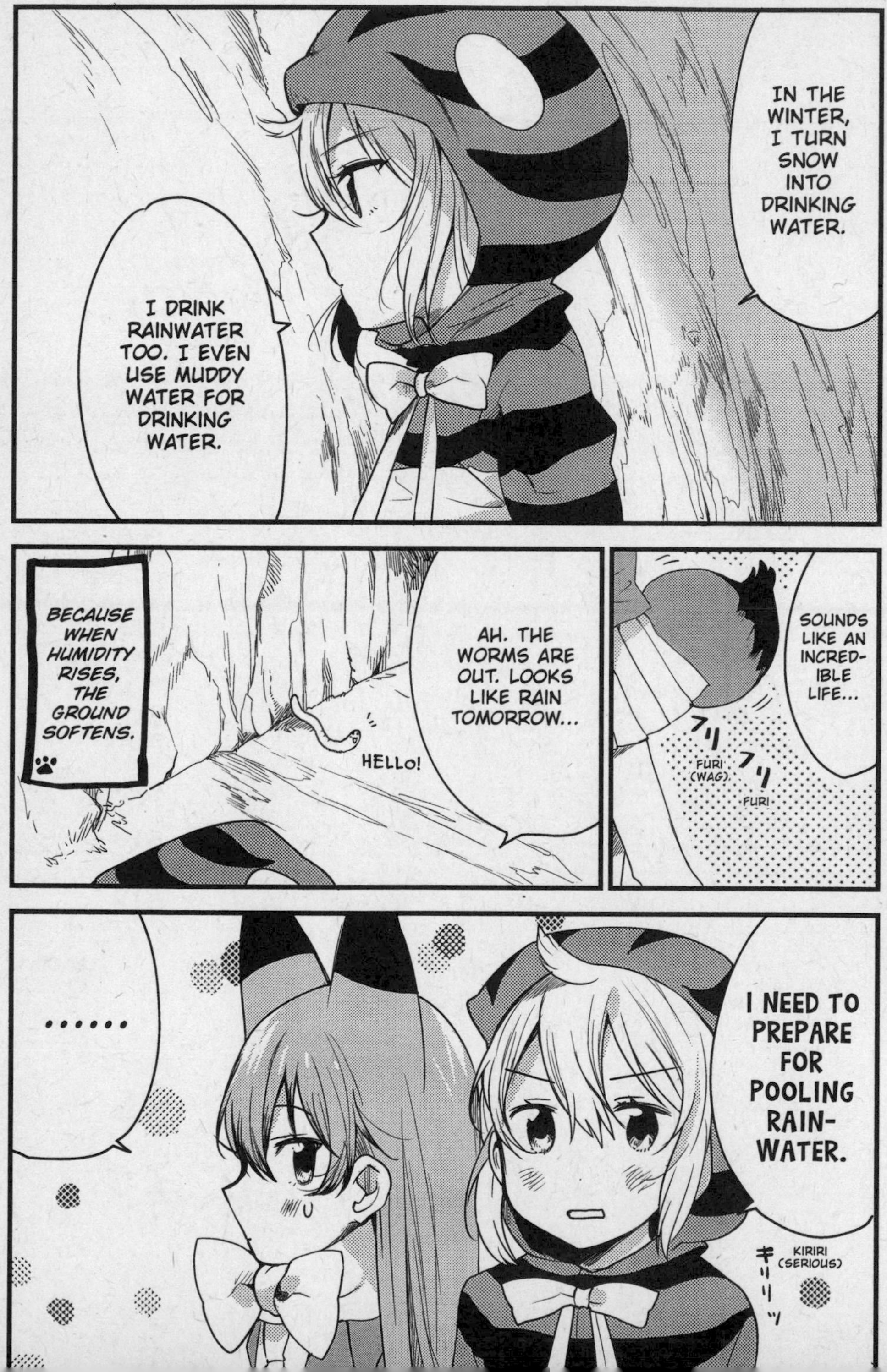
IN THE WINTER, I TURN SNOW INTO DRINKING WATER.
I DRINK RAINWATER TOO. I EVEN USE MUDDY WATER FOR DRINKING WATER.
SOUNDS LIKE AN INCRED-IBLE LIFE...
フリ
FURI (WAG)
フリ
FURI
AH. THE WORMS ARE OUT. LOOKS LIKE RAIN TOMORROW...
HELLO!
BECAUSE WHEN HUMIDITY RISES, THE GROUND SOFTENS.
I NEED TO PREPARE FOR POOLING RAIN-WATER.
キリリッ
KIRIRI (SERIOUS)
......

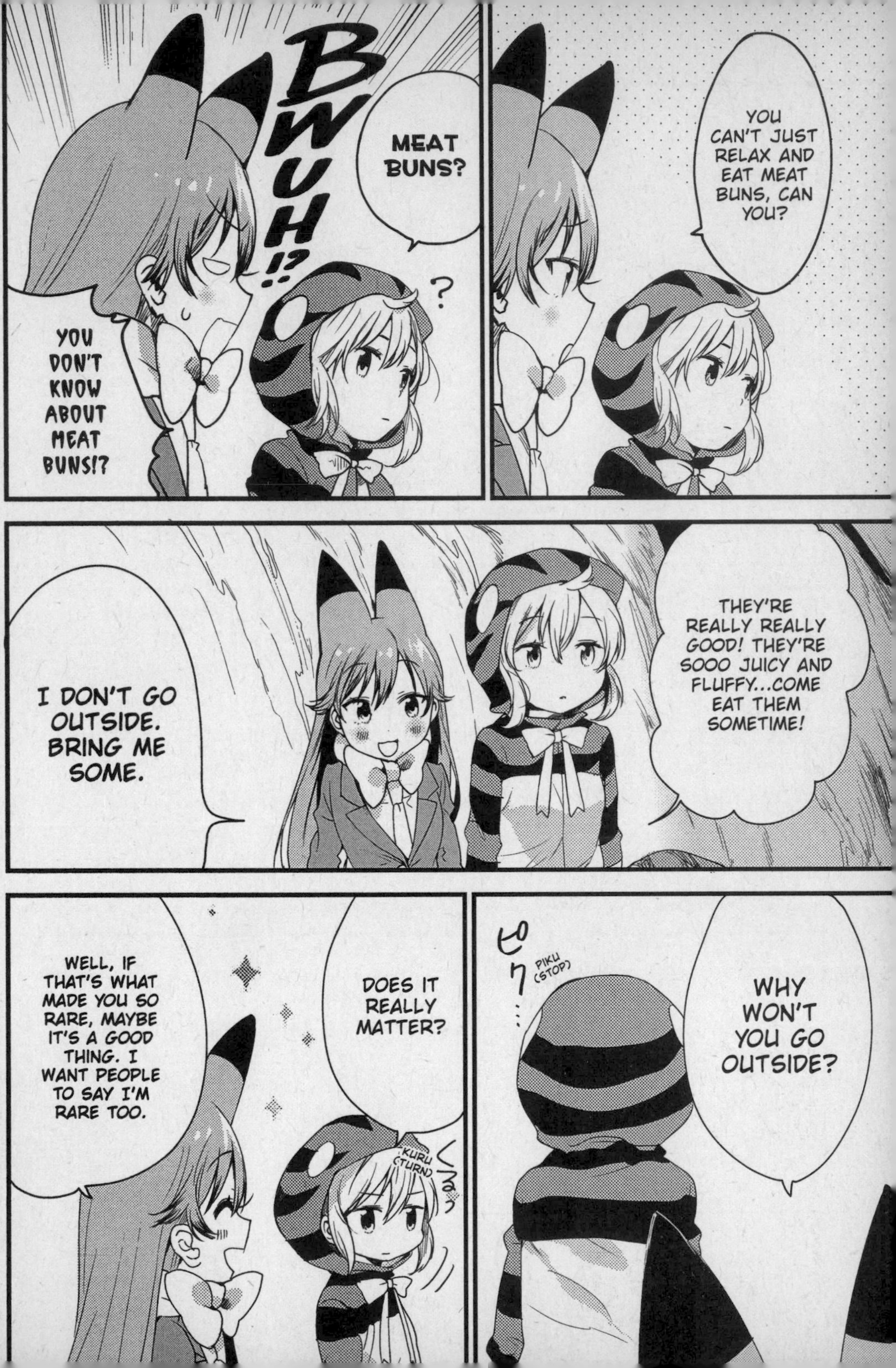
YOU CAN'T JUST RELAX AND EAT MEAT BUNS, CAN YOU?
MEAT BUNS?
BWUH!?
?
YOU DON'T KNOW ABOUT MEAT BUNS!?
THEY'RE REALLY REALLY GOOD! THEY'RE SOOO JUICY AND FLUFFY...COME EAT THEM SOMETIME!
I DON'T GO OUTSIDE. BRING ME SOME.
ピク…
PIKU (STOP)
WHY WON'T YOU GO OUTSIDE?
DOES IT REALLY MATTER?
くるっ
KURU (TURN)
WELL, IF THAT'S WHAT MADE YOU SO RARE, MAYBE IT'S A GOOD THING. I WANT PEOPLE TO SAY I'M RARE TOO.

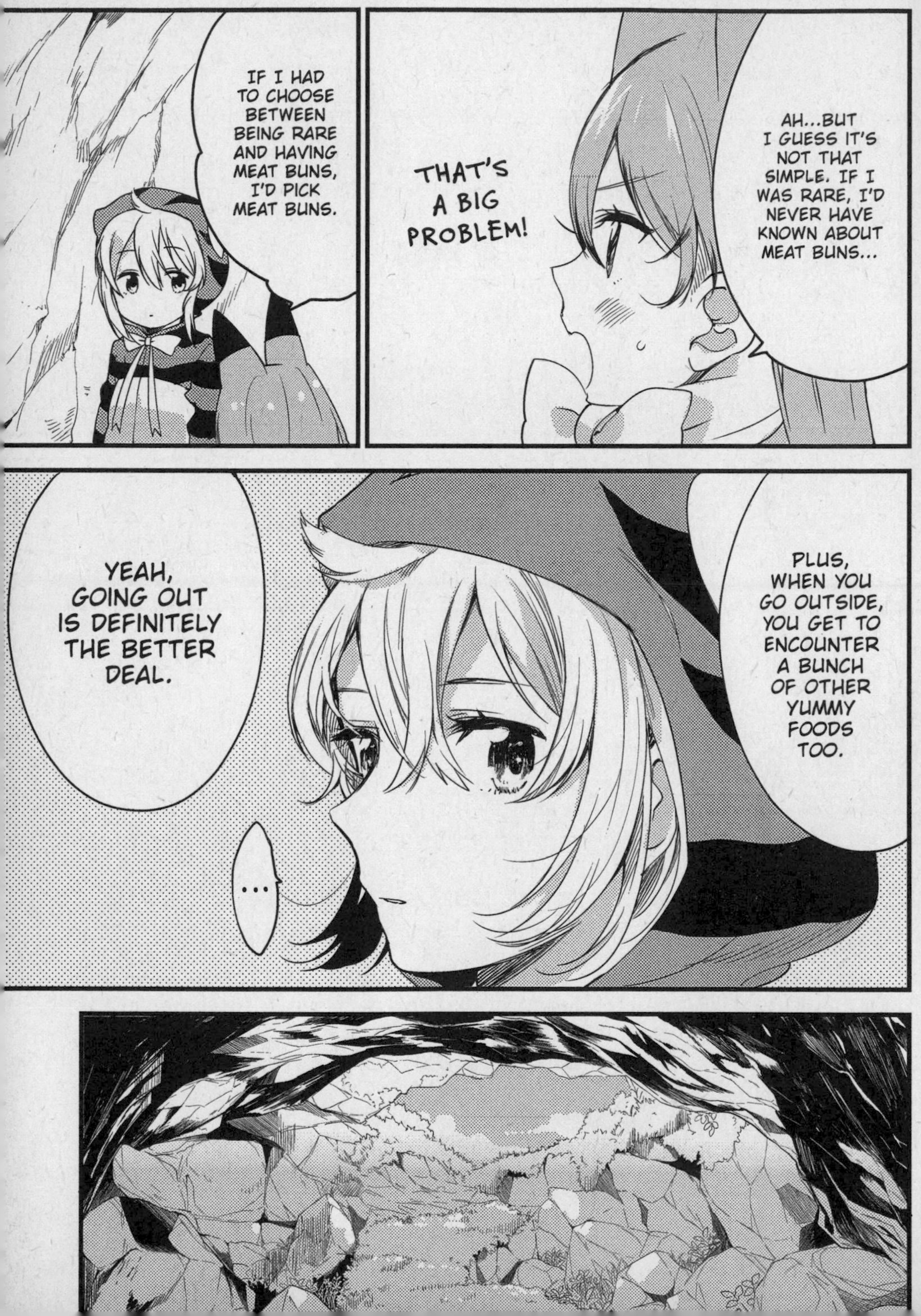
AH...BUT I GUESS IT'S NOT THAT SIMPLE. IF I WAS RARE, I'D NEVER HAVE KNOWN ABOUT MEAT BUNS...
THAT'S A BIG PROBLEM!
IF I HAD TO CHOOSE BETWEEN BEING RARE AND HAVING MEAT BUNS, I'D PICK MEAT BUNS.
PLUS, WHEN YOU GO OUTSIDE, YOU GET TO ENCOUNTER A BUNCH OF OTHER YUMMY FOODS TOO.
YEAH, GOING OUT IS DEFINITELY THE BETTER DEAL.
...

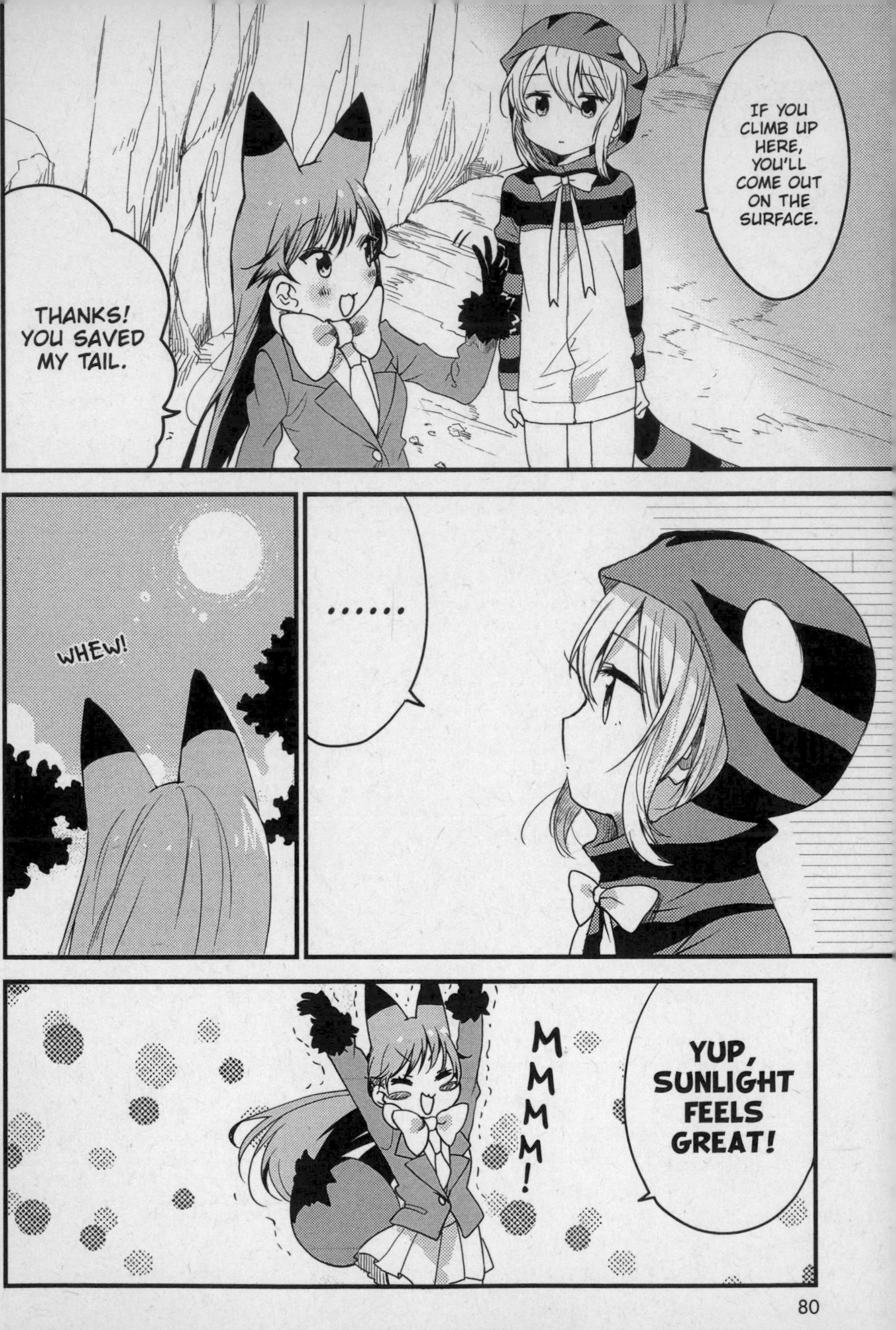
IF YOU CLIMB UP HERE, YOU'LL COME OUT ON THE SURFACE.
THANKS! YOU SAVED MY TAIL.
......
WHEW!
YUP, SUNLIGHT FEELS GREAT!
MMMM!

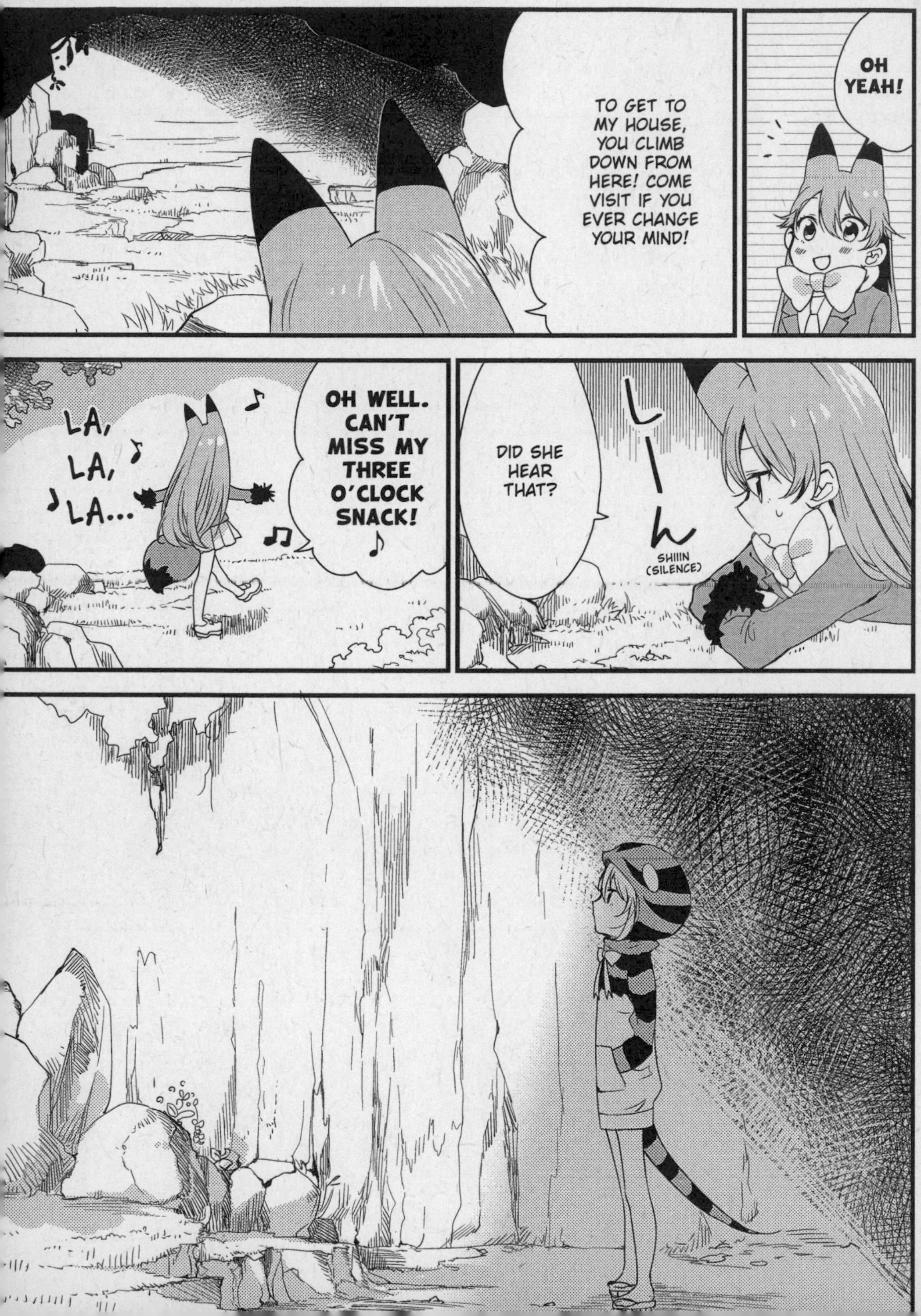
OH YEAH!
TO GET TO MY HOUSE, YOU CLIMB DOWN FROM HERE! COME VISIT IF YOU EVER CHANGE YOUR MIND!
しーん
SHIIIN (SILENCE)
DID SHE HEAR THAT?
OH WELL. CAN'T MISS MY THREE O'CLOCK SNACK! ♪
LA, LA, LA...

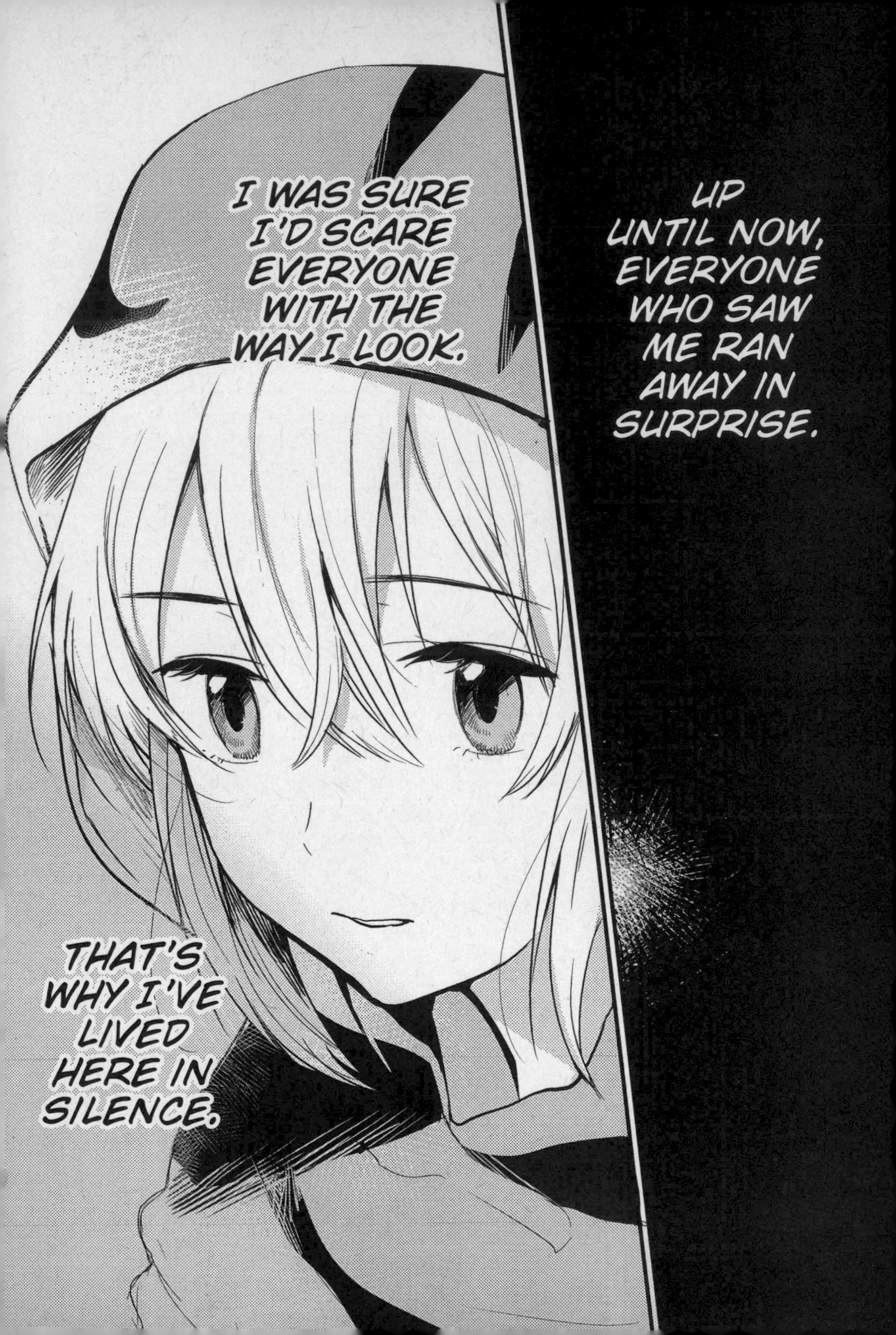
UP UNTIL NOW, EVERYONE WHO SAW ME RAN AWAY IN SURPRISE.
I WAS SURE I'D SCARE EVERYONE WITH THE WAY I LOOK.
THAT'S WHY I'VE LIVED HERE IN SILENCE.

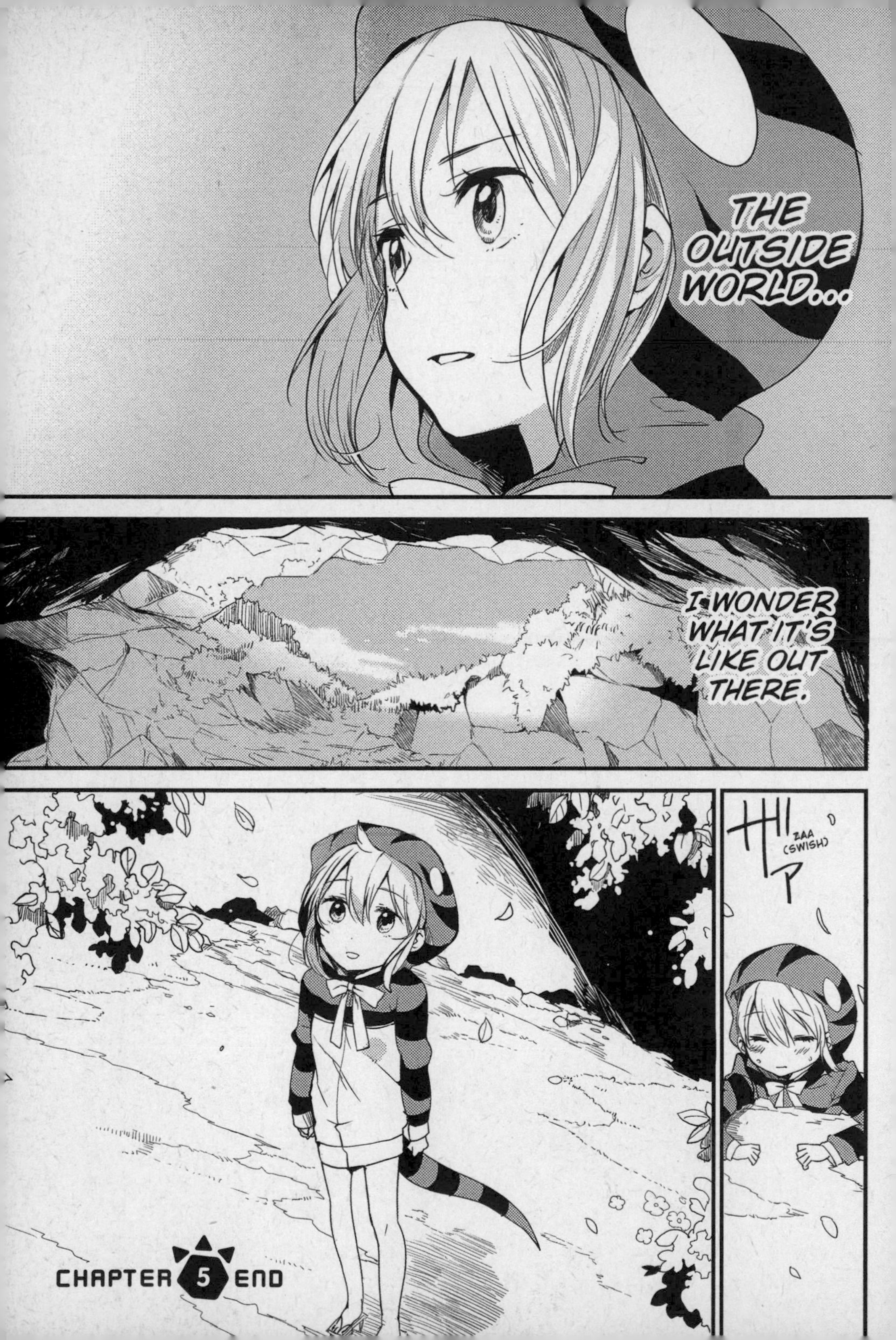
THE OUTSIDE WORLD...
I WONDER WHAT IT'S LIKE OUT THERE.
ザア
ZAA (SWISH)
CHAPTER 5 END

CHAPTER 6

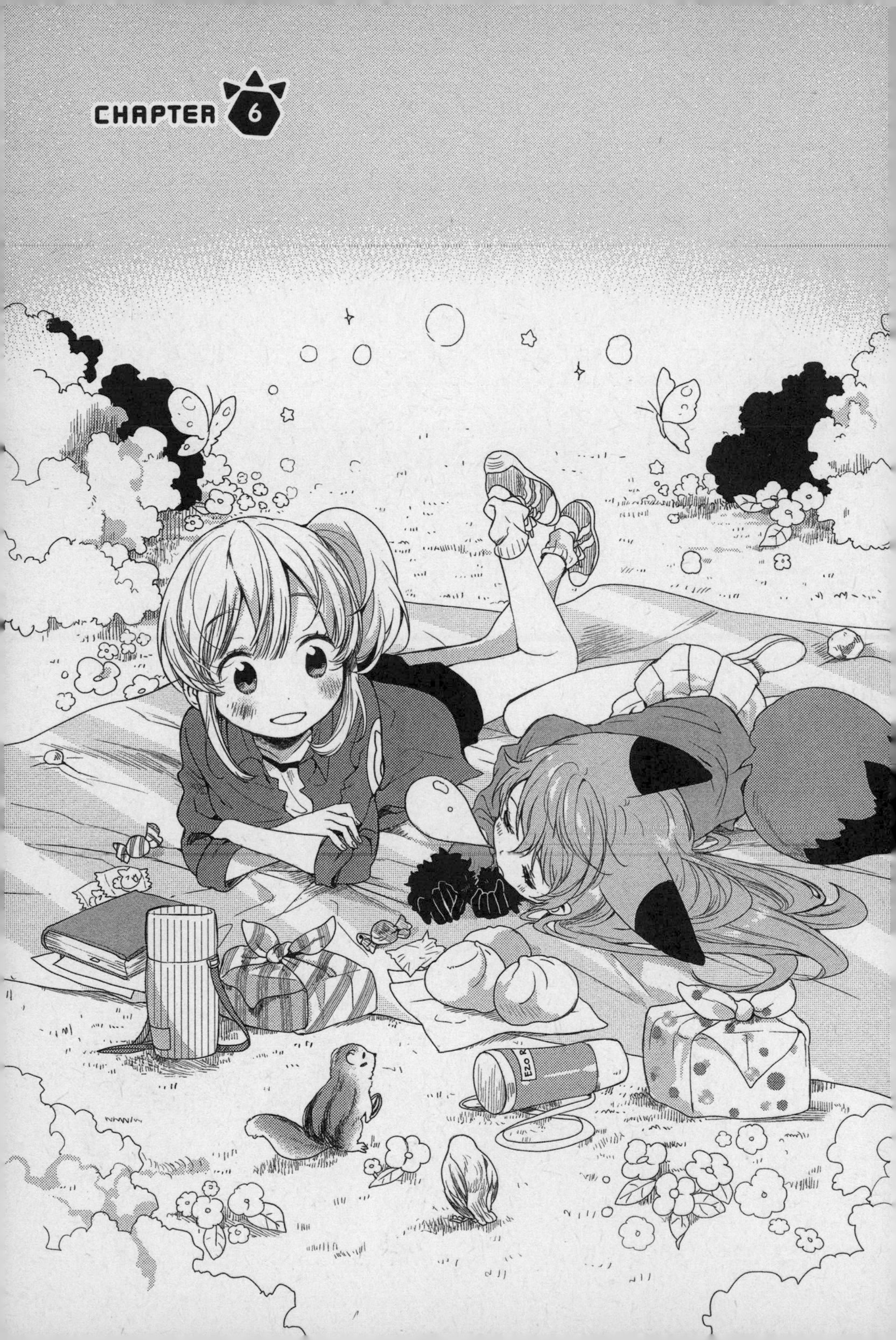

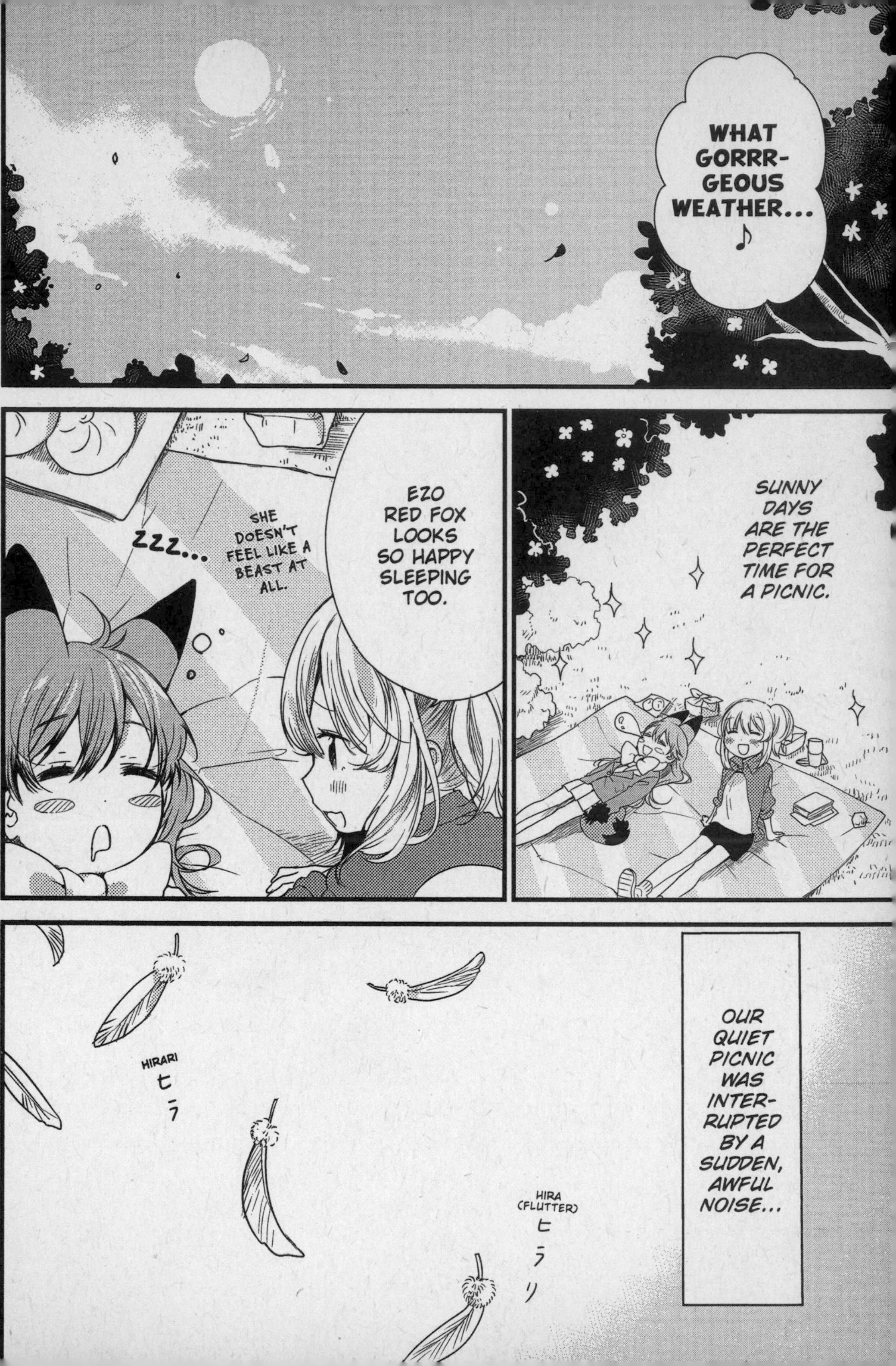
WHAT GORRR-GEOUS WEATHER... ♪
SUNNY DAYS ARE THE PERFECT TIME FOR A PICNIC.
EZO RED FOX LOOKS SO HAPPY SLEEPING TOO.
SHE DOESN'T FEEL LIKE A BEAST AT ALL.
ZZZ...
OUR QUIET PICNIC WAS INTER-RUPTED BY A SUDDEN, AWFUL NOISE...
HIRA (FLUTTER)
ヒラリ
HIRARI
ヒラ

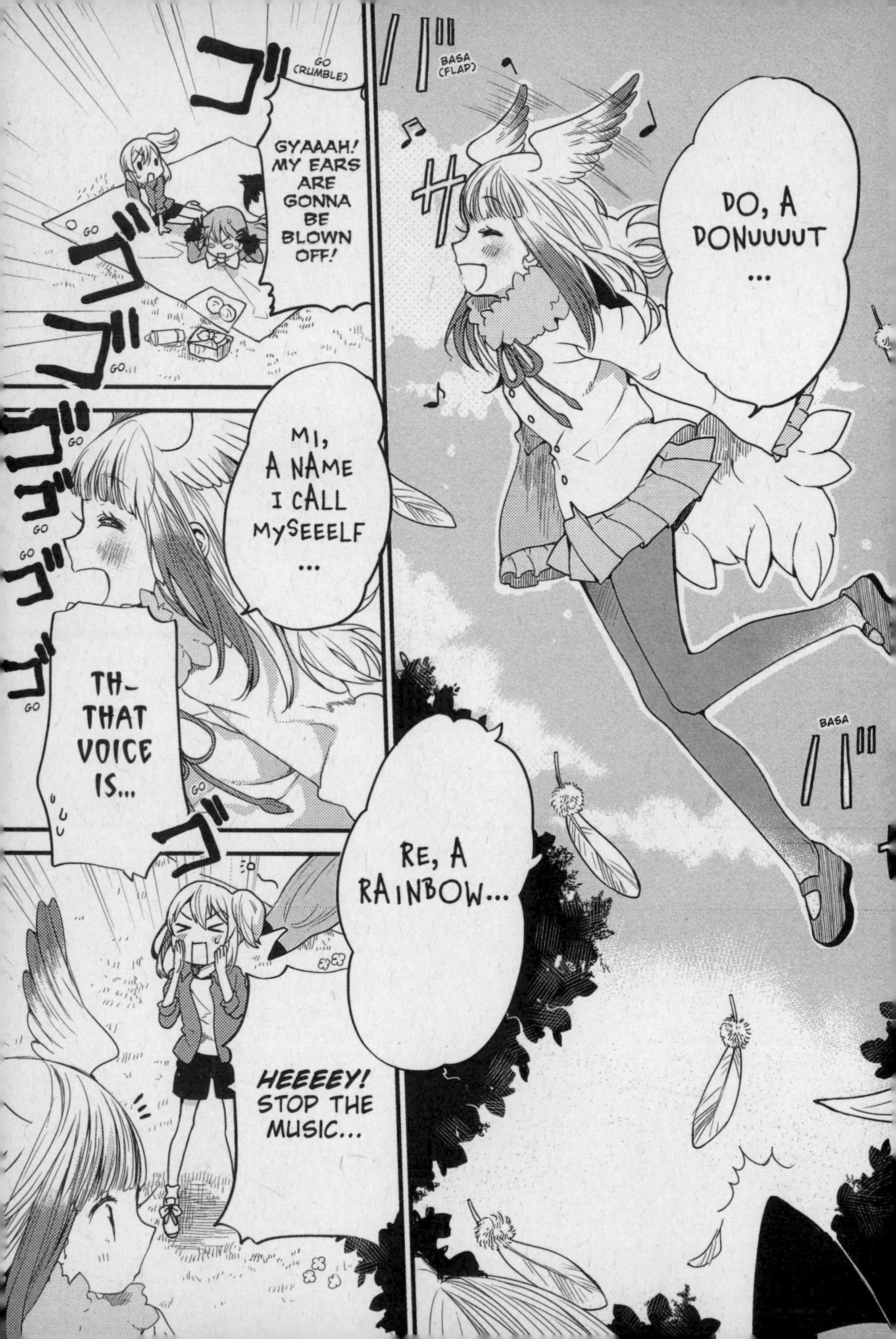
BASA (FLAP)
DO, A DONUUUUT ...
RE, A RAINBOW...
BASA
GO (RUMBLE)
GYAAAH! MY EARS ARE GONNA BE BLOWN OFF!
GO
GO...
MI, A NAME I CALL MYSEEELF ...
GO
GO
GO
GO
TH-THAT VOICE IS...
GO
HEEEEY! STOP THE MUSIC...

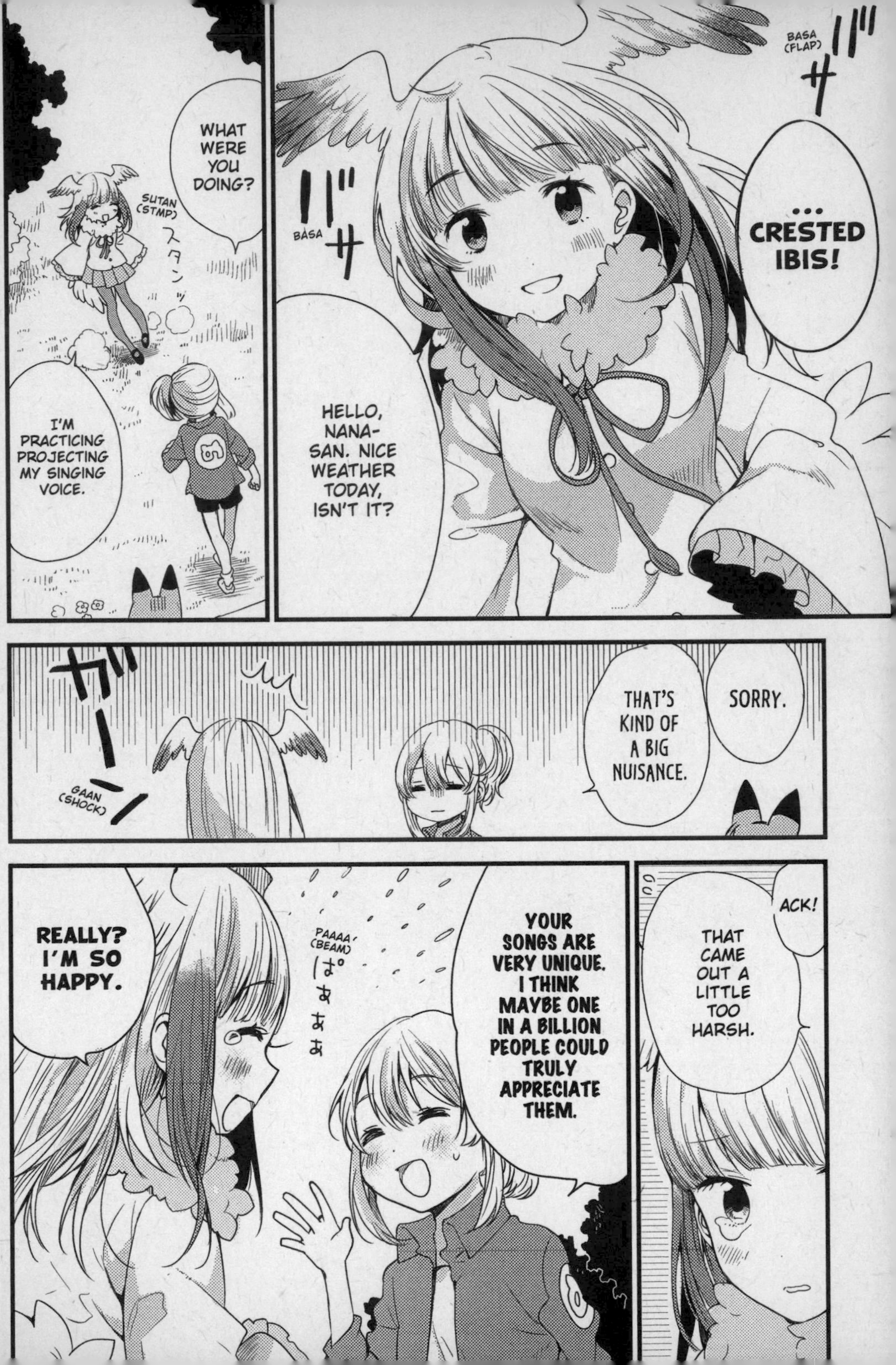
BASA (FLAP)
バサ
... CRESTED IBIS!
バサ
BASA
HELLO, NANA-SAN. NICE WEATHER TODAY, ISN'T IT?
WHAT WERE YOU DOING?
SUTAN (STMP)
スタンッ
I'M PRACTICING PROJECTING MY SINGING VOICE.
SORRY.
THAT'S KIND OF A BIG NUISANCE.
ガーン
GAAN (SHOCK)
ACK!
THAT CAME OUT A LITTLE TOO HARSH.
YOUR SONGS ARE VERY UNIQUE. I THINK MAYBE ONE IN A BILLION PEOPLE COULD TRULY APPRECIATE THEM.
PAAAA (BEAM)
ぱぁぁぁ
REALLY? I'M SO HAPPY.

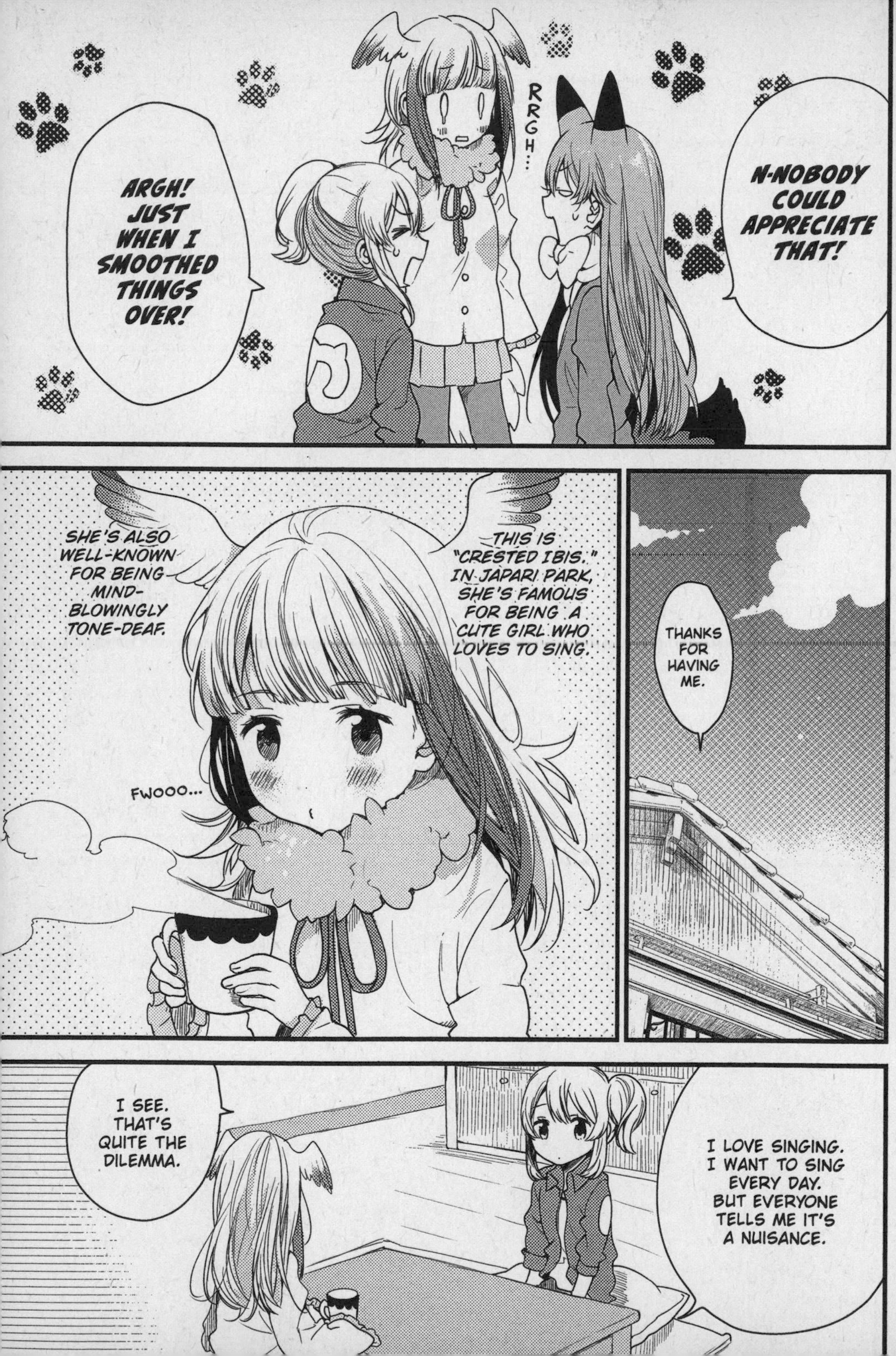
N-NOBODY COULD APPRECIATE THAT!
RRGH...
ARGH! JUST WHEN I SMOOTHED THINGS OVER!
THANKS FOR HAVING ME.
THIS IS "CRESTED IBIS." IN JAPARI PARK, SHE'S FAMOUS FOR BEING A CUTE GIRL WHO LOVES TO SING.
SHE'S ALSO WELL-KNOWN FOR BEING MIND-BLOWINGLY TONE-DEAF.
FWOOO...
I LOVE SINGING. I WANT TO SING EVERY DAY. BUT EVERYONE TELLS ME IT'S A NUISANCE.
I SEE. THAT'S QUITE THE DILEMMA.

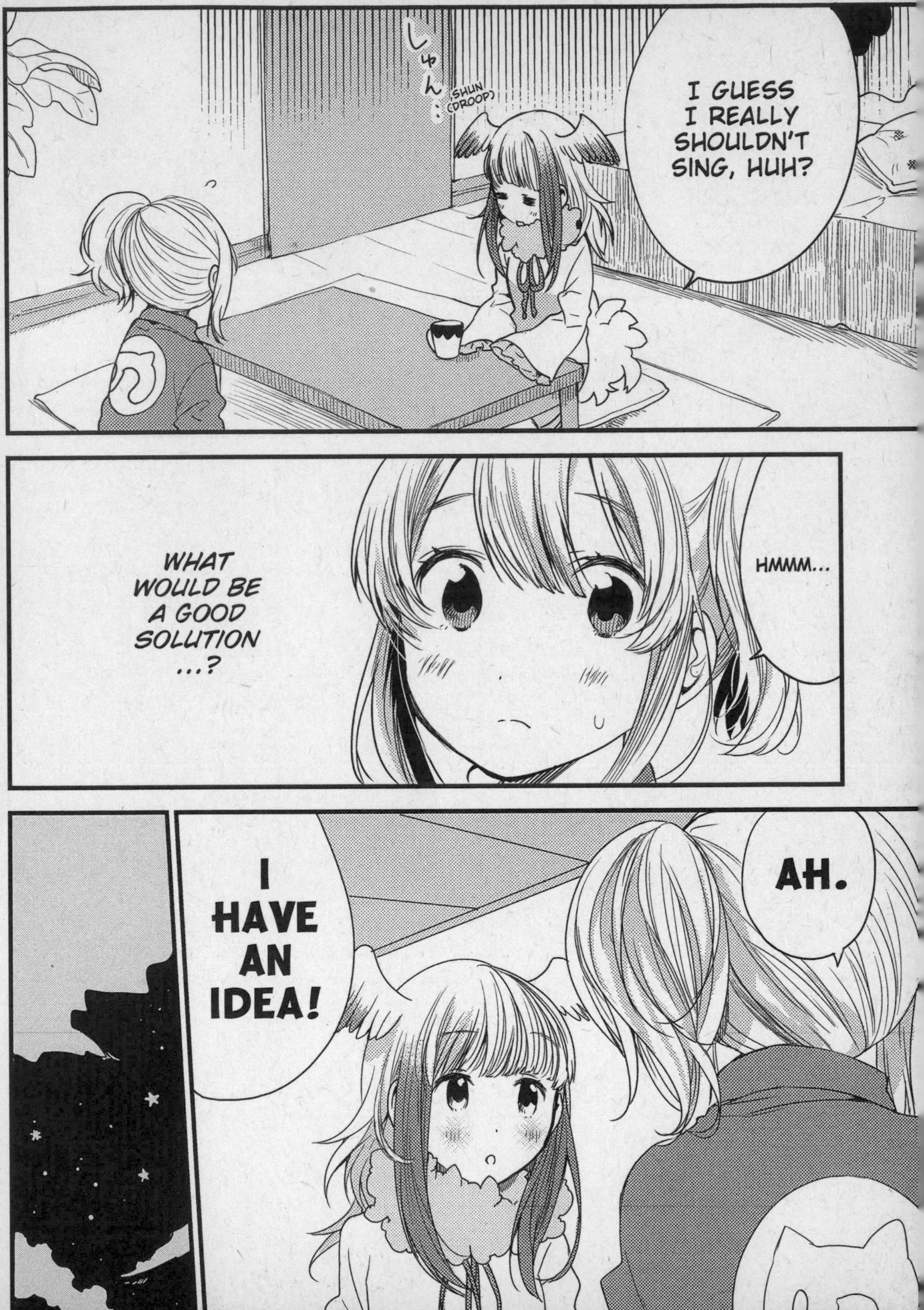
I GUESS I REALLY SHOULDN'T SING, HUH?
しゅん…
SHUN (DROOP)
HMMM...
WHAT WOULD BE A GOOD SOLUTION ...?
AH.
I HAVE AN IDEA!

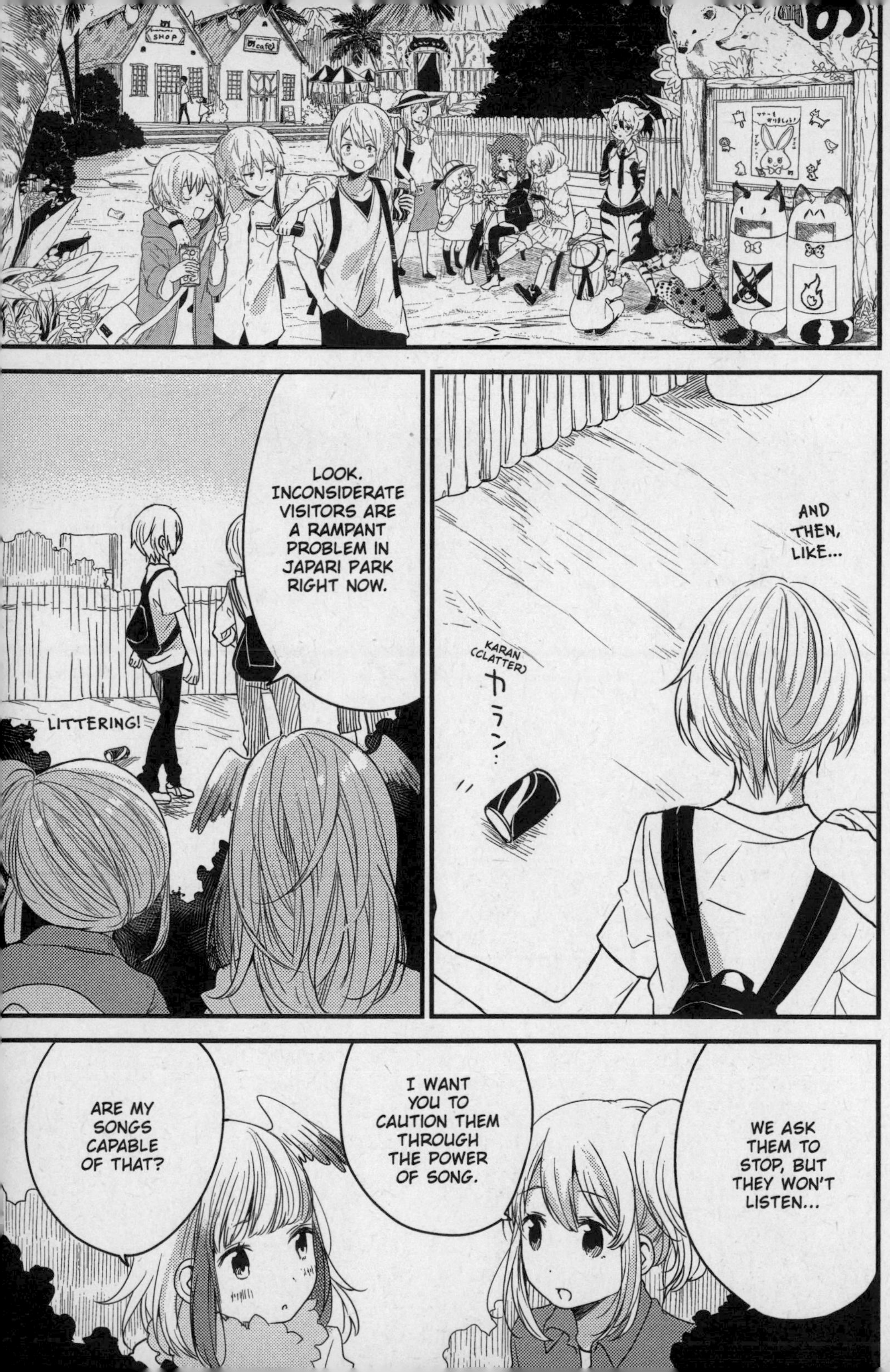
SHOP
cafe
AND THEN, LIKE...
KARAN (CLATTER)
カラン…
LOOK. INCONSIDERATE VISITORS ARE A RAMPANT PROBLEM IN JAPARI PARK RIGHT NOW.
LITTERING!
WE ASK THEM TO STOP, BUT THEY WON'T LISTEN...
I WANT YOU TO CAUTION THEM THROUGH THE POWER OF SONG.
ARE MY SONGS CAPABLE OF THAT?

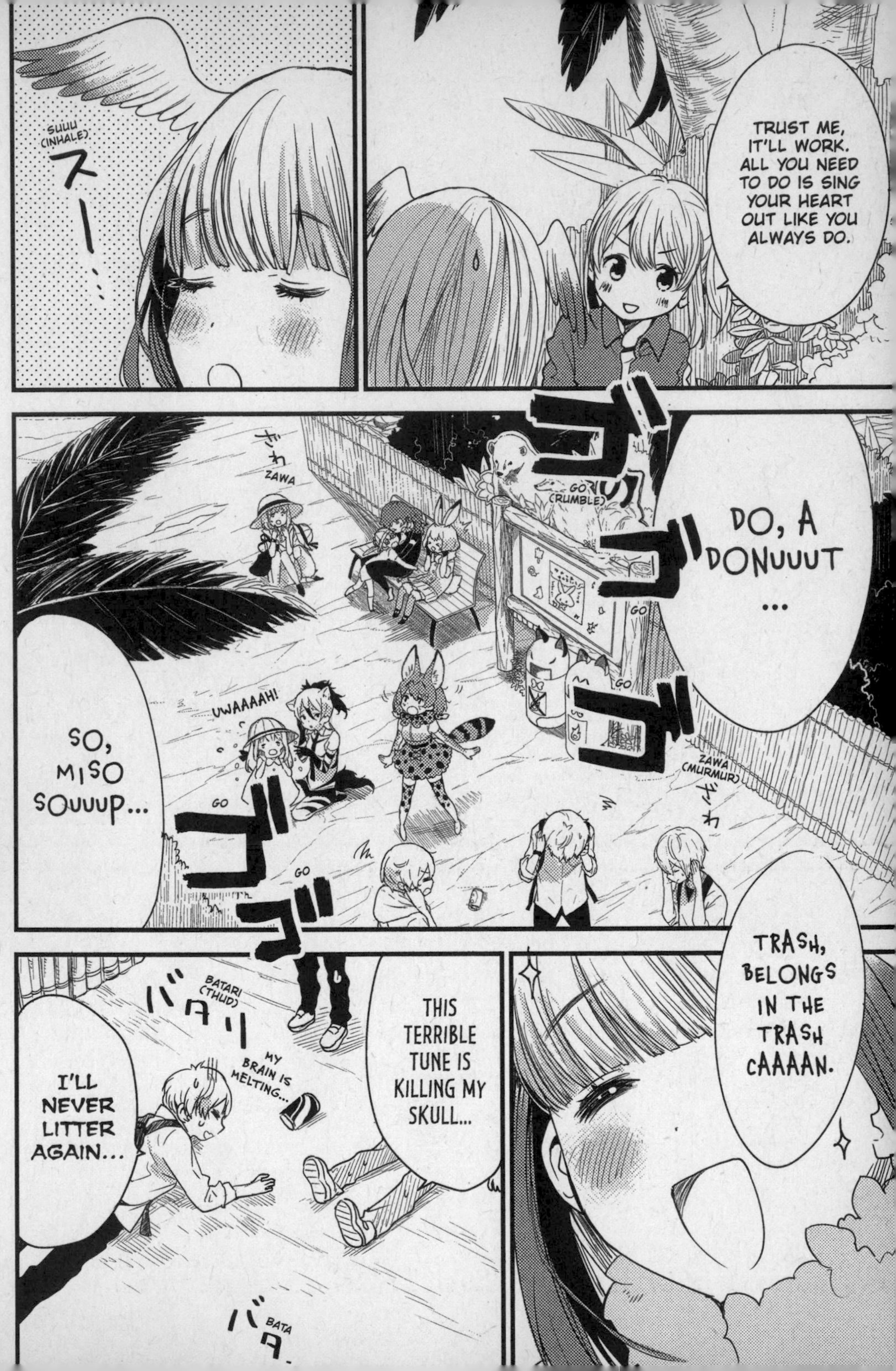
TRUST ME, IT'LL WORK. ALL YOU NEED TO DO IS SING YOUR HEART OUT LIKE YOU ALWAYS DO.
SUUU (INHALE)
スー…
DO, A DONUUUT...
GO (RUMBLE)
ざわ ZAWA
UWAAAAH!
SO, MISO SOUUUP...
ZAWA (MURMUR) ざわ
GO
TRASH, BELONGS IN THE TRASH CAAAAN.
THIS TERRIBLE TUNE IS KILLING MY SKULL...
BATARI (THUD) バタリ
MY BRAIN IS MELTING...
I'LL NEVER LITTER AGAIN...
BATA バタ

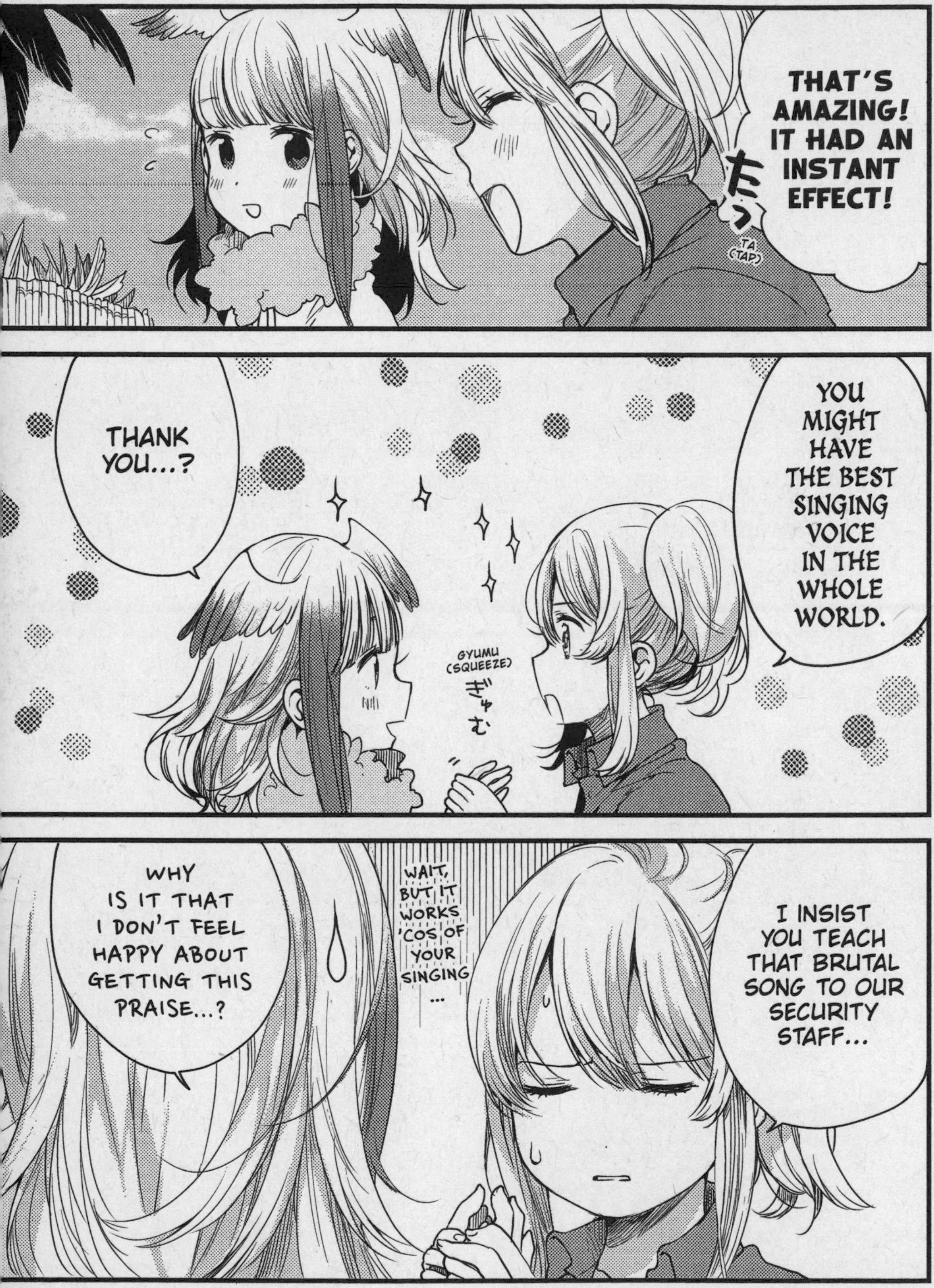

THAT'S AMAZING! IT HAD AN INSTANT EFFECT!
たっ
TA (TAP)
YOU MIGHT HAVE THE BEST SINGING VOICE IN THE WHOLE WORLD.
GYUMU (SQUEEZE)
ぎゅむ
THANK YOU...?
I INSIST YOU TEACH THAT BRUTAL SONG TO OUR SECURITY STAFF...
WAIT, BUT IT WORKS 'COS OF YOUR SINGING...
WHY IS IT THAT I DON'T FEEL HAPPY ABOUT GETTING THIS PRAISE...?

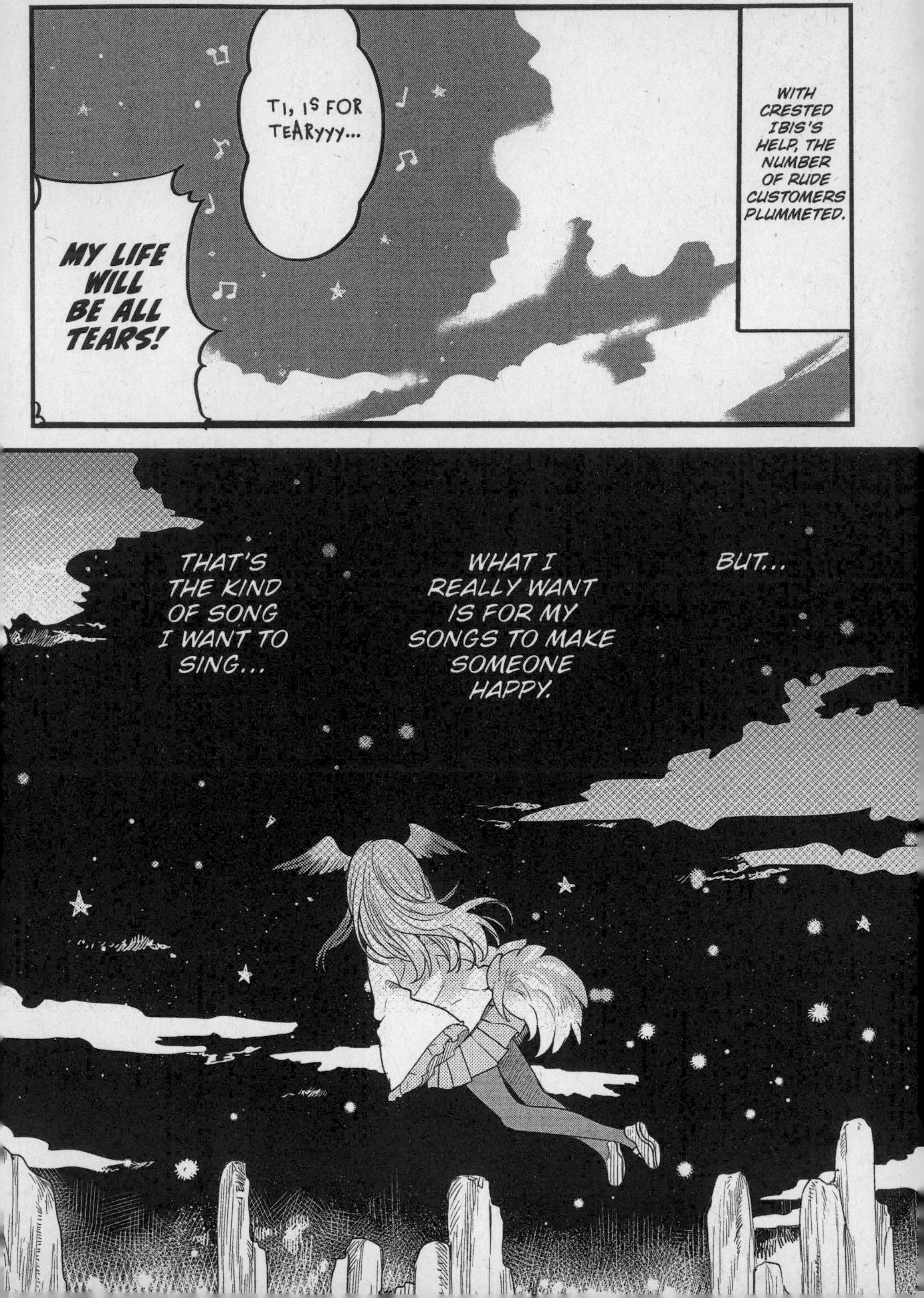
WITH CRESTED IBIS'S HELP, THE NUMBER OF RUDE CUSTOMERS PLUMMETED.
TI, IS FOR TEARyyy...
MY LIFE WILL BE ALL TEARS!
BUT...
WHAT I REALLY WANT IS FOR MY SONGS TO MAKE SOMEONE HAPPY.
THAT'S THE KIND OF SONG I WANT TO SING...

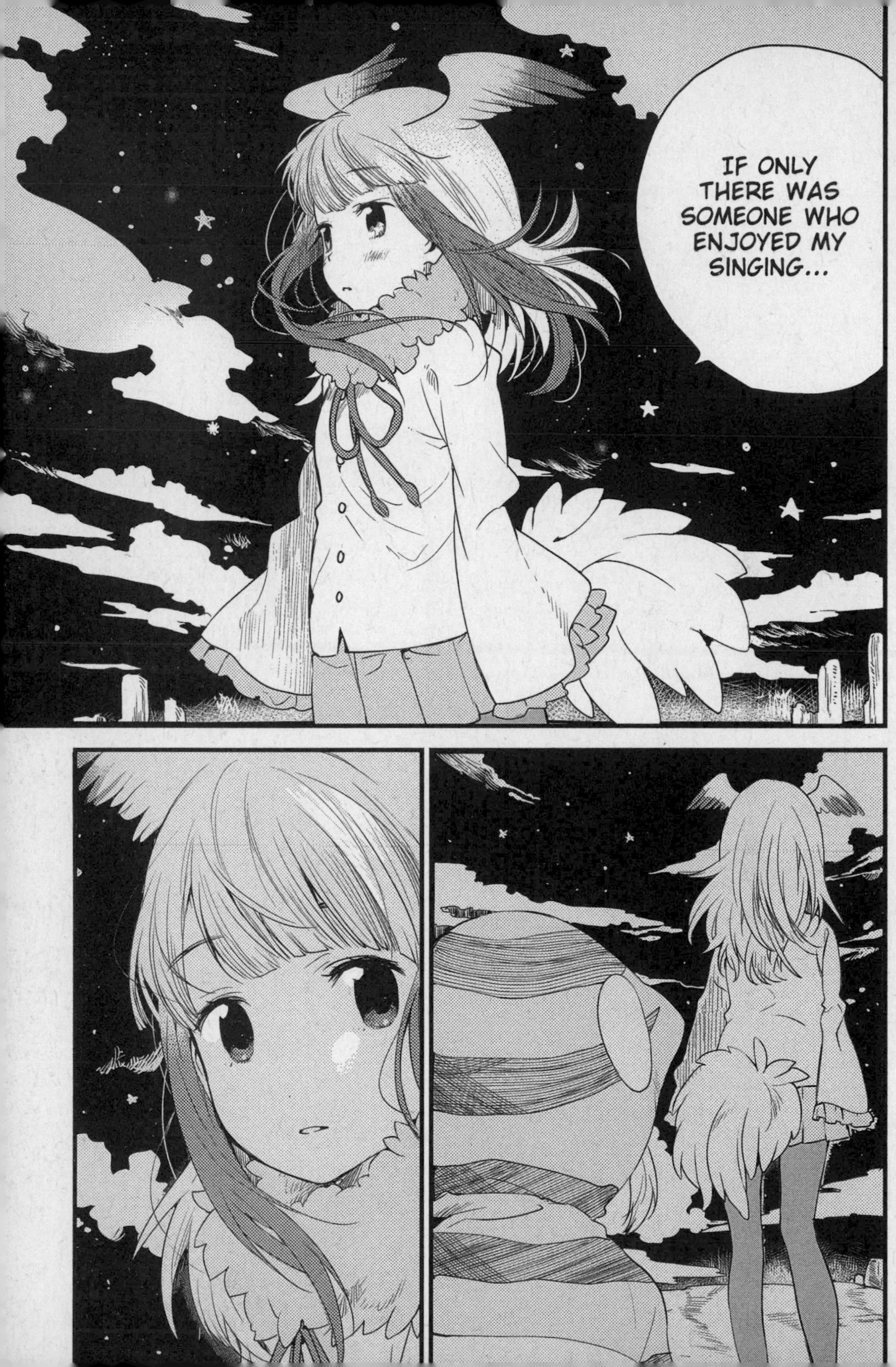
IF ONLY THERE WAS SOMEONE WHO ENJOYED MY SINGING...

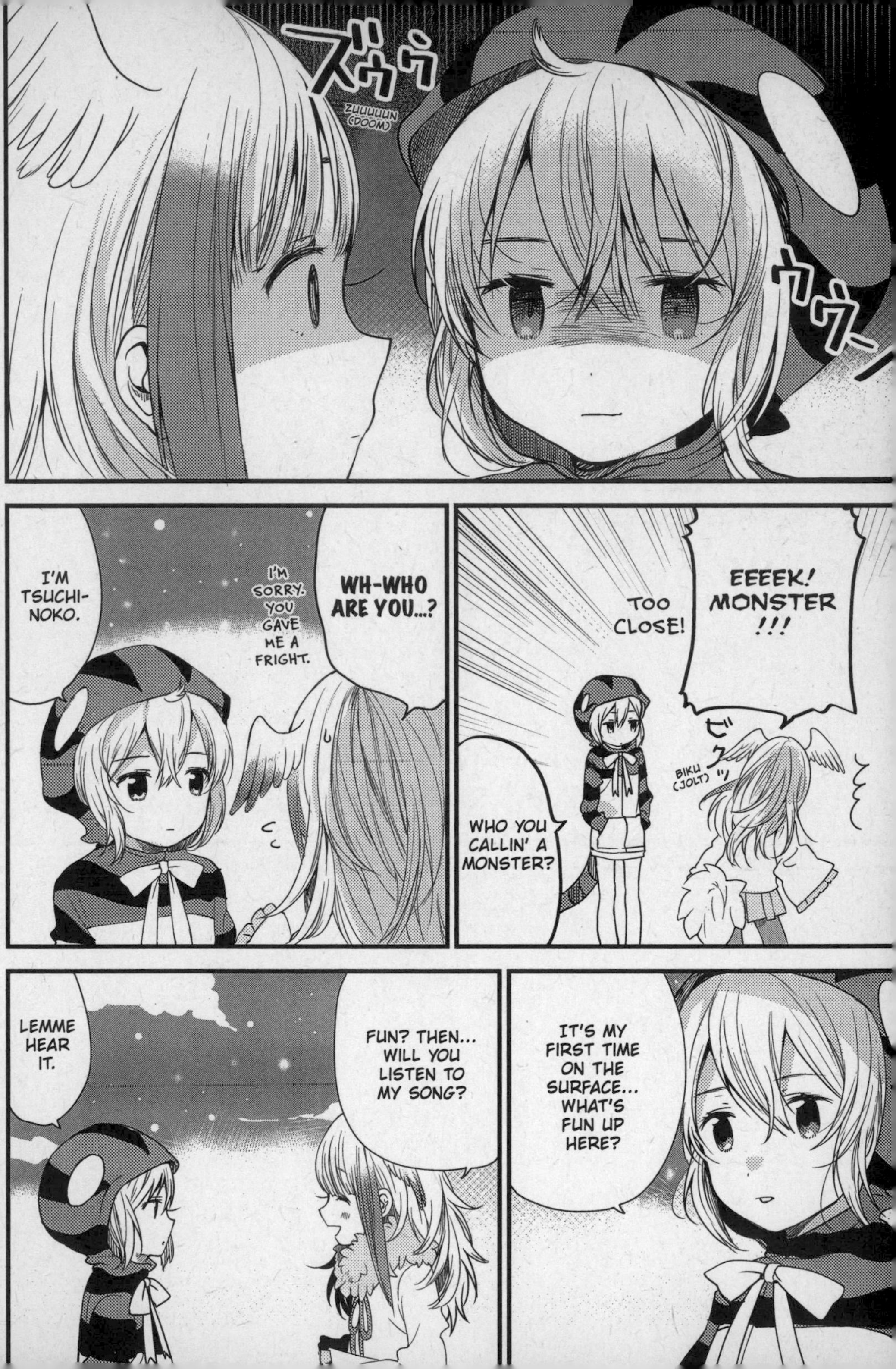
ズゥゥ
ZUUUUUN (DOOM)
ウウー
EEEEK! MONSTER !!!
ビクッ
BIKU (JOLT)
TOO CLOSE!
WHO YOU CALLIN' A MONSTER?
WH-WHO ARE YOU...?
I'M SORRY. YOU GAVE ME A FRIGHT.
I'M TSUCHI-NOKO.
IT'S MY FIRST TIME ON THE SURFACE... WHAT'S FUN UP HERE?
FUN? THEN... WILL YOU LISTEN TO MY SONG?
LEMME HEAR IT.

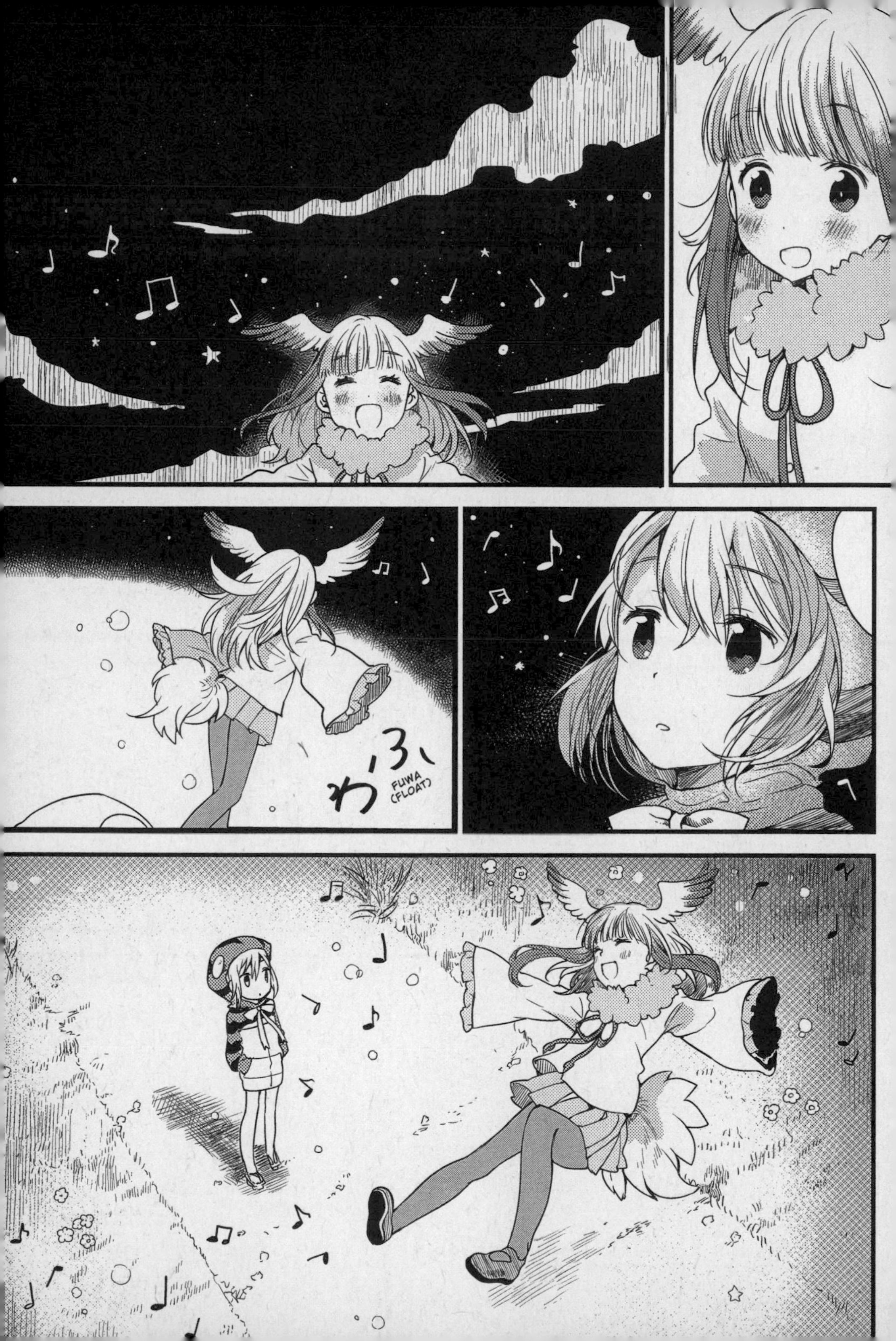
ふわ
FUWA
(FLOAT)

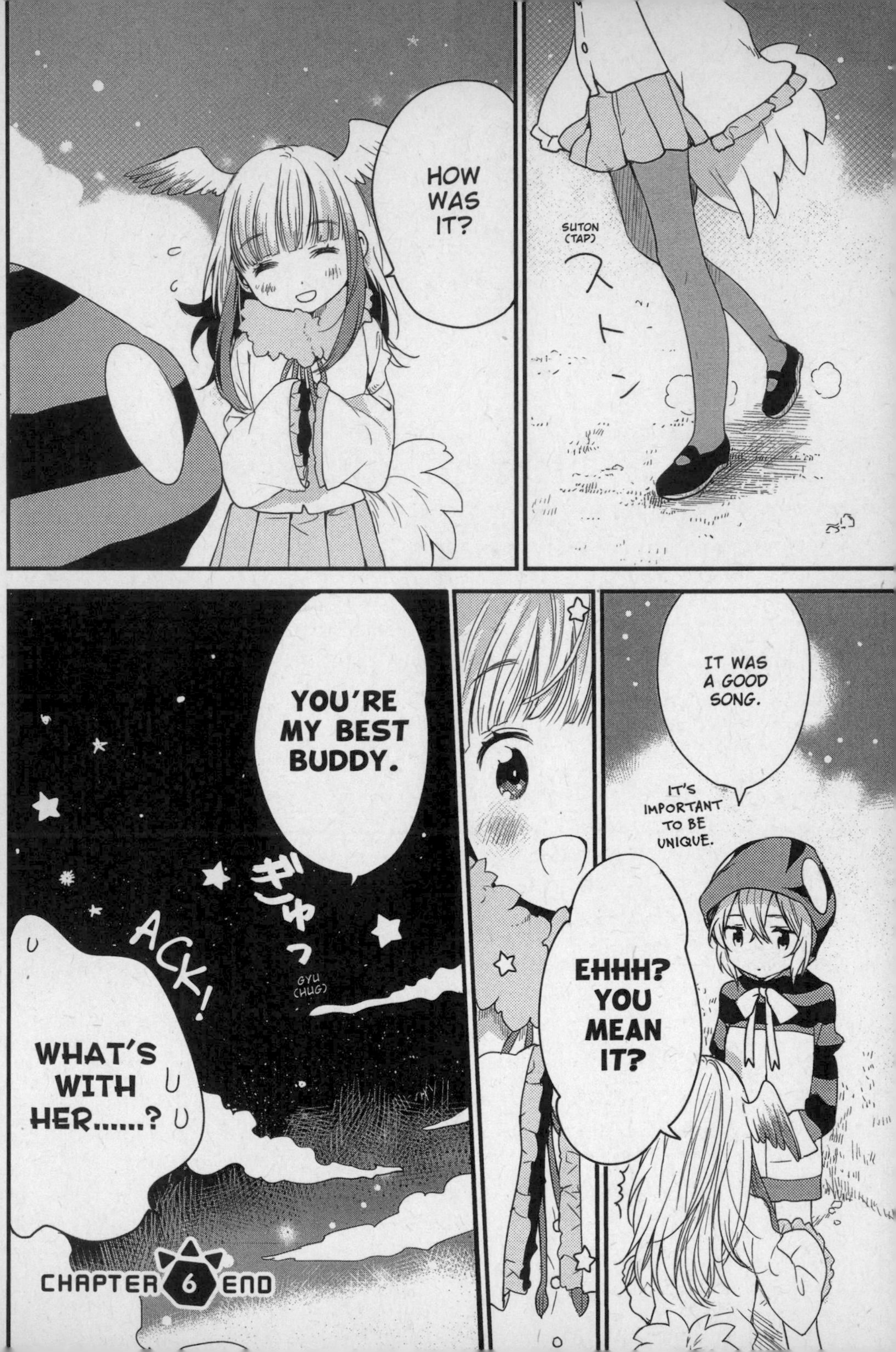
SUTON (TAP)
ストーン
HOW WAS IT?
IT WAS A GOOD SONG.
IT'S IMPORTANT TO BE UNIQUE.
EHHH? YOU MEAN IT?
YOU'RE MY BEST BUDDY.
ぎゅっ
GYU (HUG)
ACK!
WHAT'S WITH HER......?
CHAPTER 6 END

KEMONO FRIENDS
WELCOME TO JAPARI PARK!

CHAPTER 7

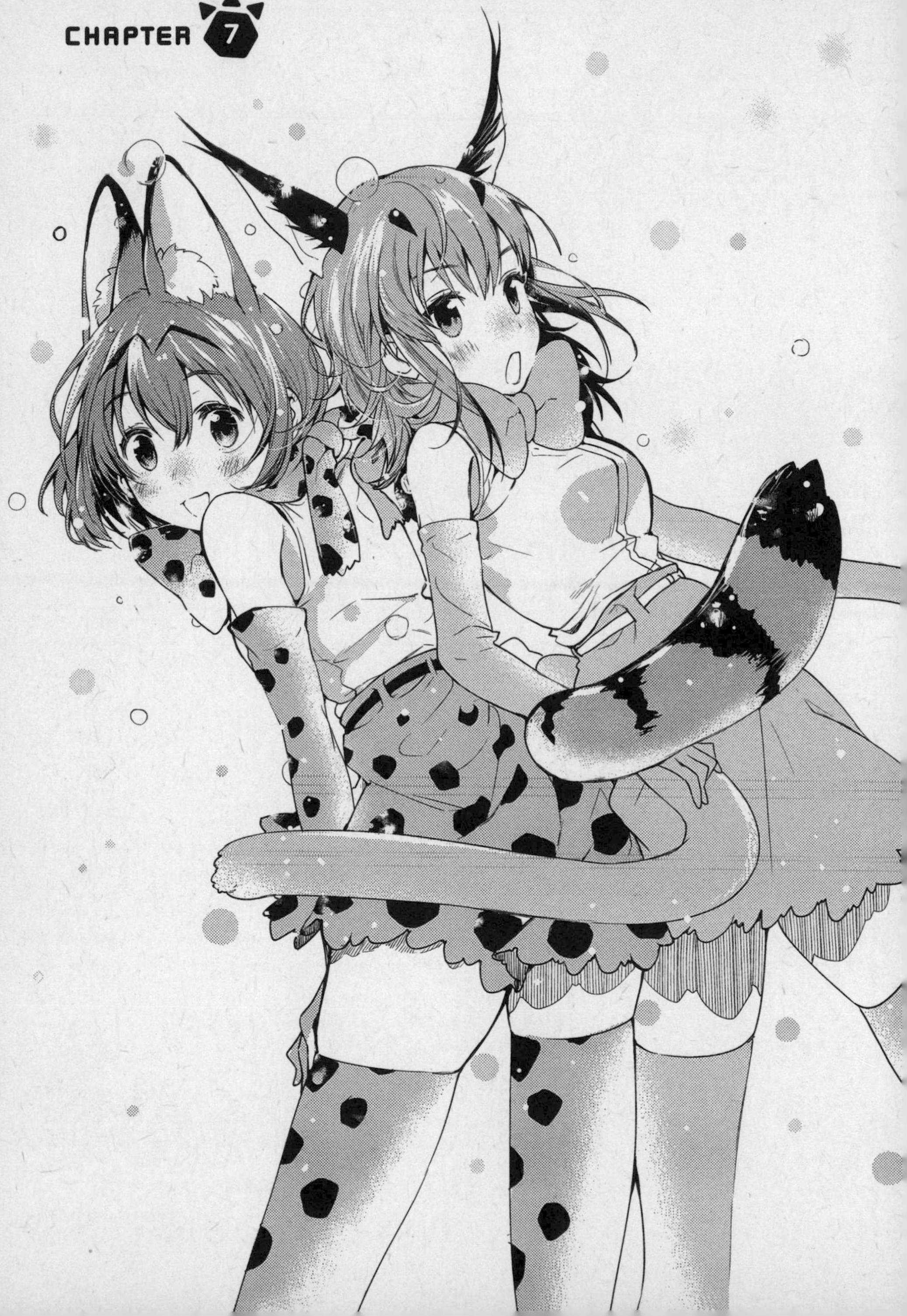

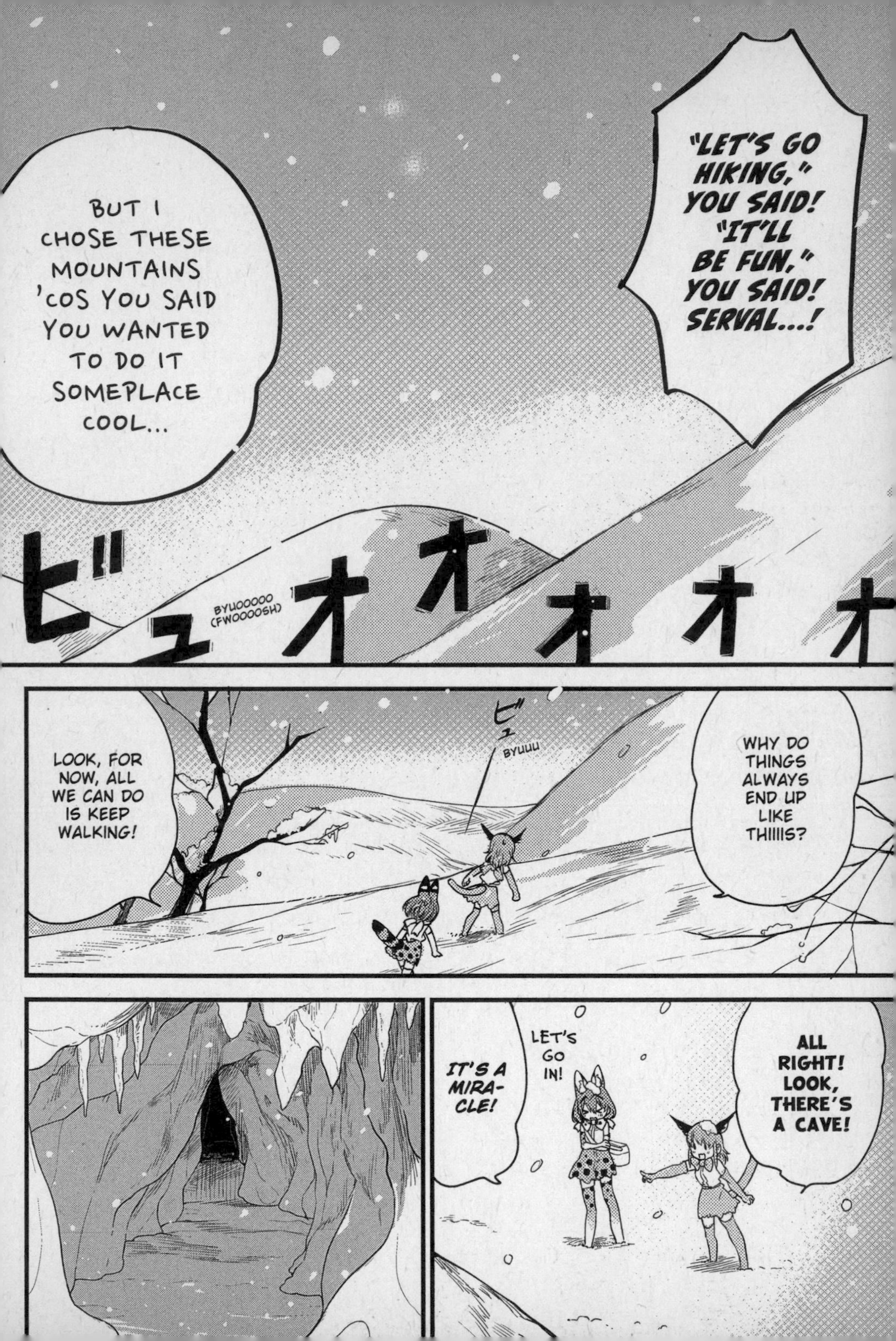
"LET'S GO HIKING," YOU SAID! "IT'LL BE FUN," YOU SAID! SERVAL...!
BUT I CHOSE THESE MOUNTAINS 'COS YOU SAID YOU WANTED TO DO IT SOMEPLACE COOL...
ビュオオォオォ
BYUOOOOO (FWOOOOSH)
WHY DO THINGS ALWAYS END UP LIKE THIIIIS?
ビュ
BYUUU
LOOK, FOR NOW, ALL WE CAN DO IS KEEP WALKING!
ALL RIGHT! LOOK, THERE'S A CAVE!
LET'S GO IN!
IT'S A MIRA-CLE!

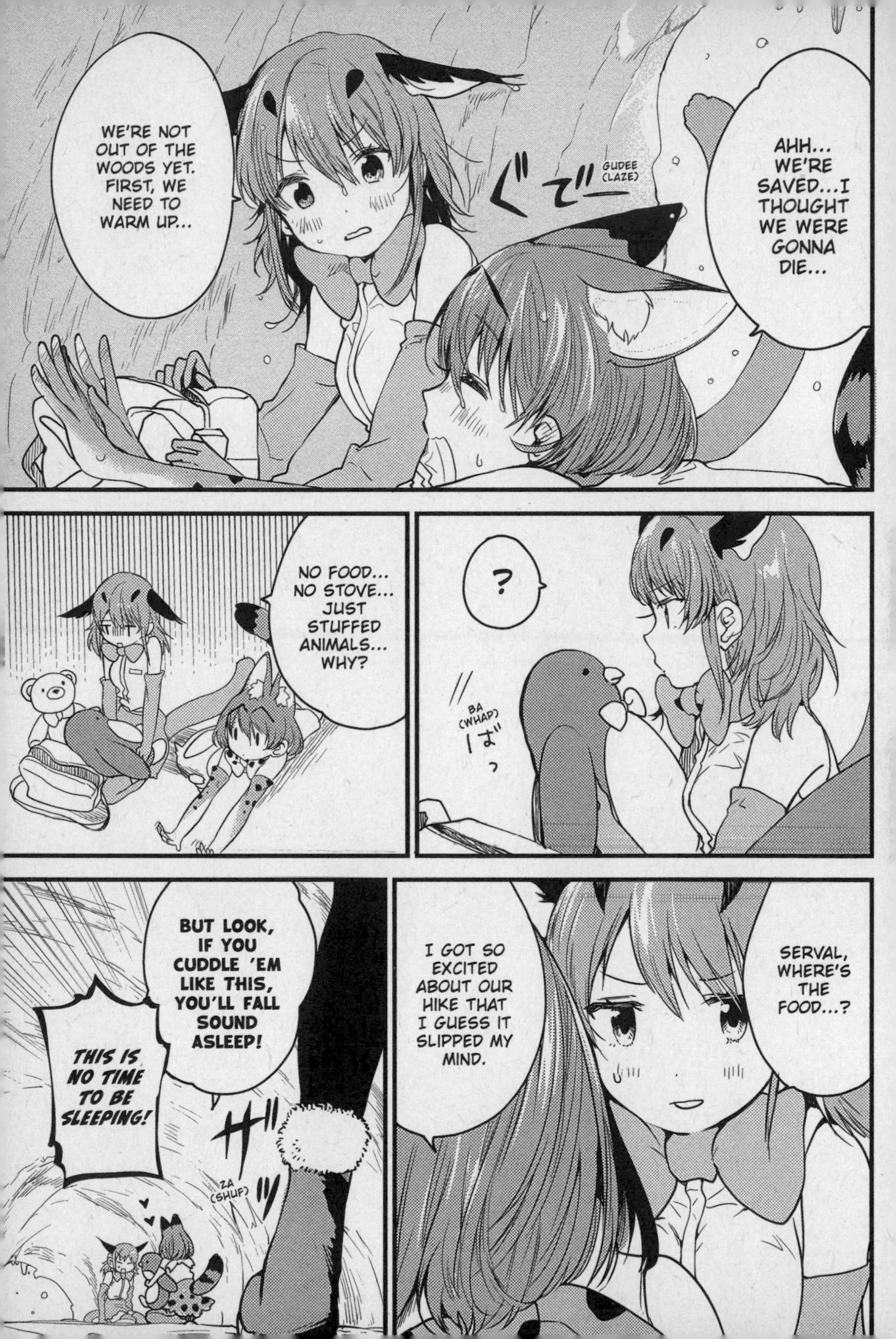
AHH... WE'RE SAVED...I THOUGHT WE WERE GONNA DIE...
GUDEE (LAZE)
WE'RE NOT OUT OF THE WOODS YET. FIRST, WE NEED TO WARM UP...
?
BA (WHAP)
NO FOOD... NO STOVE... JUST STUFFED ANIMALS... WHY?
SERVAL, WHERE'S THE FOOD...?
I GOT SO EXCITED ABOUT OUR HIKE THAT I GUESS IT SLIPPED MY MIND.
BUT LOOK, IF YOU CUDDLE 'EM LIKE THIS, YOU'LL FALL SOUND ASLEEP!
THIS IS NO TIME TO BE SLEEPING!
ZA (SHUF)

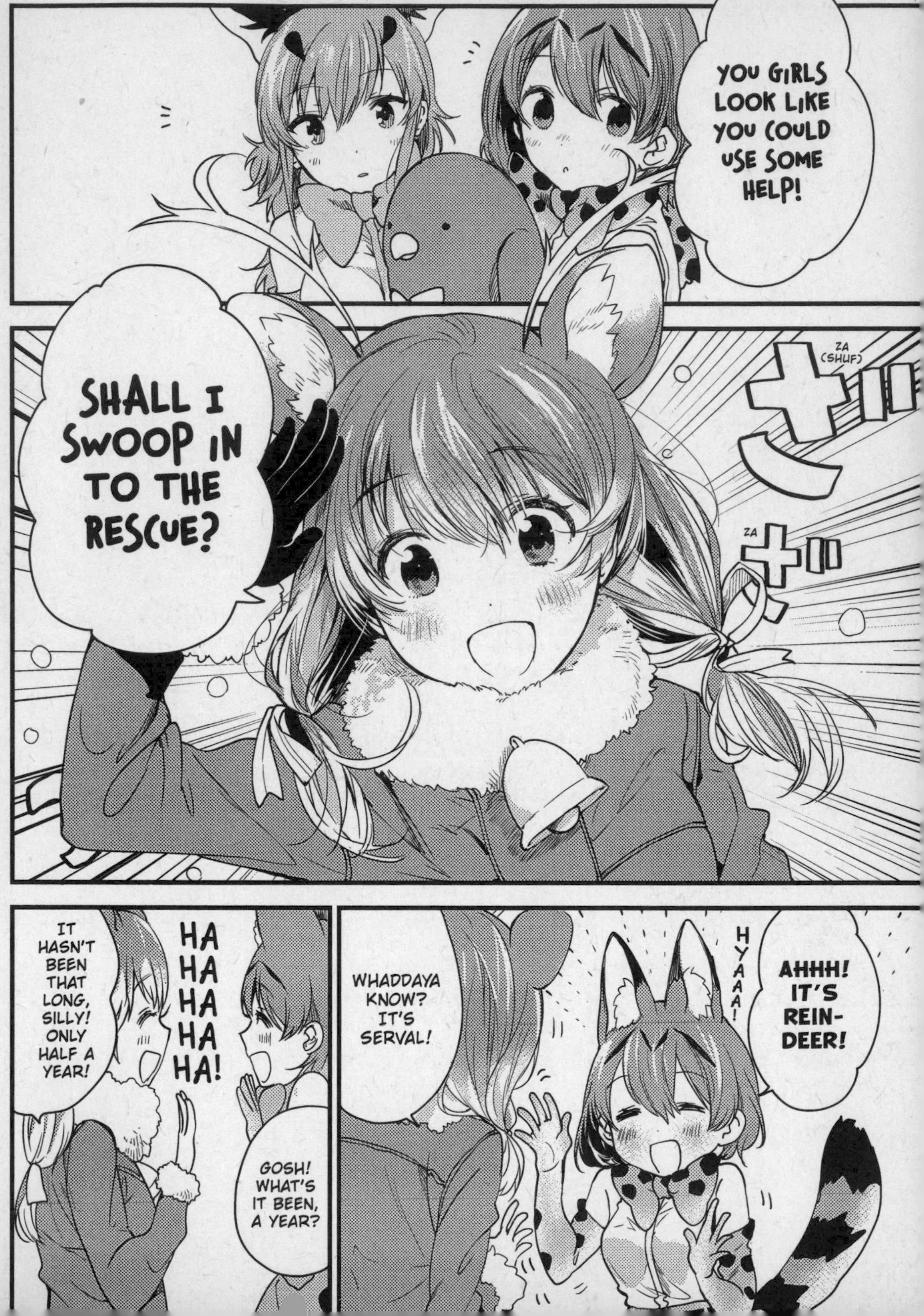
YOU GIRLS LOOK LIKE YOU COULD USE SOME HELP!
ZA (SHUF)
ZA
SHALL I SWOOP IN TO THE RESCUE?
AHHH! IT'S REIN-DEER!
HYAAA!
WHADDAYA KNOW? IT'S SERVAL!
GOSH! WHAT'S IT BEEN, A YEAR?
HA HA HA HA HA!
IT HASN'T BEEN THAT LONG, SILLY! ONLY HALF A YEAR!

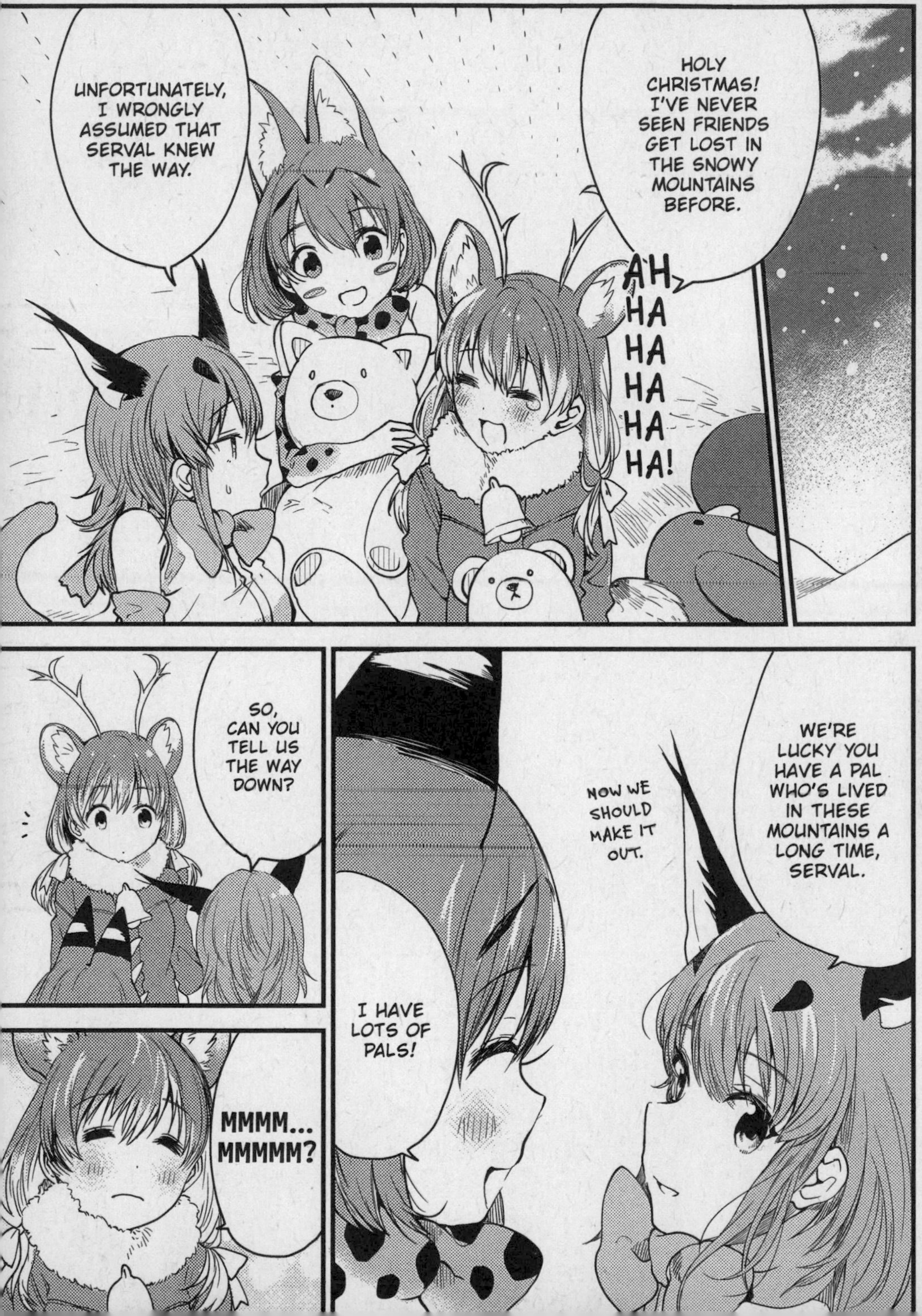
HOLY CHRISTMAS! I'VE NEVER SEEN FRIENDS GET LOST IN THE SNOWY MOUNTAINS BEFORE.
AHHAHAHAHAHAHAHA!
UNFORTUNATELY, I WRONGLY ASSUMED THAT SERVAL KNEW THE WAY.
WE'RE LUCKY YOU HAVE A PAL WHO'S LIVED IN THESE MOUNTAINS A LONG TIME, SERVAL.
NOW WE SHOULD MAKE IT OUT.
I HAVE LOTS OF PALS!
SO, CAN YOU TELL US THE WAY DOWN?
MMMM... MMMMM?

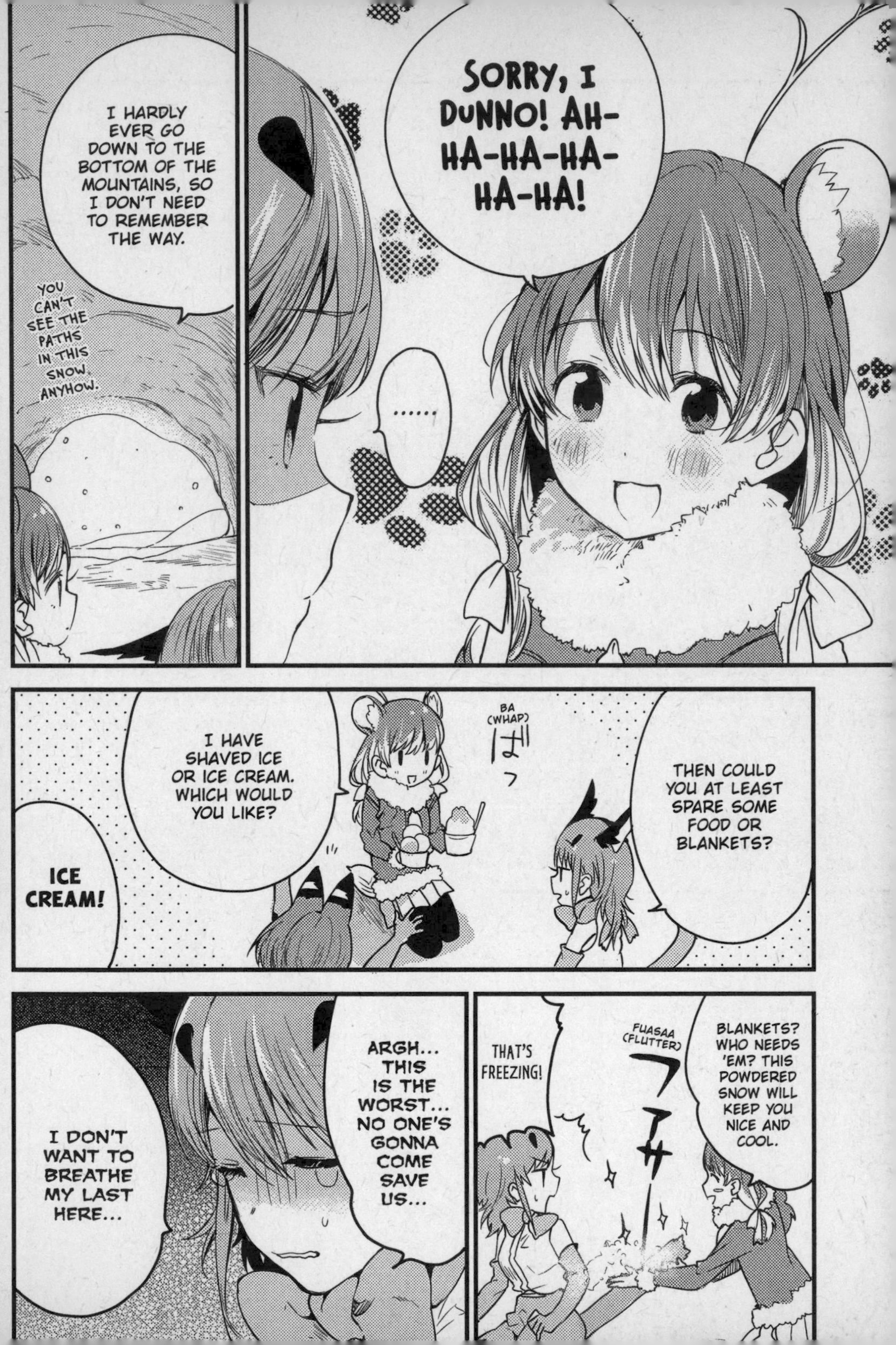
SORRY, I DUNNO! AH-HA-HA-HA-HA-HA!
......
I HARDLY EVER GO DOWN TO THE BOTTOM OF THE MOUNTAINS, SO I DON'T NEED TO REMEMBER THE WAY.
YOU CAN'T SEE THE PATHS IN THIS SNOW ANYHOW.
THEN COULD YOU AT LEAST SPARE SOME FOOD OR BLANKETS?
BA (WHAP)
ばっ
I HAVE SHAVED ICE OR ICE CREAM. WHICH WOULD YOU LIKE?
ICE CREAM!
BLANKETS? WHO NEEDS 'EM? THIS POWDERED SNOW WILL KEEP YOU NICE AND COOL.
FUASAA (FLUTTER)
ファサ
THAT'S FREEZING!
ARGH... THIS IS THE WORST... NO ONE'S GONNA COME SAVE US...
I DON'T WANT TO BREATHE MY LAST HERE...

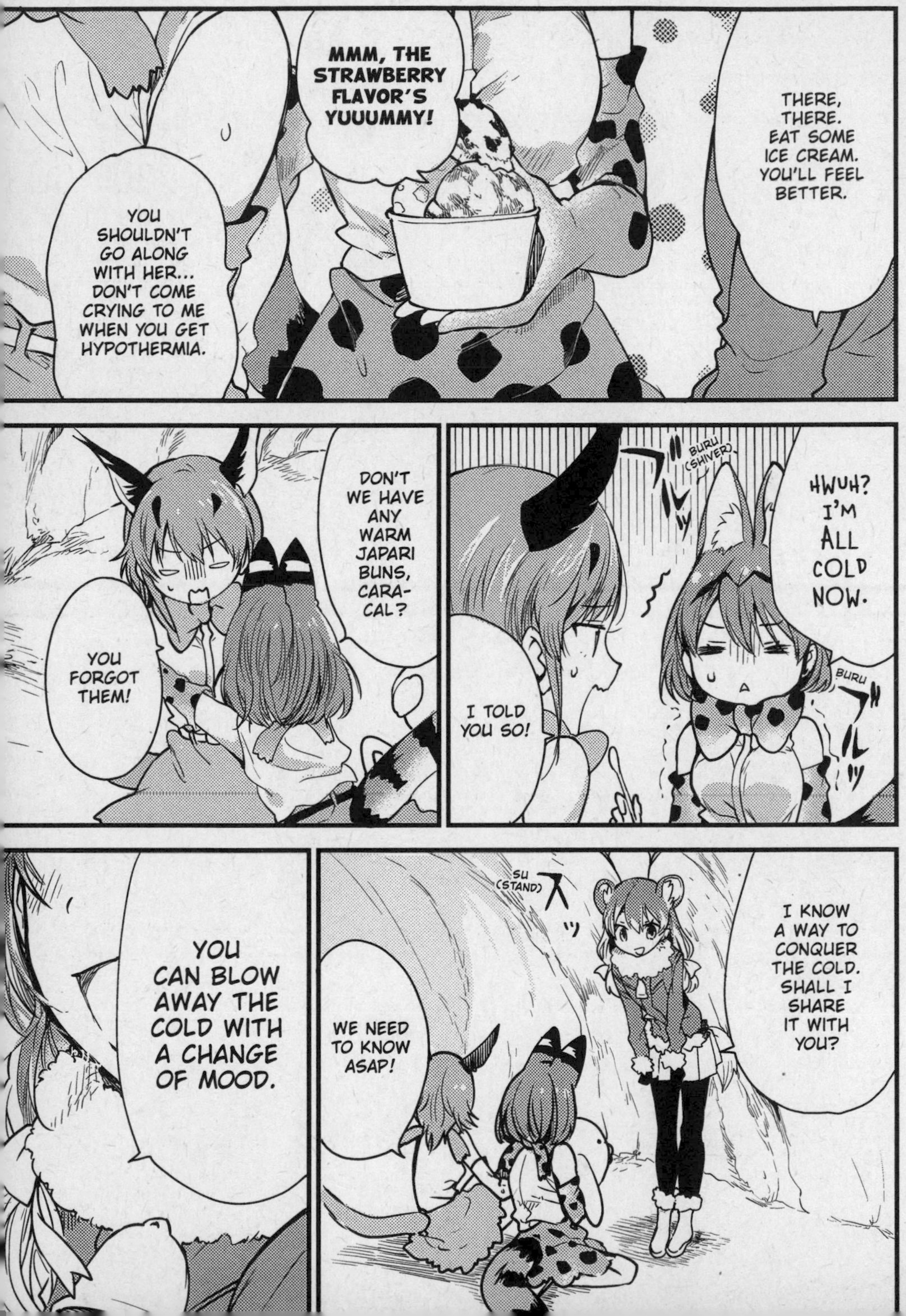
THERE, THERE. EAT SOME ICE CREAM. YOU'LL FEEL BETTER.
MMM, THE STRAWBERRY FLAVOR'S YUUUMMY!
YOU SHOULDN'T GO ALONG WITH HER... DON'T COME CRYING TO ME WHEN YOU GET HYPOTHERMIA.
BURU (SHIVER)
HWUH? I'M ALL COLD NOW.
BURU
I TOLD YOU SO!
DON'T WE HAVE ANY WARM JAPARI BUNS, CARA-CAL?
YOU FORGOT THEM!
SU (STAND)
I KNOW A WAY TO CONQUER THE COLD. SHALL I SHARE IT WITH YOU?
WE NEED TO KNOW ASAP!
YOU CAN BLOW AWAY THE COLD WITH A CHANGE OF MOOD.

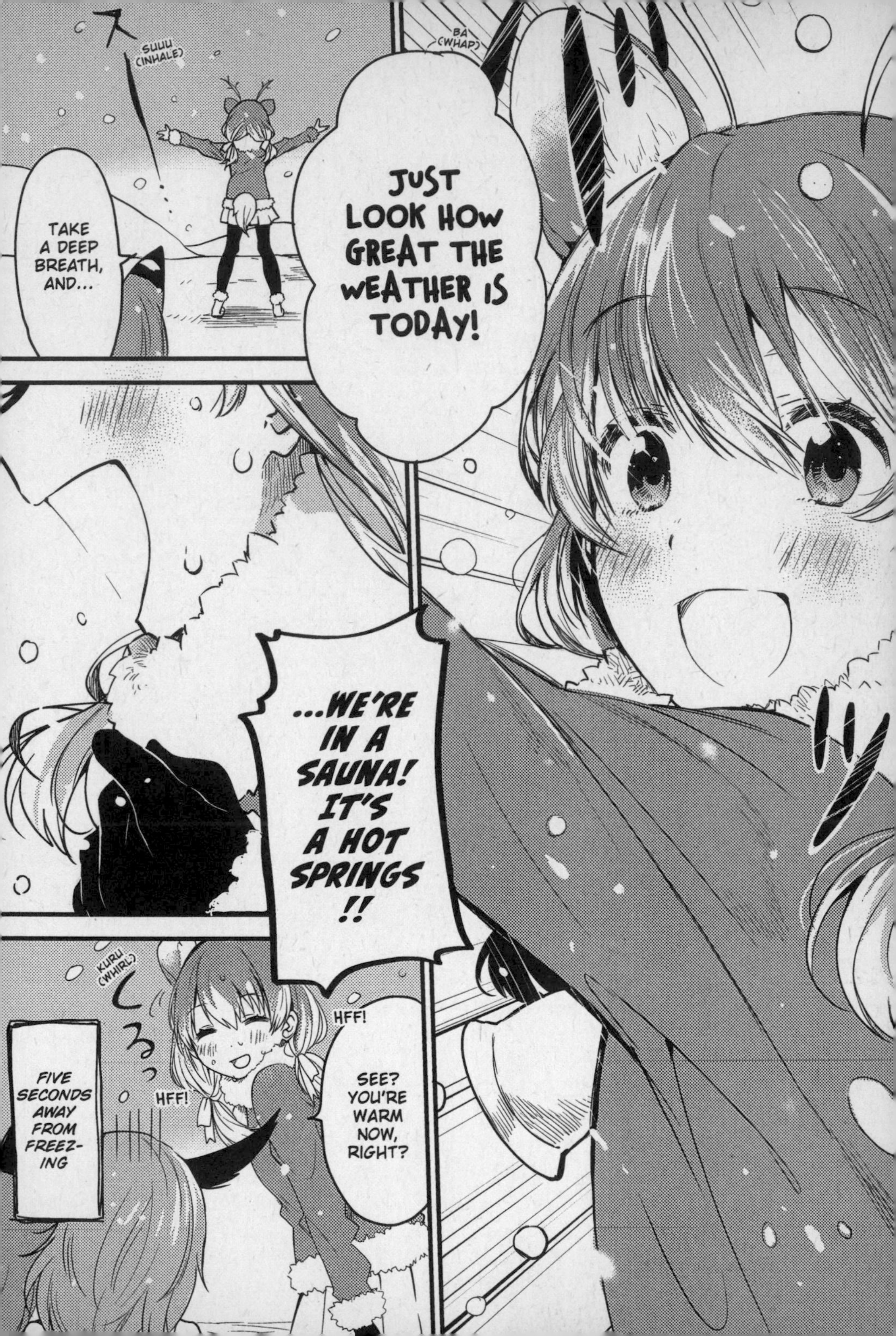
BA (WHAP)
JUST LOOK HOW GREAT THE WEATHER IS TODAY!
...WE'RE IN A SAUNA! IT'S A HOT SPRINGS!!
SUUU (INHALE)
TAKE A DEEP BREATH, AND...
KURU (WHIRL)
HFF!
SEE? YOU'RE WARM NOW, RIGHT?
HFF!
FIVE SECONDS AWAY FROM FREEZ-ING

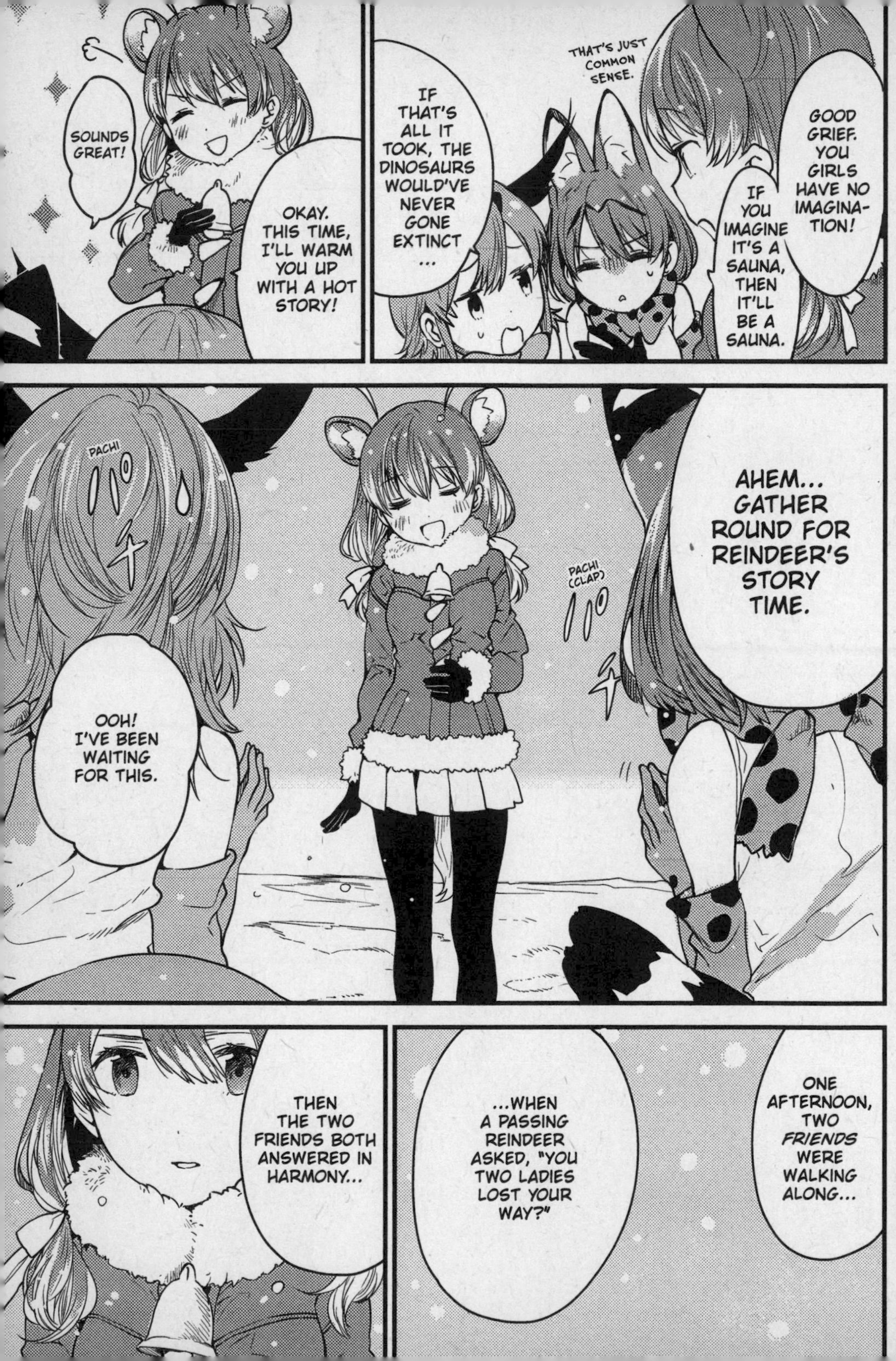
GOOD GRIEF. YOU GIRLS HAVE NO IMAGINATION!
IF YOU IMAGINE IT'S A SAUNA, THEN IT'LL BE A SAUNA.
THAT'S JUST COMMON SENSE.
IF THAT'S ALL IT TOOK, THE DINOSAURS WOULD'VE NEVER GONE EXTINCT...
OKAY. THIS TIME, I'LL WARM YOU UP WITH A HOT STORY!
SOUNDS GREAT!
AHEM... GATHER ROUND FOR REINDEER'S STORY TIME.
PACHI (CLAP)
PACHI
OOH! I'VE BEEN WAITING FOR THIS.
ONE AFTERNOON, TWO *FRIENDS* WERE WALKING ALONG...
...WHEN A PASSING REINDEER ASKED, "YOU TWO LADIES LOST YOUR WAY?"
THEN THE TWO FRIENDS BOTH ANSWERED IN HARMONY...

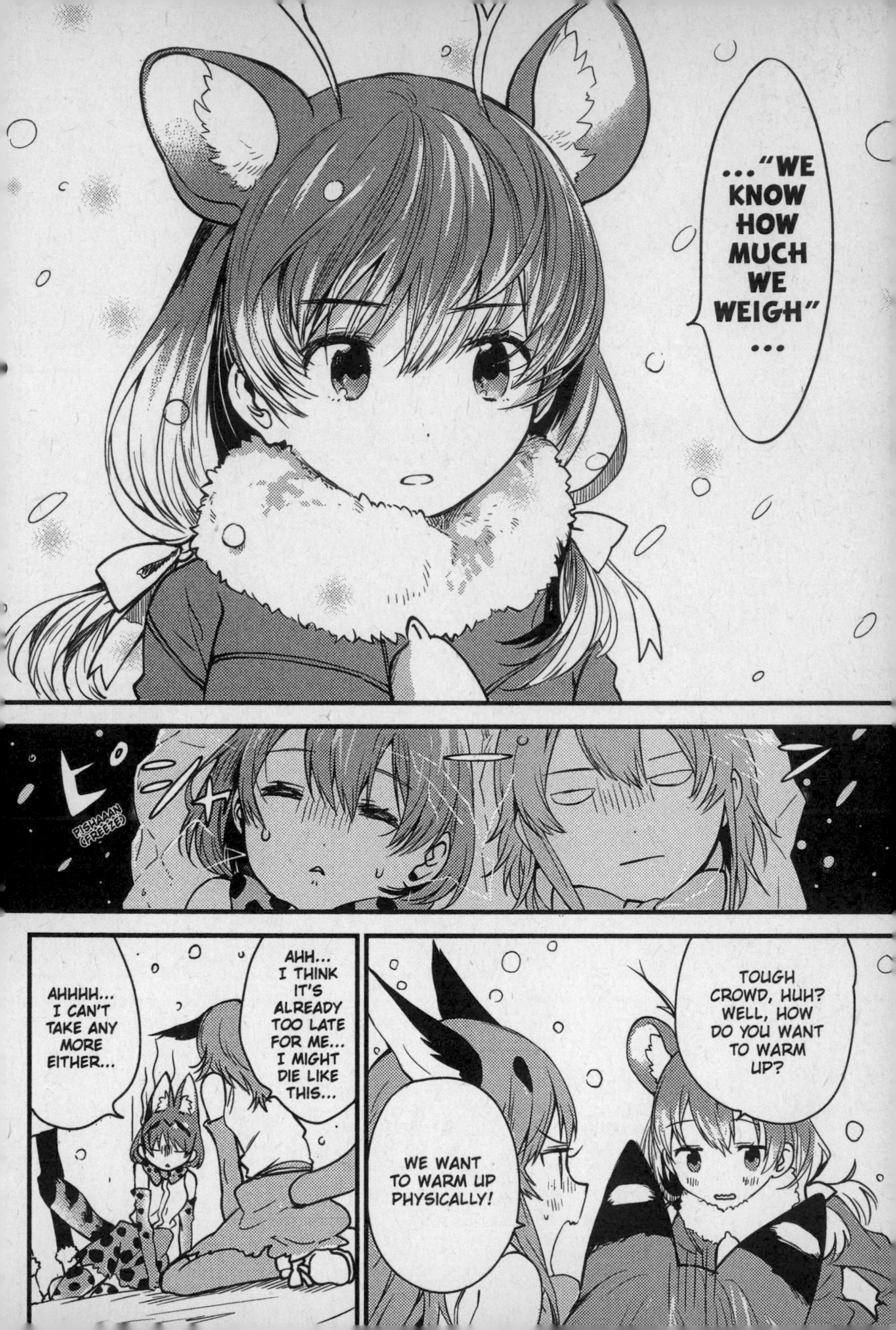
..."WE KNOW HOW MUCH WE WEIGH"...
PISHAAAN (FREEZE)
TOUGH CROWD, HUH? WELL, HOW DO YOU WANT TO WARM UP?
WE WANT TO WARM UP PHYSICALLY!
AHH... I THINK IT'S ALREADY TOO LATE FOR ME... I MIGHT DIE LIKE THIS...
AHHHH... I CAN'T TAKE ANY MORE EITHER...

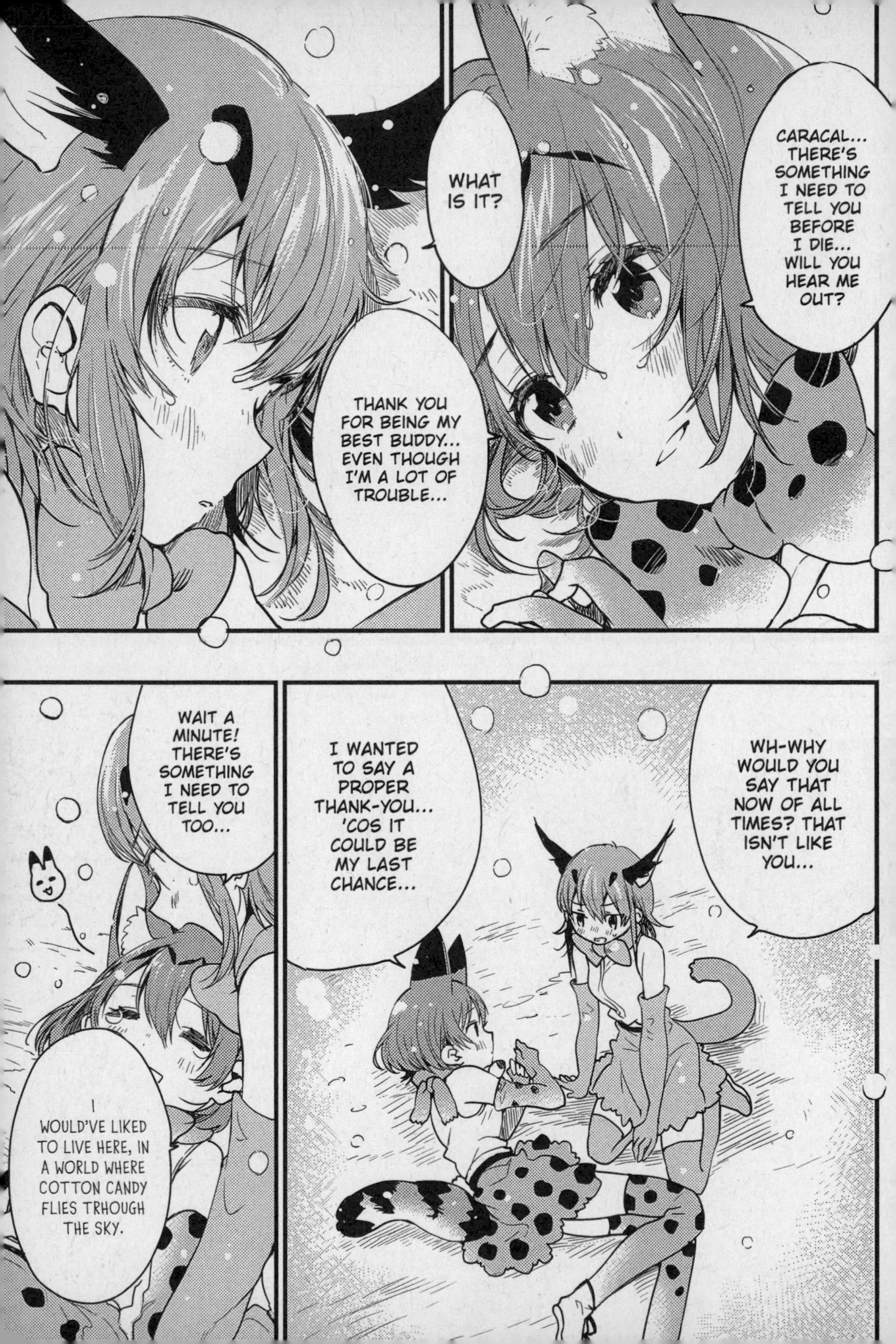

CARACAL... THERE'S SOMETHING I NEED TO TELL YOU BEFORE I DIE... WILL YOU HEAR ME OUT?
WHAT IS IT?
THANK YOU FOR BEING MY BEST BUDDY... EVEN THOUGH I'M A LOT OF TROUBLE...
WH-WHY WOULD YOU SAY THAT NOW OF ALL TIMES? THAT ISN'T LIKE YOU...
I WANTED TO SAY A PROPER THANK-YOU... 'COS IT COULD BE MY LAST CHANCE...
WAIT A MINUTE! THERE'S SOMETHING I NEED TO TELL YOU TOO...
I WOULD'VE LIKED TO LIVE HERE, IN A WORLD WHERE COTTON CANDY FLIES TRHOUGH THE SKY.

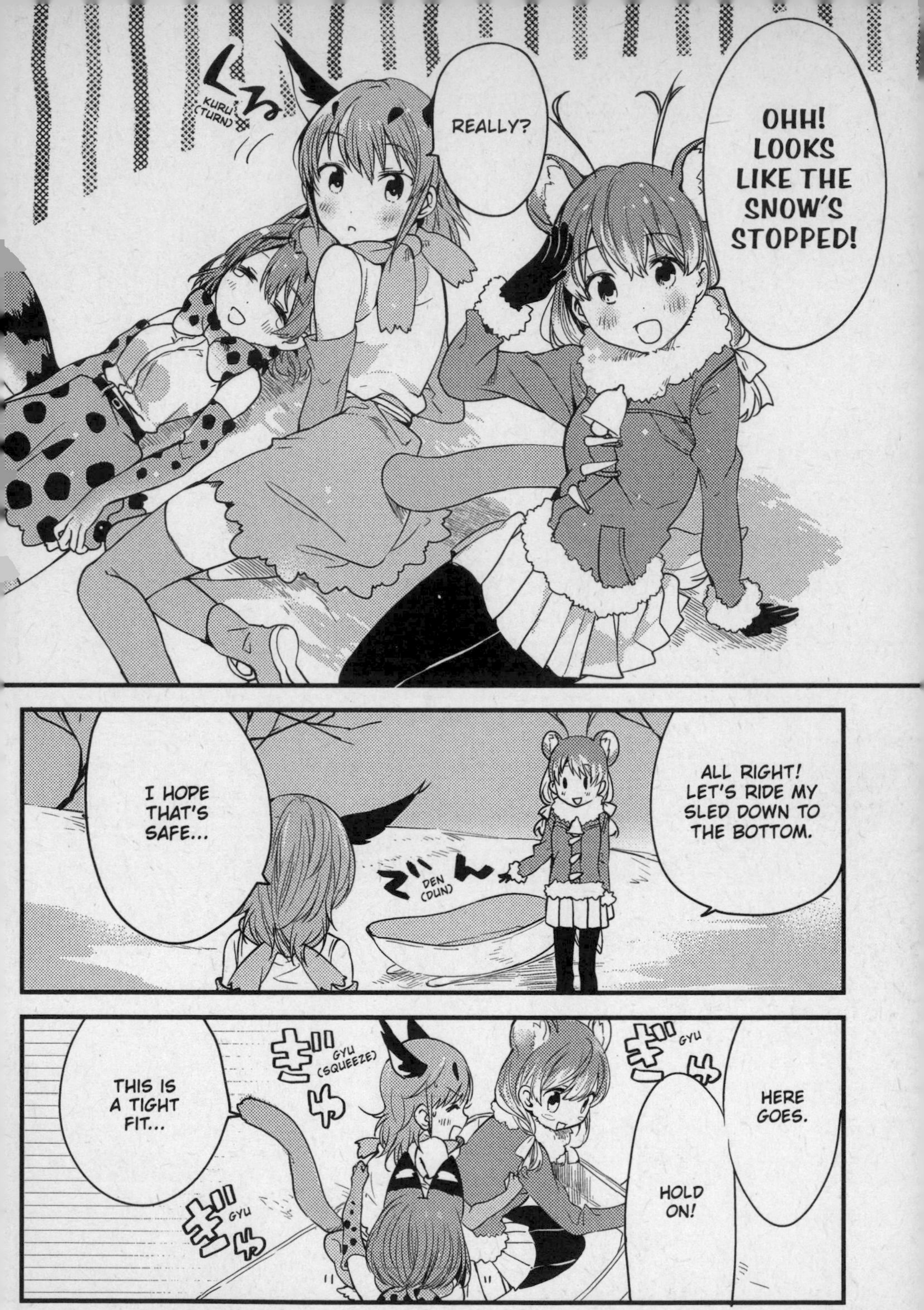
OHH! LOOKS LIKE THE SNOW'S STOPPED!
REALLY?
KURU (TURN)
ALL RIGHT! LET'S RIDE MY SLED DOWN TO THE BOTTOM.
DEN (DUN)
I HOPE THAT'S SAFE...
GYU
HERE GOES.
HOLD ON!
GYU (SQUEEZE)
THIS IS A TIGHT FIT...
GYU

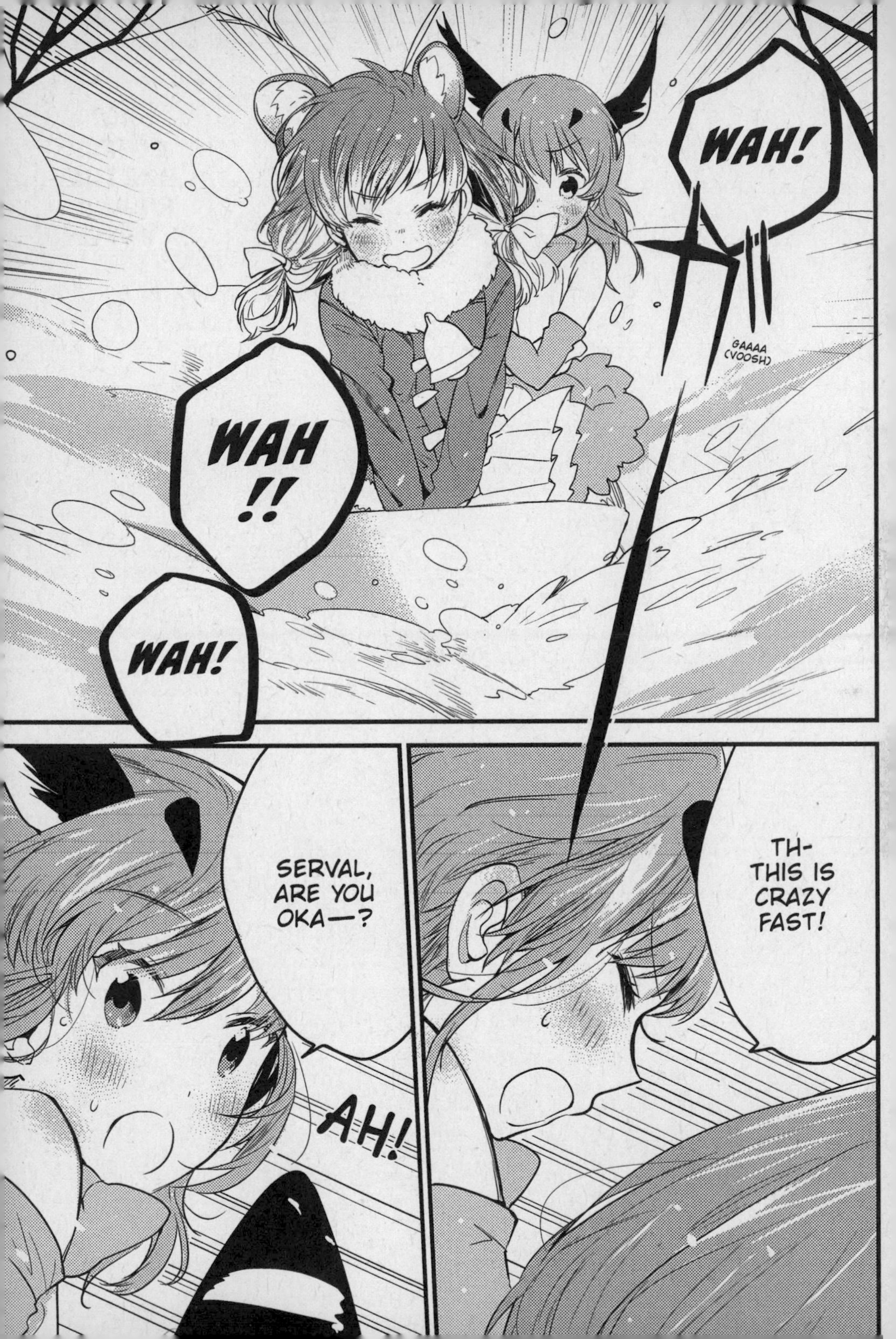
WAH!
GAAAA (VOOSH)
WAH !!
WAH!
TH- THIS IS CRAZY FAST!
SERVAL, ARE YOU OKA—?
AH!

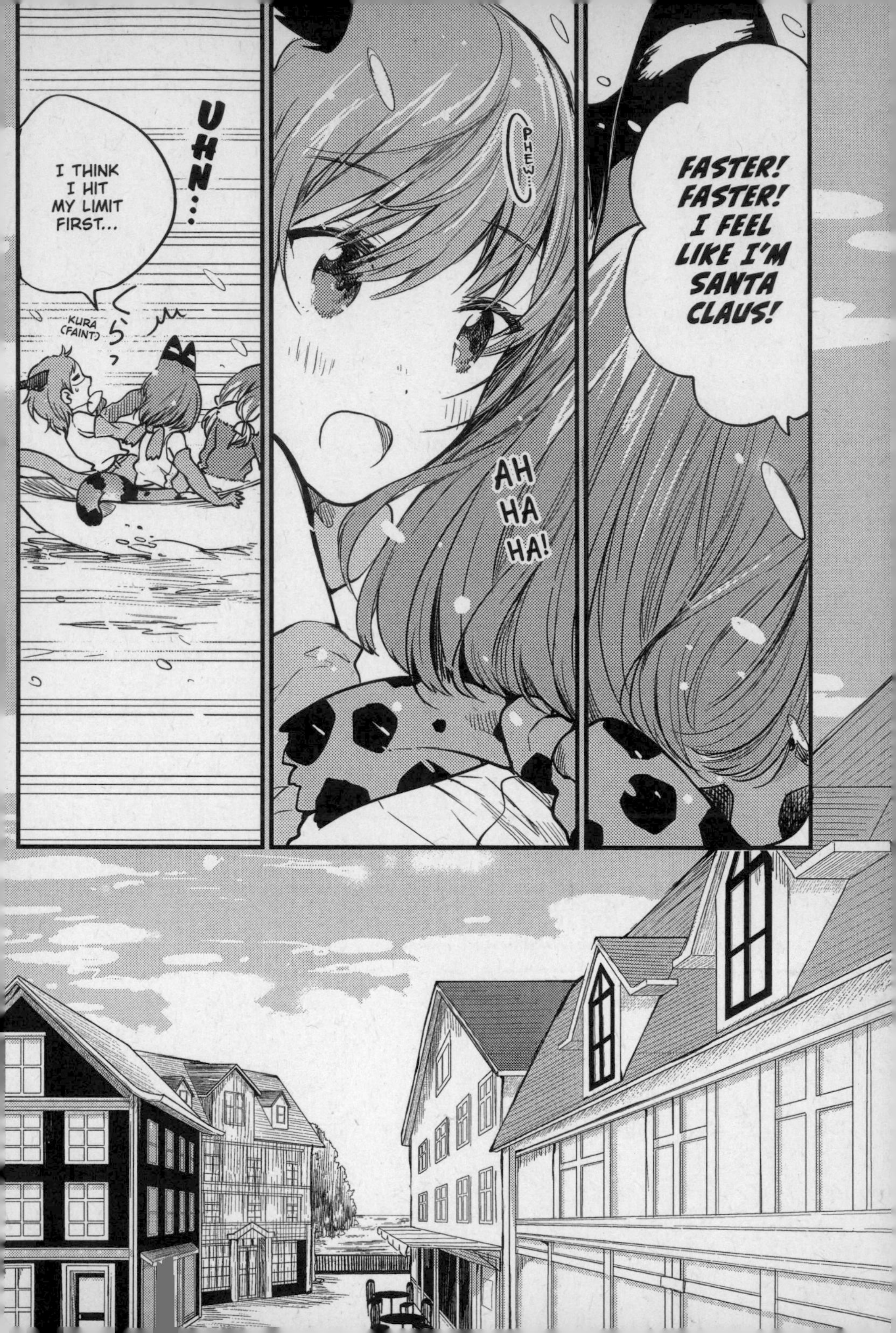
FASTER! FASTER! I FEEL LIKE I'M SANTA CLAUS!
PHEW...
AH HA HA!
UHN...
I THINK I HIT MY LIMIT FIRST...
KURA (FAINT)

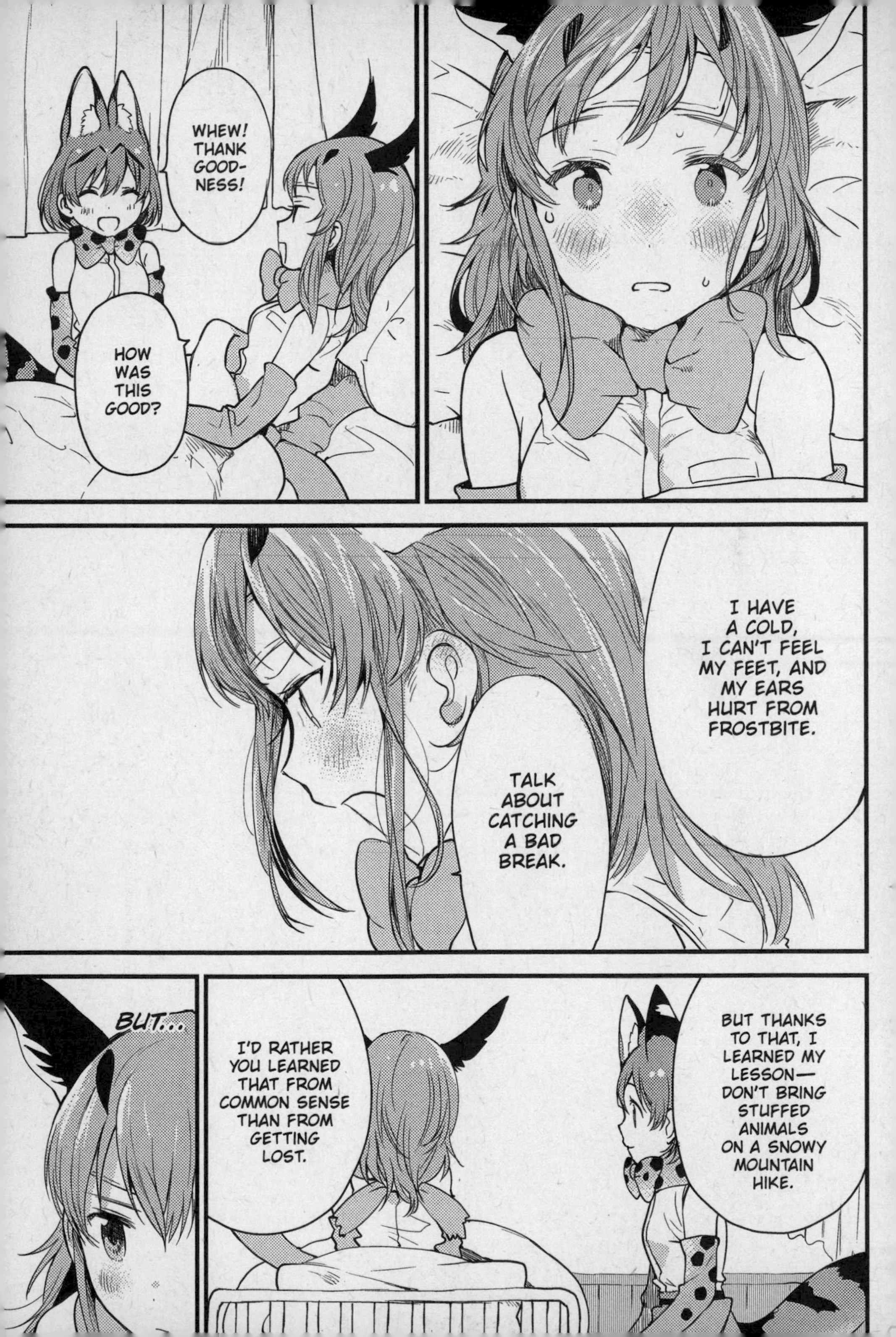
WHEW! THANK GOODNESS!
HOW WAS THIS GOOD?
I HAVE A COLD, I CAN'T FEEL MY FEET, AND MY EARS HURT FROM FROSTBITE.
TALK ABOUT CATCHING A BAD BREAK.
BUT THANKS TO THAT, I LEARNED MY LESSON—DON'T BRING STUFFED ANIMALS ON A SNOWY MOUNTAIN HIKE.
I'D RATHER YOU LEARNED THAT FROM COMMON SENSE THAN FROM GETTING LOST.
BUT...

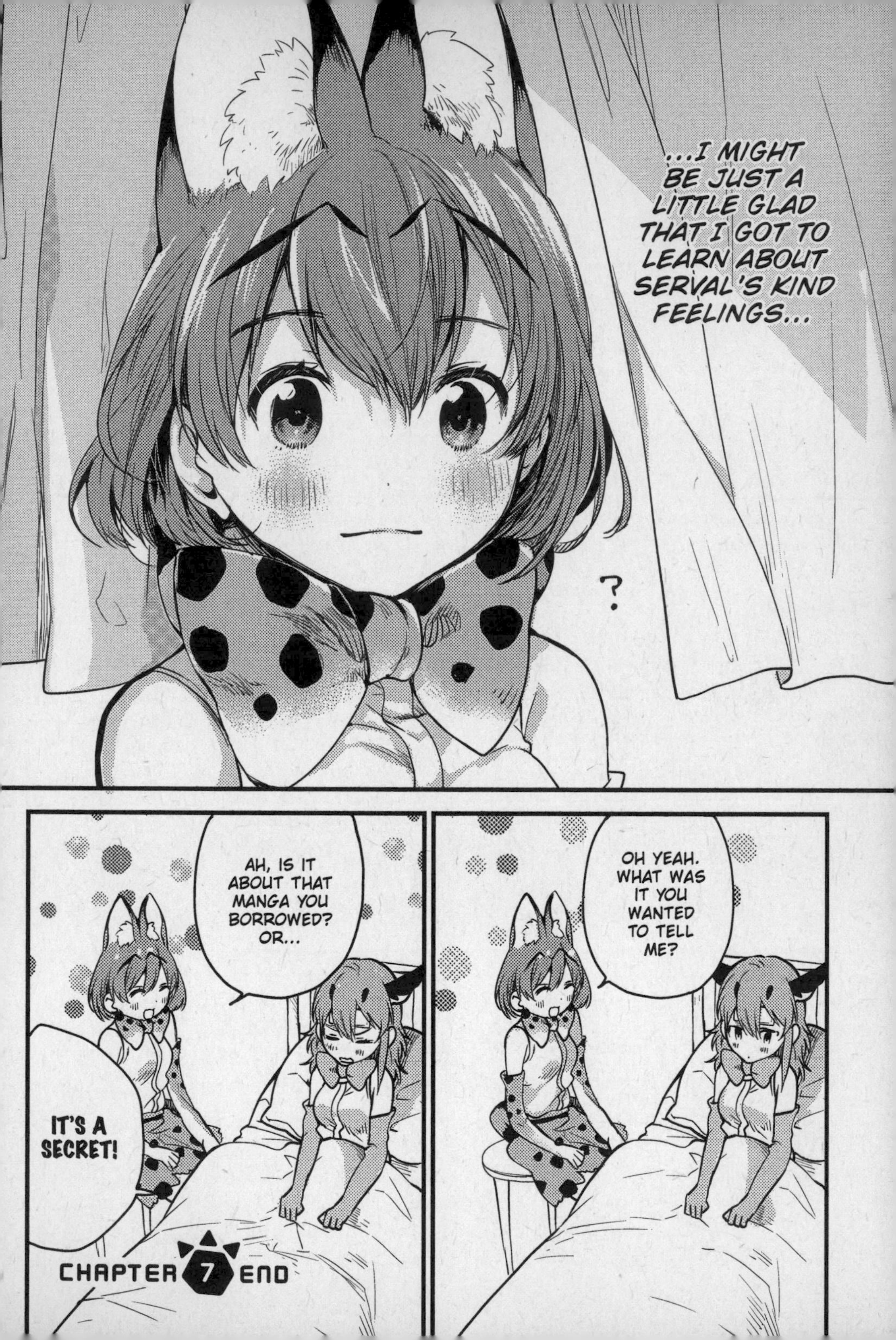
...I MIGHT BE JUST A LITTLE GLAD THAT I GOT TO LEARN ABOUT SERVAL'S KIND FEELINGS...
?
OH YEAH. WHAT WAS IT YOU WANTED TO TELL ME?
AH, IS IT ABOUT THAT MANGA YOU BORROWED? OR...
IT'S A SECRET!
CHAPTER 7 END

KEMONO FRIENDS
WELCOME TO JAPARI PARK!

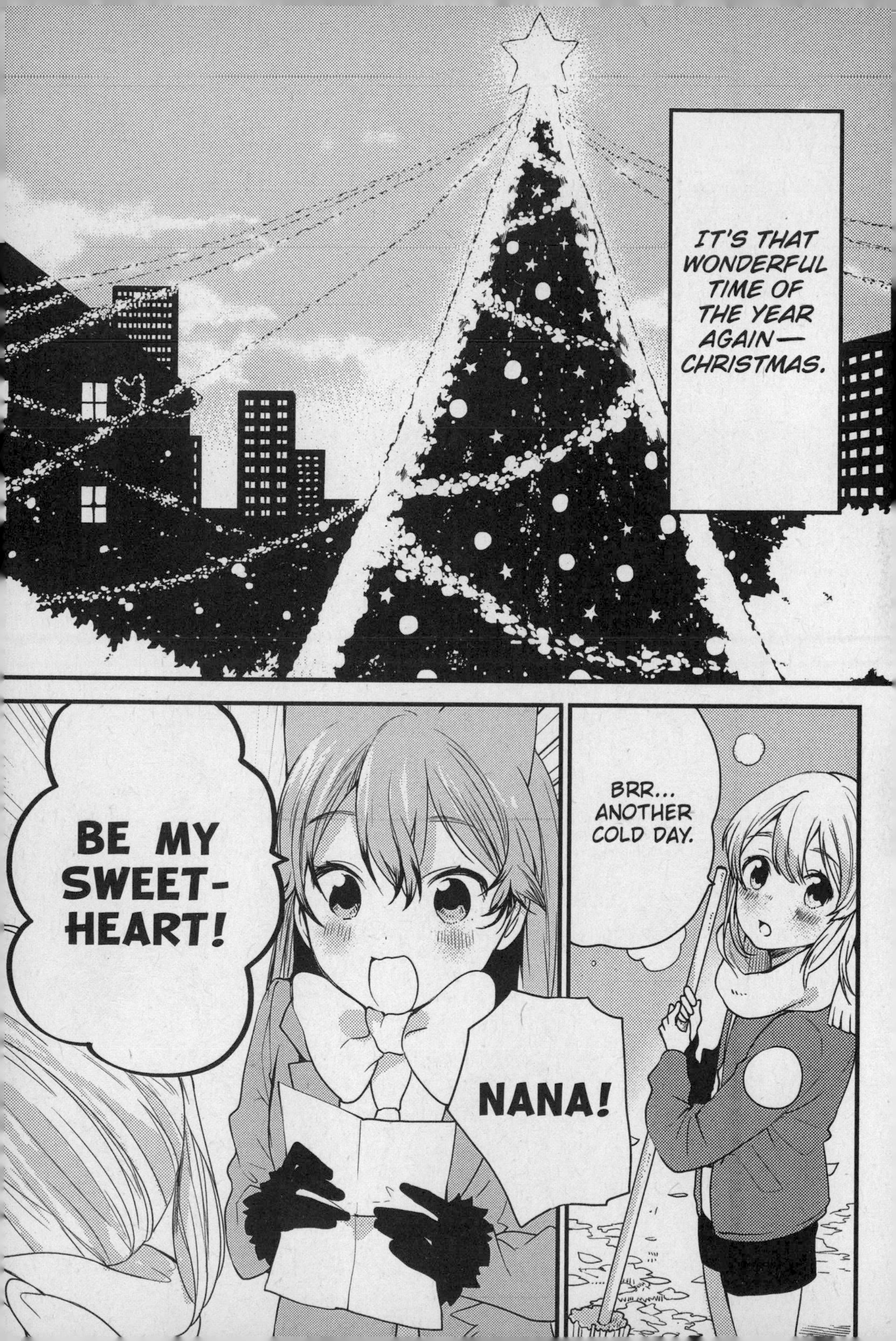
IT'S THAT WONDERFUL TIME OF THE YEAR AGAIN— CHRISTMAS.
BRR... ANOTHER COLD DAY.
BE MY SWEET-HEART!
NANA!

CHAPTER 8

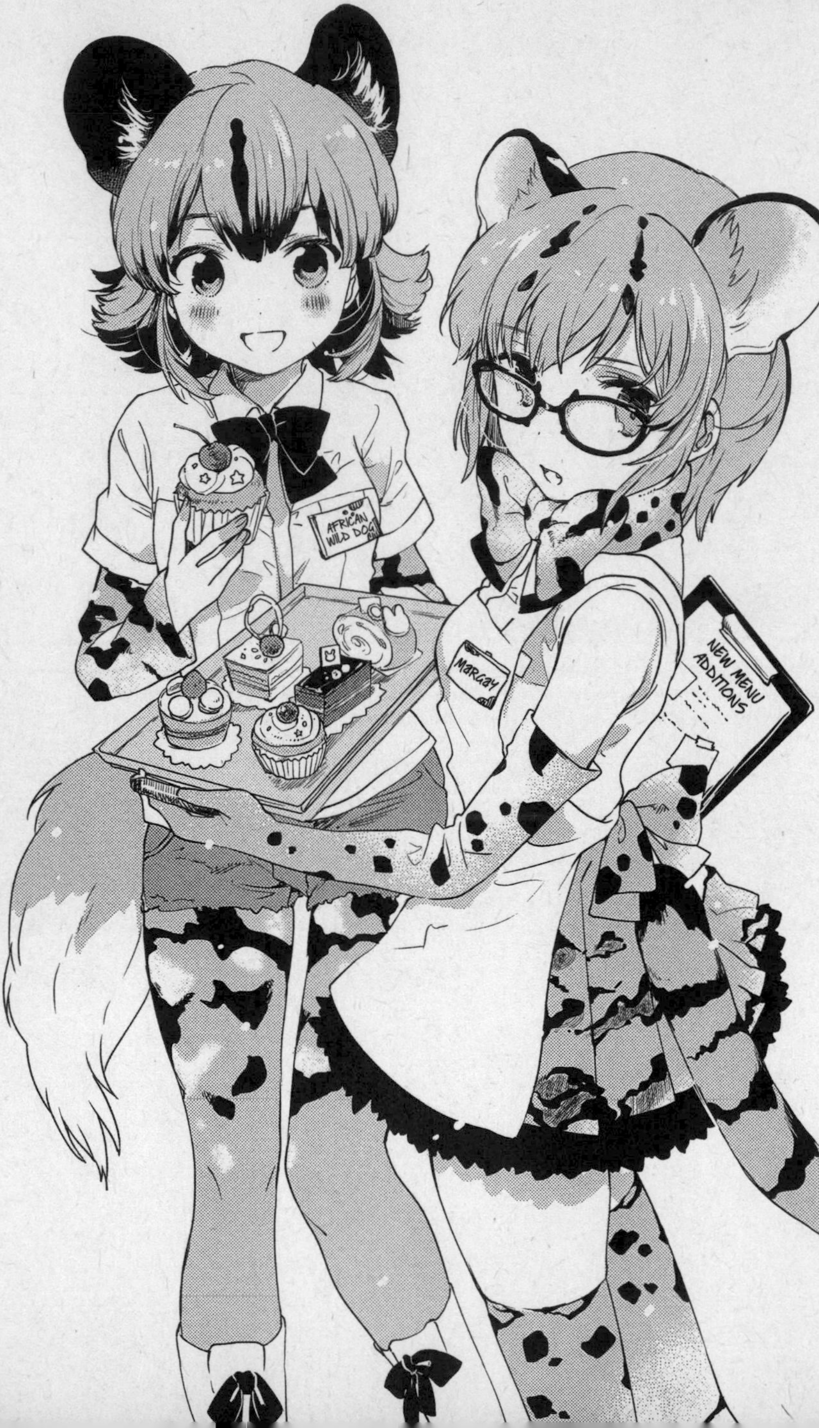
AFRICAN WILD DOG
Margay
NEW MENU ADDITIONS

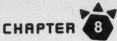

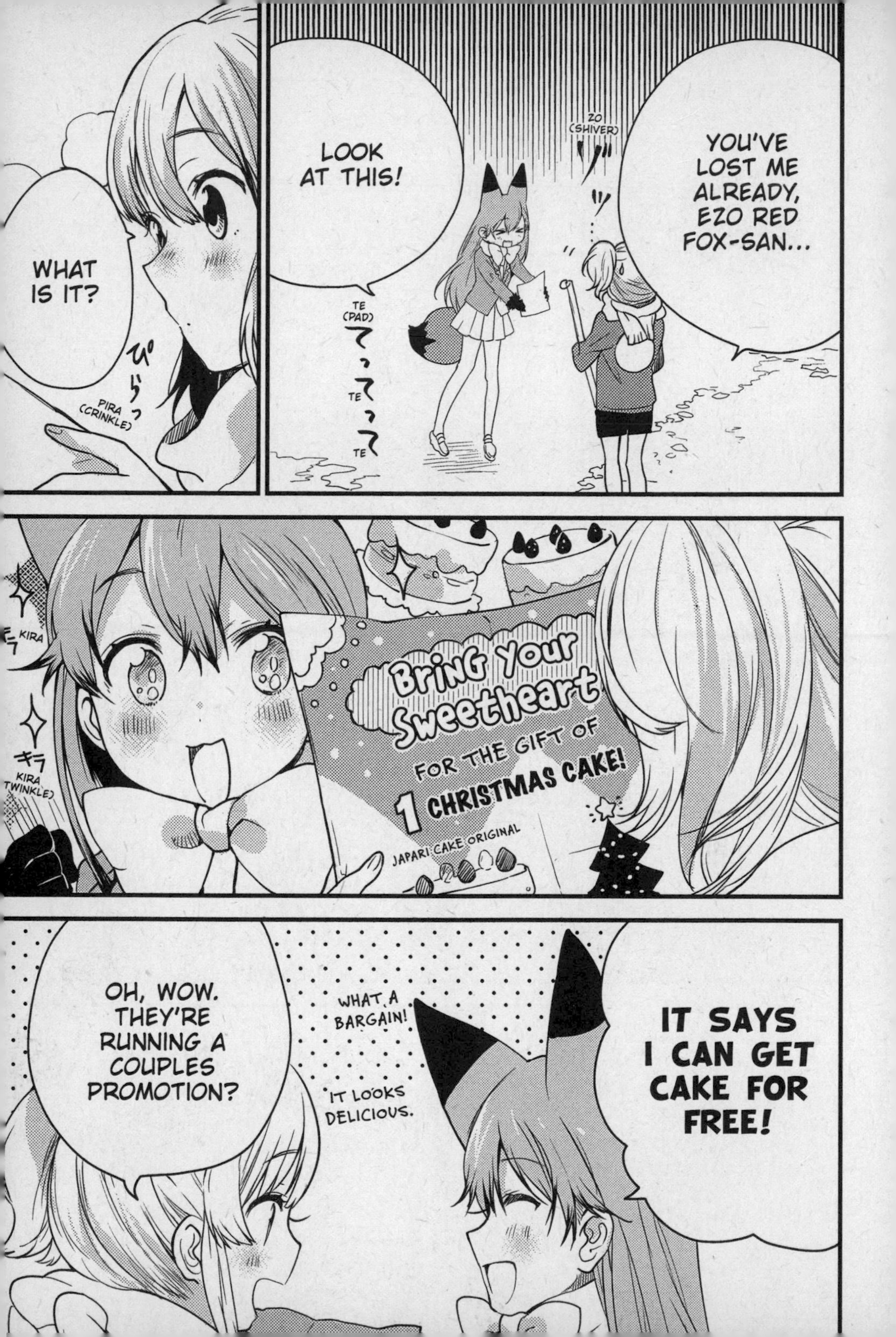
YOU'VE LOST ME ALREADY, EZO RED FOX-SAN...
ZO (SHIVER)
LOOK AT THIS!
てってって
TE (PAD) TE TE
WHAT IS IT?
ぴらっ
PIRA (CRINKLE)
キラ KIRA
キラ KIRA (TWINKLE)
Bring your Sweetheart
FOR THE GIFT OF
1 CHRISTMAS CAKE!
JAPARI CAKE ORIGINAL
IT SAYS I CAN GET CAKE FOR FREE!
WHAT A BARGAIN!
IT LOOKS DELICIOUS.
OH, WOW. THEY'RE RUNNING A COUPLES PROMOTION?

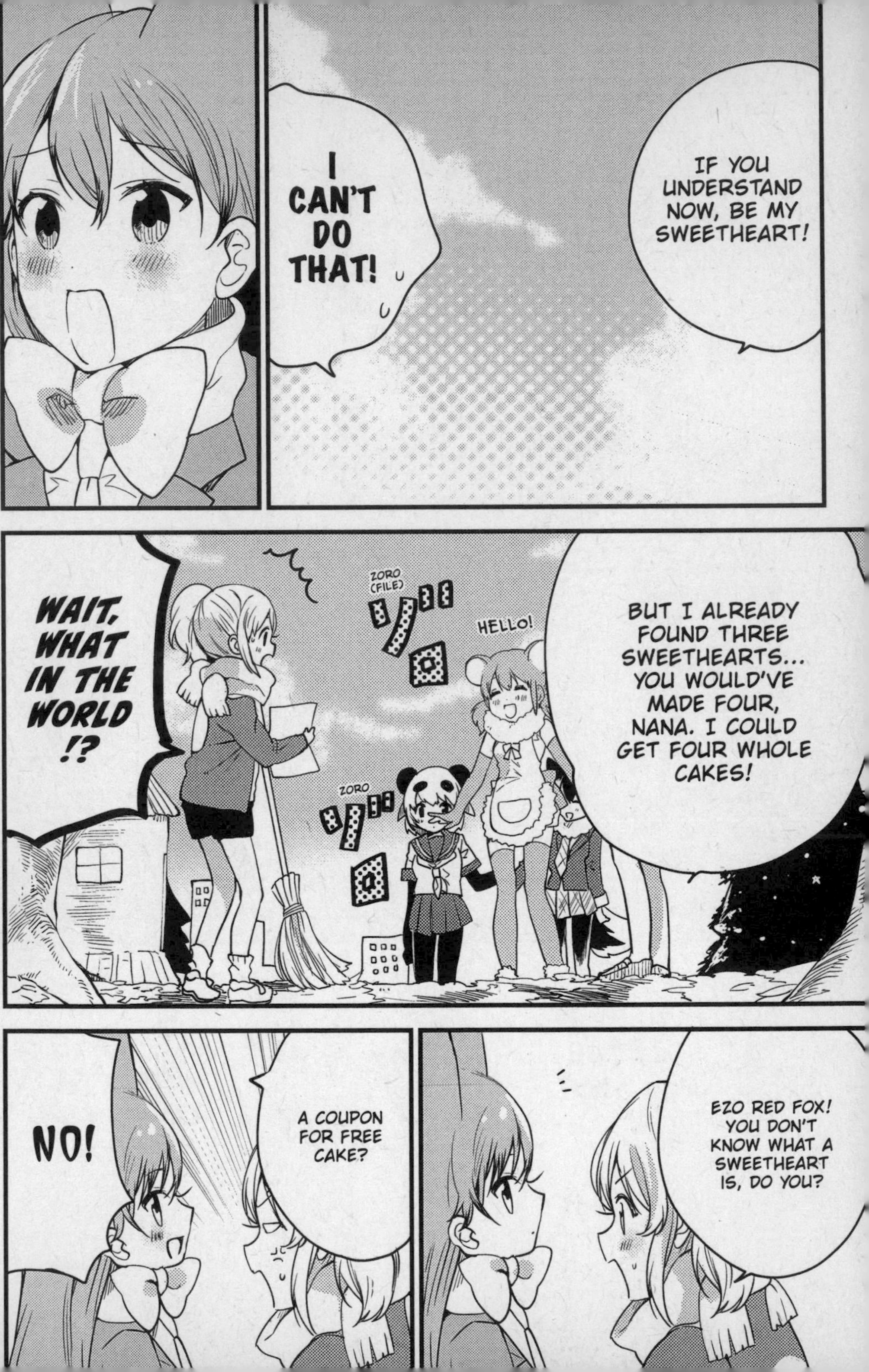
IF YOU UNDERSTAND NOW, BE MY SWEETHEART!
I CAN'T DO THAT!
BUT I ALREADY FOUND THREE SWEETHEARTS... YOU WOULD'VE MADE FOUR, NANA. I COULD GET FOUR WHOLE CAKES!
HELLO!
ZORO (FILE)
ZORO
WAIT, WHAT IN THE WORLD!?
EZO RED FOX! YOU DON'T KNOW WHAT A SWEETHEART IS, DO YOU?
A COUPON FOR FREE CAKE?
NO!

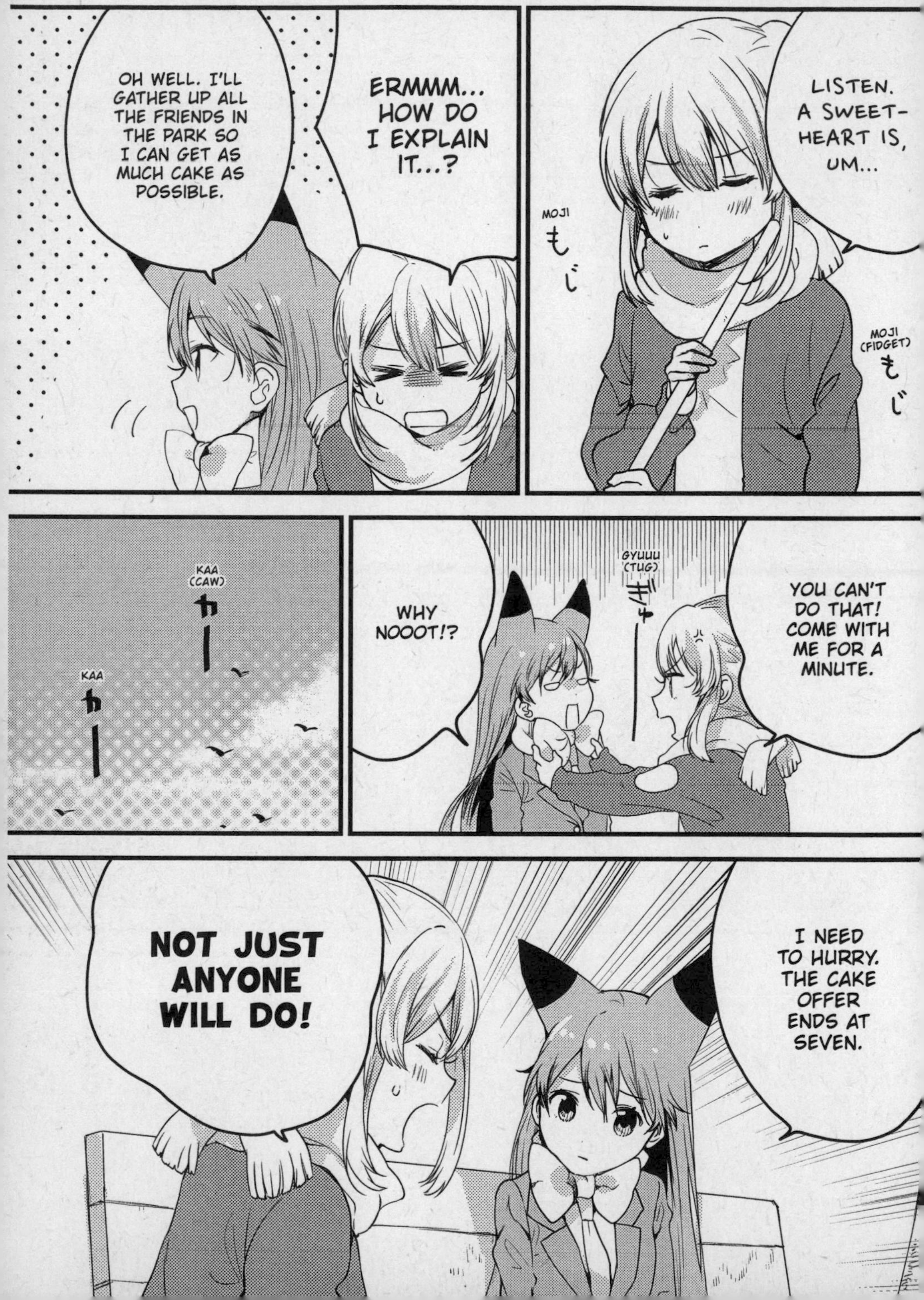
LISTEN. A SWEET-HEART IS, UM...
MOJI
もじ
MOJI (FIDGET)
もじ
ERMMM... HOW DO I EXPLAIN IT...?
OH WELL. I'LL GATHER UP ALL THE FRIENDS IN THE PARK SO I CAN GET AS MUCH CAKE AS POSSIBLE.
YOU CAN'T DO THAT! COME WITH ME FOR A MINUTE.
GYUUU (TUG)
ギュー
WHY NOOOT!?
KAA (CAW)
カー
KAA
カー
I NEED TO HURRY. THE CAKE OFFER ENDS AT SEVEN.
NOT JUST ANYONE WILL DO!

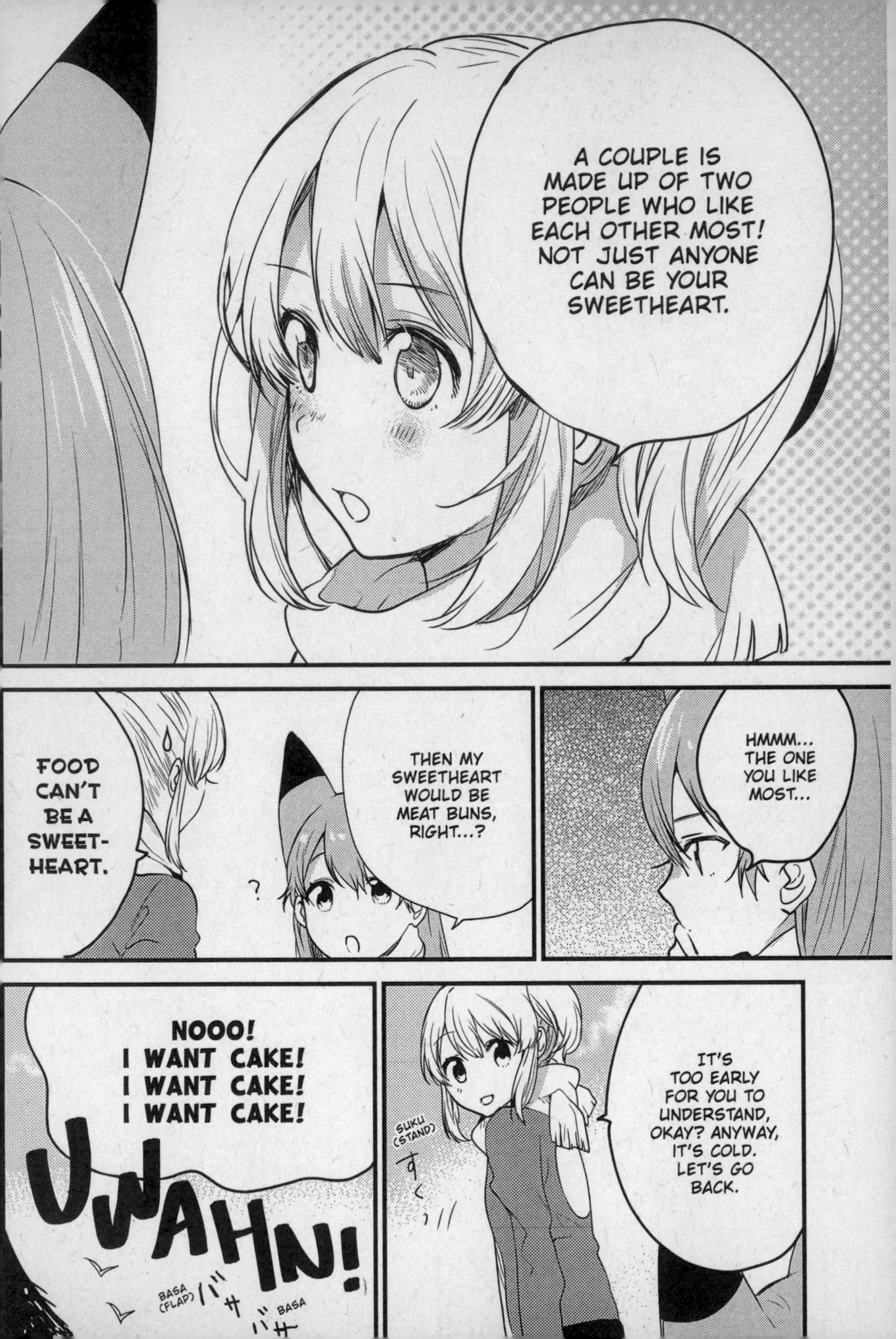
A COUPLE IS MADE UP OF TWO PEOPLE WHO LIKE EACH OTHER MOST! NOT JUST ANYONE CAN BE YOUR SWEETHEART.
HMMM... THE ONE YOU LIKE MOST...
THEN MY SWEETHEART WOULD BE MEAT BUNS, RIGHT...?
?
FOOD CAN'T BE A SWEET-HEART.
SUKU (STAND)
IT'S TOO EARLY FOR YOU TO UNDERSTAND, OKAY? ANYWAY, IT'S COLD. LET'S GO BACK.
NOOO! I WANT CAKE! I WANT CAKE! I WANT CAKE!
UWAHN!
BASA (FLAP)
BASA

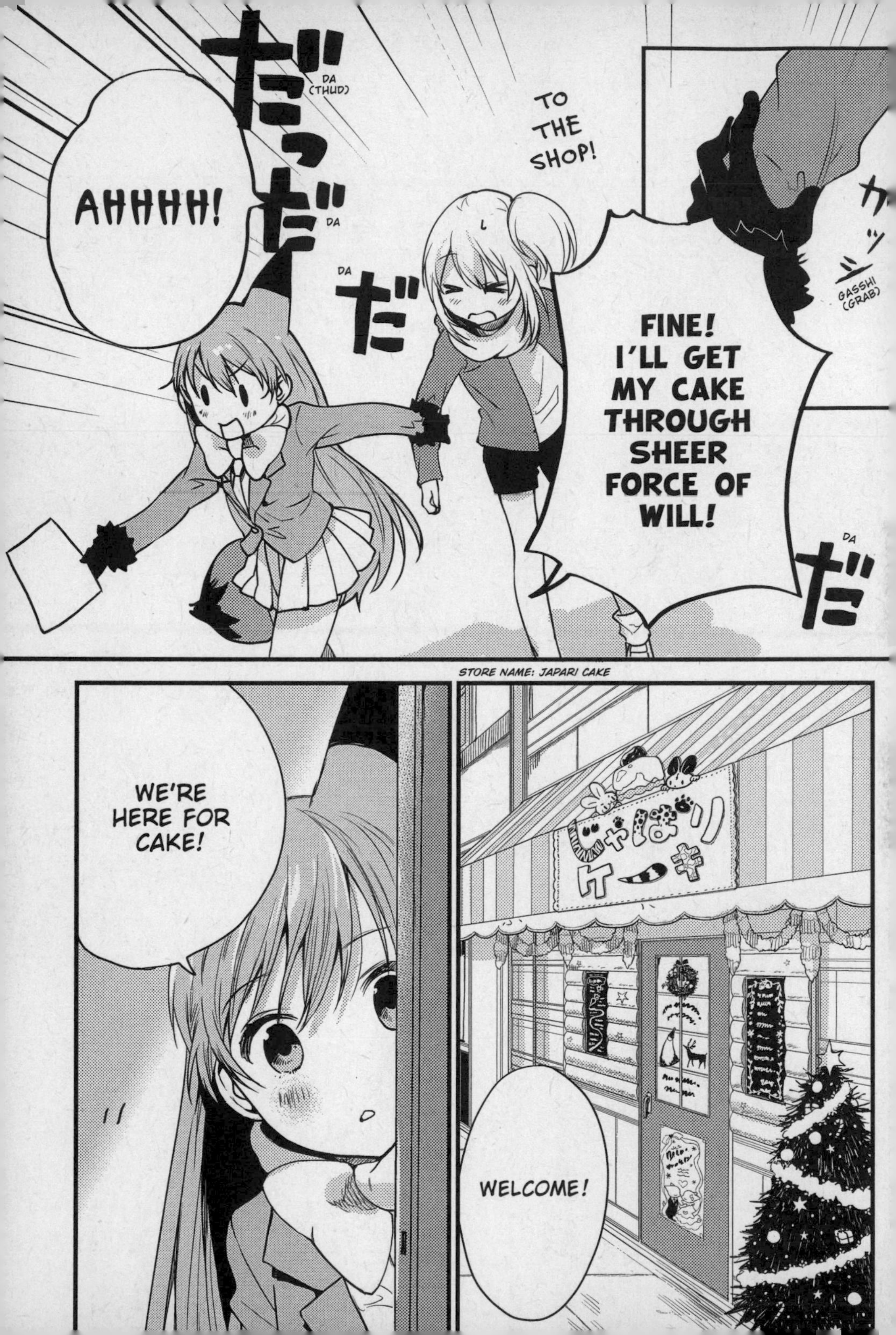
ガッ
GASSHI (GRAB)
FINE! I'LL GET MY CAKE THROUGH SHEER FORCE OF WILL!
だ
DA
TO THE SHOP!
だ
DA
だっだ
DA (THUD) DA
AHHHH!
STORE NAME: JAPARI CAKE
じゃぱり ケーキ
WELCOME!
WE'RE HERE FOR CAKE!

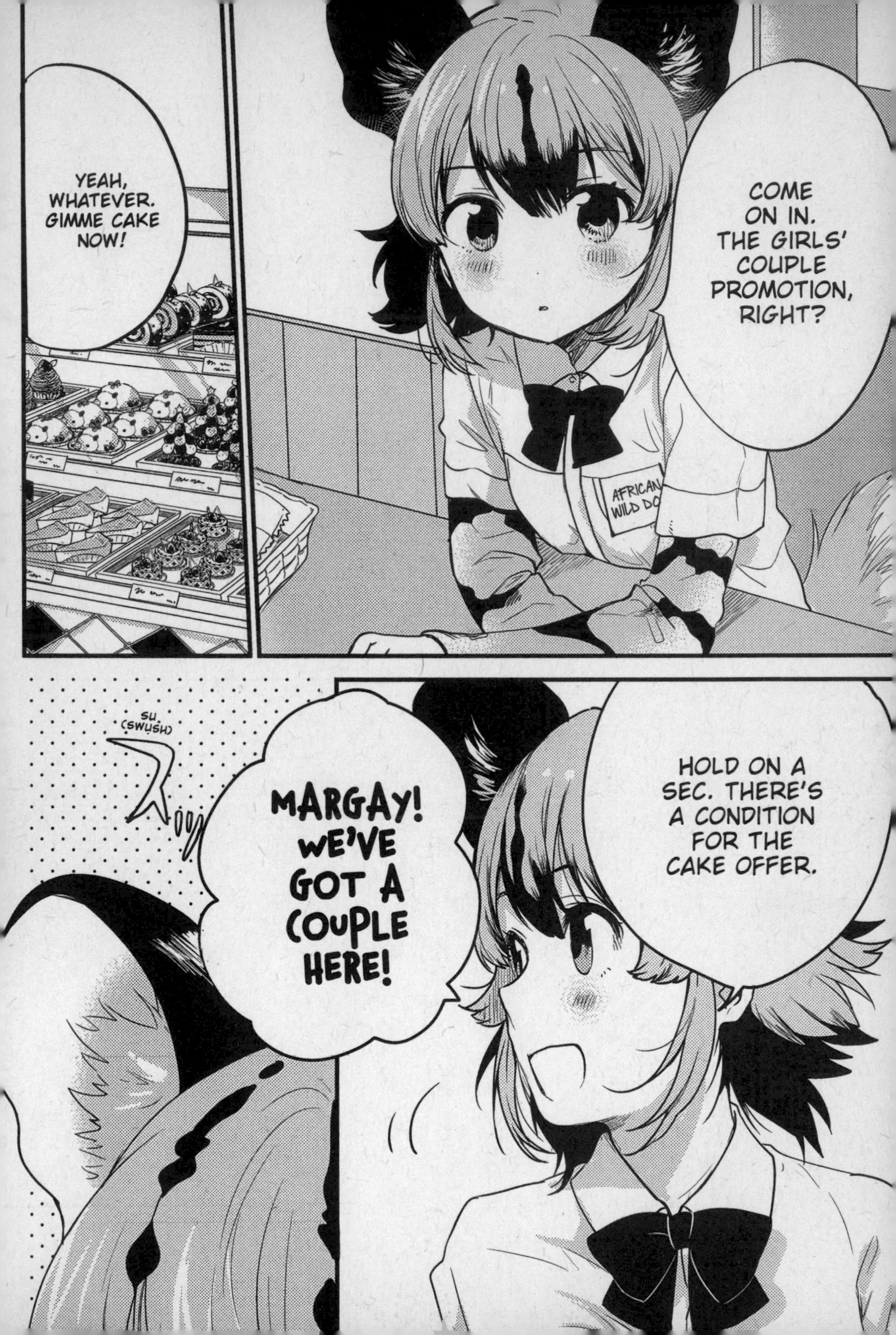
COME ON IN. THE GIRLS' COUPLE PROMOTION, RIGHT?
YEAH, WHATEVER. GIMME CAKE NOW!
HOLD ON A SEC. THERE'S A CONDITION FOR THE CAKE OFFER.
MARGAY! WE'VE GOT A COUPLE HERE!
SU (SWUSH)

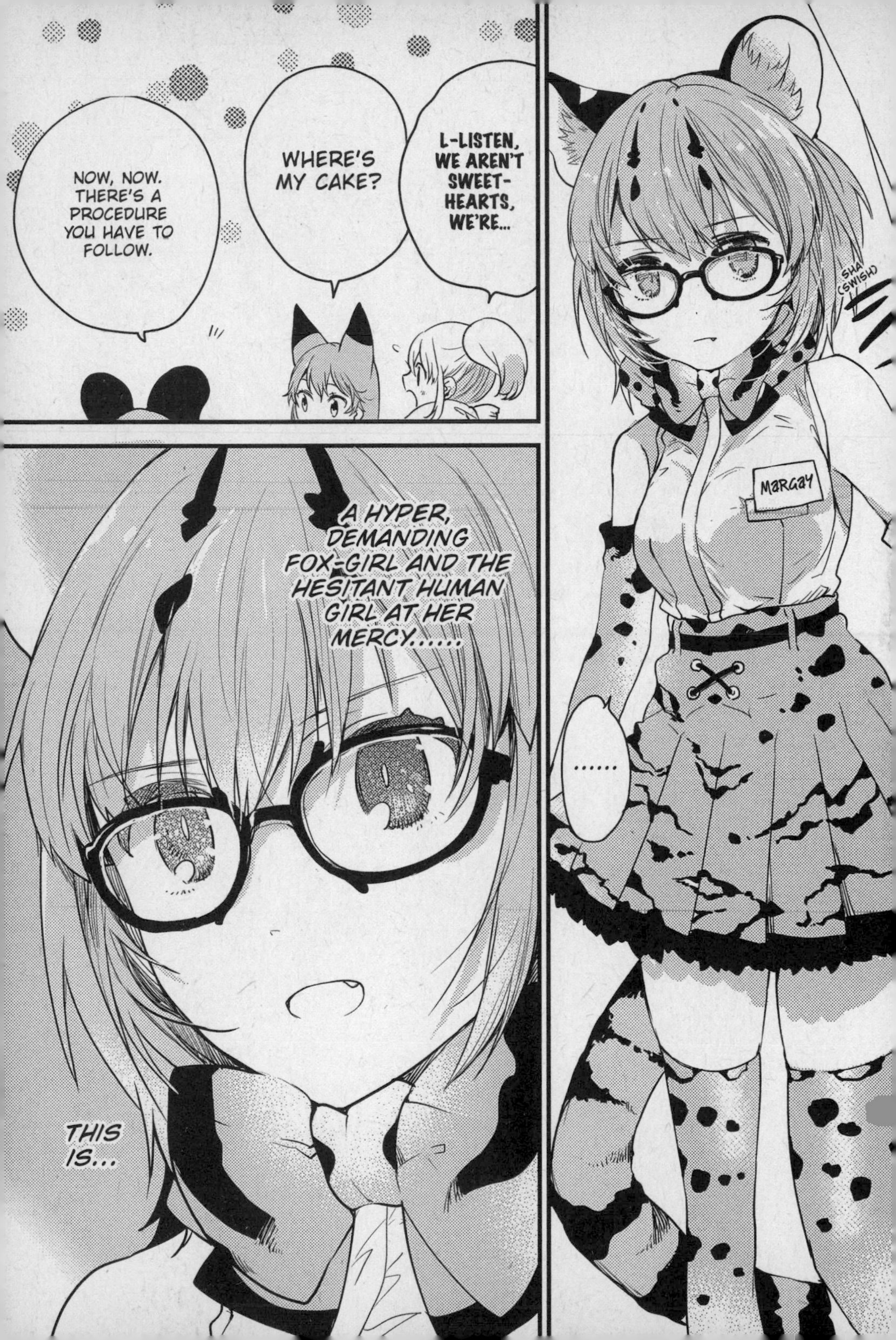
SHA (SWISH)
Margay
......
L-LISTEN, WE AREN'T SWEET-HEARTS, WE'RE...
WHERE'S MY CAKE?
NOW, NOW. THERE'S A PROCEDURE YOU HAVE TO FOLLOW.
A HYPER, DEMANDING FOX-GIRL AND THE HESITANT HUMAN GIRL AT HER MERCY......
THIS IS...

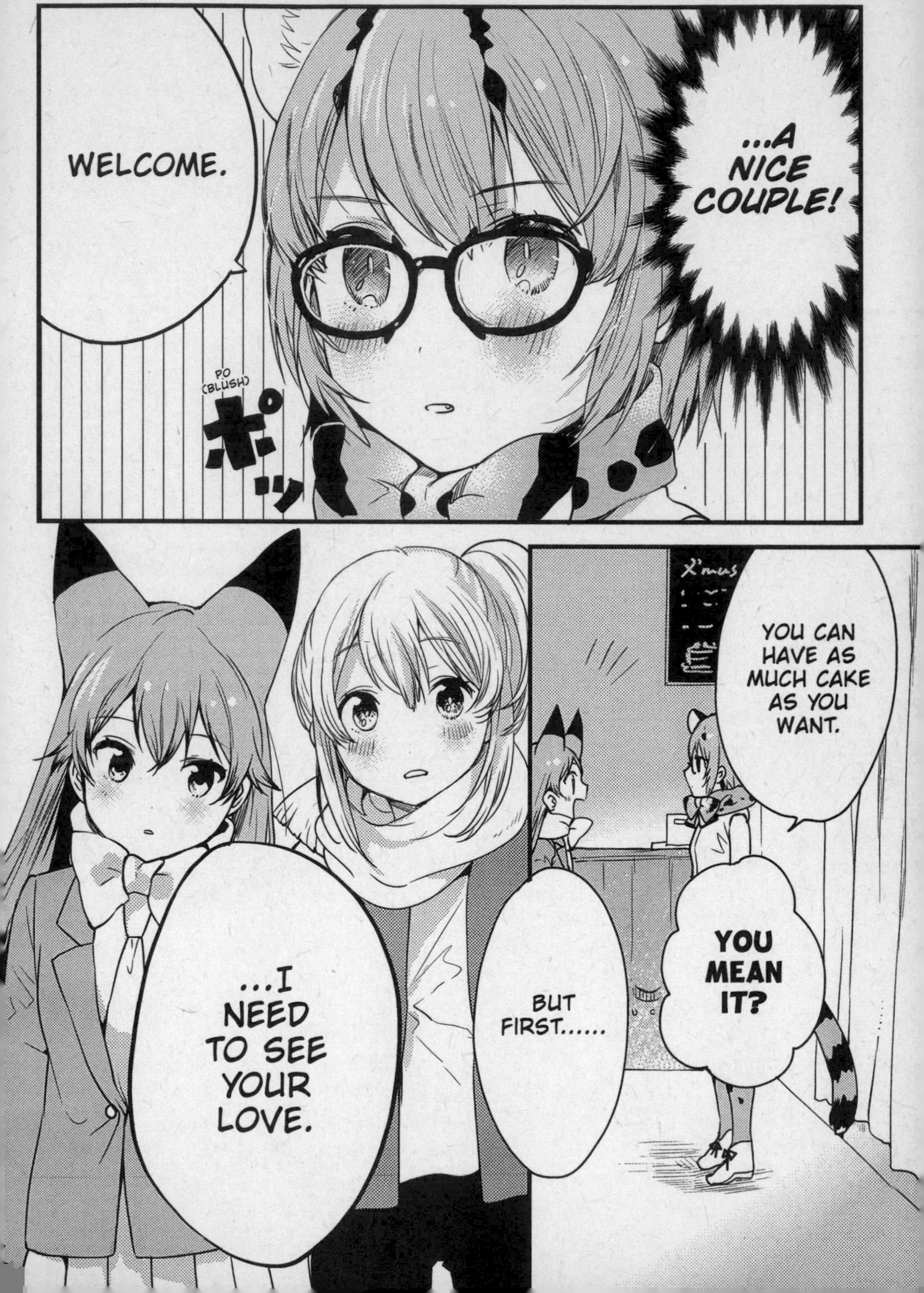
...A NICE COUPLE!
WELCOME.
PO (BLUSH)
ポッ
X'mas
YOU CAN HAVE AS MUCH CAKE AS YOU WANT.
YOU MEAN IT?
BUT FIRST......
...I NEED TO SEE YOUR LOVE.

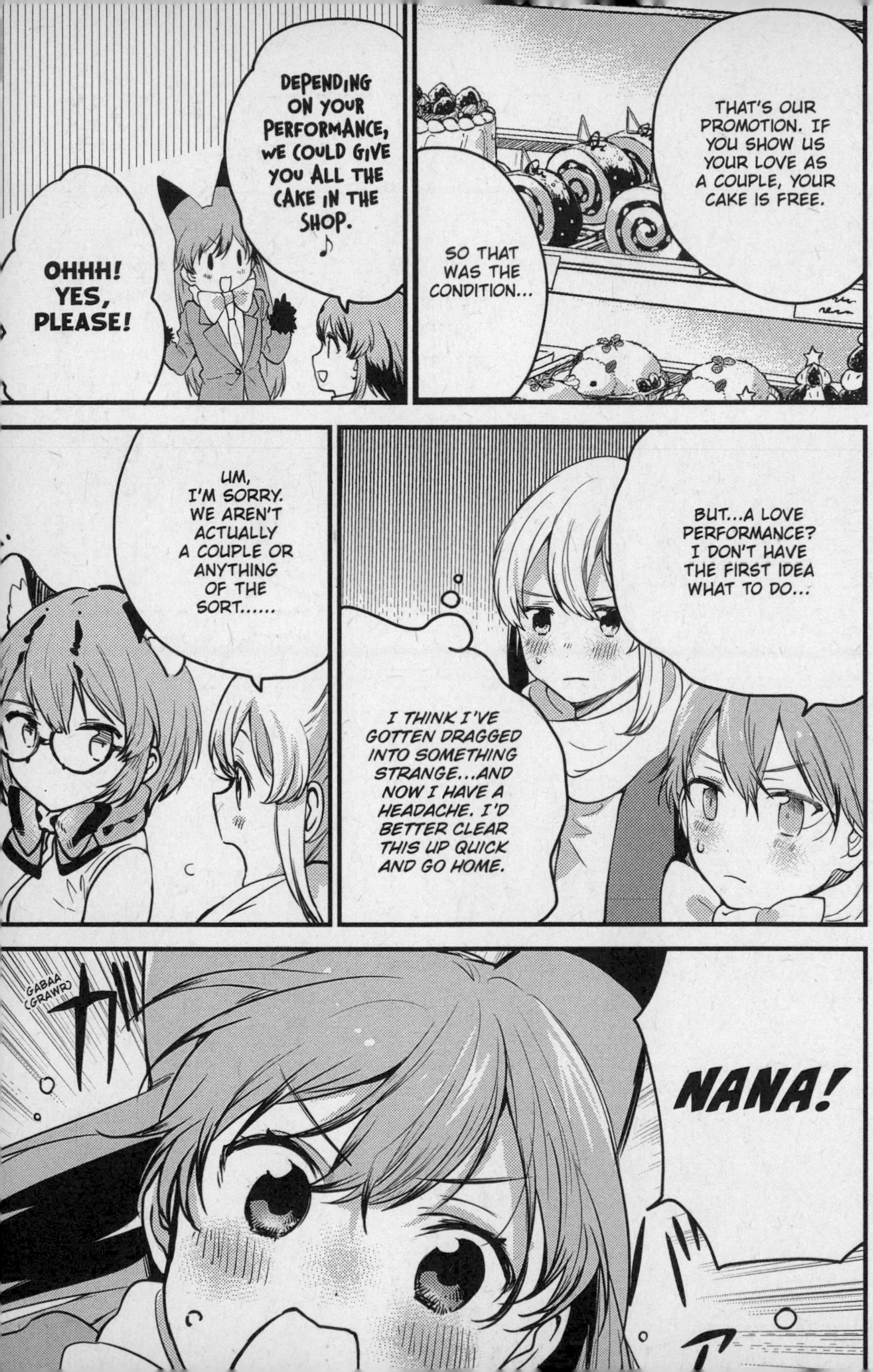
THAT'S OUR PROMOTION. IF YOU SHOW US YOUR LOVE AS A COUPLE, YOUR CAKE IS FREE.
SO THAT WAS THE CONDITION...
DEPENDING ON YOUR PERFORMANCE, WE COULD GIVE YOU ALL THE CAKE IN THE SHOP. ♪
OHHH! YES, PLEASE!
BUT...A LOVE PERFORMANCE? I DON'T HAVE THE FIRST IDEA WHAT TO DO...
I THINK I'VE GOTTEN DRAGGED INTO SOMETHING STRANGE...AND NOW I HAVE A HEADACHE. I'D BETTER CLEAR THIS UP QUICK AND GO HOME.
UM, I'M SORRY. WE AREN'T ACTUALLY A COUPLE OR ANYTHING OF THE SORT......
NANA!
GABAA (GRAWR)

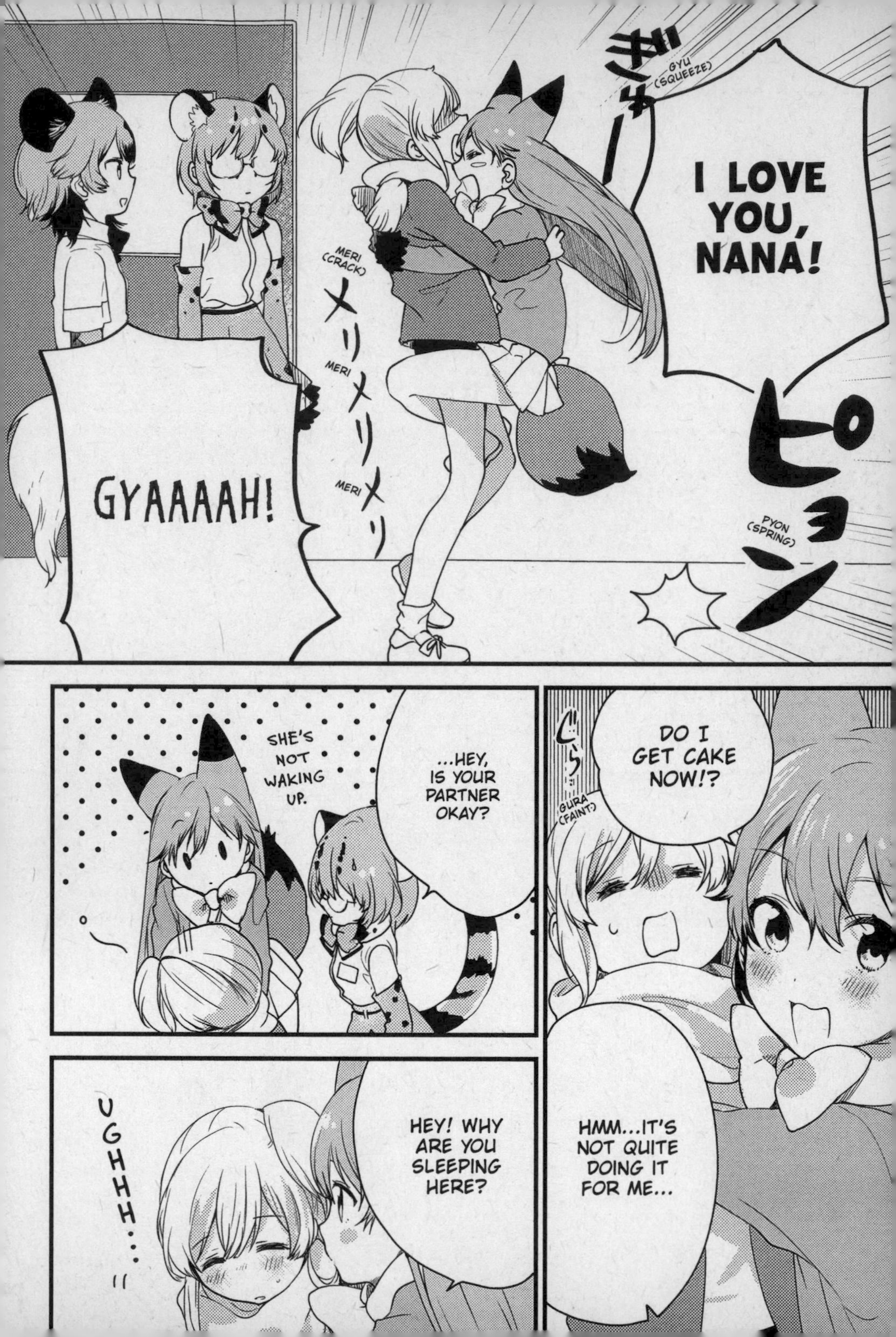

ぎゅー
GYU (SQUEEZE)
I LOVE YOU, NANA!
ピョン
PYON (SPRING)
MERI (CRACK)
メリ
MERI
メリ
MERI
メリ
GYAAAAH!
DO I GET CAKE NOW!?
ぐら
GURA (FAINT)
HMM...IT'S NOT QUITE DOING IT FOR ME...
...HEY, IS YOUR PARTNER OKAY?
SHE'S NOT WAKING UP.
HEY! WHY ARE YOU SLEEPING HERE?
UGHHH...

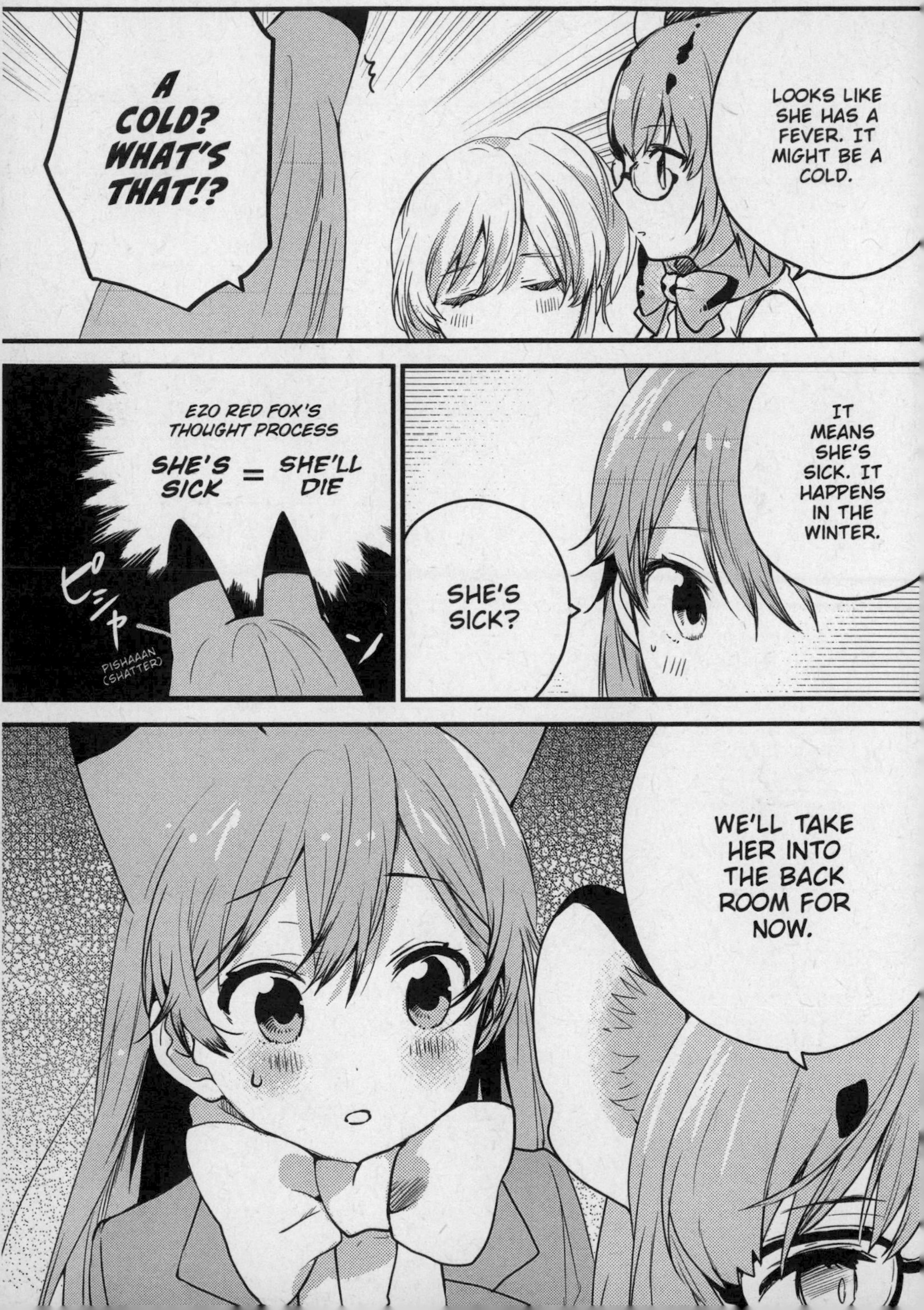
LOOKS LIKE SHE HAS A FEVER. IT MIGHT BE A COLD.
A COLD? WHAT'S THAT!?
IT MEANS SHE'S SICK. IT HAPPENS IN THE WINTER.
SHE'S SICK?
EZO RED FOX'S THOUGHT PROCESS
SHE'S SICK = SHE'LL DIE
ピシャ
PISHAAAN (SHATTER)
WE'LL TAKE HER INTO THE BACK ROOM FOR NOW.

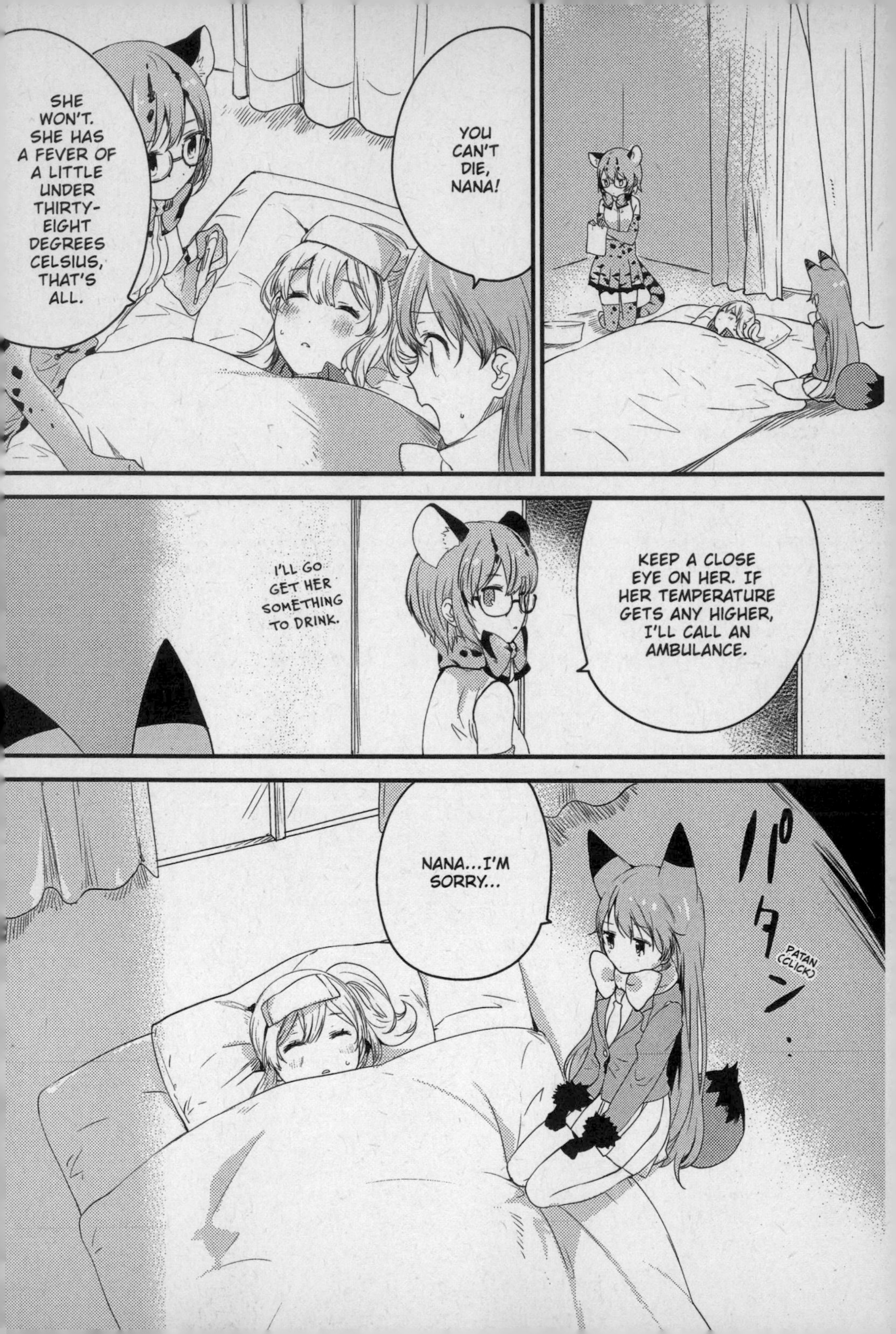
YOU CAN'T DIE, NANA!
SHE WON'T. SHE HAS A FEVER OF A LITTLE UNDER THIRTY-EIGHT DEGREES CELSIUS, THAT'S ALL.
KEEP A CLOSE EYE ON HER. IF HER TEMPERATURE GETS ANY HIGHER, I'LL CALL AN AMBULANCE.
I'LL GO GET HER SOMETHING TO DRINK.
NANA...I'M SORRY...
パタン
PATAN (CLICK)

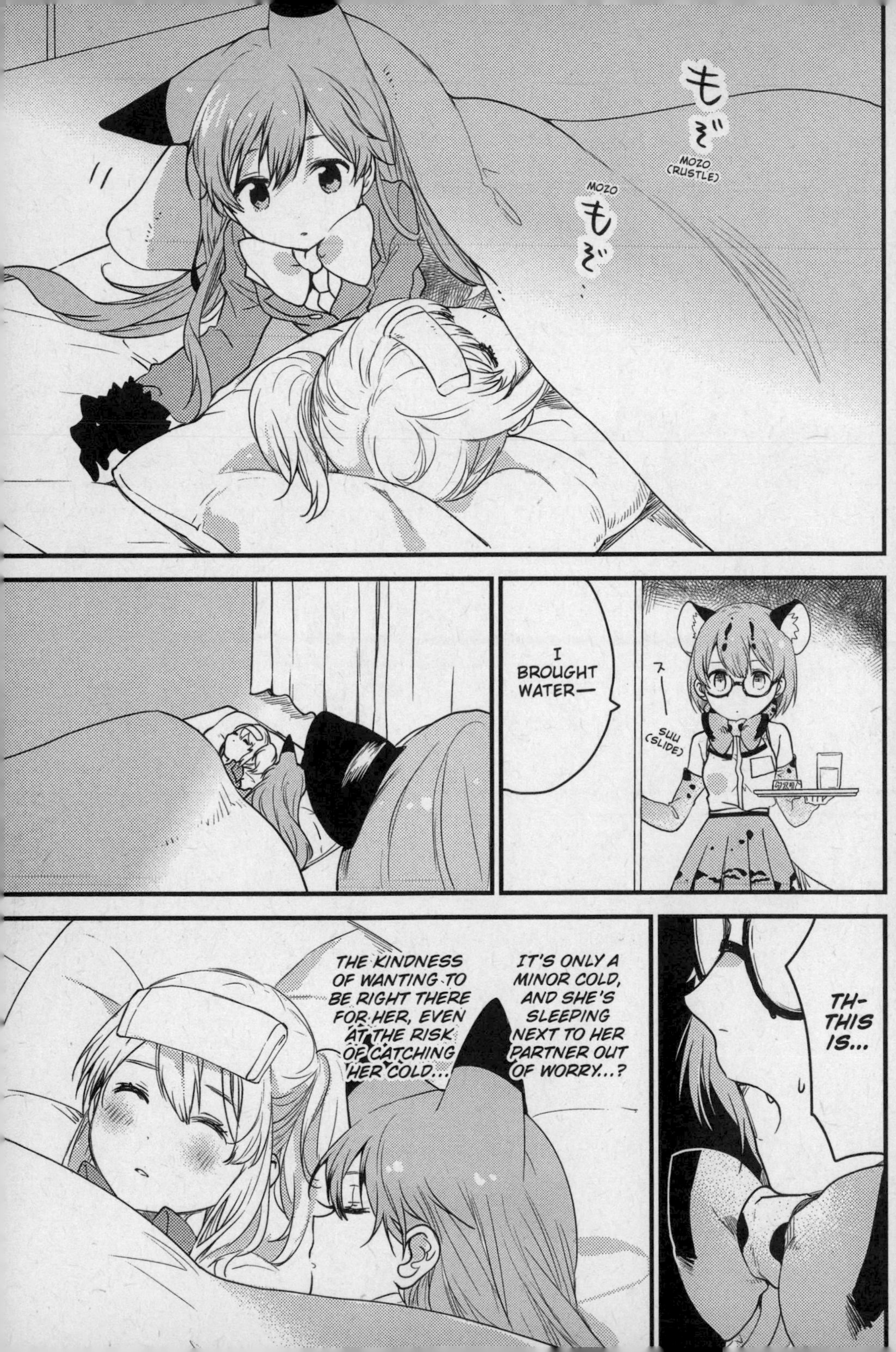
もぞ
MOZO (RUSTLE)
MOZO
もぞ
I BROUGHT WATER—
スー
SUU (SLIDE)
TH-THIS IS...
IT'S ONLY A MINOR COLD, AND SHE'S SLEEPING NEXT TO HER PARTNER OUT OF WORRY...?
THE KINDNESS OF WANTING TO BE RIGHT THERE FOR HER, EVEN AT THE RISK OF CATCHING HER COLD...

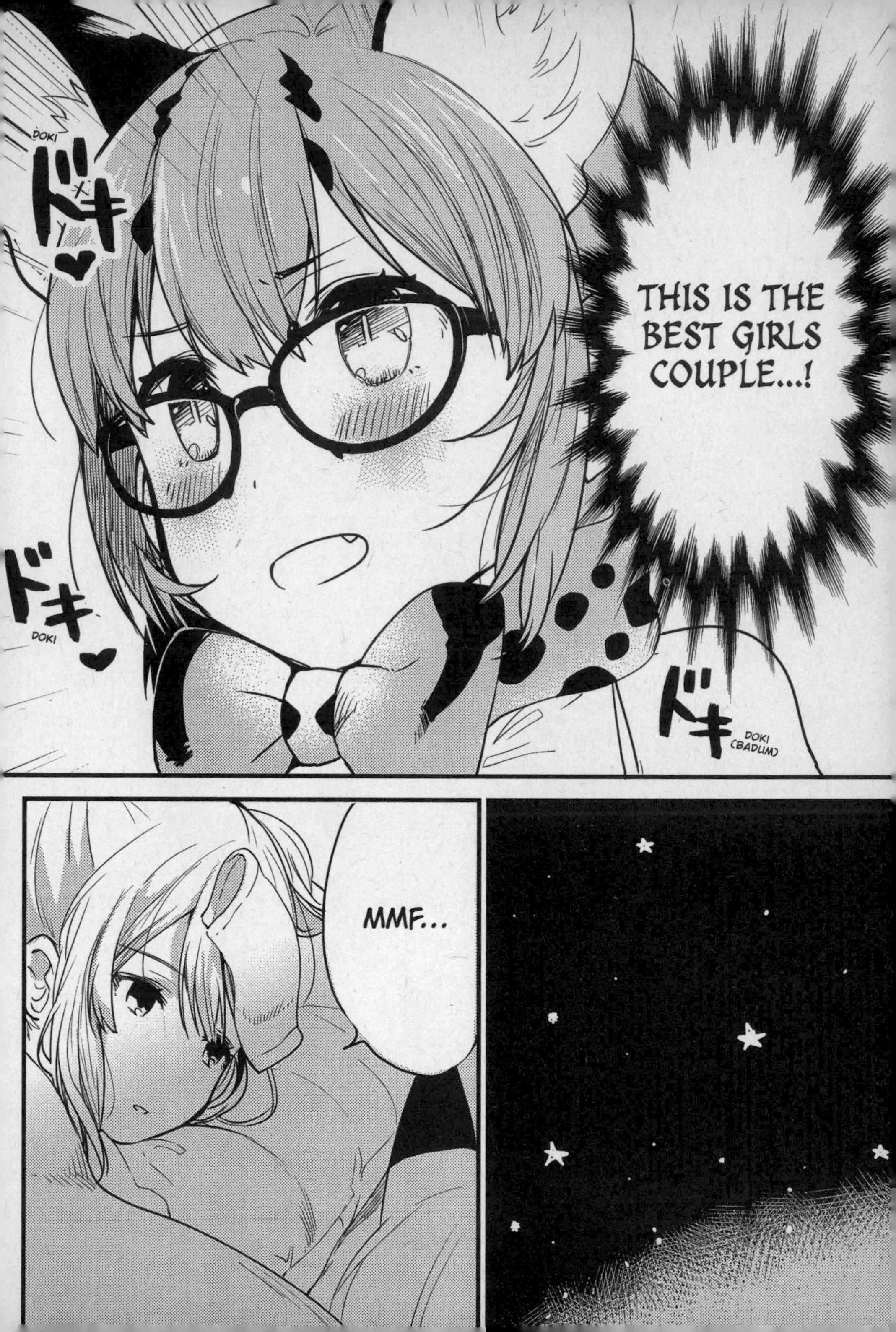
THIS IS THE BEST GIRLS COUPLE...!
ドキ DOKI (BADUM)
DOKI ドキ
ドキ DOKI
MMF...

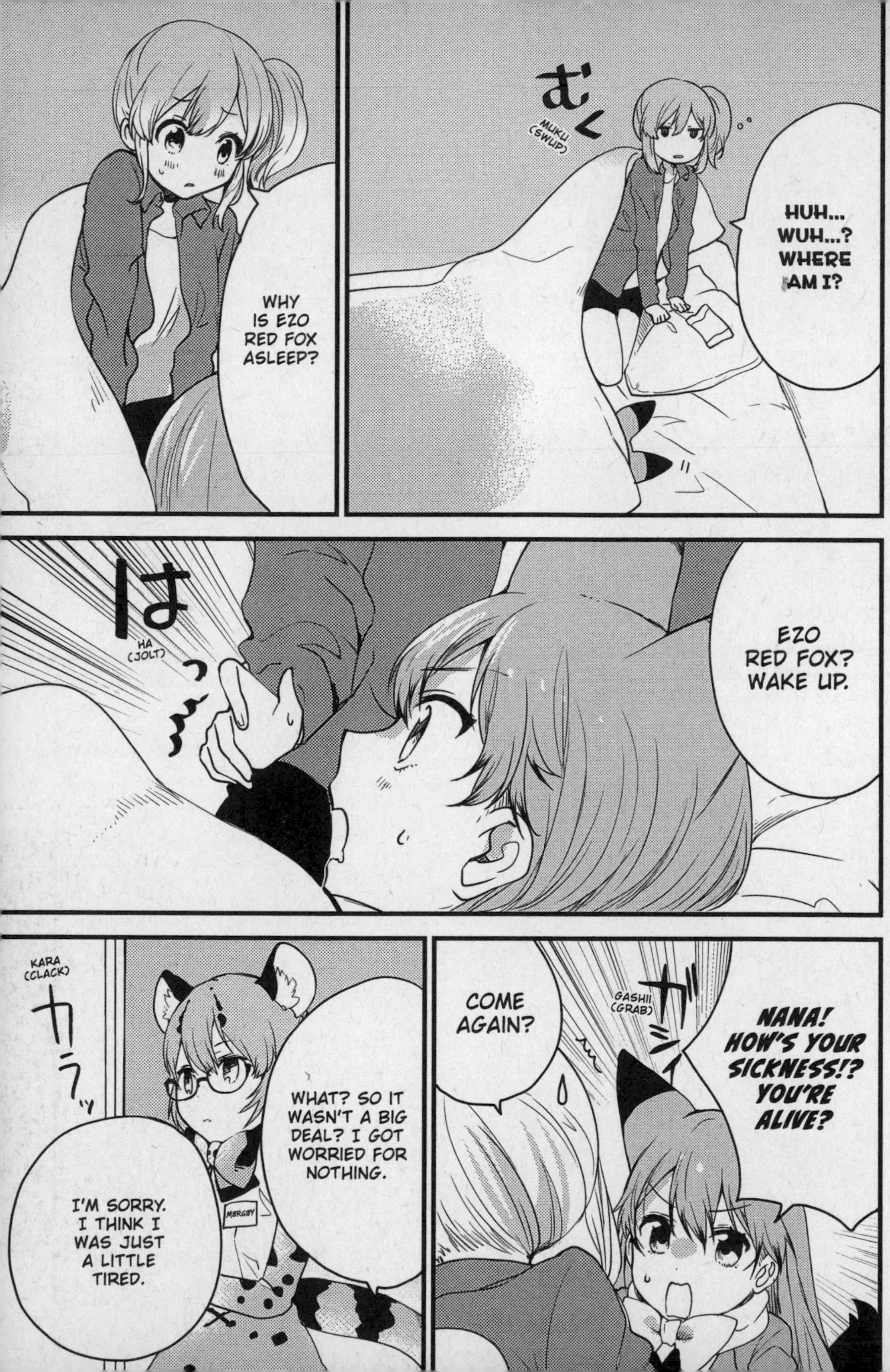
むく
MUKU (SWUP)
HUH... WUH...? WHERE AM I?
WHY IS EZO RED FOX ASLEEP?
EZO RED FOX? WAKE UP.
はっ
HA (JOLT)
NANA! HOW'S YOUR SICKNESS!? YOU'RE ALIVE?
ガシッ
GASHII (GRAB)
COME AGAIN?
WHAT? SO IT WASN'T A BIG DEAL? I GOT WORRIED FOR NOTHING.
カラッ
KARA (CLACK)
I'M SORRY. I THINK I WAS JUST A LITTLE TIRED.

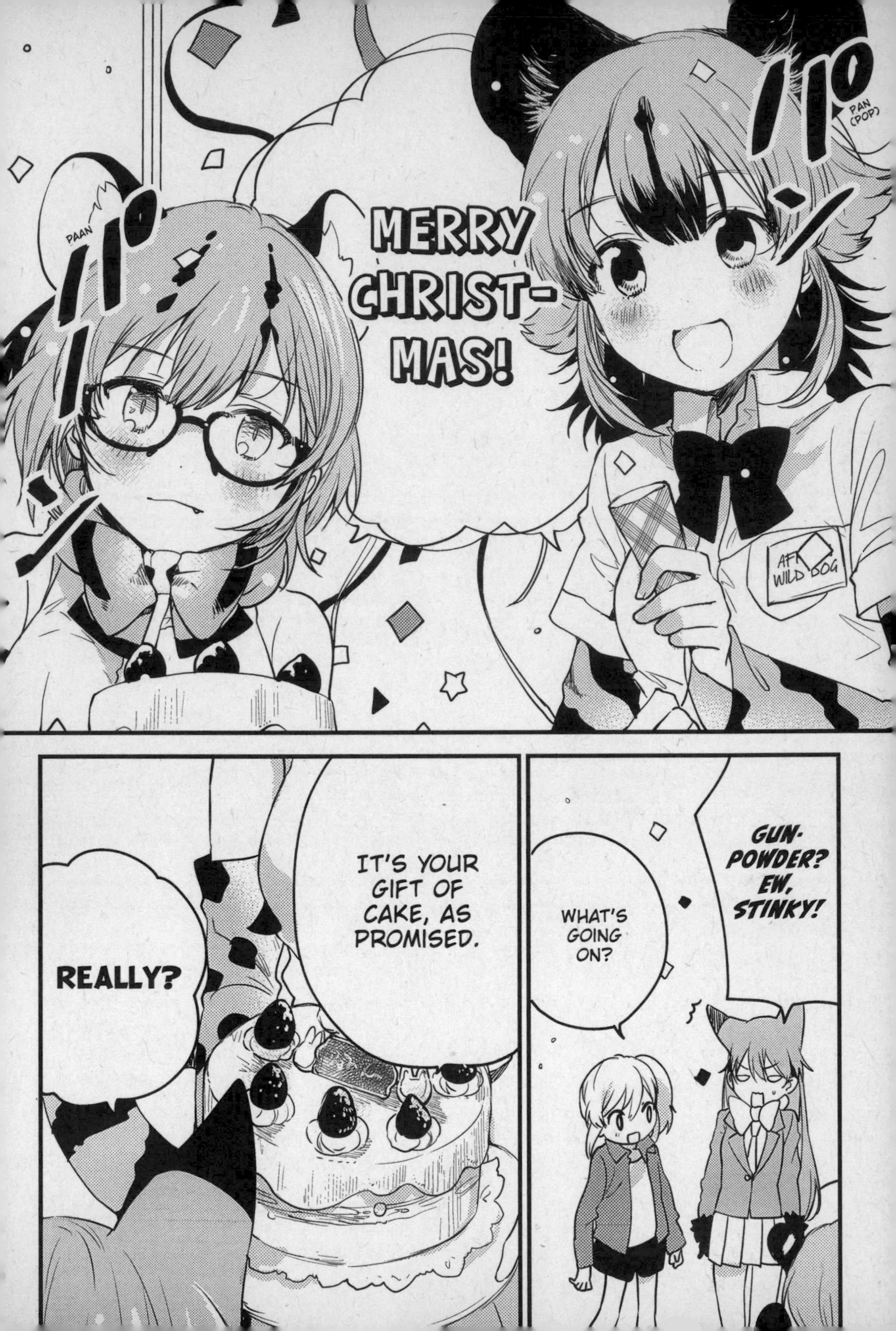
PAN (POP)
MERRY CHRIST-MAS!
PAAN
GUN-POWDER? EW, STINKY!
WHAT'S GOING ON?
IT'S YOUR GIFT OF CAKE, AS PROMISED.
REALLY?

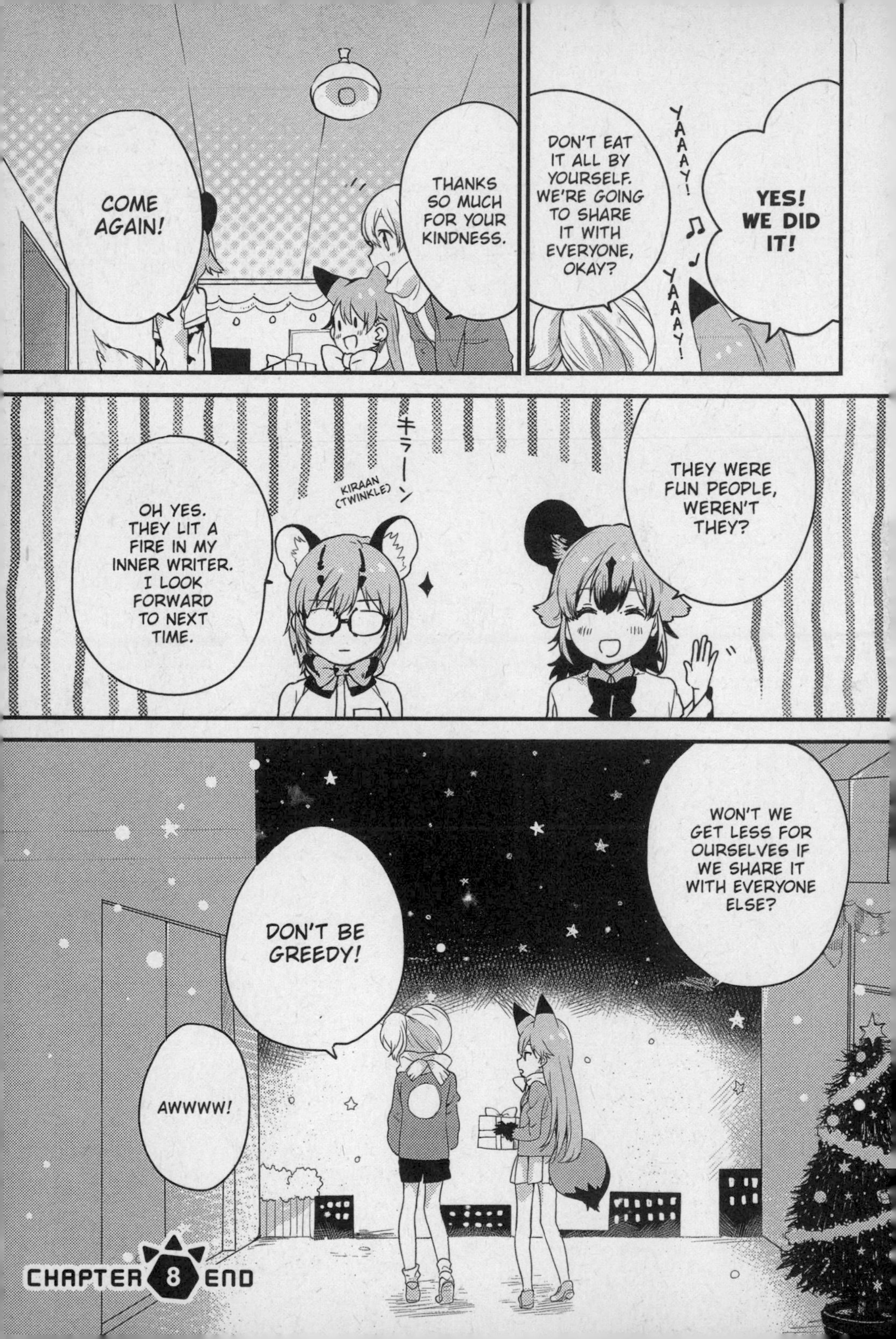
YES! WE DID IT!
YAAAAY!
YAAAAY!
DON'T EAT IT ALL BY YOURSELF. WE'RE GOING TO SHARE IT WITH EVERYONE, OKAY?
THANKS SO MUCH FOR YOUR KINDNESS.
COME AGAIN!
THEY WERE FUN PEOPLE, WEREN'T THEY?
キラーン
KIRAAN (TWINKLE)
OH YES. THEY LIT A FIRE IN MY INNER WRITER. I LOOK FORWARD TO NEXT TIME.
WON'T WE GET LESS FOR OURSELVES IF WE SHARE IT WITH EVERYONE ELSE?
DON'T BE GREEDY!
AWWWW!
CHAPTER 8 END

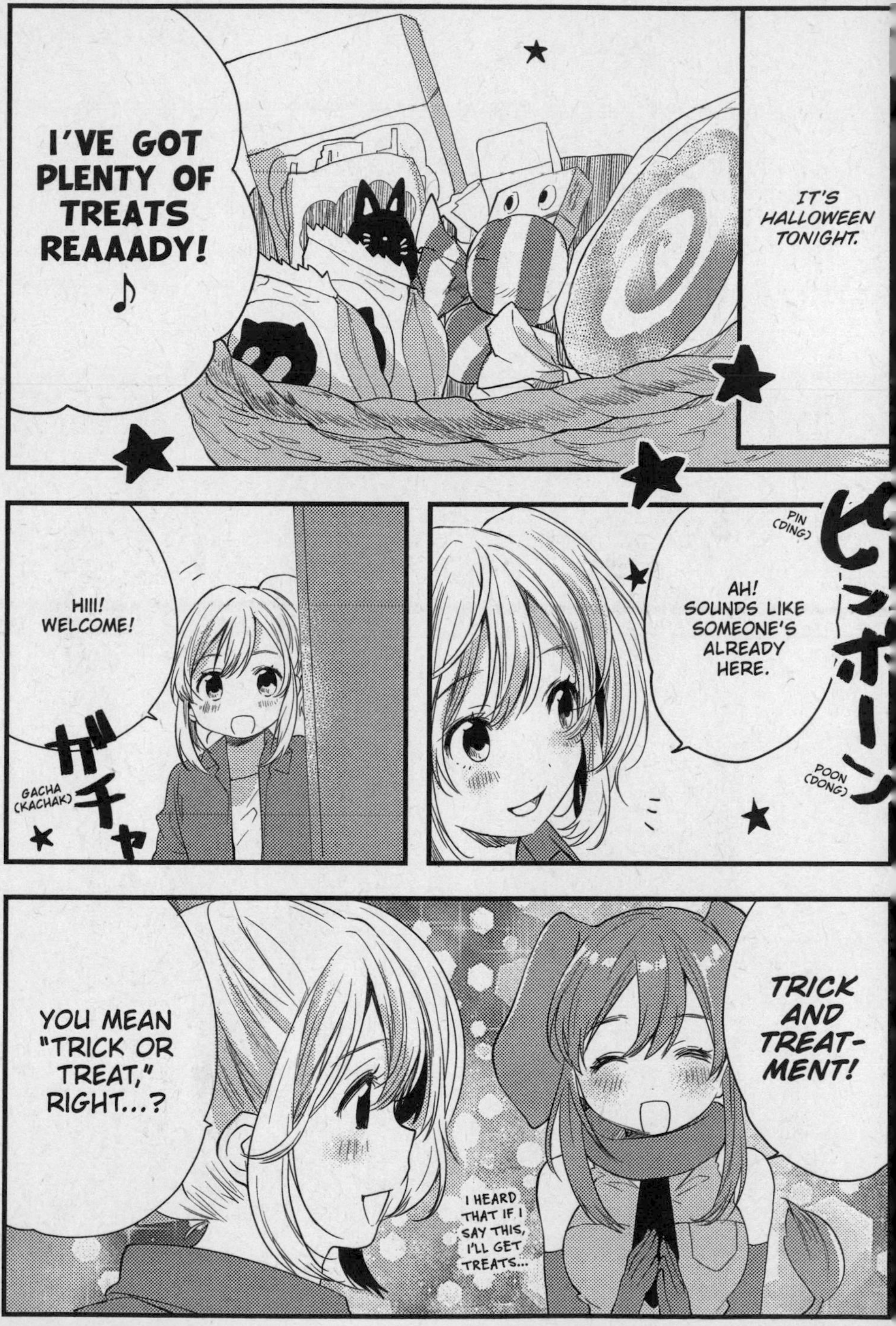
IT'S HALLOWEEN TONIGHT.
I'VE GOT PLENTY OF TREATS REAAADY! ♪
ピンポーン
PIN (DING)
POON (DONG)
AH! SOUNDS LIKE SOMEONE'S ALREADY HERE.
HIII! WELCOME!
ガチャ
GACHA (KACHAK)
TRICK AND TREAT-MENT!
I HEARD THAT IF I SAY THIS, I'LL GET TREATS...
YOU MEAN "TRICK OR TREAT," RIGHT...?

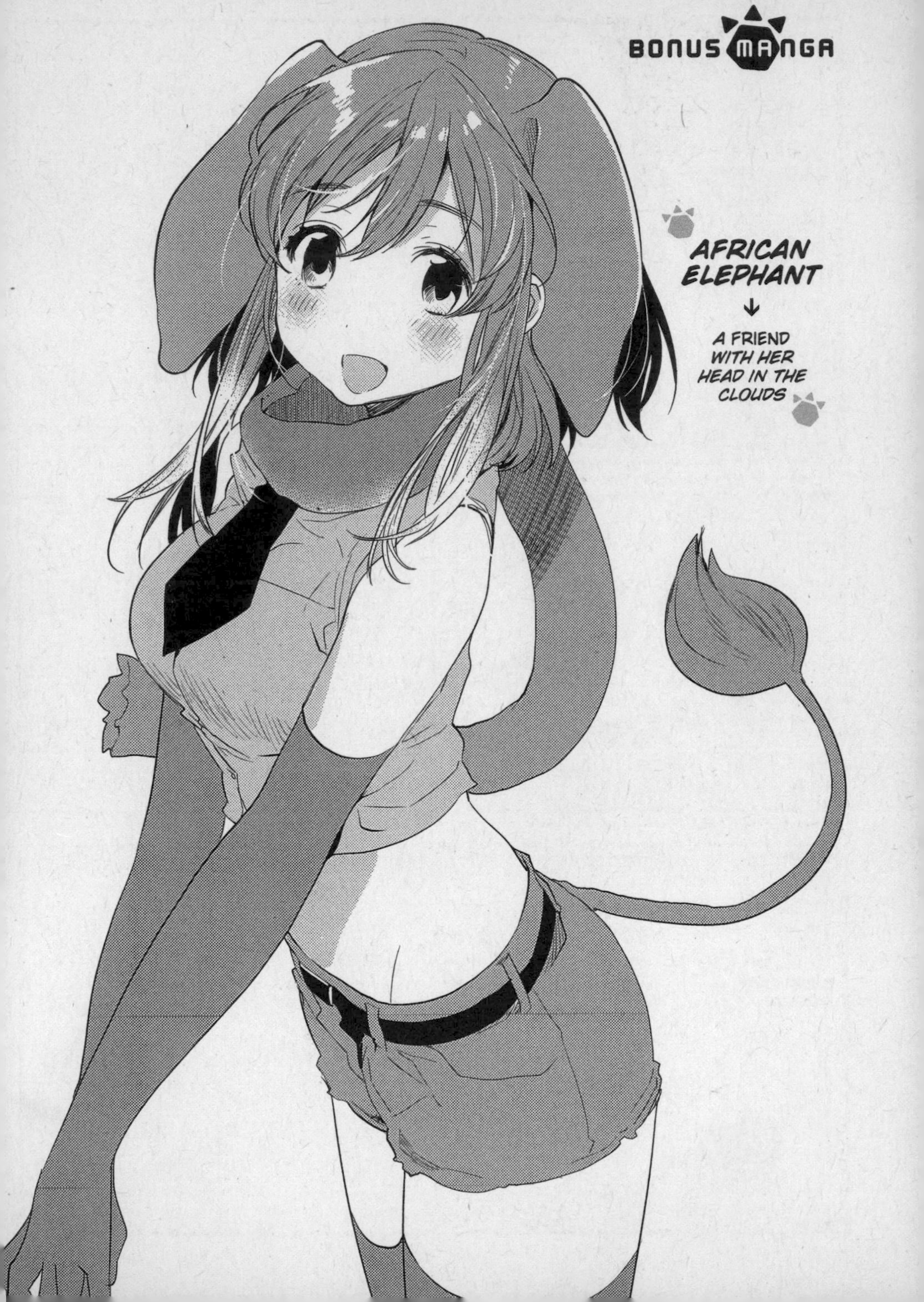
BONUS MANGA
AFRICAN ELEPHANT
↓
A FRIEND WITH HER HEAD IN THE CLOUDS

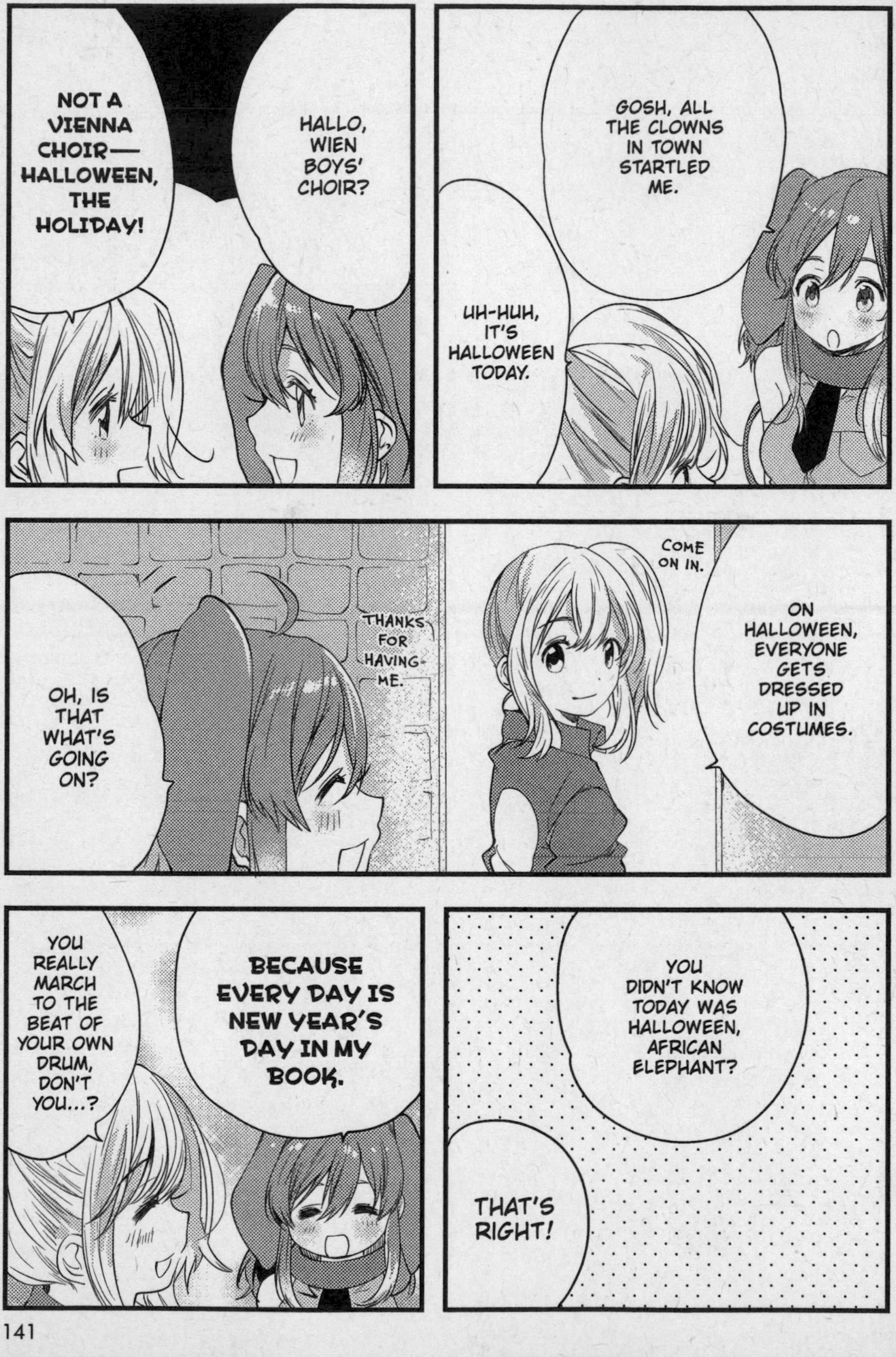
GOSH, ALL THE CLOWNS IN TOWN STARTLED ME.
UH-HUH, IT'S HALLOWEEN TODAY.
HALLO, WIEN BOYS' CHOIR?
NOT A VIENNA CHOIR—HALLOWEEN, THE HOLIDAY!
COME ON IN.
ON HALLOWEEN, EVERYONE GETS DRESSED UP IN COSTUMES.
THANKS FOR HAVING-ME.
OH, IS THAT WHAT'S GOING ON?
YOU DIDN'T KNOW TODAY WAS HALLOWEEN, AFRICAN ELEPHANT?
THAT'S RIGHT!
BECAUSE EVERY DAY IS NEW YEAR'S DAY IN MY BOOK.
YOU REALLY MARCH TO THE BEAT OF YOUR OWN DRUM, DON'T YOU...?

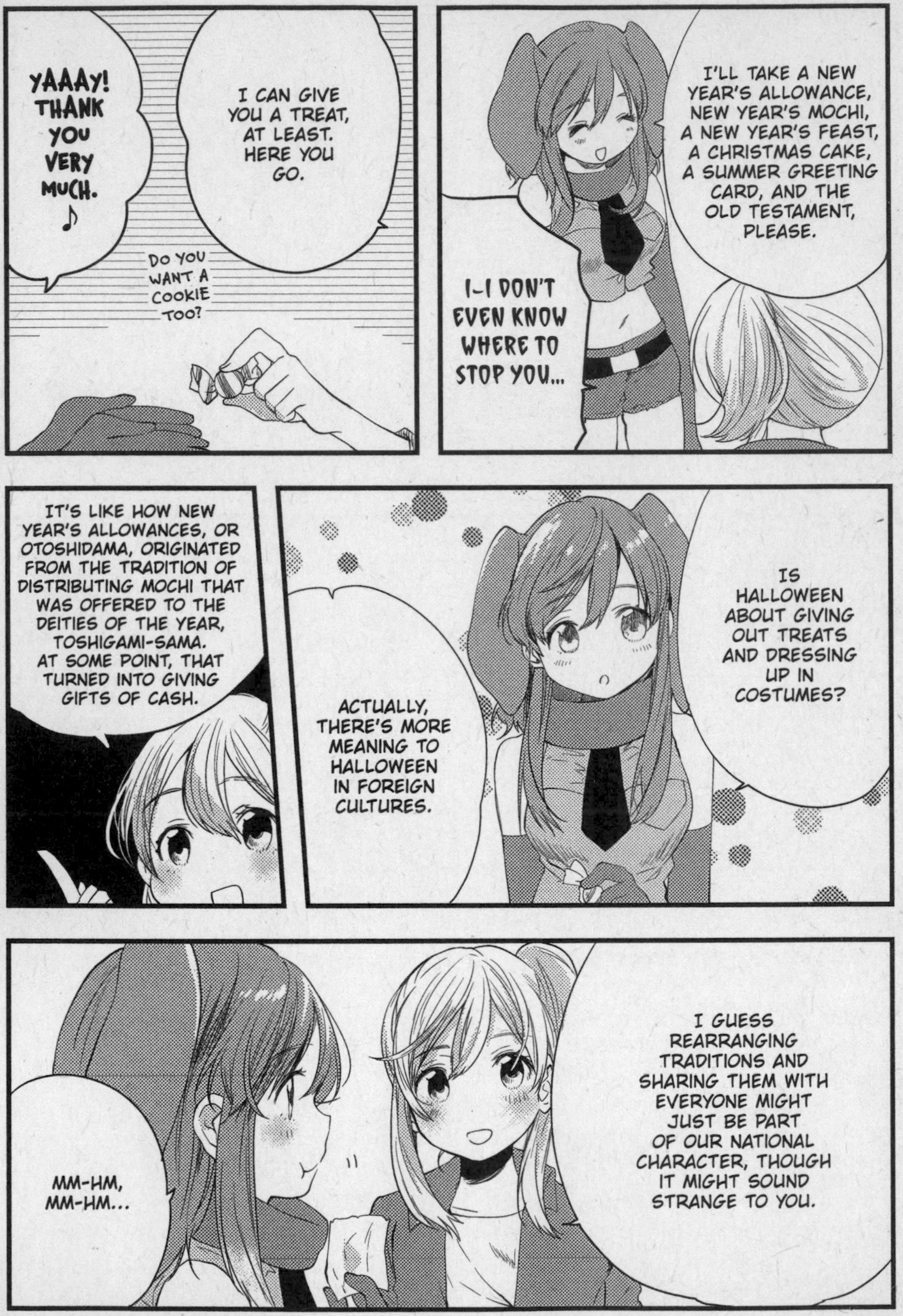
I'LL TAKE A NEW YEAR'S ALLOWANCE, NEW YEAR'S MOCHI, A NEW YEAR'S FEAST, A CHRISTMAS CAKE, A SUMMER GREETING CARD, AND THE OLD TESTAMENT, PLEASE.
I-I DON'T EVEN KNOW WHERE TO STOP YOU...
I CAN GIVE YOU A TREAT, AT LEAST. HERE YOU GO.
YAAAY! THANK YOU VERY MUCH. ♪
DO YOU WANT A COOKIE TOO?
IS HALLOWEEN ABOUT GIVING OUT TREATS AND DRESSING UP IN COSTUMES?
ACTUALLY, THERE'S MORE MEANING TO HALLOWEEN IN FOREIGN CULTURES.
IT'S LIKE HOW NEW YEAR'S ALLOWANCES, OR OTOSHIDAMA, ORIGINATED FROM THE TRADITION OF DISTRIBUTING MOCHI THAT WAS OFFERED TO THE DEITIES OF THE YEAR, TOSHIGAMI-SAMA. AT SOME POINT, THAT TURNED INTO GIVING GIFTS OF CASH.
I GUESS REARRANGING TRADITIONS AND SHARING THEM WITH EVERYONE MIGHT JUST BE PART OF OUR NATIONAL CHARACTER, THOUGH IT MIGHT SOUND STRANGE TO YOU.
MM-HM, MM-HM...

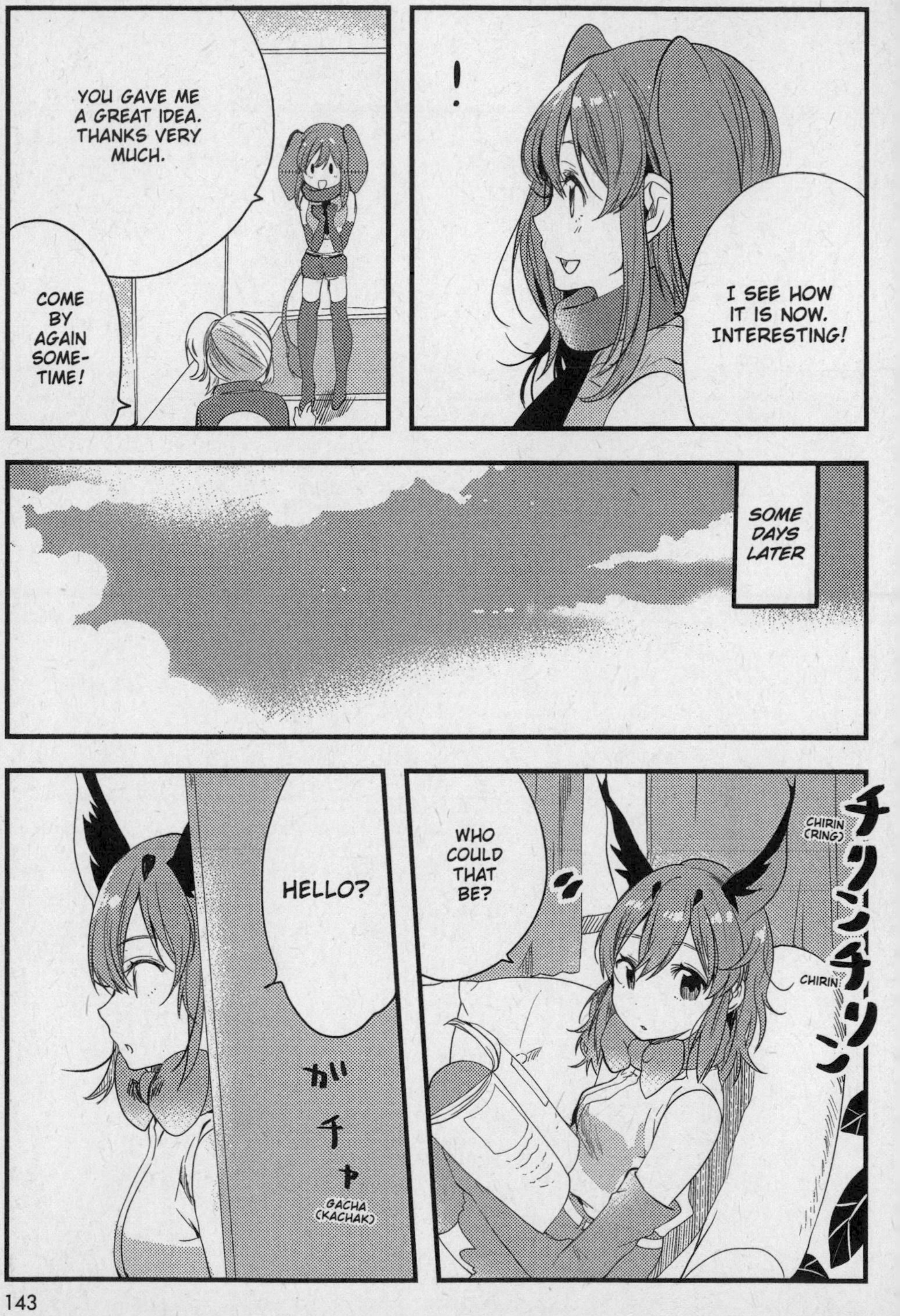
!
I SEE HOW IT IS NOW. INTERESTING!
YOU GAVE ME A GREAT IDEA. THANKS VERY MUCH.
COME BY AGAIN SOME-TIME!
SOME DAYS LATER
チリン
CHIRIN (RING)
チリン
CHIRIN
WHO COULD THAT BE?
HELLO?
ガチャ
GACHA (KACHAK)

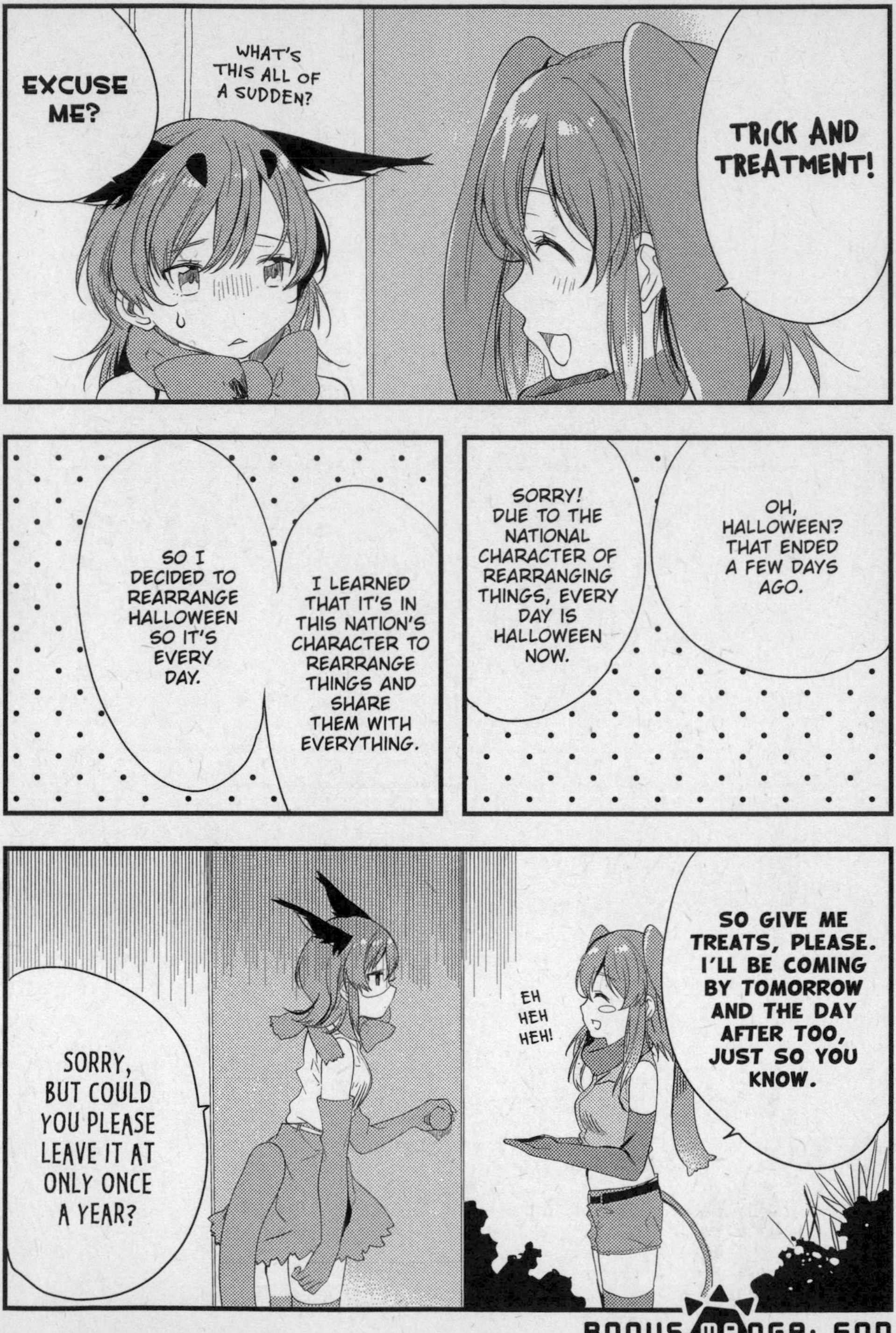

TRICK AND TREATMENT!
EXCUSE ME?
WHAT'S THIS ALL OF A SUDDEN?
OH, HALLOWEEN? THAT ENDED A FEW DAYS AGO.
SORRY! DUE TO THE NATIONAL CHARACTER OF REARRANGING THINGS, EVERY DAY IS HALLOWEEN NOW.
I LEARNED THAT IT'S IN THIS NATION'S CHARACTER TO REARRANGE THINGS AND SHARE THEM WITH EVERYTHING.
SO I DECIDED TO REARRANGE HALLOWEEN SO IT'S EVERY DAY.
SO GIVE ME TREATS, PLEASE. I'LL BE COMING BY TOMORROW AND THE DAY AFTER TOO, JUST SO YOU KNOW.
EH HEH HEH!
SORRY, BUT COULD YOU PLEASE LEAVE IT AT ONLY ONCE A YEAR?

BONUS MANGA: END

KEMONO FRIENDS
WELCOME TO JAPARI PARK!

KEMONO FRIENDS

WELCOME TO JAPARI PARK!

AFTERWORD

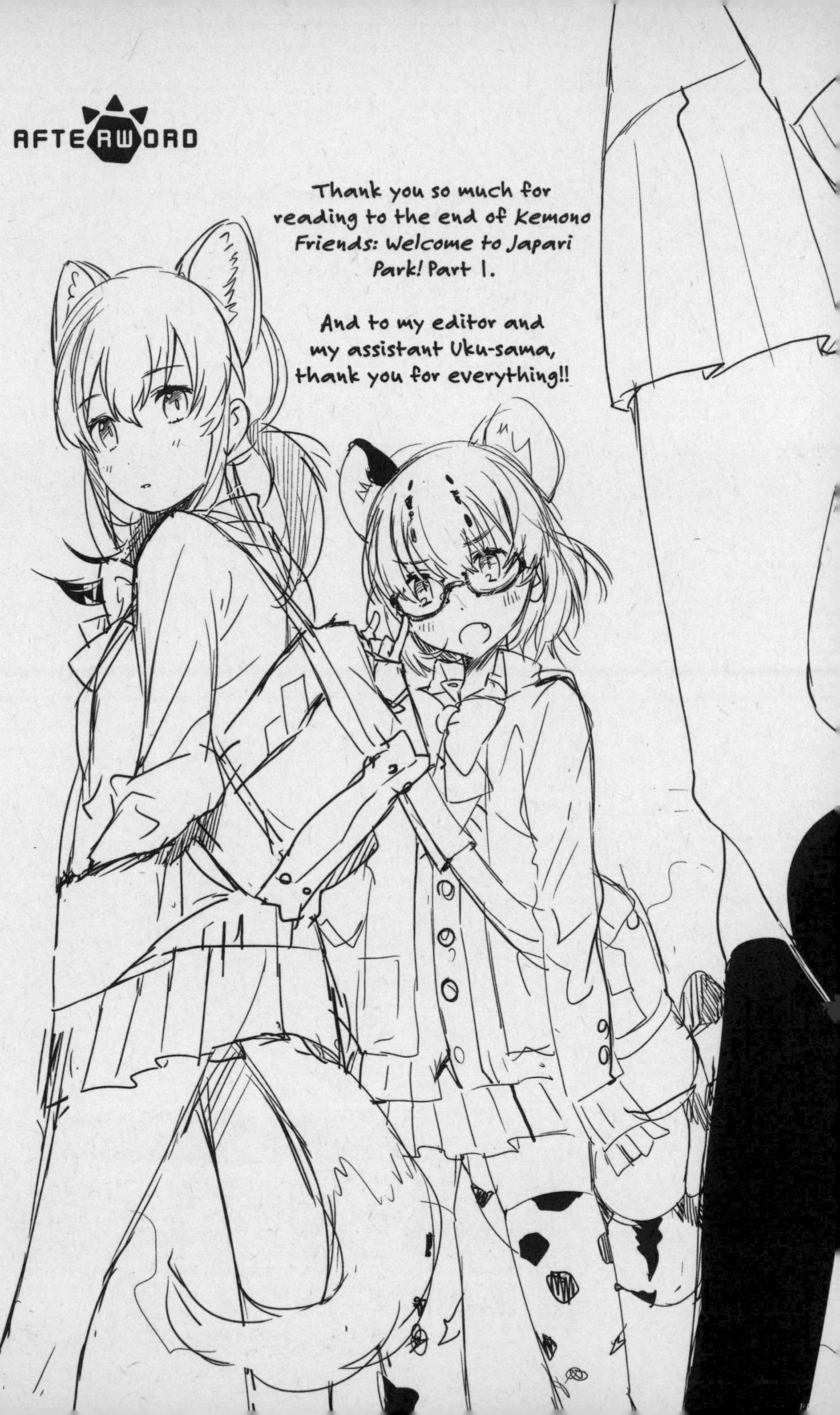
Thank you so much for reading to the end of Kemono Friends: Welcome to Japari Park! Part 1.
And to my editor and my assistant Uku-sama, thank you for everything!!

KEMONO FRIENDS

WELCOME TO JAPARI PARK!

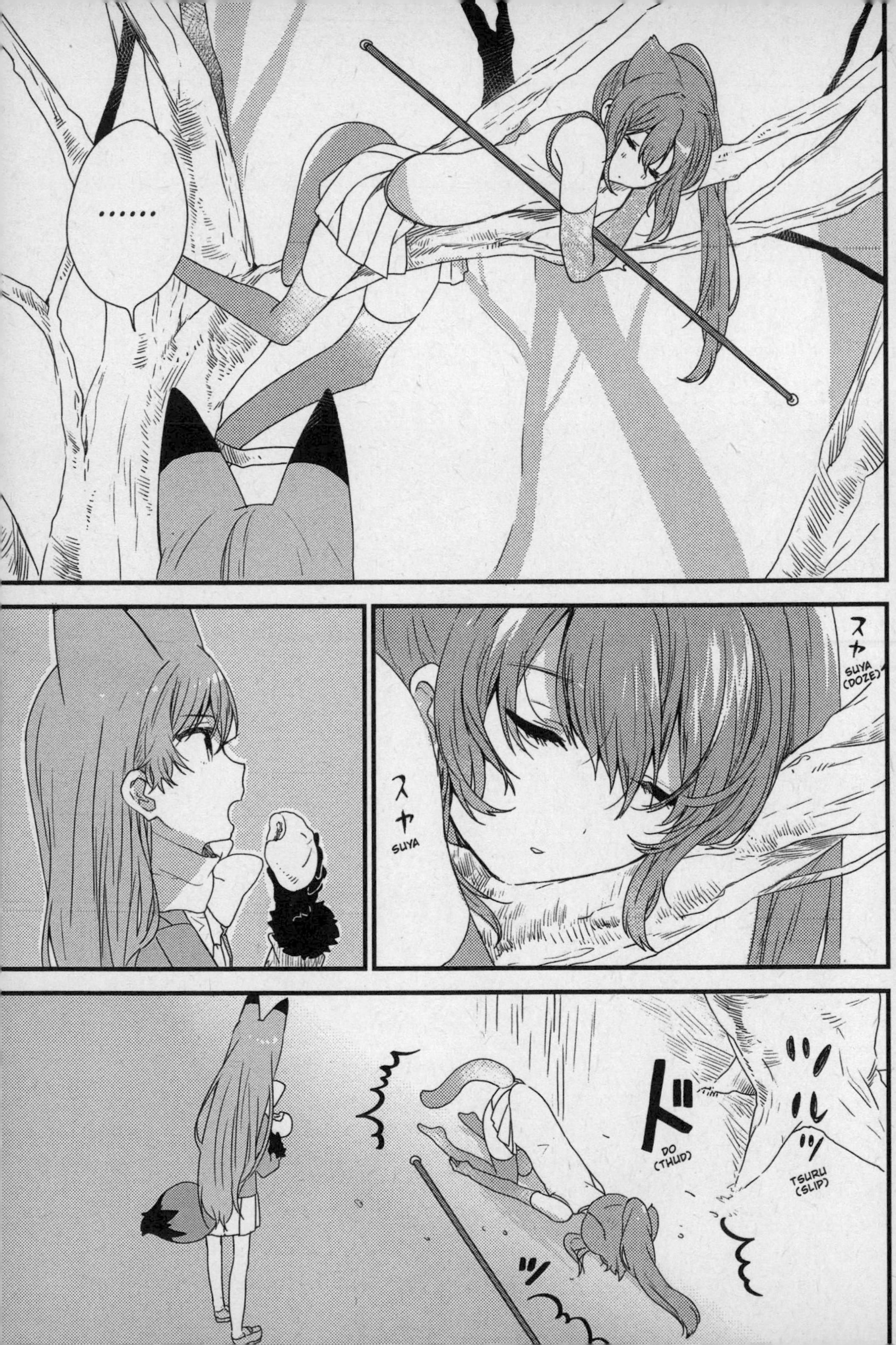

......
スヤ
SUYA (DOZE)
スヤ
SUYA
ツル
TSURU (SLIP)
ド
DO (THUD)

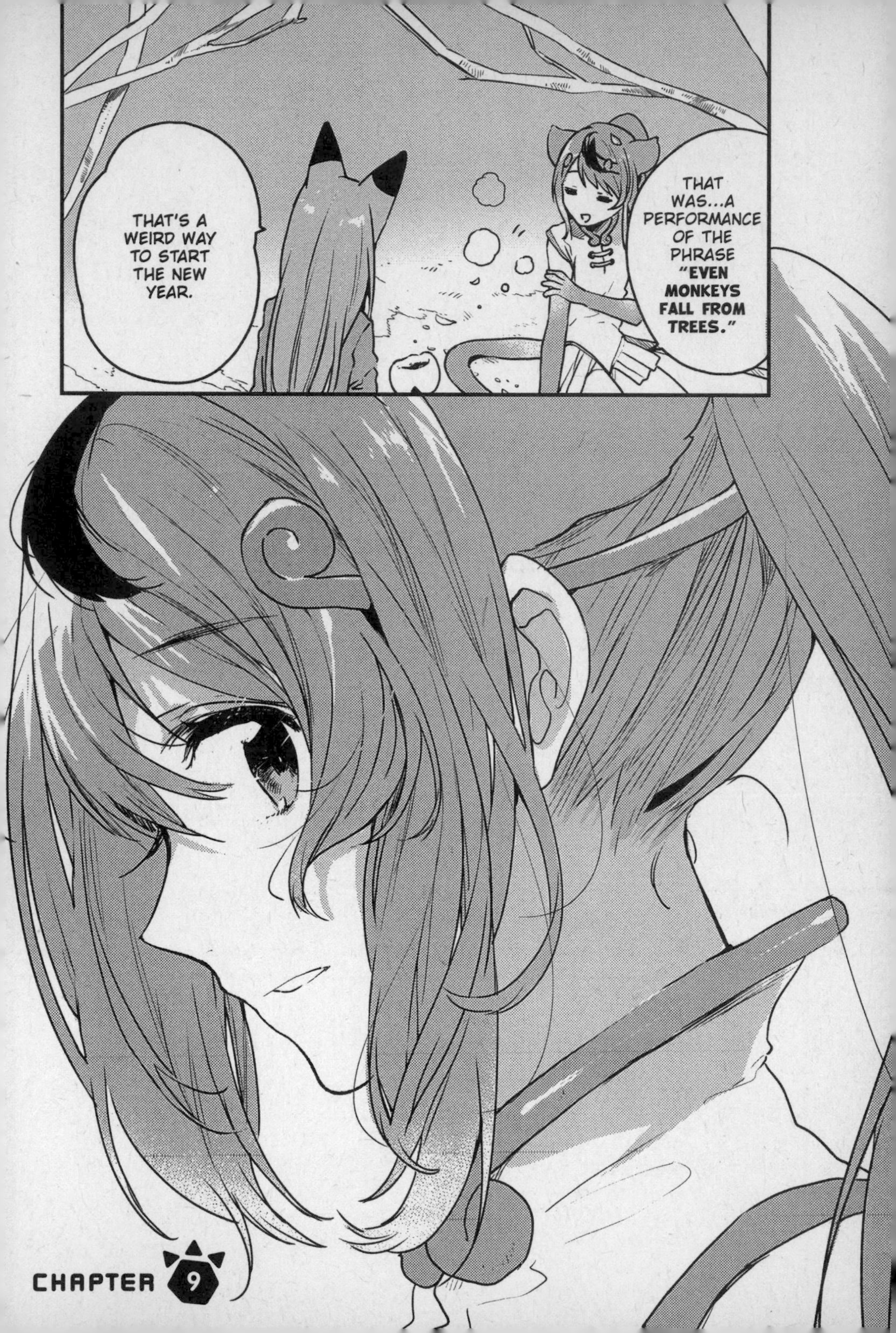
THAT WAS...A PERFORMANCE OF THE PHRASE "EVEN MONKEYS FALL FROM TREES."
THAT'S A WEIRD WAY TO START THE NEW YEAR.
CHAPTER 9

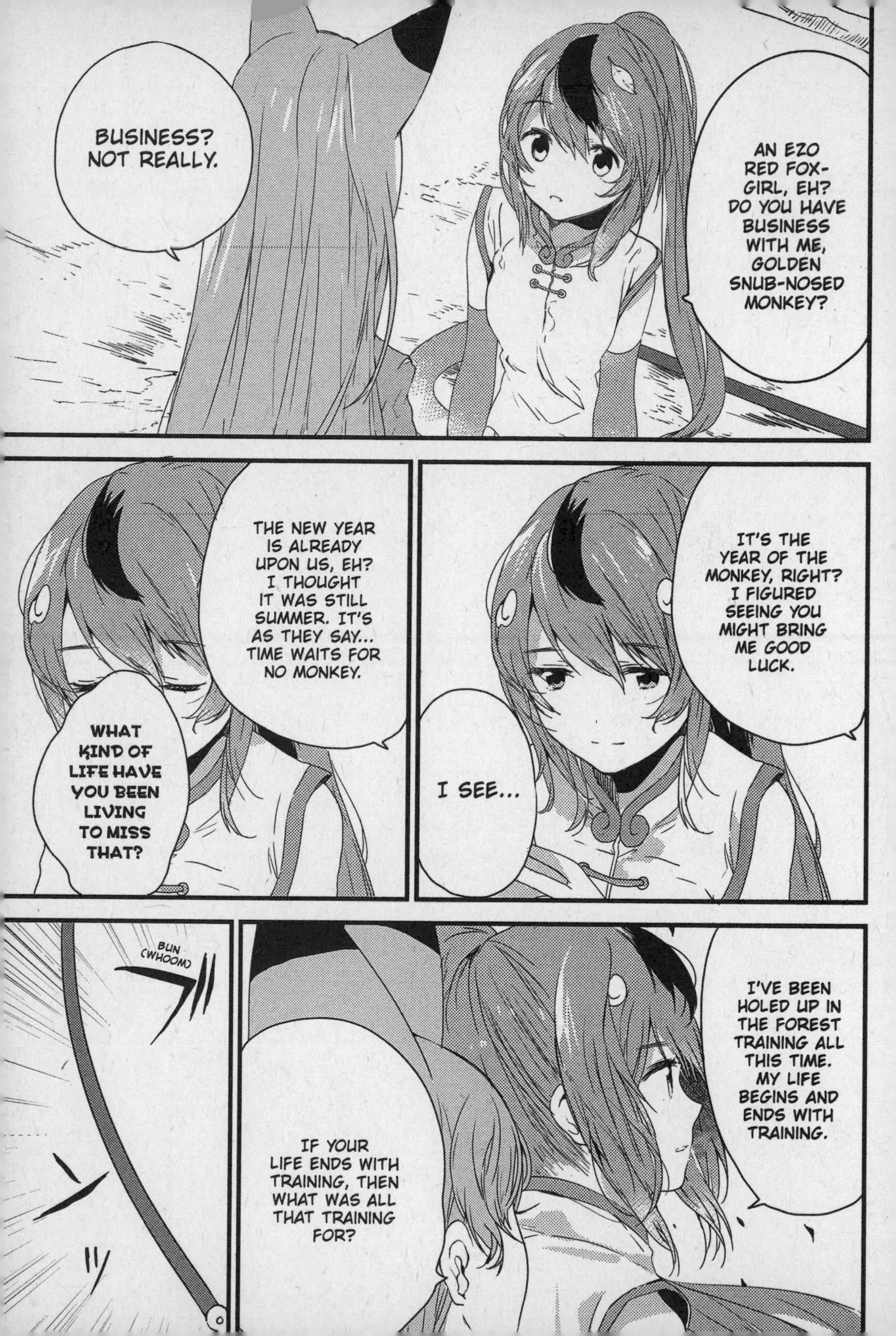
AN EZO RED FOX-GIRL, EH? DO YOU HAVE BUSINESS WITH ME, GOLDEN SNUB-NOSED MONKEY?
BUSINESS? NOT REALLY.
IT'S THE YEAR OF THE MONKEY, RIGHT? I FIGURED SEEING YOU MIGHT BRING ME GOOD LUCK.
I SEE...
THE NEW YEAR IS ALREADY UPON US, EH? I THOUGHT IT WAS STILL SUMMER. IT'S AS THEY SAY... TIME WAITS FOR NO MONKEY.
WHAT KIND OF LIFE HAVE YOU BEEN LIVING TO MISS THAT?
I'VE BEEN HOLED UP IN THE FOREST TRAINING ALL THIS TIME. MY LIFE BEGINS AND ENDS WITH TRAINING.
IF YOUR LIFE ENDS WITH TRAINING, THEN WHAT WAS ALL THAT TRAINING FOR?
BUN (WHOOM)

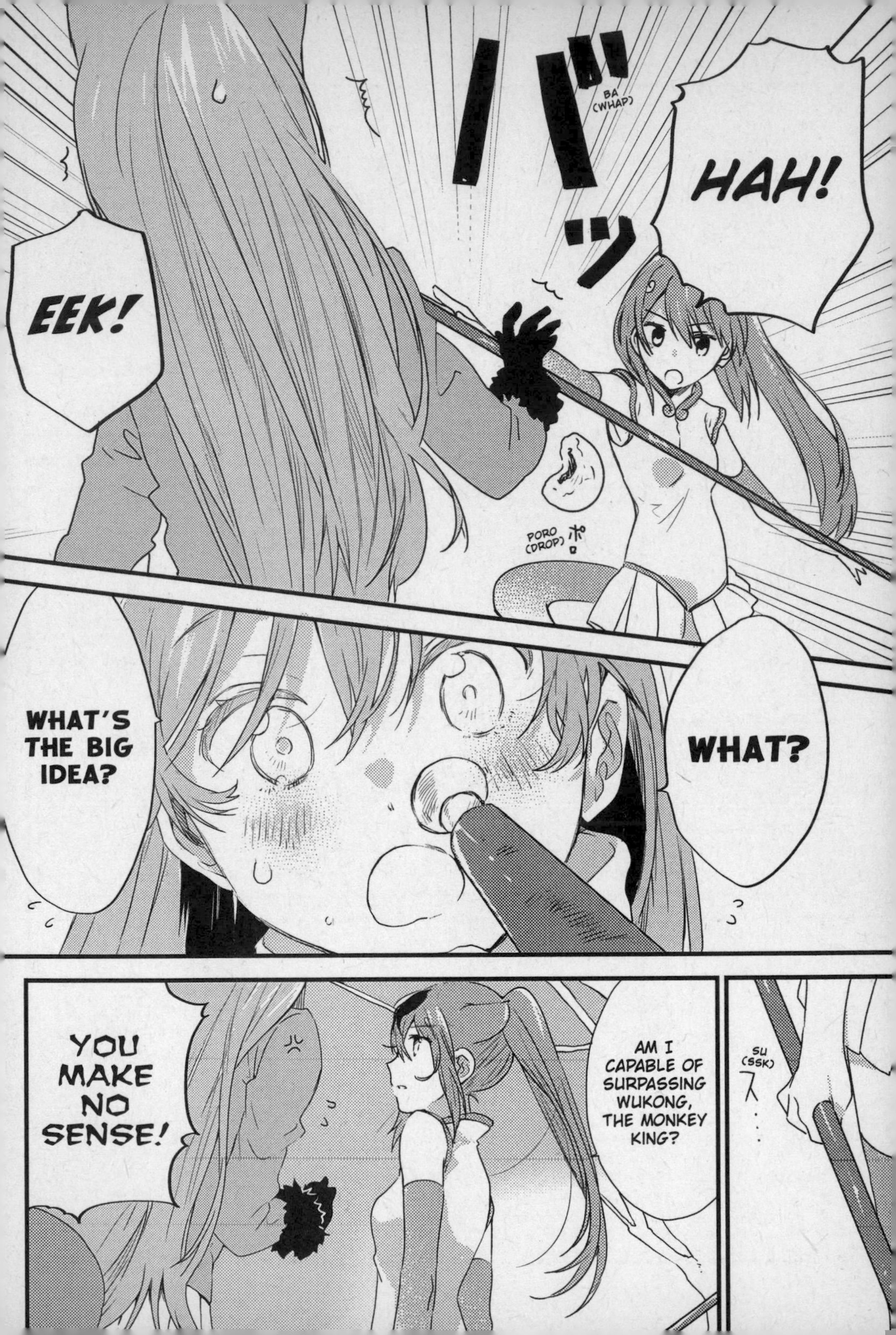
HAH!
バッ
BA (WHAP)
EEK!
ポロ
PORO (DROP)
WHAT?
WHAT'S THE BIG IDEA?
ス
SU (SSK)
AM I CAPABLE OF SURPASSING WUKONG, THE MONKEY KING?
YOU MAKE NO SENSE!

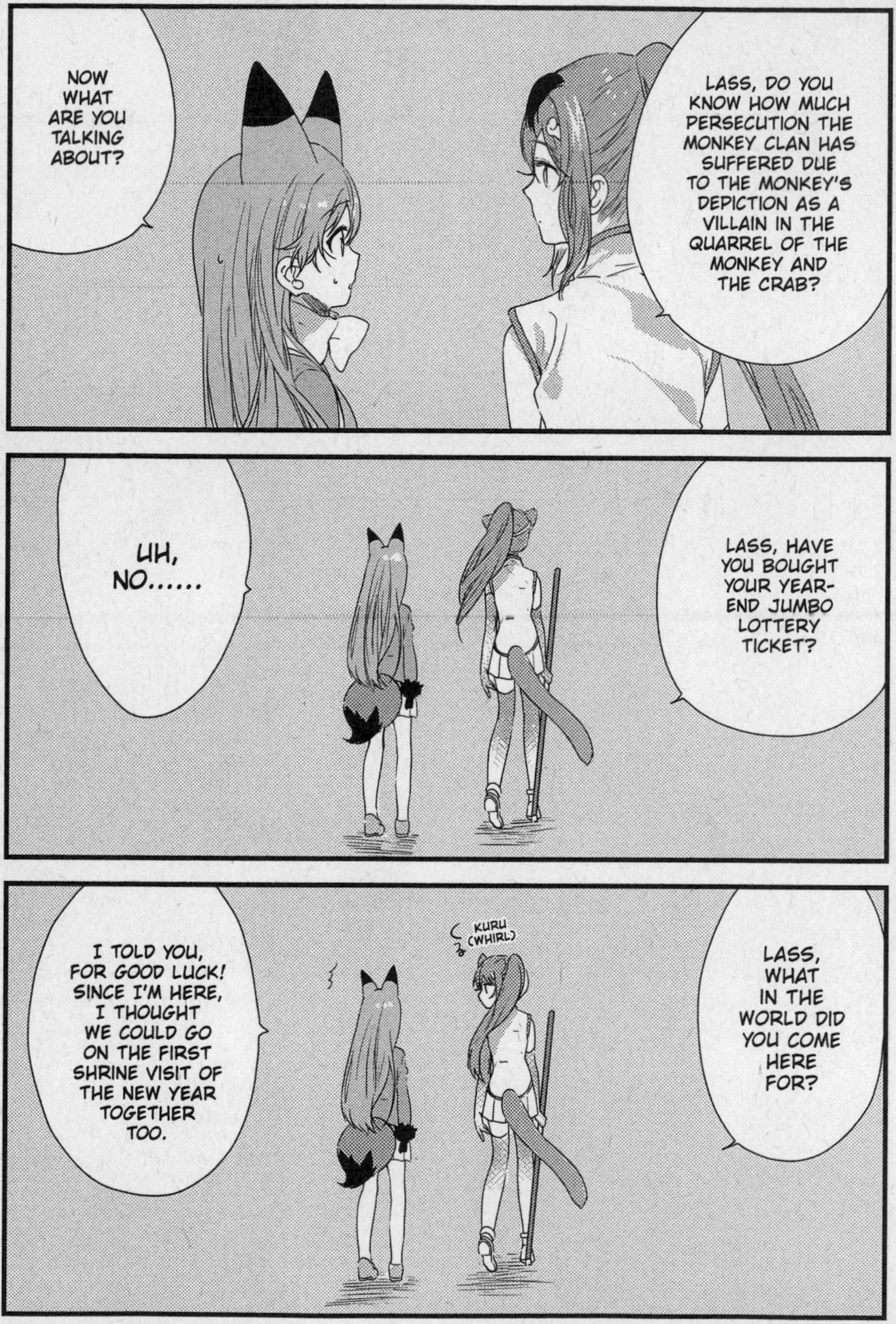
LASS, DO YOU KNOW HOW MUCH PERSECUTION THE MONKEY CLAN HAS SUFFERED DUE TO THE MONKEY'S DEPICTION AS A VILLAIN IN THE QUARREL OF THE MONKEY AND THE CRAB?
NOW WHAT ARE YOU TALKING ABOUT?
LASS, HAVE YOU BOUGHT YOUR YEAR-END JUMBO LOTTERY TICKET?
UH, NO......
LASS, WHAT IN THE WORLD DID YOU COME HERE FOR?
KURU (WHIRL)
I TOLD YOU, FOR GOOD LUCK! SINCE I'M HERE, I THOUGHT WE COULD GO ON THE FIRST SHRINE VISIT OF THE NEW YEAR TOGETHER TOO.

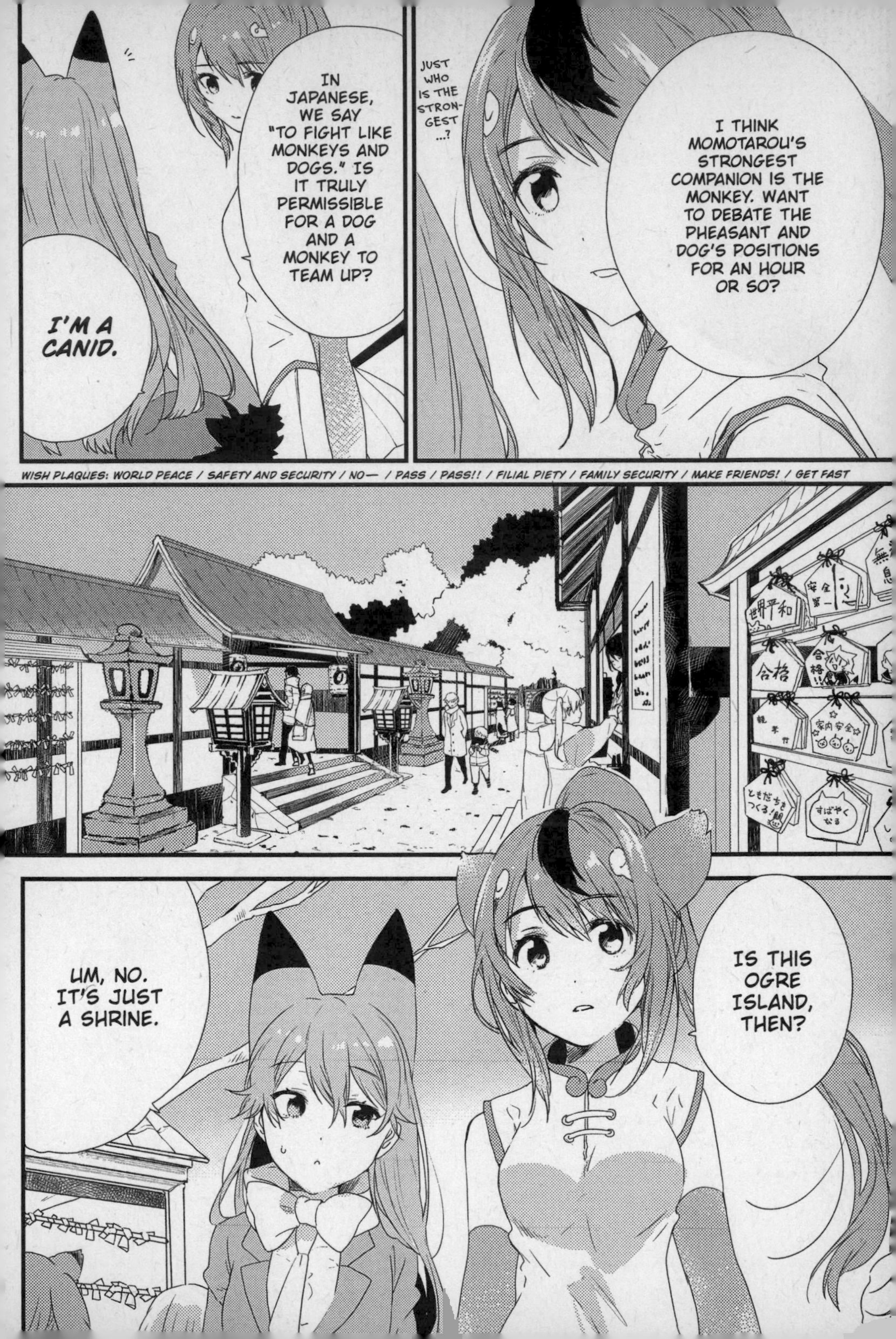

I THINK MOMOTAROU'S STRONGEST COMPANION IS THE MONKEY. WANT TO DEBATE THE PHEASANT AND DOG'S POSITIONS FOR AN HOUR OR SO?
JUST WHO IS THE STRONGEST ...?
IN JAPANESE, WE SAY "TO FIGHT LIKE MONKEYS AND DOGS." IS IT TRULY PERMISSIBLE FOR A DOG AND A MONKEY TO TEAM UP?
I'M A CANID.
WISH PLAQUES: WORLD PEACE / SAFETY AND SECURITY / NO— / PASS / PASS!! / FILIAL PIETY / FAMILY SECURITY / MAKE FRIENDS! / GET FAST
IS THIS OGRE ISLAND, THEN?
UM, NO. IT'S JUST A SHRINE.

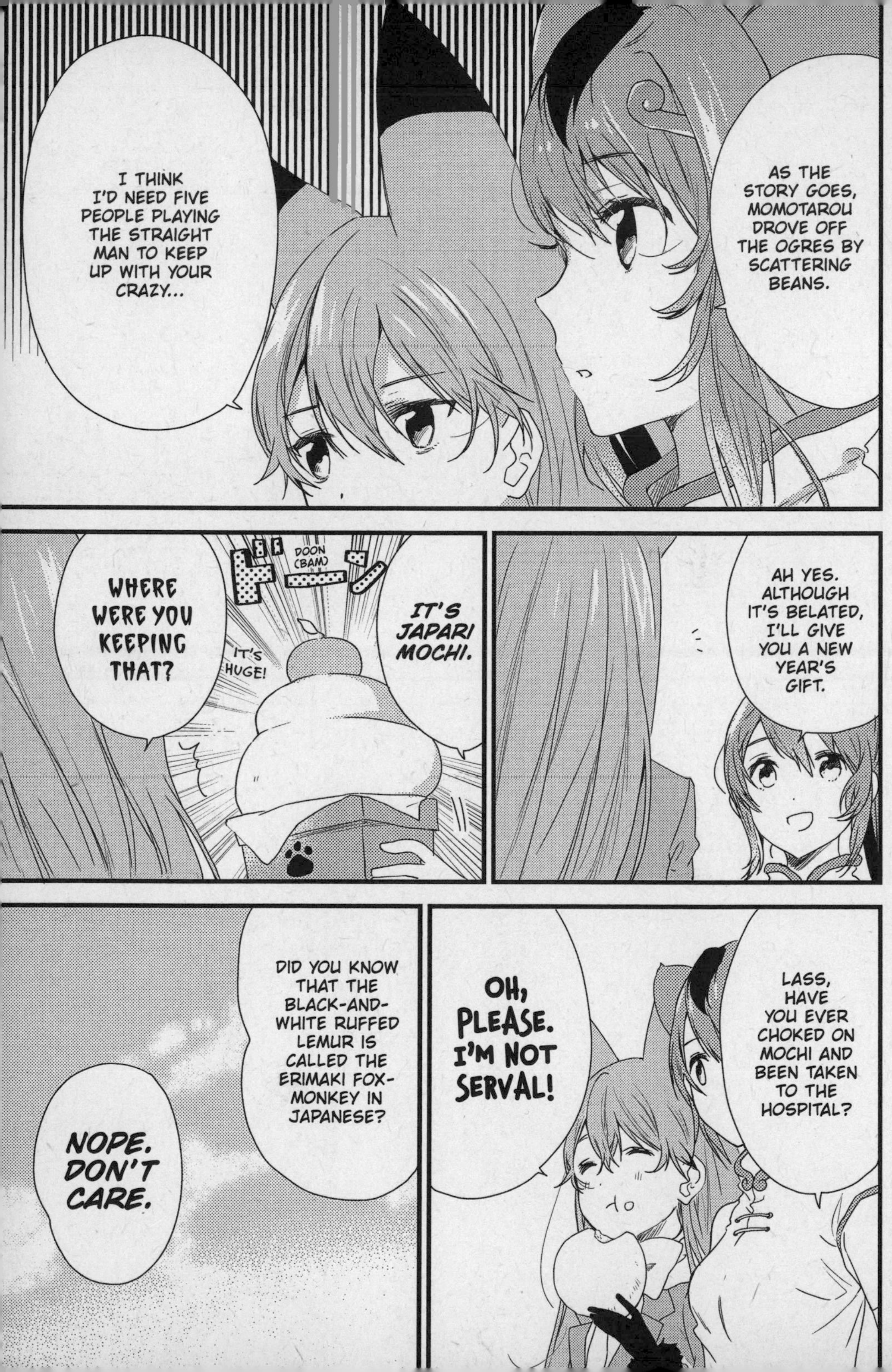
AS THE STORY GOES, MOMOTAROU DROVE OFF THE OGRES BY SCATTERING BEANS.
I THINK I'D NEED FIVE PEOPLE PLAYING THE STRAIGHT MAN TO KEEP UP WITH YOUR CRAZY...
AH YES. ALTHOUGH IT'S BELATED, I'LL GIVE YOU A NEW YEAR'S GIFT.
IT'S JAPARI MOCHI.
DOON (BAM)
IT'S HUGE!
WHERE WERE YOU KEEPING THAT?
LASS, HAVE YOU EVER CHOKED ON MOCHI AND BEEN TAKEN TO THE HOSPITAL?
OH, PLEASE. I'M NOT SERVAL!
DID YOU KNOW THAT THE BLACK-AND-WHITE RUFFED LEMUR IS CALLED THE ERIMAKI FOX-MONKEY IN JAPANESE?
NOPE. DON'T CARE.

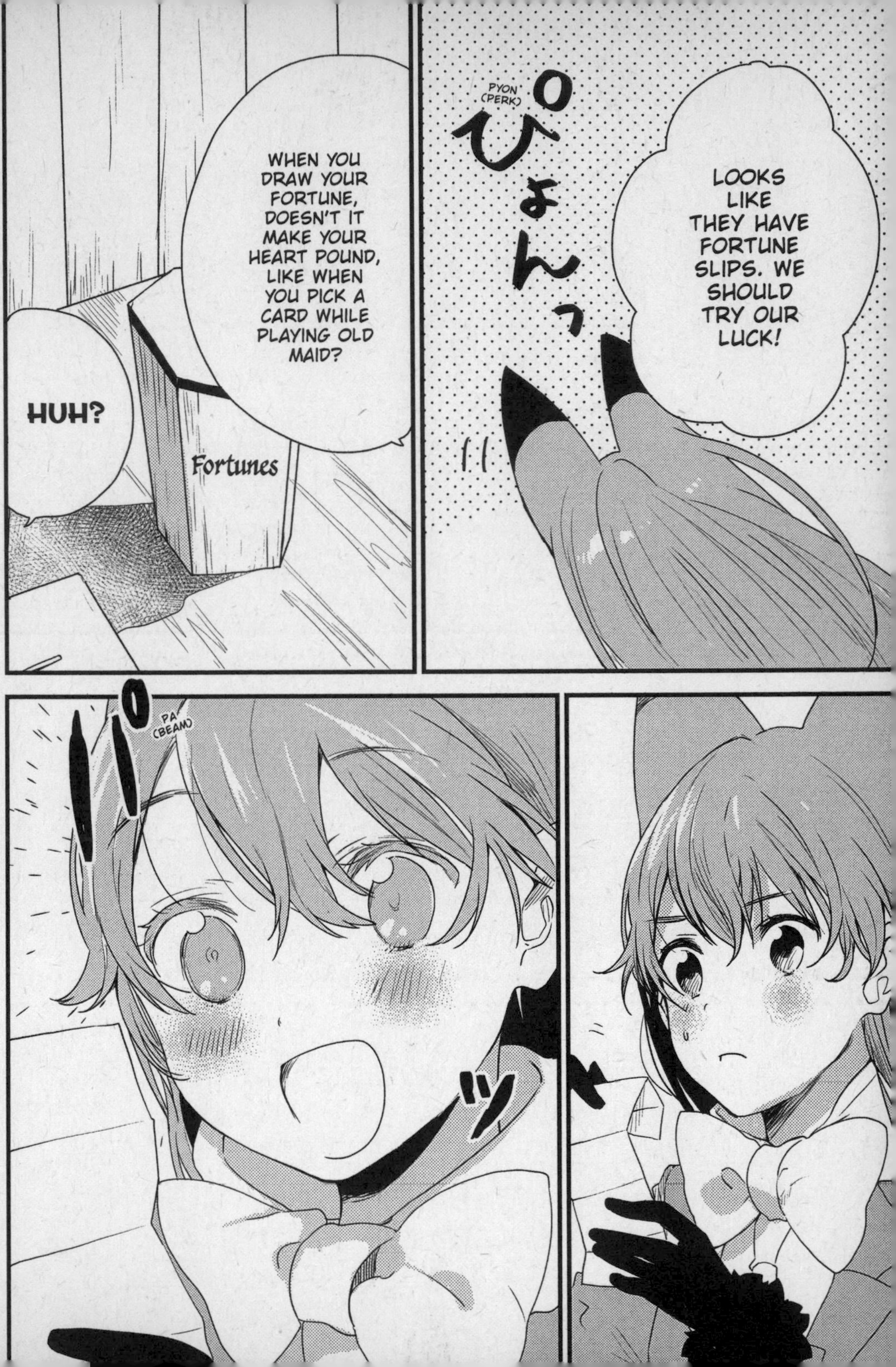
PYON (PERK)
ぴょんっ
LOOKS LIKE THEY HAVE FORTUNE SLIPS. WE SHOULD TRY OUR LUCK!
WHEN YOU DRAW YOUR FORTUNE, DOESN'T IT MAKE YOUR HEART POUND, LIKE WHEN YOU PICK A CARD WHILE PLAYING OLD MAID?
HUH?
Fortunes
PA (BEAM)

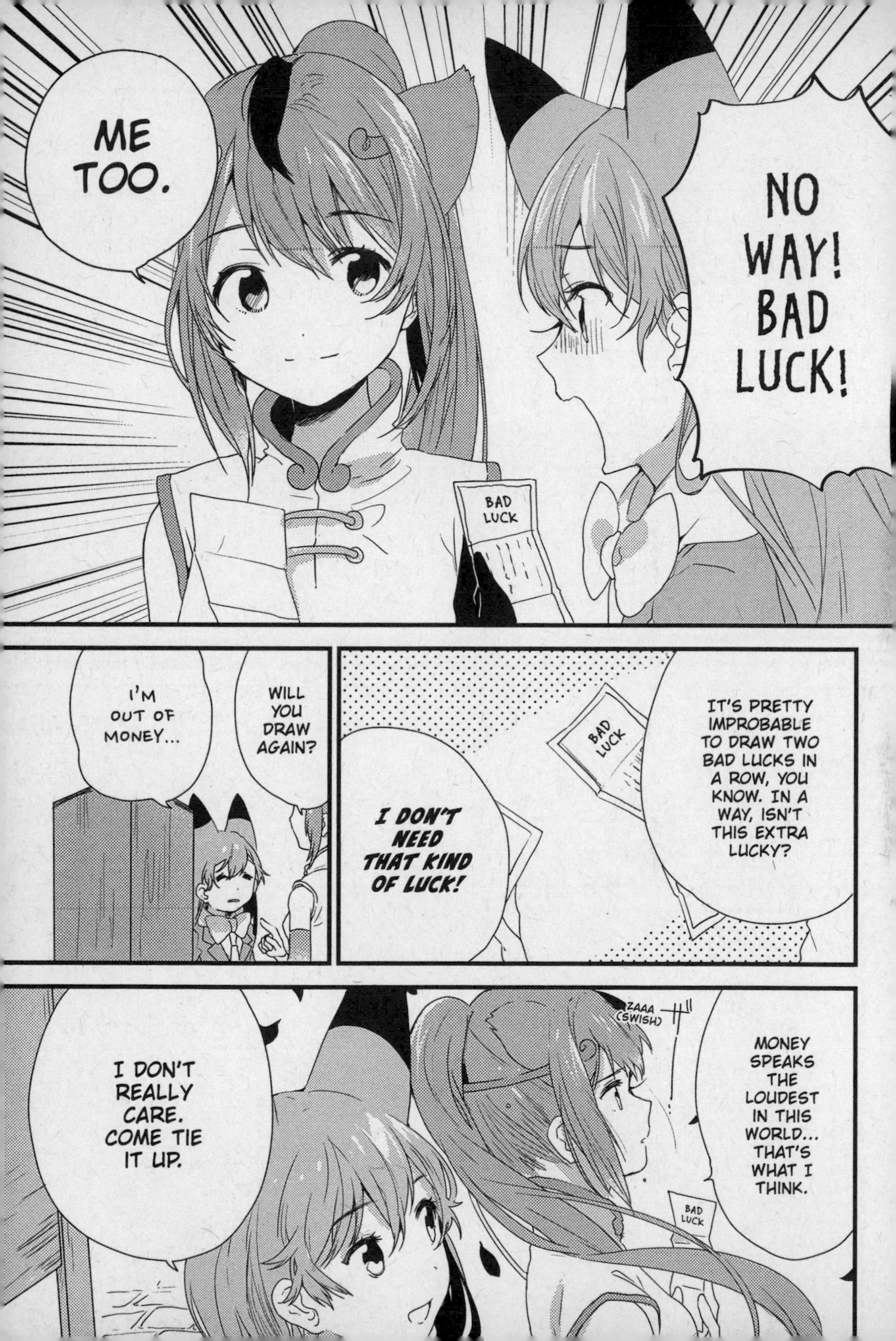
NO WAY! BAD LUCK!
ME TOO.
BAD LUCK
IT'S PRETTY IMPROBABLE TO DRAW TWO BAD LUCKS IN A ROW, YOU KNOW. IN A WAY, ISN'T THIS EXTRA LUCKY?
BAD LUCK
I DON'T NEED THAT KIND OF LUCK!
WILL YOU DRAW AGAIN?
I'M OUT OF MONEY...
MONEY SPEAKS THE LOUDEST IN THIS WORLD... THAT'S WHAT I THINK.
ZAAA (SWISH)
BAD LUCK
I DON'T REALLY CARE. COME TIE IT UP.

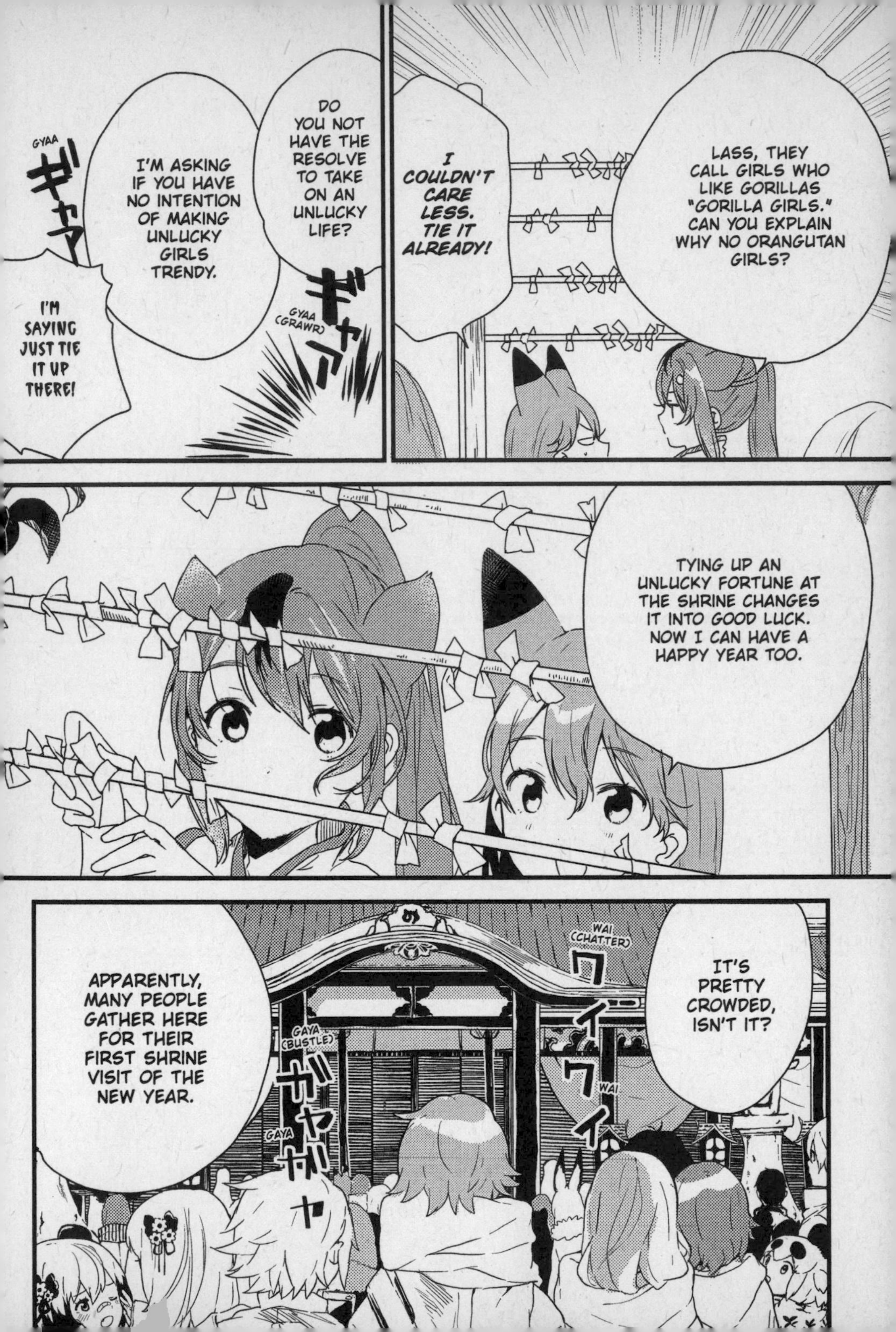
LASS, THEY CALL GIRLS WHO LIKE GORILLAS "GORILLA GIRLS." CAN YOU EXPLAIN WHY NO ORANGUTAN GIRLS?
I COULDN'T CARE LESS. TIE IT ALREADY!
DO YOU NOT HAVE THE RESOLVE TO TAKE ON AN UNLUCKY LIFE?
GYAA (GRAWR)
I'M ASKING IF YOU HAVE NO INTENTION OF MAKING UNLUCKY GIRLS TRENDY.
GYAA
I'M SAYING JUST TIE IT UP THERE!
TYING UP AN UNLUCKY FORTUNE AT THE SHRINE CHANGES IT INTO GOOD LUCK. NOW I CAN HAVE A HAPPY YEAR TOO.
IT'S PRETTY CROWDED, ISN'T IT?
WAI (CHATTER)
WAI
GAYA (BUSTLE)
GAYA
APPARENTLY, MANY PEOPLE GATHER HERE FOR THEIR FIRST SHRINE VISIT OF THE NEW YEAR.

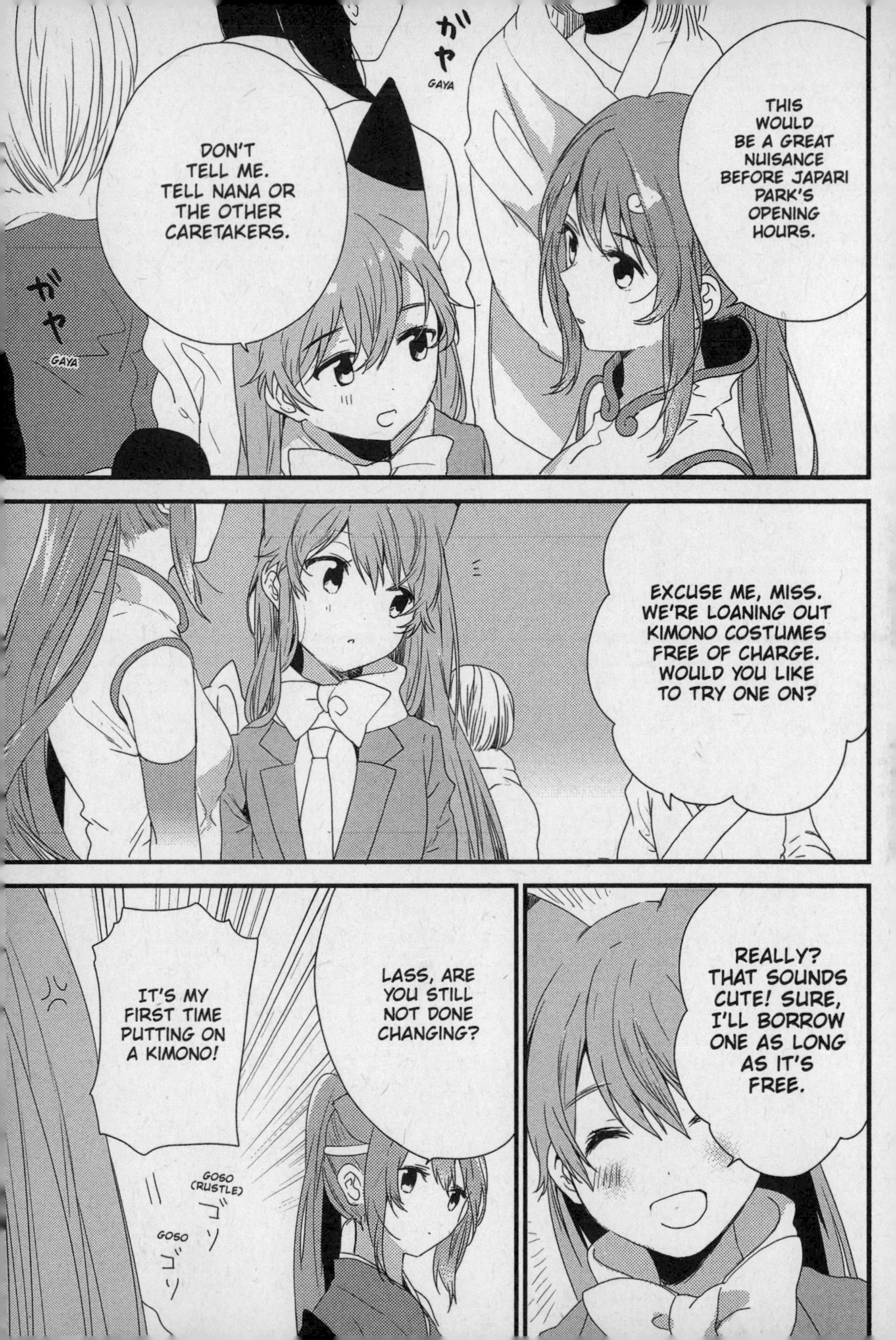
THIS WOULD BE A GREAT NUISANCE BEFORE JAPARI PARK'S OPENING HOURS.
ガヤ
GAYA
DON'T TELL ME. TELL NANA OR THE OTHER CARETAKERS.
ガヤ
GAYA
EXCUSE ME, MISS. WE'RE LOANING OUT KIMONO COSTUMES FREE OF CHARGE. WOULD YOU LIKE TO TRY ONE ON?
REALLY? THAT SOUNDS CUTE! SURE, I'LL BORROW ONE AS LONG AS IT'S FREE.
LASS, ARE YOU STILL NOT DONE CHANGING?
IT'S MY FIRST TIME PUTTING ON A KIMONO!
ゴソ
GOSO (RUSTLE)
ゴソ
GOSO

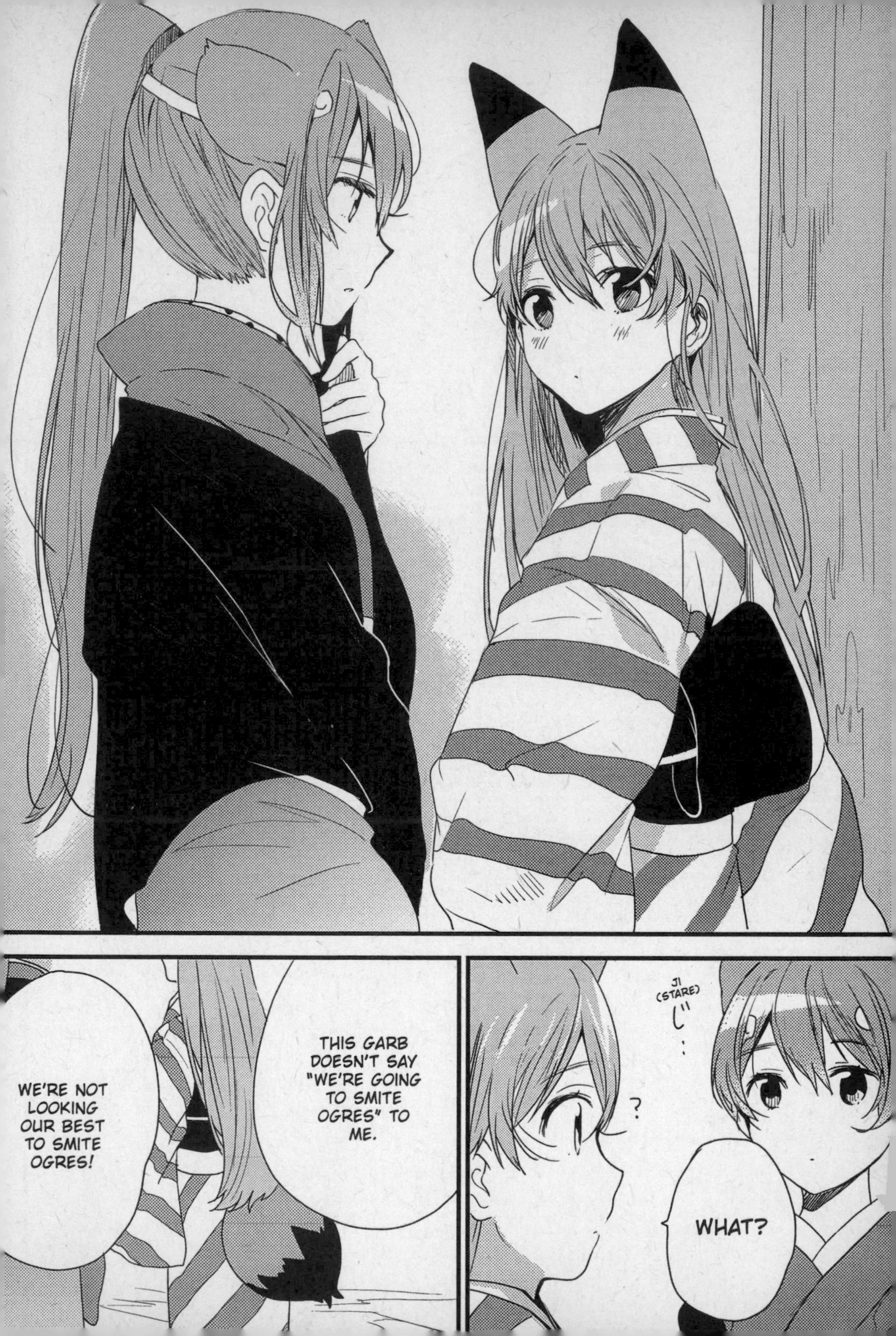
JI (STARE)
?
WHAT?
THIS GARB DOESN'T SAY "WE'RE GOING TO SMITE OGRES" TO ME.
WE'RE NOT LOOKING OUR BEST TO SMITE OGRES!

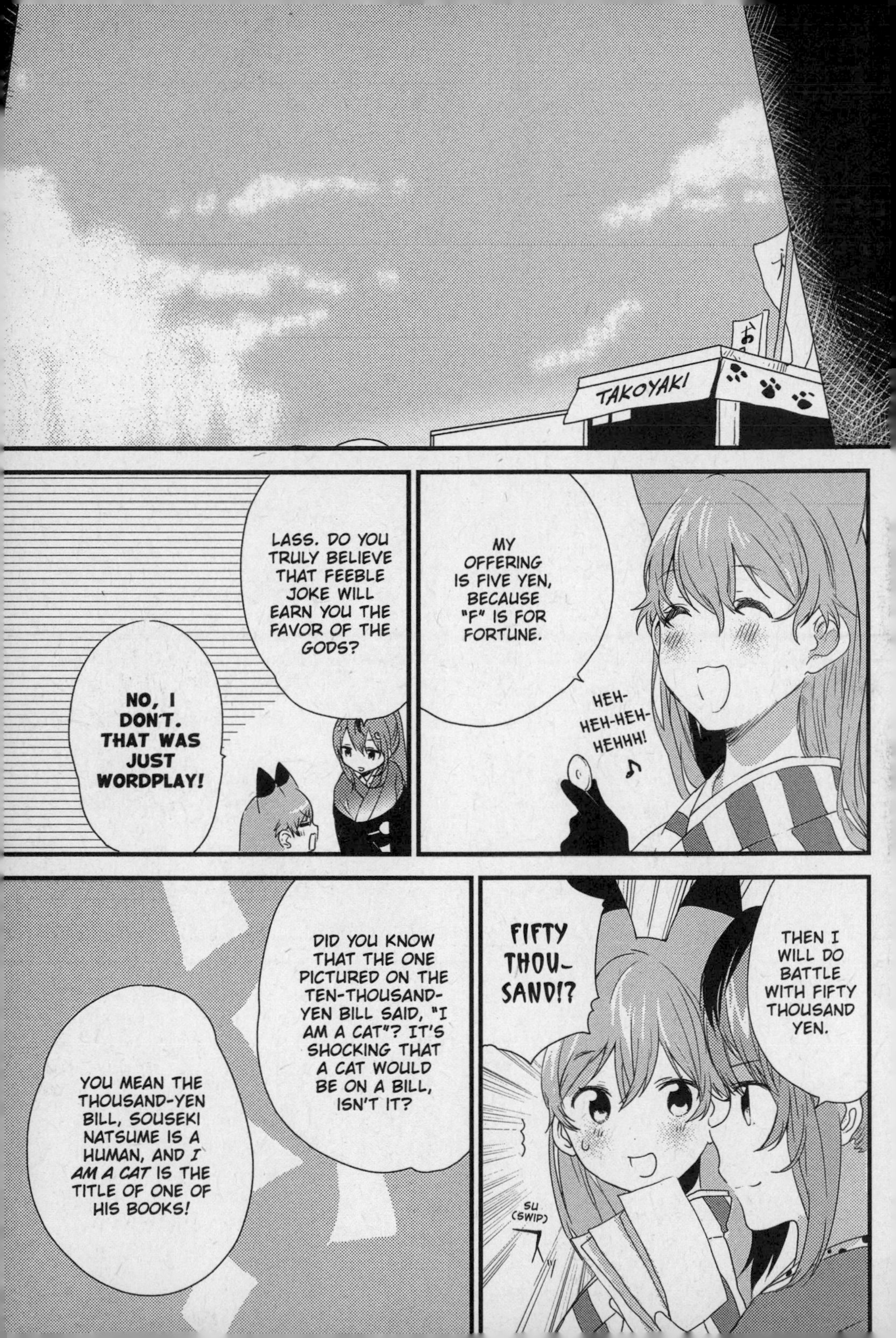
TAKOYAKI
MY OFFERING IS FIVE YEN, BECAUSE "F" IS FOR FORTUNE.
HEH-HEH-HEH-HEHHH! ♪
LASS. DO YOU TRULY BELIEVE THAT FEEBLE JOKE WILL EARN YOU THE FAVOR OF THE GODS?
NO, I DON'T. THAT WAS JUST WORDPLAY!
THEN I WILL DO BATTLE WITH FIFTY THOUSAND YEN.
FIFTY THOU-SAND!?
SU (SWIP)
DID YOU KNOW THAT THE ONE PICTURED ON THE TEN-THOUSAND-YEN BILL SAID, "I AM A CAT"? IT'S SHOCKING THAT A CAT WOULD BE ON A BILL, ISN'T IT?
YOU MEAN THE THOUSAND-YEN BILL, SOUSEKI NATSUME IS A HUMAN, AND *I AM A CAT* IS THE TITLE OF ONE OF HIS BOOKS!

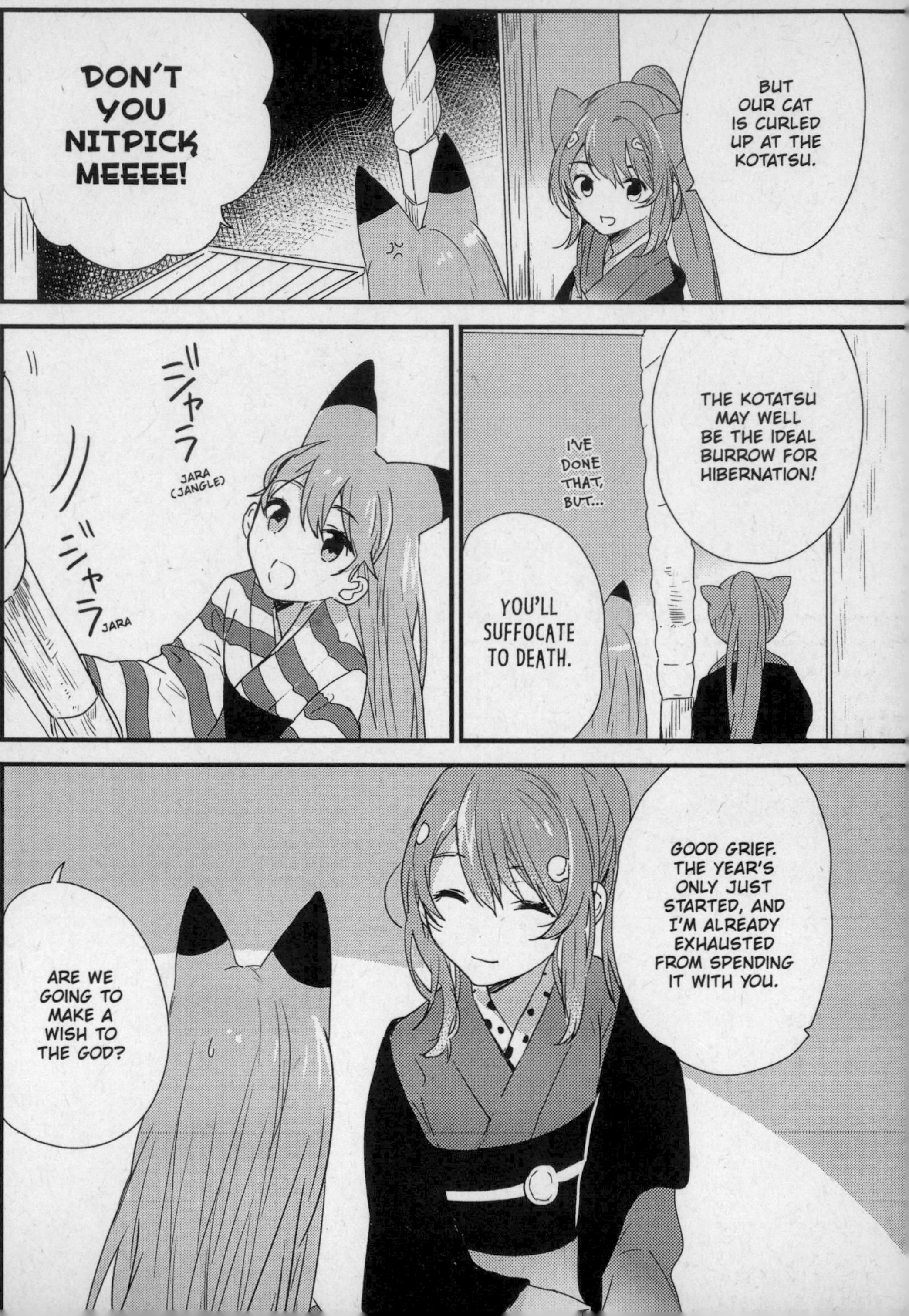
BUT OUR CAT IS CURLED UP AT THE KOTATSU.
DON'T YOU NITPICK MEEEE!
THE KOTATSU MAY WELL BE THE IDEAL BURROW FOR HIBERNATION!
I'VE DONE THAT, BUT...
YOU'LL SUFFOCATE TO DEATH.
ジャラ
JARA (JANGLE)
ジャラ
JARA
GOOD GRIEF. THE YEAR'S ONLY JUST STARTED, AND I'M ALREADY EXHAUSTED FROM SPENDING IT WITH YOU.
ARE WE GOING TO MAKE A WISH TO THE GOD?

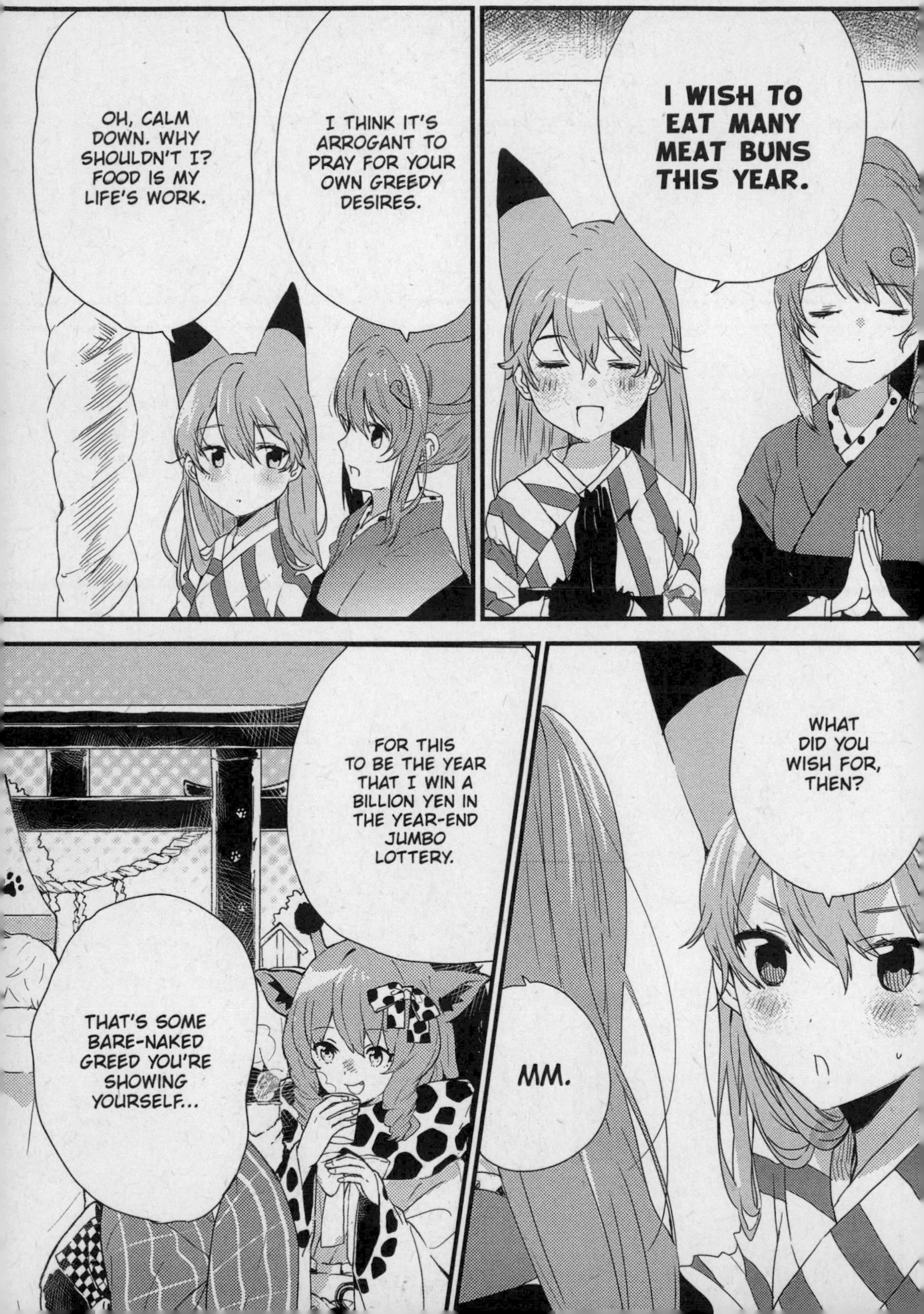
I WISH TO EAT MANY MEAT BUNS THIS YEAR.
I THINK IT'S ARROGANT TO PRAY FOR YOUR OWN GREEDY DESIRES.
OH, CALM DOWN. WHY SHOULDN'T I? FOOD IS MY LIFE'S WORK.
WHAT DID YOU WISH FOR, THEN?
MM.
FOR THIS TO BE THE YEAR THAT I WIN A BILLION YEN IN THE YEAR-END JUMBO LOTTERY.
THAT'S SOME BARE-NAKED GREED YOU'RE SHOWING YOURSELF...

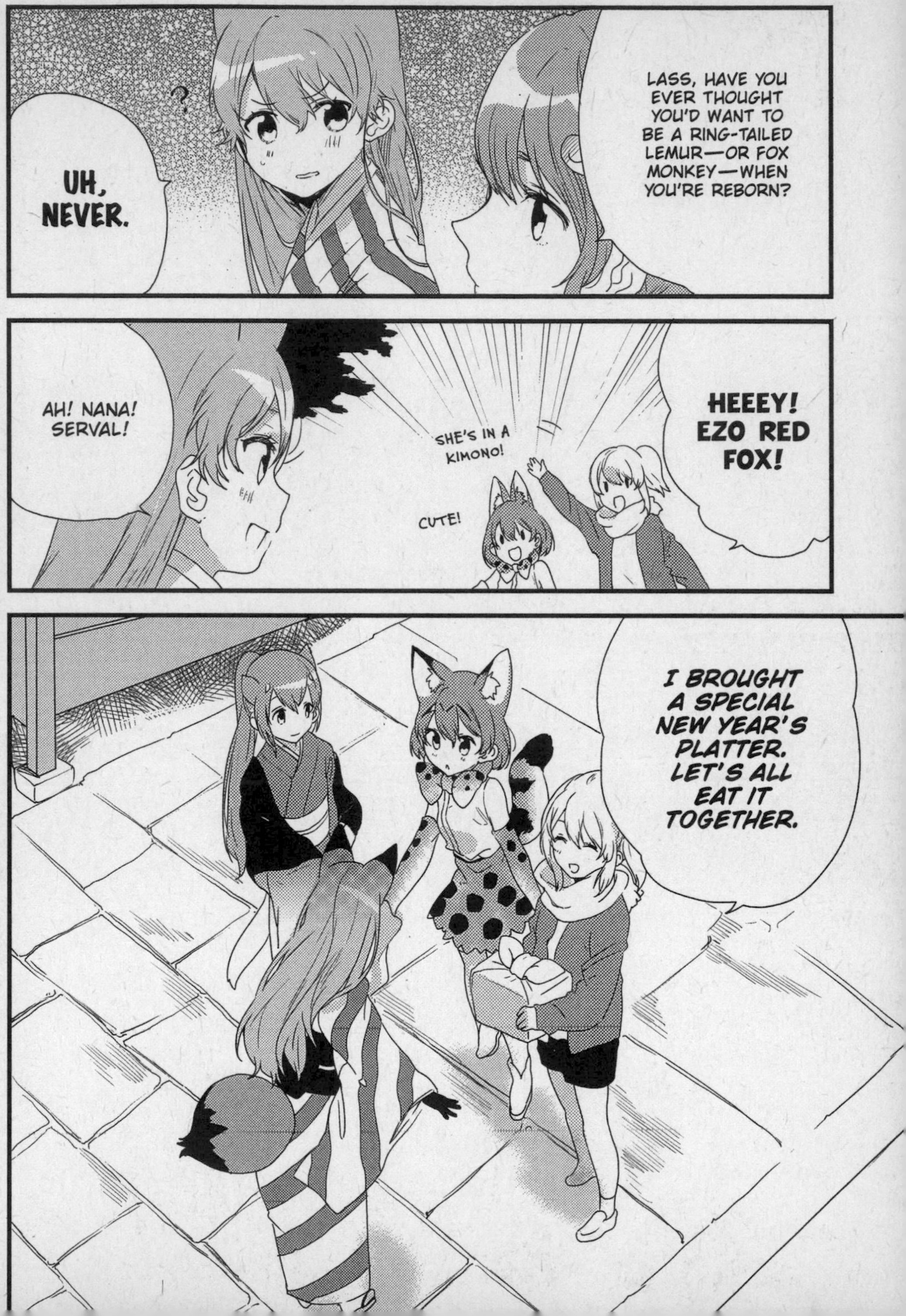
LASS, HAVE YOU EVER THOUGHT YOU'D WANT TO BE A RING-TAILED LEMUR—OR FOX MONKEY—WHEN YOU'RE REBORN?
UH, NEVER.
HEEEY! EZO RED FOX!
SHE'S IN A KIMONO!
CUTE!
AH! NANA! SERVAL!
I BROUGHT A SPECIAL NEW YEAR'S PLATTER. LET'S ALL EAT IT TOGETHER.

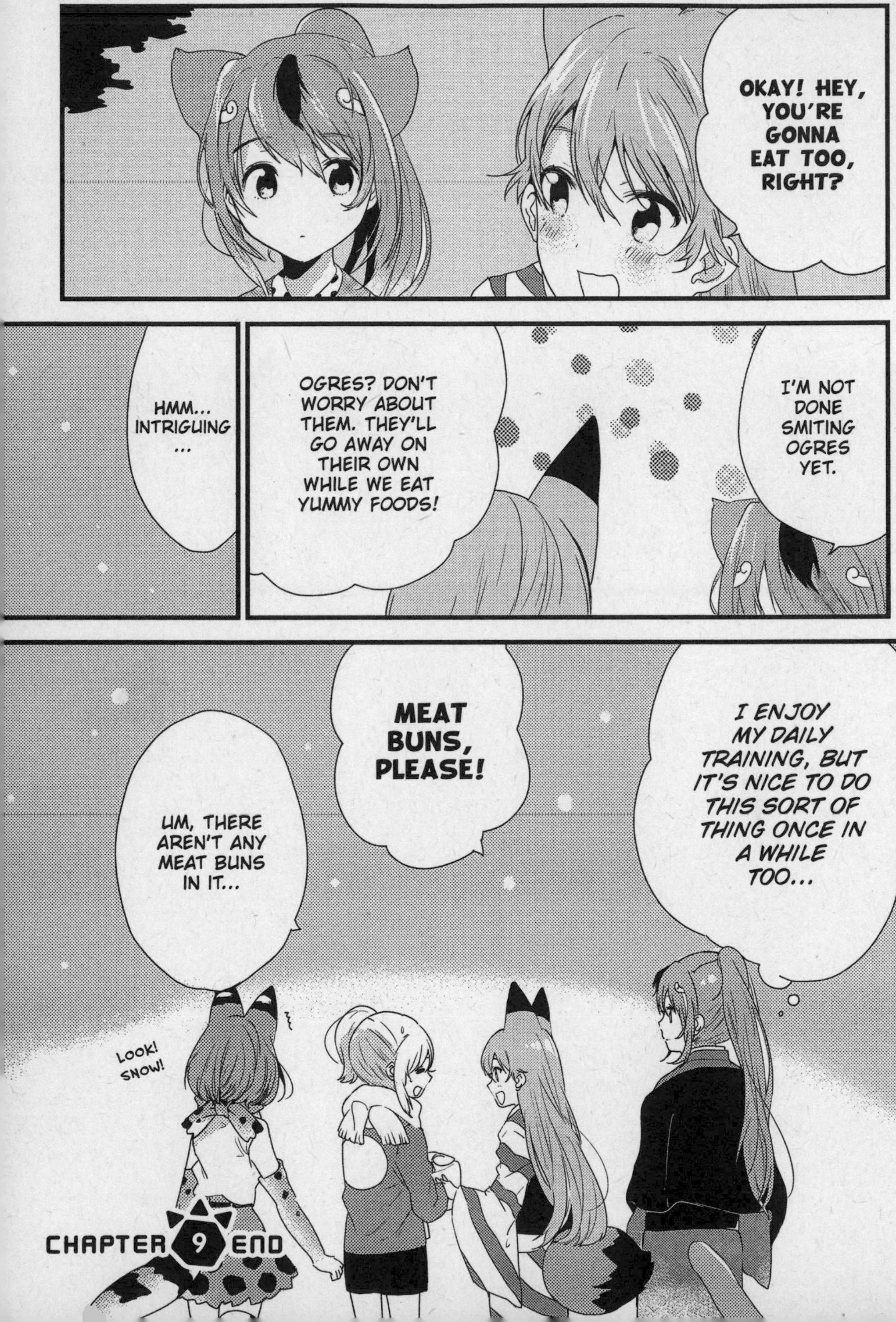
OKAY! HEY, YOU'RE GONNA EAT TOO, RIGHT?
I'M NOT DONE SMITING OGRES YET.
OGRES? DON'T WORRY ABOUT THEM. THEY'LL GO AWAY ON THEIR OWN WHILE WE EAT YUMMY FOODS!
HMM... INTRIGUING ...
I ENJOY MY DAILY TRAINING, BUT IT'S NICE TO DO THIS SORT OF THING ONCE IN A WHILE TOO...
MEAT BUNS, PLEASE!
UM, THERE AREN'T ANY MEAT BUNS IN IT...
LOOK! SNOW!
CHAPTER 9 END

KEMONO FRIENDS

WELCOME TO JAPARI PARK!

CHAPTER 10

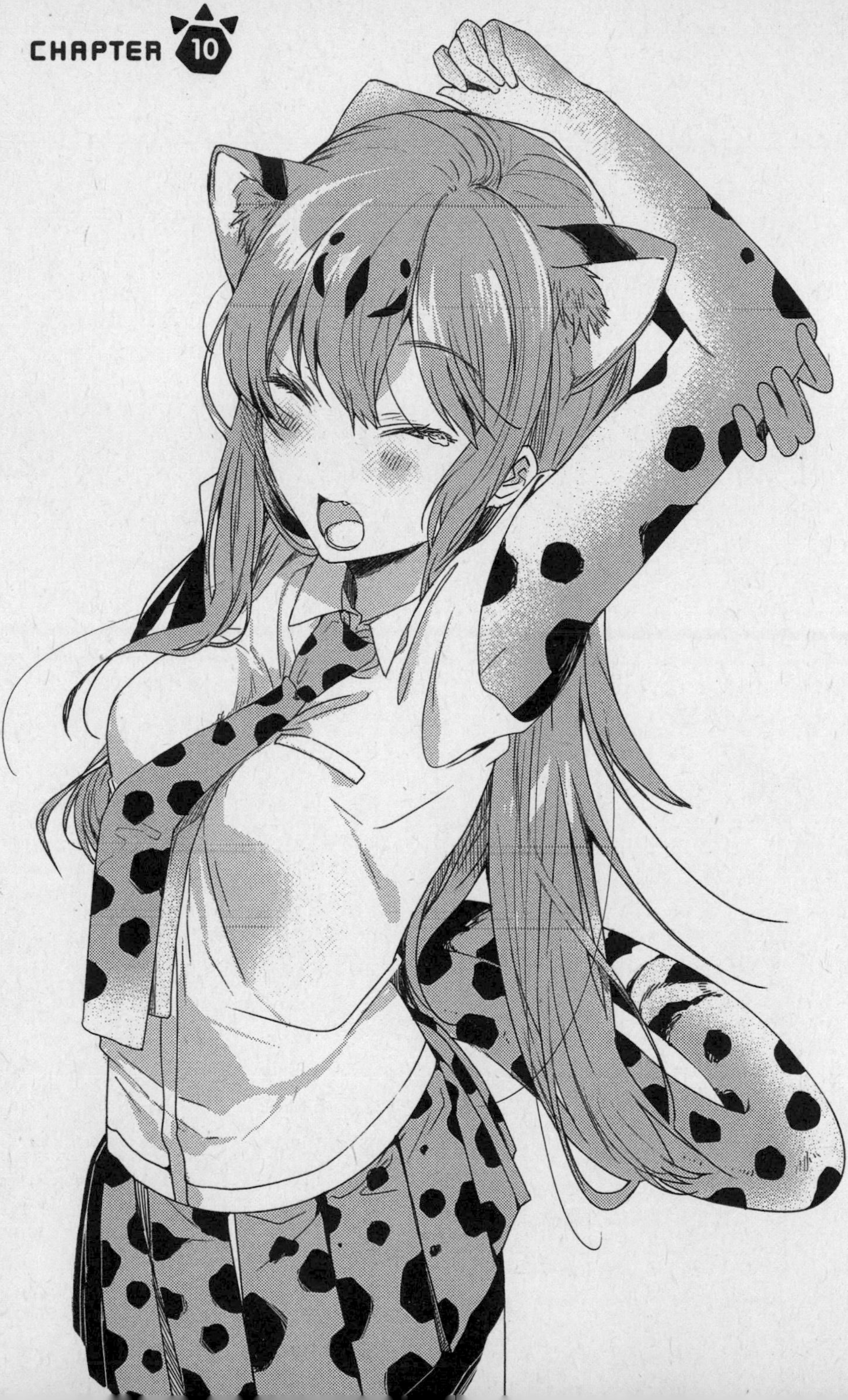

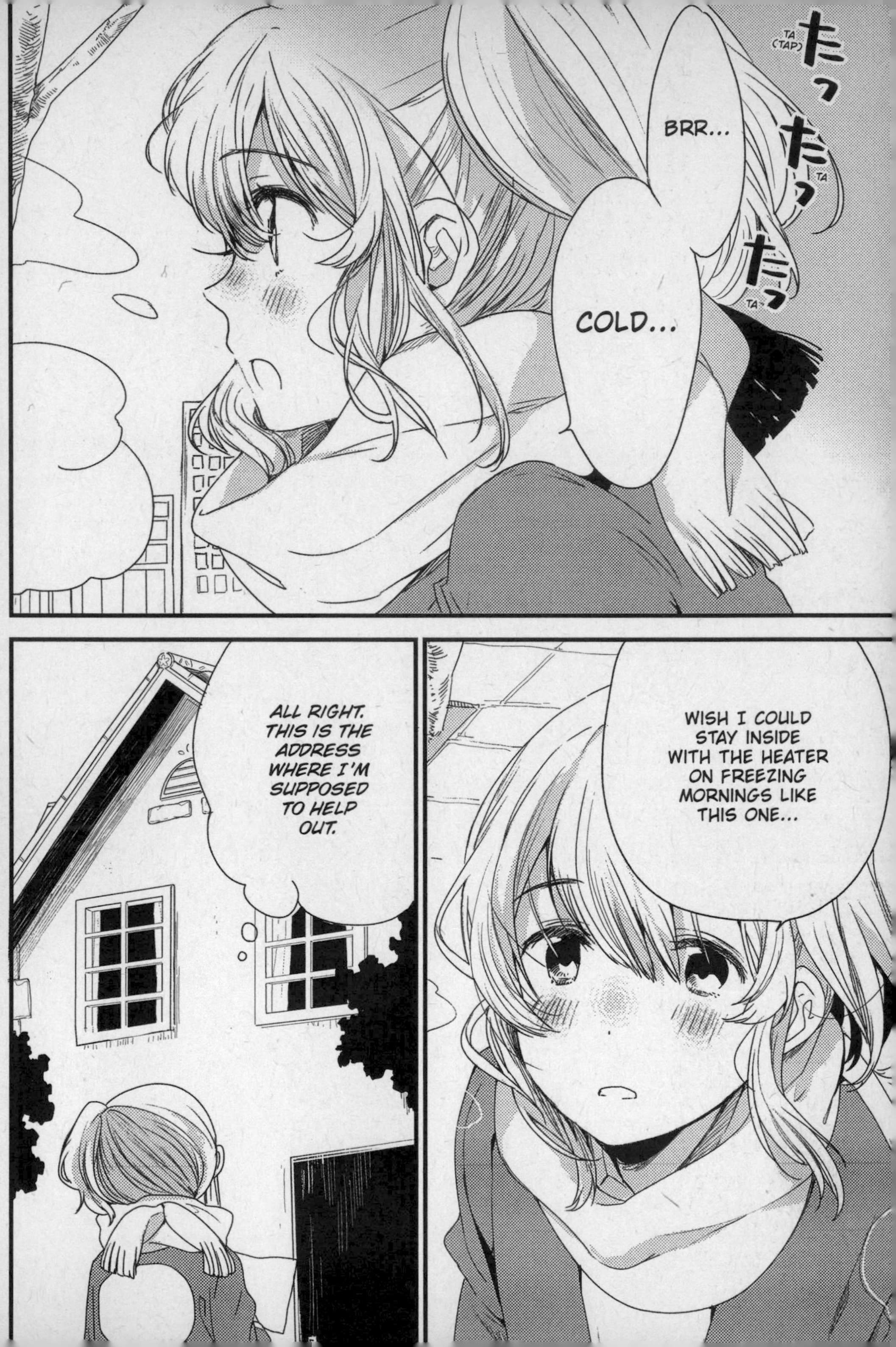
たっ
TA (TAP)
たっ
TA
たっ
TA
BRR...
COLD...
WISH I COULD STAY INSIDE WITH THE HEATER ON FREEZING MORNINGS LIKE THIS ONE...
ALL RIGHT. THIS IS THE ADDRESS WHERE I'M SUPPOSED TO HELP OUT.

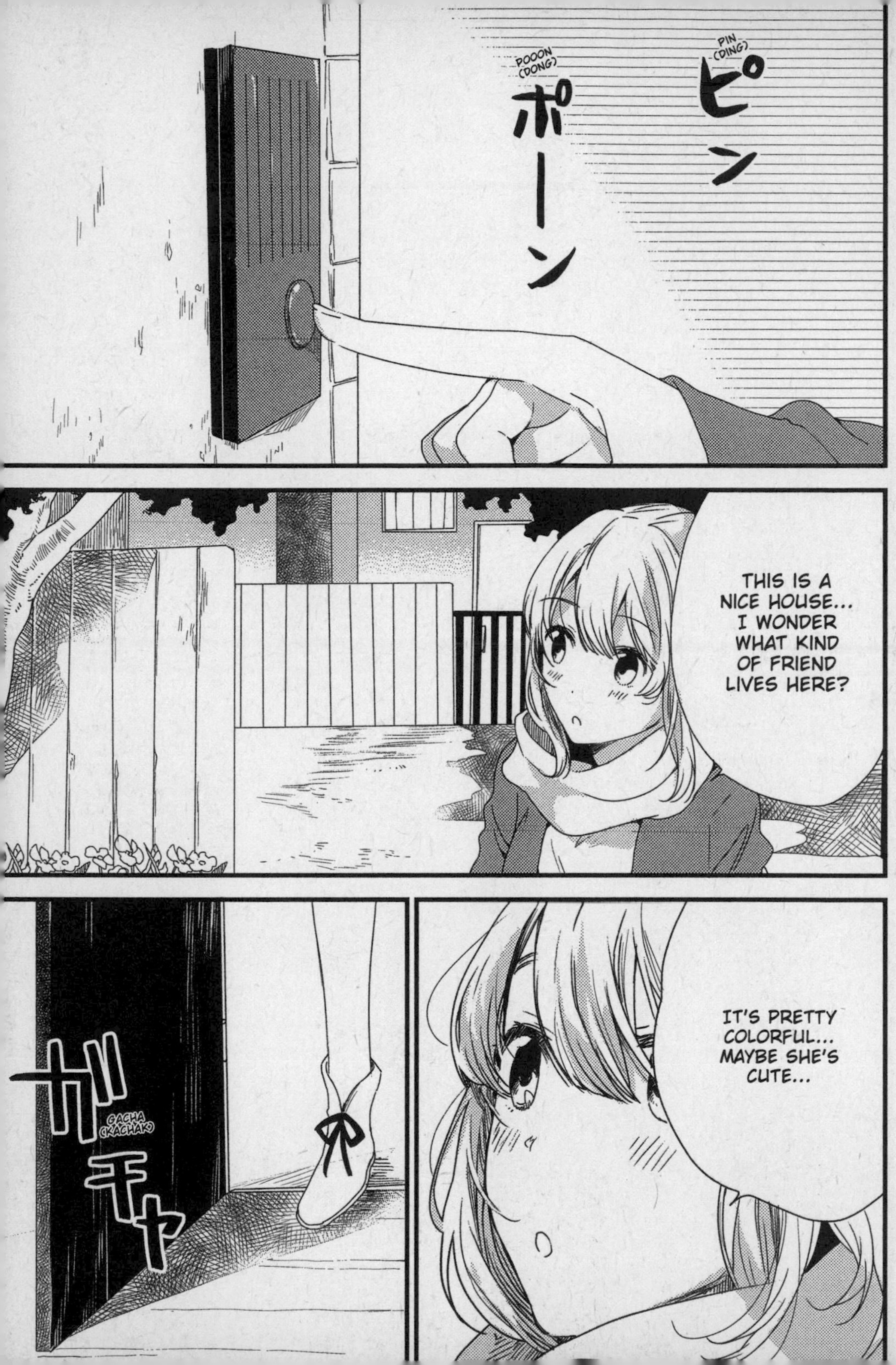
ピン
PIN (DING)
ポーン
POOON (DONG)
THIS IS A NICE HOUSE... I WONDER WHAT KIND OF FRIEND LIVES HERE?
IT'S PRETTY COLORFUL... MAYBE SHE'S CUTE...
ガチャ
GACHA (KACHAK)

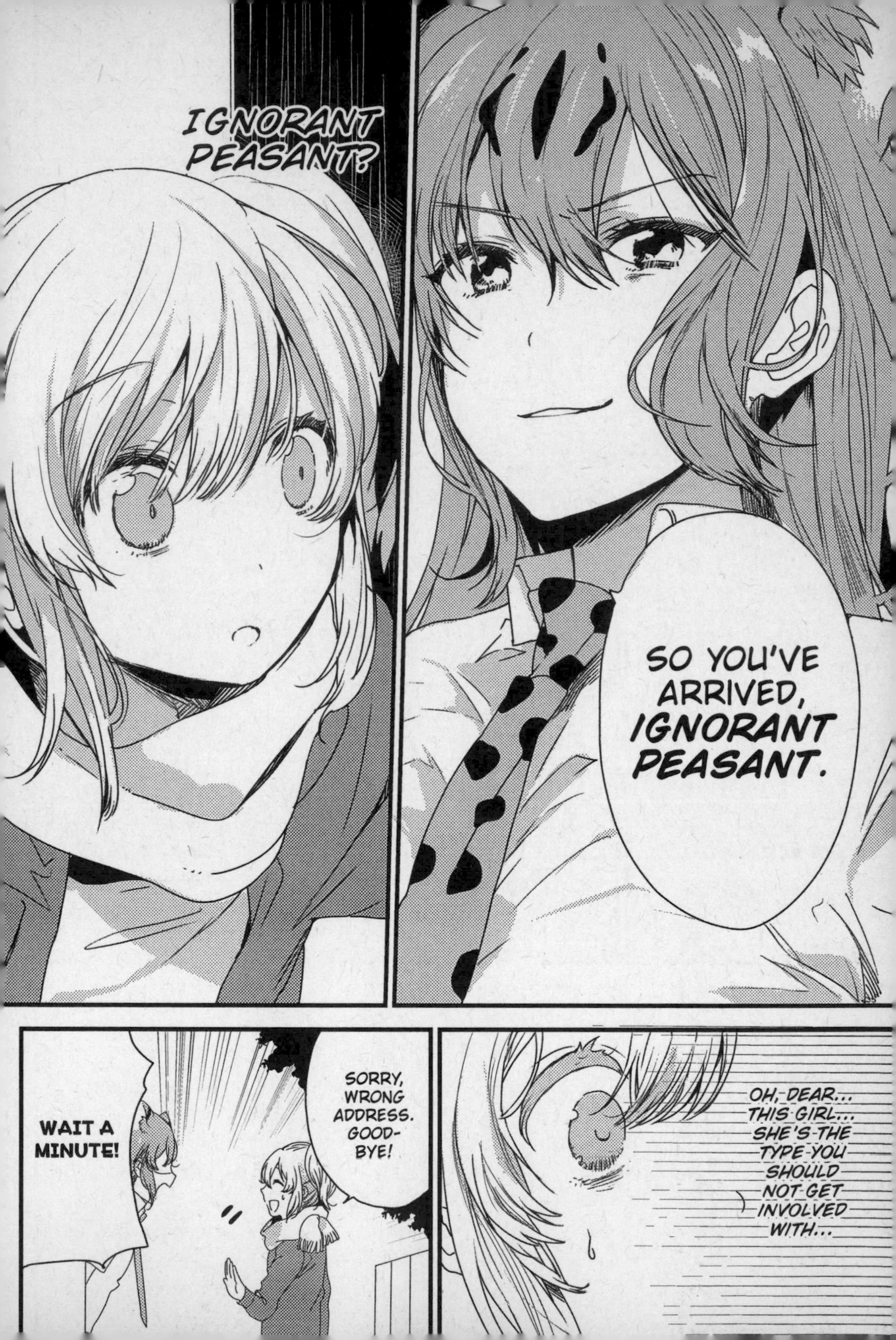
SO YOU'VE ARRIVED, IGNORANT PEASANT.
IGNORANT PEASANT?
OH, DEAR... THIS GIRL... SHE'S THE TYPE YOU SHOULD NOT GET INVOLVED WITH...
SORRY, WRONG ADDRESS. GOOD-BYE!
WAIT A MINUTE!

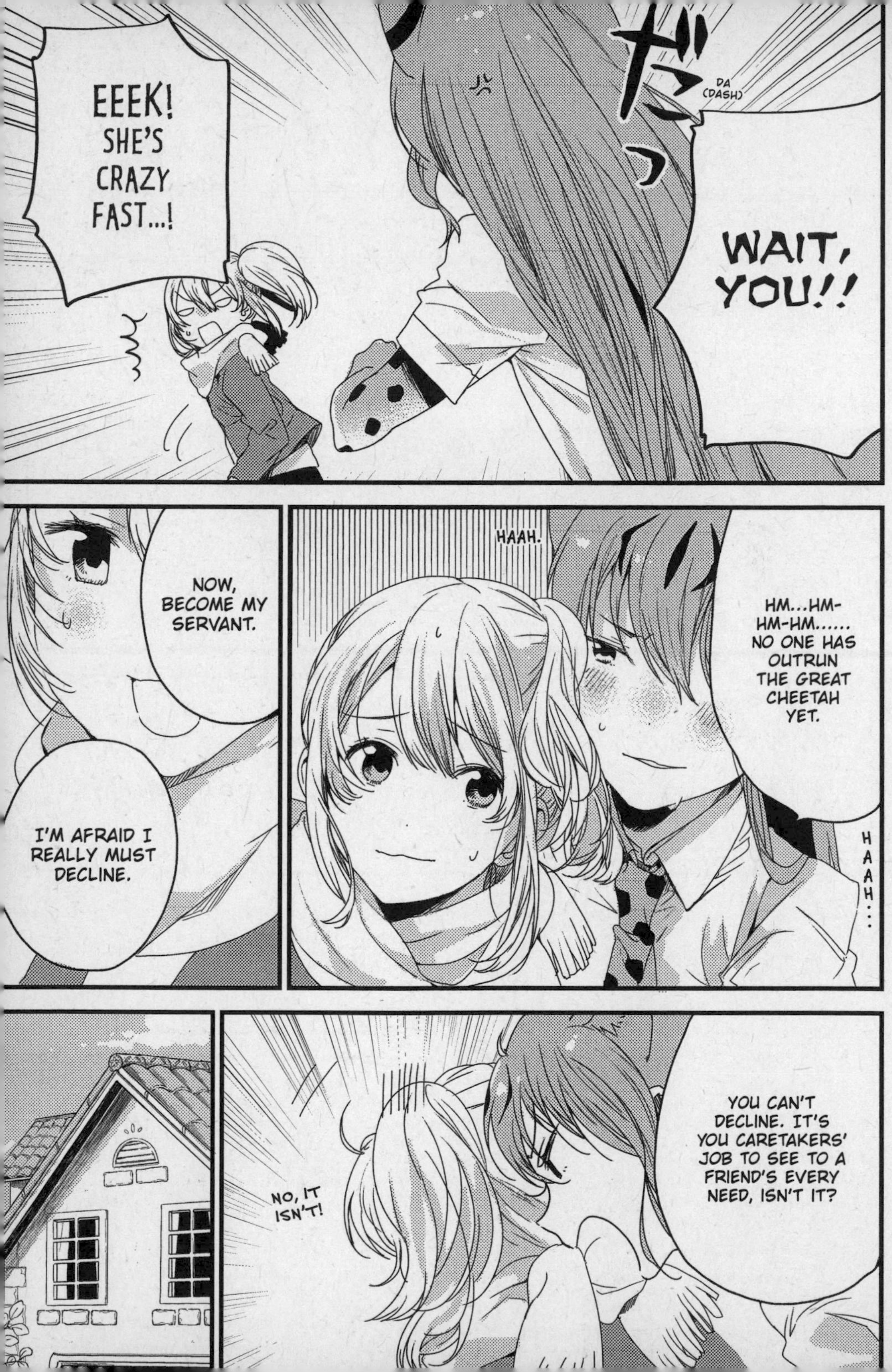

DA (DASH)
WAIT, YOU!!
EEEK! SHE'S CRAZY FAST...!
HAAH.
HM...HM-HM-HM...... NO ONE HAS OUTRUN THE GREAT CHEETAH YET.
HAAH...
NOW, BECOME MY SERVANT.
I'M AFRAID I REALLY MUST DECLINE.
YOU CAN'T DECLINE. IT'S YOU CARETAKERS' JOB TO SEE TO A FRIEND'S EVERY NEED, ISN'T IT?
NO, IT ISN'T!

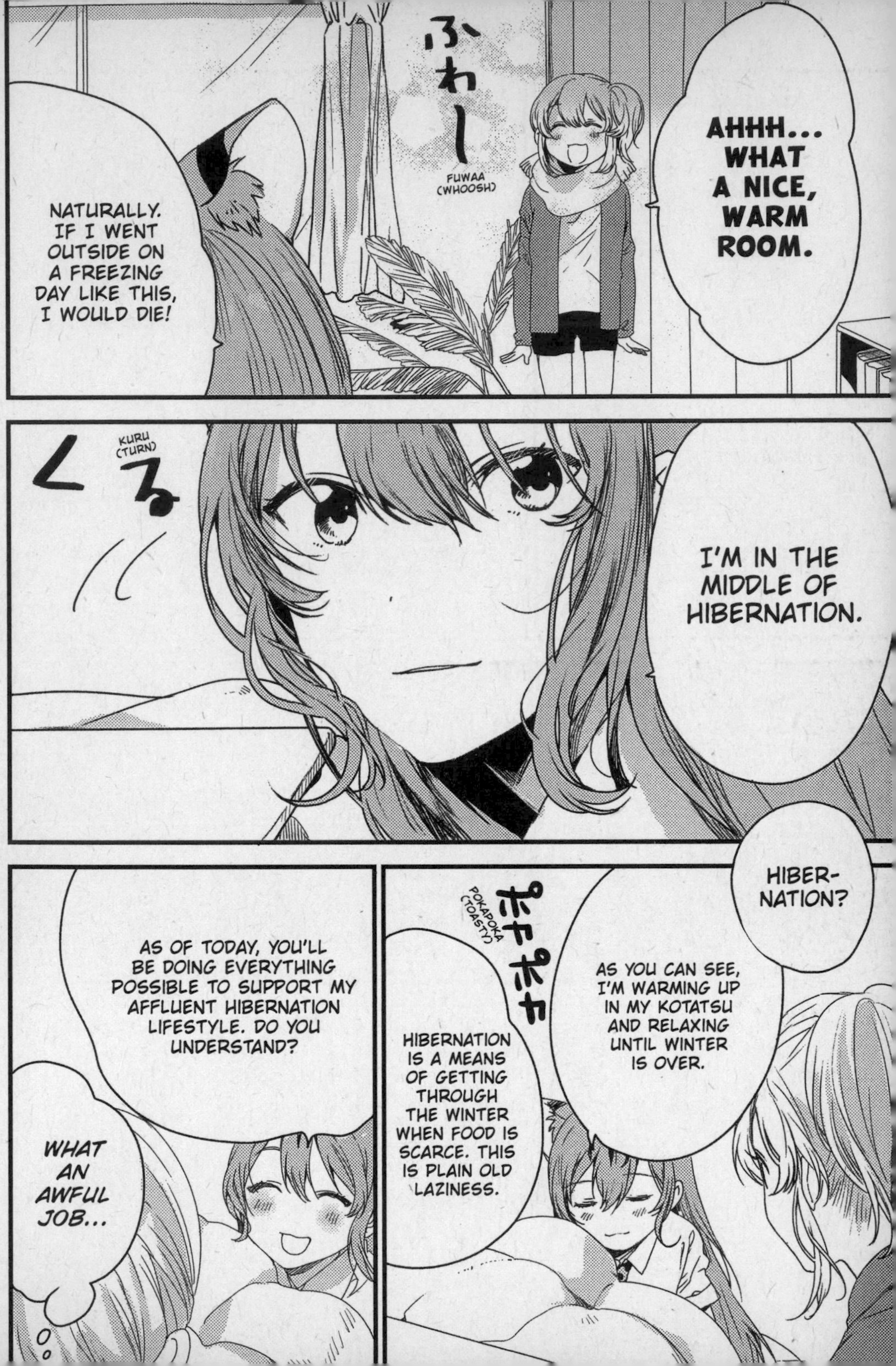
AHHH... WHAT A NICE, WARM ROOM.
ふわー
FUWAA (WHOOSH)
NATURALLY. IF I WENT OUTSIDE ON A FREEZING DAY LIKE THIS, I WOULD DIE!
I'M IN THE MIDDLE OF HIBERNATION.
くる
KURU (TURN)
HIBER-NATION?
AS YOU CAN SEE, I'M WARMING UP IN MY KOTATSU AND RELAXING UNTIL WINTER IS OVER.
HIBERNATION IS A MEANS OF GETTING THROUGH THE WINTER WHEN FOOD IS SCARCE. THIS IS PLAIN OLD LAZINESS.
ポカポカ
POKAPOKA (TOASTY)
AS OF TODAY, YOU'LL BE DOING EVERYTHING POSSIBLE TO SUPPORT MY AFFLUENT HIBERNATION LIFESTYLE. DO YOU UNDERSTAND?
WHAT AN AWFUL JOB...

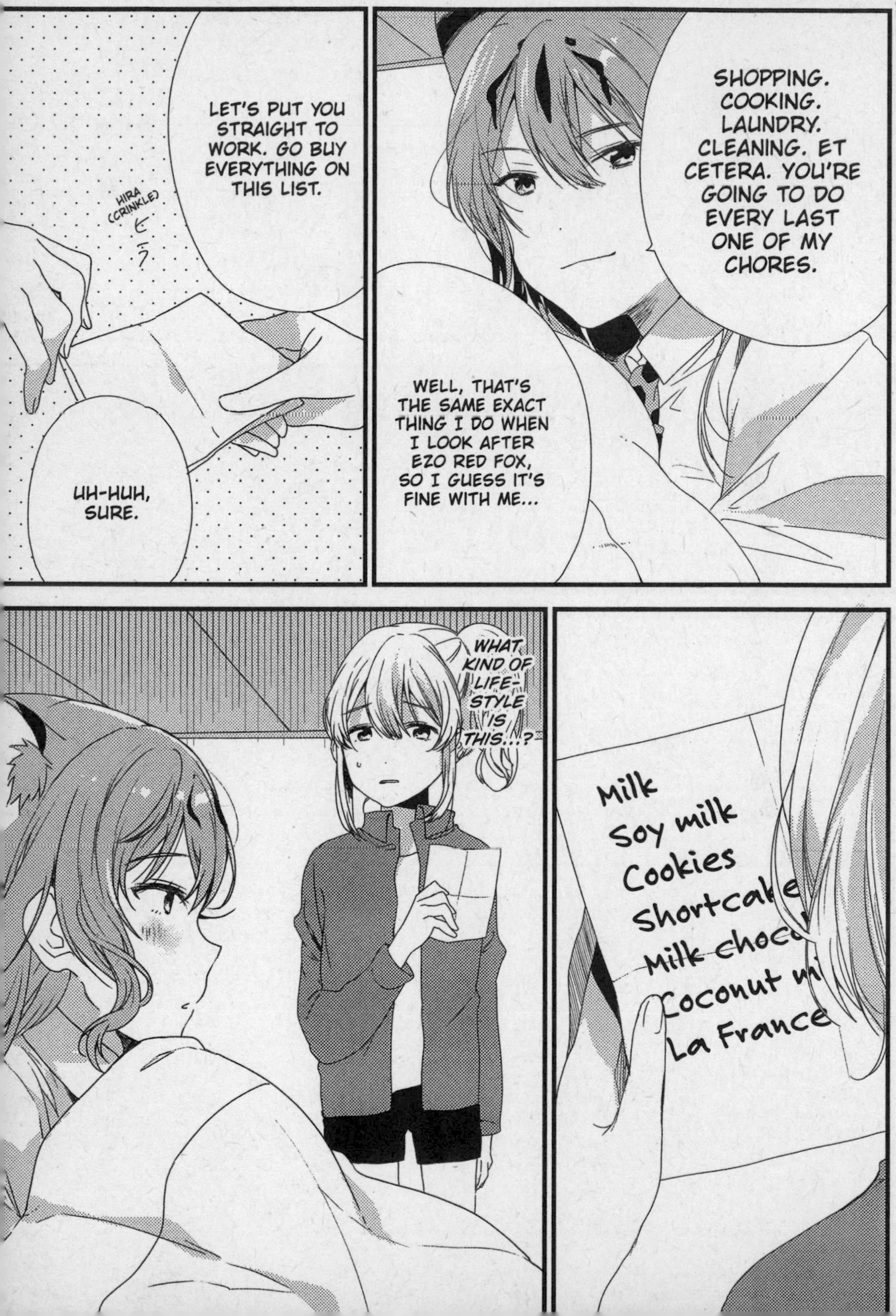

SHOPPING. COOKING. LAUNDRY. CLEANING. ET CETERA. YOU'RE GOING TO DO EVERY LAST ONE OF MY CHORES.
WELL, THAT'S THE SAME EXACT THING I DO WHEN I LOOK AFTER EZO RED FOX, SO I GUESS IT'S FINE WITH ME...
LET'S PUT YOU STRAIGHT TO WORK. GO BUY EVERYTHING ON THIS LIST.
HIRA (CRINKLE)
UH-HUH, SURE.
Milk
Soy milk
Cookies
Shortcak
Milk choco
Coconut mi
La France
WHAT KIND OF LIFE-STYLE IS THIS...?

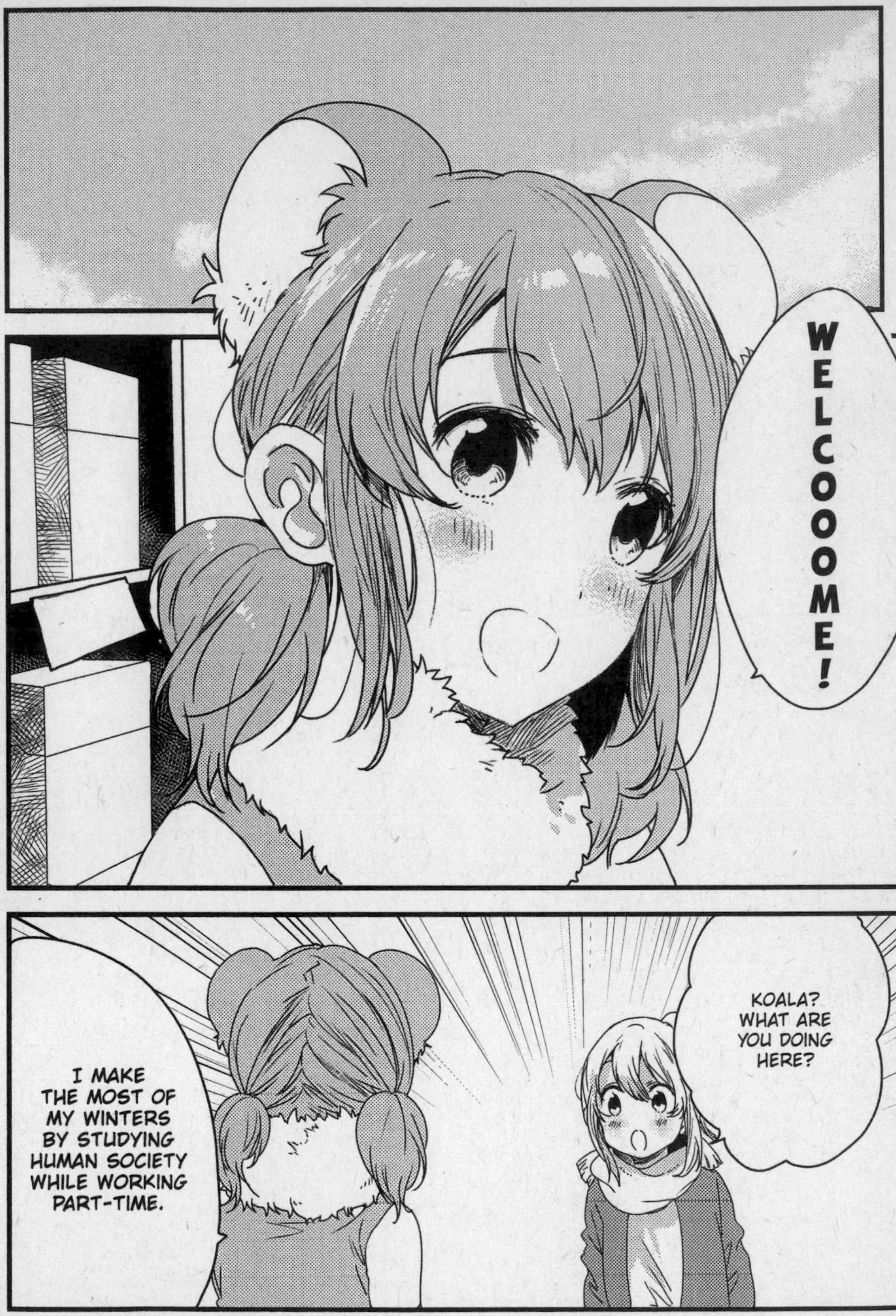
WELCOOOME!
KOALA? WHAT ARE YOU DOING HERE?
I MAKE THE MOST OF MY WINTERS BY STUDYING HUMAN SOCIETY WHILE WORKING PART-TIME.

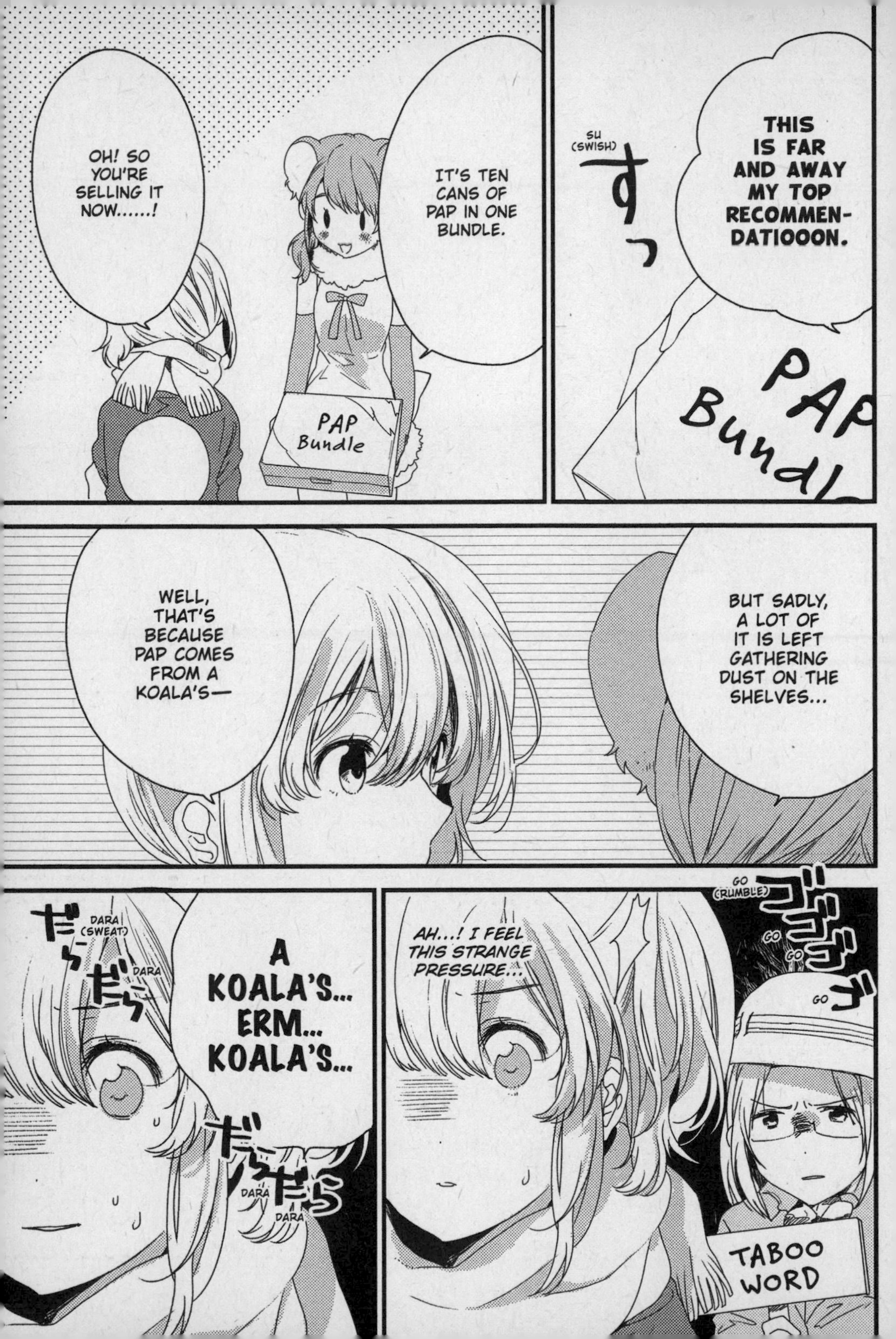
SU (SWISH)
すっ
THIS IS FAR AND AWAY MY TOP RECOMMEN-DATIOOON.
PAP Bundl
IT'S TEN CANS OF PAP IN ONE BUNDLE.
OH! SO YOU'RE SELLING IT NOW......!
PAP Bundle
BUT SADLY, A LOT OF IT IS LEFT GATHERING DUST ON THE SHELVES...
WELL, THAT'S BECAUSE PAP COMES FROM A KOALA'S—
GO (RUMBLE)
GO
GO
GO
AH...! I FEEL THIS STRANGE PRESSURE...
TABOO WORD
DARA (SWEAT)
DARA
A KOALA'S... ERM... KOALA'S...
DARA
DARA

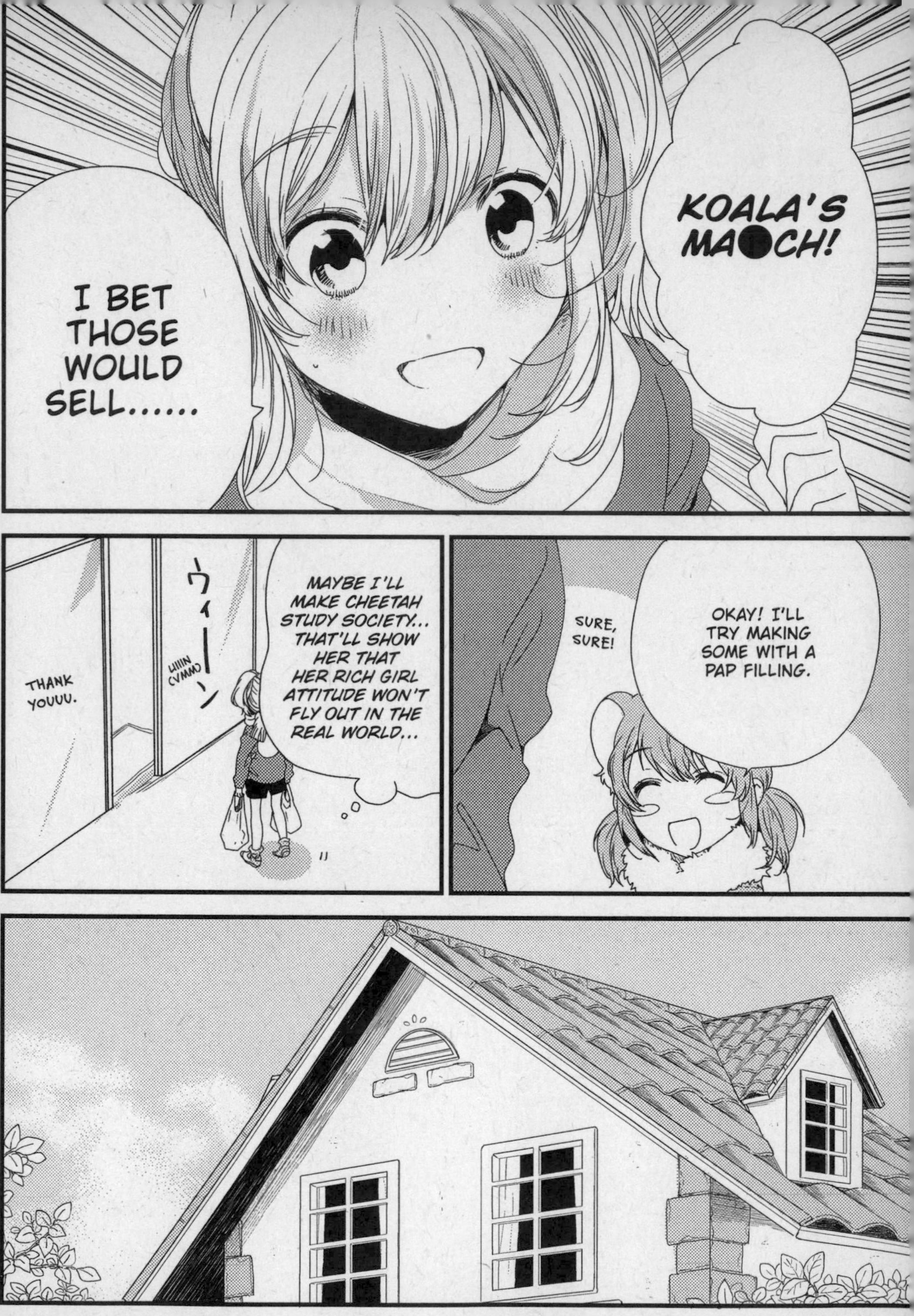
KOALA'S MA●CH!
I BET THOSE WOULD SELL......
OKAY! I'LL TRY MAKING SOME WITH A PAP FILLING.
SURE, SURE!
MAYBE I'LL MAKE CHEETAH STUDY SOCIETY... THAT'LL SHOW HER THAT HER RICH GIRL ATTITUDE WON'T FLY OUT IN THE REAL WORLD...
ウィーン
UIIIN (VMM)
THANK YOUUU.

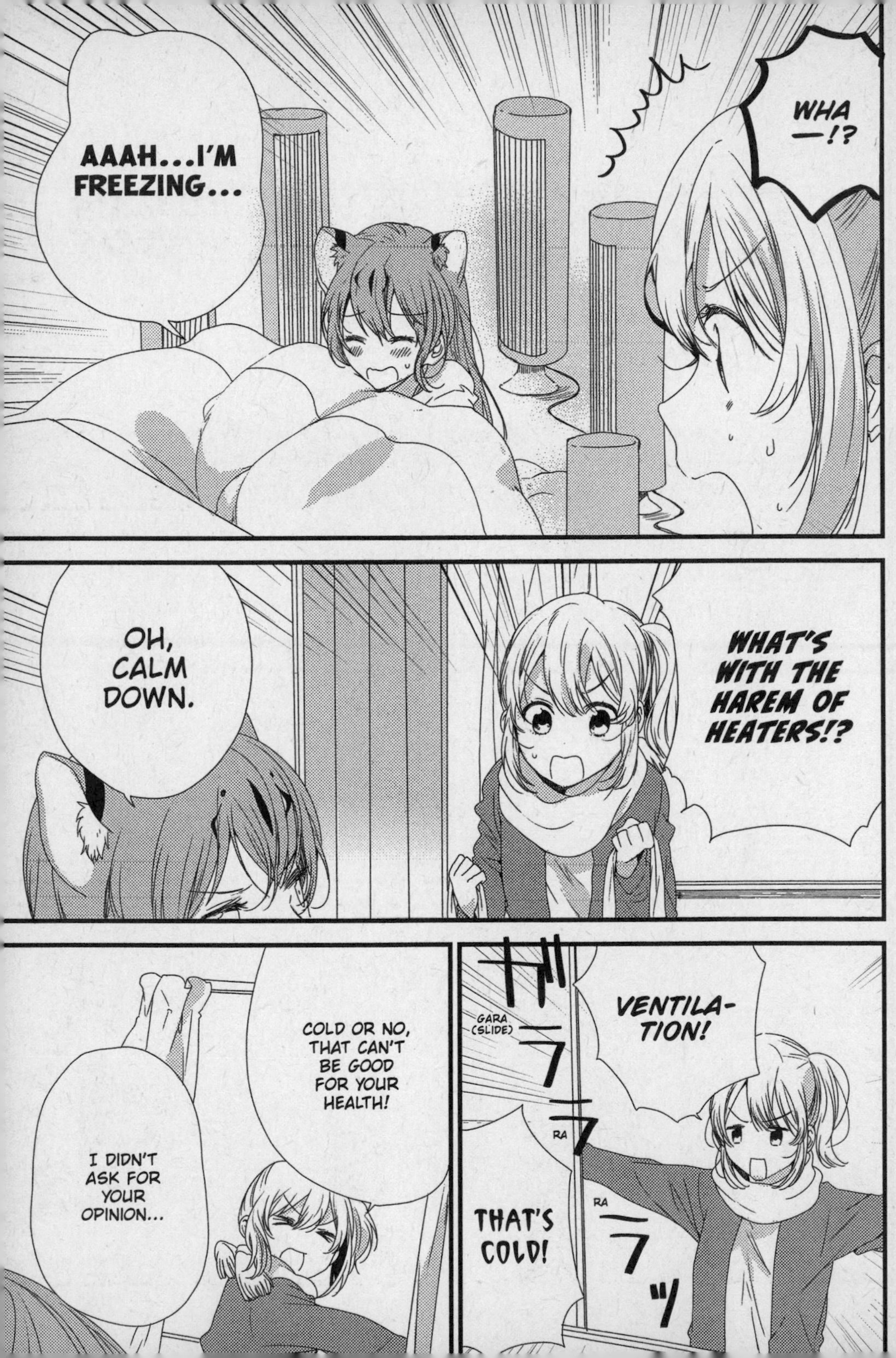
WHA—!?
AAAH...I'M FREEZING...
WHAT'S WITH THE HAREM OF HEATERS!?
OH, CALM DOWN.
VENTILATION!
GARA (SLIDE)
RA
RA
THAT'S COLD!
COLD OR NO, THAT CAN'T BE GOOD FOR YOUR HEALTH!
I DIDN'T ASK FOR YOUR OPINION...

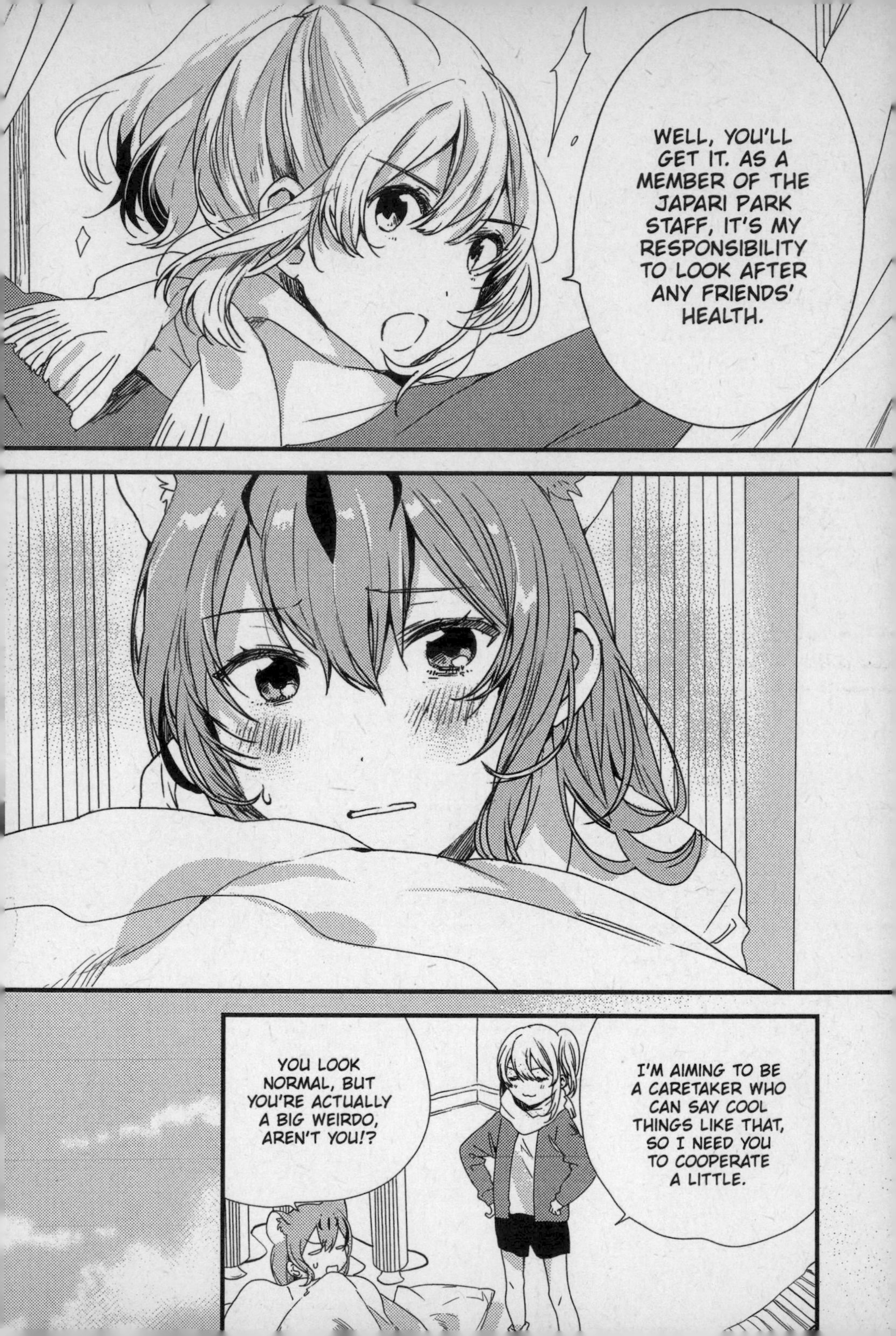
WELL, YOU'LL GET IT. AS A MEMBER OF THE JAPARI PARK STAFF, IT'S MY RESPONSIBILITY TO LOOK AFTER ANY FRIENDS' HEALTH.
I'M AIMING TO BE A CARETAKER WHO CAN SAY COOL THINGS LIKE THAT, SO I NEED YOU TO COOPERATE A LITTLE.
YOU LOOK NORMAL, BUT YOU'RE ACTUALLY A BIG WEIRDO, AREN'T YOU!?

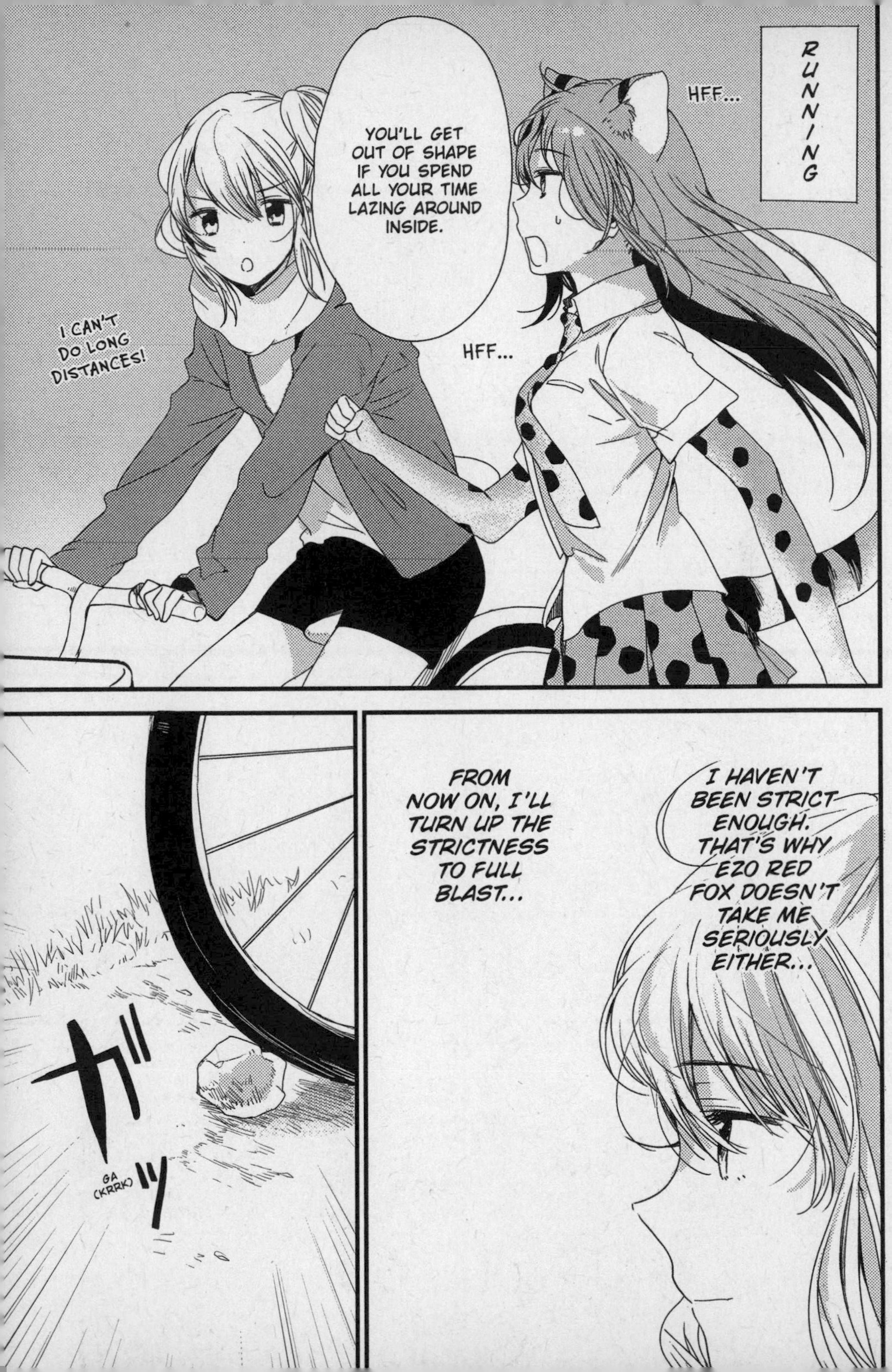
RUNNING
HFF...
YOU'LL GET OUT OF SHAPE IF YOU SPEND ALL YOUR TIME LAZING AROUND INSIDE.
HFF...
I CAN'T DO LONG DISTANCES!
I HAVEN'T BEEN STRICT ENOUGH. THAT'S WHY EZO RED FOX DOESN'T TAKE ME SERIOUSLY EITHER...
FROM NOW ON, I'LL TURN UP THE STRICTNESS TO FULL BLAST...
ガッ
GA (KRRK)

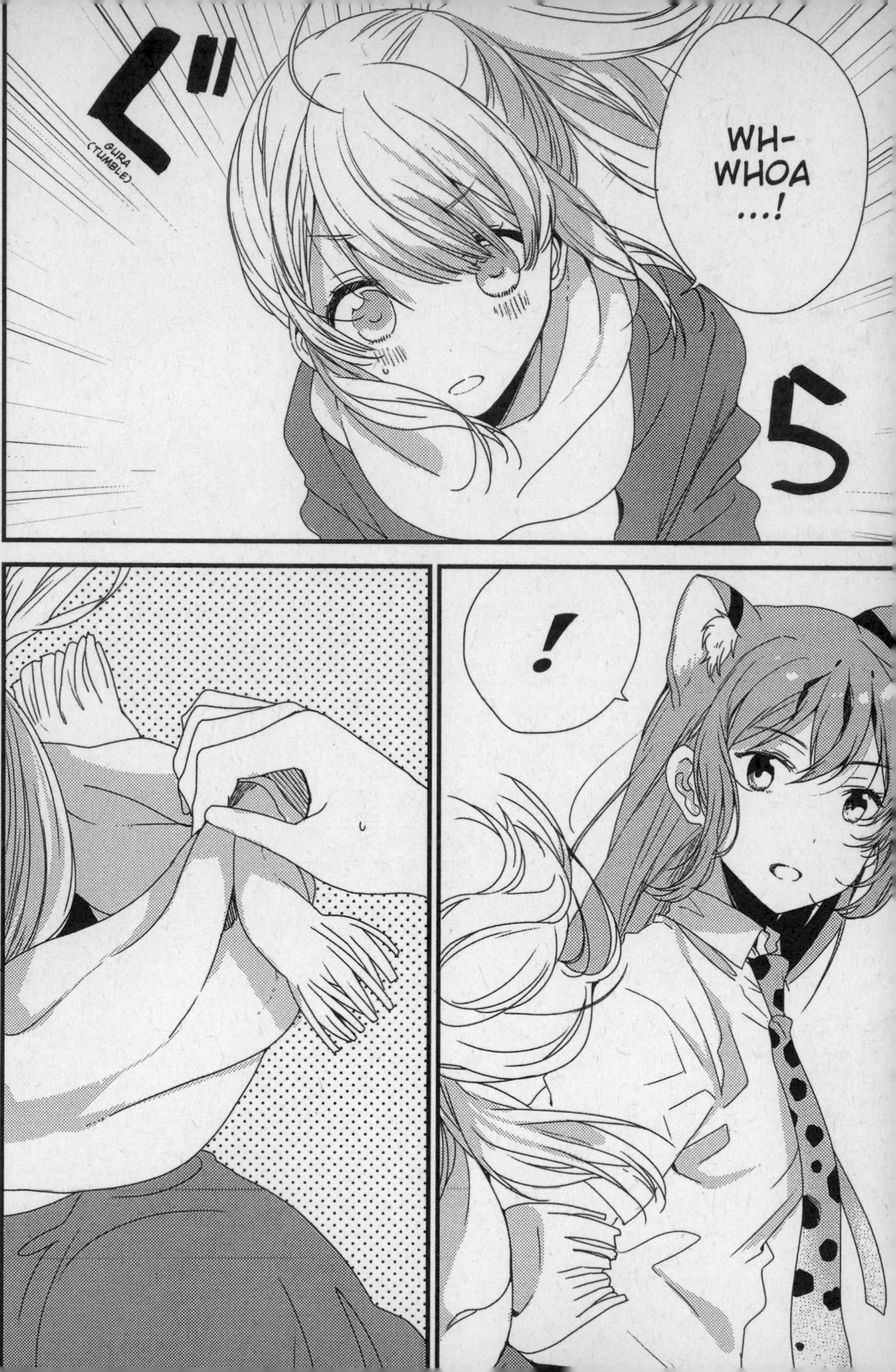
WH-WHOA...!
GURA (TUMBLE)
!

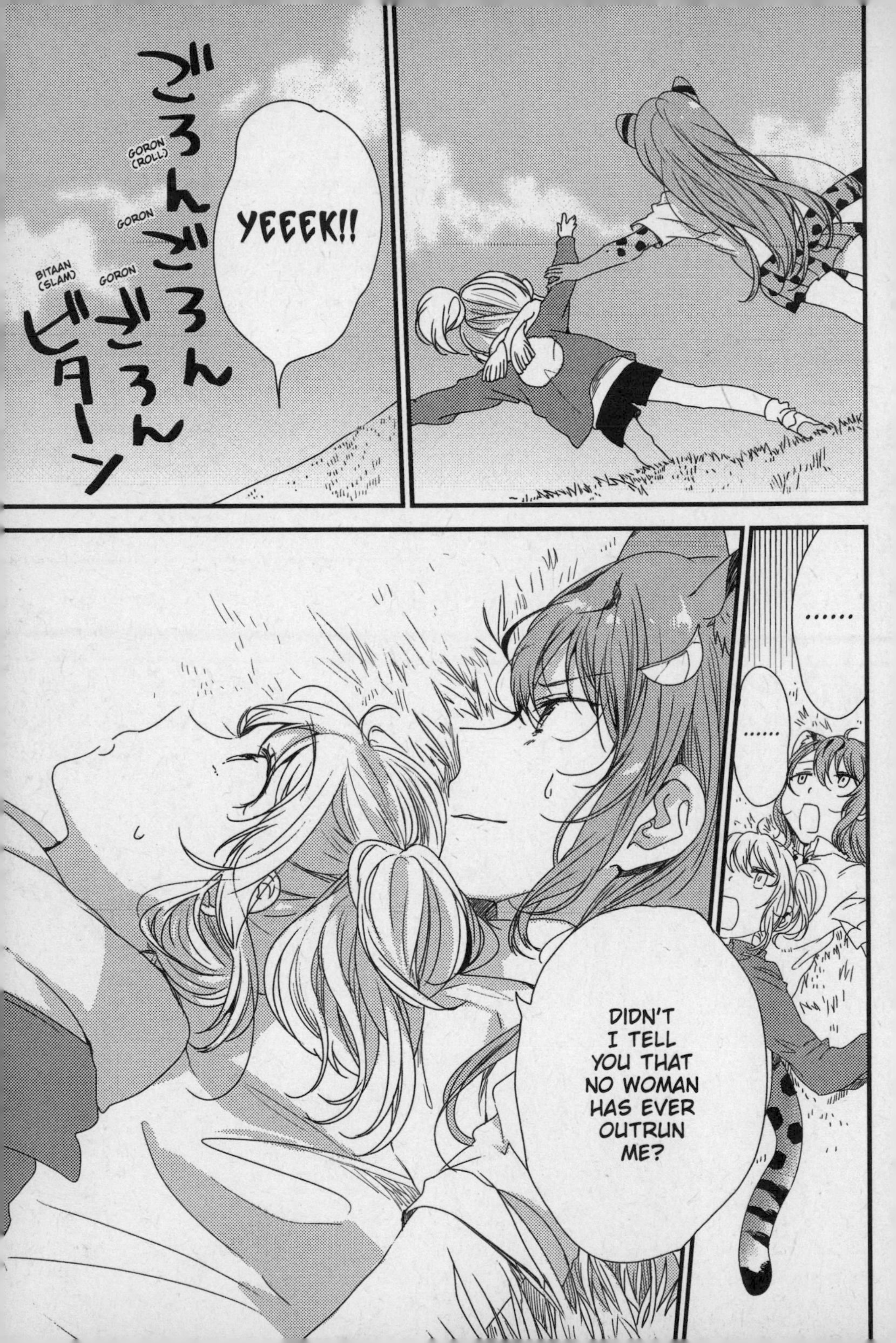

YEEEK!!
ごろんごろん
GORON (ROLL)
GORON
ごろんごろん
GORON
ビターン
BITAAN (SLAM)
......
......
DIDN'T I TELL YOU THAT NO WOMAN HAS EVER OUTRUN ME?

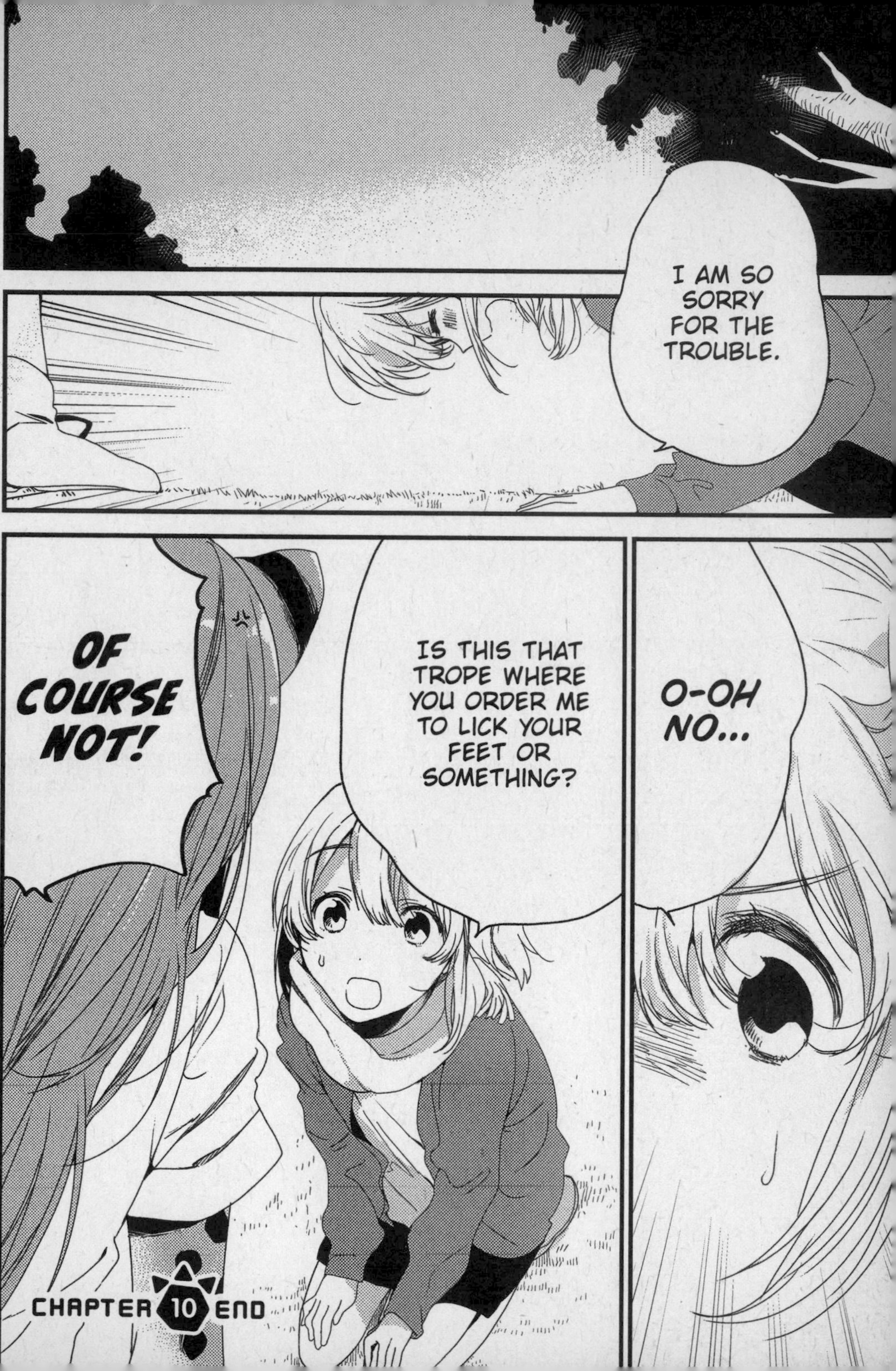
I AM SO SORRY FOR THE TROUBLE.
O-OH NO...
IS THIS THAT TROPE WHERE YOU ORDER ME TO LICK YOUR FEET OR SOMETHING?
OF COURSE NOT!
CHAPTER 10 END

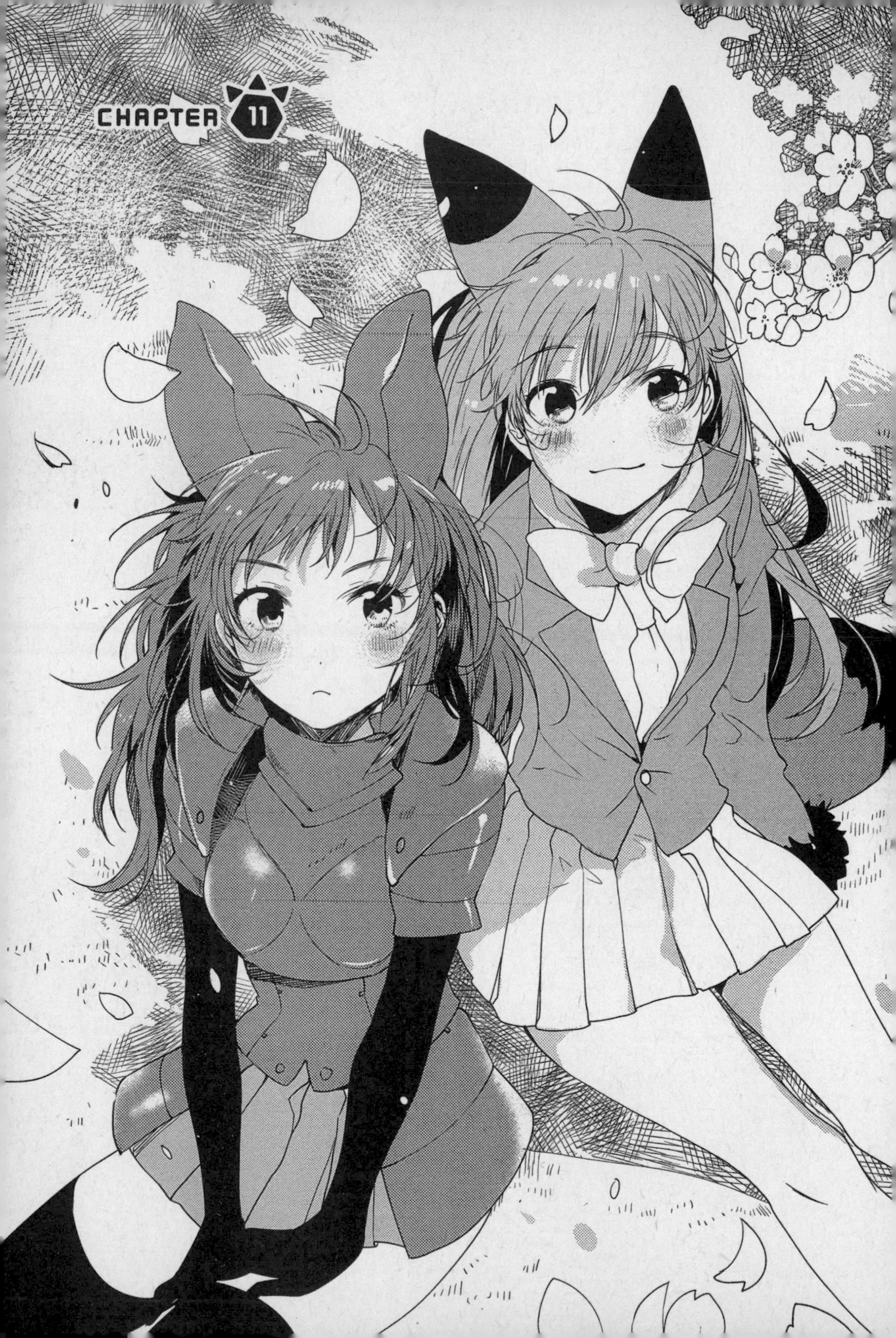
CHAPTER 11

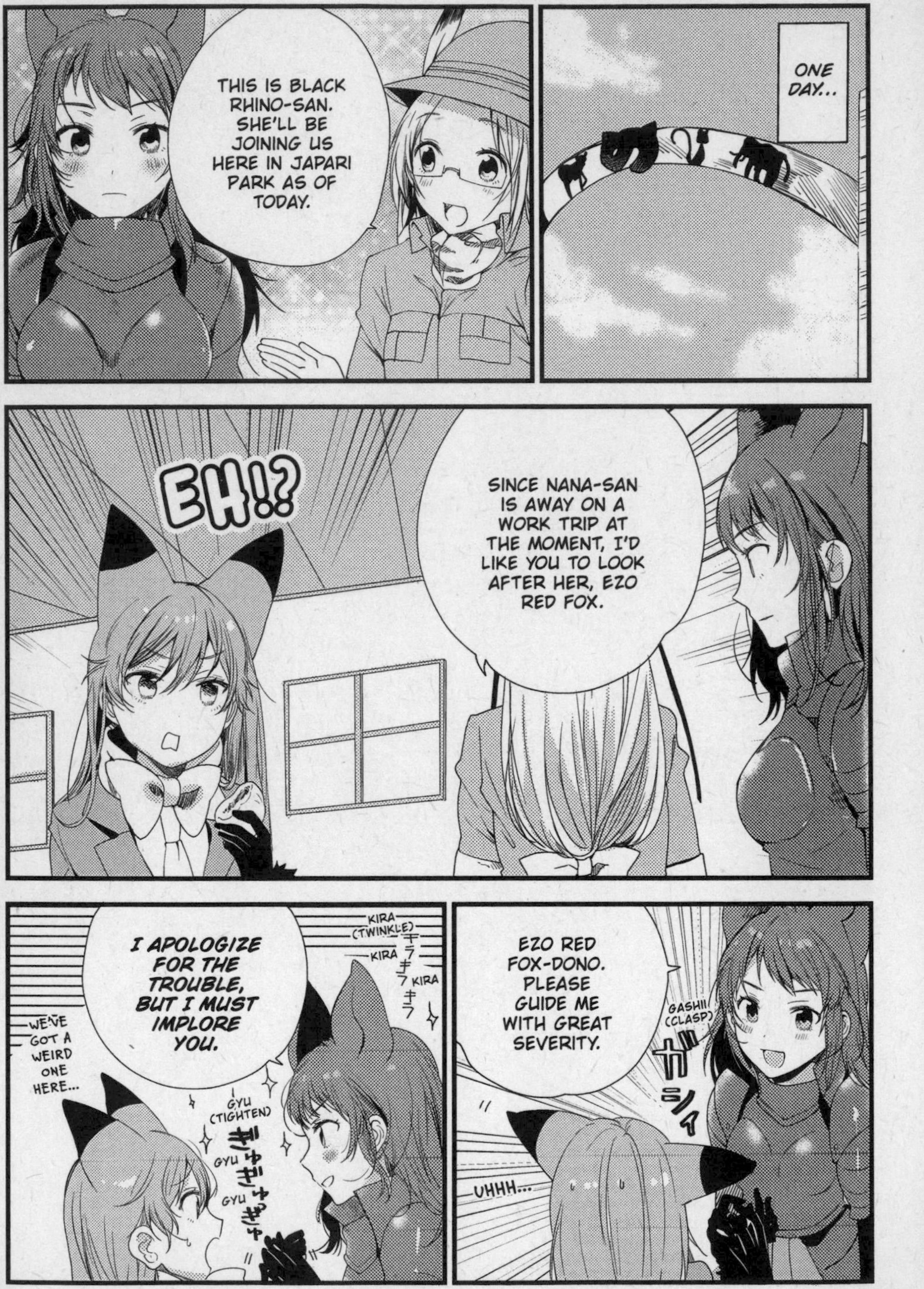

ONE DAY...
THIS IS BLACK RHINO-SAN. SHE'LL BE JOINING US HERE IN JAPARI PARK AS OF TODAY.
SINCE NANA-SAN IS AWAY ON A WORK TRIP AT THE MOMENT, I'D LIKE YOU TO LOOK AFTER HER, EZO RED FOX.
EH!?
EZO RED FOX-DONO. PLEASE GUIDE ME WITH GREAT SEVERITY.
GASHI! (CLASP)
UHHH...
I APOLOGIZE FOR THE TROUBLE, BUT I MUST IMPLORE YOU.
KIRA (TWINKLE)
KIRA
KIRA
WE'VE GOT A WEIRD ONE HERE...
GYU (TIGHTEN)
GYU
GYU

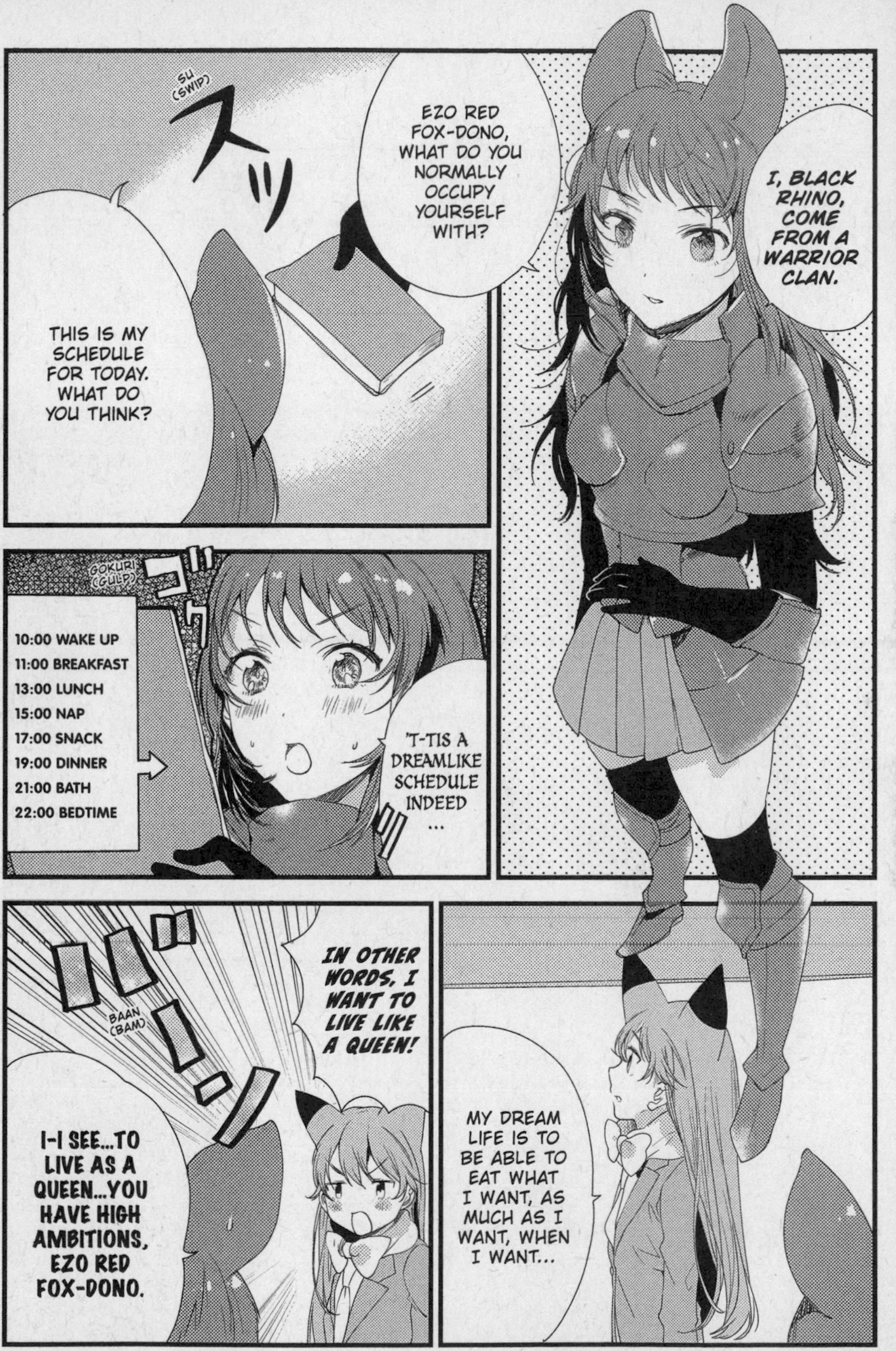
I, BLACK RHINO, COME FROM A WARRIOR CLAN.
EZO RED FOX-DONO, WHAT DO YOU NORMALLY OCCUPY YOURSELF WITH?
SU (SWIP)
THIS IS MY SCHEDULE FOR TODAY. WHAT DO YOU THINK?
GOKURI (GULP)
'T-TIS A DREAMLIKE SCHEDULE INDEED ...
10:00 WAKE UP
11:00 BREAKFAST
13:00 LUNCH
15:00 NAP
17:00 SNACK
19:00 DINNER
21:00 BATH
22:00 BEDTIME
MY DREAM LIFE IS TO BE ABLE TO EAT WHAT I WANT, AS MUCH AS I WANT, WHEN I WANT...
IN OTHER WORDS, I WANT TO LIVE LIKE A QUEEN!
BAAN (BAM)
I-I SEE...TO LIVE AS A QUEEN...YOU HAVE HIGH AMBITIONS, EZO RED FOX-DONO.

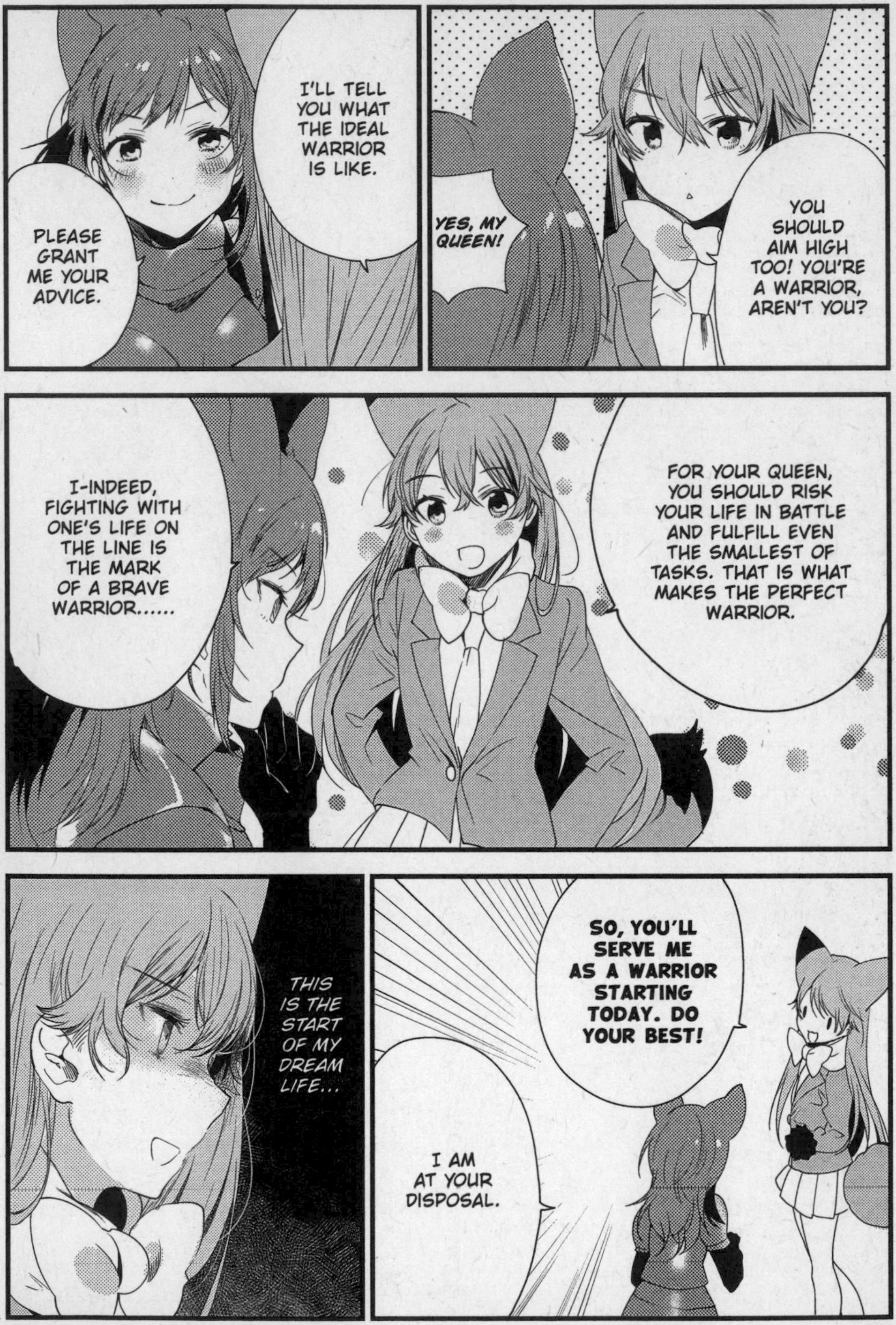
YOU SHOULD AIM HIGH TOO! YOU'RE A WARRIOR, AREN'T YOU?
YES, MY QUEEN!
I'LL TELL YOU WHAT THE IDEAL WARRIOR IS LIKE.
PLEASE GRANT ME YOUR ADVICE.
FOR YOUR QUEEN, YOU SHOULD RISK YOUR LIFE IN BATTLE AND FULFILL EVEN THE SMALLEST OF TASKS. THAT IS WHAT MAKES THE PERFECT WARRIOR.
I-INDEED, FIGHTING WITH ONE'S LIFE ON THE LINE IS THE MARK OF A BRAVE WARRIOR......
SO, YOU'LL SERVE ME AS A WARRIOR STARTING TODAY. DO YOUR BEST!
I AM AT YOUR DISPOSAL.
THIS IS THE START OF MY DREAM LIFE...

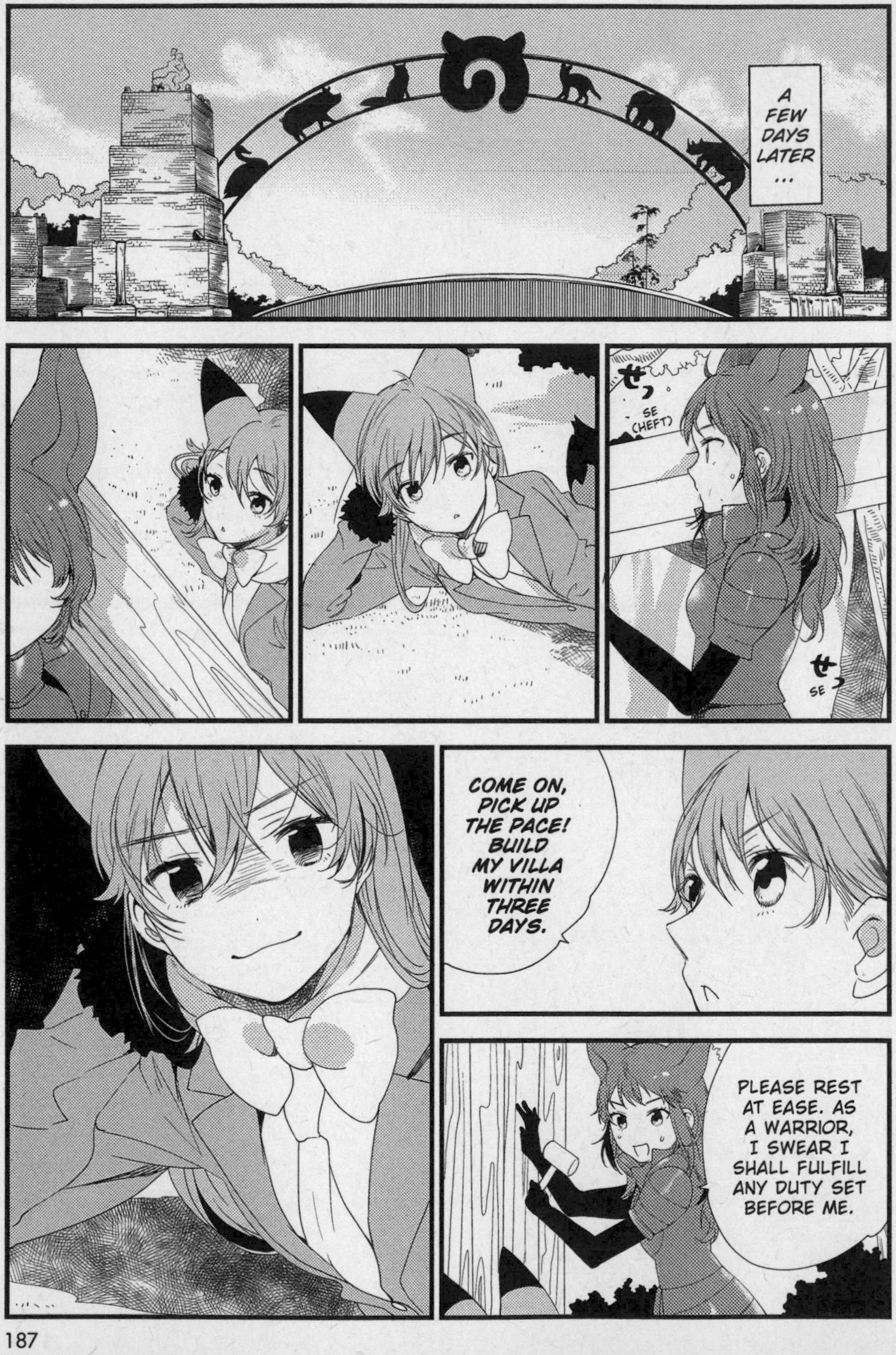
A FEW DAYS LATER ...
せっ
SE (HEFT)
せっ
SE
COME ON, PICK UP THE PACE! BUILD MY VILLA WITHIN THREE DAYS.
PLEASE REST AT EASE. AS A WARRIOR, I SWEAR I SHALL FULFILL ANY DUTY SET BEFORE ME.

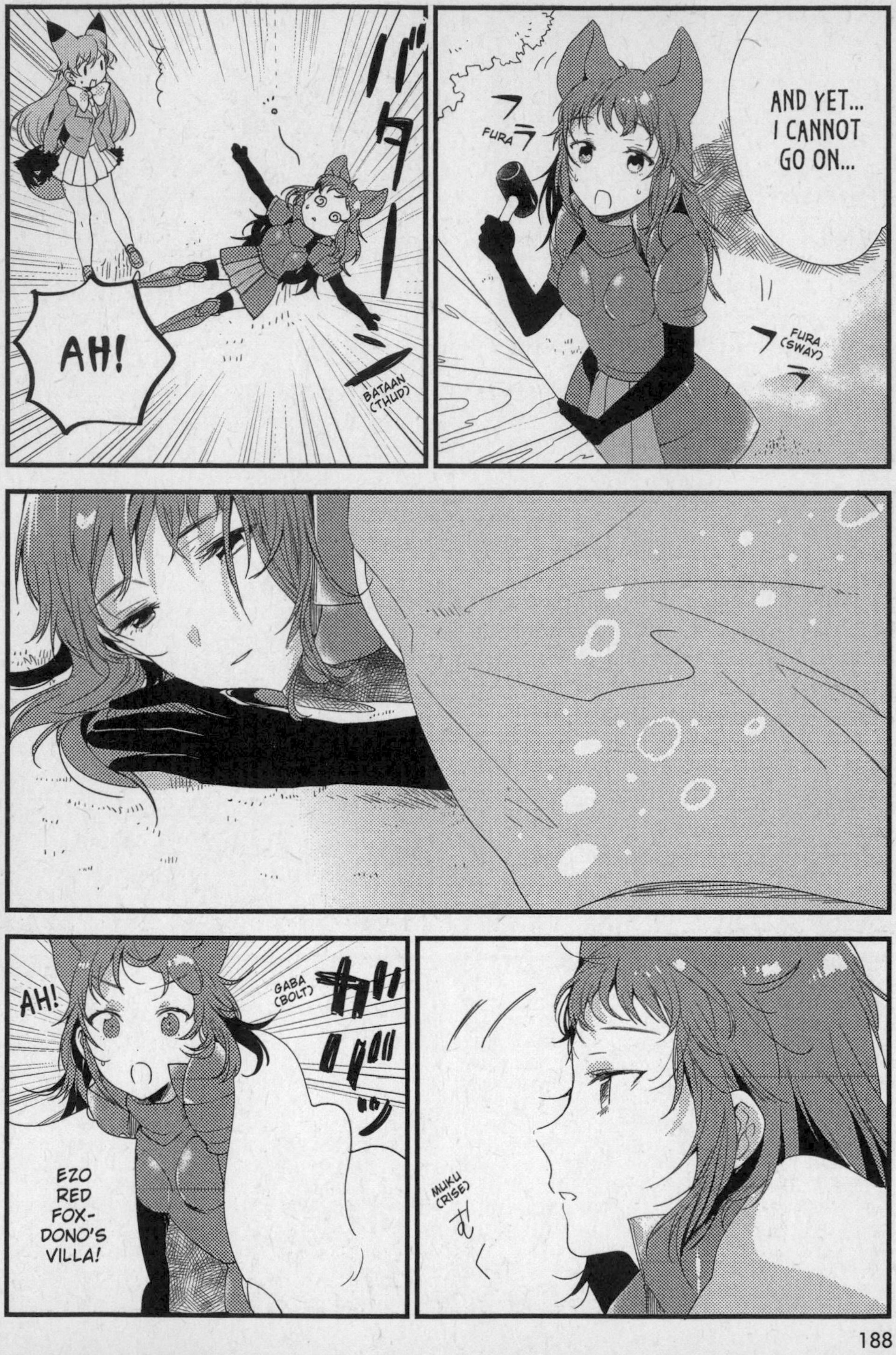
AND YET... I CANNOT GO ON...
FURA (SWAY)
FURA
AH!
BATAAN (THUD)
MUKU (RISE)
GABA (BOLT)
AH!
EZO RED FOX-DONO'S VILLA!

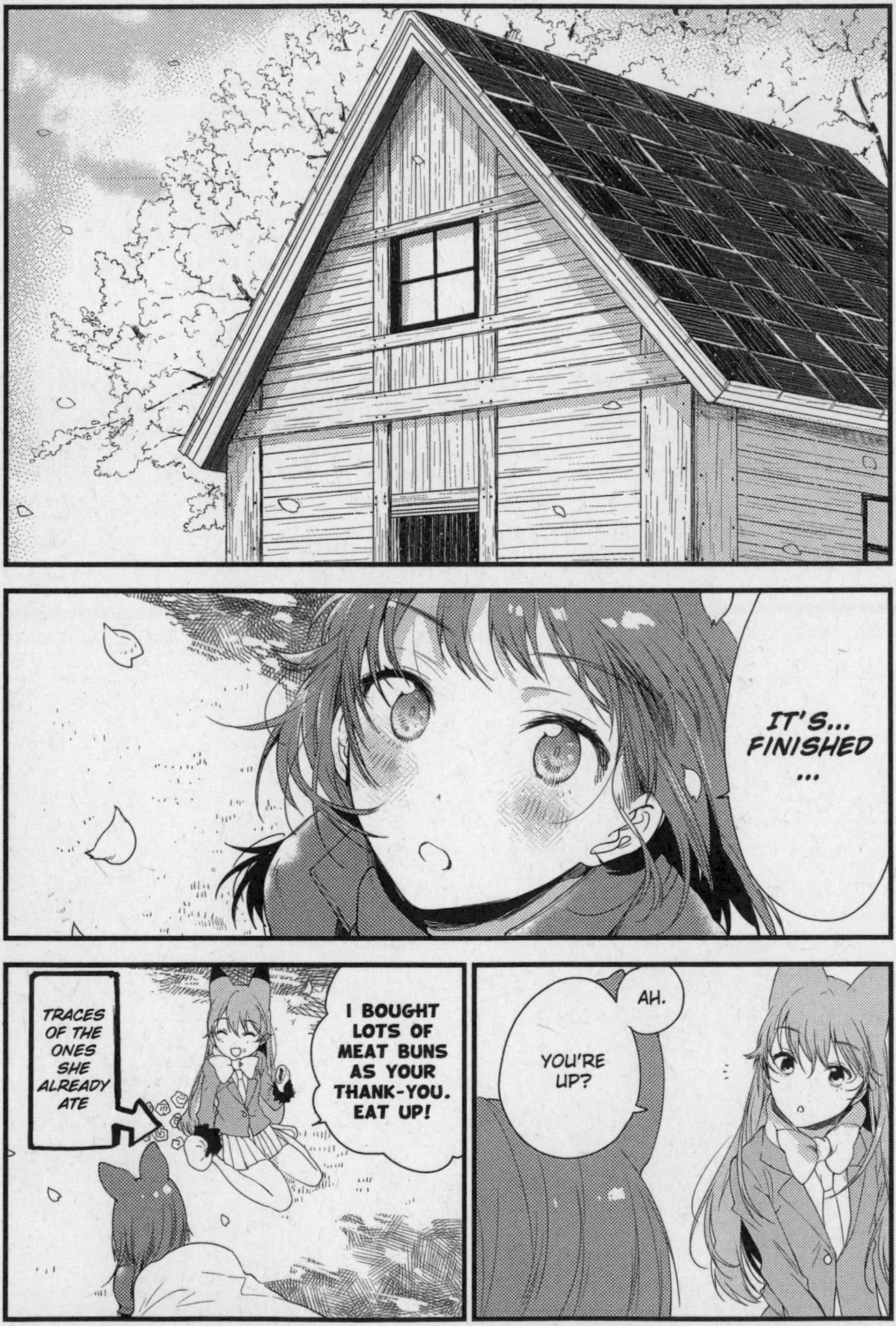
IT'S... FINISHED ...
AH.
YOU'RE UP?
I BOUGHT LOTS OF MEAT BUNS AS YOUR THANK-YOU. EAT UP!
TRACES OF THE ONES SHE ALREADY ATE

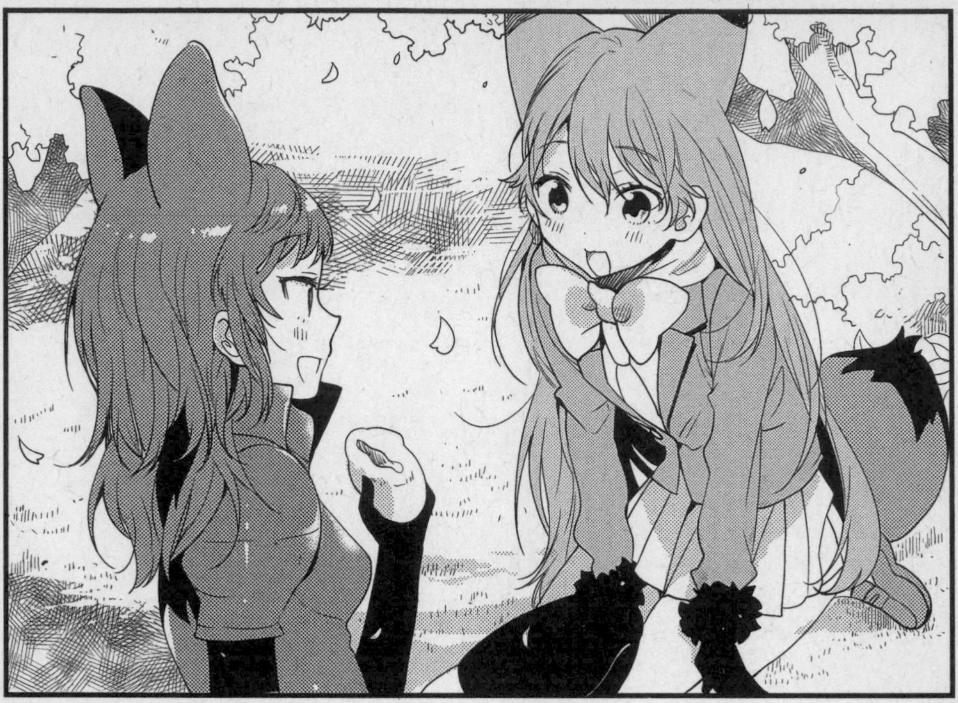

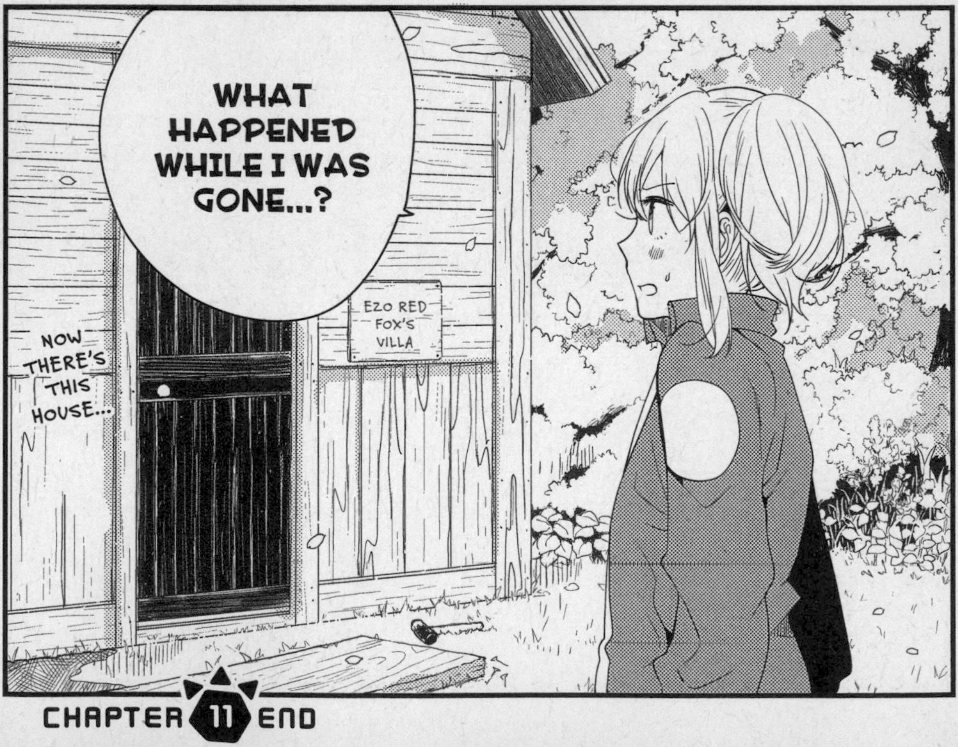
WHAT HAPPENED WHILE I WAS GONE...?
EZO RED FOX'S VILLA
NOW THERE'S THIS HOUSE...

CHAPTER 11 END

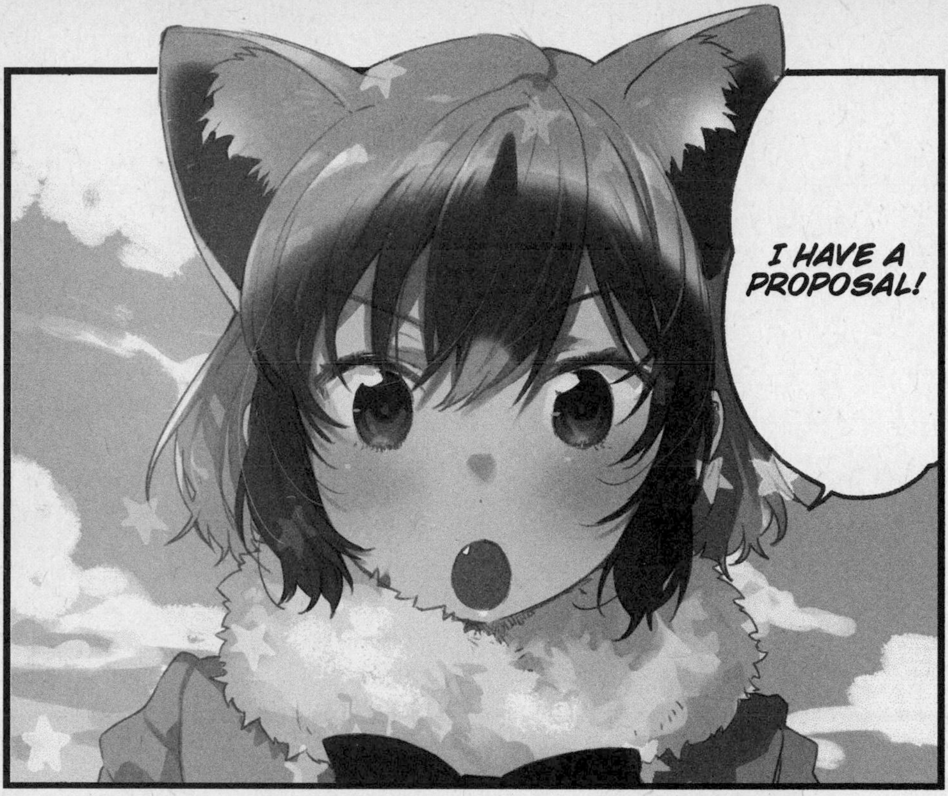
I HAVE A PROPOSAL!

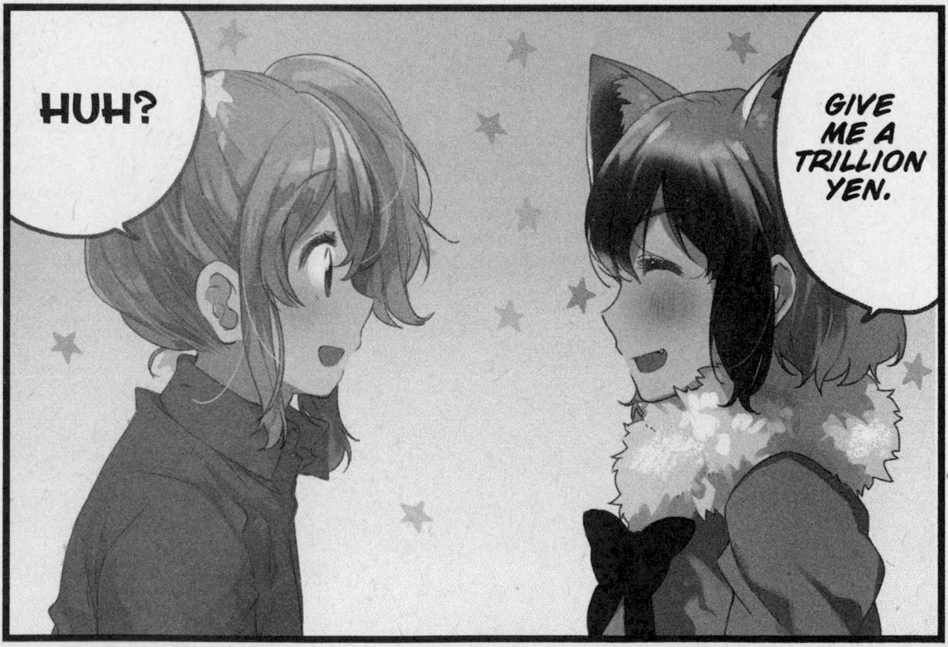
GIVE ME A TRILLION YEN.
HUH?

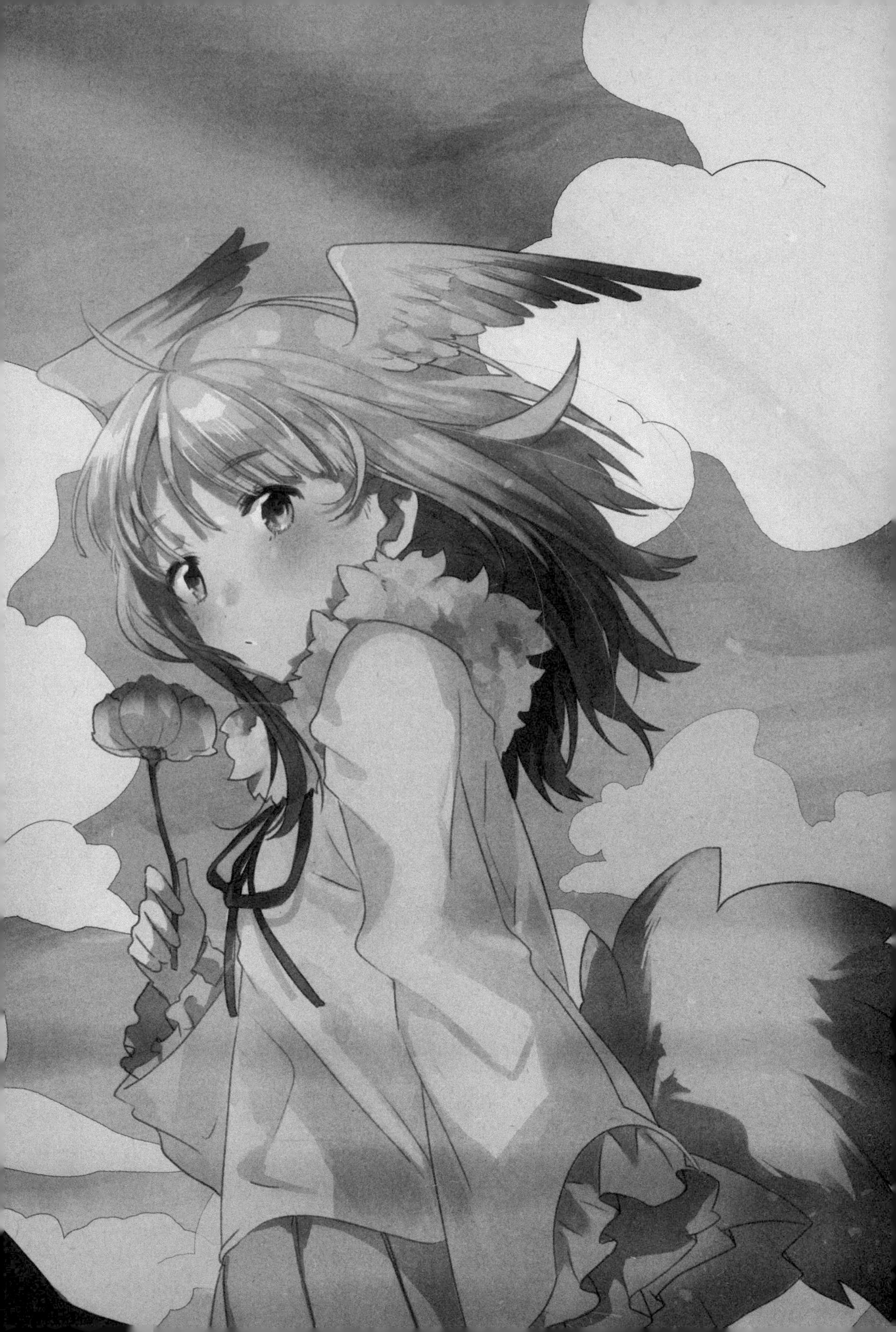

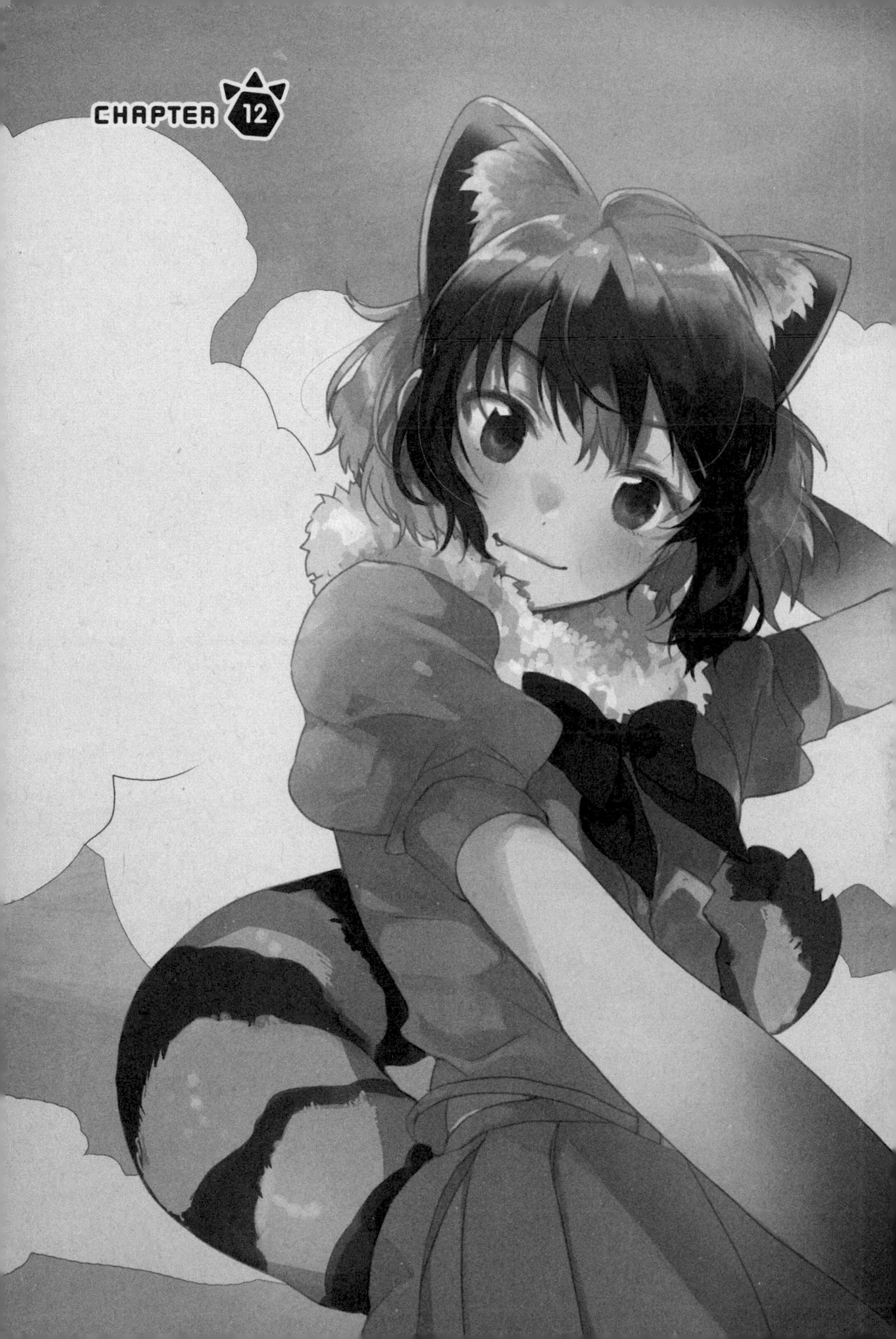
CHAPTER 12

KEMONO FRIENDS

WELCOME TO JAPARI PARK!

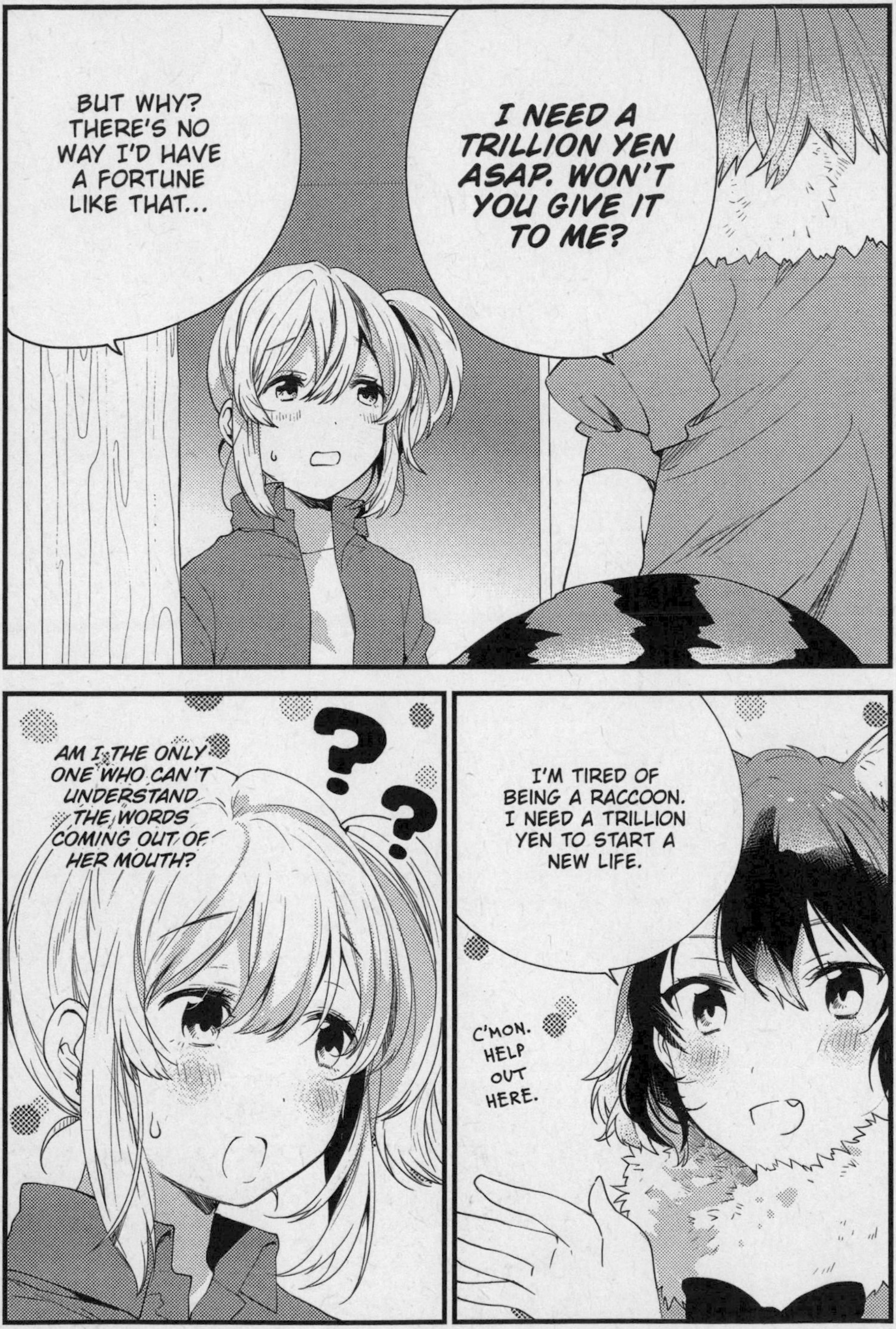
I NEED A TRILLION YEN ASAP. WON'T YOU GIVE IT TO ME?
BUT WHY? THERE'S NO WAY I'D HAVE A FORTUNE LIKE THAT...
I'M TIRED OF BEING A RACCOON. I NEED A TRILLION YEN TO START A NEW LIFE.
C'MON. HELP OUT HERE.
AM I THE ONLY ONE WHO CAN'T UNDERSTAND THE WORDS COMING OUT OF HER MOUTH?

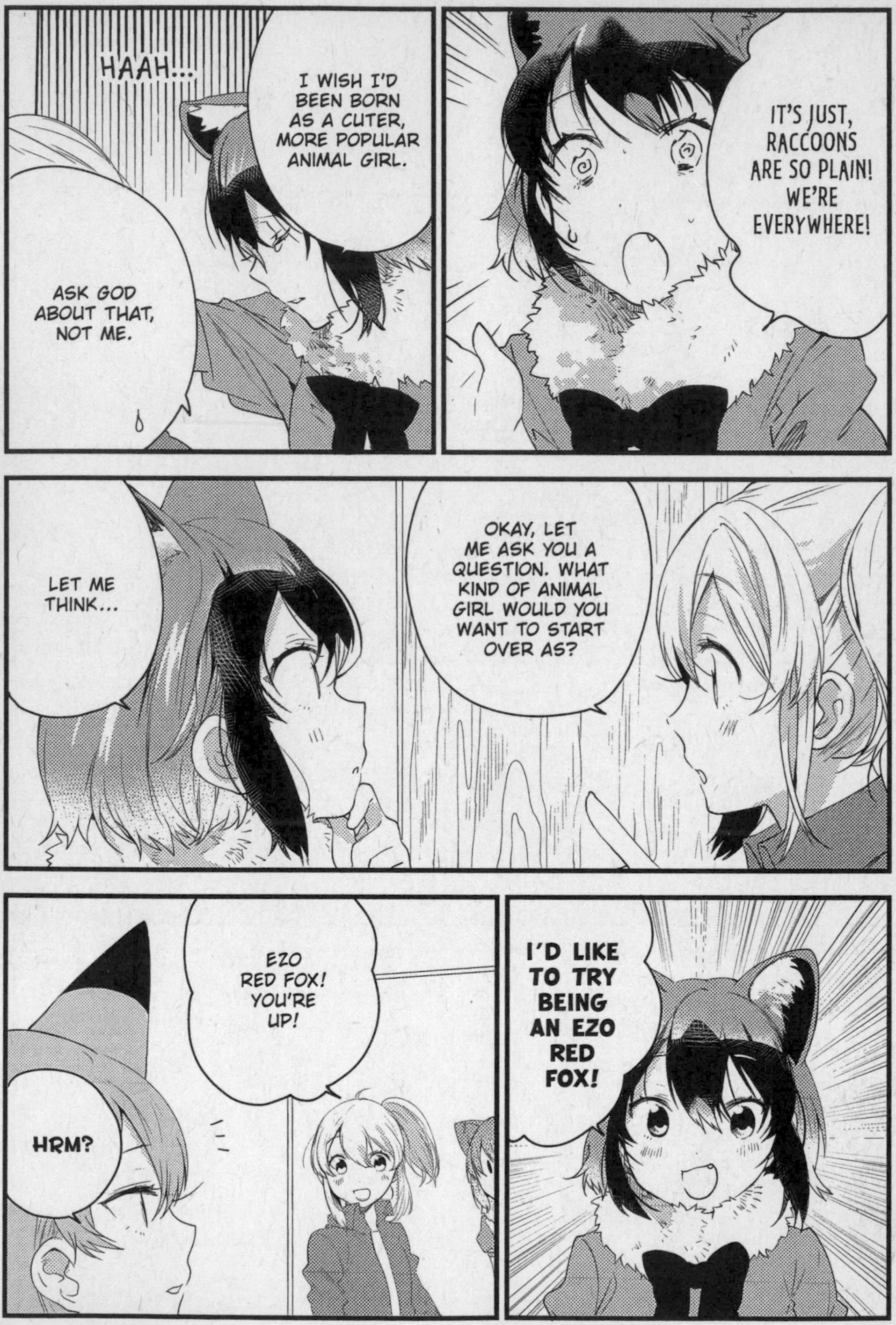

IT'S JUST, RACCOONS ARE SO PLAIN! WE'RE EVERYWHERE!
HAAH...
I WISH I'D BEEN BORN AS A CUTER, MORE POPULAR ANIMAL GIRL.
ASK GOD ABOUT THAT, NOT ME.
OKAY, LET ME ASK YOU A QUESTION. WHAT KIND OF ANIMAL GIRL WOULD YOU WANT TO START OVER AS?
LET ME THINK...
I'D LIKE TO TRY BEING AN EZO RED FOX!
EZO RED FOX! YOU'RE UP!
HRM?

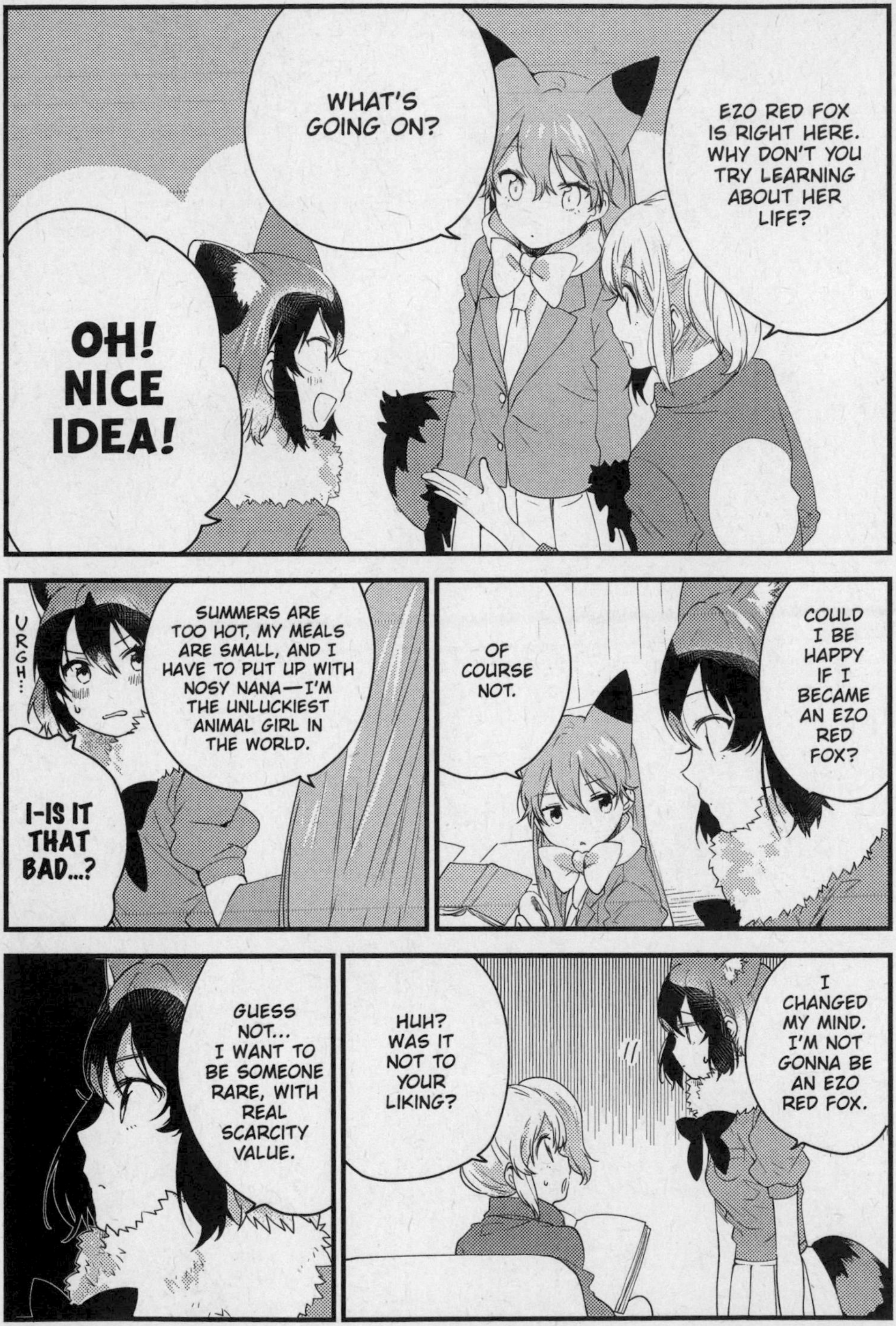
EZO RED FOX IS RIGHT HERE. WHY DON'T YOU TRY LEARNING ABOUT HER LIFE?
WHAT'S GOING ON?
OH! NICE IDEA!
COULD I BE HAPPY IF I BECAME AN EZO RED FOX?
OF COURSE NOT.
SUMMERS ARE TOO HOT, MY MEALS ARE SMALL, AND I HAVE TO PUT UP WITH NOSY NANA—I'M THE UNLUCKIEST ANIMAL GIRL IN THE WORLD.
URGH...
I-IS IT THAT BAD...?
I CHANGED MY MIND. I'M NOT GONNA BE AN EZO RED FOX.
HUH? WAS IT NOT TO YOUR LIKING?
GUESS NOT... I WANT TO BE SOMEONE RARE, WITH REAL SCARCITY VALUE.

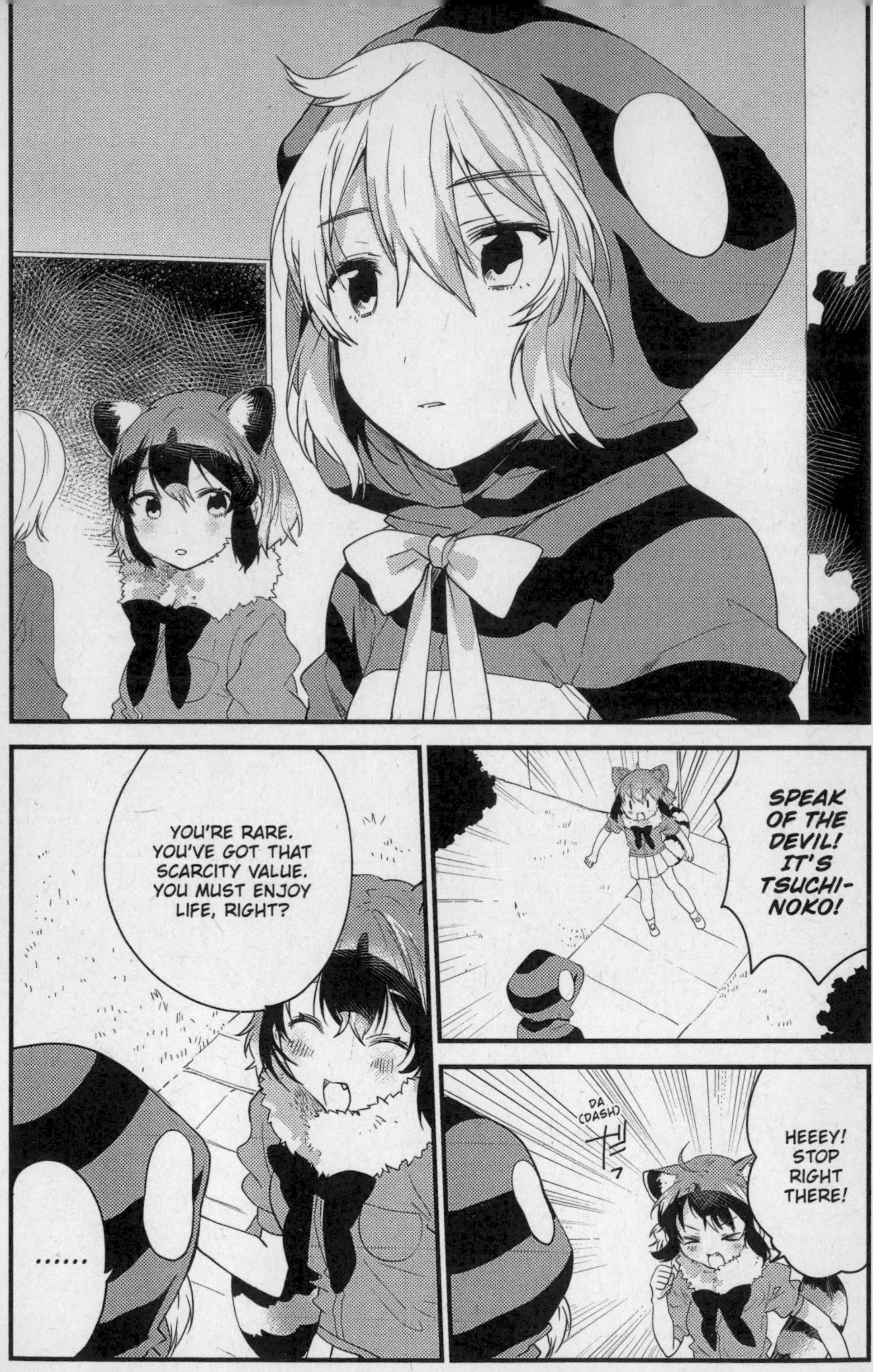

SPEAK OF THE DEVIL! IT'S TSUCHI-NOKO!
DA (DASH)
HEEEY! STOP RIGHT THERE!
YOU'RE RARE. YOU'VE GOT THAT SCARCITY VALUE. YOU MUST ENJOY LIFE, RIGHT?
......

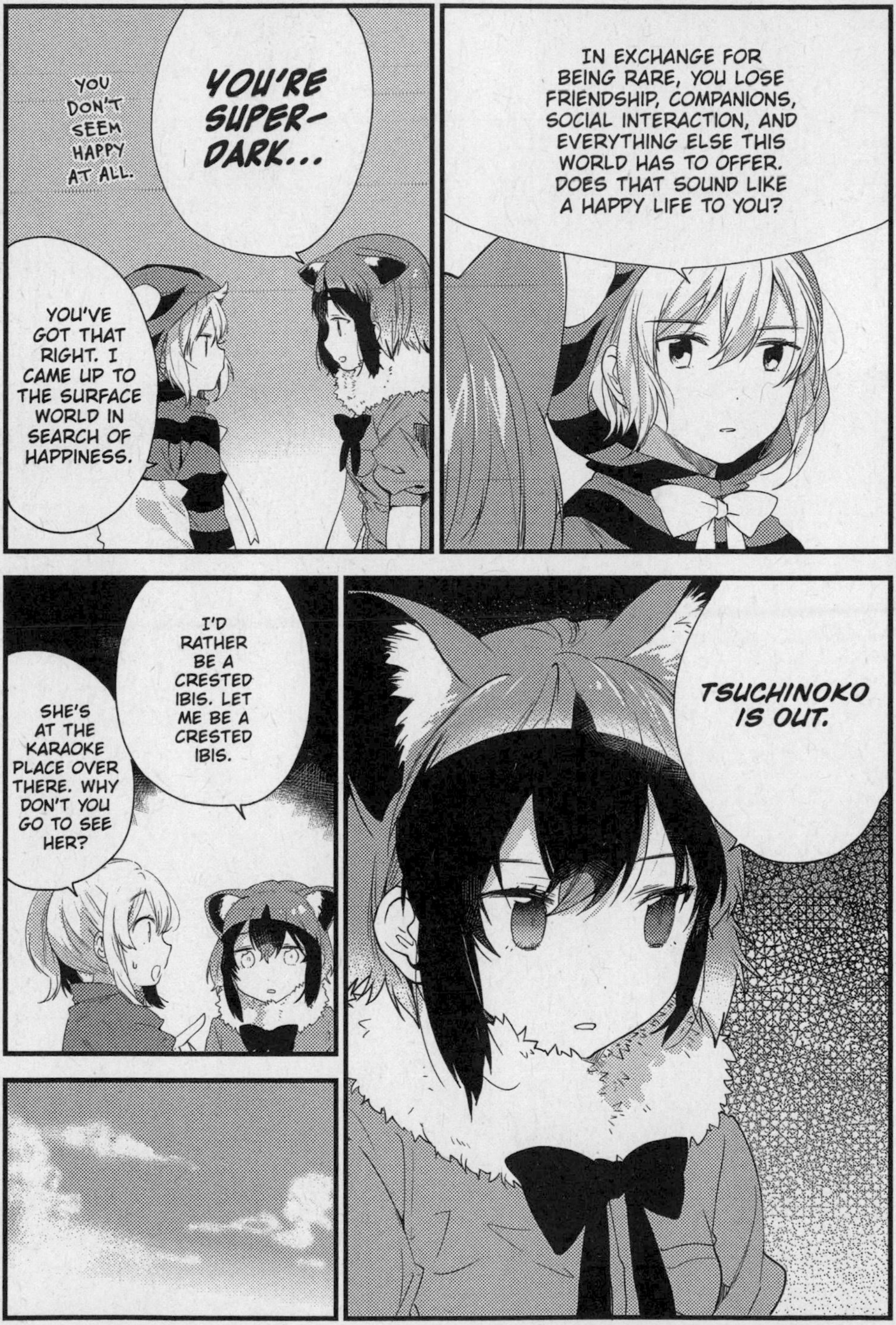
IN EXCHANGE FOR BEING RARE, YOU LOSE FRIENDSHIP, COMPANIONS, SOCIAL INTERACTION, AND EVERYTHING ELSE THIS WORLD HAS TO OFFER. DOES THAT SOUND LIKE A HAPPY LIFE TO YOU?
YOU'RE SUPER-DARK...
YOU DON'T SEEM HAPPY AT ALL.
YOU'VE GOT THAT RIGHT. I CAME UP TO THE SURFACE WORLD IN SEARCH OF HAPPINESS.
TSUCHINOKO IS OUT.
I'D RATHER BE A CRESTED IBIS. LET ME BE A CRESTED IBIS.
SHE'S AT THE KARAOKE PLACE OVER THERE. WHY DON'T YOU GO TO SEE HER?

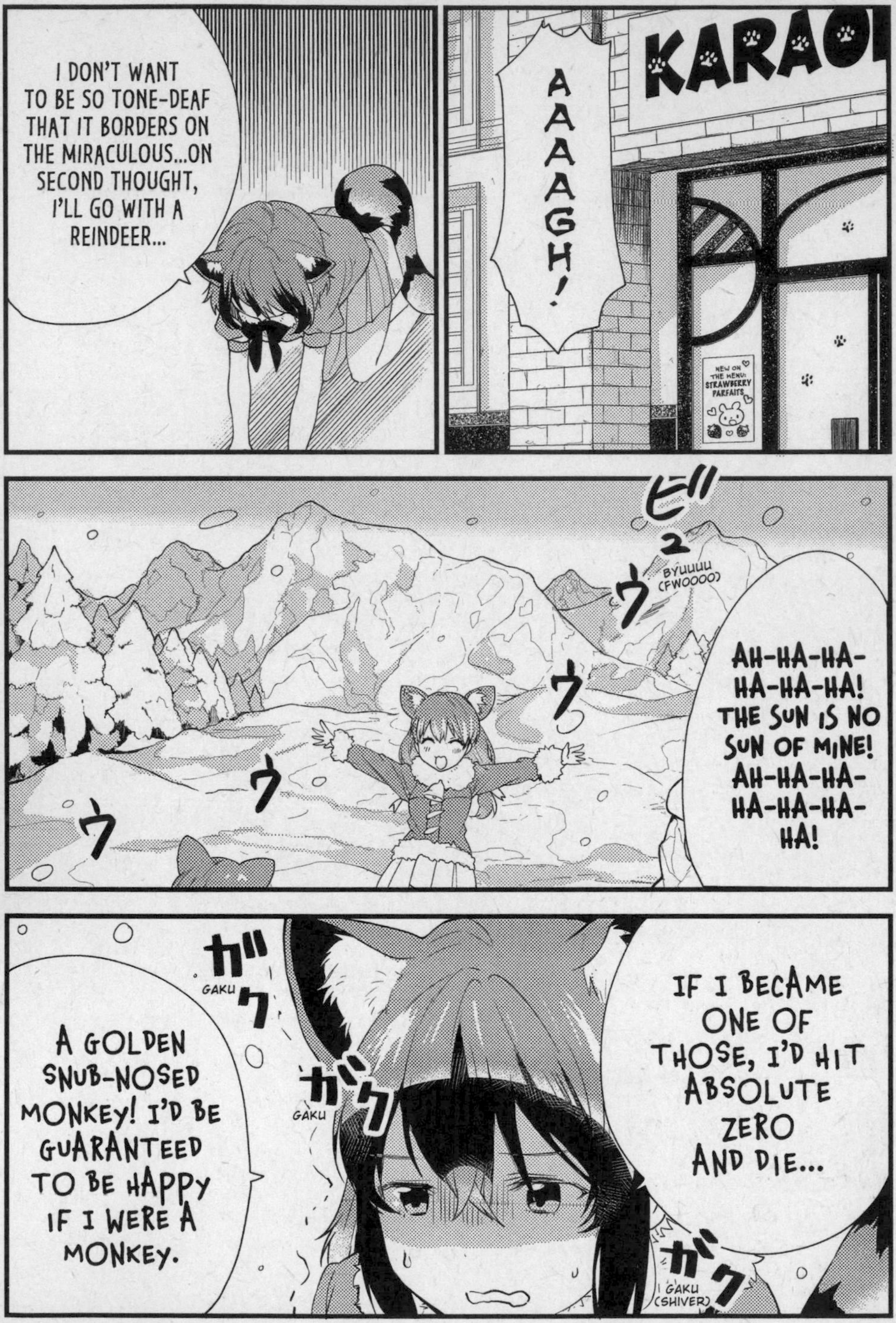
KARAO
AAAAAGH!
NEW ON THE MENU: STRAWBERRY PARFAITS
I DON'T WANT TO BE SO TONE-DEAF THAT IT BORDERS ON THE MIRACULOUS...ON SECOND THOUGHT, I'LL GO WITH A REINDEER...
ビュウウウウ
BYUUUU (FWOOOO)
AH-HA-HA-HA-HA-HA! THE SUN IS NO SUN OF MINE! AH-HA-HA-HA-HA-HA-HA!
IF I BECAME ONE OF THOSE, I'D HIT ABSOLUTE ZERO AND DIE...
ガク
GAKU (SHIVER)
ガク
GAKU
ガク
GAKU
A GOLDEN SNUB-NOSED MONKEY! I'D BE GUARANTEED TO BE HAPPY IF I WERE A MONKEY.

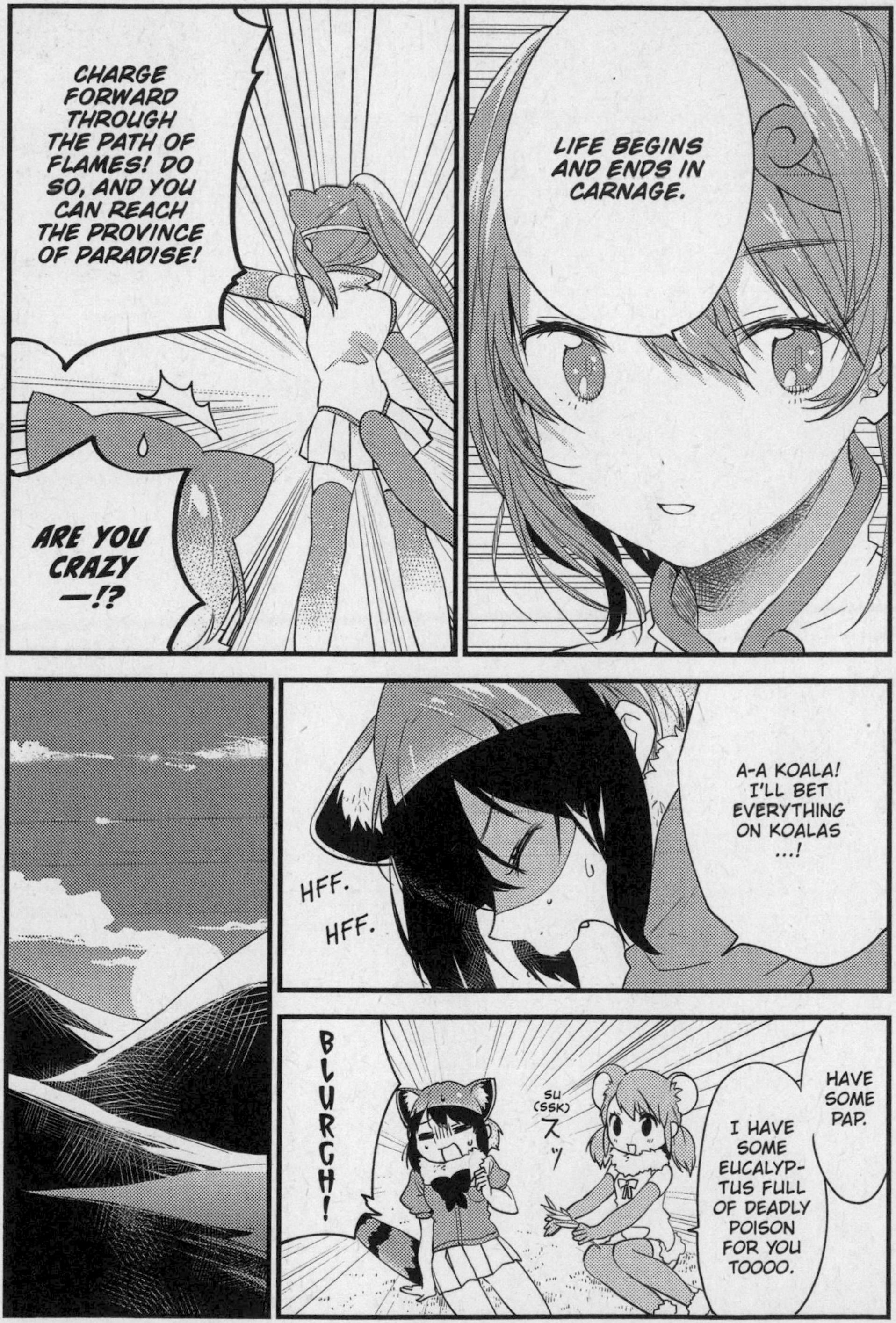
LIFE BEGINS AND ENDS IN CARNAGE.
CHARGE FORWARD THROUGH THE PATH OF FLAMES! DO SO, AND YOU CAN REACH THE PROVINCE OF PARADISE!
ARE YOU CRAZY —!?
A-A KOALA! I'LL BET EVERYTHING ON KOALAS ...!
HFF.
HFF.
HAVE SOME PAP.
I HAVE SOME EUCALYPTUS FULL OF DEADLY POISON FOR YOU TOOOO.
SU (SSK)
スッ
BLURGH!

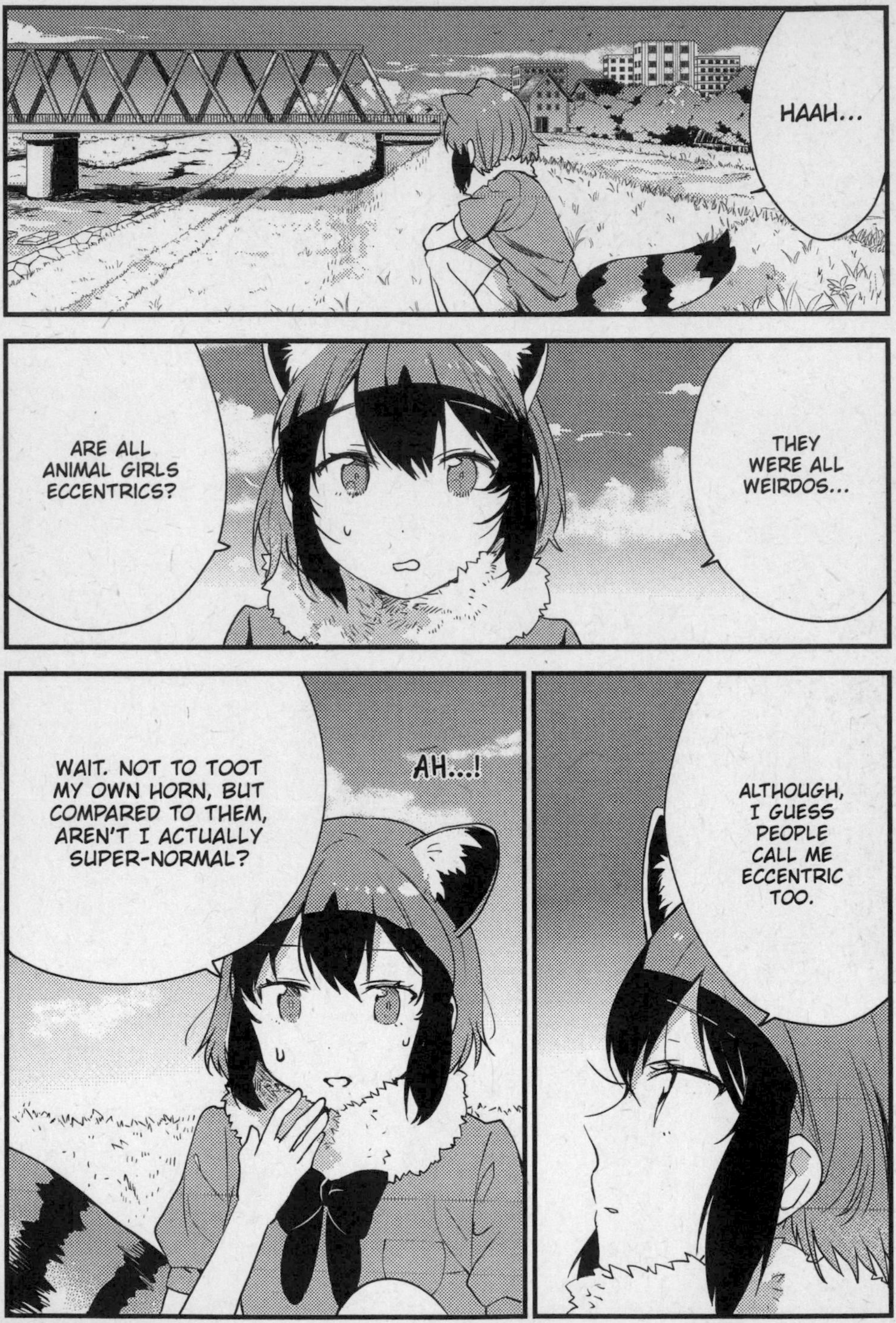
HAAH...
THEY WERE ALL WEIRDOS...
ARE ALL ANIMAL GIRLS ECCENTRICS?
ALTHOUGH, I GUESS PEOPLE CALL ME ECCENTRIC TOO.
AH...!
WAIT. NOT TO TOOT MY OWN HORN, BUT COMPARED TO THEM, AREN'T I ACTUALLY SUPER-NORMAL?

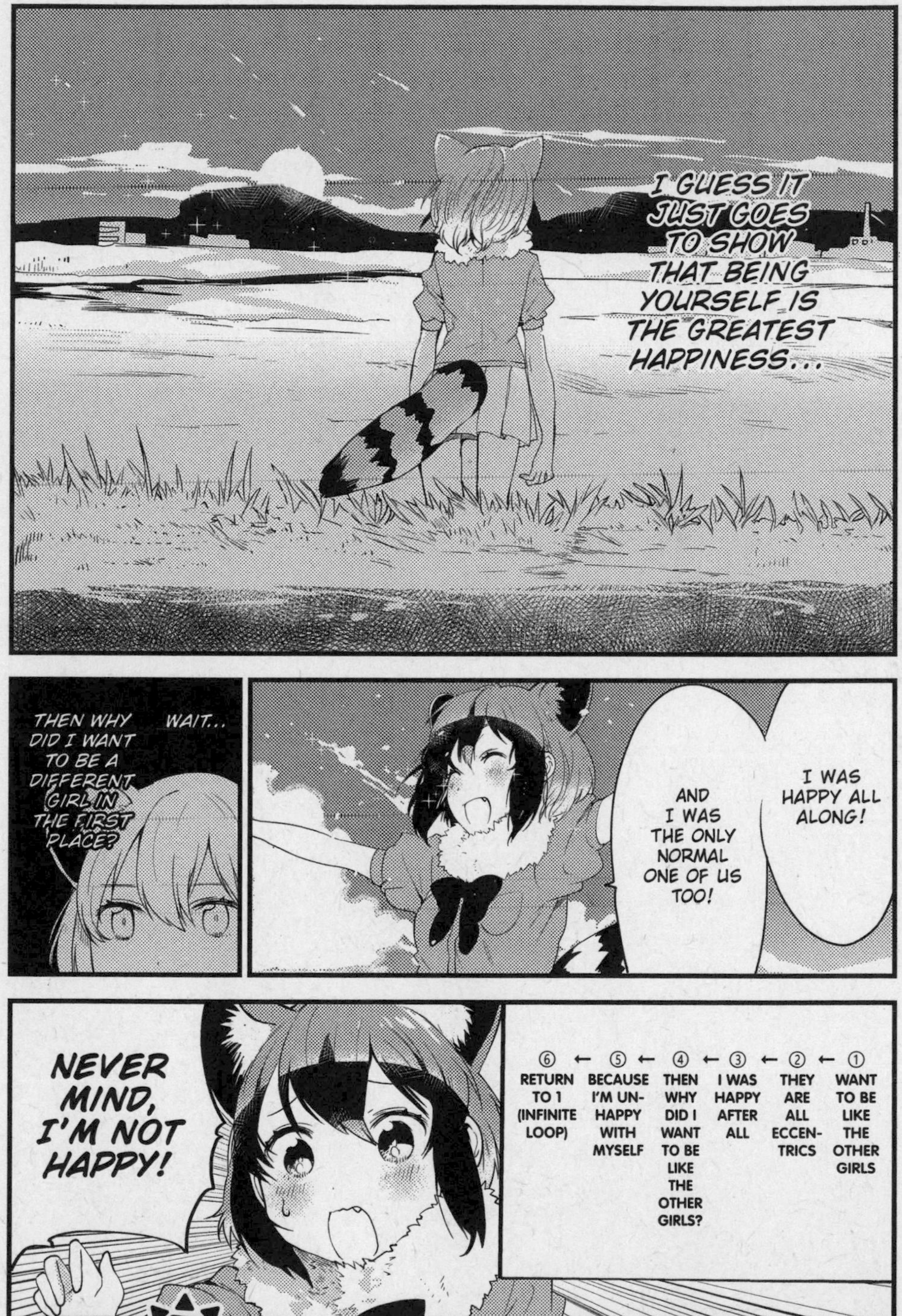
I GUESS IT JUST GOES TO SHOW THAT BEING YOURSELF IS THE GREATEST HAPPINESS...
I WAS HAPPY ALL ALONG!
AND I WAS THE ONLY NORMAL ONE OF US TOO!
WAIT...
THEN WHY DID I WANT TO BE A DIFFERENT GIRL IN THE FIRST PLACE?
① WANT TO BE LIKE THE OTHER GIRLS
← ② THEY ARE ALL ECCENTRICS
← ③ I WAS HAPPY AFTER ALL
← ④ THEN WHY DID I WANT TO BE LIKE THE OTHER GIRLS?
← ⑤ BECAUSE I'M UNHAPPY WITH MYSELF
← ⑥ RETURN TO 1 (INFINITE LOOP)
NEVER MIND, I'M NOT HAPPY!

CHAPTER 12 END

KEMONO FRIENDS

WELCOME TO JAPARI PARK!

CHAPTER 13

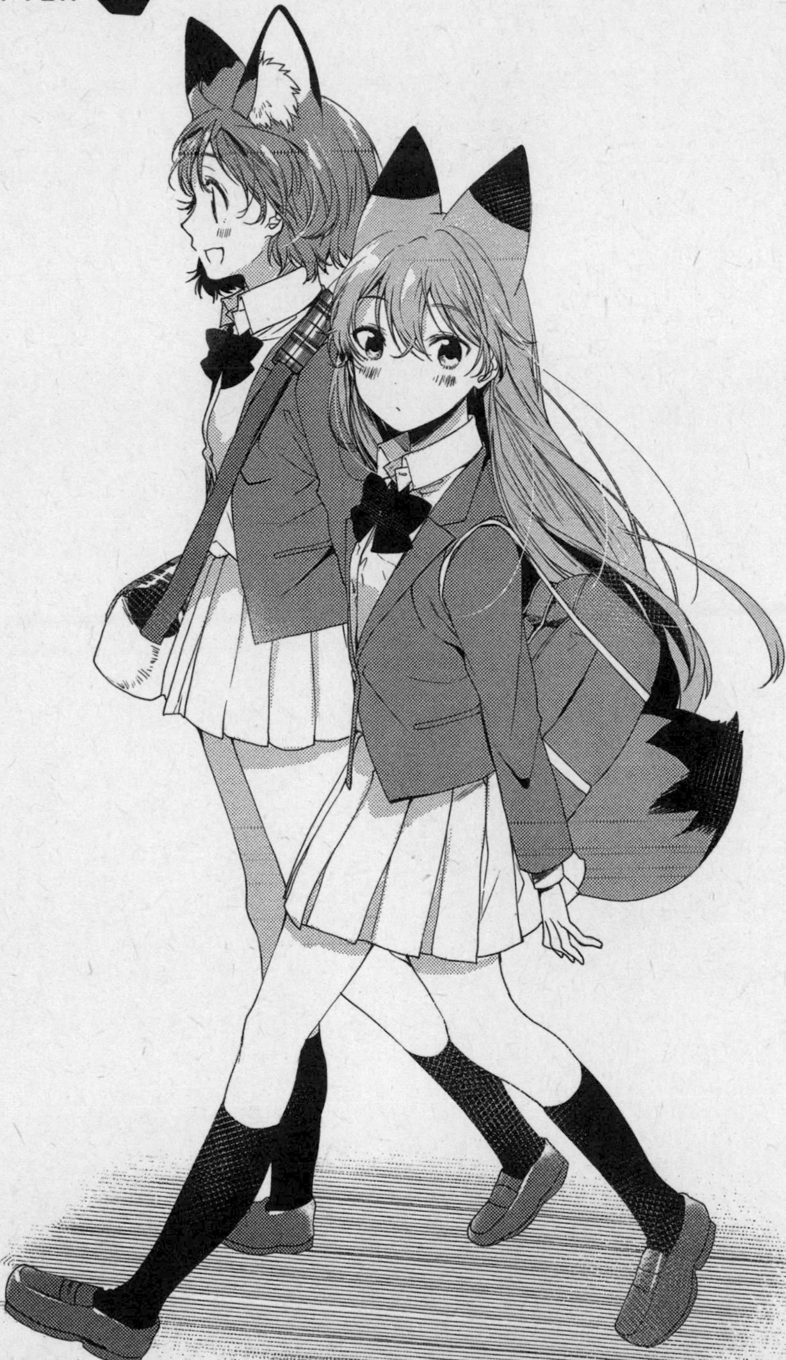

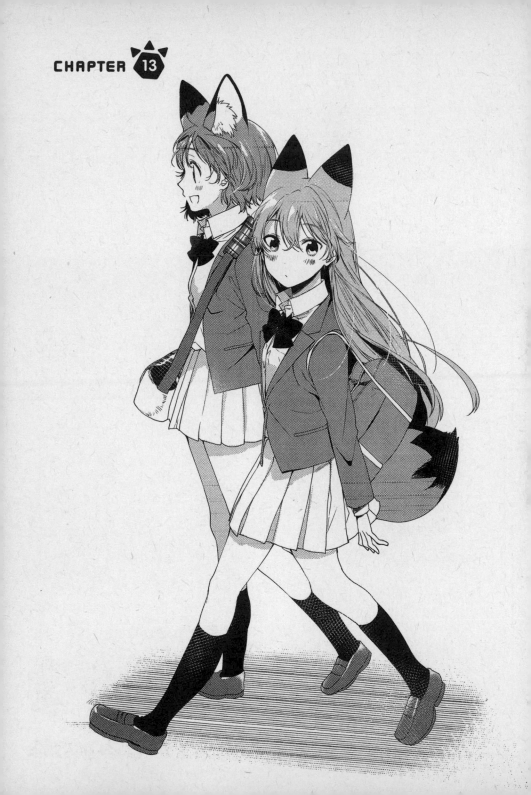

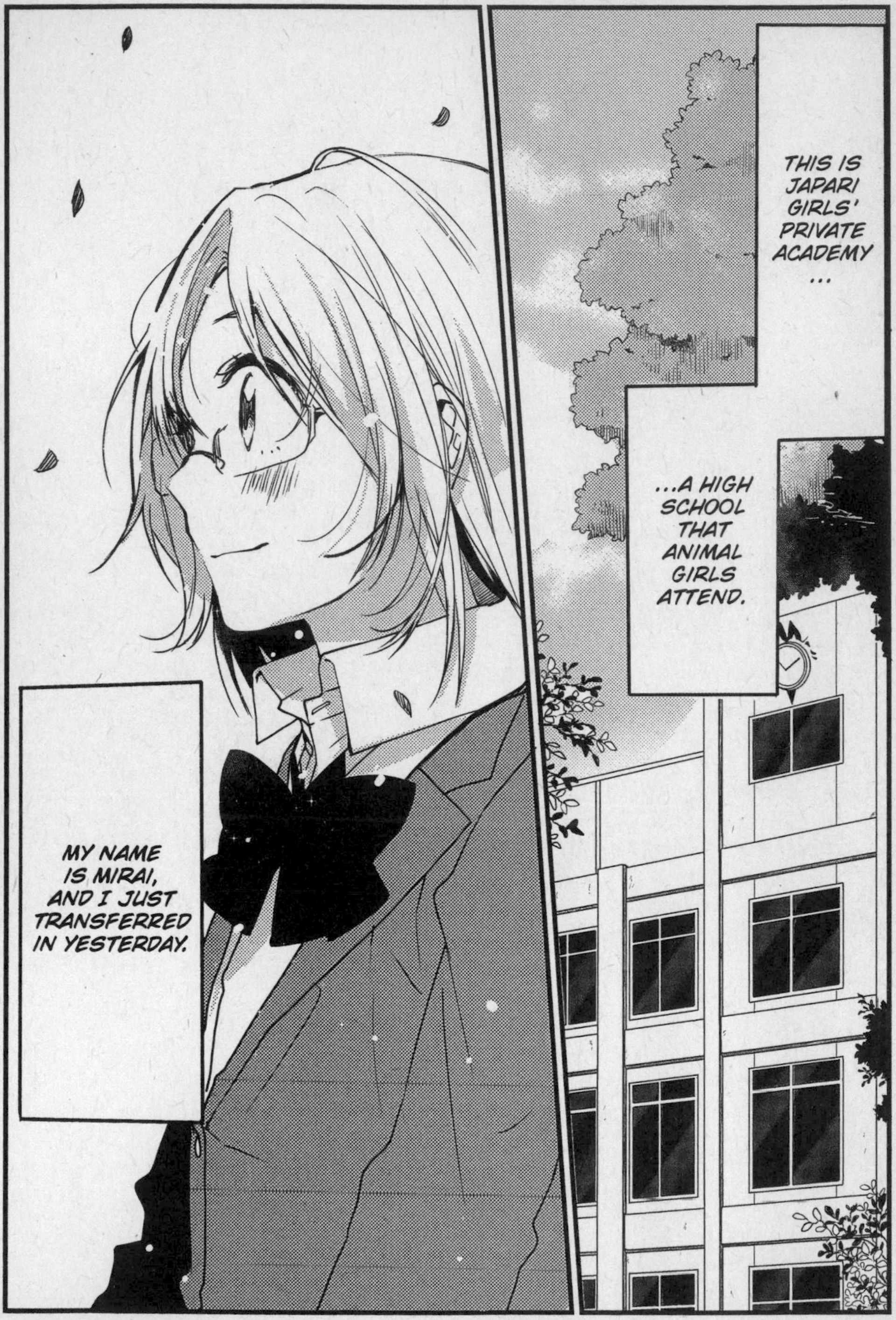
THIS IS JAPARI GIRLS' PRIVATE ACADEMY ...
...A HIGH SCHOOL THAT ANIMAL GIRLS ATTEND.
MY NAME IS MIRAI, AND I JUST TRANSFERRED IN YESTERDAY.

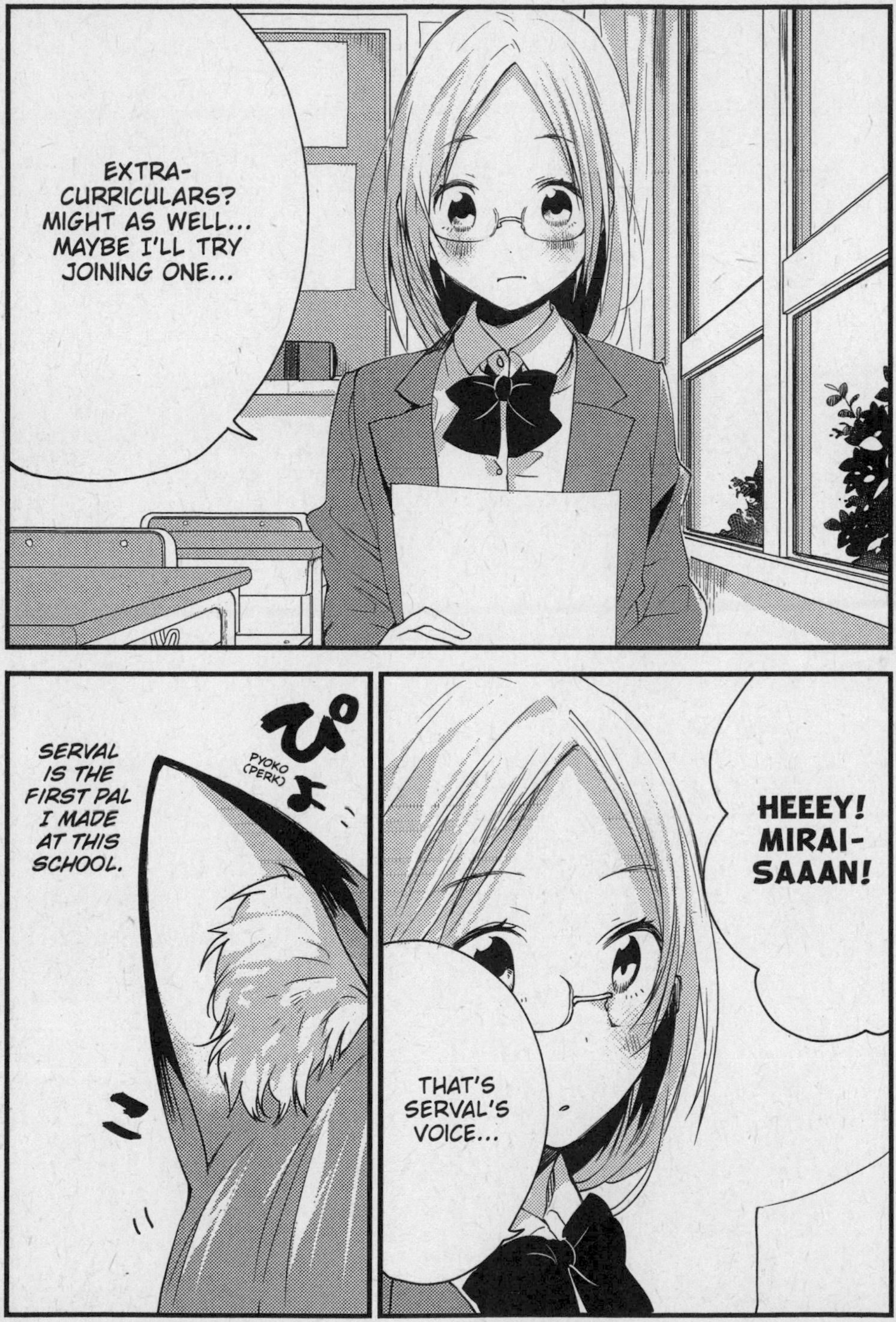
EXTRA-CURRICULARS? MIGHT AS WELL... MAYBE I'LL TRY JOINING ONE...
HEEEY! MIRAI-SAAAN!
THAT'S SERVAL'S VOICE...
ぴょ
PYOKO (PERK)
SERVAL IS THE FIRST PAL I MADE AT THIS SCHOOL.

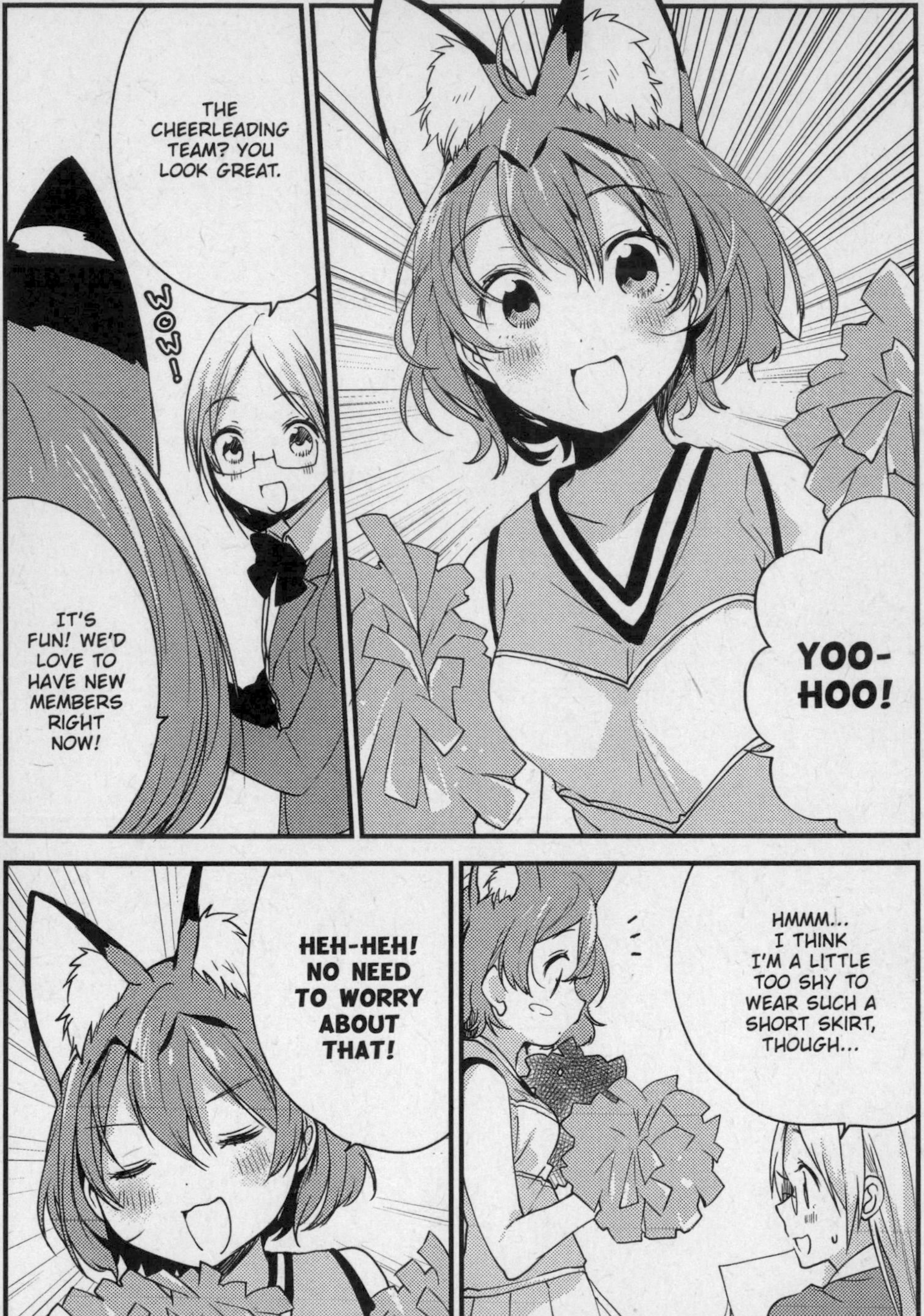
YOO-HOO!
THE CHEERLEADING TEAM? YOU LOOK GREAT.
WOW!
IT'S FUN! WE'D LOVE TO HAVE NEW MEMBERS RIGHT NOW!
HMMM... I THINK I'M A LITTLE TOO SHY TO WEAR SUCH A SHORT SKIRT, THOUGH...
HEH-HEH! NO NEED TO WORRY ABOUT THAT!

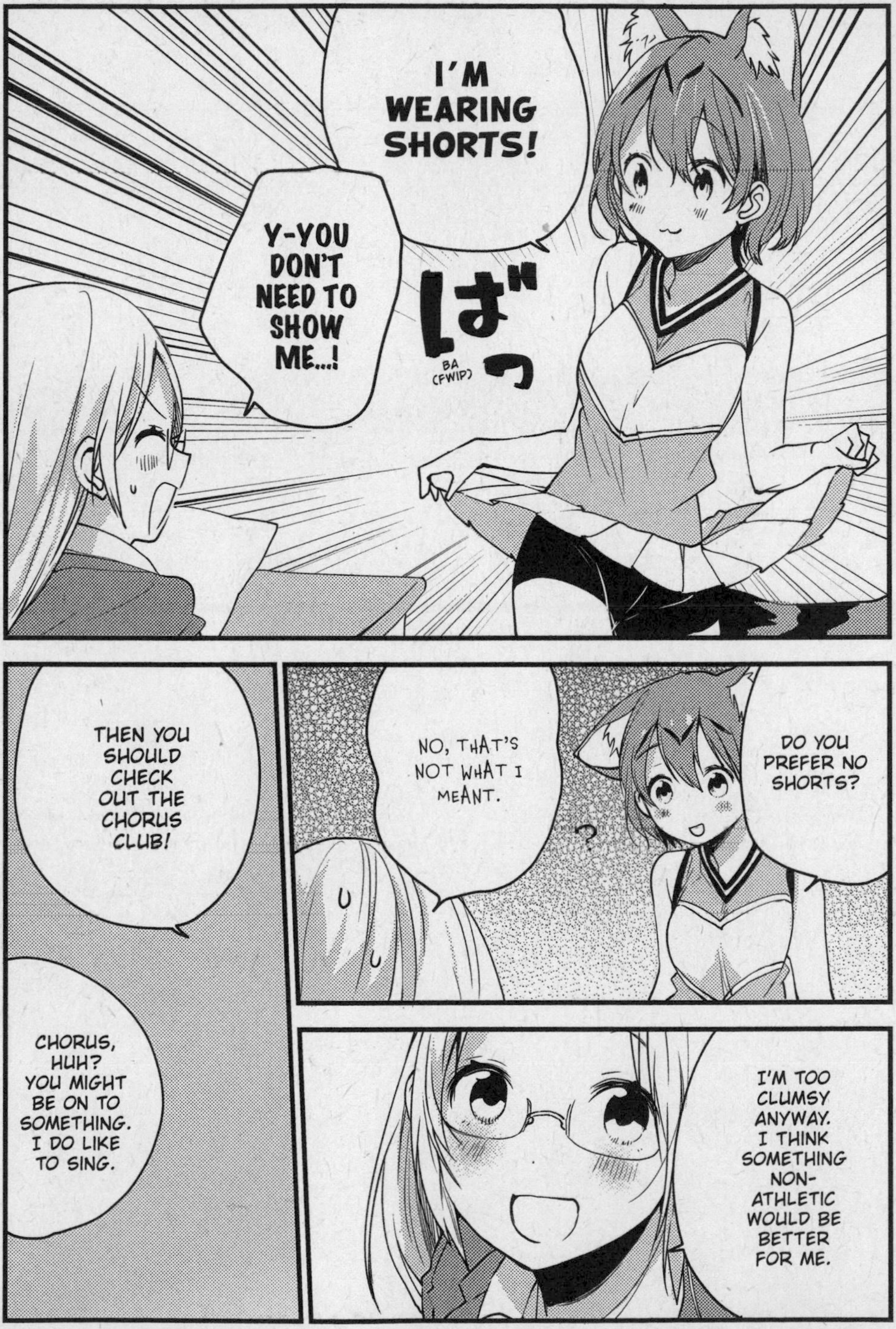
I'M WEARING SHORTS!
ばっ
BA (FWIP)
Y-YOU DON'T NEED TO SHOW ME...!
DO YOU PREFER NO SHORTS?
?
NO, THAT'S NOT WHAT I MEANT.
I'M TOO CLUMSY ANYWAY. I THINK SOMETHING NON-ATHLETIC WOULD BE BETTER FOR ME.
THEN YOU SHOULD CHECK OUT THE CHORUS CLUB!
CHORUS, HUH? YOU MIGHT BE ON TO SOMETHING. I DO LIKE TO SING.

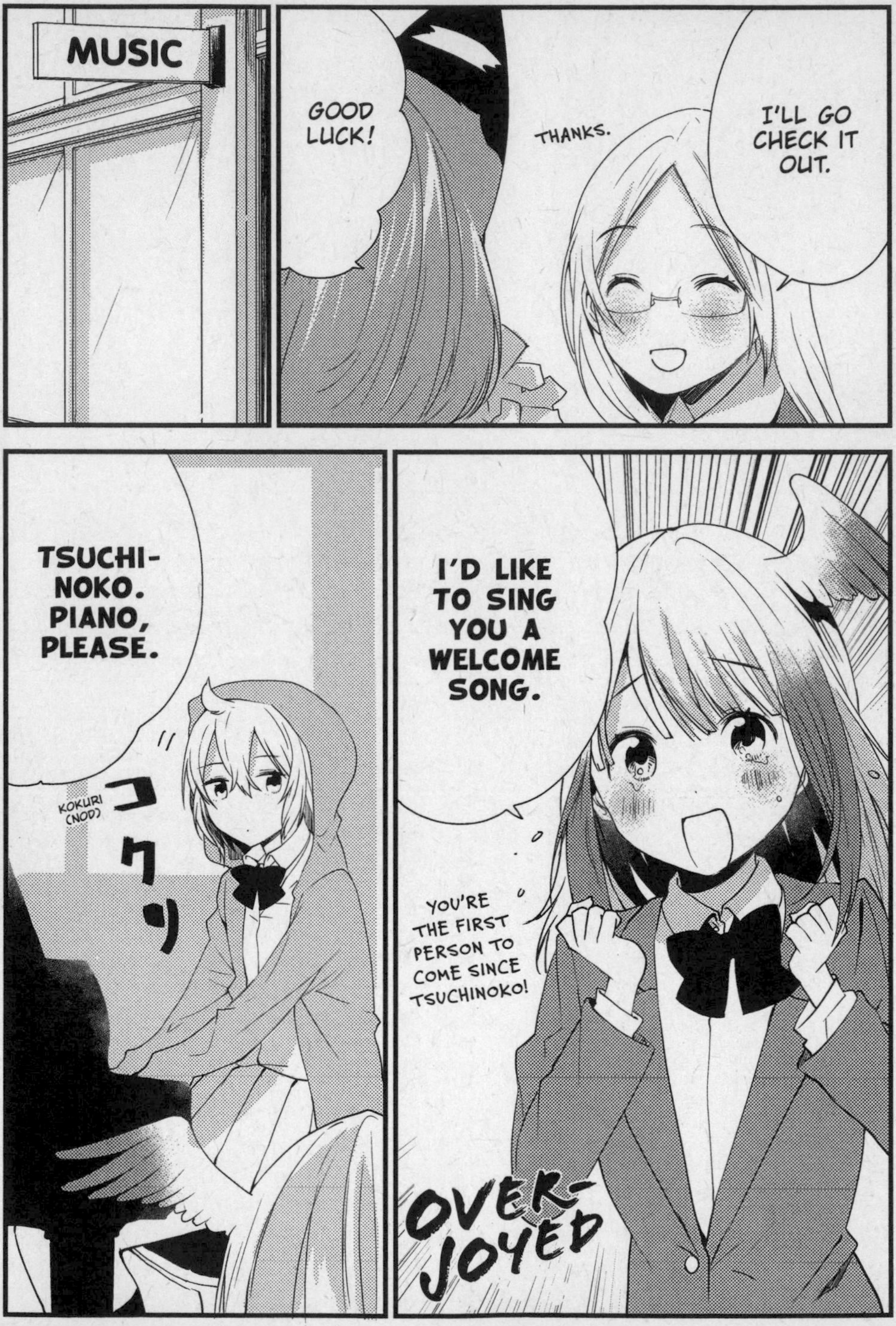
I'LL GO CHECK IT OUT.
THANKS.
GOOD LUCK!
MUSIC
I'D LIKE TO SING YOU A WELCOME SONG.
YOU'RE THE FIRST PERSON TO COME SINCE TSUCHINOKO!
OVER-JOYED
TSUCHI-NOKO. PIANO, PLEASE.
コクリ
KOKURI (NOD)

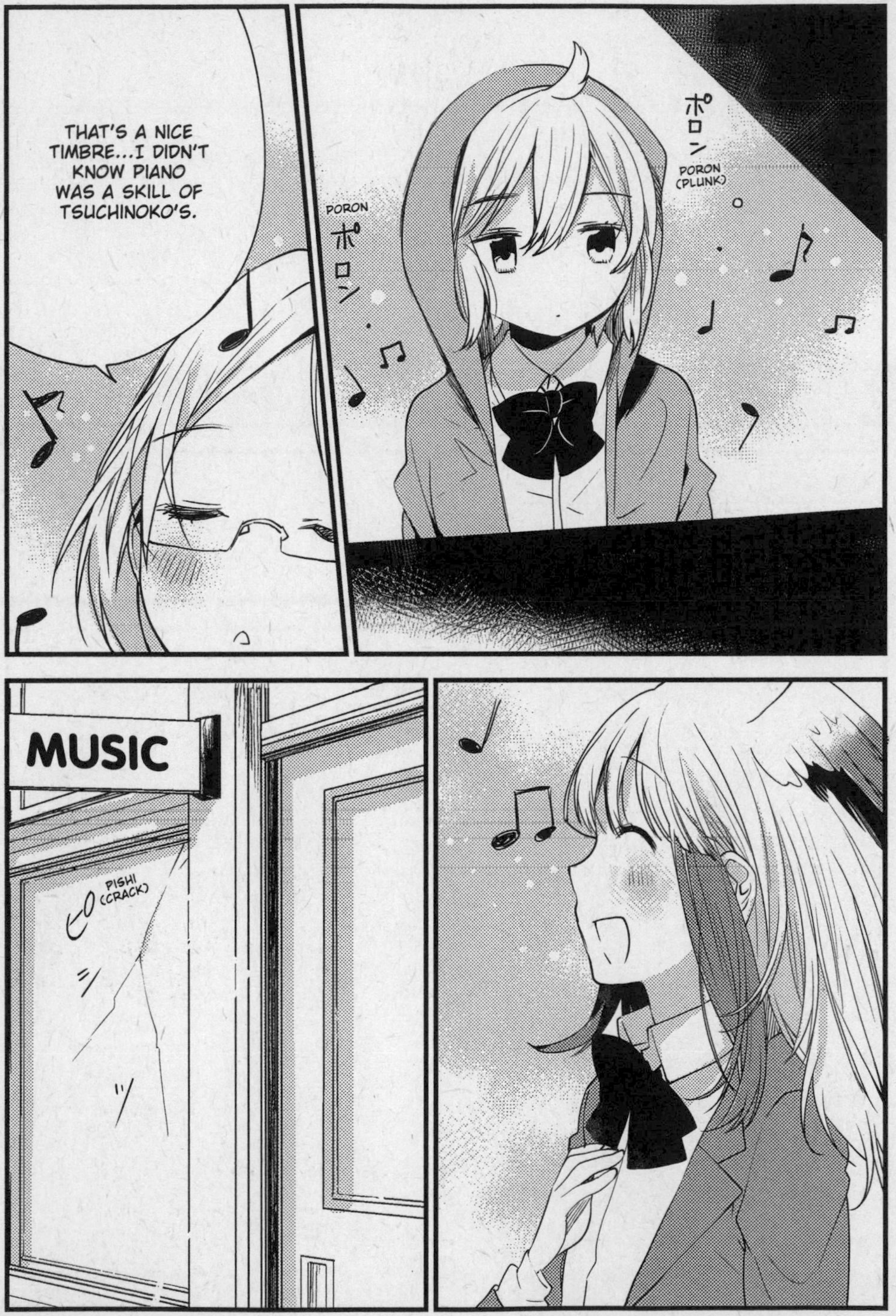
ポロン
PORON (PLUNK)
PORON
ポロン
THAT'S A NICE TIMBRE...I DIDN'T KNOW PIANO WAS A SKILL OF TSUCHINOKO'S.
MUSIC
PISHI (CRACK)

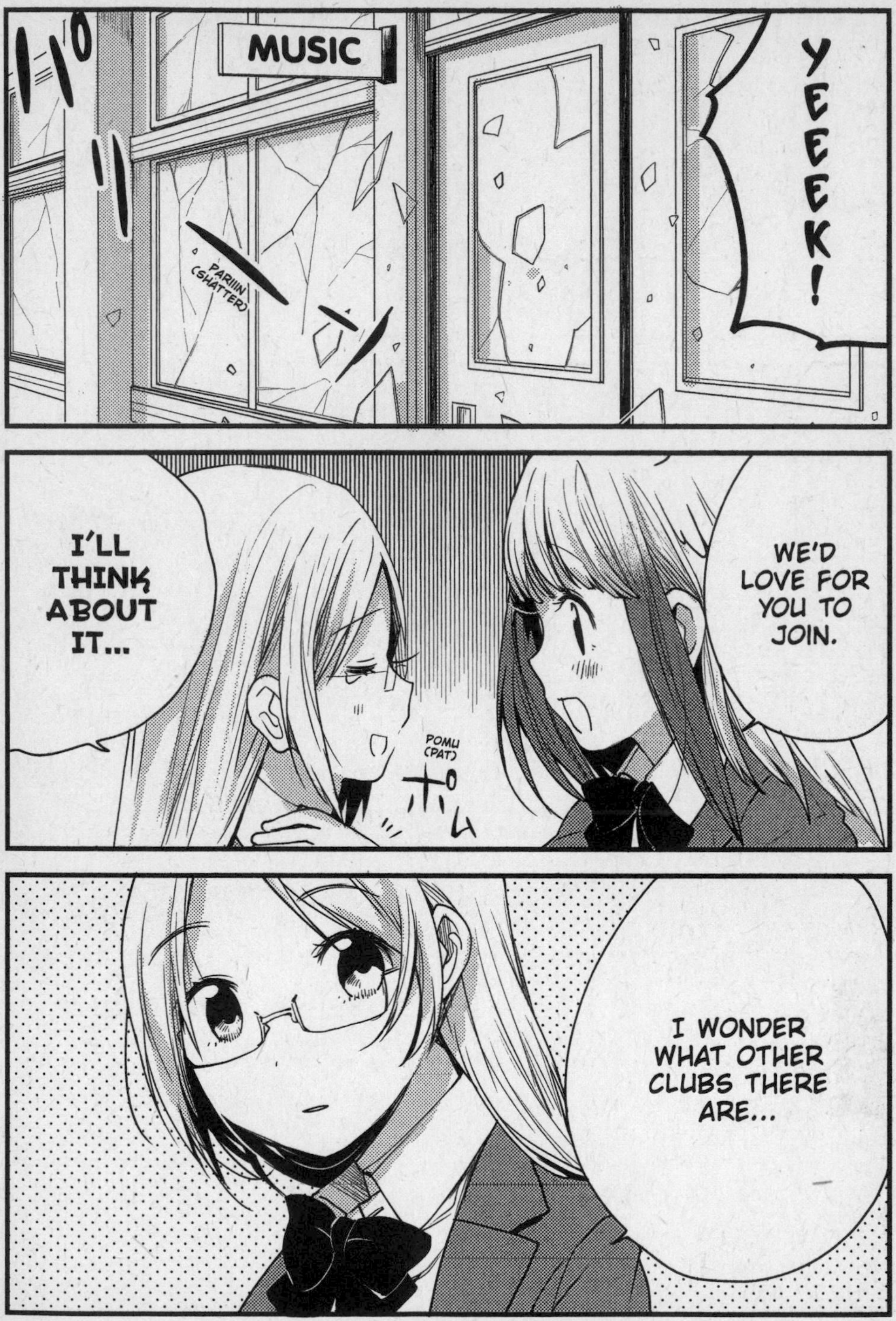
YEEEK!
MUSIC
PARIIN (SHATTER)
WE'D LOVE FOR YOU TO JOIN.
I'LL THINK ABOUT IT...
POMU (PAT)
I WONDER WHAT OTHER CLUBS THERE ARE...

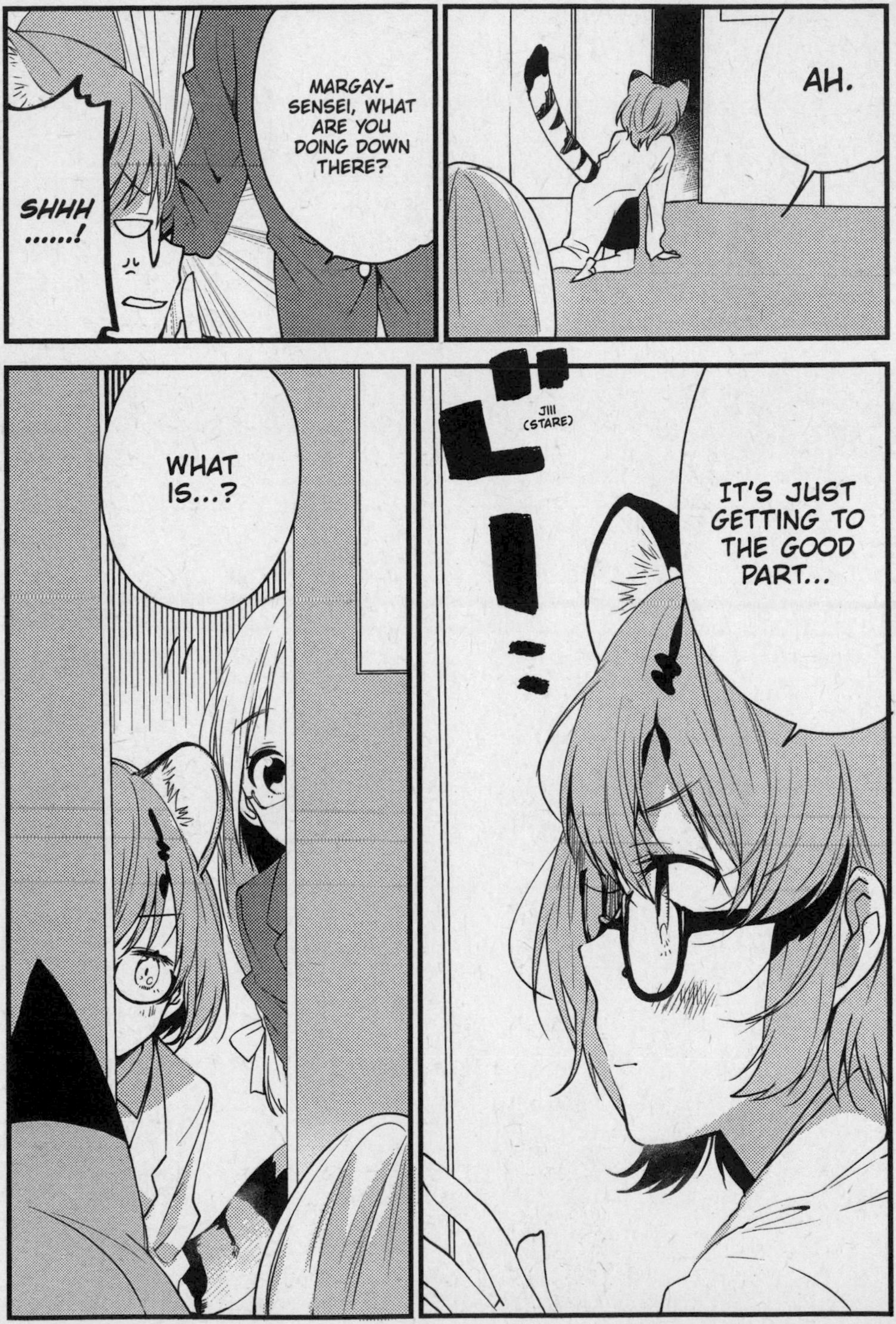
AH.
MARGAY-SENSEI, WHAT ARE YOU DOING DOWN THERE?
SHHH ......!
JIII (STARE)
IT'S JUST GETTING TO THE GOOD PART...
WHAT IS...?

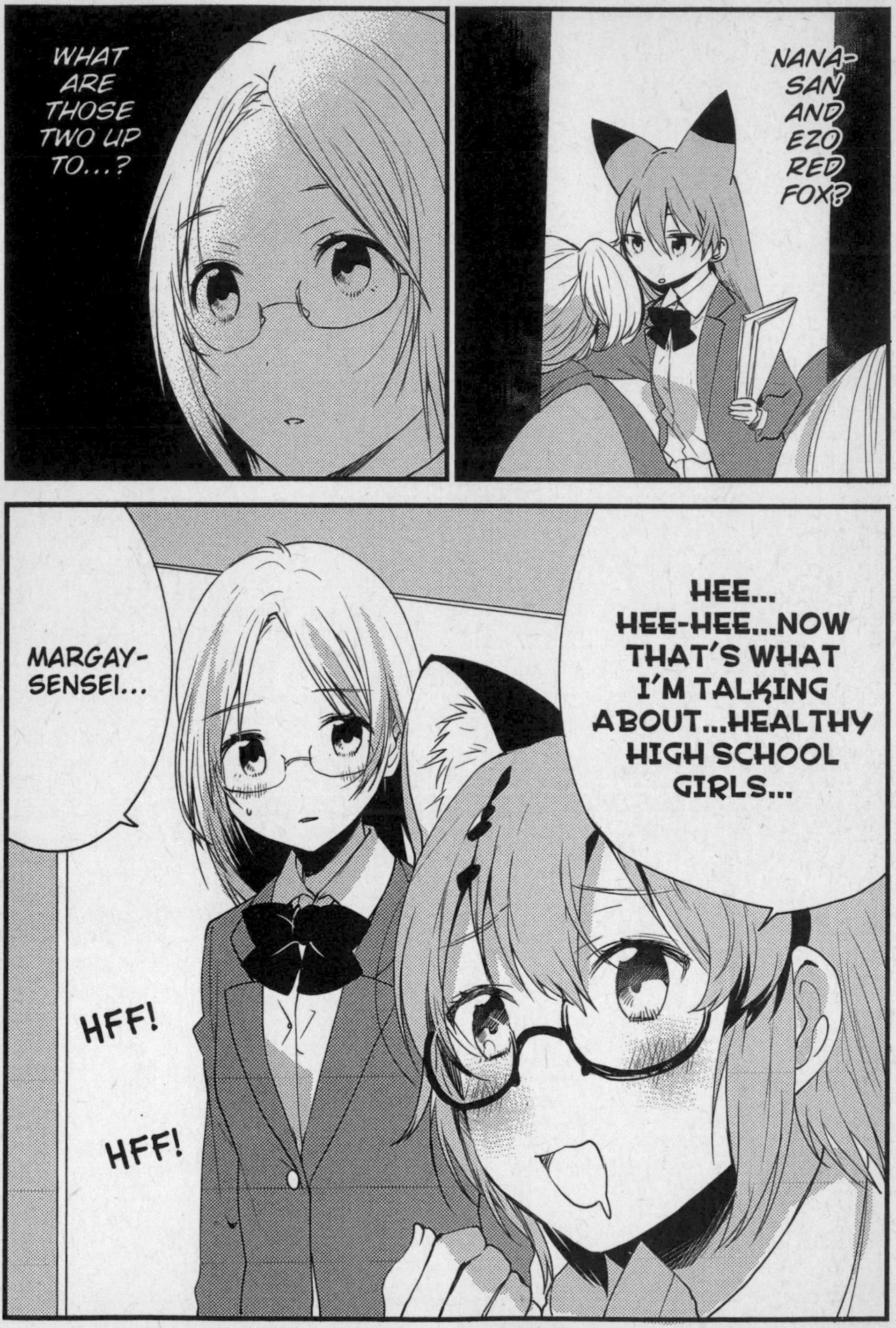
NANA-SAN AND EZO RED FOX?
WHAT ARE THOSE TWO UP TO...?
HEE... HEE-HEE...NOW THAT'S WHAT I'M TALKING ABOUT...HEALTHY HIGH SCHOOL GIRLS...
MARGAY-SENSEI...
HFF!
HFF!

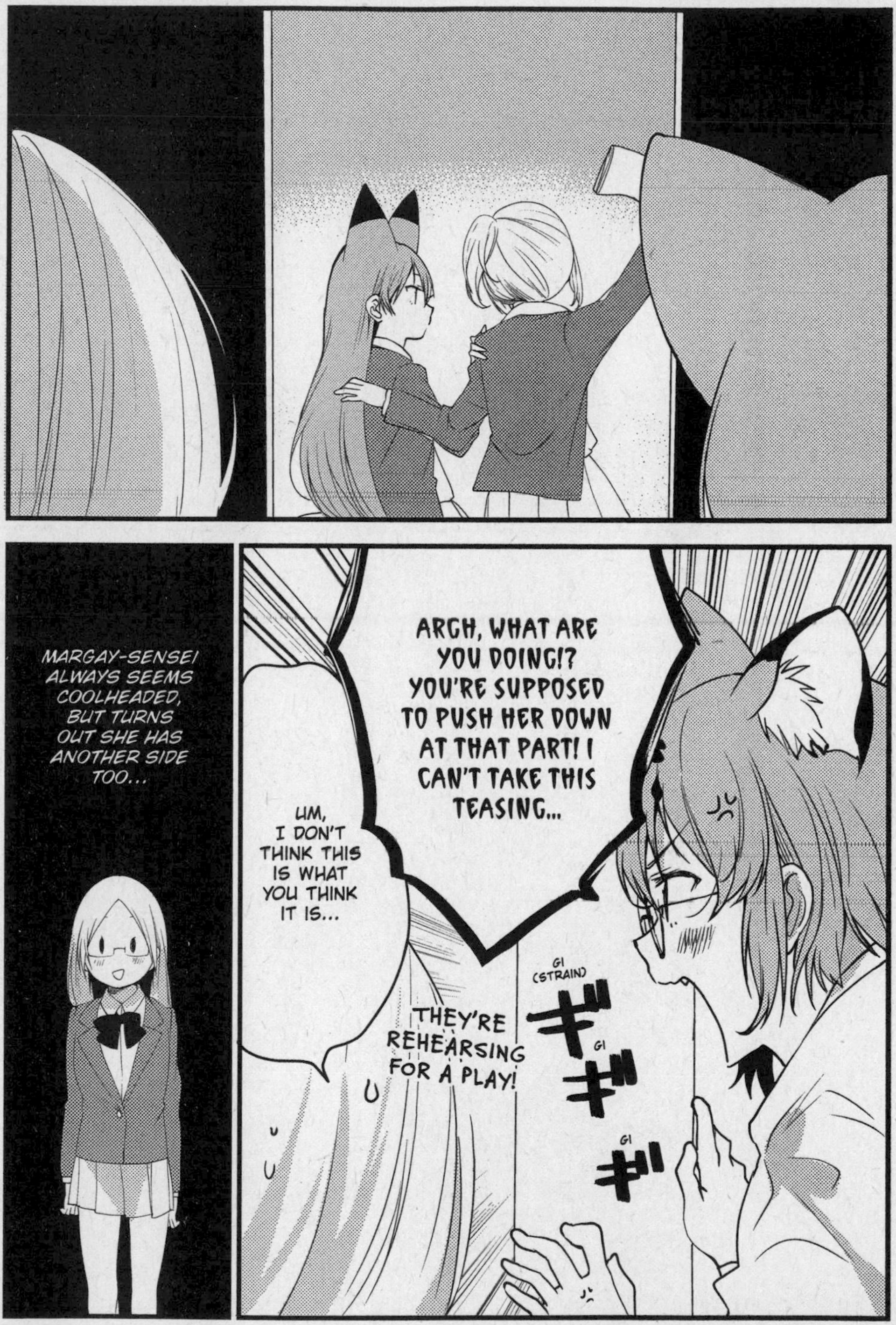
ARGH, WHAT ARE YOU DOING!? YOU'RE SUPPOSED TO PUSH HER DOWN AT THAT PART! I CAN'T TAKE THIS TEASING...
GI (STRAIN)
GI
GI
UM, I DON'T THINK THIS IS WHAT YOU THINK IT IS...
THEY'RE REHEARSING FOR A PLAY!
MARGAY-SENSEI ALWAYS SEEMS COOLHEADED, BUT TURNS OUT SHE HAS ANOTHER SIDE TOO...

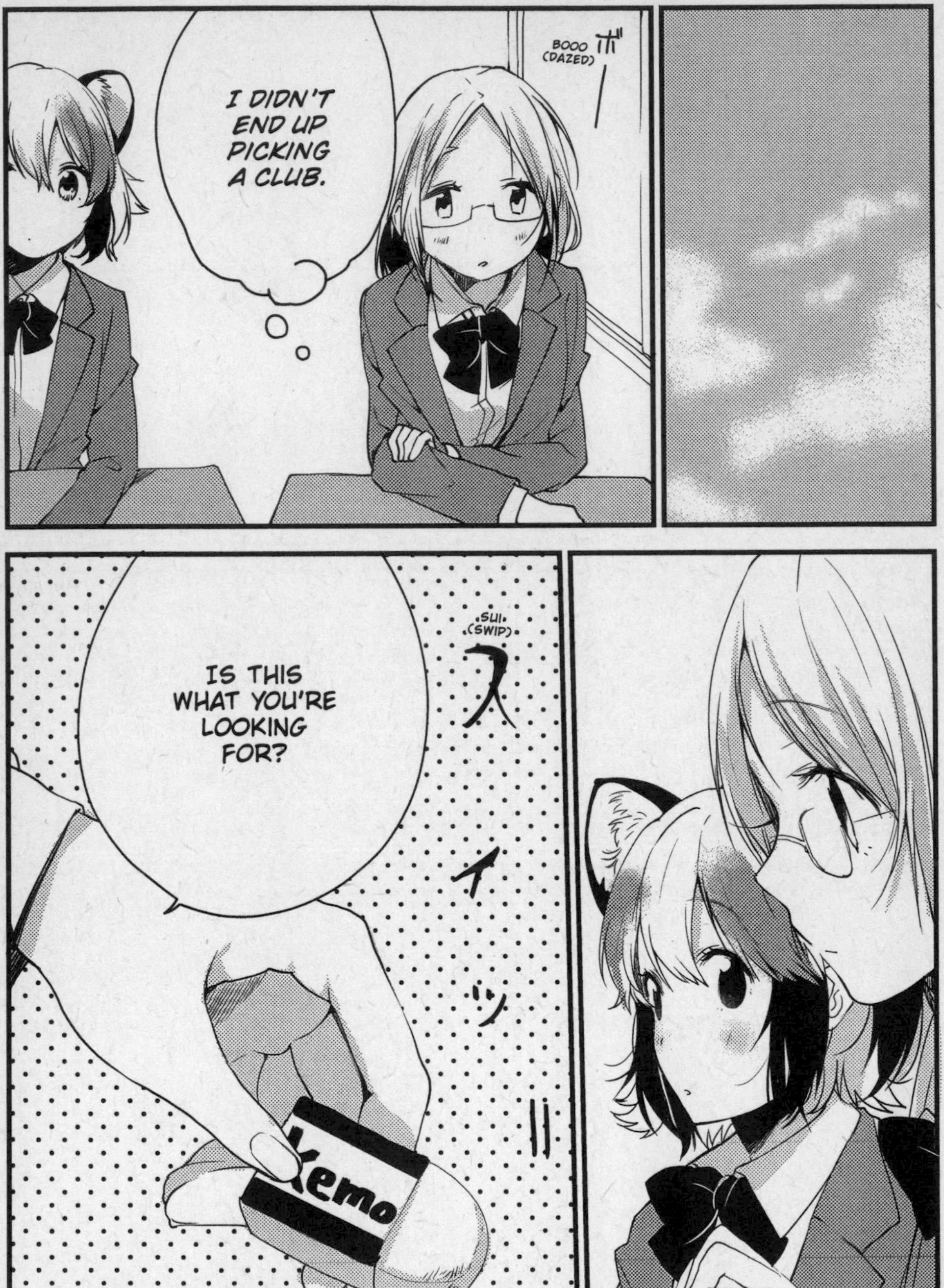
ボー
BOOO (DAZED)
I DIDN'T END UP PICKING A CLUB.
スイッ
SUI (SWIP)
IS THIS WHAT YOU'RE LOOKING FOR?
Kemo

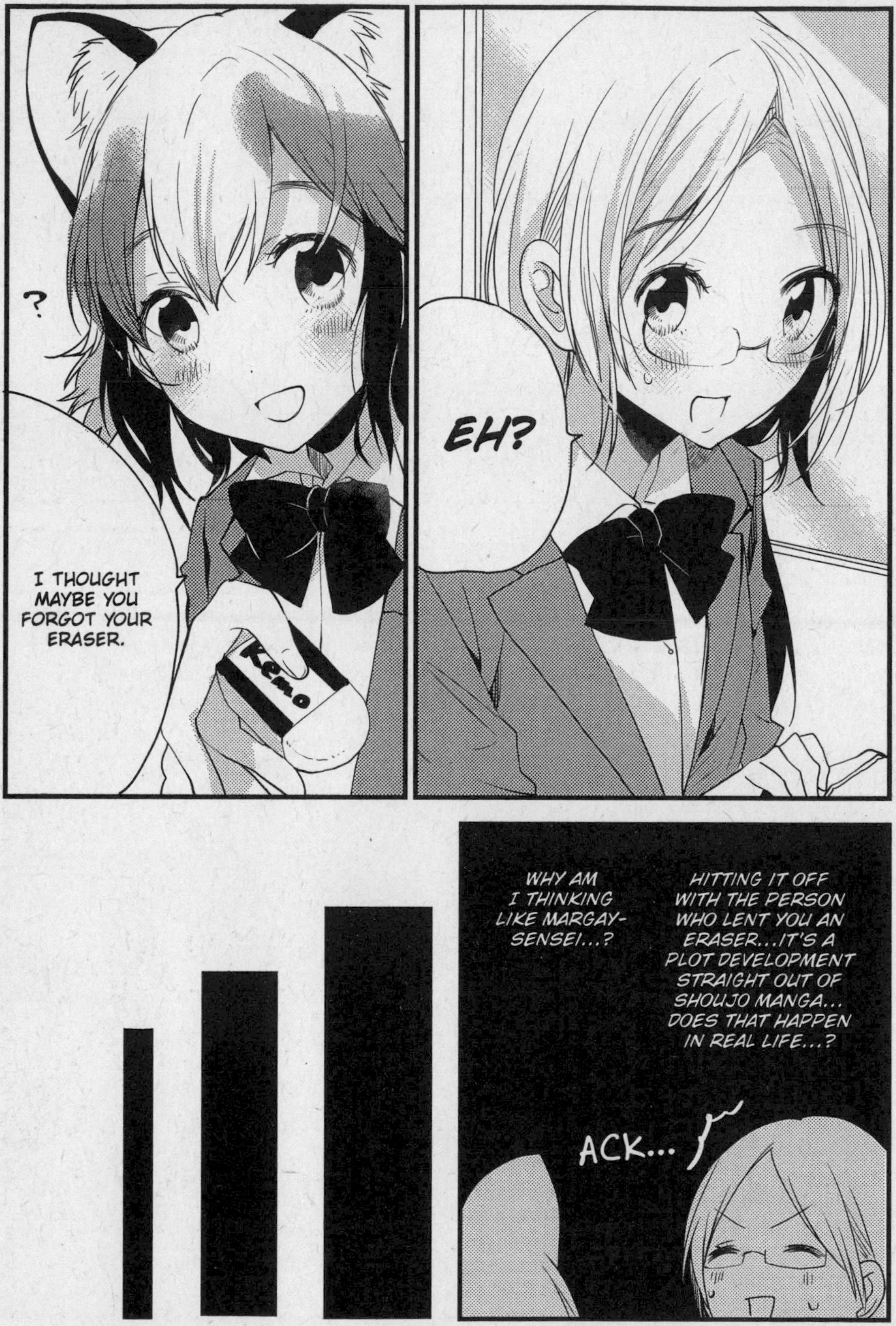
EH?
?
I THOUGHT MAYBE YOU FORGOT YOUR ERASER.
Kemo
HITTING IT OFF WITH THE PERSON WHO LENT YOU AN ERASER...IT'S A PLOT DEVELOPMENT STRAIGHT OUT OF SHOUJO MANGA... DOES THAT HAPPEN IN REAL LIFE...?
WHY AM I THINKING LIKE MARGAY-SENSEI...?
ACK...

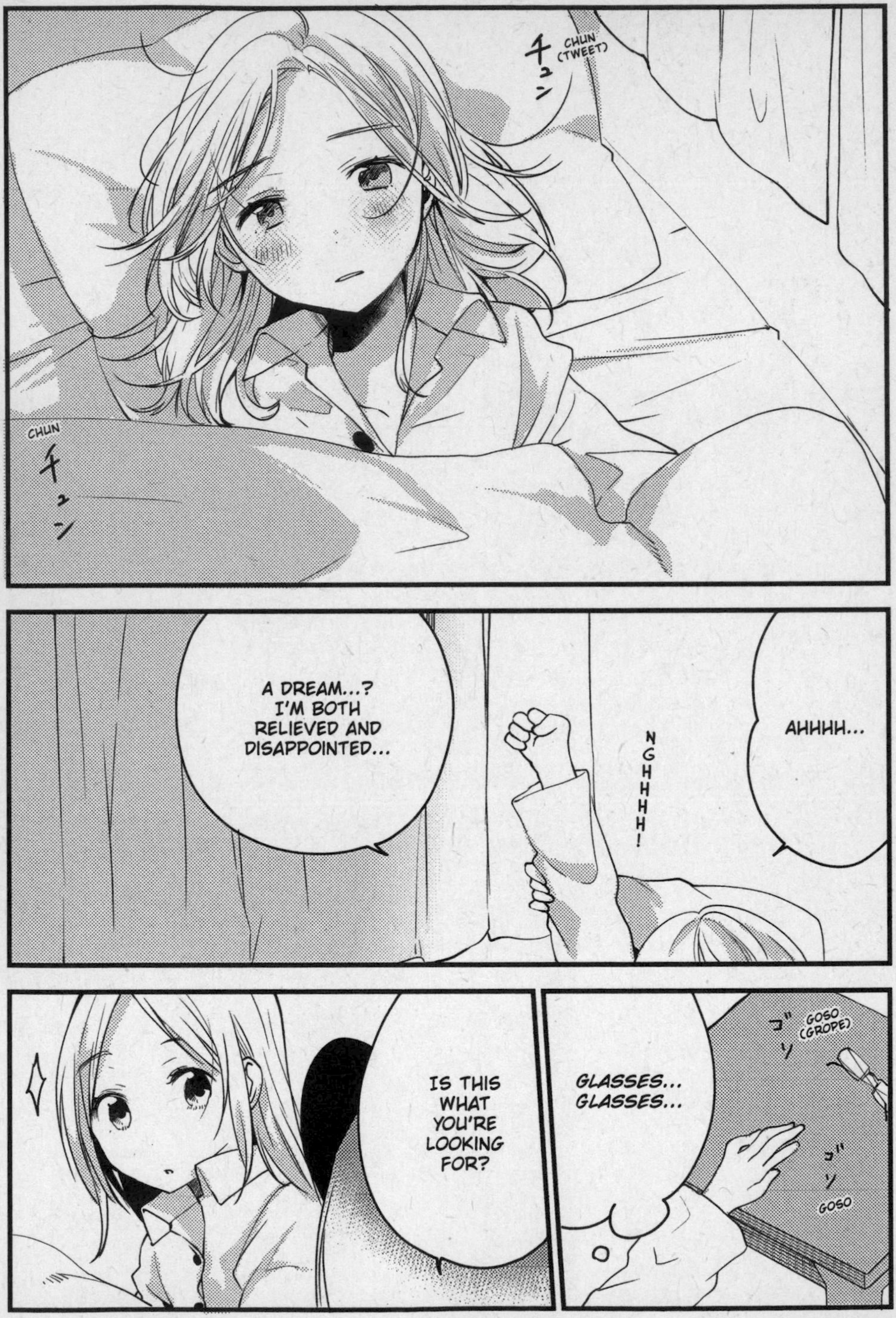
チュン
CHUN (TWEET)
CHUN
チュン
AHHHH...
NGHHHHH!
A DREAM...? I'M BOTH RELIEVED AND DISAPPOINTED...
ゴソ
GOSO (GROPE)
GLASSES... GLASSES...
ゴソ
GOSO
IS THIS WHAT YOU'RE LOOKING FOR?

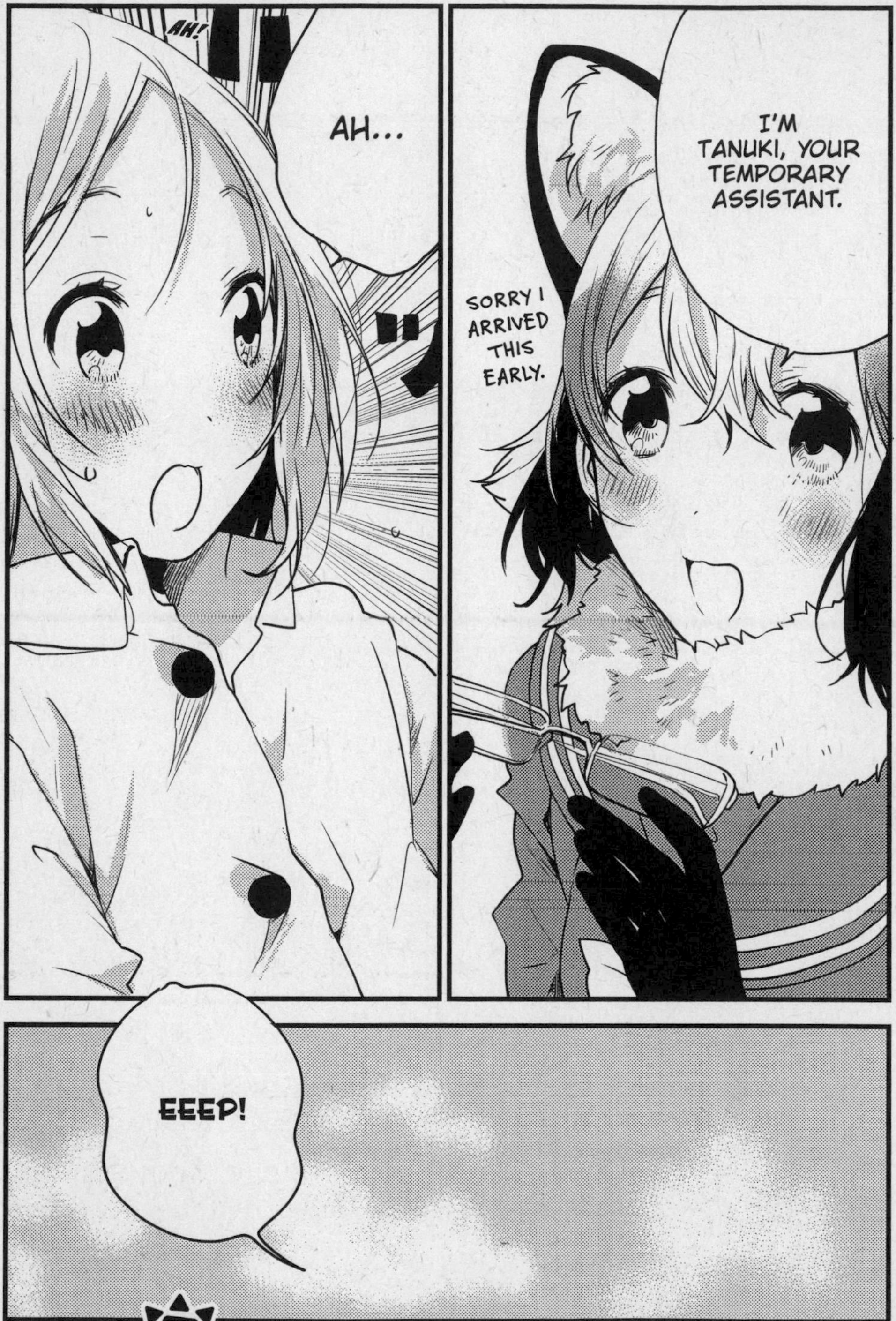
I'M TANUKI, YOUR TEMPORARY ASSISTANT.
SORRY I ARRIVED THIS EARLY.
AH!
AH...
EEEP!

CHAPTER 13 END

KEMONO FRIENDS

WELCOME TO JAPARI PARK!

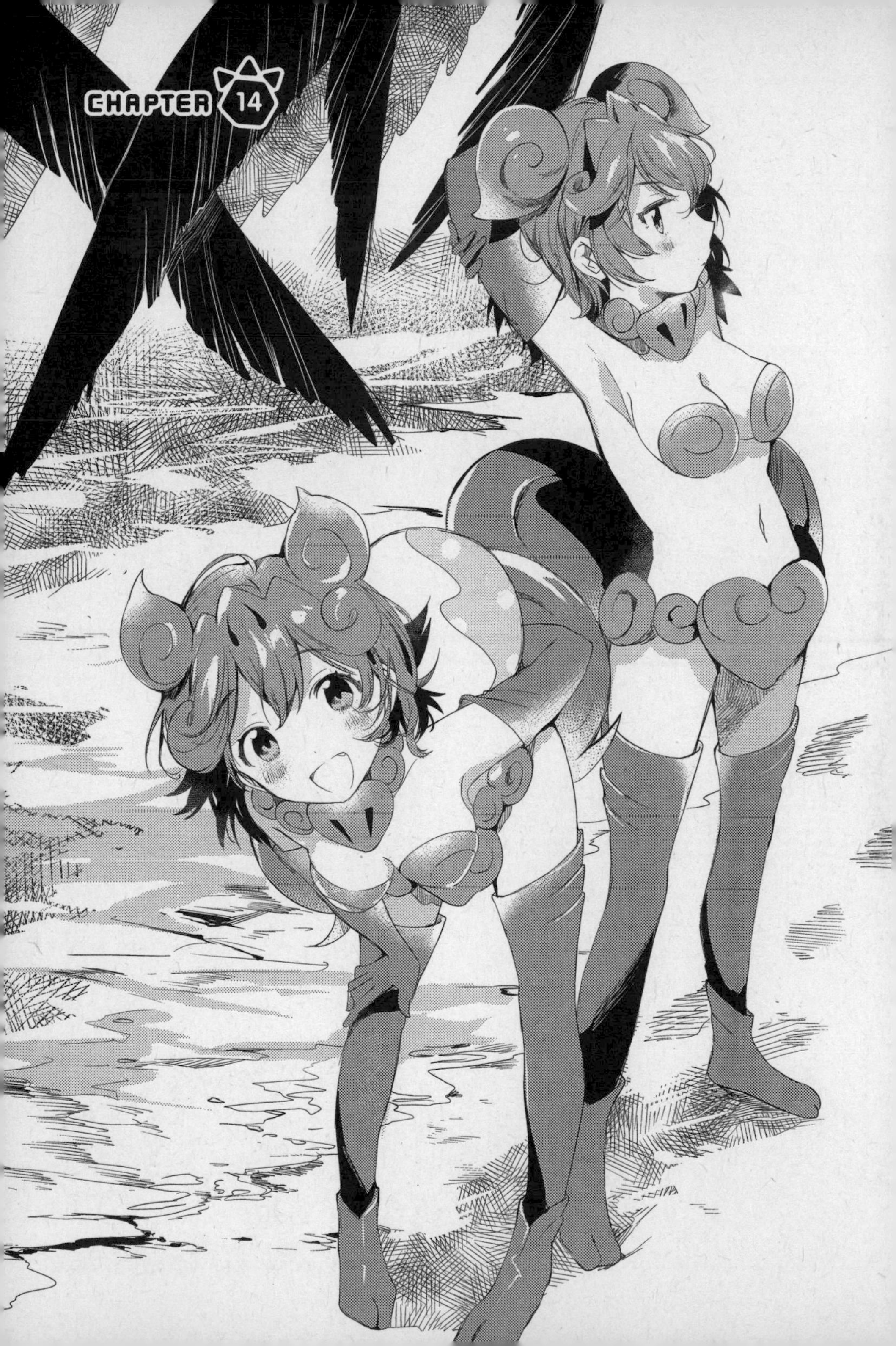
CHAPTER 14

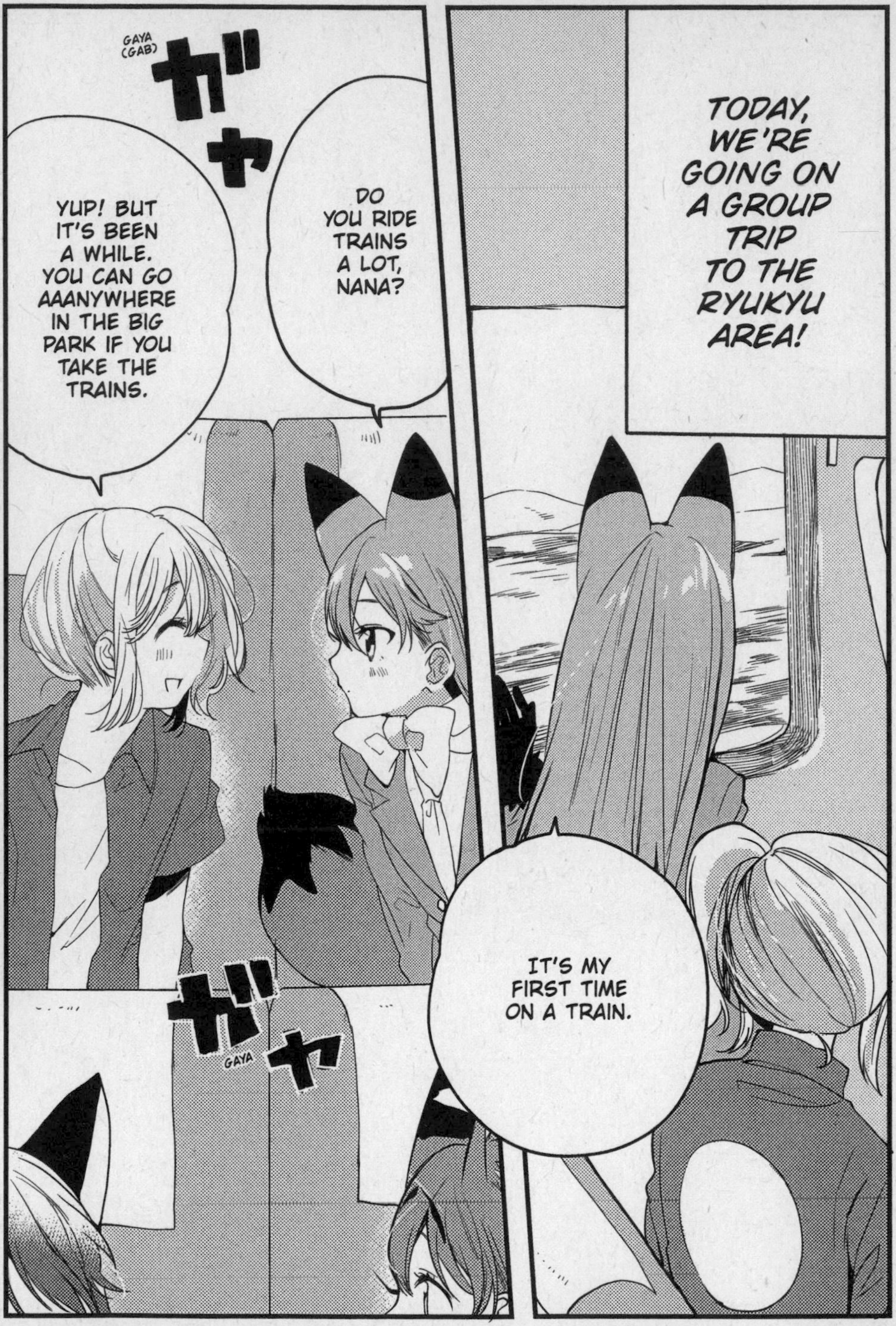
TODAY, WE'RE GOING ON A GROUP TRIP TO THE RYUKYU AREA!
IT'S MY FIRST TIME ON A TRAIN.
GAYA (GAB)
DO YOU RIDE TRAINS A LOT, NANA?
YUP! BUT IT'S BEEN A WHILE. YOU CAN GO AAANYWHERE IN THE BIG PARK IF YOU TAKE THE TRAINS.
GAYA

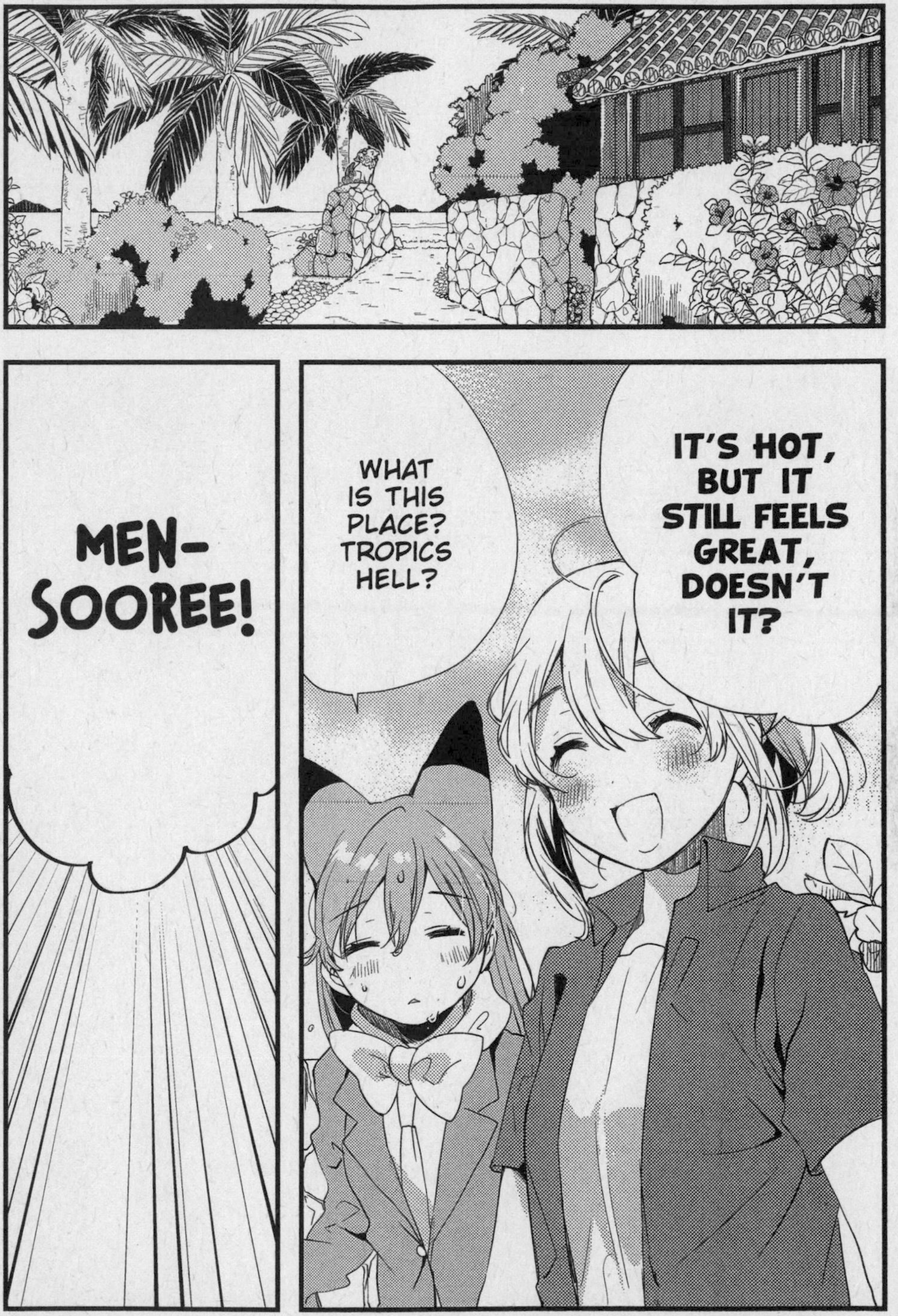
IT'S HOT, BUT IT STILL FEELS GREAT, DOESN'T IT?
WHAT IS THIS PLACE? TROPICS HELL?
MEN-SOOREE!

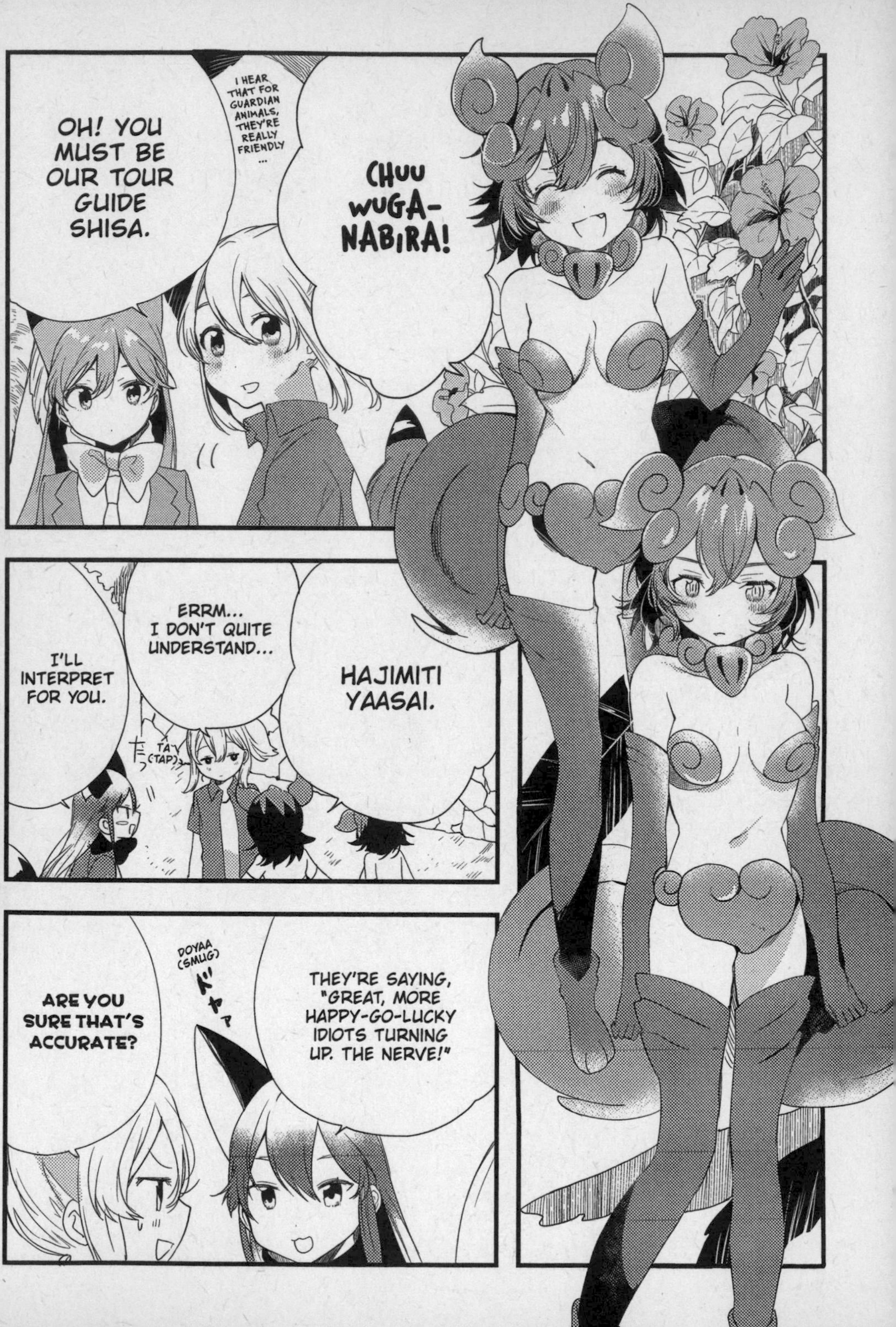
CHUU WUGA-NABIRA!
I HEAR THAT FOR GUARDIAN ANIMALS, THEY'RE REALLY FRIENDLY ...
OH! YOU MUST BE OUR TOUR GUIDE SHISA.
HAJIMITI YAASAI.
ERRM... I DON'T QUITE UNDERSTAND...
TA (TAP)
I'LL INTERPRET FOR YOU.
THEY'RE SAYING, "GREAT, MORE HAPPY-GO-LUCKY IDIOTS TURNING UP. THE NERVE!"
DOYAA (SMUG)
ARE YOU SURE THAT'S ACCURATE?

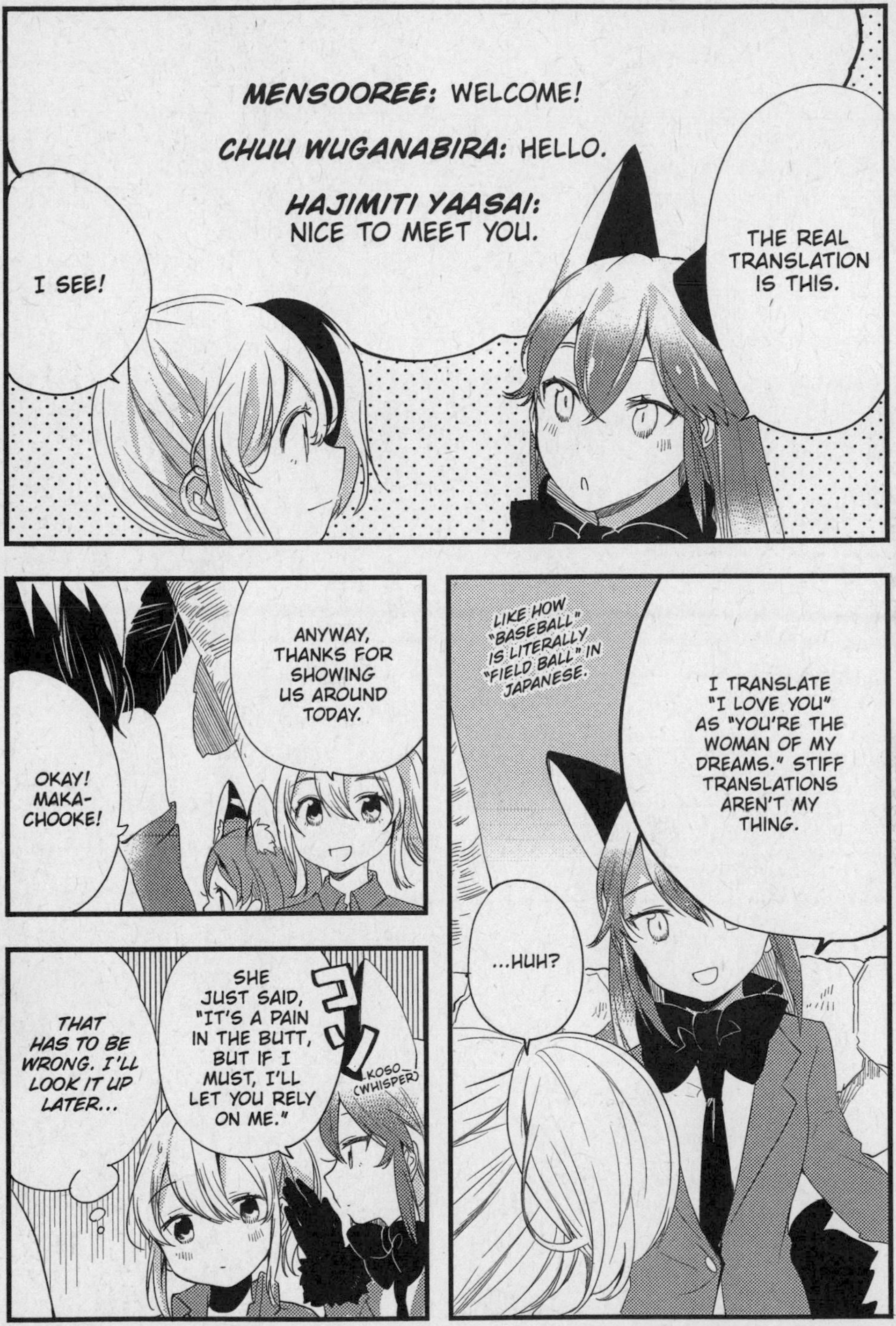
THE REAL TRANSLATION IS THIS.
MENSOOREE: WELCOME!
CHUU WUGANABIRA: HELLO.
HAJIMITI YAASAI: NICE TO MEET YOU.
I SEE!
I TRANSLATE "I LOVE YOU" AS "YOU'RE THE WOMAN OF MY DREAMS." STIFF TRANSLATIONS AREN'T MY THING.
LIKE HOW "BASEBALL" IS LITERALLY "FIELD BALL" IN JAPANESE.
...HUH?
ANYWAY, THANKS FOR SHOWING US AROUND TODAY.
OKAY! MAKA-CHOOKE!
SHE JUST SAID, "IT'S A PAIN IN THE BUTT, BUT IF I MUST, I'LL LET YOU RELY ON ME."
KOSO (WHISPER)
THAT HAS TO BE WRONG. I'LL LOOK IT UP LATER...

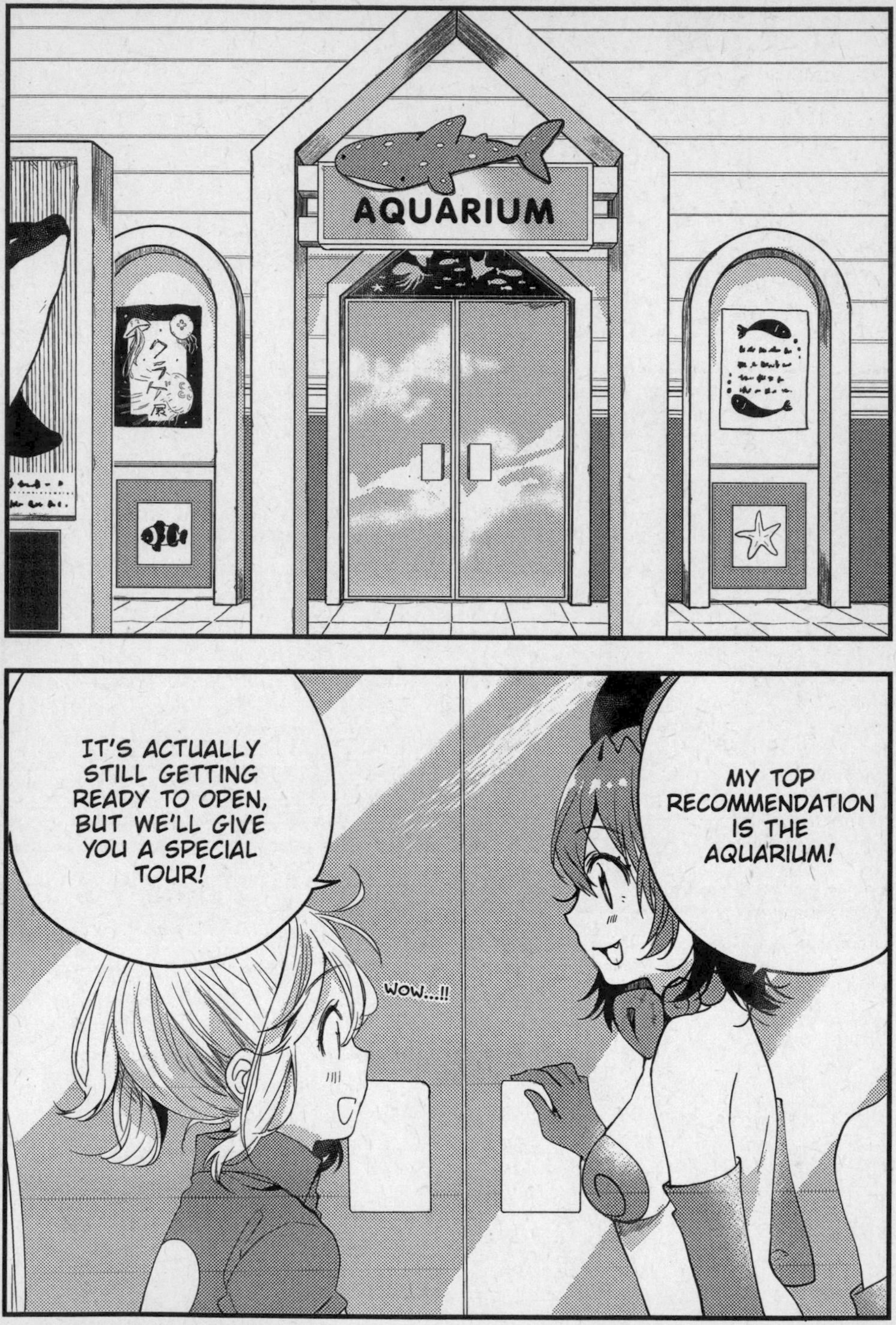
AQUARIUM
クラゲ展
MY TOP RECOMMENDATION IS THE AQUARIUM!
IT'S ACTUALLY STILL GETTING READY TO OPEN, BUT WE'LL GIVE YOU A SPECIAL TOUR!
WOW...!!

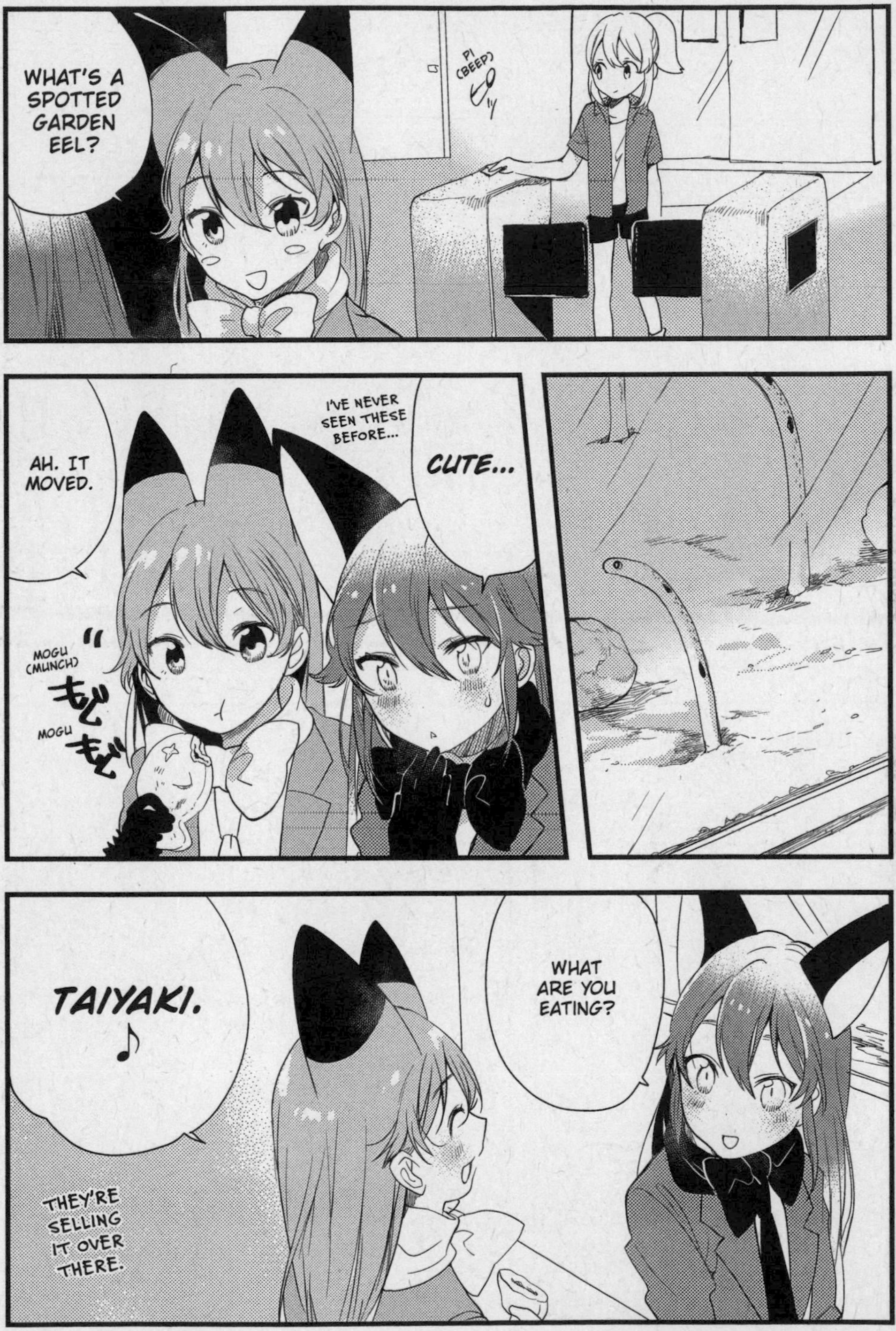
PI (BEEP)
WHAT'S A SPOTTED GARDEN EEL?
I'VE NEVER SEEN THESE BEFORE...
CUTE...
AH. IT MOVED.
MOGU (MUNCH)
MOGU
WHAT ARE YOU EATING?
TAIYAKI. ♪
THEY'RE SELLING IT OVER THERE.

GIFT SHOP
WE'D BETTER BRING SOUVENIRS BACK FOR EVERYONE.
NOW WHAT WOULD BE GOOD...?
LET'S BUY UP ALL THE YUMMY-LOOKING FOODS AND TAKE THEM HOME WITH US.
WE RECOMMEND THE SHIKWASA JUICE.
I'LL GET SOME FOR THE STAFF, THEN.
SHIKWASA JUICE
I WANT THIS.
A SHISA ORNAMENT.

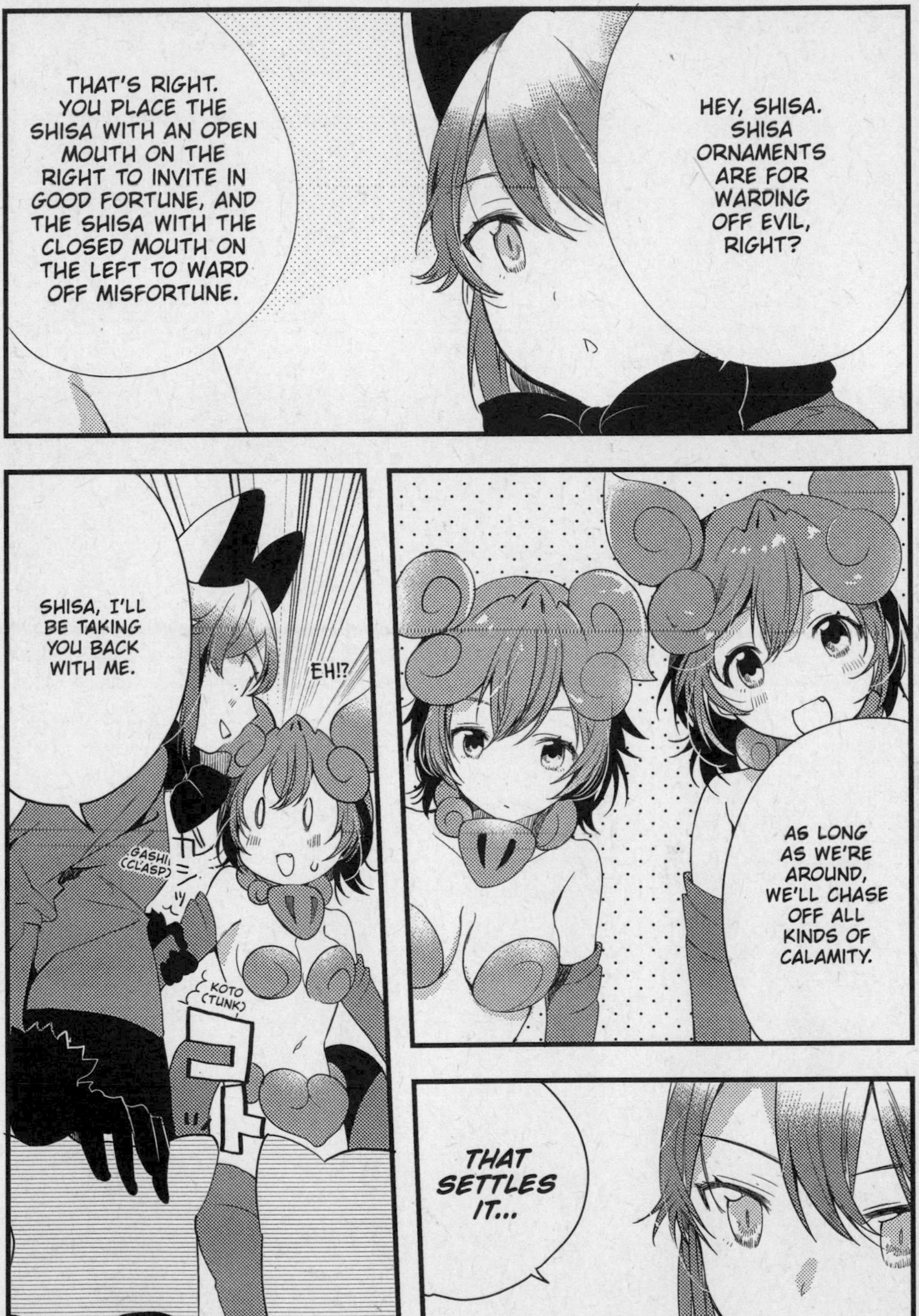
HEY, SHISA. SHISA ORNAMENTS ARE FOR WARDING OFF EVIL, RIGHT?
THAT'S RIGHT. YOU PLACE THE SHISA WITH AN OPEN MOUTH ON THE RIGHT TO INVITE IN GOOD FORTUNE, AND THE SHISA WITH THE CLOSED MOUTH ON THE LEFT TO WARD OFF MISFORTUNE.
AS LONG AS WE'RE AROUND, WE'LL CHASE OFF ALL KINDS OF CALAMITY.
THAT SETTLES IT...
SHISA, I'LL BE TAKING YOU BACK WITH ME.
EH!?
GASHI (CLASP)
KOTO (TUNK)

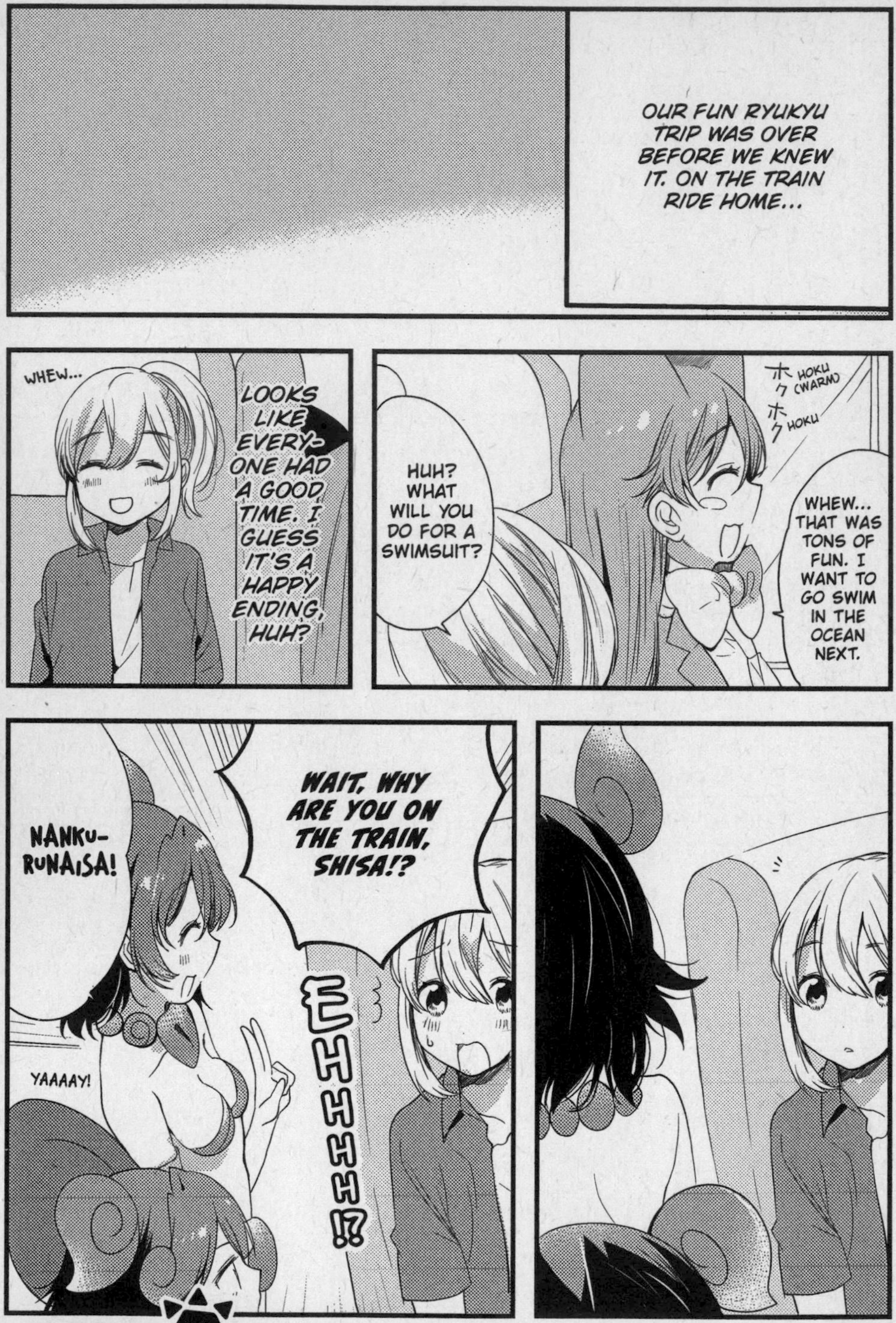
OUR FUN RYUKYU TRIP WAS OVER BEFORE WE KNEW IT. ON THE TRAIN RIDE HOME...
ホクホク HOKU (WARM) HOKU
WHEW... THAT WAS TONS OF FUN. I WANT TO GO SWIM IN THE OCEAN NEXT.
HUH? WHAT WILL YOU DO FOR A SWIMSUIT?
WHEW...
LOOKS LIKE EVERYONE HAD A GOOD TIME. I GUESS IT'S A HAPPY ENDING, HUH?
WAIT, WHY ARE YOU ON THE TRAIN, SHISA!?
EHHHHHH!?
NANKU-RUNAISA!
YAAAAY!

CHAPTER 14 END

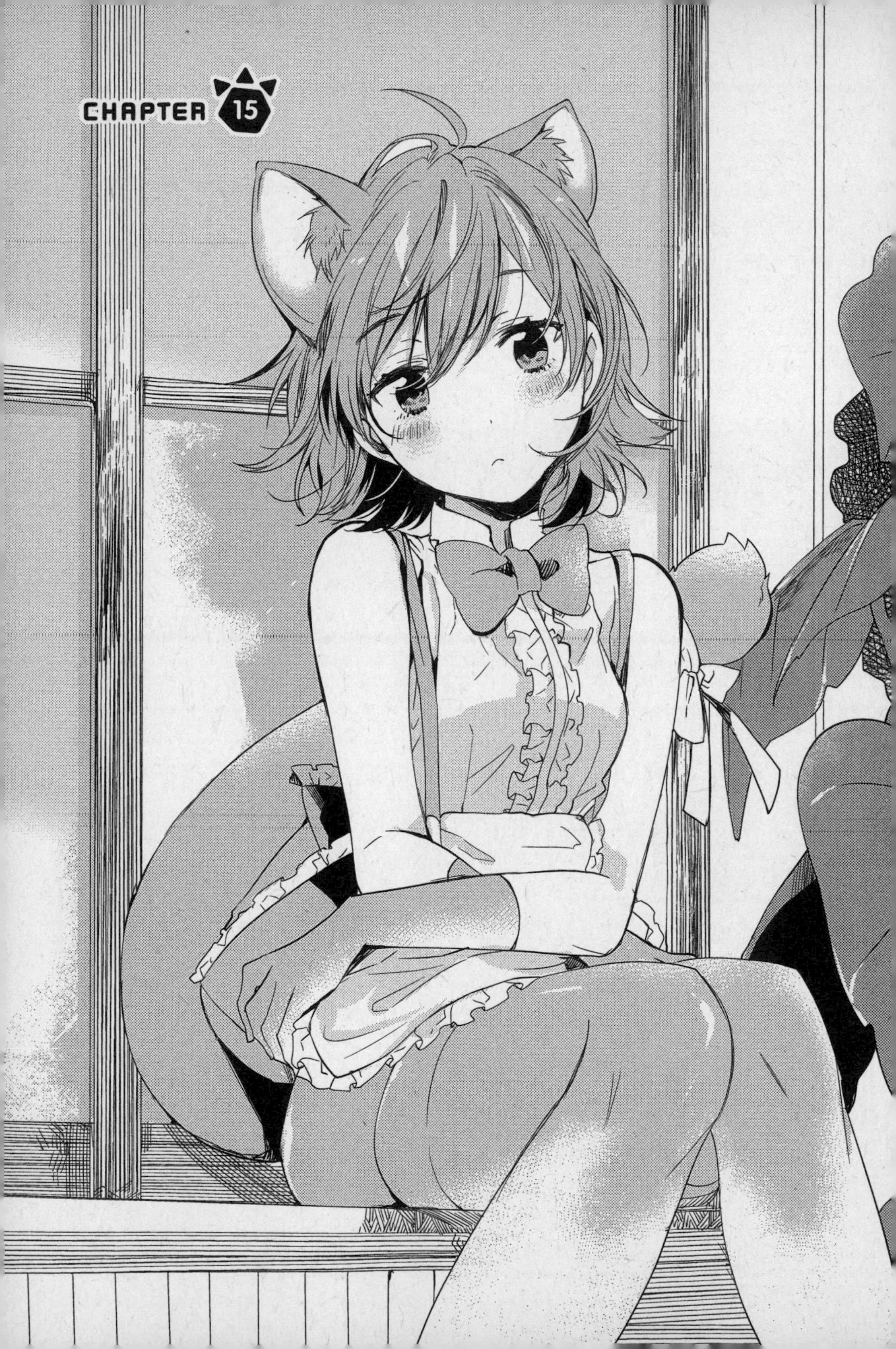
CHAPTER 15

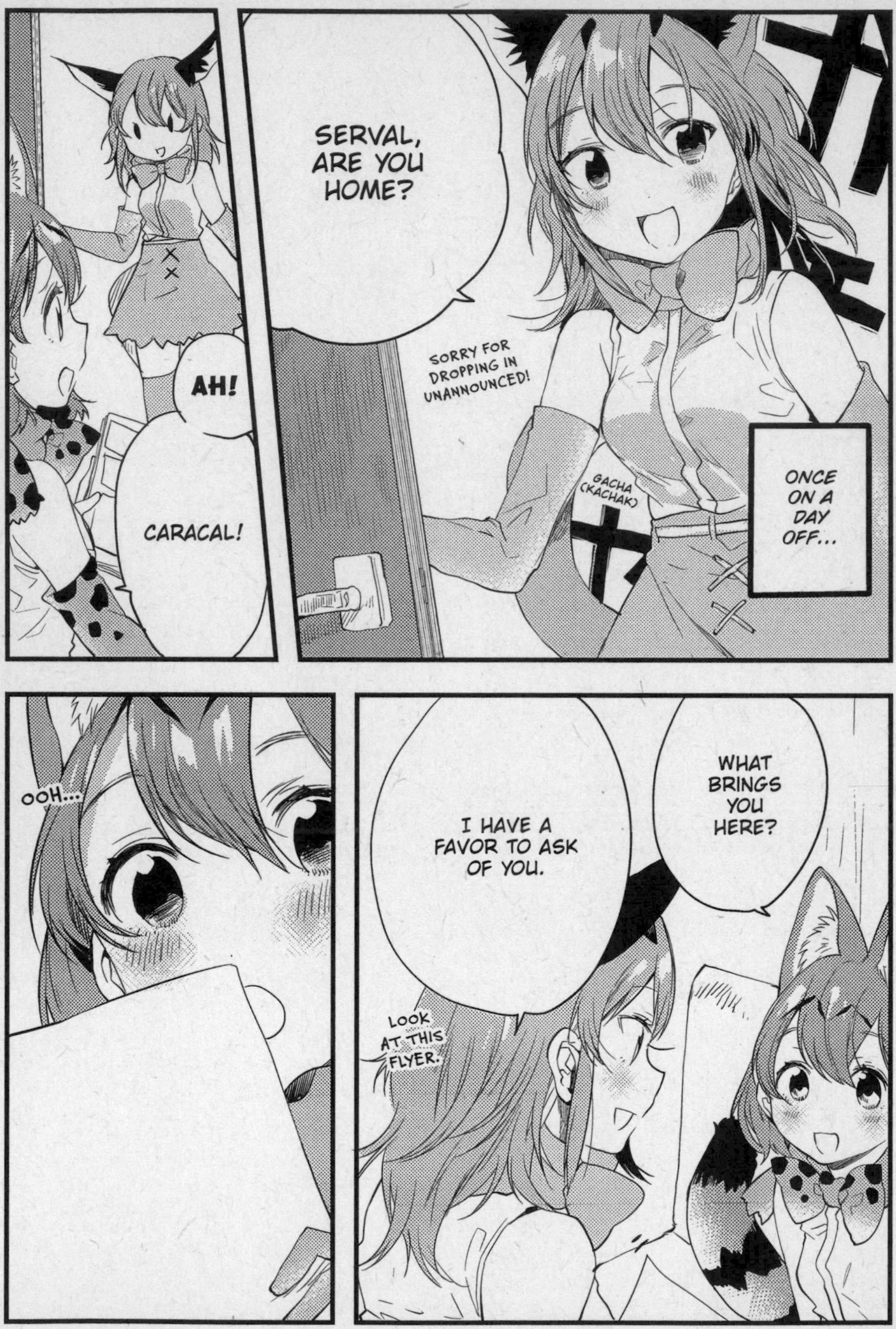
ONCE ON A DAY OFF...
GACHA (KACHAK)
SERVAL, ARE YOU HOME?
SORRY FOR DROPPING IN UNANNOUNCED!
AH!
CARACAL!
WHAT BRINGS YOU HERE?
I HAVE A FAVOR TO ASK OF YOU.
LOOK AT THIS FLYER.
OOH...

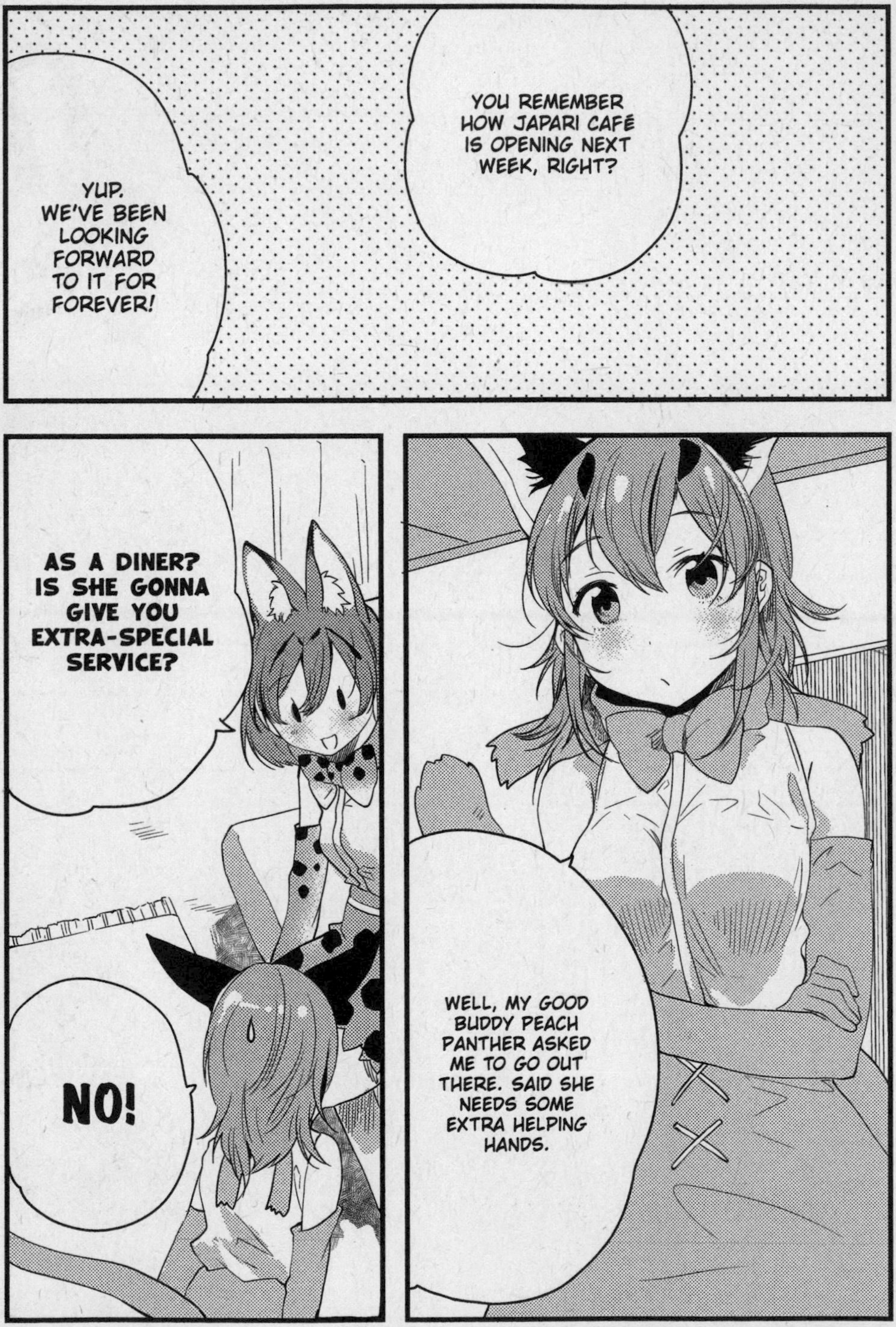
YOU REMEMBER HOW JAPARI CAFÉ IS OPENING NEXT WEEK, RIGHT?
YUP. WE'VE BEEN LOOKING FORWARD TO IT FOR FOREVER!
WELL, MY GOOD BUDDY PEACH PANTHER ASKED ME TO GO OUT THERE. SAID SHE NEEDS SOME EXTRA HELPING HANDS.
AS A DINER? IS SHE GONNA GIVE YOU EXTRA-SPECIAL SERVICE?
NO!

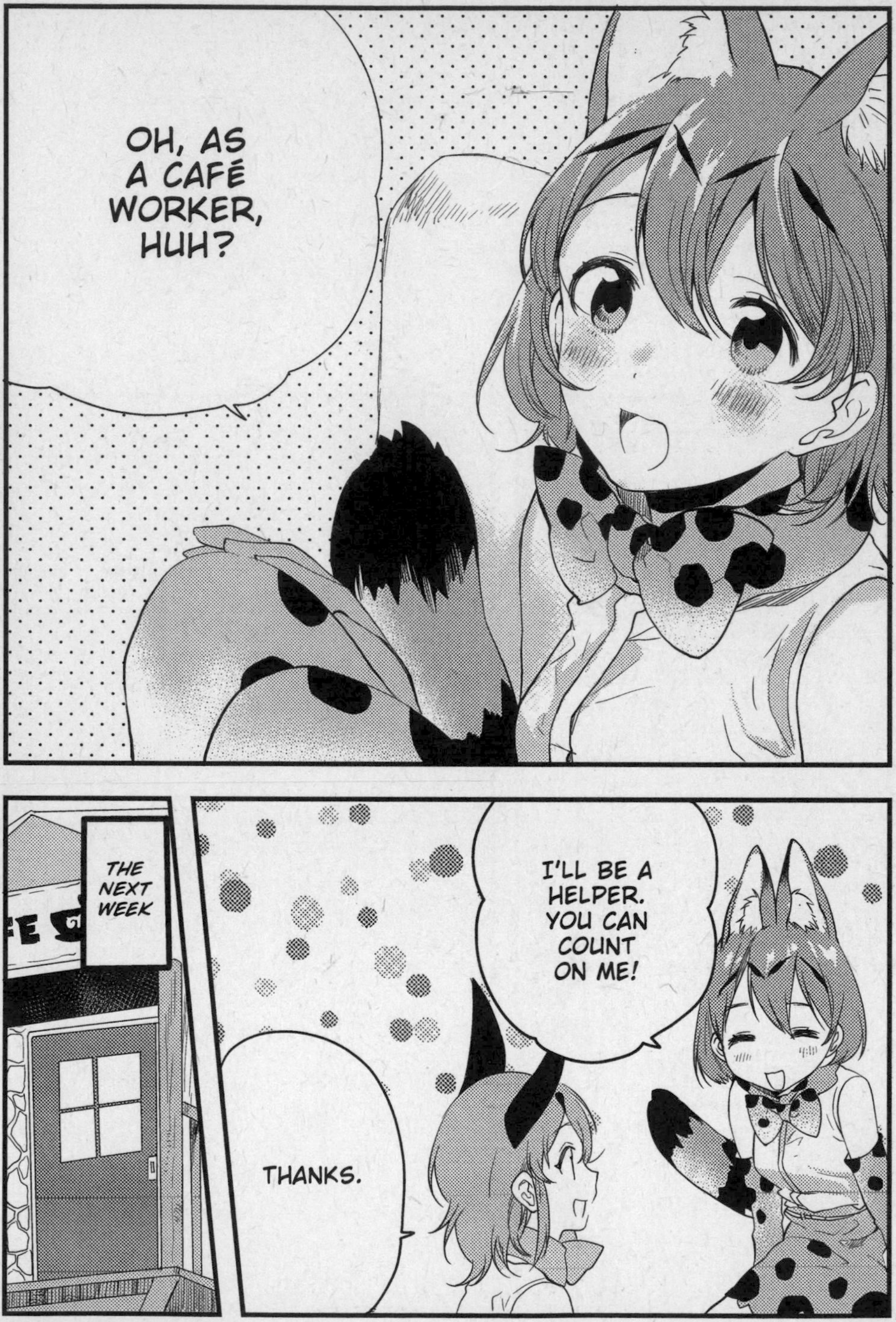
OH, AS A CAFÉ WORKER, HUH?
I'LL BE A HELPER. YOU CAN COUNT ON ME!
THANKS.
THE NEXT WEEK

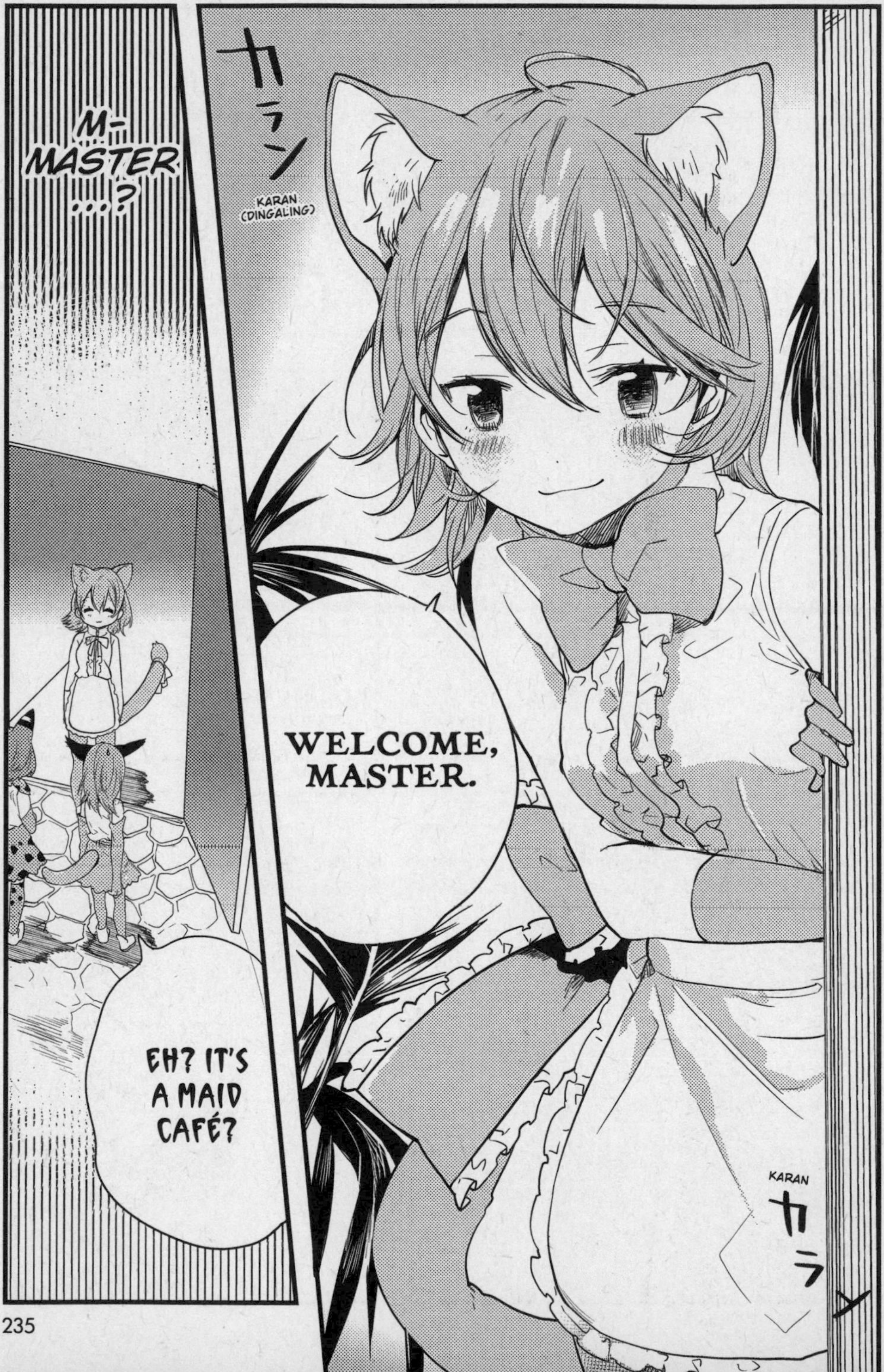
カラン
KARAN (DINGALING)
WELCOME, MASTER.
KARAN
カラン
M-MASTER...?
EH? IT'S A MAID CAFÉ?

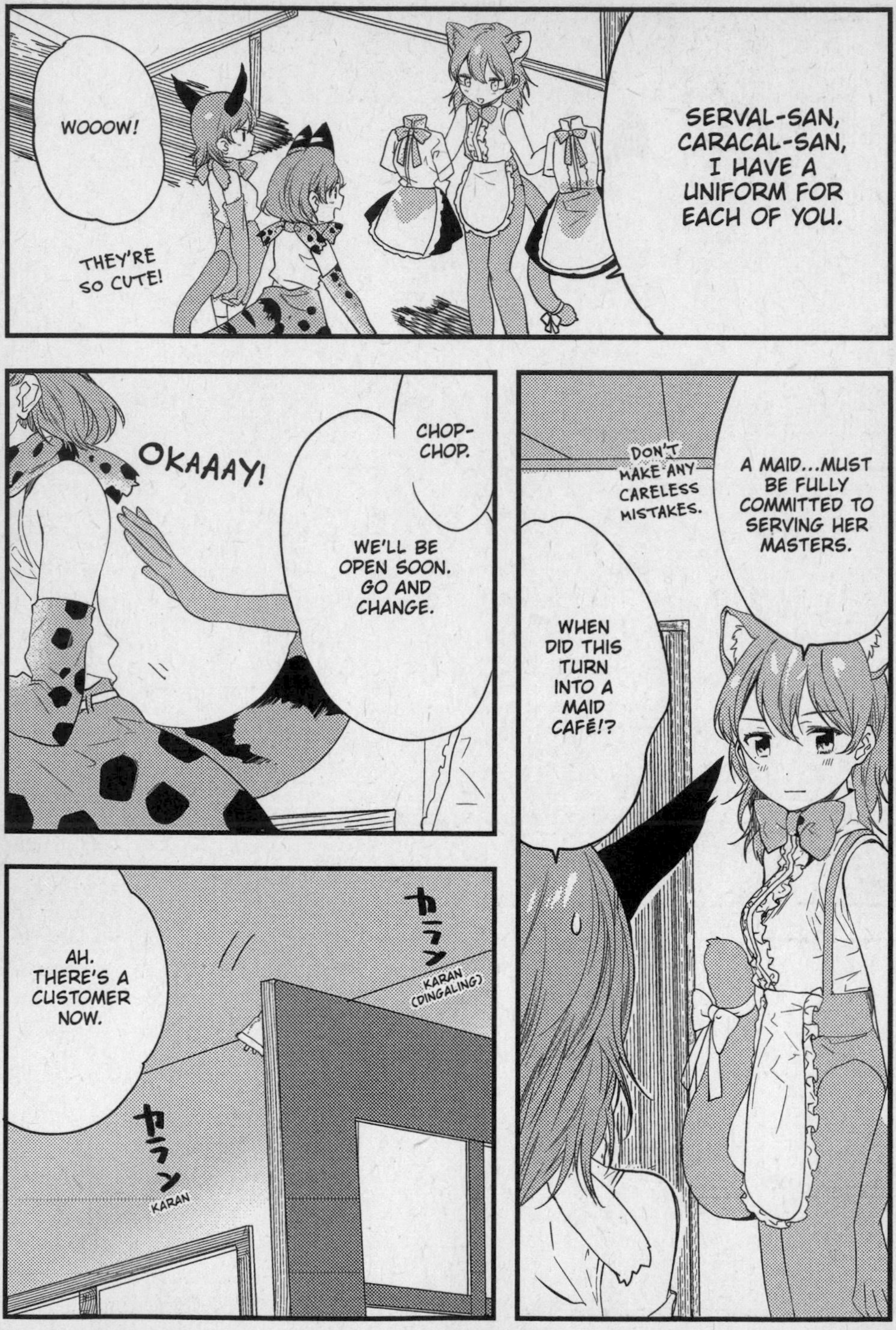

SERVAL-SAN, CARACAL-SAN, I HAVE A UNIFORM FOR EACH OF YOU.
WOOOW!
THEY'RE SO CUTE!
A MAID...MUST BE FULLY COMMITTED TO SERVING HER MASTERS.
DON'T MAKE ANY CARELESS MISTAKES.
WHEN DID THIS TURN INTO A MAID CAFÉ!?
CHOP-CHOP.
WE'LL BE OPEN SOON. GO AND CHANGE.
OKAAAY!
カラン
KARAN (DINGALING)
AH. THERE'S A CUSTOMER NOW.
カラン
KARAN

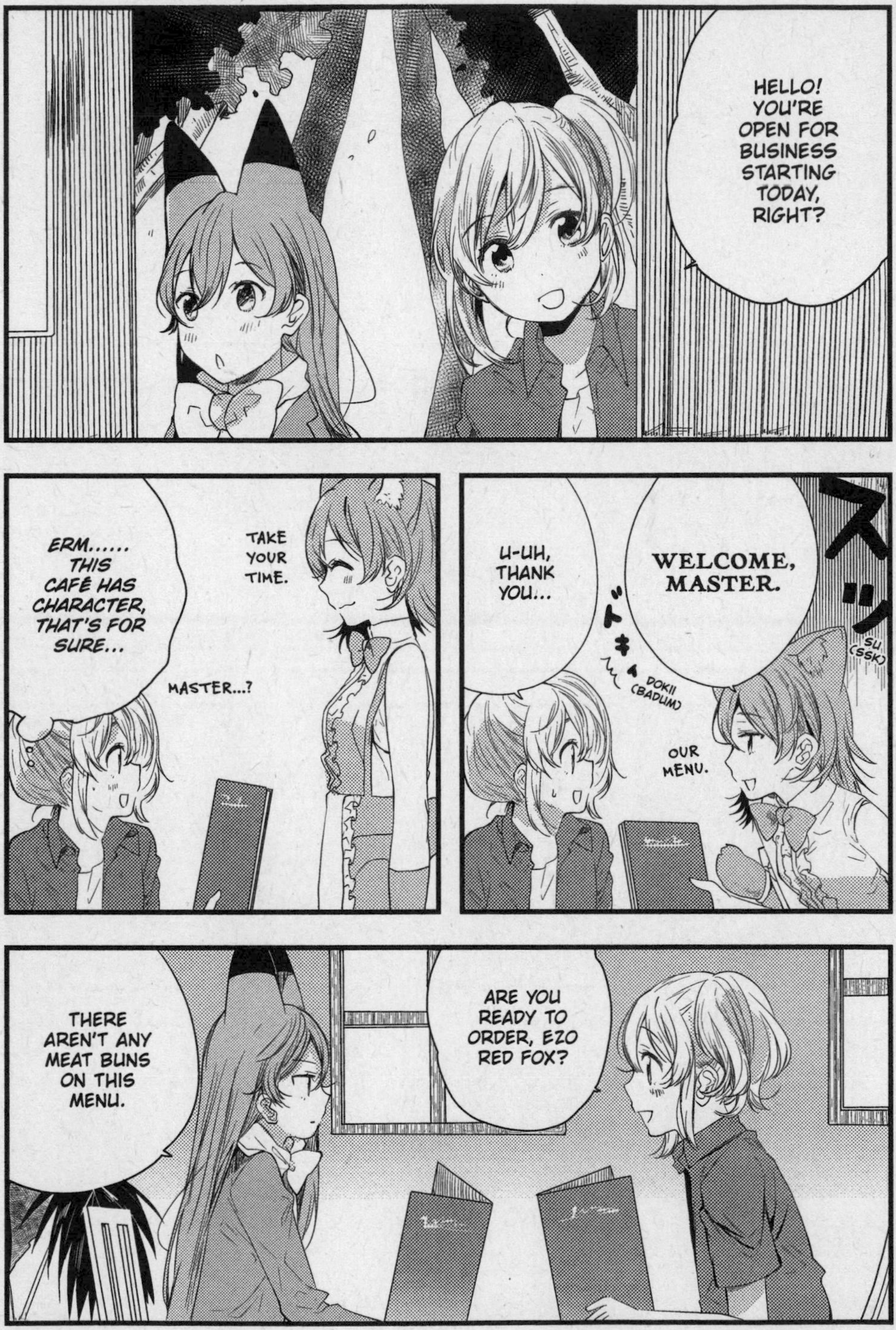
HELLO! YOU'RE OPEN FOR BUSINESS STARTING TODAY, RIGHT?
スッ
SU (SSK)
WELCOME, MASTER.
U-UH, THANK YOU...
DOKII (BADUM)
OUR MENU.
TAKE YOUR TIME.
ERM...... THIS CAFÉ HAS CHARACTER, THAT'S FOR SURE...
MASTER...?
ARE YOU READY TO ORDER, EZO RED FOX?
THERE AREN'T ANY MEAT BUNS ON THIS MENU.

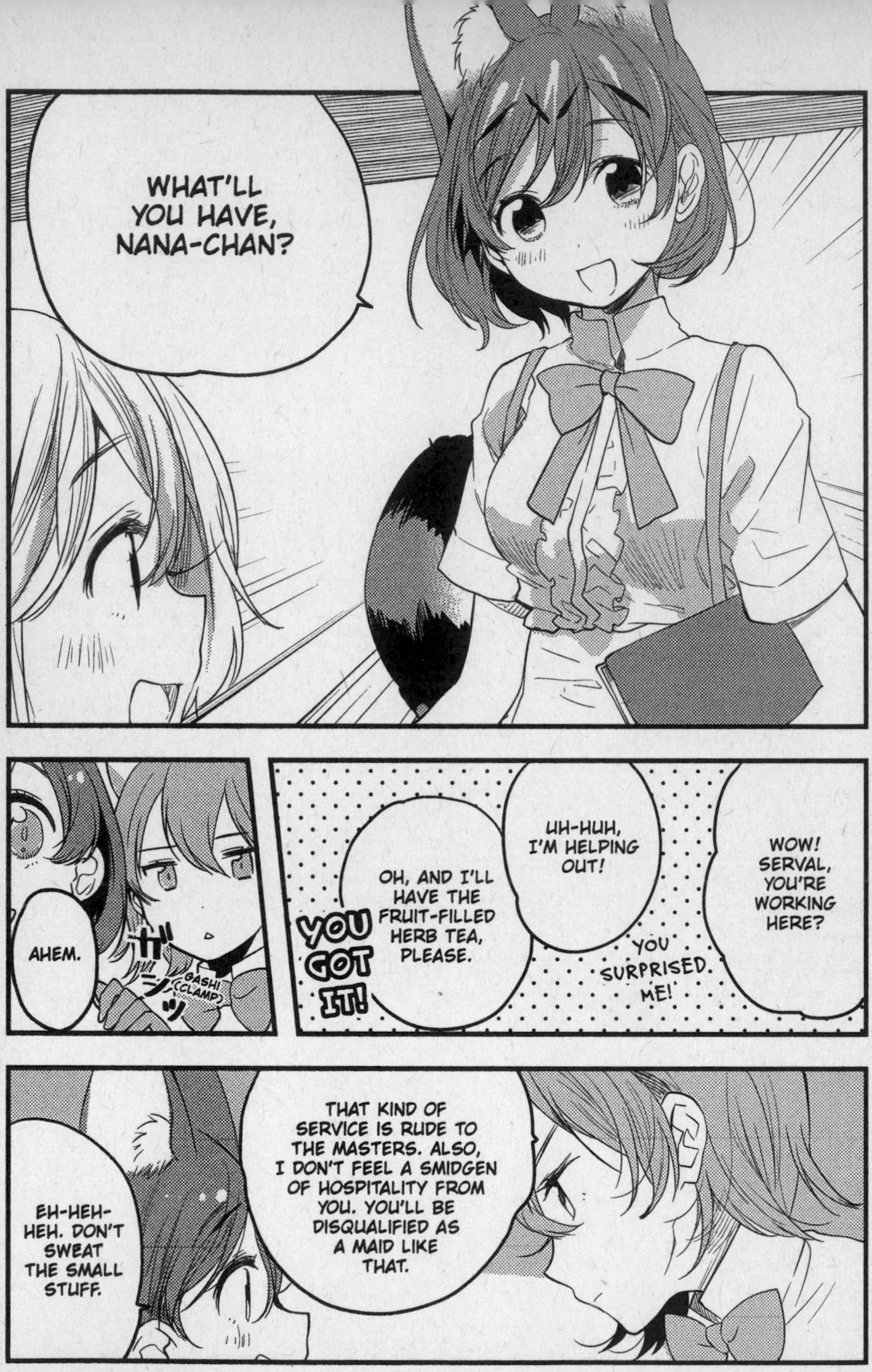
WHAT'LL YOU HAVE, NANA-CHAN?
WOW! SERVAL, YOU'RE WORKING HERE?
UH-HUH, I'M HELPING OUT!
YOU SURPRISED ME!
OH, AND I'LL HAVE THE FRUIT-FILLED HERB TEA, PLEASE.
YOU GOT IT!
GASHI (CLAMP)
AHEM.
THAT KIND OF SERVICE IS RUDE TO THE MASTERS. ALSO, I DON'T FEEL A SMIDGEN OF HOSPITALITY FROM YOU. YOU'LL BE DISQUALIFIED AS A MAID LIKE THAT.
EH-HEH-HEH. DON'T SWEAT THE SMALL STUFF.

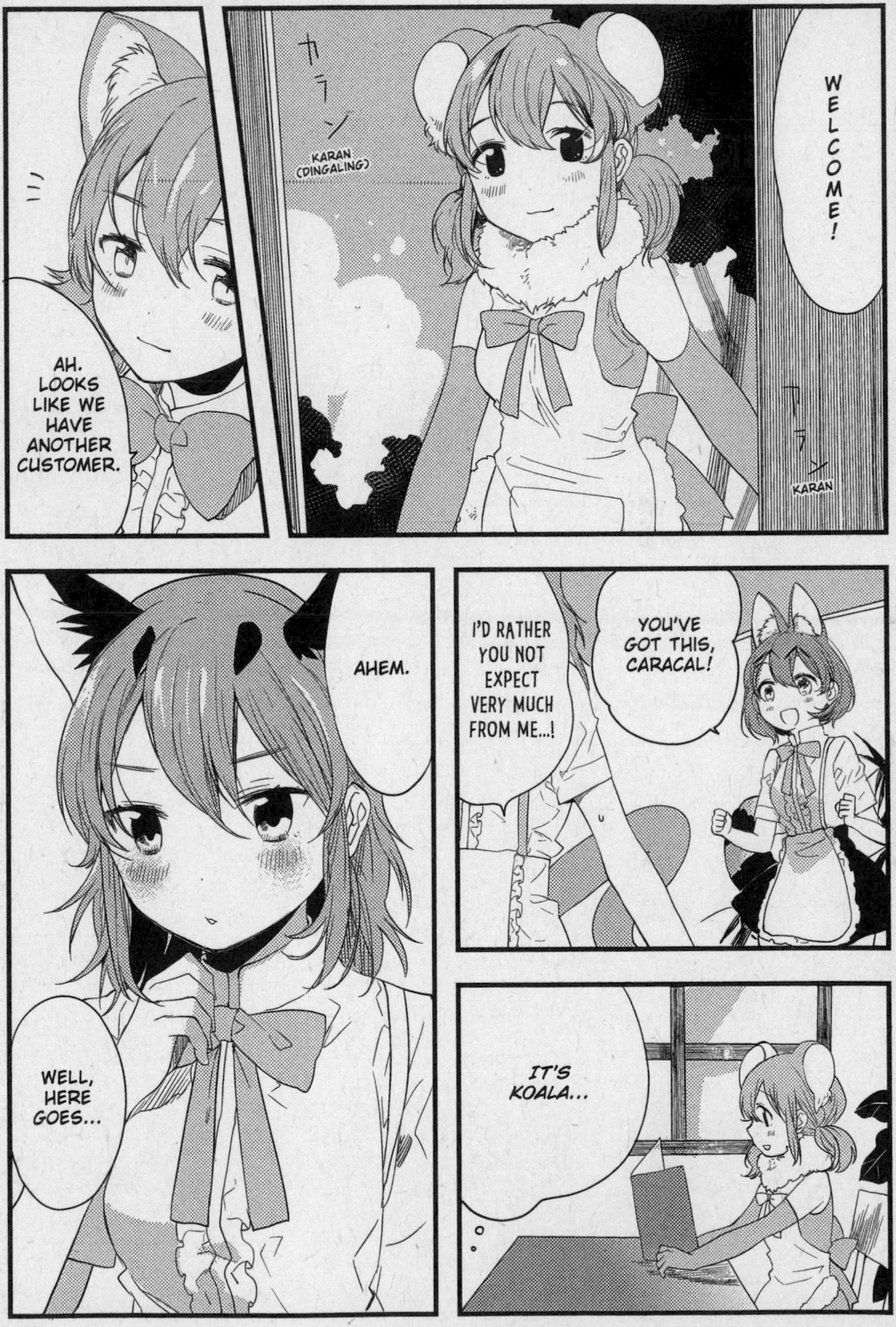
WELCOME!
カラン
KARAN
カラン
KARAN (DINGALING)
AH. LOOKS LIKE WE HAVE ANOTHER CUSTOMER.
YOU'VE GOT THIS, CARACAL!
I'D RATHER YOU NOT EXPECT VERY MUCH FROM ME...!
IT'S KOALA...
AHEM.
WELL, HERE GOES...

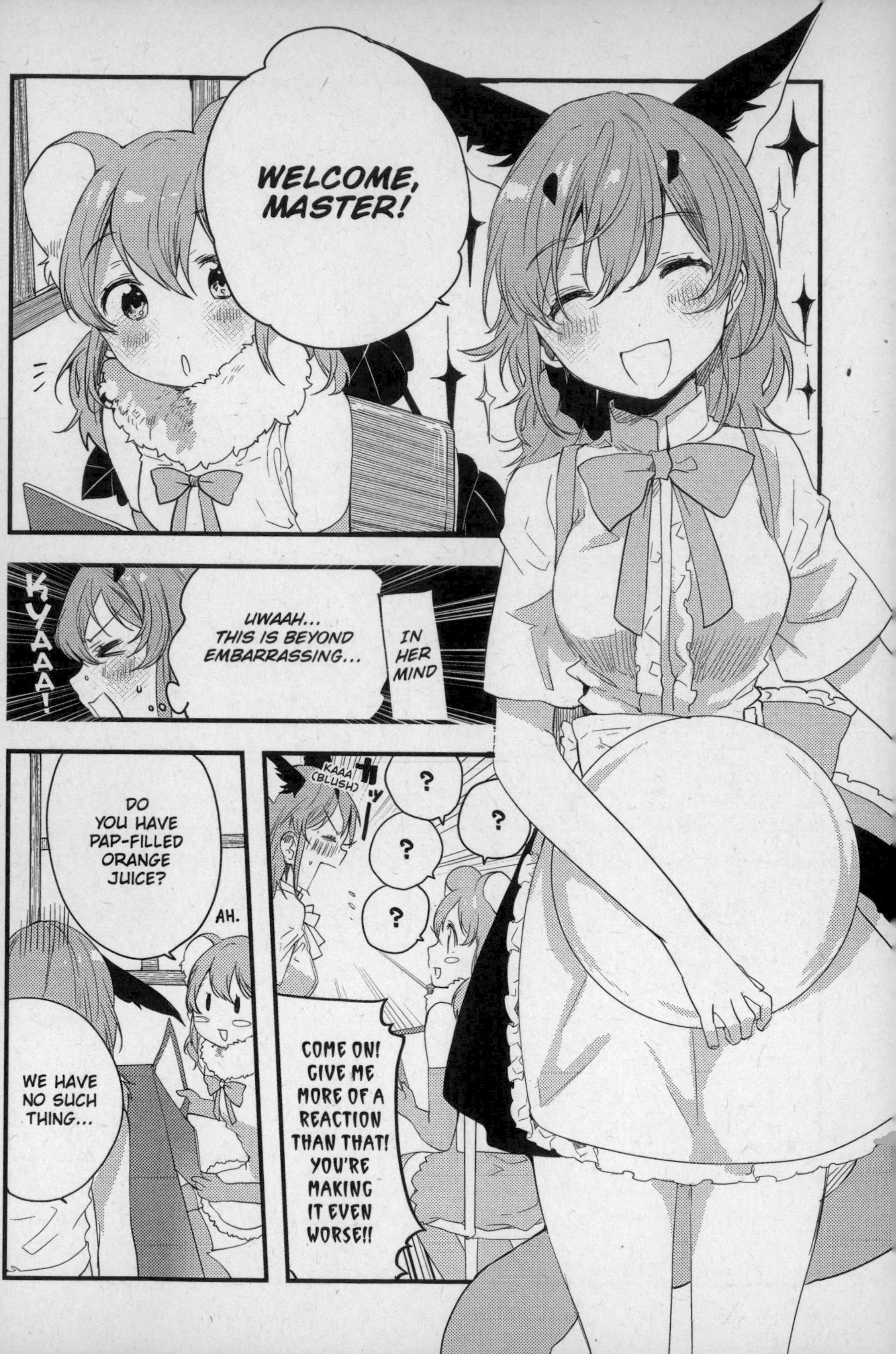
WELCOME, MASTER!
KYAAA!
UWAAH... THIS IS BEYOND EMBARRASSING...
IN HER MIND
KAAA (BLUSH)
?
?
?
?
COME ON! GIVE ME MORE OF A REACTION THAN THAT! YOU'RE MAKING IT EVEN WORSE!!
DO YOU HAVE PAP-FILLED ORANGE JUICE?
AH.
WE HAVE NO SUCH THING...

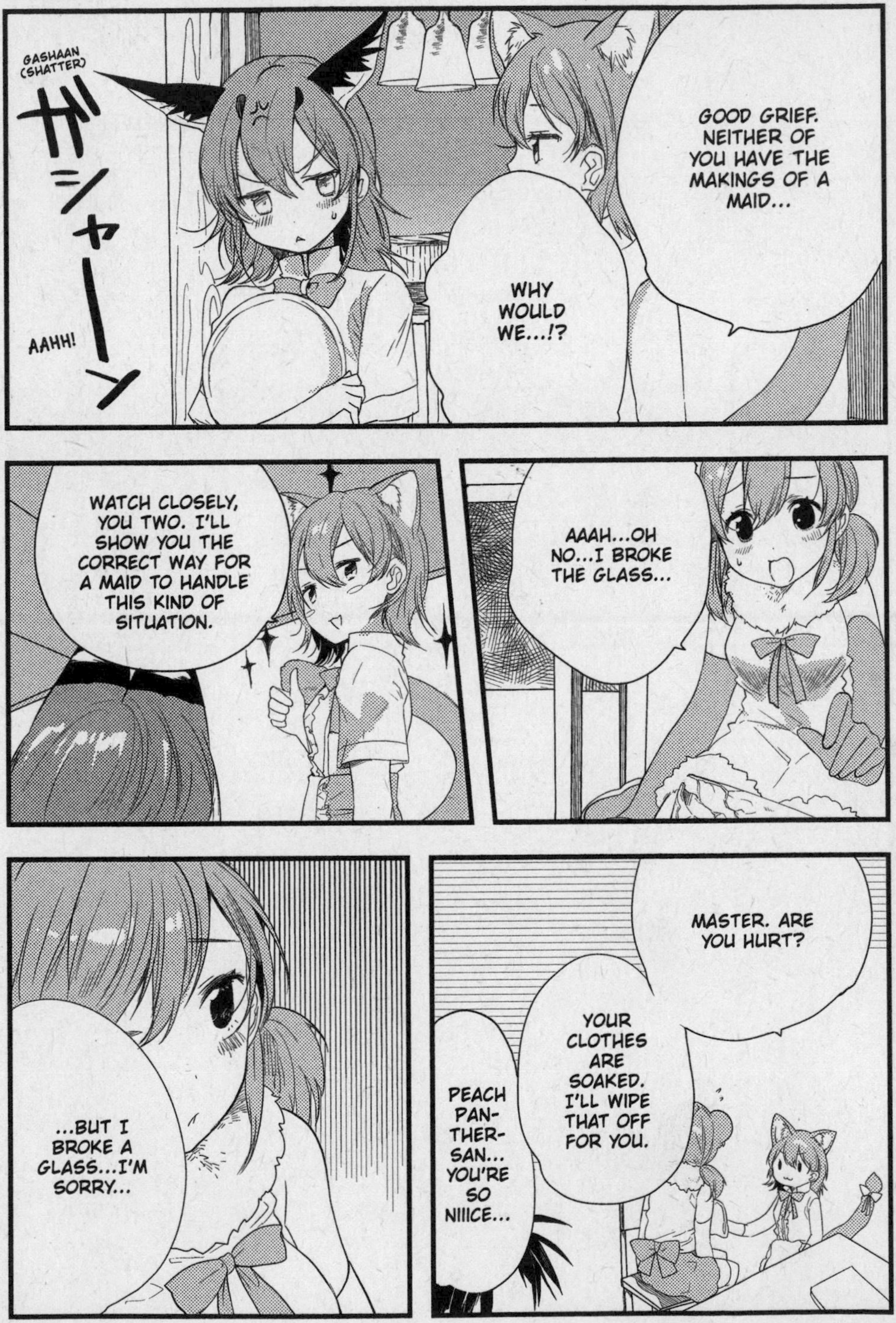
GOOD GRIEF. NEITHER OF YOU HAVE THE MAKINGS OF A MAID...
WHY WOULD WE...!?
ガシャーン
GASHAAN (SHATTER)
AAHH!
AAAH...OH NO...I BROKE THE GLASS...
WATCH CLOSELY, YOU TWO. I'LL SHOW YOU THE CORRECT WAY FOR A MAID TO HANDLE THIS KIND OF SITUATION.
MASTER. ARE YOU HURT?
YOUR CLOTHES ARE SOAKED. I'LL WIPE THAT OFF FOR YOU.
PEACH PANTHER-SAN... YOU'RE SO NIIICE...
...BUT I BROKE A GLASS...I'M SORRY...

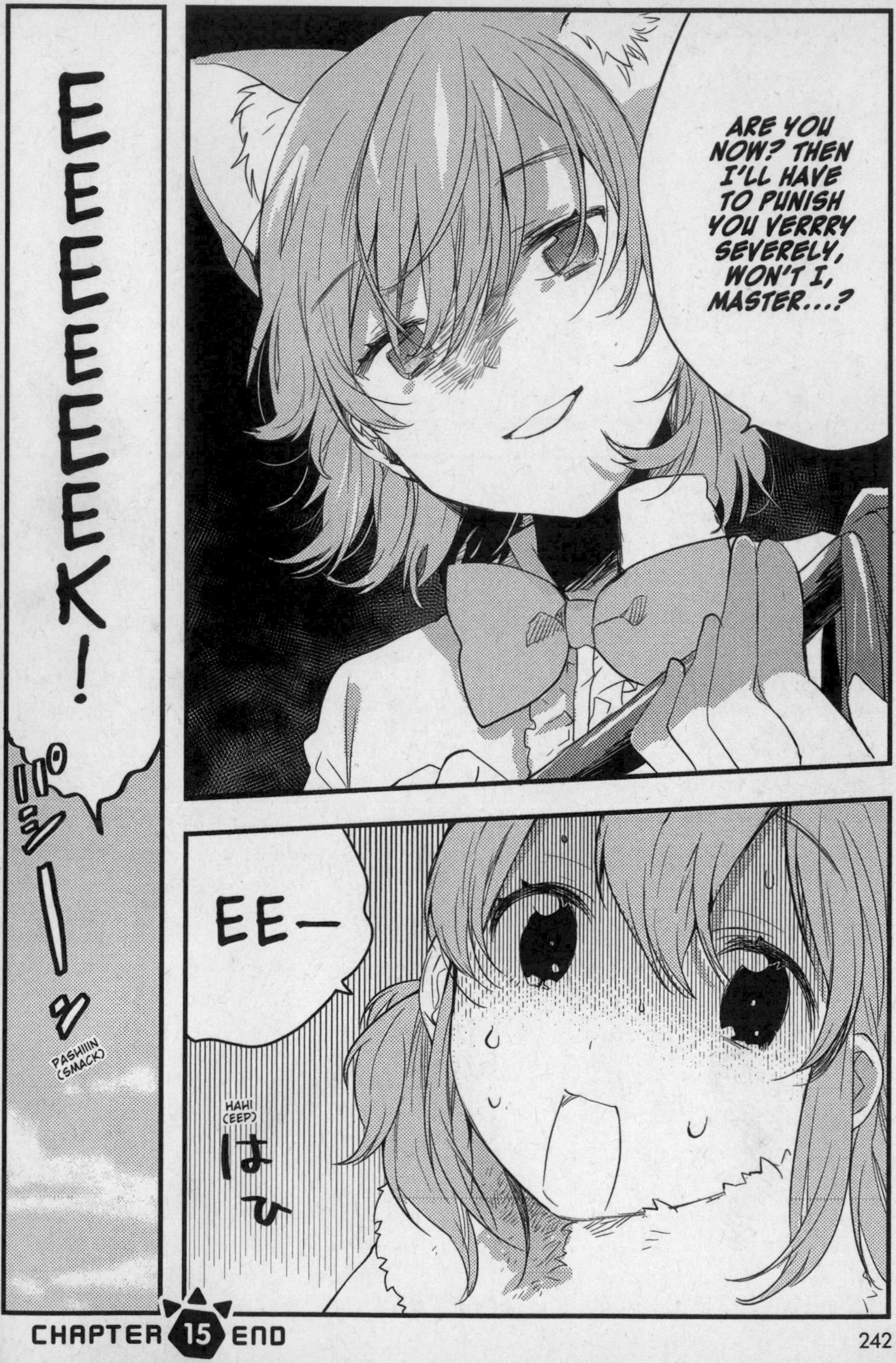
ARE YOU NOW? THEN I'LL HAVE TO PUNISH YOU VERRRY SEVERELY, WON'T I, MASTER...?
EE—
HAHI (EEP)
はひ
EEEEEEEK!
パシーン
PASHIIIN (SMACK)

CHAPTER 15 END

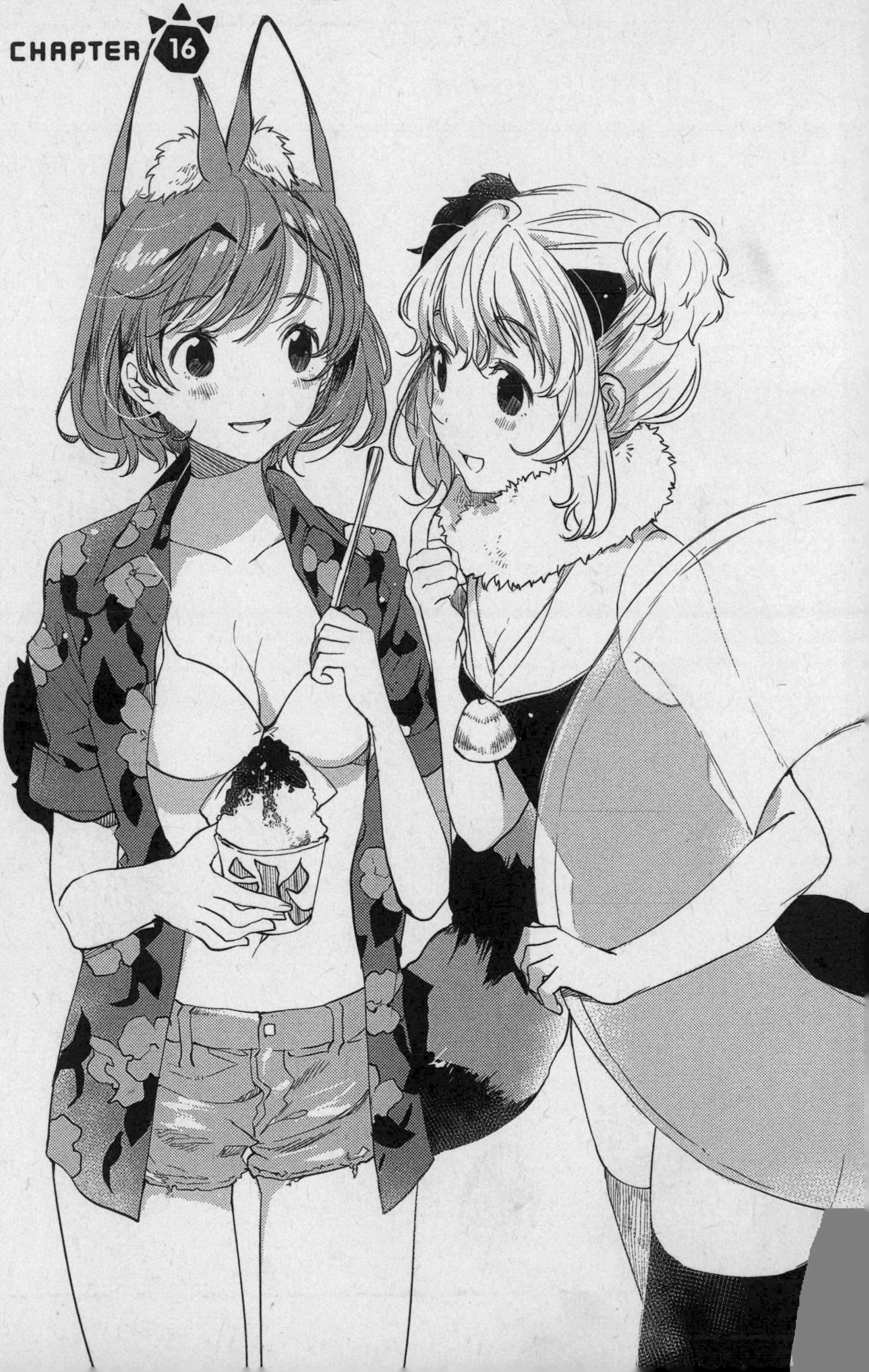
CHAPTER 16

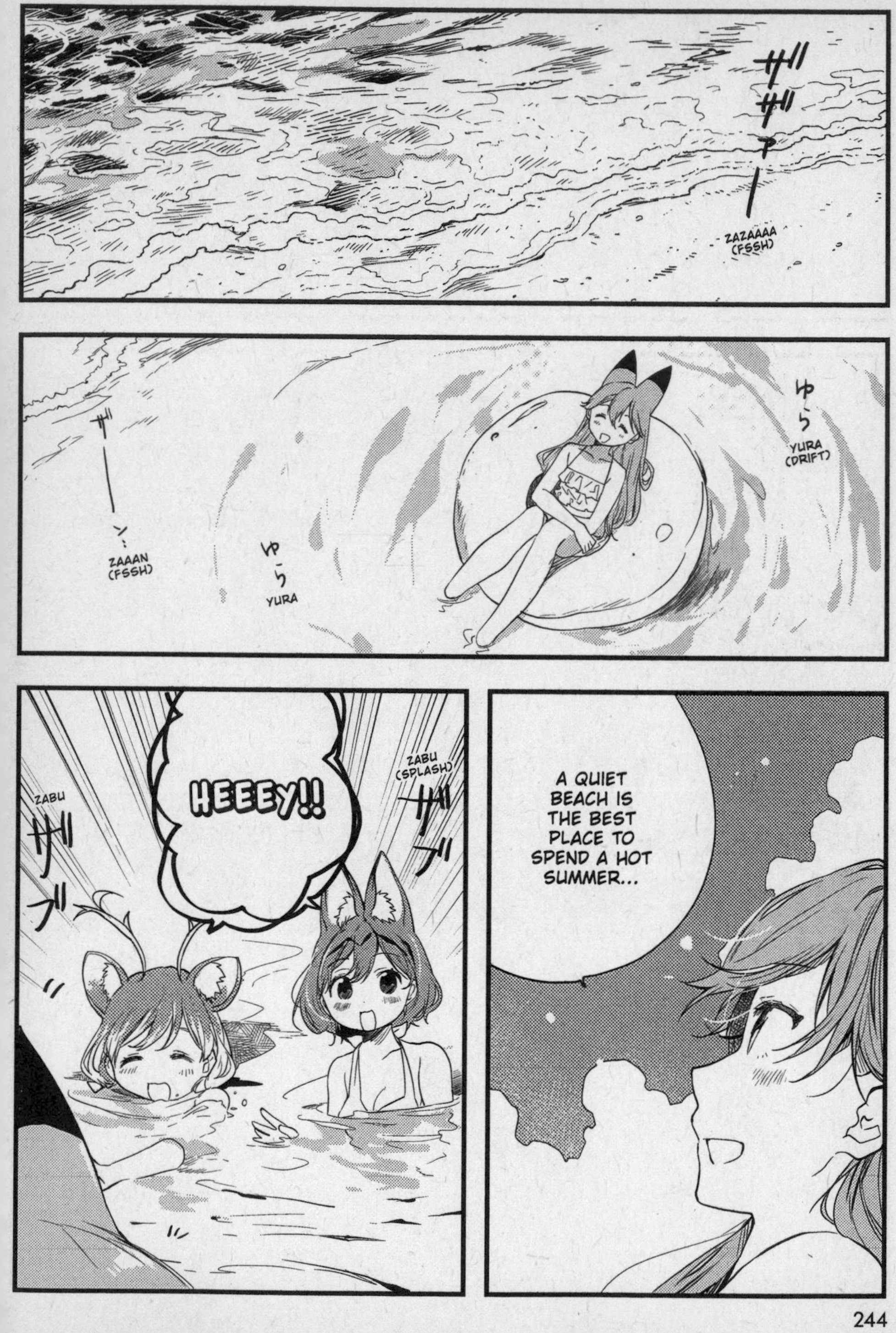
ザザァー
ZAZAAAA (FSSH)
ゆら
YURA (DRIFT)
ゆら
YURA
ザーン
ZAAAN (FSSH)
A QUIET BEACH IS THE BEST PLACE TO SPEND A HOT SUMMER...
ザブ
ZABU (SPLASH)
HEEEY!!
ザブ
ZABU

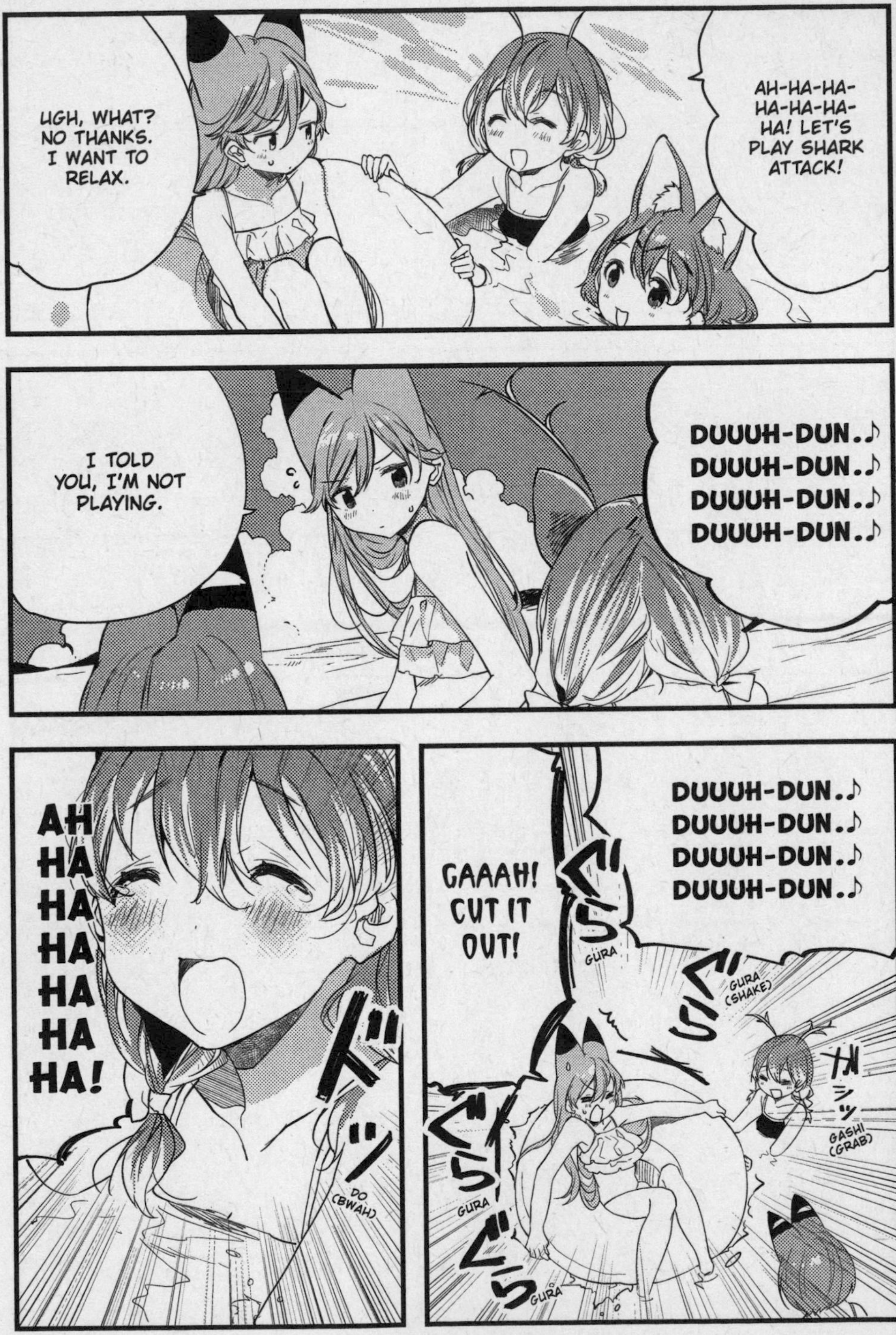
AH-HA-HA-HA-HA-HA-HA! LET'S PLAY SHARK ATTACK!
UGH, WHAT? NO THANKS. I WANT TO RELAX.
DUUUH-DUN.♪ DUUUH-DUN.♪ DUUUH-DUN.♪ DUUUH-DUN.♪
I TOLD YOU, I'M NOT PLAYING.
DUUUH-DUN.♪ DUUUH-DUN.♪ DUUUH-DUN.♪ DUUUH-DUN.♪
GAAAH! CUT IT OUT!
GURA
GURA (SHAKE)
GASHI (GRAB)
GURA
GURA
AH HA HA HA HA HA HA HA!
DO (BWAH)

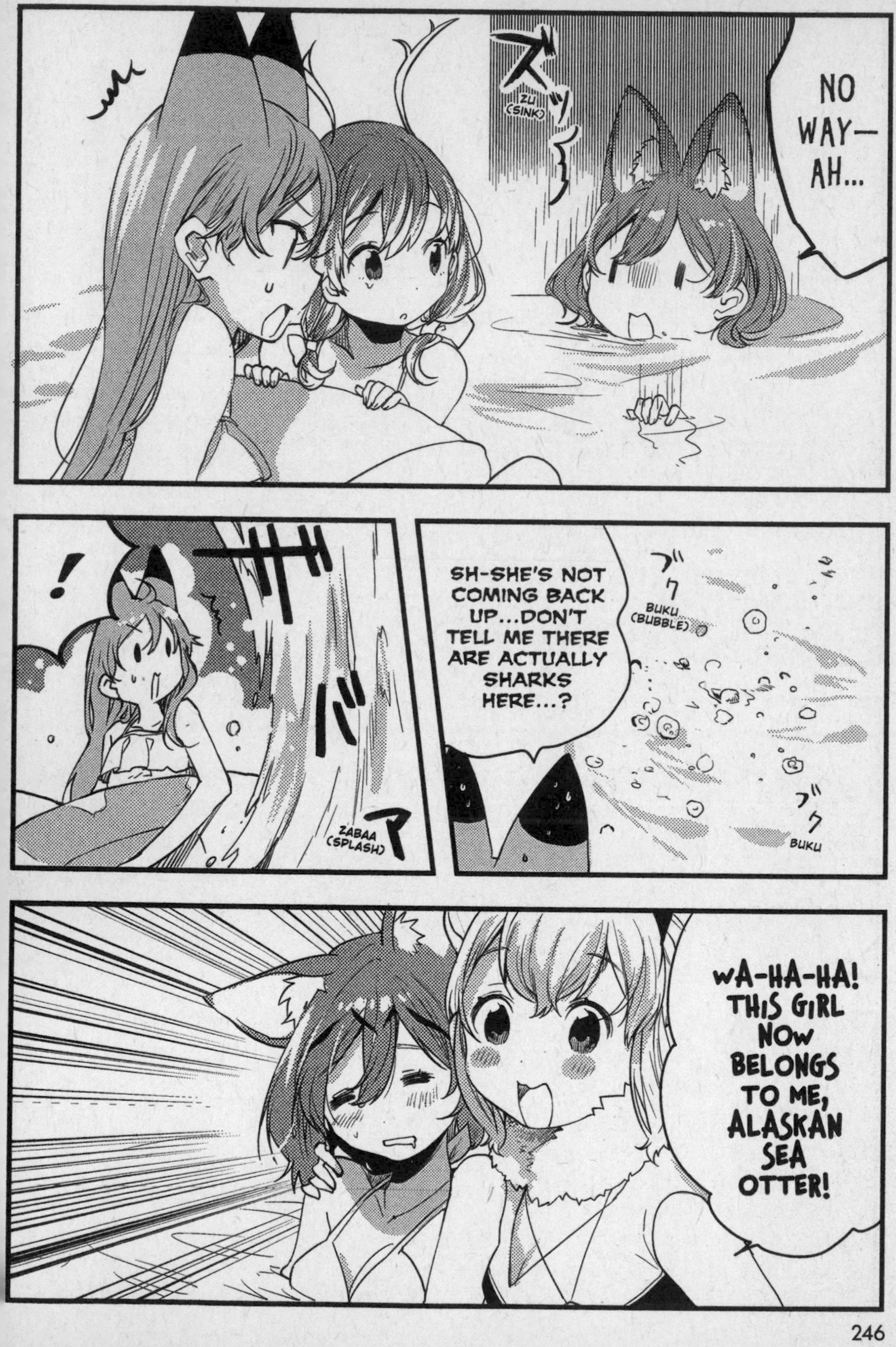
NO WAY—AH...
ZU (SINK)
SH-SHE'S NOT COMING BACK UP...DON'T TELL ME THERE ARE ACTUALLY SHARKS HERE...?
BUKU (BUBBLE)
BUKU
!
ZABAA (SPLASH)
WA-HA-HA! THIS GIRL NOW BELONGS TO ME, ALASKAN SEA OTTER!

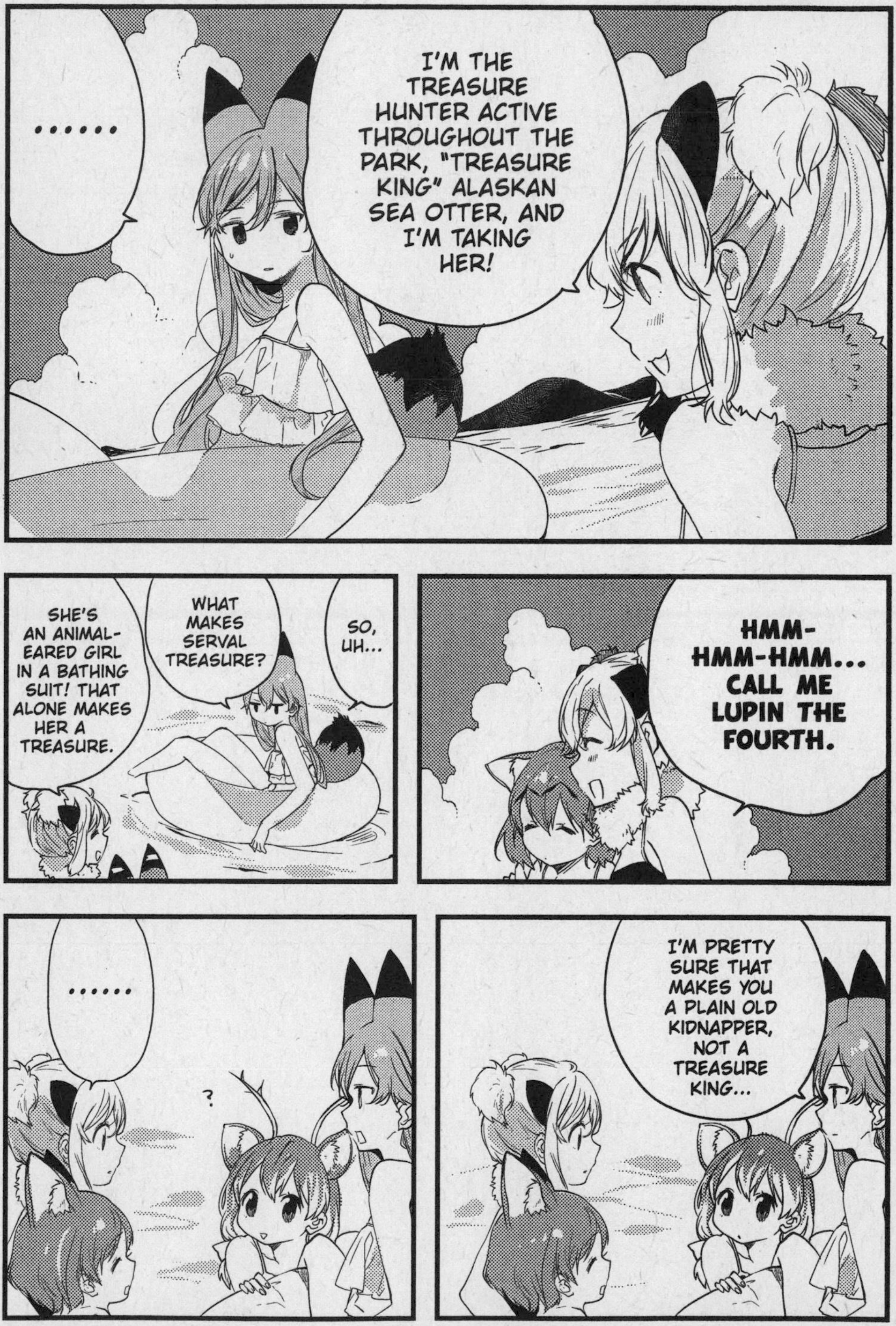
I'M THE TREASURE HUNTER ACTIVE THROUGHOUT THE PARK, "TREASURE KING" ALASKAN SEA OTTER, AND I'M TAKING HER!
......
HMM-HMM-HMM... CALL ME LUPIN THE FOURTH.
SO, UH...
WHAT MAKES SERVAL TREASURE?
SHE'S AN ANIMAL-EARED GIRL IN A BATHING SUIT! THAT ALONE MAKES HER A TREASURE.
I'M PRETTY SURE THAT MAKES YOU A PLAIN OLD KIDNAPPER, NOT A TREASURE KING...
......
?

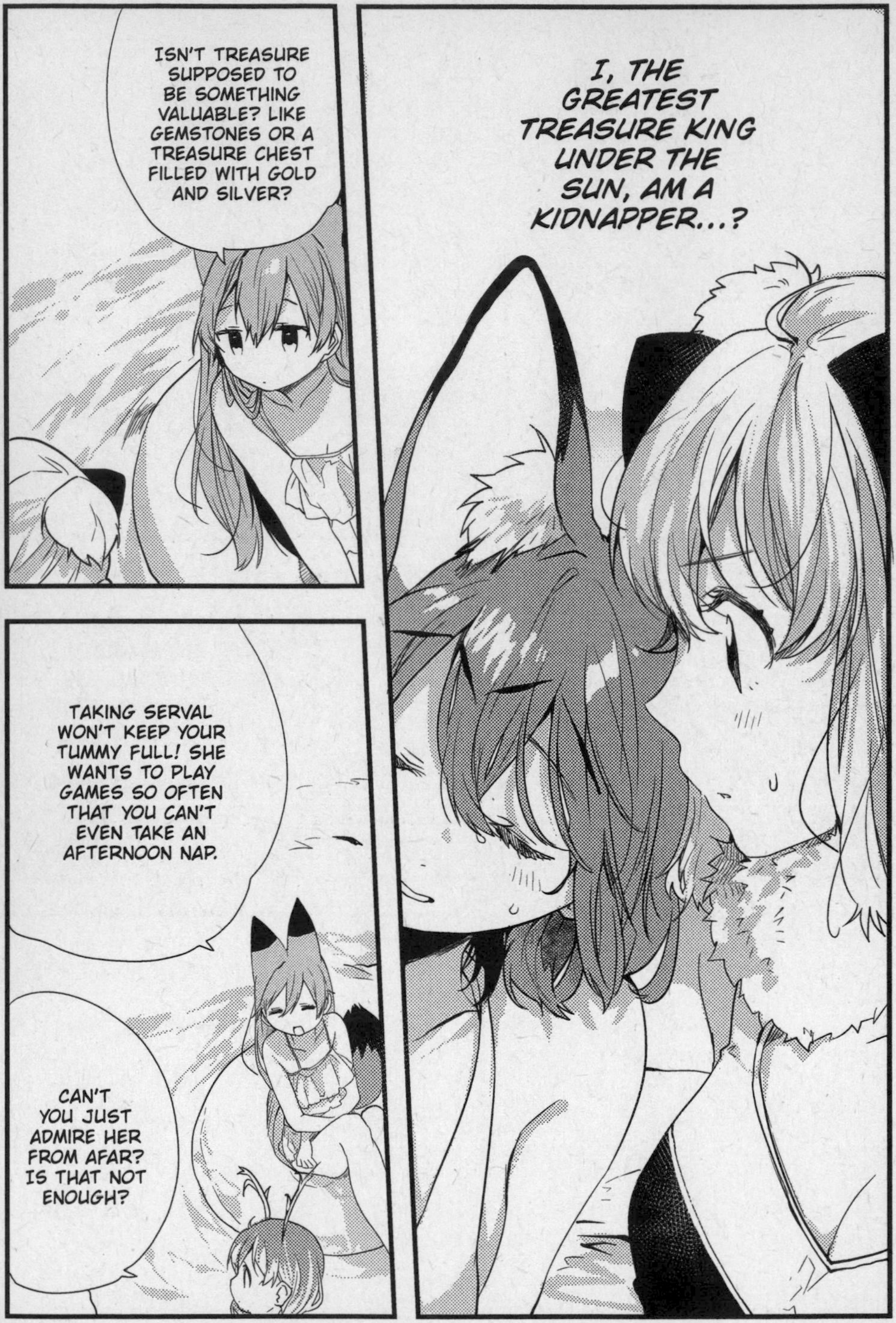
I, THE GREATEST TREASURE KING UNDER THE SUN, AM A KIDNAPPER...?
ISN'T TREASURE SUPPOSED TO BE SOMETHING VALUABLE? LIKE GEMSTONES OR A TREASURE CHEST FILLED WITH GOLD AND SILVER?
TAKING SERVAL WON'T KEEP YOUR TUMMY FULL! SHE WANTS TO PLAY GAMES SO OFTEN THAT YOU CAN'T EVEN TAKE AN AFTERNOON NAP.
CAN'T YOU JUST ADMIRE HER FROM AFAR? IS THAT NOT ENOUGH?

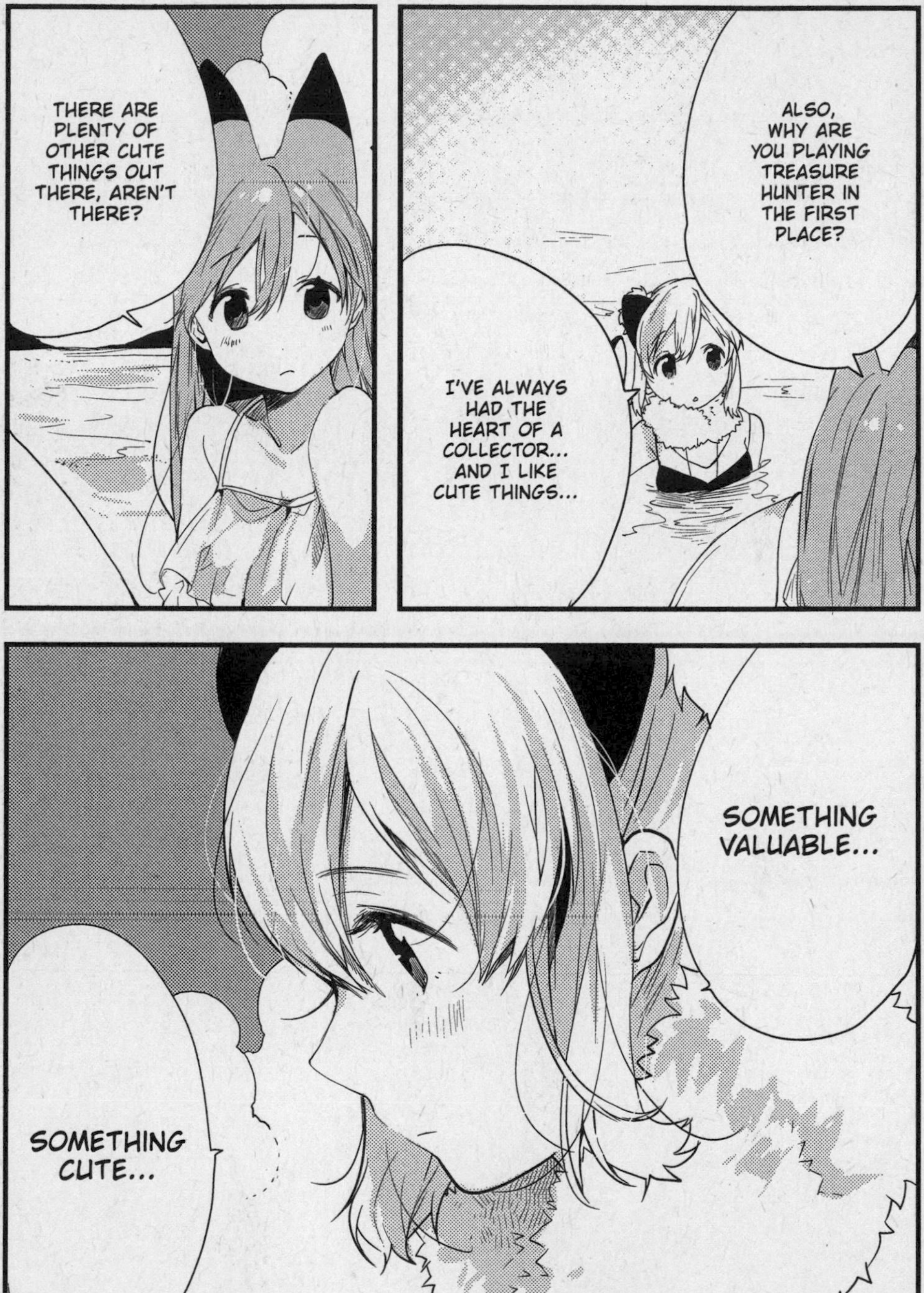
ALSO, WHY ARE YOU PLAYING TREASURE HUNTER IN THE FIRST PLACE?
I'VE ALWAYS HAD THE HEART OF A COLLECTOR... AND I LIKE CUTE THINGS...
THERE ARE PLENTY OF OTHER CUTE THINGS OUT THERE, AREN'T THERE?
SOMETHING VALUABLE...
SOMETHING CUTE...

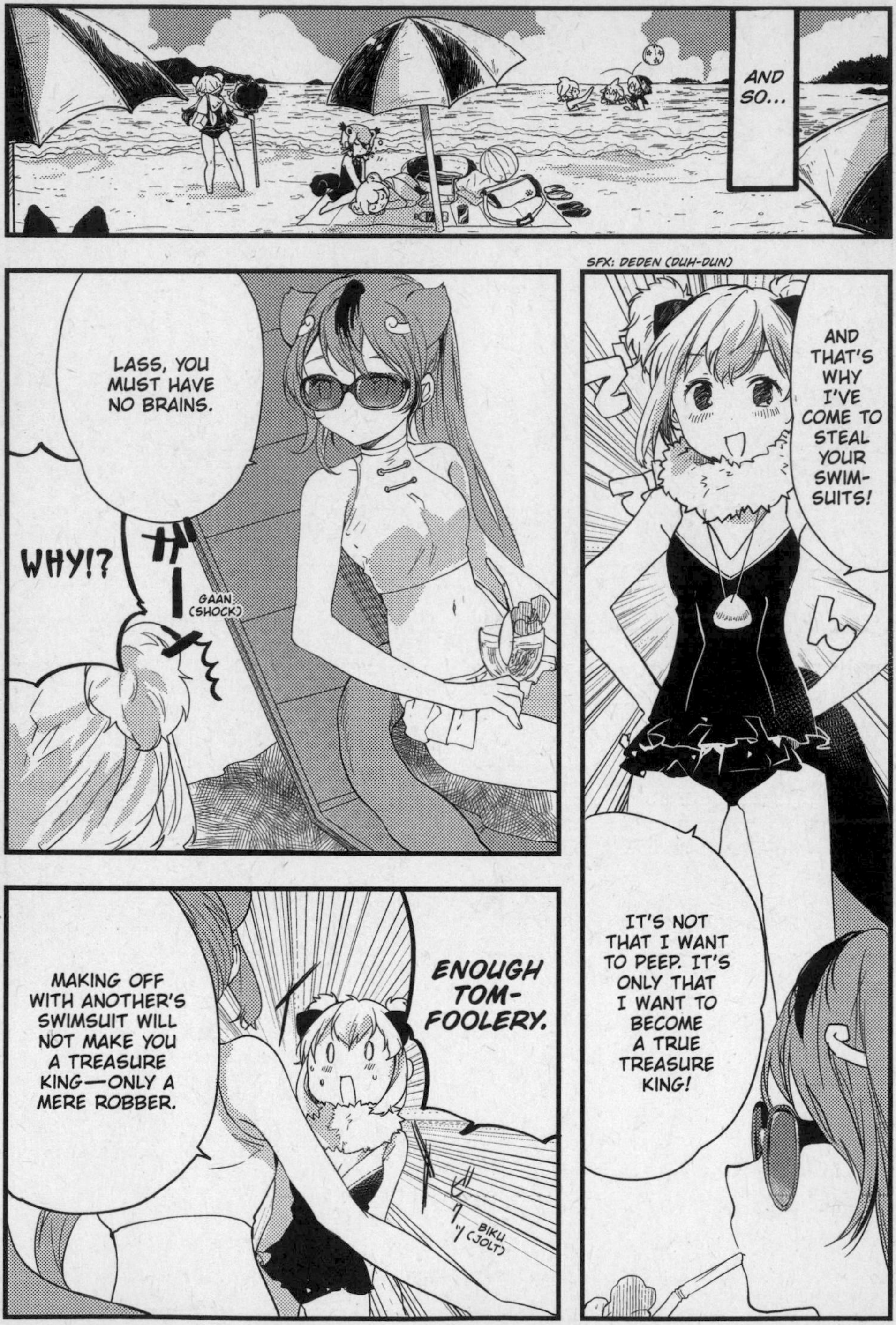
AND SO...
SFX: DEDEN (DUH-DUN)
AND THAT'S WHY I'VE COME TO STEAL YOUR SWIM-SUITS!
IT'S NOT THAT I WANT TO PEEP. IT'S ONLY THAT I WANT TO BECOME A TRUE TREASURE KING!
LASS, YOU MUST HAVE NO BRAINS.
WHY!?
GAAN (SHOCK)
ENOUGH TOM-FOOLERY.
MAKING OFF WITH ANOTHER'S SWIMSUIT WILL NOT MAKE YOU A TREASURE KING—ONLY A MERE ROBBER.
BIKU (JOLT)

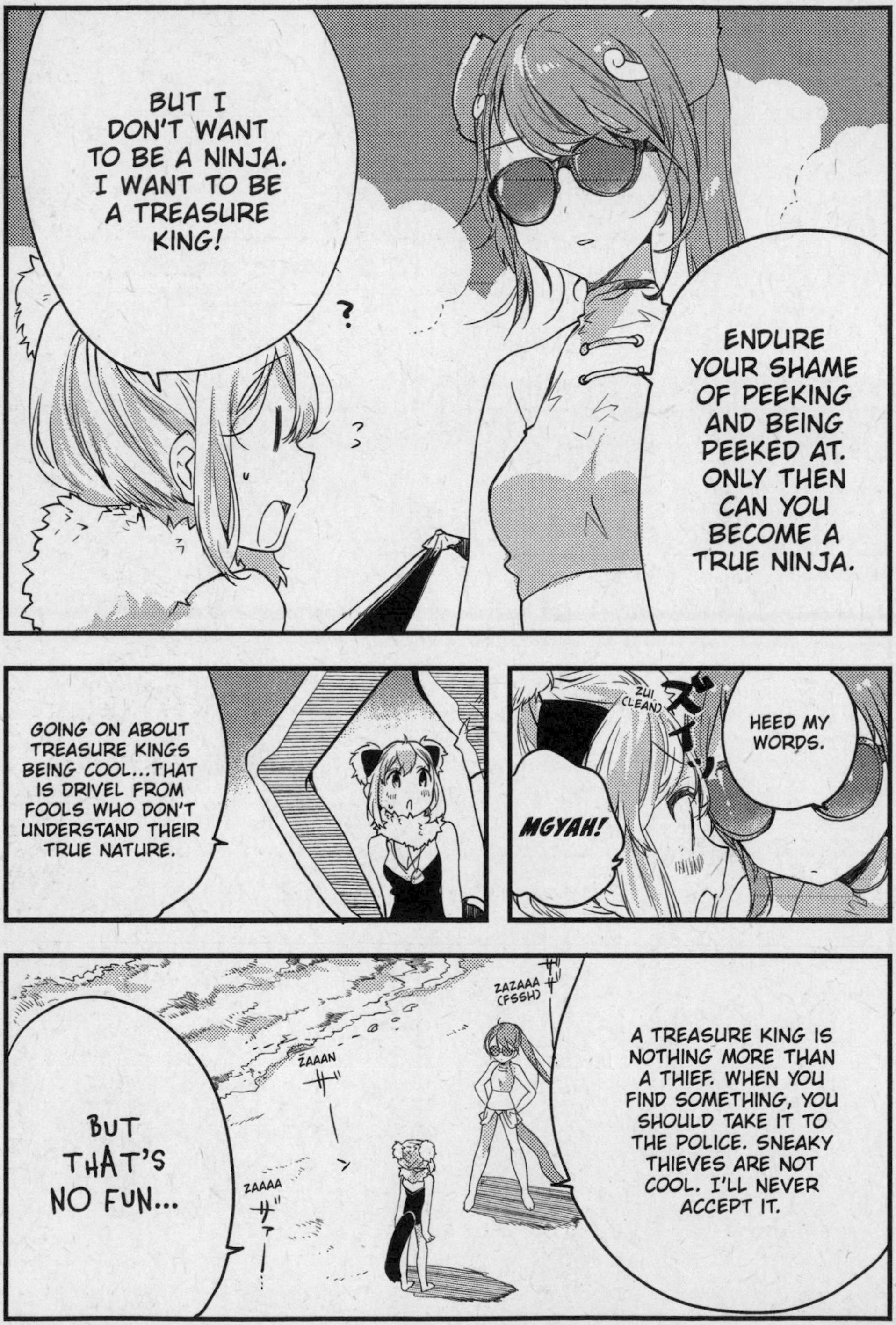
ENDURE YOUR SHAME OF PEEKING AND BEING PEEKED AT. ONLY THEN CAN YOU BECOME A TRUE NINJA.
BUT I DON'T WANT TO BE A NINJA. I WANT TO BE A TREASURE KING!
ZUI (LEAN)
HEED MY WORDS.
MGYAH!
GOING ON ABOUT TREASURE KINGS BEING COOL...THAT IS DRIVEL FROM FOOLS WHO DON'T UNDERSTAND THEIR TRUE NATURE.
ZAZAAA (FSSH)
A TREASURE KING IS NOTHING MORE THAN A THIEF. WHEN YOU FIND SOMETHING, YOU SHOULD TAKE IT TO THE POLICE. SNEAKY THIEVES ARE NOT COOL. I'LL NEVER ACCEPT IT.
ZAAAN
ZAAAA
BUT THAT'S NO FUN...

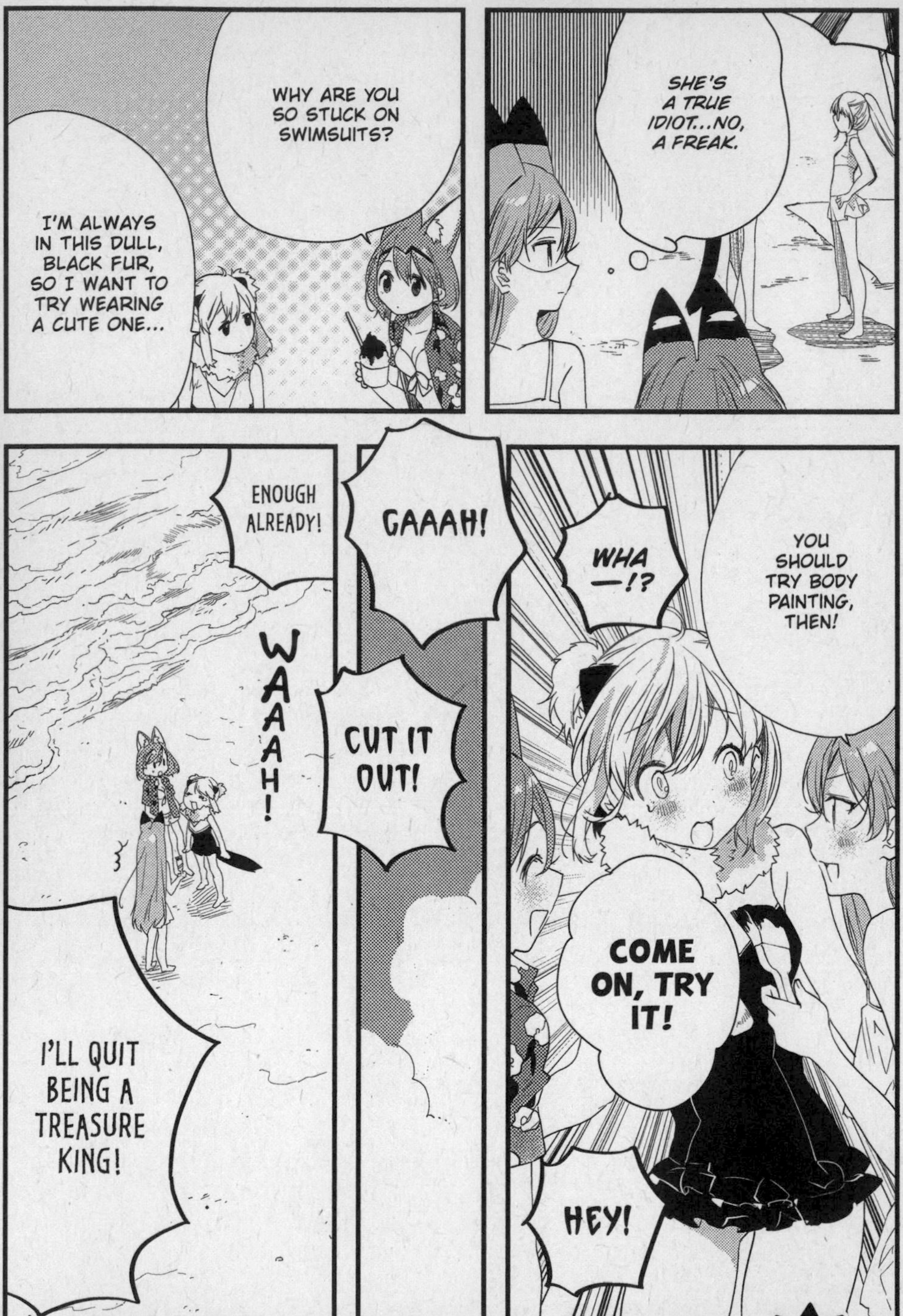
SHE'S A TRUE IDIOT...NO, A FREAK.
WHY ARE YOU SO STUCK ON SWIMSUITS?
I'M ALWAYS IN THIS DULL, BLACK FUR, SO I WANT TO TRY WEARING A CUTE ONE...
YOU SHOULD TRY BODY PAINTING, THEN!
WHA—!?
COME ON, TRY IT!
HEY!
GAAAH!
CUT IT OUT!
ENOUGH ALREADY!
WAAAAH!
I'LL QUIT BEING A TREASURE KING!

CHAPTER 16 END

KEMONO FRIENDS

WELCOME TO JAPARI PARK!

KEMONO FRIENDS
WELCOME TO JAPARI PARK!

CHAPTER 17

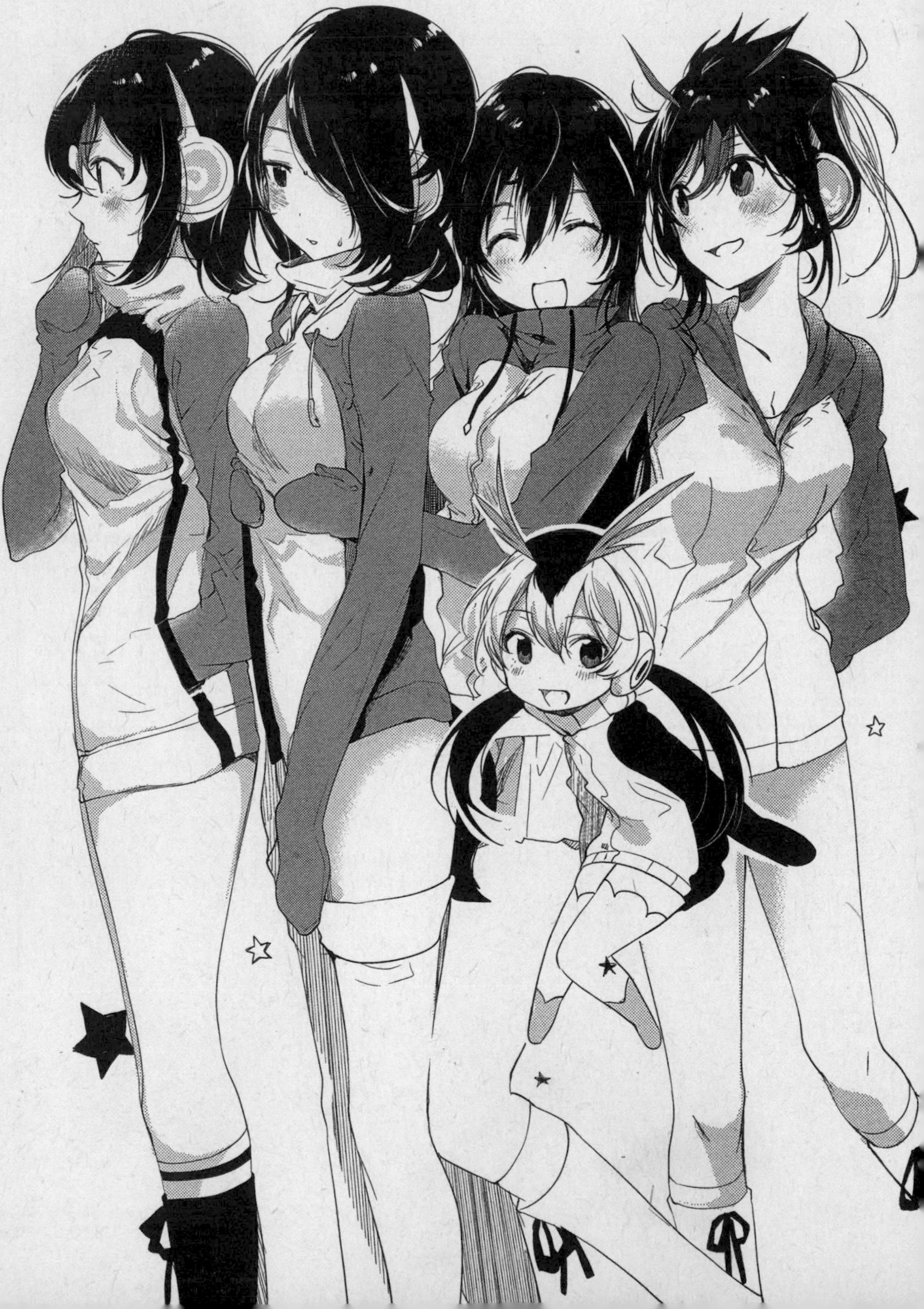

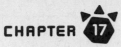

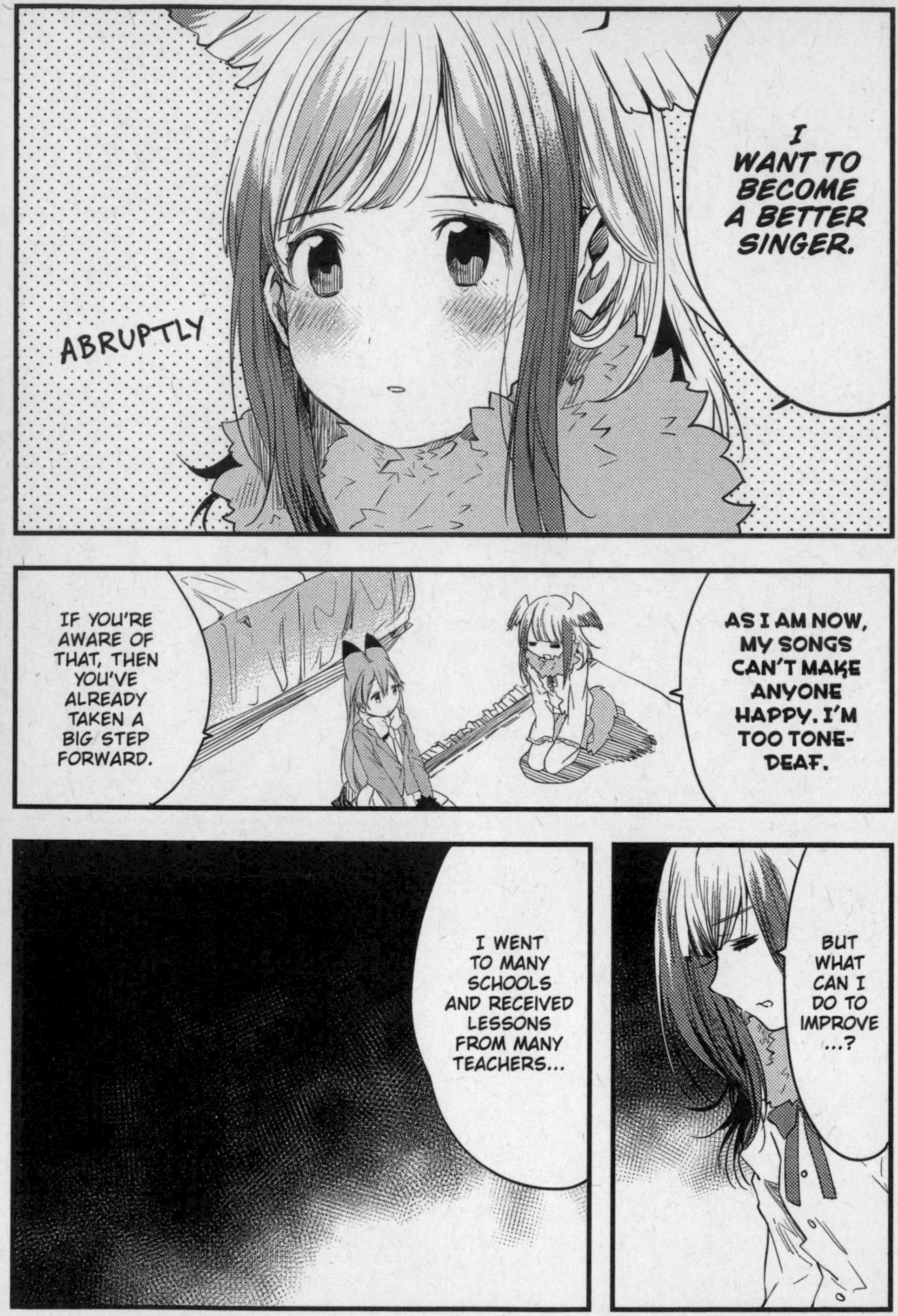
I WANT TO BECOME A BETTER SINGER.
ABRUPTLY
AS I AM NOW, MY SONGS CAN'T MAKE ANYONE HAPPY. I'M TOO TONE-DEAF.
IF YOU'RE AWARE OF THAT, THEN YOU'VE ALREADY TAKEN A BIG STEP FORWARD.
BUT WHAT CAN I DO TO IMPROVE ...?
I WENT TO MANY SCHOOLS AND RECEIVED LESSONS FROM MANY TEACHERS...

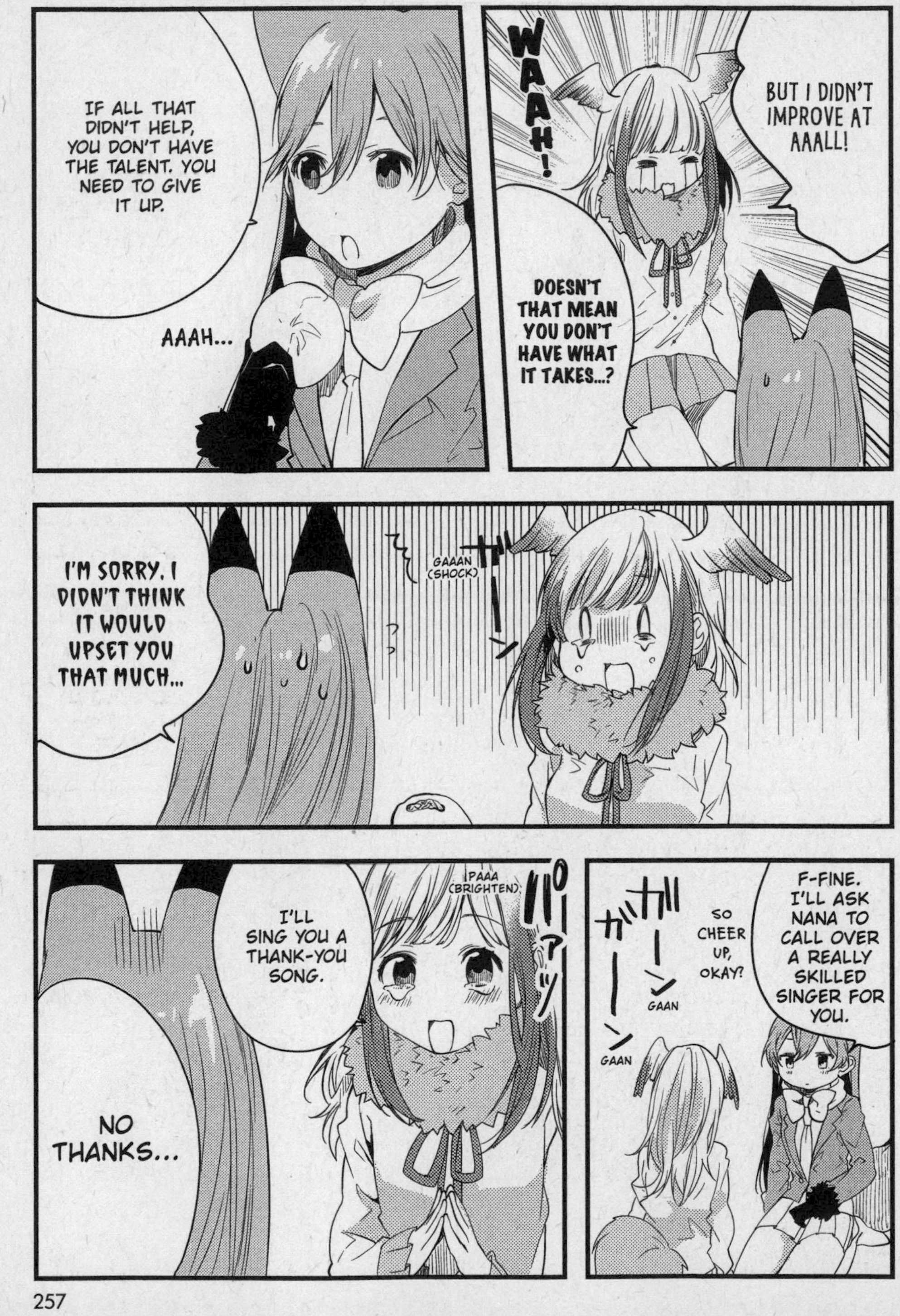
BUT I DIDN'T IMPROVE AT AAALL!
WAAH!
DOESN'T THAT MEAN YOU DON'T HAVE WHAT IT TAKES...?
IF ALL THAT DIDN'T HELP, YOU DON'T HAVE THE TALENT. YOU NEED TO GIVE IT UP.
AAAH...
GAAAN (SHOCK)
I'M SORRY. I DIDN'T THINK IT WOULD UPSET YOU THAT MUCH...
F-FINE. I'LL ASK NANA TO CALL OVER A REALLY SKILLED SINGER FOR YOU.
SO CHEER UP, OKAY?
GAAN
GAAN
PAAA (BRIGHTEN)
I'LL SING YOU A THANK-YOU SONG.
NO THANKS...

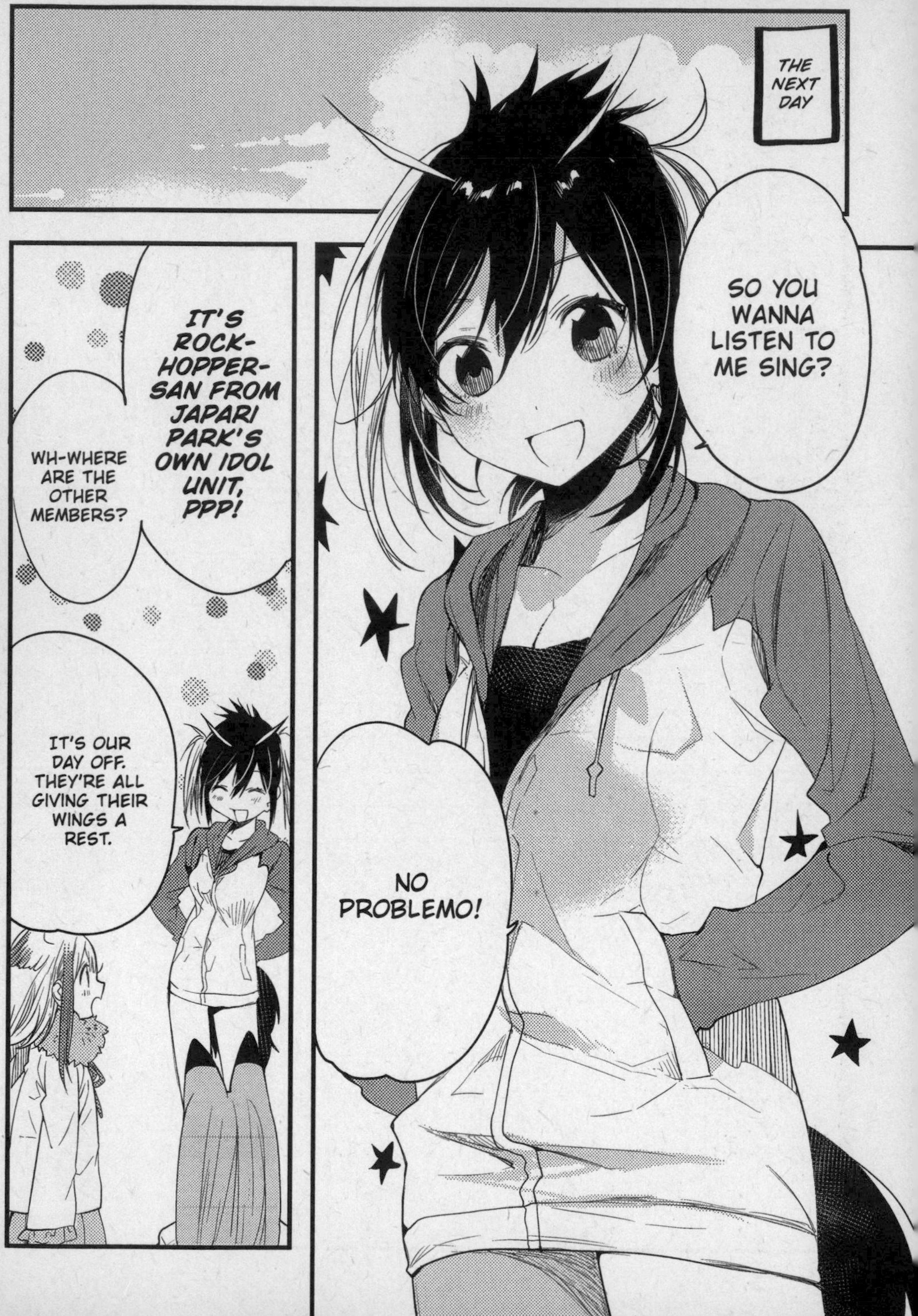
THE NEXT DAY
SO YOU WANNA LISTEN TO ME SING?
NO PROBLEMO!
IT'S ROCK-HOPPER-SAN FROM JAPARI PARK'S OWN IDOL UNIT, PPP!
WH-WHERE ARE THE OTHER MEMBERS?
IT'S OUR DAY OFF. THEY'RE ALL GIVING THEIR WINGS A REST.

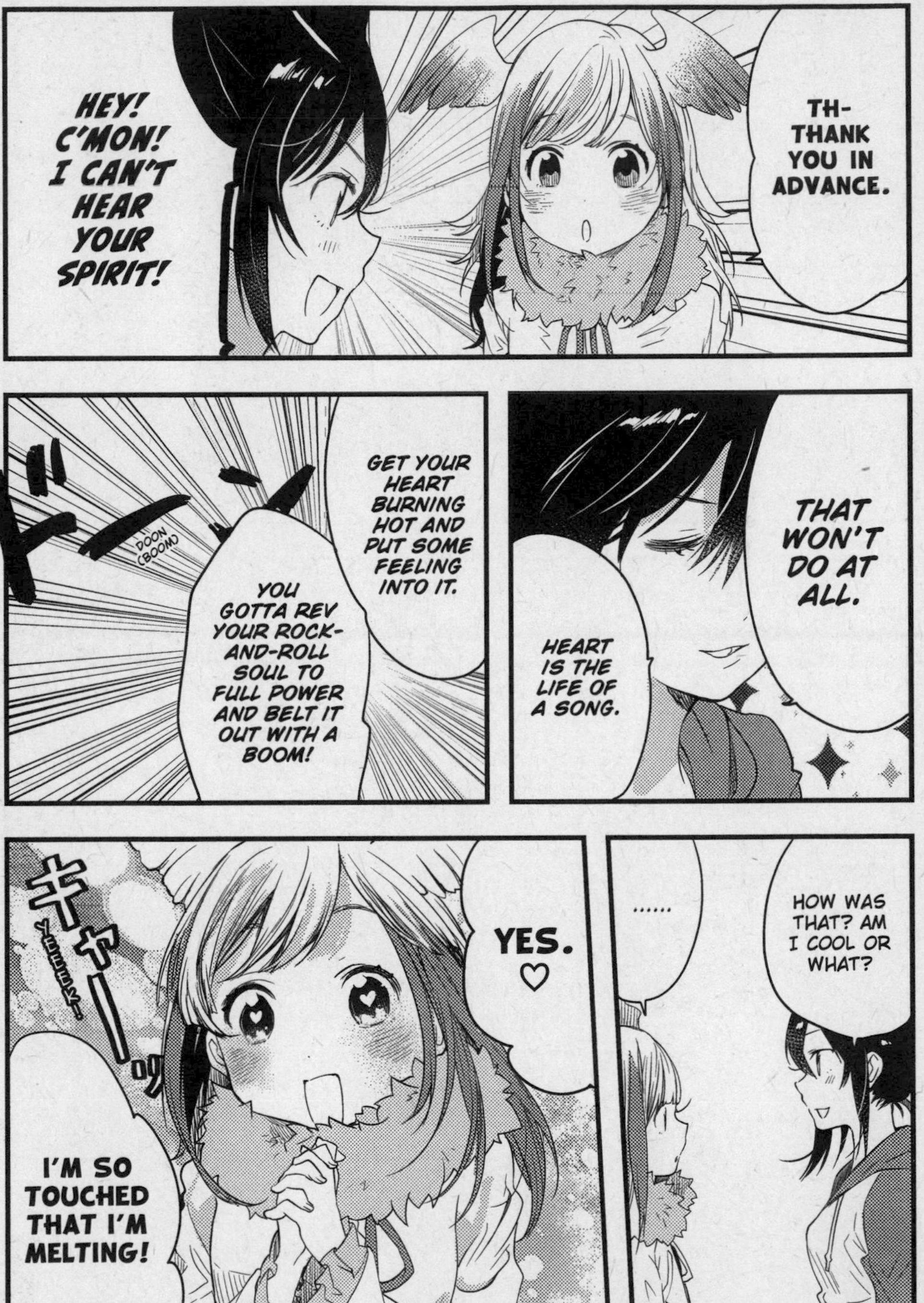
TH- THANK YOU IN ADVANCE.
HEY! C'MON! I CAN'T HEAR YOUR SPIRIT!
THAT WON'T DO AT ALL.
HEART IS THE LIFE OF A SONG.
GET YOUR HEART BURNING HOT AND PUT SOME FEELING INTO IT.
YOU GOTTA REV YOUR ROCK-AND-ROLL SOUL TO FULL POWER AND BELT IT OUT WITH A BOOM!
DOON (BOOM)
HOW WAS THAT? AM I COOL OR WHAT?
......
YES. ♡
I'M SO TOUCHED THAT I'M MELTING!

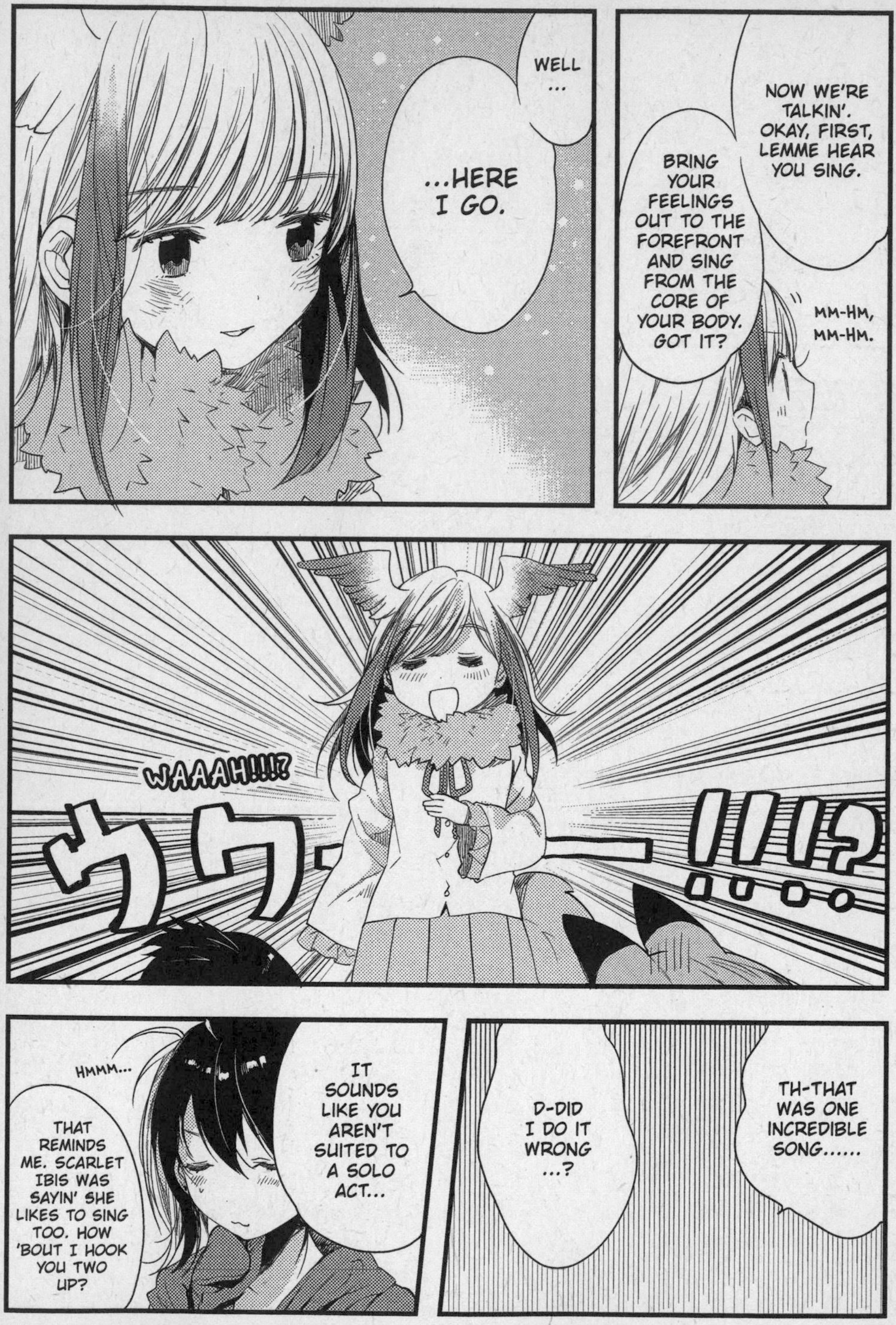
NOW WE'RE TALKIN'. OKAY, FIRST, LEMME HEAR YOU SING.
BRING YOUR FEELINGS OUT TO THE FOREFRONT AND SING FROM THE CORE OF YOUR BODY. GOT IT?
MM-HM, MM-HM.
WELL...
...HERE I GO.
ウウー—!!!?
WAAAH!!!?
TH-THAT WAS ONE INCREDIBLE SONG......
D-DID I DO IT WRONG...?
IT SOUNDS LIKE YOU AREN'T SUITED TO A SOLO ACT...
HMMM...
THAT REMINDS ME. SCARLET IBIS WAS SAYIN' SHE LIKES TO SING TOO. HOW 'BOUT I HOOK YOU TWO UP?

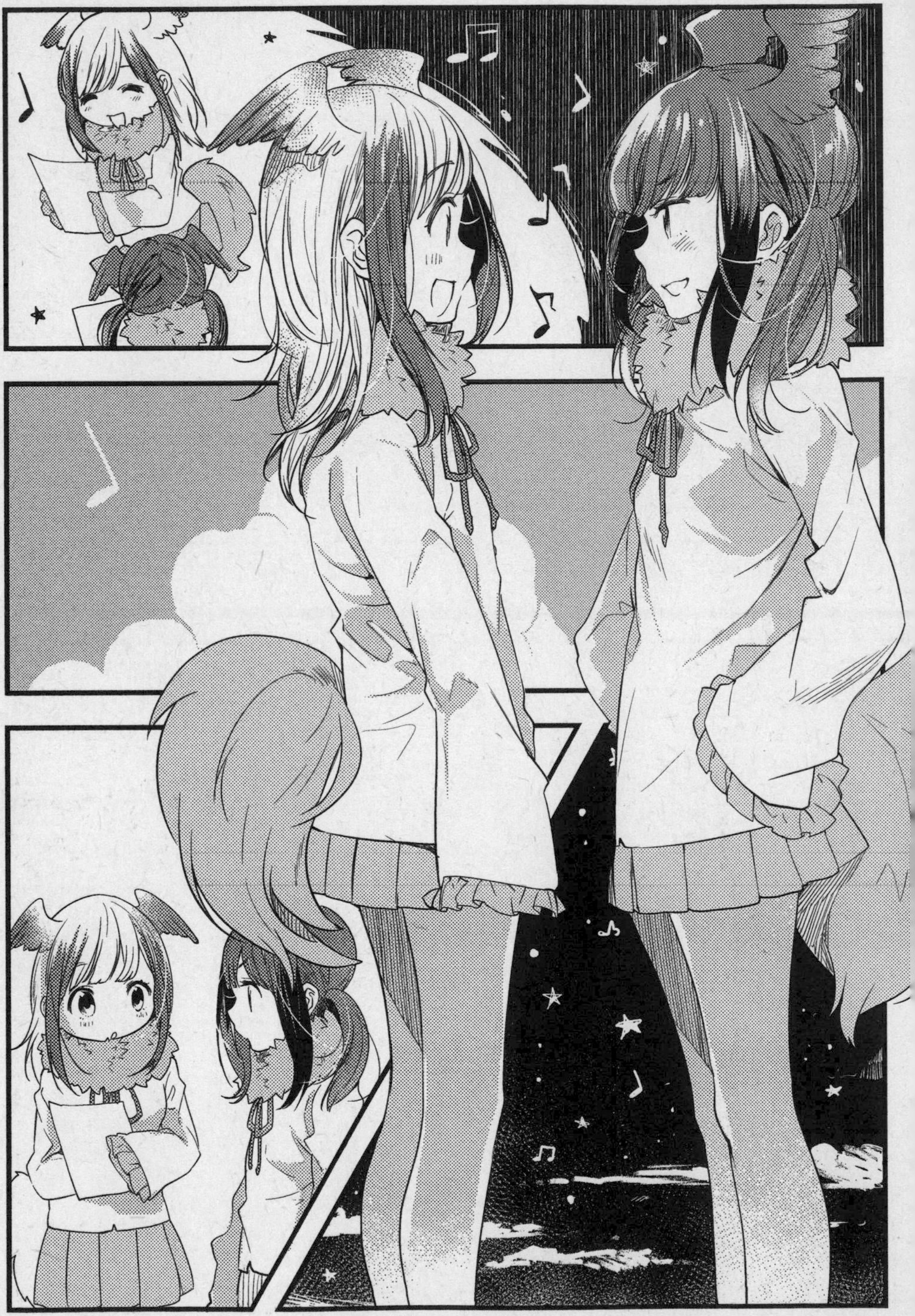

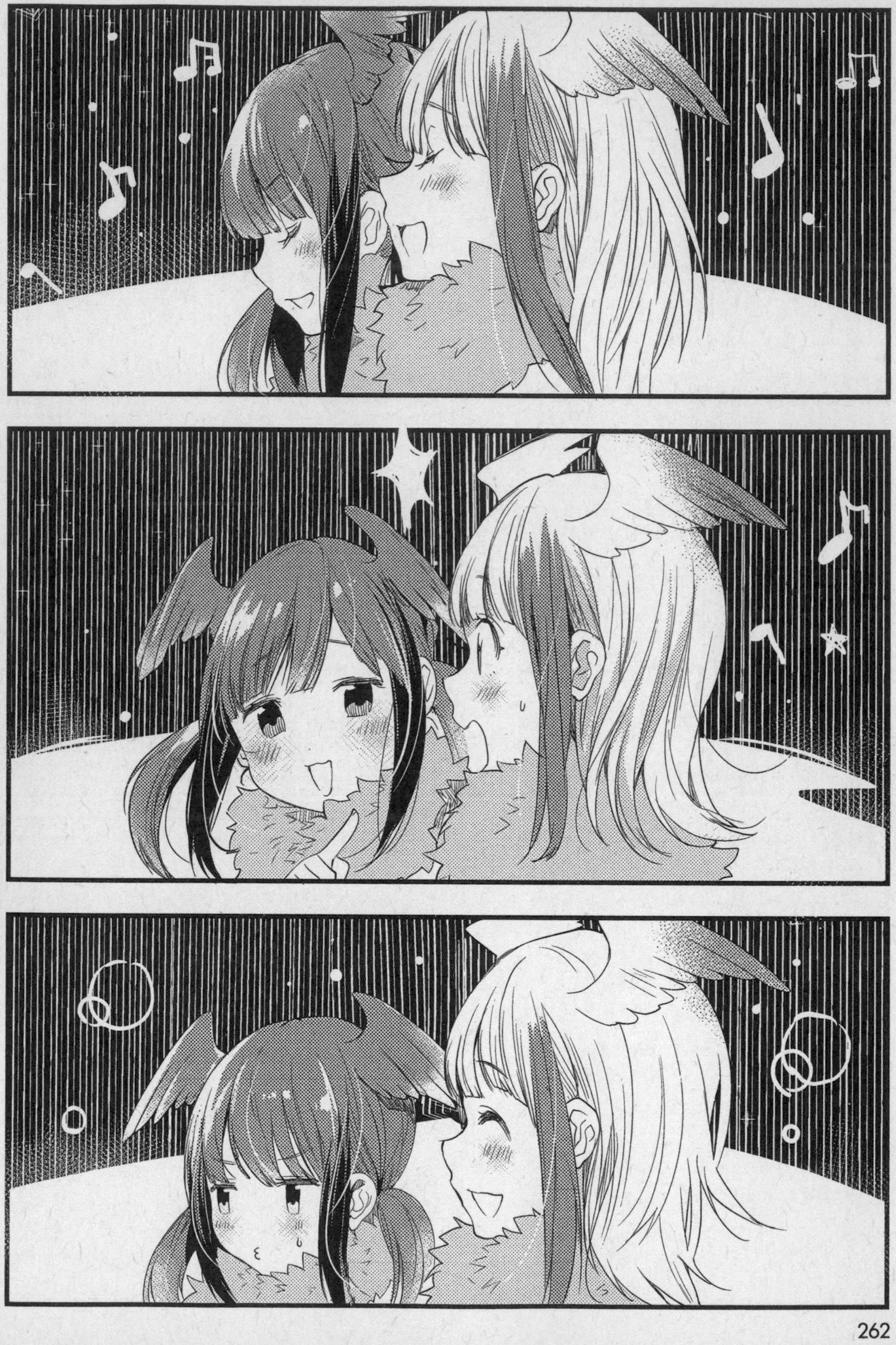

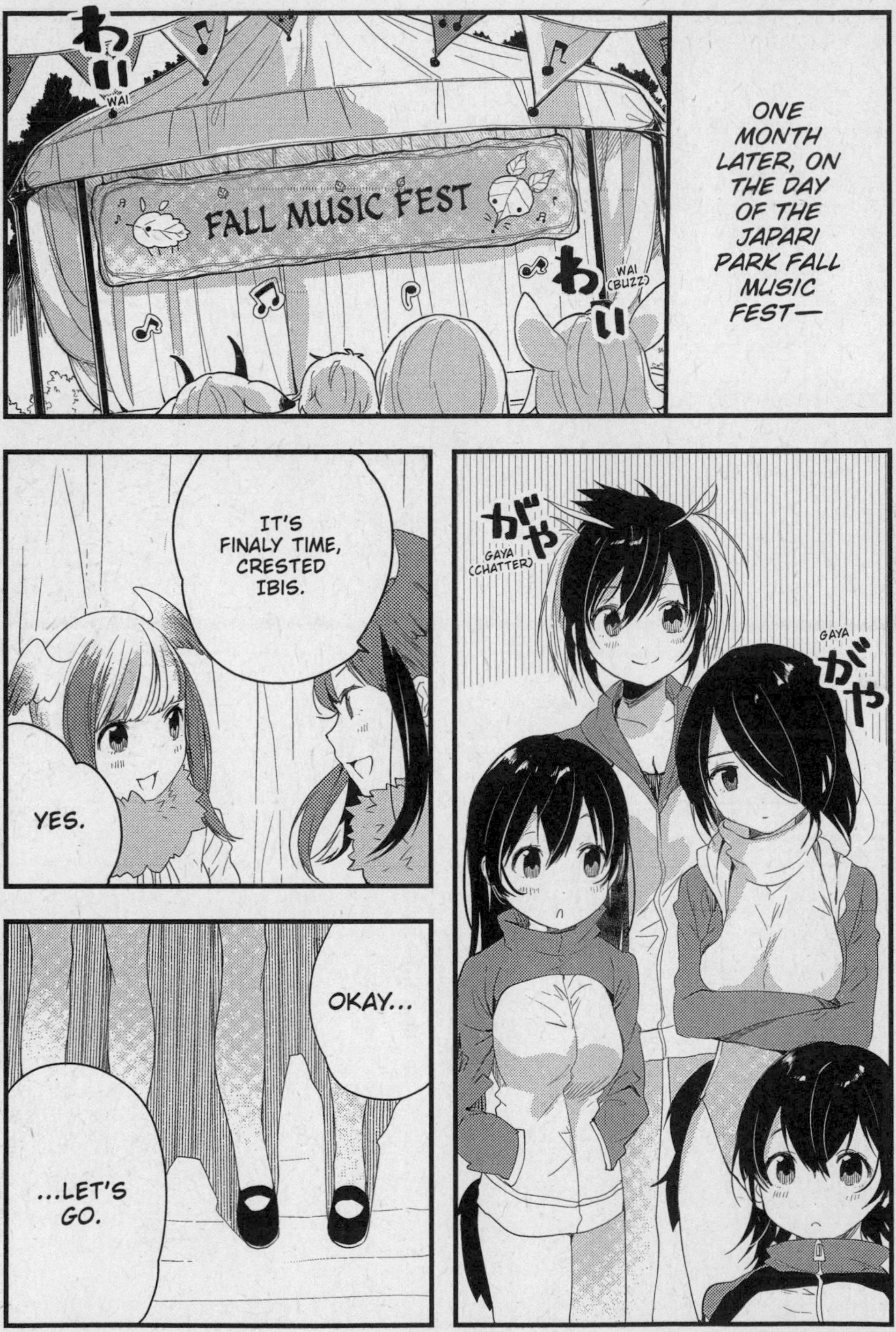
ONE MONTH LATER, ON THE DAY OF THE JAPARI PARK FALL MUSIC FEST—
わい
WAI
FALL MUSIC FEST
わい
WAI (BUZZ)
がや
GAYA (CHATTER)
がや
GAYA
IT'S FINALY TIME, CRESTED IBIS.
YES.
OKAY...
...LET'S GO.

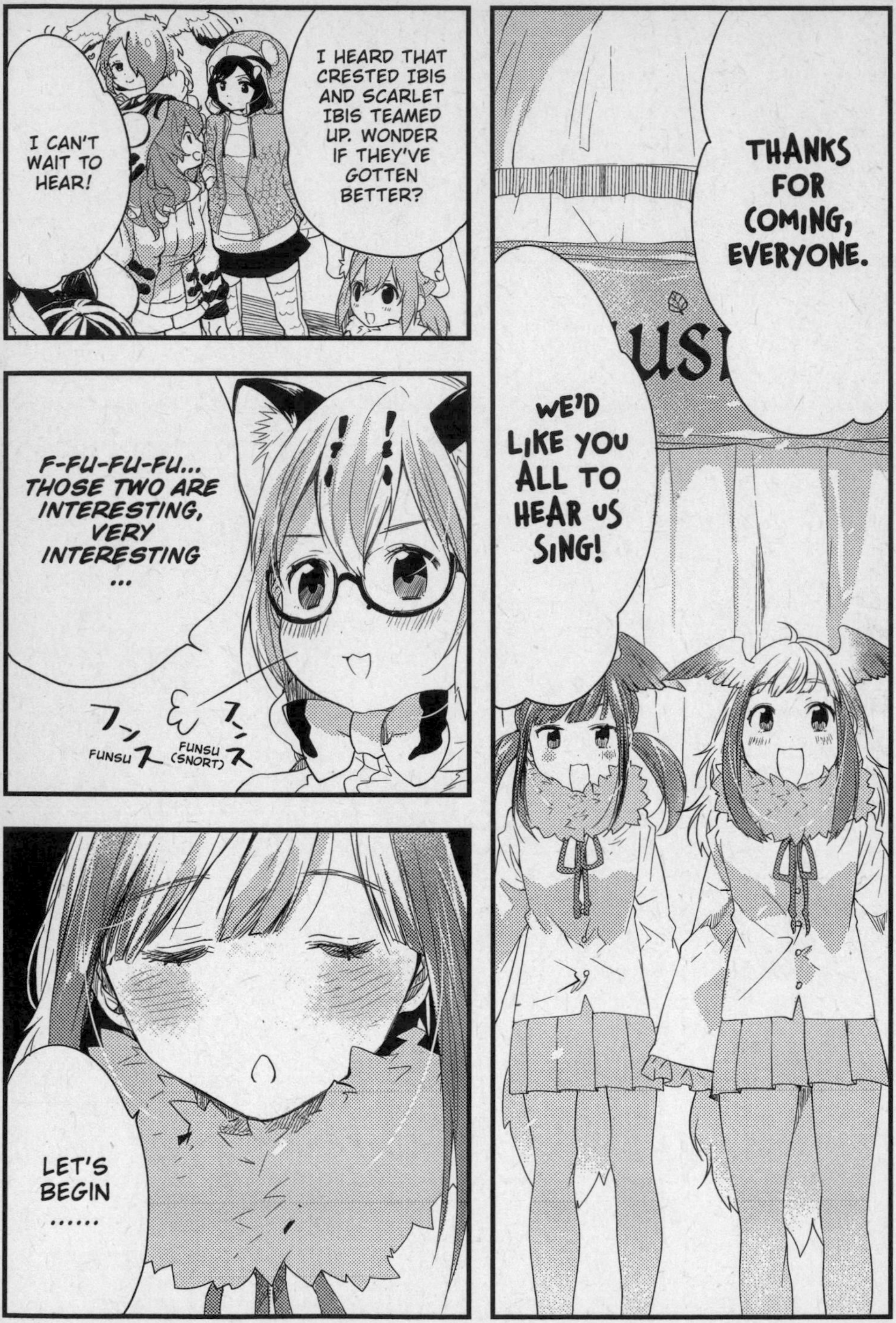
THANKS FOR COMING, EVERYONE.
WE'D LIKE YOU ALL TO HEAR US SING!
I HEARD THAT CRESTED IBIS AND SCARLET IBIS TEAMED UP. WONDER IF THEY'VE GOTTEN BETTER?
I CAN'T WAIT TO HEAR!
F-FU-FU-FU... THOSE TWO ARE INTERESTING, VERY INTERESTING ...
フンス
FUNSU (SNORT)
フンス
FUNSU
LET'S BEGIN ......

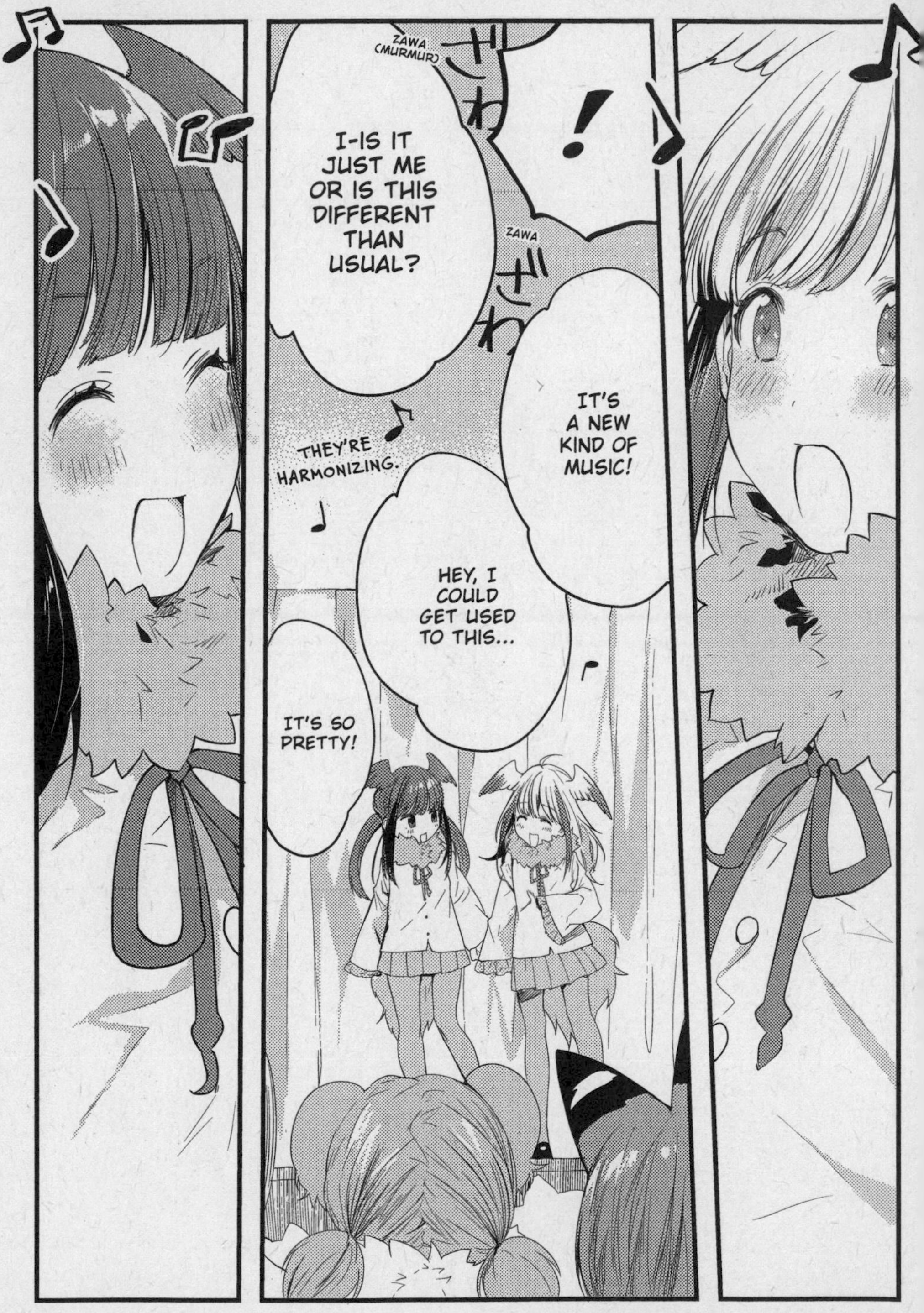
ざわ
ZAWA (MURMUR)
!
I-IS IT JUST ME OR IS THIS DIFFERENT THAN USUAL?
ざわ
ZAWA
IT'S A NEW KIND OF MUSIC!
THEY'RE HARMONIZING.
HEY, I COULD GET USED TO THIS...
IT'S SO PRETTY!

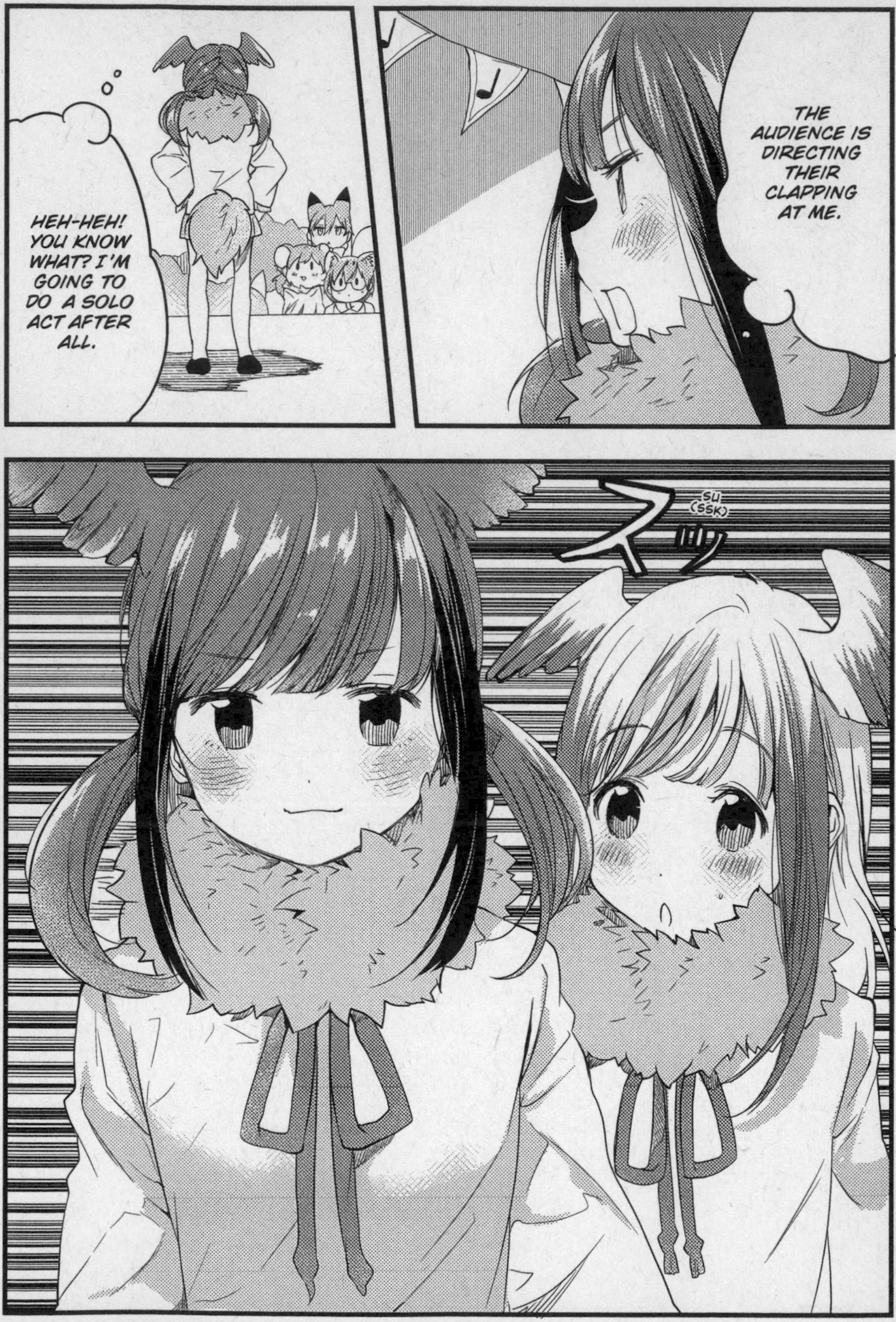
THE AUDIENCE IS DIRECTING THEIR CLAPPING AT ME.
HEH-HEH! YOU KNOW WHAT? I'M GOING TO DO A SOLO ACT AFTER ALL.
スッ
SU (SSK)

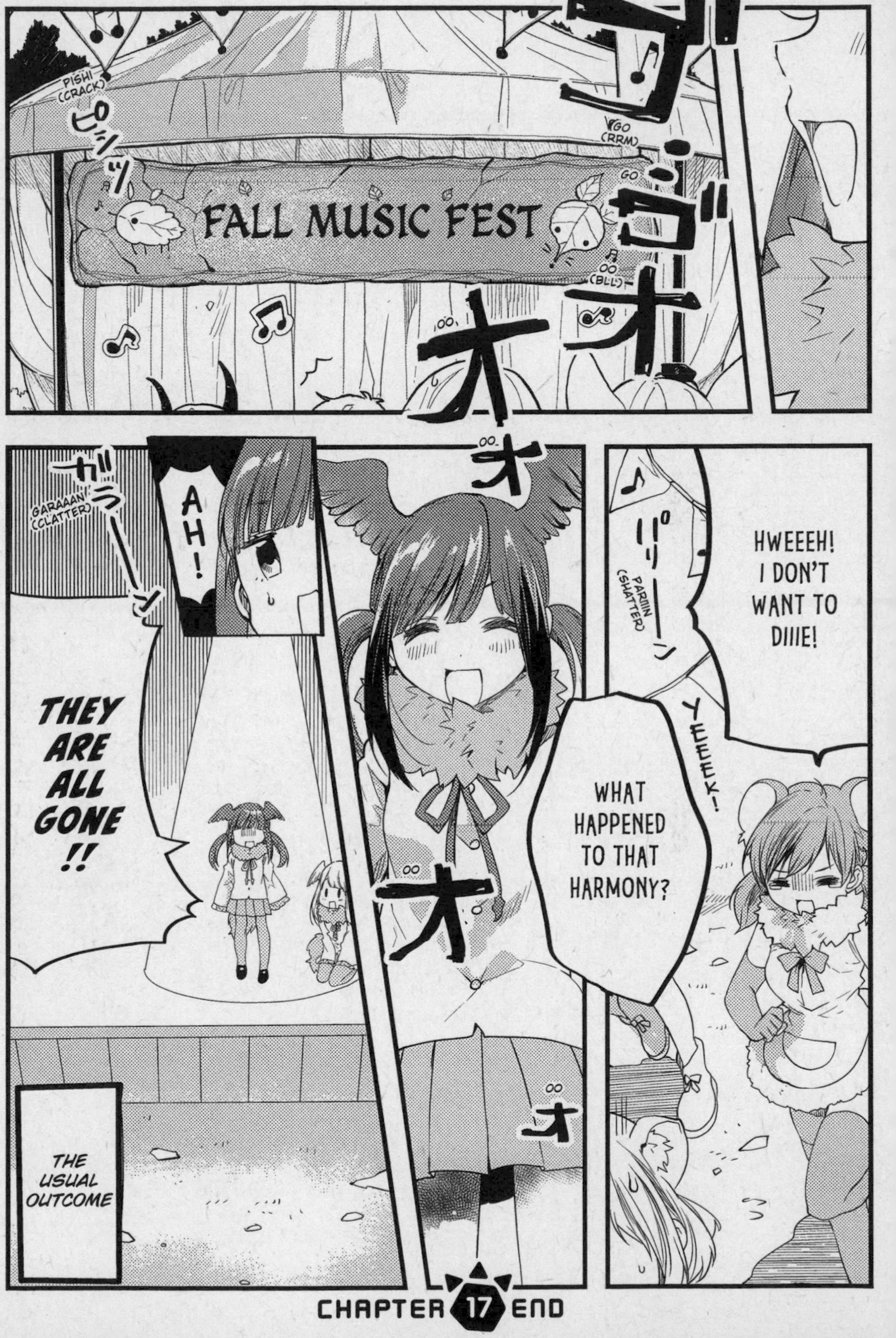
GO (RRM)
GO
OO (BL-L)
FALL MUSIC FEST
PISHI (CRACK)
HWEEEH! I DON'T WANT TO DIIIE!
PARIIIN (SHATTER)
YEEEK!
WHAT HAPPENED TO THAT HARMONY?
AH!
GARAAAN (CLATTER)
THEY ARE ALL GONE!!
THE USUAL OUTCOME

CHAPTER 17 END

KEMONO FRIENDS

WELCOME TO JAPARI PARK!

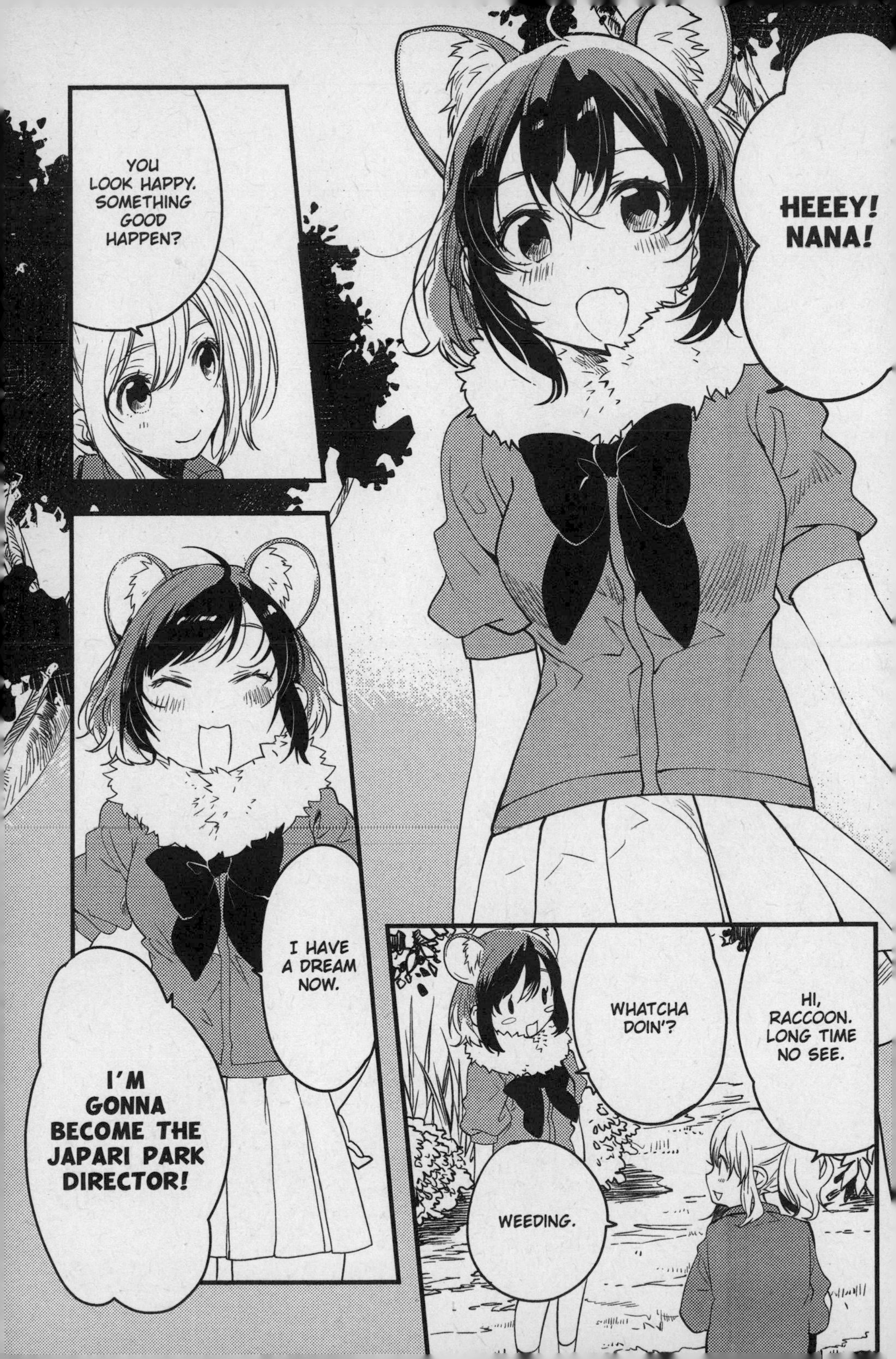
HEEEY! NANA!
YOU LOOK HAPPY. SOMETHING GOOD HAPPEN?
I HAVE A DREAM NOW.
I'M GONNA BECOME THE JAPARI PARK DIRECTOR!
HI, RACCOON. LONG TIME NO SEE.
WHATCHA DOIN'?
WEEDING.

CHAPTER 18

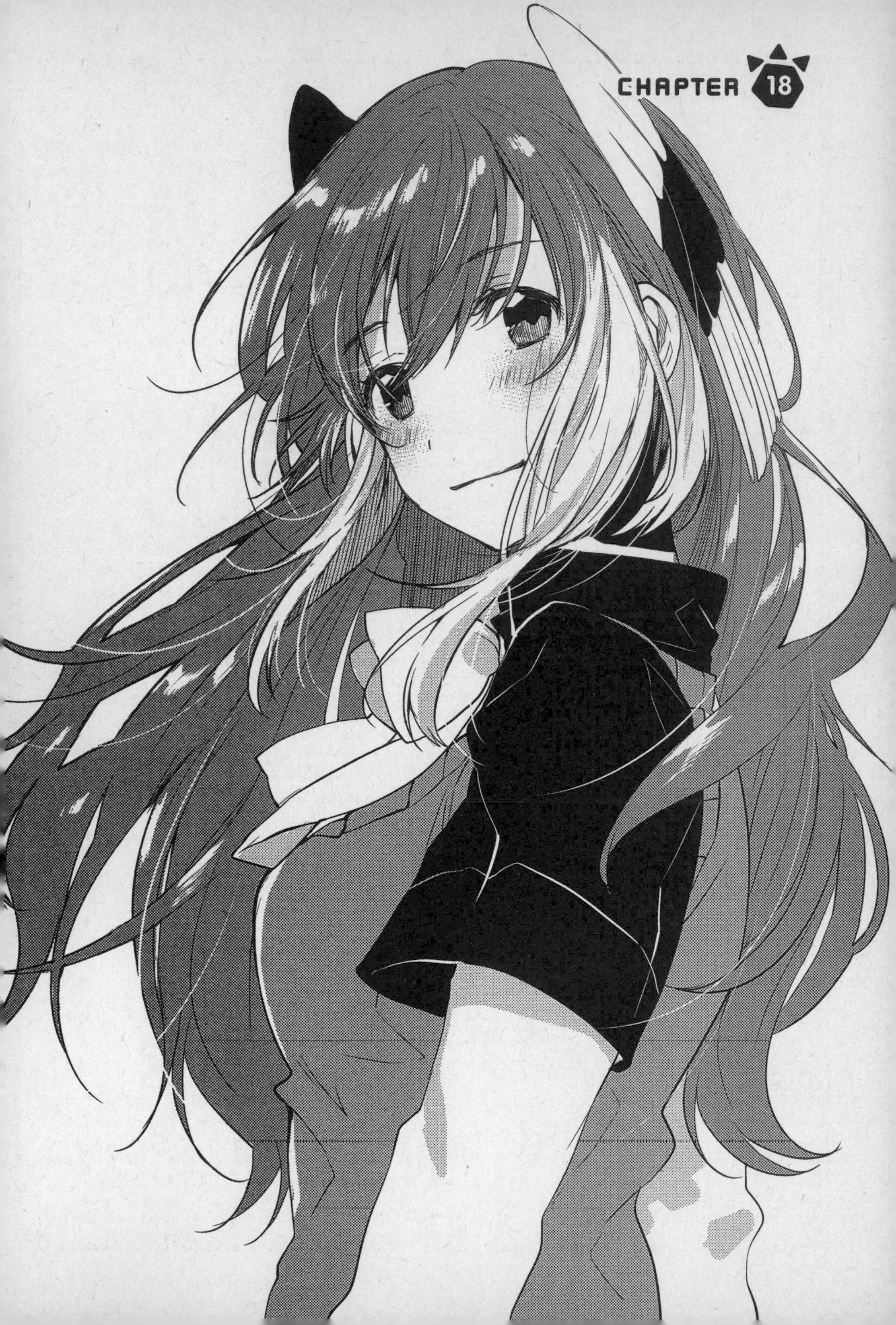

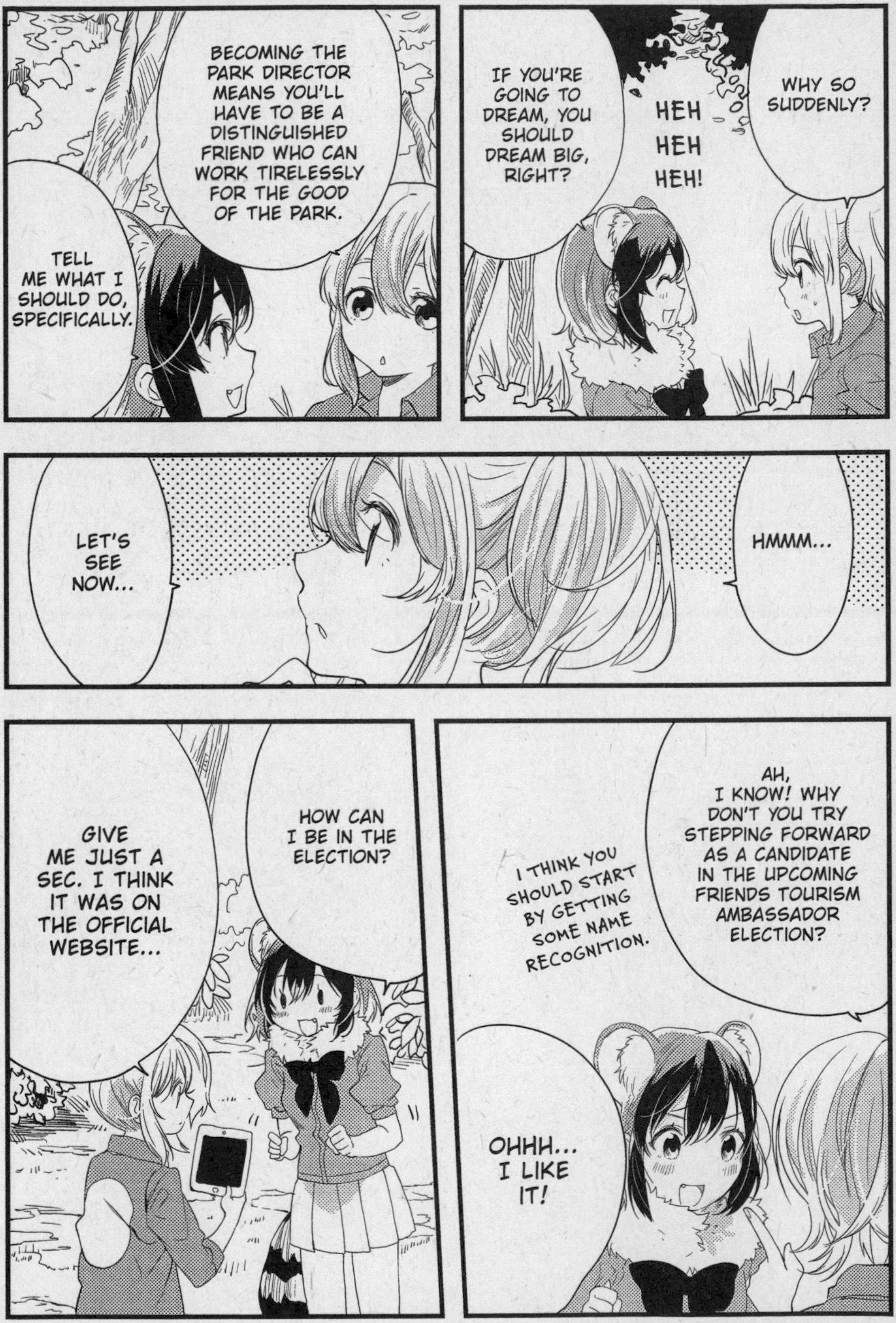
WHY SO SUDDENLY?
HEH HEH HEH!
IF YOU'RE GOING TO DREAM, YOU SHOULD DREAM BIG, RIGHT?
BECOMING THE PARK DIRECTOR MEANS YOU'LL HAVE TO BE A DISTINGUISHED FRIEND WHO CAN WORK TIRELESSLY FOR THE GOOD OF THE PARK.
TELL ME WHAT I SHOULD DO, SPECIFICALLY.
HMMM...
LET'S SEE NOW...
AH, I KNOW! WHY DON'T YOU TRY STEPPING FORWARD AS A CANDIDATE IN THE UPCOMING FRIENDS TOURISM AMBASSADOR ELECTION?
I THINK YOU SHOULD START BY GETTING SOME NAME RECOGNITION.
OHHH... I LIKE IT!
HOW CAN I BE IN THE ELECTION?
GIVE ME JUST A SEC. I THINK IT WAS ON THE OFFICIAL WEBSITE...

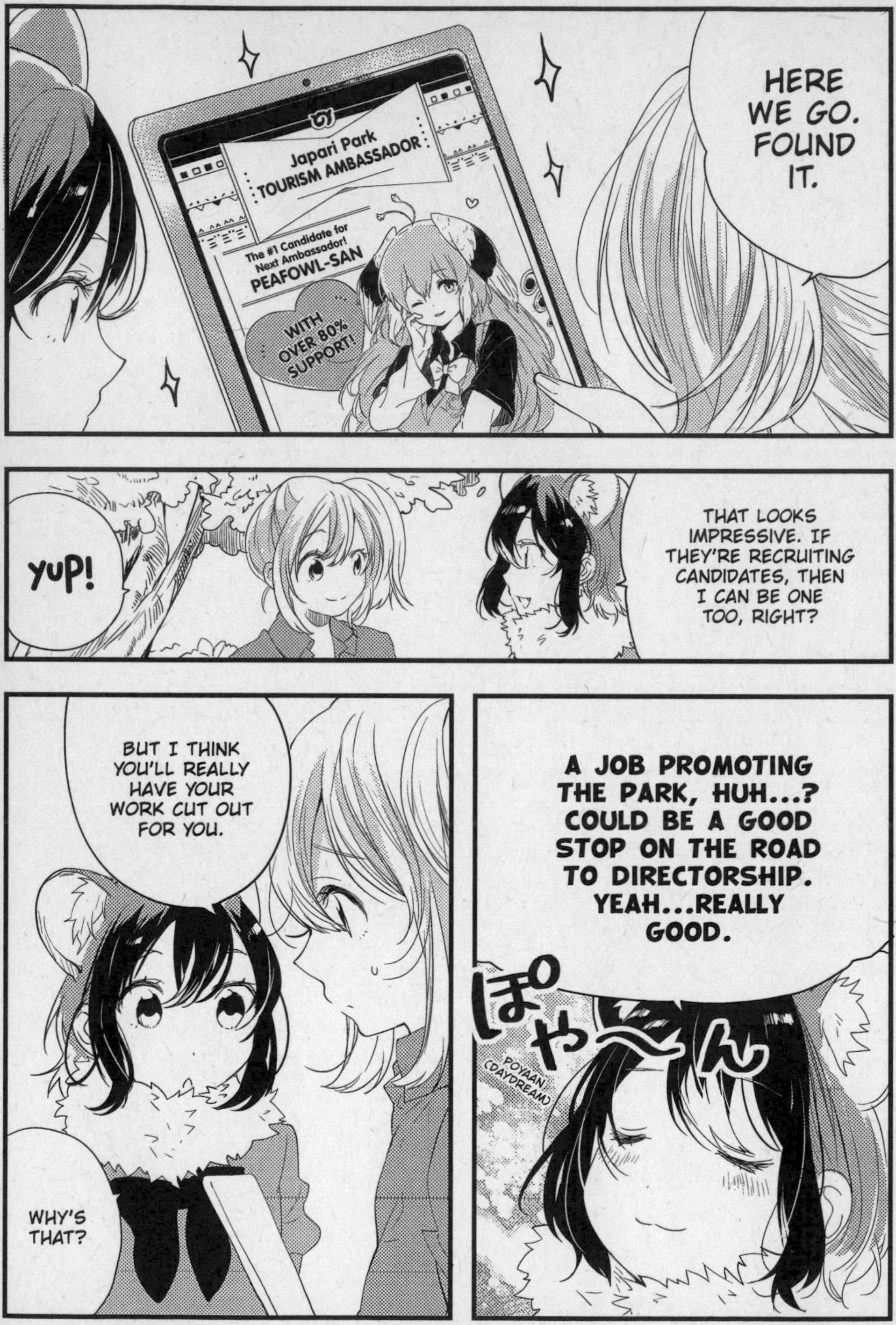
HERE WE GO. FOUND IT.
Japari Park
TOURISM AMBASSADOR
The #1 Candidate for Next Ambassador!
PEAFOWL-SAN
WITH OVER 80% SUPPORT!
THAT LOOKS IMPRESSIVE. IF THEY'RE RECRUITING CANDIDATES, THEN I CAN BE ONE TOO, RIGHT?
YUP!
A JOB PROMOTING THE PARK, HUH...? COULD BE A GOOD STOP ON THE ROAD TO DIRECTORSHIP. YEAH...REALLY GOOD.
ぽや〜ん
POYAAN (DAYDREAM)
BUT I THINK YOU'LL REALLY HAVE YOUR WORK CUT OUT FOR YOU.
WHY'S THAT?

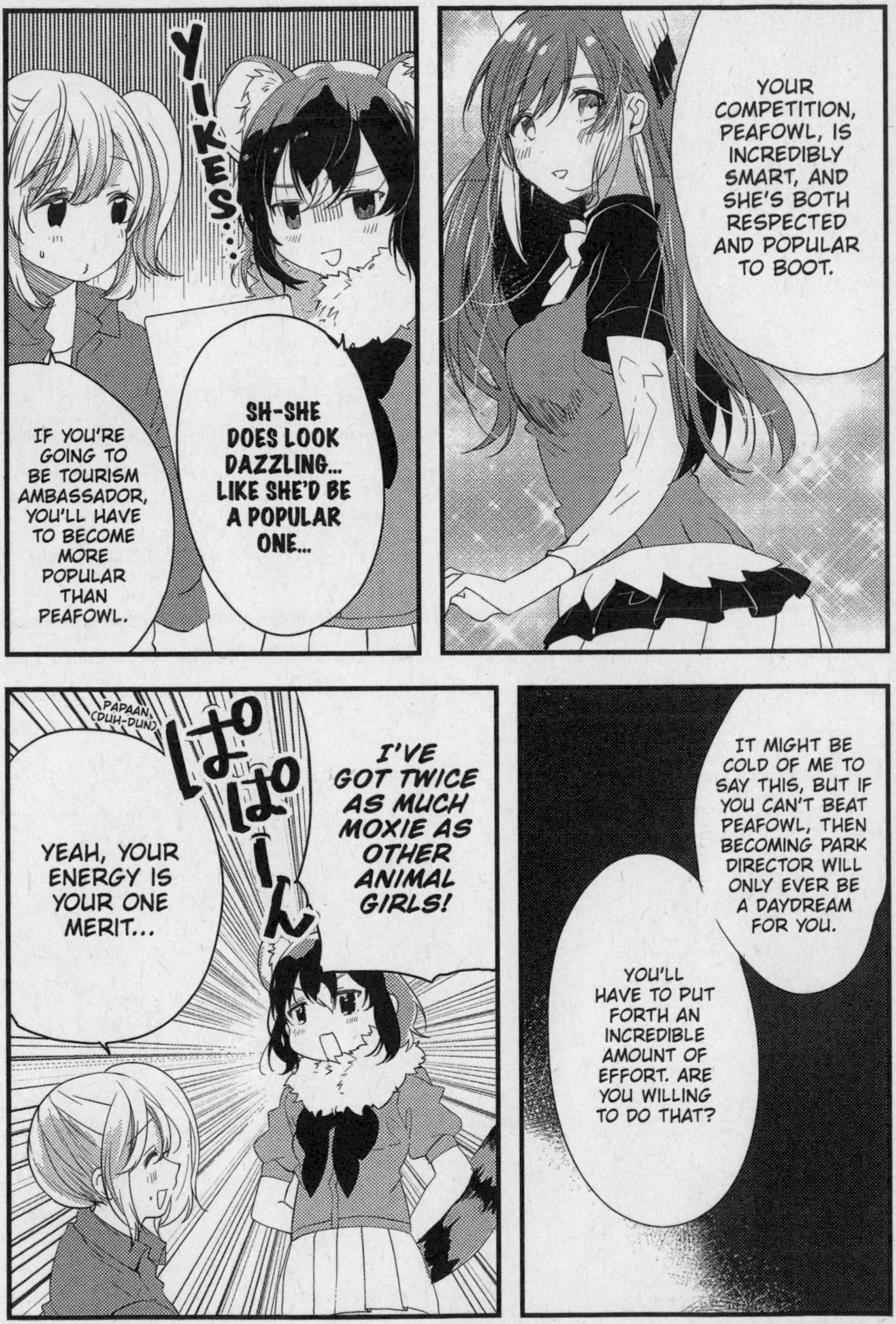
YOUR COMPETITION, PEAFOWL, IS INCREDIBLY SMART, AND SHE'S BOTH RESPECTED AND POPULAR TO BOOT.
YIKES...
SH-SHE DOES LOOK DAZZLING... LIKE SHE'D BE A POPULAR ONE...
IF YOU'RE GOING TO BE TOURISM AMBASSADOR, YOU'LL HAVE TO BECOME MORE POPULAR THAN PEAFOWL.
IT MIGHT BE COLD OF ME TO SAY THIS, BUT IF YOU CAN'T BEAT PEAFOWL, THEN BECOMING PARK DIRECTOR WILL ONLY EVER BE A DAYDREAM FOR YOU.
YOU'LL HAVE TO PUT FORTH AN INCREDIBLE AMOUNT OF EFFORT. ARE YOU WILLING TO DO THAT?
I'VE GOT TWICE AS MUCH MOXIE AS OTHER ANIMAL GIRLS!
ぱぱーん
PAPAAN (DUH-DUN)
YEAH, YOUR ENERGY IS YOUR ONE MERIT...

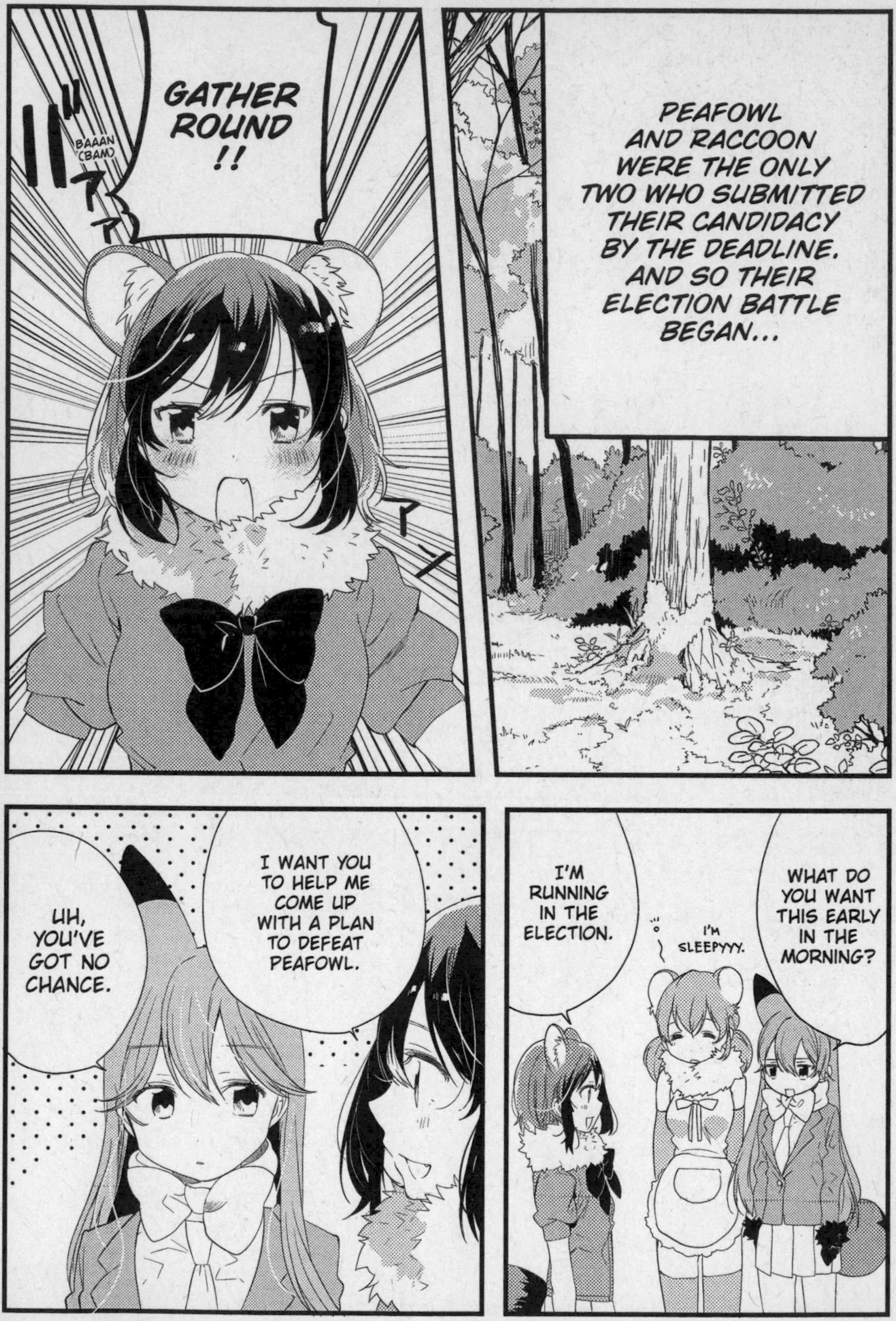
PEAFOWL AND RACCOON WERE THE ONLY TWO WHO SUBMITTED THEIR CANDIDACY BY THE DEADLINE. AND SO THEIR ELECTION BATTLE BEGAN...
GATHER ROUND !!
BAAAN (BAM)
WHAT DO YOU WANT THIS EARLY IN THE MORNING?
I'M SLEEPYYY.
I'M RUNNING IN THE ELECTION.
I WANT YOU TO HELP ME COME UP WITH A PLAN TO DEFEAT PEAFOWL.
UH, YOU'VE GOT NO CHANCE.

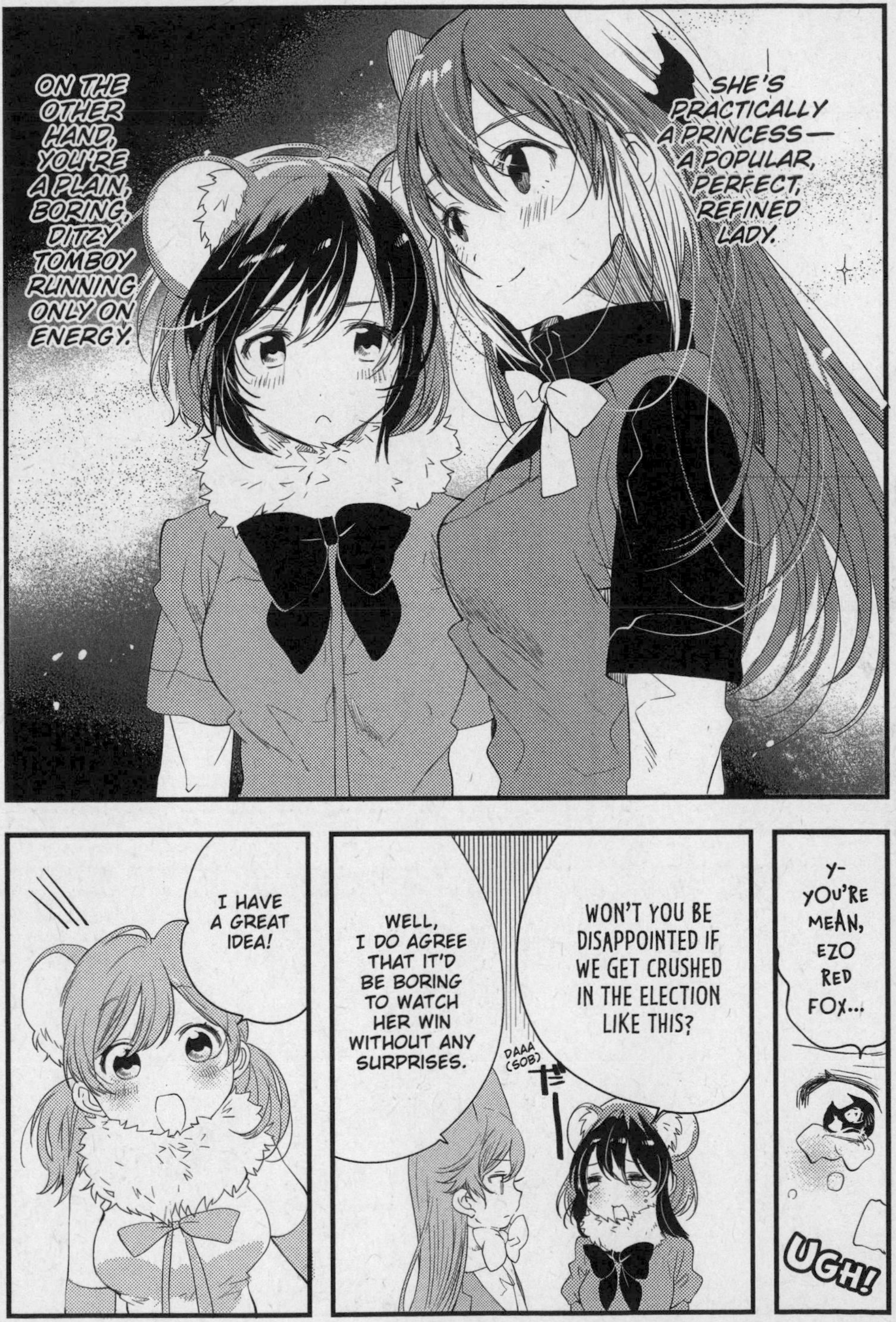
SHE'S PRACTICALLY A PRINCESS—A POPULAR, PERFECT, REFINED LADY.
ON THE OTHER HAND, YOU'RE A PLAIN, BORING, DITZY TOMBOY RUNNING ONLY ON ENERGY.
Y-YOU'RE MEAN, EZO RED FOX...
UGH!
WON'T YOU BE DISAPPOINTED IF WE GET CRUSHED IN THE ELECTION LIKE THIS?
DAAA (SOB)
WELL, I DO AGREE THAT IT'D BE BORING TO WATCH HER WIN WITHOUT ANY SURPRISES.
I HAVE A GREAT IDEA!

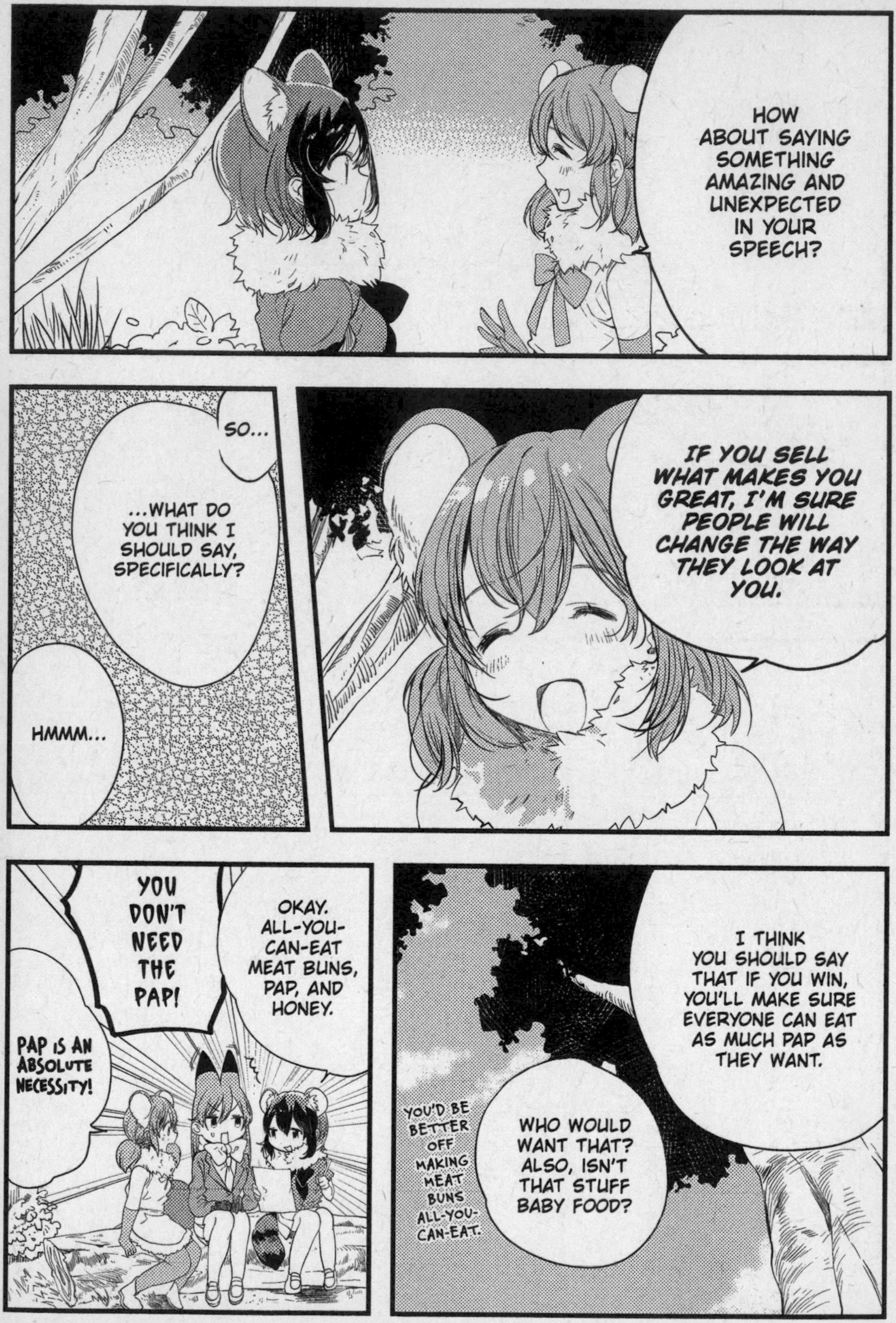
HOW ABOUT SAYING SOMETHING AMAZING AND UNEXPECTED IN YOUR SPEECH?
IF YOU SELL WHAT MAKES YOU GREAT, I'M SURE PEOPLE WILL CHANGE THE WAY THEY LOOK AT YOU.
SO...
...WHAT DO YOU THINK I SHOULD SAY, SPECIFICALLY?
HMMM...
I THINK YOU SHOULD SAY THAT IF YOU WIN, YOU'LL MAKE SURE EVERYONE CAN EAT AS MUCH PAP AS THEY WANT.
WHO WOULD WANT THAT? ALSO, ISN'T THAT STUFF BABY FOOD?
YOU'D BE BETTER OFF MAKING MEAT BUNS ALL-YOU-CAN-EAT.
OKAY. ALL-YOU-CAN-EAT MEAT BUNS, PAP, AND HONEY.
YOU DON'T NEED THE PAP!
PAP IS AN ABSOLUTE NECESSITY!

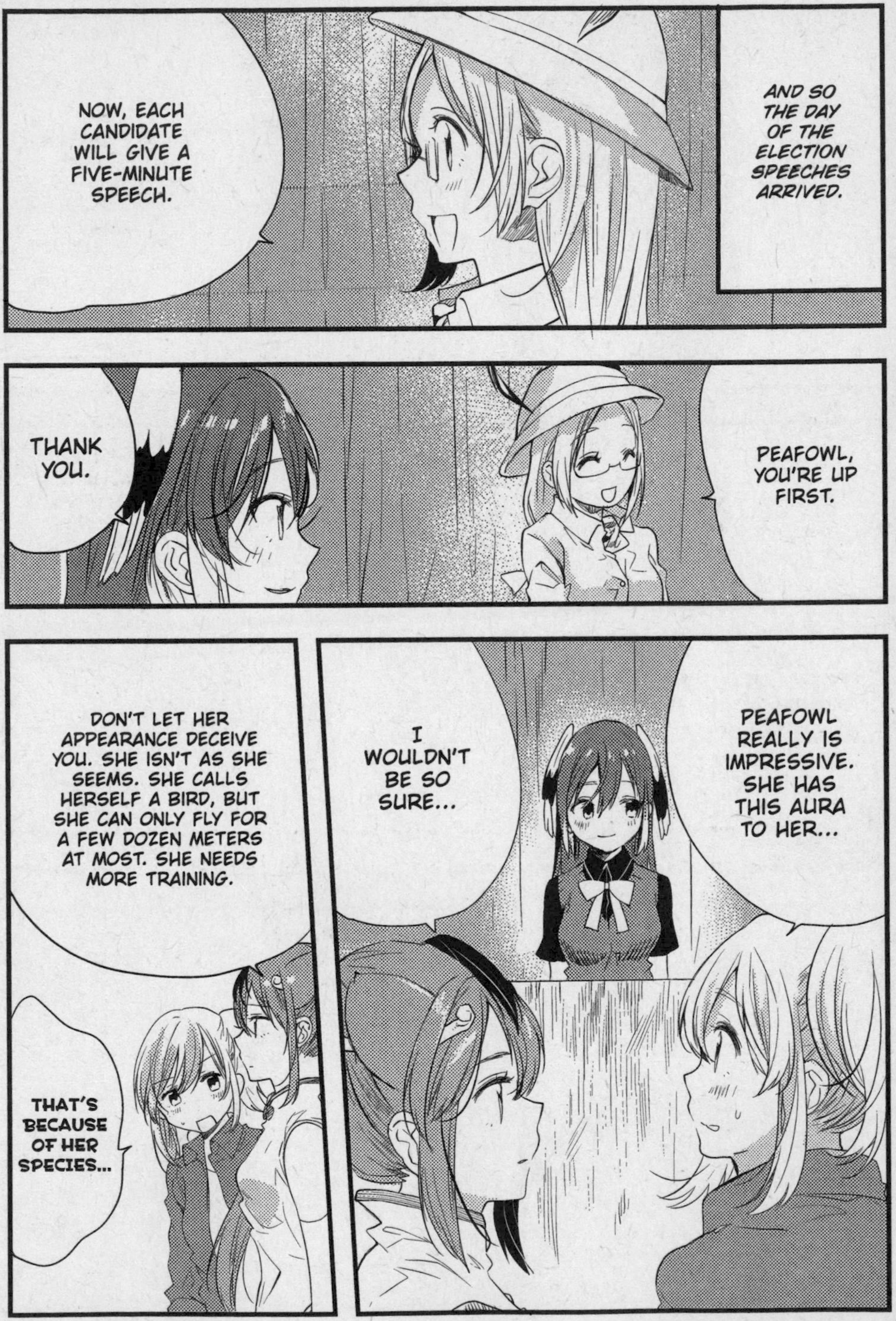
AND SO THE DAY OF THE ELECTION SPEECHES ARRIVED.
NOW, EACH CANDIDATE WILL GIVE A FIVE-MINUTE SPEECH.
PEAFOWL, YOU'RE UP FIRST.
THANK YOU.
PEAFOWL REALLY IS IMPRESSIVE. SHE HAS THIS AURA TO HER...
I WOULDN'T BE SO SURE...
DON'T LET HER APPEARANCE DECEIVE YOU. SHE ISN'T AS SHE SEEMS. SHE CALLS HERSELF A BIRD, BUT SHE CAN ONLY FLY FOR A FEW DOZEN METERS AT MOST. SHE NEEDS MORE TRAINING.
THAT'S BECAUSE OF HER SPECIES...

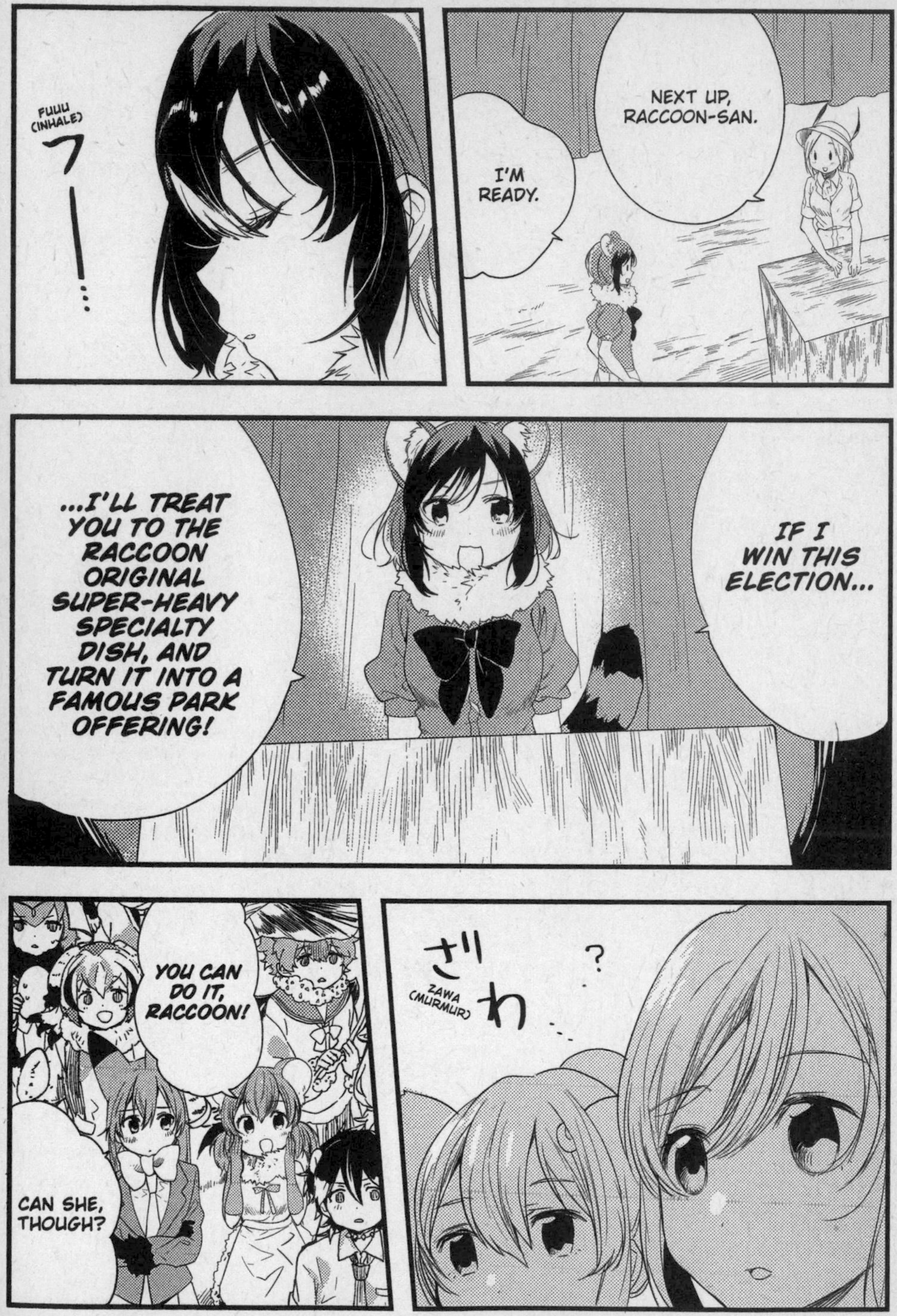
NEXT UP, RACCOON-SAN.
I'M READY.
FUUU (INHALE)
フー…
IF I WIN THIS ELECTION...
...I'LL TREAT YOU TO THE RACCOON ORIGINAL SUPER-HEAVY SPECIALTY DISH, AND TURN IT INTO A FAMOUS PARK OFFERING!
ざわ
ZAWA (MURMUR)
?
YOU CAN DO IT, RACCOON!
CAN SHE, THOUGH?

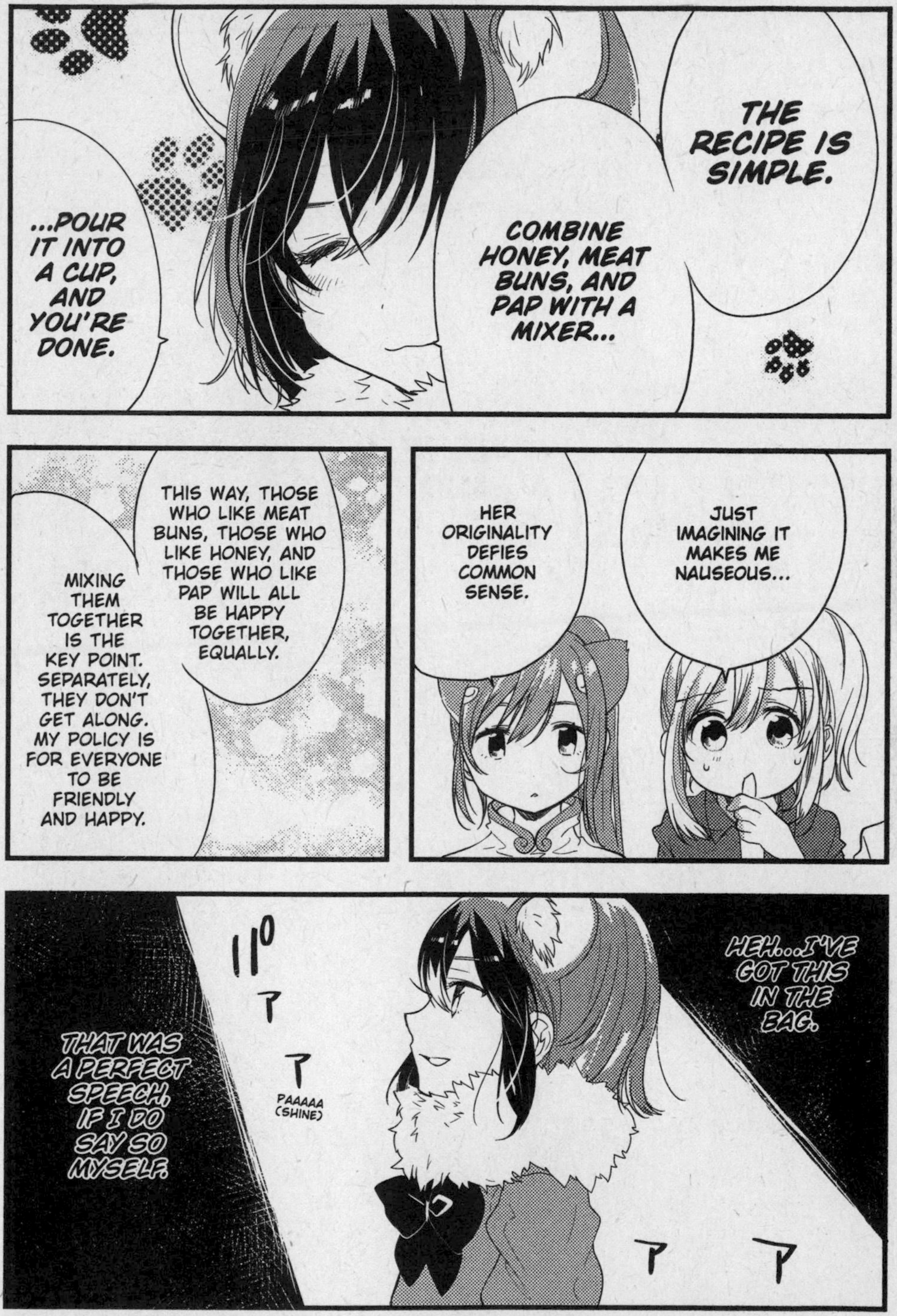
THE RECIPE IS SIMPLE.
COMBINE HONEY, MEAT BUNS, AND PAP WITH A MIXER...
...POUR IT INTO A CUP, AND YOU'RE DONE.
JUST IMAGINING IT MAKES ME NAUSEOUS...
HER ORIGINALITY DEFIES COMMON SENSE.
THIS WAY, THOSE WHO LIKE MEAT BUNS, THOSE WHO LIKE HONEY, AND THOSE WHO LIKE PAP WILL ALL BE HAPPY TOGETHER, EQUALLY.
MIXING THEM TOGETHER IS THE KEY POINT. SEPARATELY, THEY DON'T GET ALONG. MY POLICY IS FOR EVERYONE TO BE FRIENDLY AND HAPPY.
HEH...I'VE GOT THIS IN THE BAG.
PAAAAA (SHINE)
THAT WAS A PERFECT SPEECH, IF I DO SAY SO MYSELF.

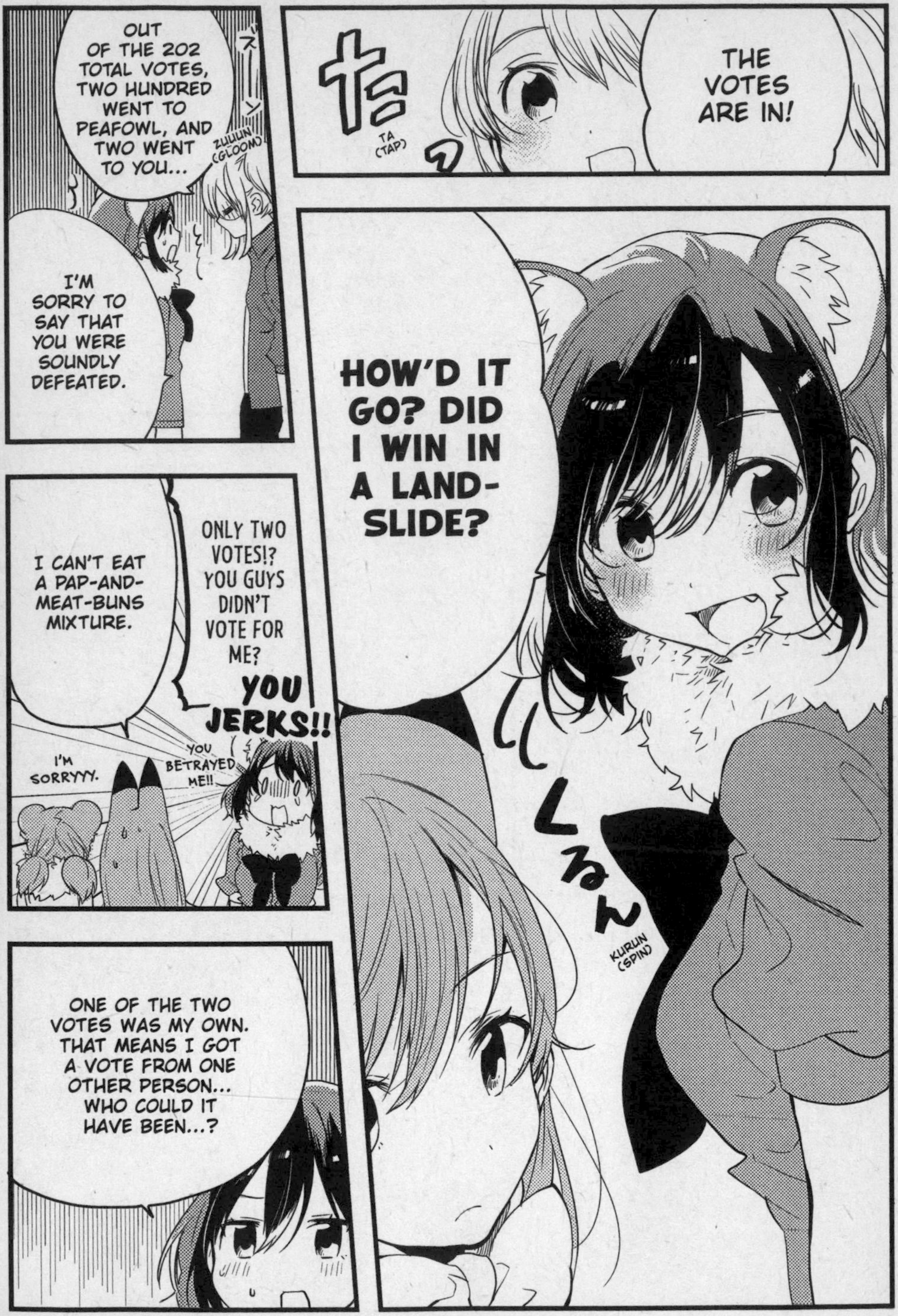
TA (TAP)
THE VOTES ARE IN!
HOW'D IT GO? DID I WIN IN A LAND-SLIDE?
KURUN (SPIN)
OUT OF THE 202 TOTAL VOTES, TWO HUNDRED WENT TO PEAFOWL, AND TWO WENT TO YOU...
ZUUUN (GLOOM)
I'M SORRY TO SAY THAT YOU WERE SOUNDLY DEFEATED.
ONLY TWO VOTES!? YOU GUYS DIDN'T VOTE FOR ME?
YOU JERKS!!
I CAN'T EAT A PAP-AND-MEAT-BUNS MIXTURE.
YOU BETRAYED ME!!
I'M SORRYYY.
ONE OF THE TWO VOTES WAS MY OWN. THAT MEANS I GOT A VOTE FROM ONE OTHER PERSON... WHO COULD IT HAVE BEEN...?

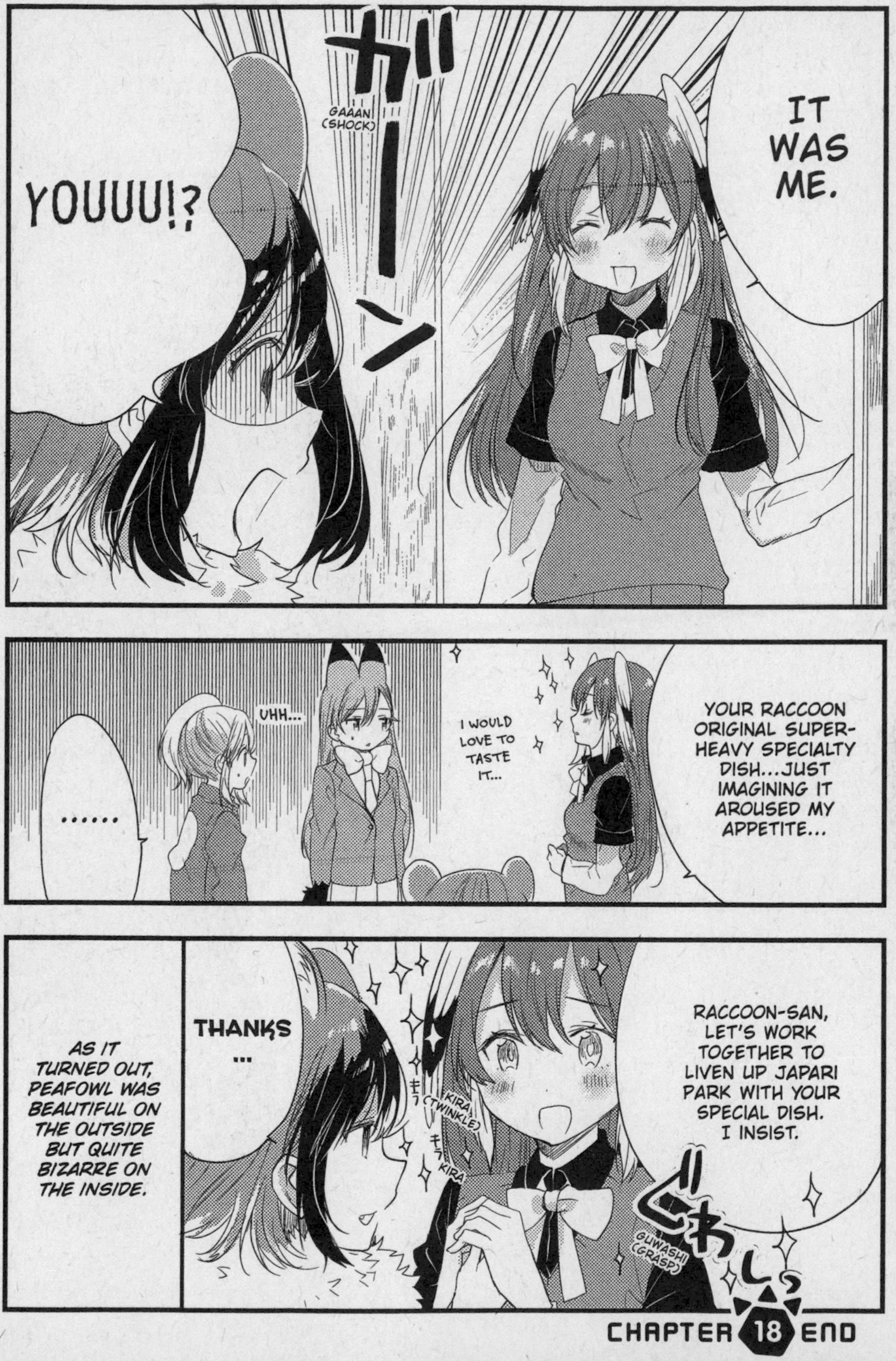
IT WAS ME.
GAAAN (SHOCK)
YOUUU!?
YOUR RACCOON ORIGINAL SUPER-HEAVY SPECIALTY DISH...JUST IMAGINING IT AROUSED MY APPETITE...
I WOULD LOVE TO TASTE IT...
UHH...
......
RACCOON-SAN, LET'S WORK TOGETHER TO LIVEN UP JAPARI PARK WITH YOUR SPECIAL DISH. I INSIST.
GUWASHI (GRASP)
KIRA (TWINKLE)
KIRA
THANKS ...
AS IT TURNED OUT, PEAFOWL WAS BEAUTIFUL ON THE OUTSIDE BUT QUITE BIZARRE ON THE INSIDE.

CHAPTER 18 END

KEMONO FRIENDS
WELCOME TO JAPARI PARK!

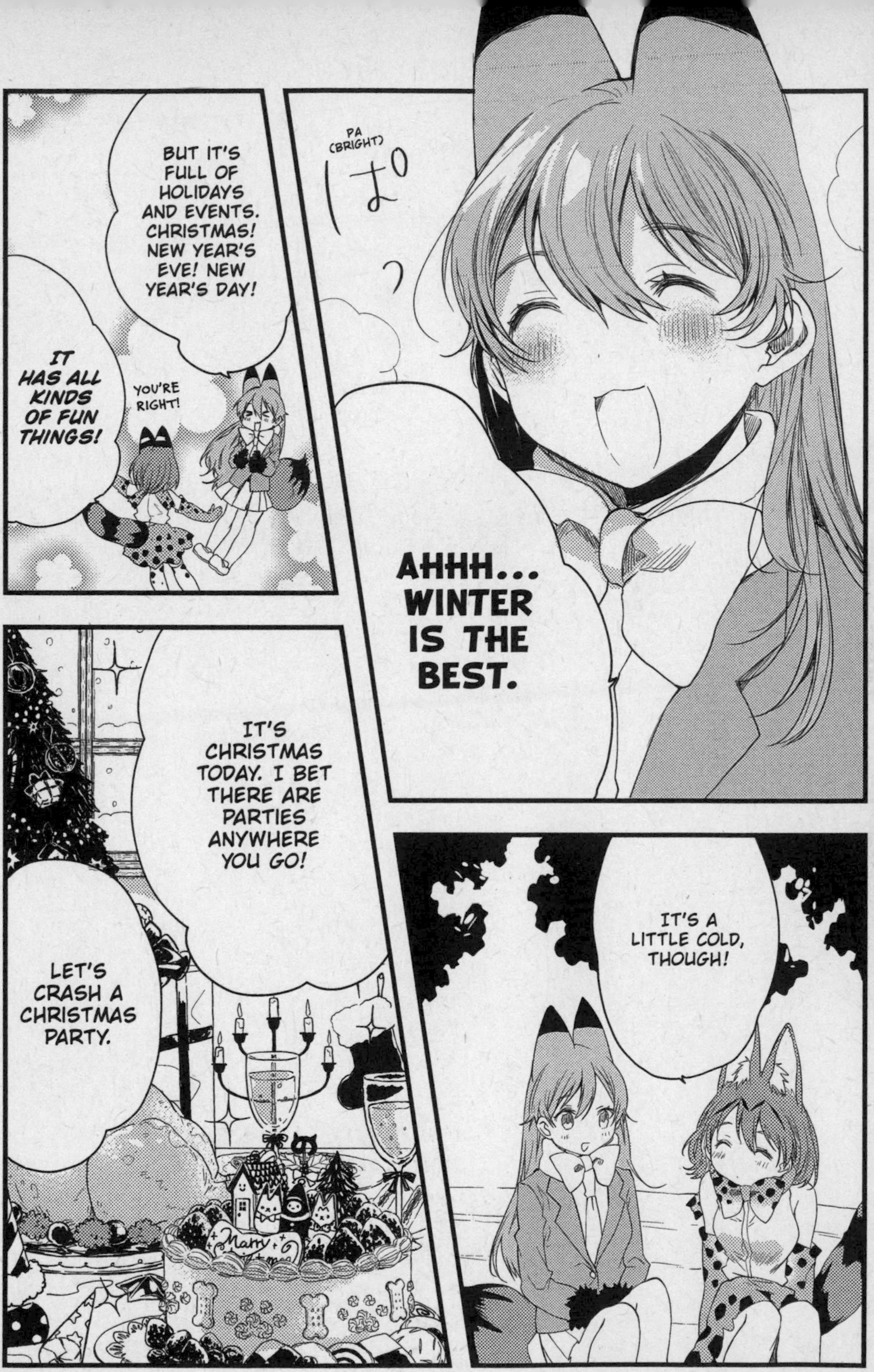
PA (BRIGHT)
ぱっ
AHHH... WINTER IS THE BEST.
IT'S A LITTLE COLD, THOUGH!
BUT IT'S FULL OF HOLIDAYS AND EVENTS. CHRISTMAS! NEW YEAR'S EVE! NEW YEAR'S DAY!
IT HAS ALL KINDS OF FUN THINGS!
YOU'RE RIGHT!
IT'S CHRISTMAS TODAY. I BET THERE ARE PARTIES ANYWHERE YOU GO!
LET'S CRASH A CHRISTMAS PARTY.

CHAPTER 19

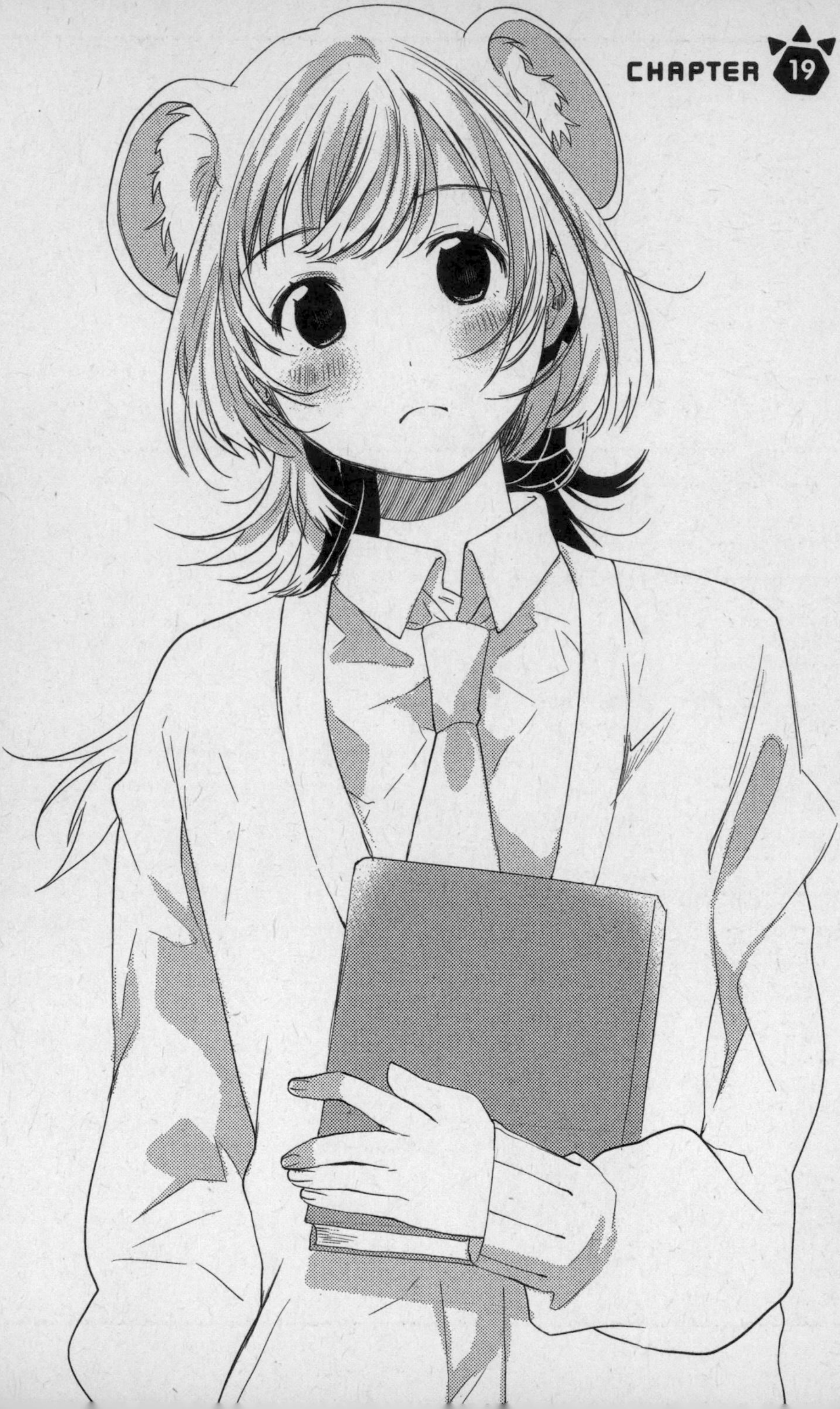

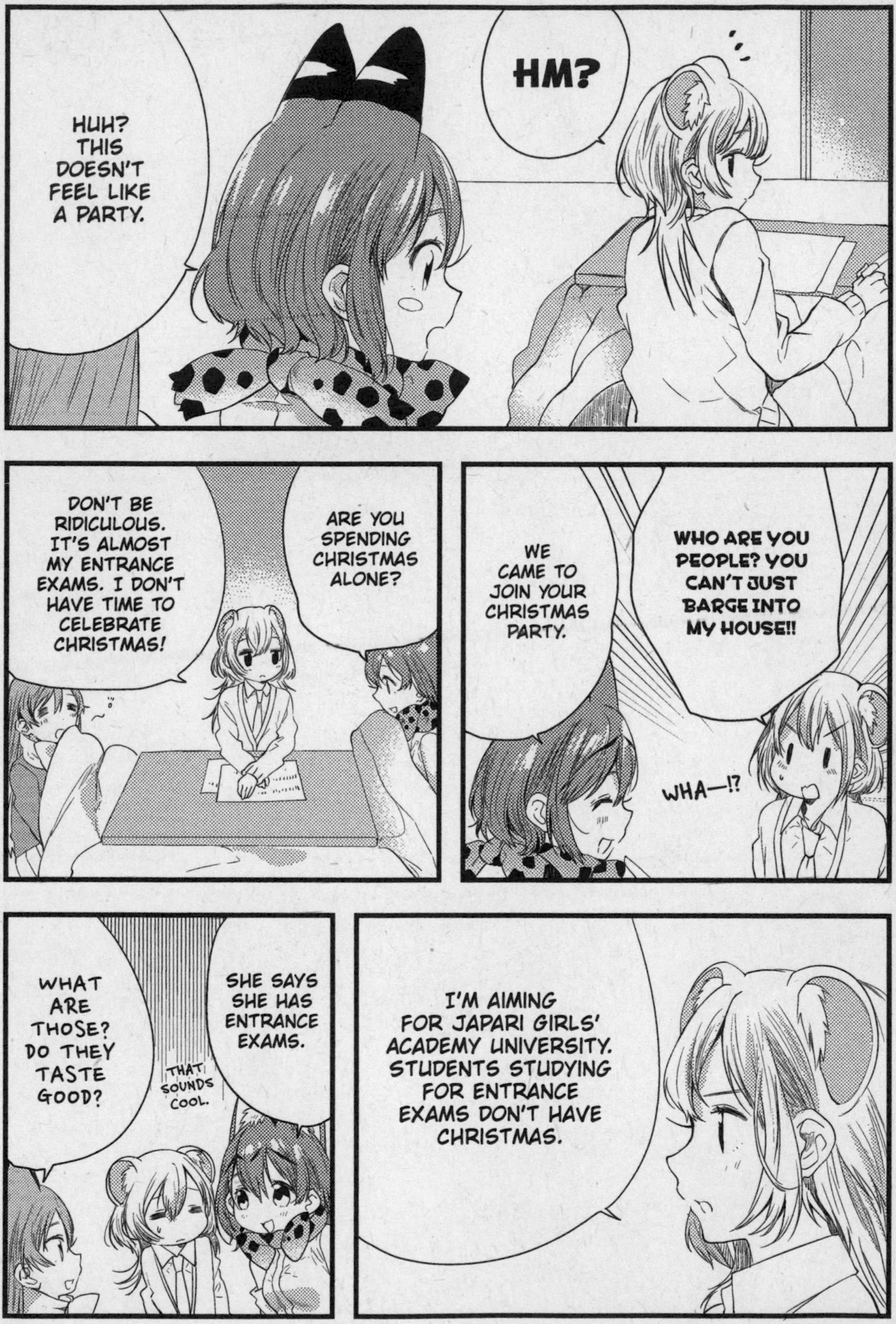
HM?
HUH? THIS DOESN'T FEEL LIKE A PARTY.
WHO ARE YOU PEOPLE? YOU CAN'T JUST BARGE INTO MY HOUSE!!
WE CAME TO JOIN YOUR CHRISTMAS PARTY.
WHA—!?
ARE YOU SPENDING CHRISTMAS ALONE?
DON'T BE RIDICULOUS. IT'S ALMOST MY ENTRANCE EXAMS. I DON'T HAVE TIME TO CELEBRATE CHRISTMAS!
I'M AIMING FOR JAPARI GIRLS' ACADEMY UNIVERSITY. STUDENTS STUDYING FOR ENTRANCE EXAMS DON'T HAVE CHRISTMAS.
SHE SAYS SHE HAS ENTRANCE EXAMS.
THAT SOUNDS COOL.
WHAT ARE THOSE? DO THEY TASTE GOOD?

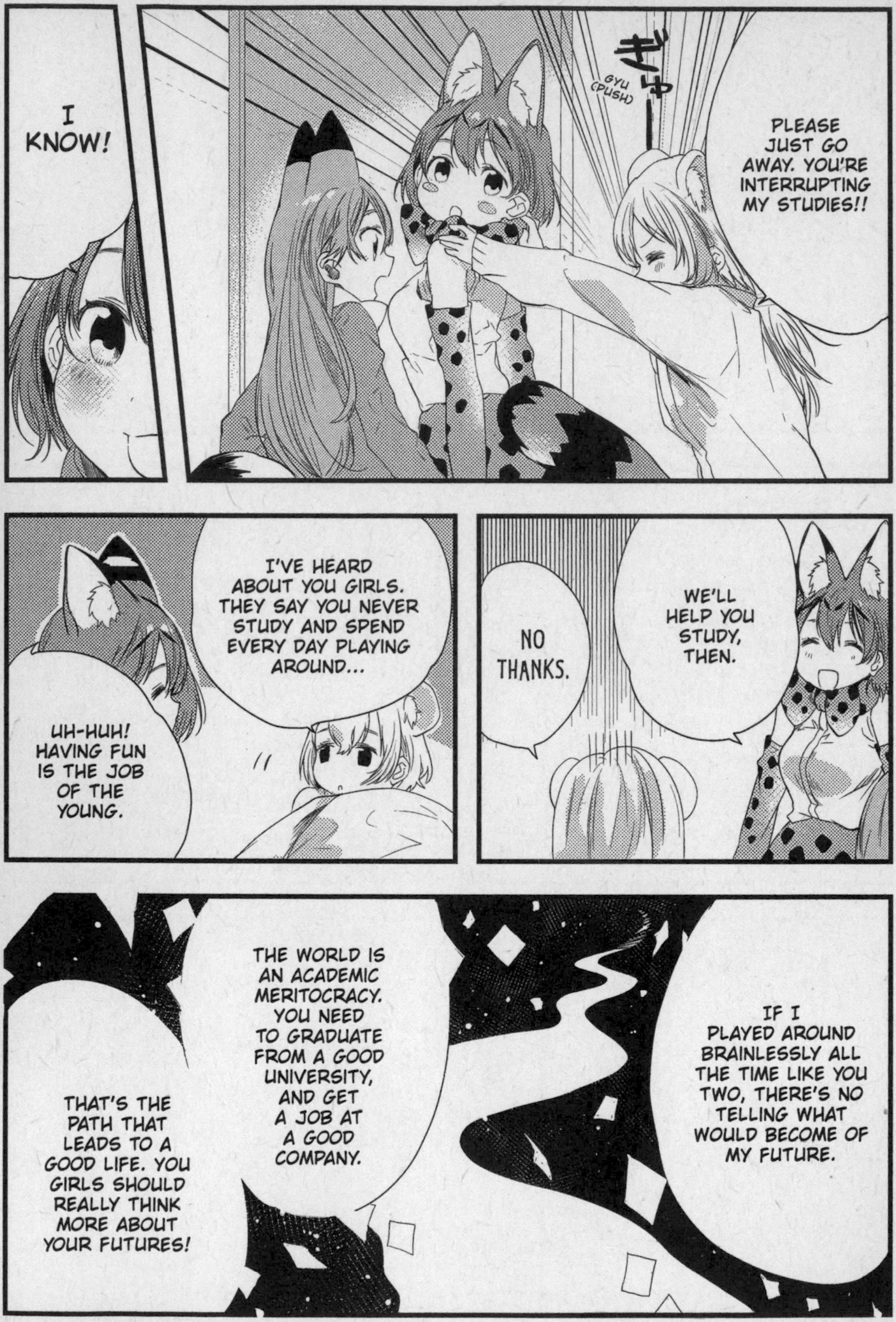
ぎゅー
GYU (PUSH)
PLEASE JUST GO AWAY. YOU'RE INTERRUPTING MY STUDIES!!
I KNOW!
WE'LL HELP YOU STUDY, THEN.
NO THANKS.
I'VE HEARD ABOUT YOU GIRLS. THEY SAY YOU NEVER STUDY AND SPEND EVERY DAY PLAYING AROUND...
UH-HUH! HAVING FUN IS THE JOB OF THE YOUNG.
IF I PLAYED AROUND BRAINLESSLY ALL THE TIME LIKE YOU TWO, THERE'S NO TELLING WHAT WOULD BECOME OF MY FUTURE.
THE WORLD IS AN ACADEMIC MERITOCRACY. YOU NEED TO GRADUATE FROM A GOOD UNIVERSITY, AND GET A JOB AT A GOOD COMPANY.
THAT'S THE PATH THAT LEADS TO A GOOD LIFE. YOU GIRLS SHOULD REALLY THINK MORE ABOUT YOUR FUTURES!

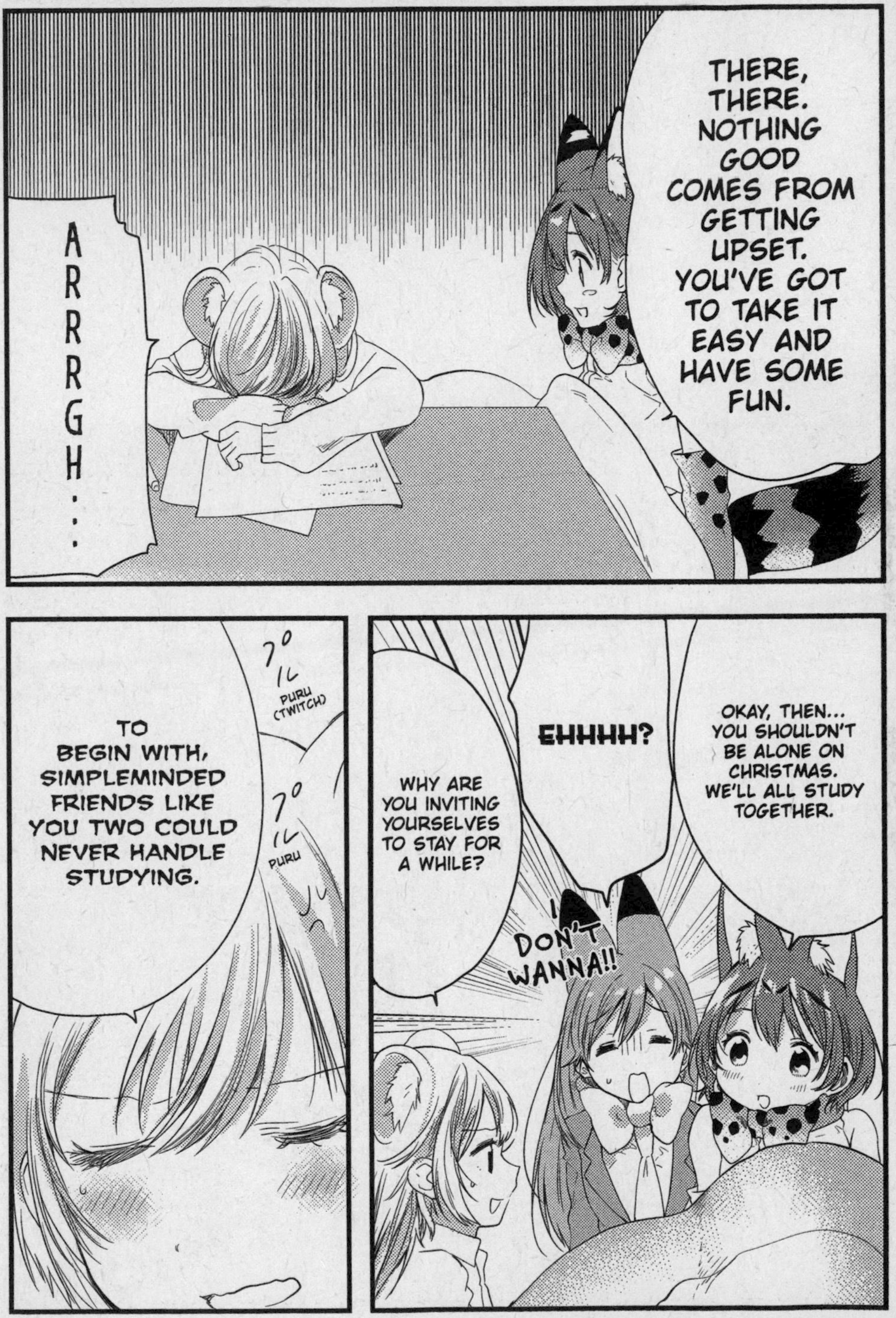
THERE, THERE. NOTHING GOOD COMES FROM GETTING UPSET. YOU'VE GOT TO TAKE IT EASY AND HAVE SOME FUN.
ARRRGH...
OKAY, THEN... YOU SHOULDN'T BE ALONE ON CHRISTMAS. WE'LL ALL STUDY TOGETHER.
EHHHH?
WHY ARE YOU INVITING YOURSELVES TO STAY FOR A WHILE?
I DON'T WANNA!!
プル
PURU (TWITCH)
プル
PURU
TO BEGIN WITH, SIMPLEMINDED FRIENDS LIKE YOU TWO COULD NEVER HANDLE STUDYING.

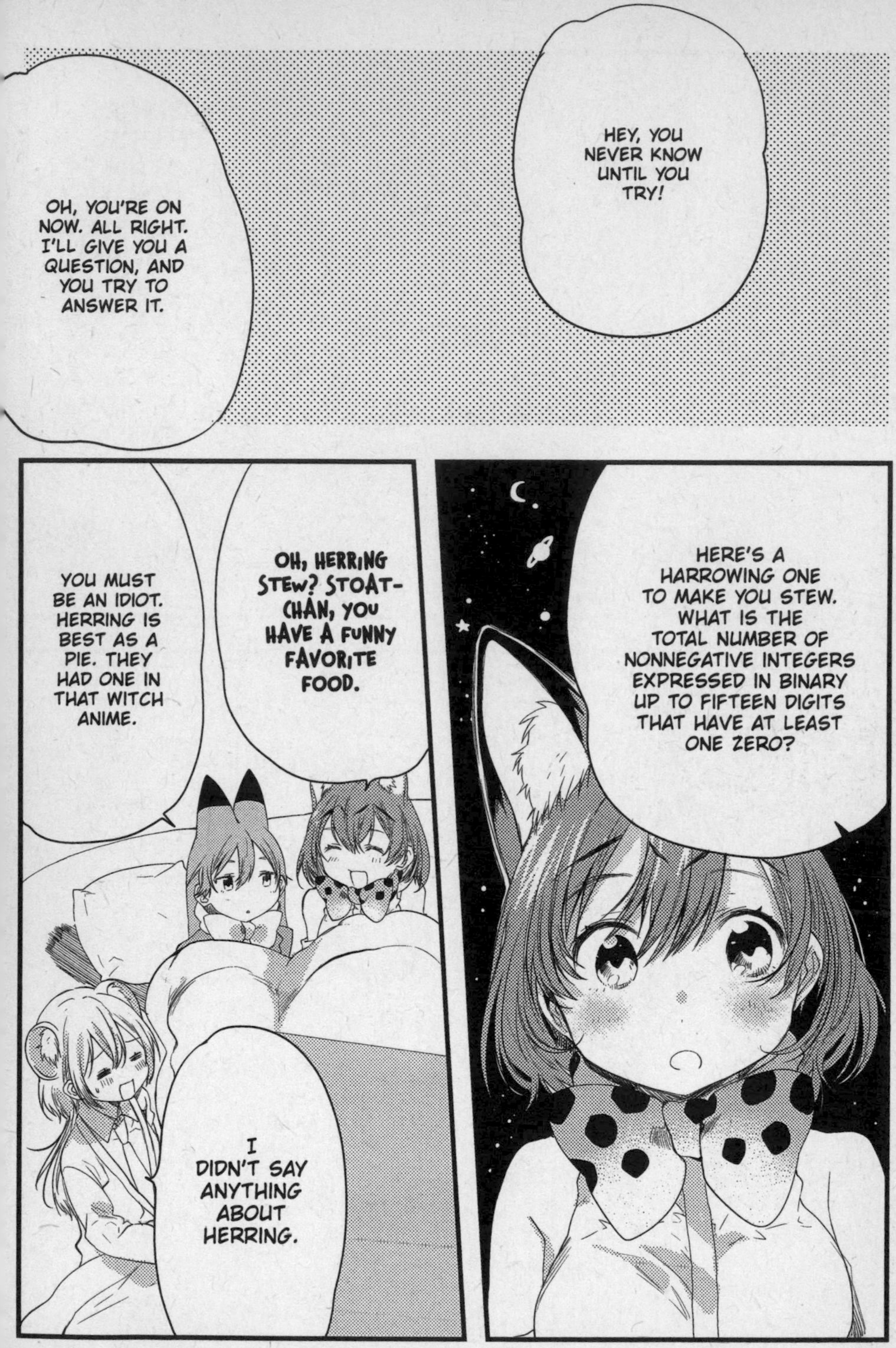
HEY, YOU NEVER KNOW UNTIL YOU TRY!
OH, YOU'RE ON NOW. ALL RIGHT. I'LL GIVE YOU A QUESTION, AND YOU TRY TO ANSWER IT.
HERE'S A HARROWING ONE TO MAKE YOU STEW. WHAT IS THE TOTAL NUMBER OF NONNEGATIVE INTEGERS EXPRESSED IN BINARY UP TO FIFTEEN DIGITS THAT HAVE AT LEAST ONE ZERO?
OH, HERRING STEW? STOAT-CHAN, YOU HAVE A FUNNY FAVORITE FOOD.
YOU MUST BE AN IDIOT. HERRING IS BEST AS A PIE. THEY HAD ONE IN THAT WITCH ANIME.
I DIDN'T SAY ANYTHING ABOUT HERRING.

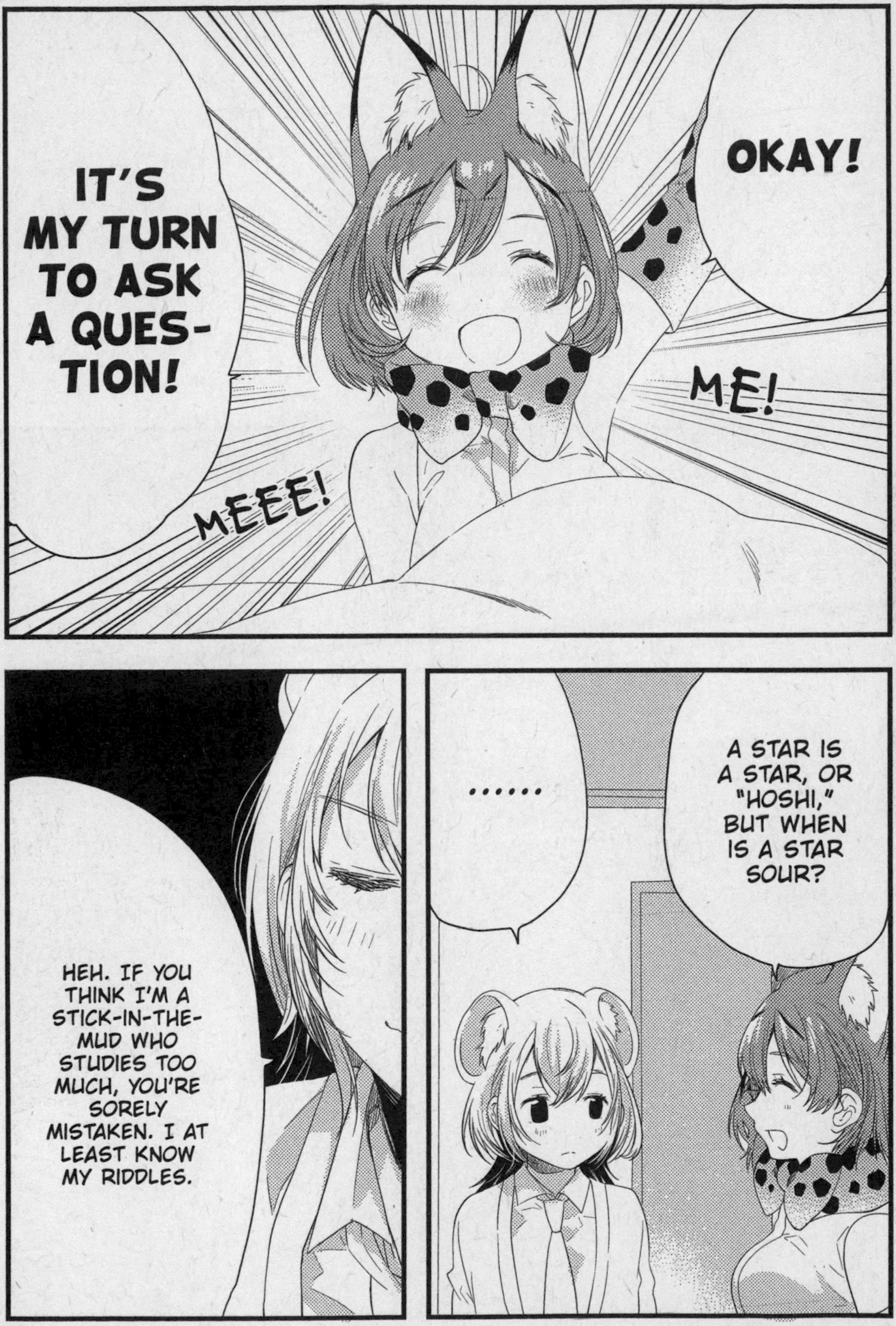
OKAY!
IT'S MY TURN TO ASK A QUES-TION!
ME!
MEEE!
A STAR IS A STAR, OR "HOSHI," BUT WHEN IS A STAR SOUR?
......
HEH. IF YOU THINK I'M A STICK-IN-THE-MUD WHO STUDIES TOO MUCH, YOU'RE SORELY MISTAKEN. I AT LEAST KNOW MY RIDDLES.

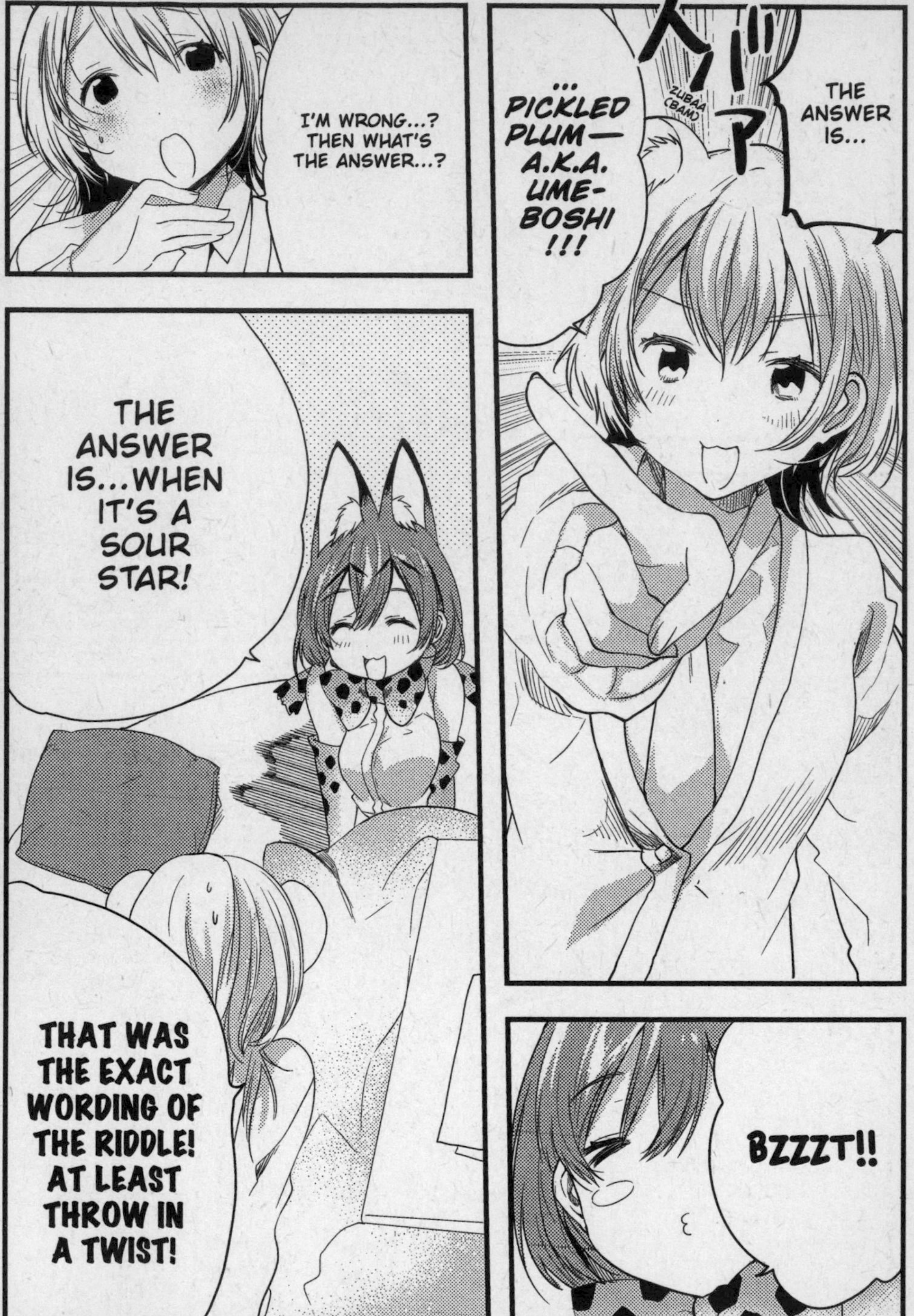
THE ANSWER IS...
ZUBAA (BAM)
... PICKLED PLUM— A.K.A. UME-BOSHI !!!
BZZZT!!
I'M WRONG...? THEN WHAT'S THE ANSWER...?
THE ANSWER IS...WHEN IT'S A SOUR STAR!
THAT WAS THE EXACT WORDING OF THE RIDDLE! AT LEAST THROW IN A TWIST!

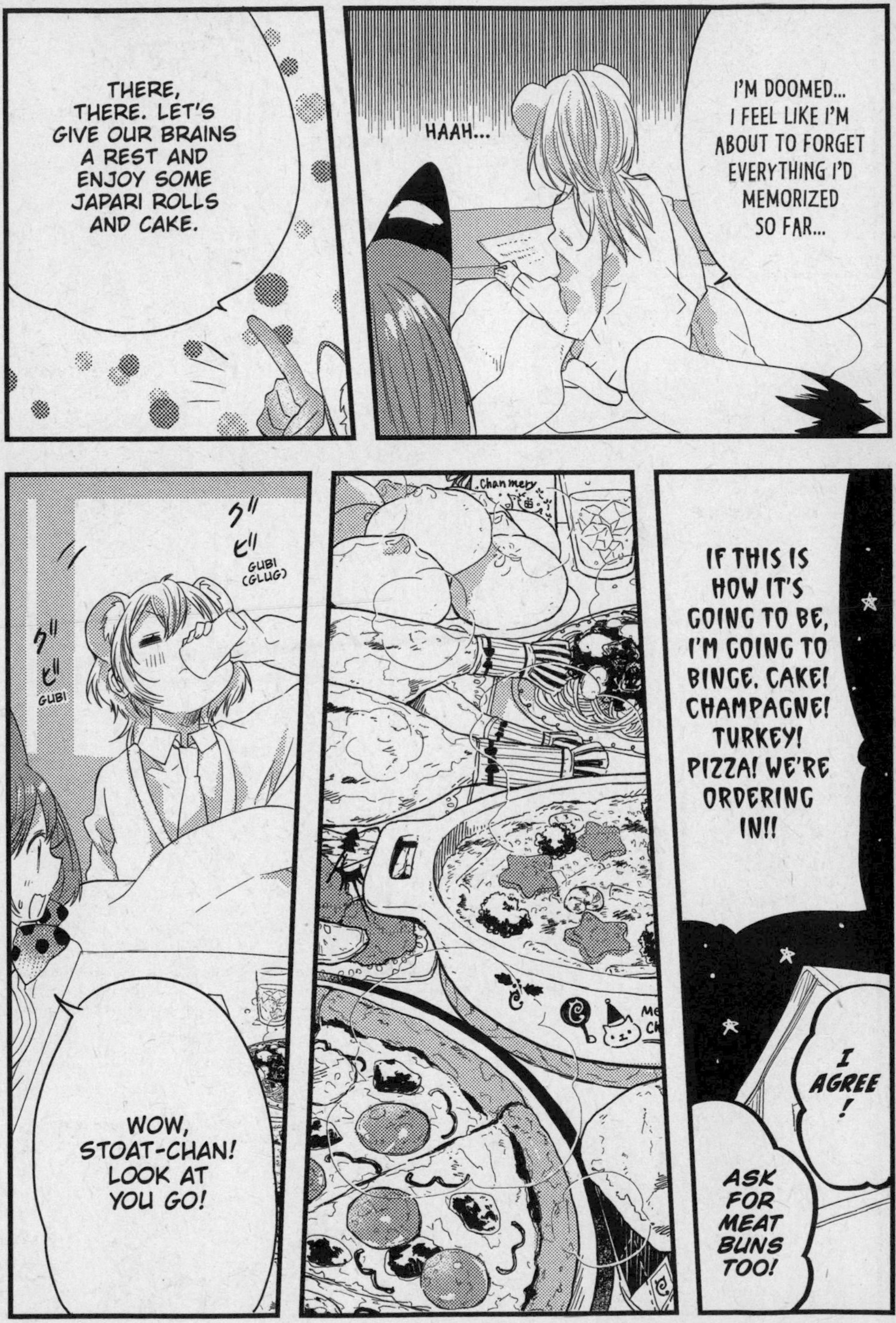
I'M DOOMED... I FEEL LIKE I'M ABOUT TO FORGET EVERYTHING I'D MEMORIZED SO FAR...
HAAH...
THERE, THERE. LET'S GIVE OUR BRAINS A REST AND ENJOY SOME JAPARI ROLLS AND CAKE.
IF THIS IS HOW IT'S GOING TO BE, I'M GOING TO BINGE. CAKE! CHAMPAGNE! TURKEY! PIZZA! WE'RE ORDERING IN!!
I AGREE!
ASK FOR MEAT BUNS TOO!
Chanmery
グビ
GUBI (GLUG)
グビ
GUBI
WOW, STOAT-CHAN! LOOK AT YOU GO!

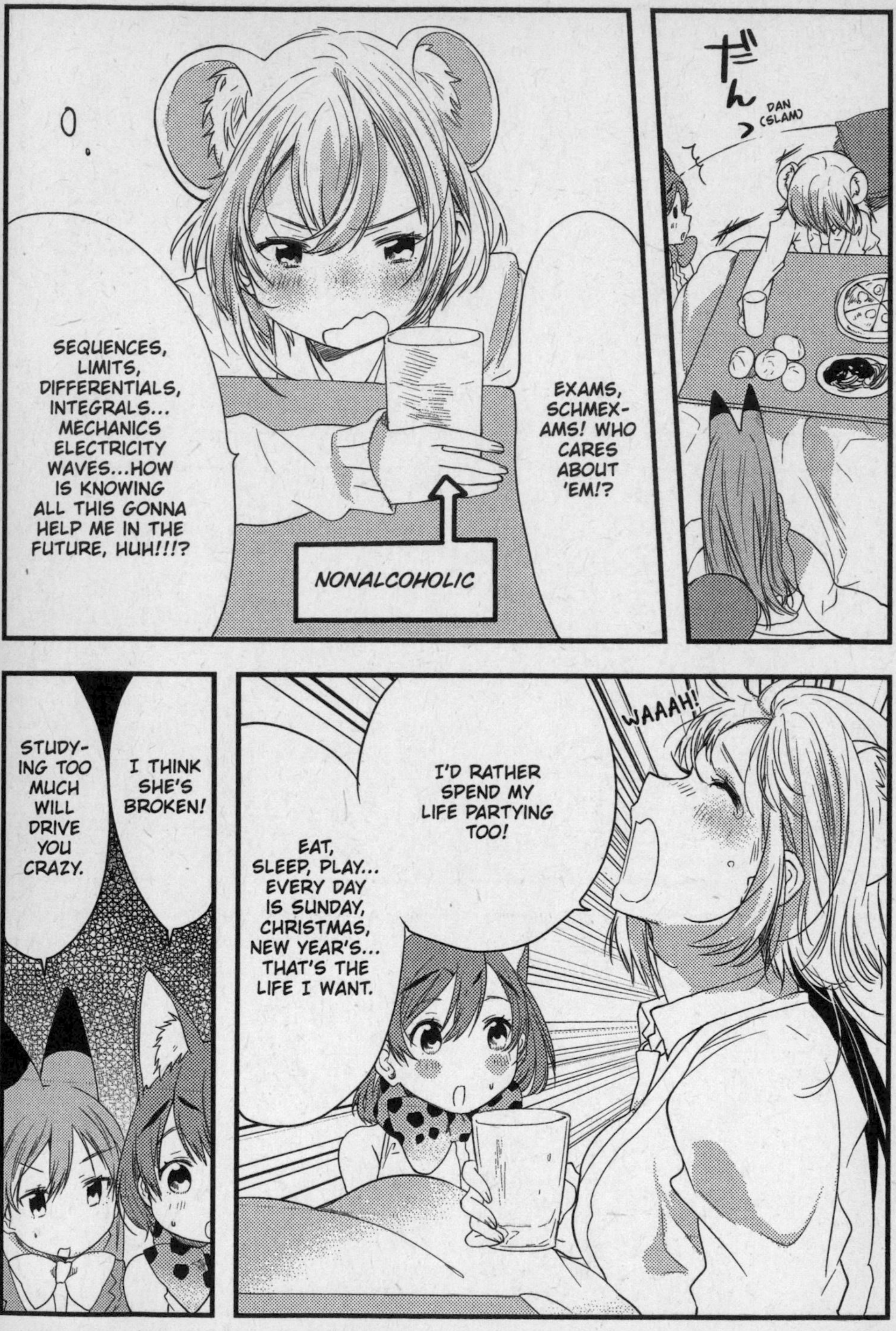
だん
DAN (SLAM)
EXAMS, SCHMEX-AMS! WHO CARES ABOUT 'EM!?
SEQUENCES, LIMITS, DIFFERENTIALS, INTEGRALS... MECHANICS ELECTRICITY WAVES...HOW IS KNOWING ALL THIS GONNA HELP ME IN THE FUTURE, HUH!!!?
NONALCOHOLIC
WAAAH!
I'D RATHER SPEND MY LIFE PARTYING TOO!
EAT, SLEEP, PLAY... EVERY DAY IS SUNDAY, CHRISTMAS, NEW YEAR'S... THAT'S THE LIFE I WANT.
I THINK SHE'S BROKEN!
STUDY-ING TOO MUCH WILL DRIVE YOU CRAZY.

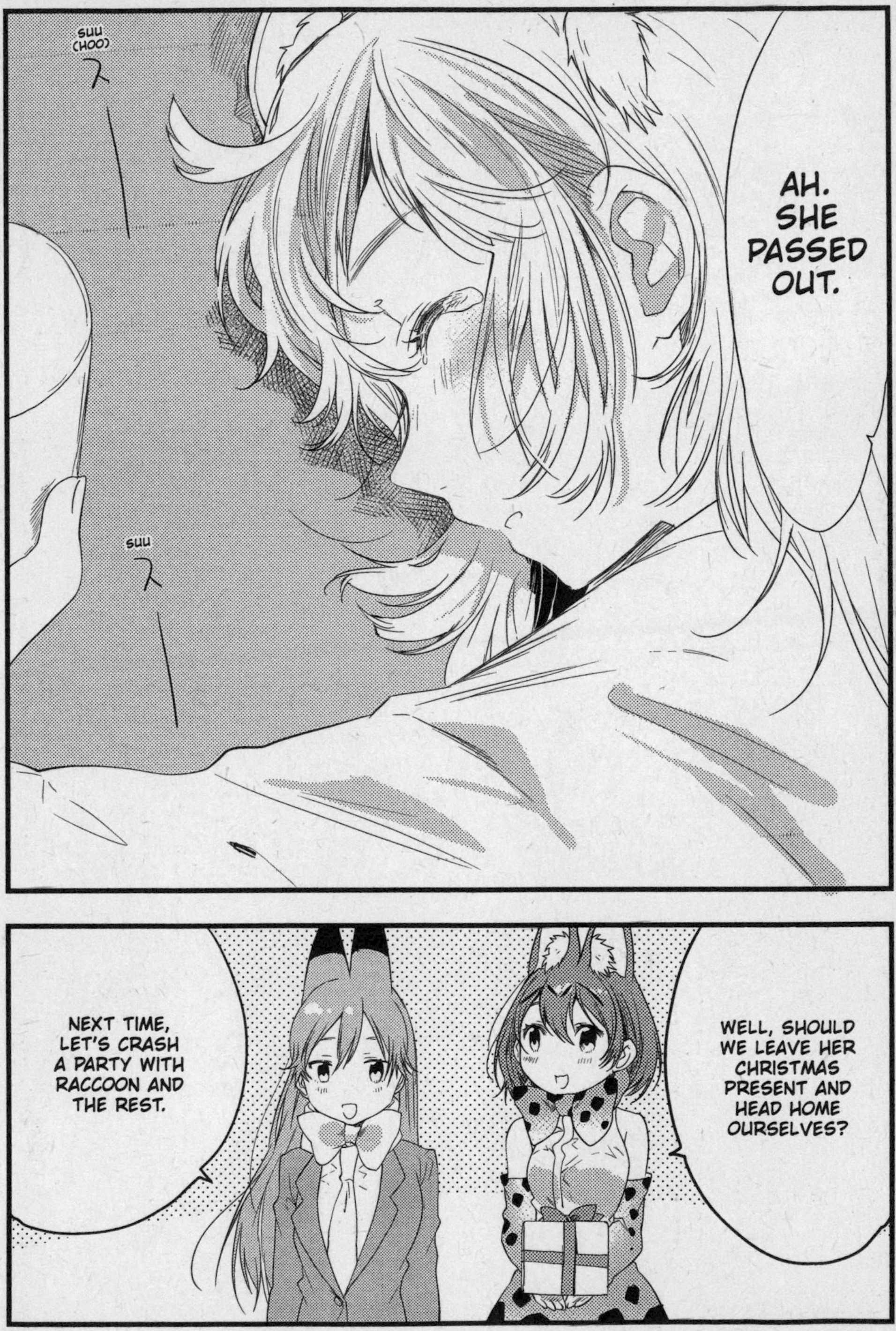
AH. SHE PASSED OUT.
SUU (HOO)
ス
SUU
ス
WELL, SHOULD WE LEAVE HER CHRISTMAS PRESENT AND HEAD HOME OURSELVES?
NEXT TIME, LET'S CRASH A PARTY WITH RACCOON AND THE REST.

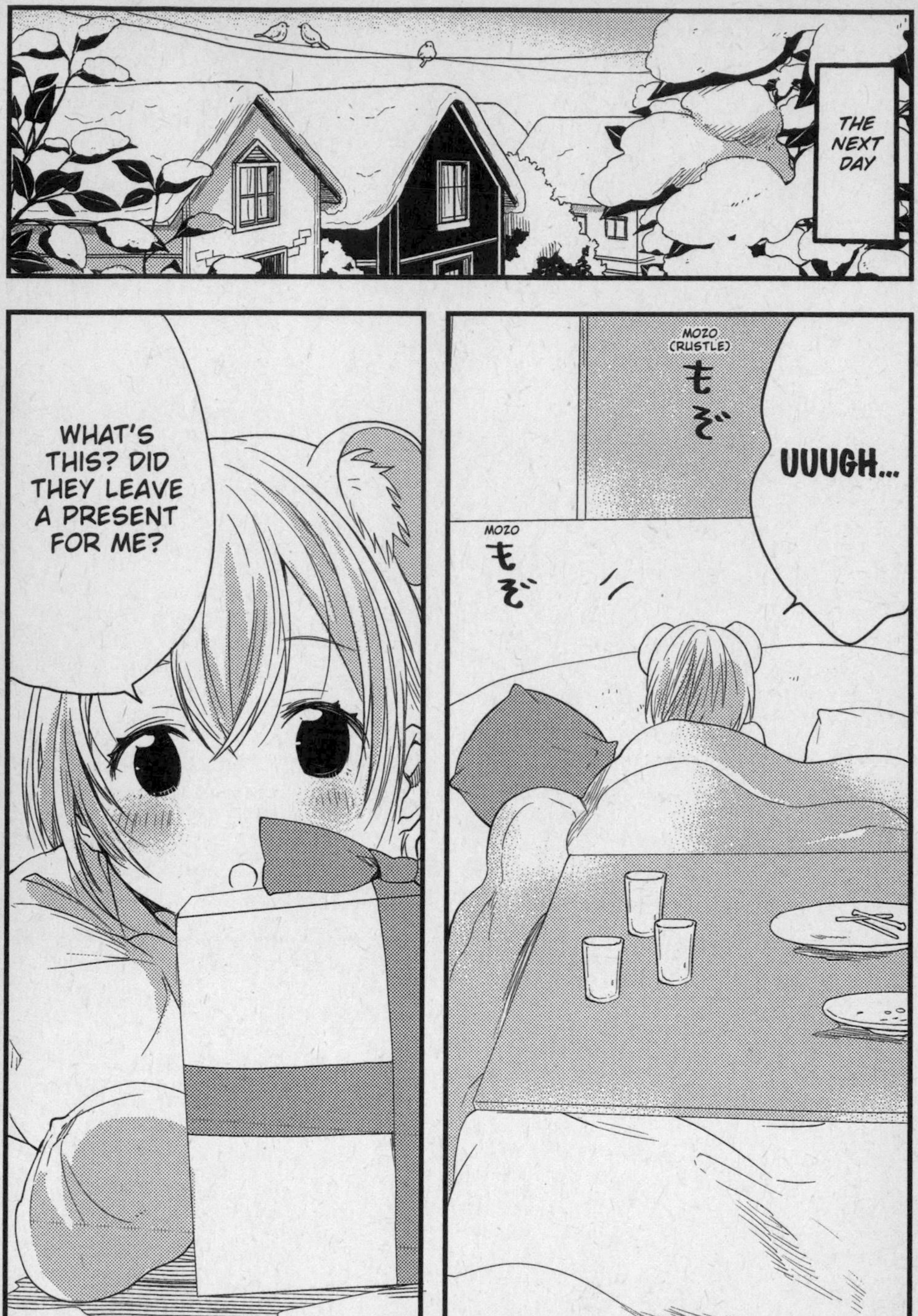
THE NEXT DAY
MOZO (RUSTLE)
もぞ
UUUGH...
MOZO
もぞ
WHAT'S THIS? DID THEY LEAVE A PRESENT FOR ME?

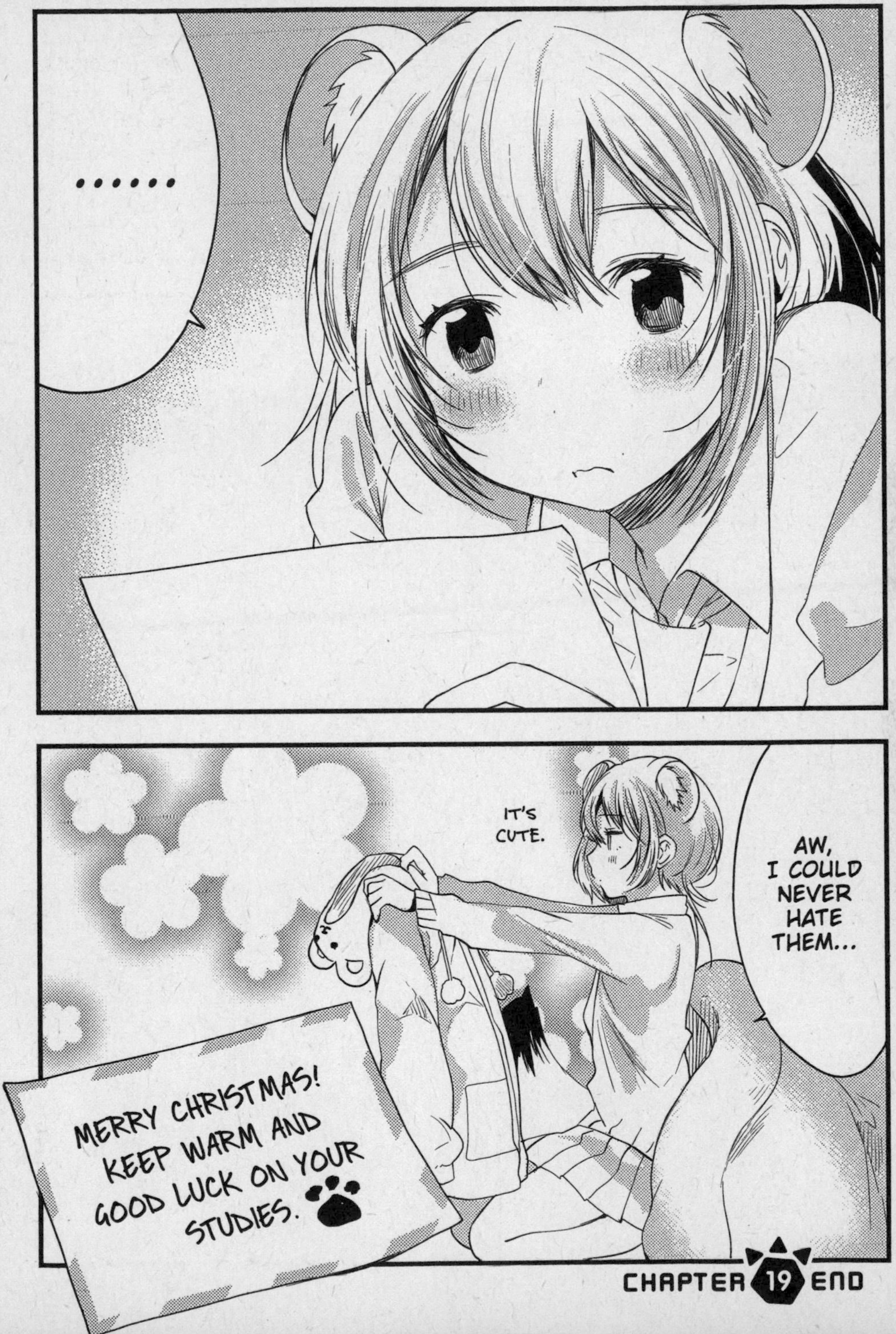
……
AW, I COULD NEVER HATE THEM…
IT'S CUTE.
MERRY CHRISTMAS! KEEP WARM AND GOOD LUCK ON YOUR STUDIES.
CHAPTER 19 END

KEMONO FRIENDS

WELCOME TO JAPARI PARK!

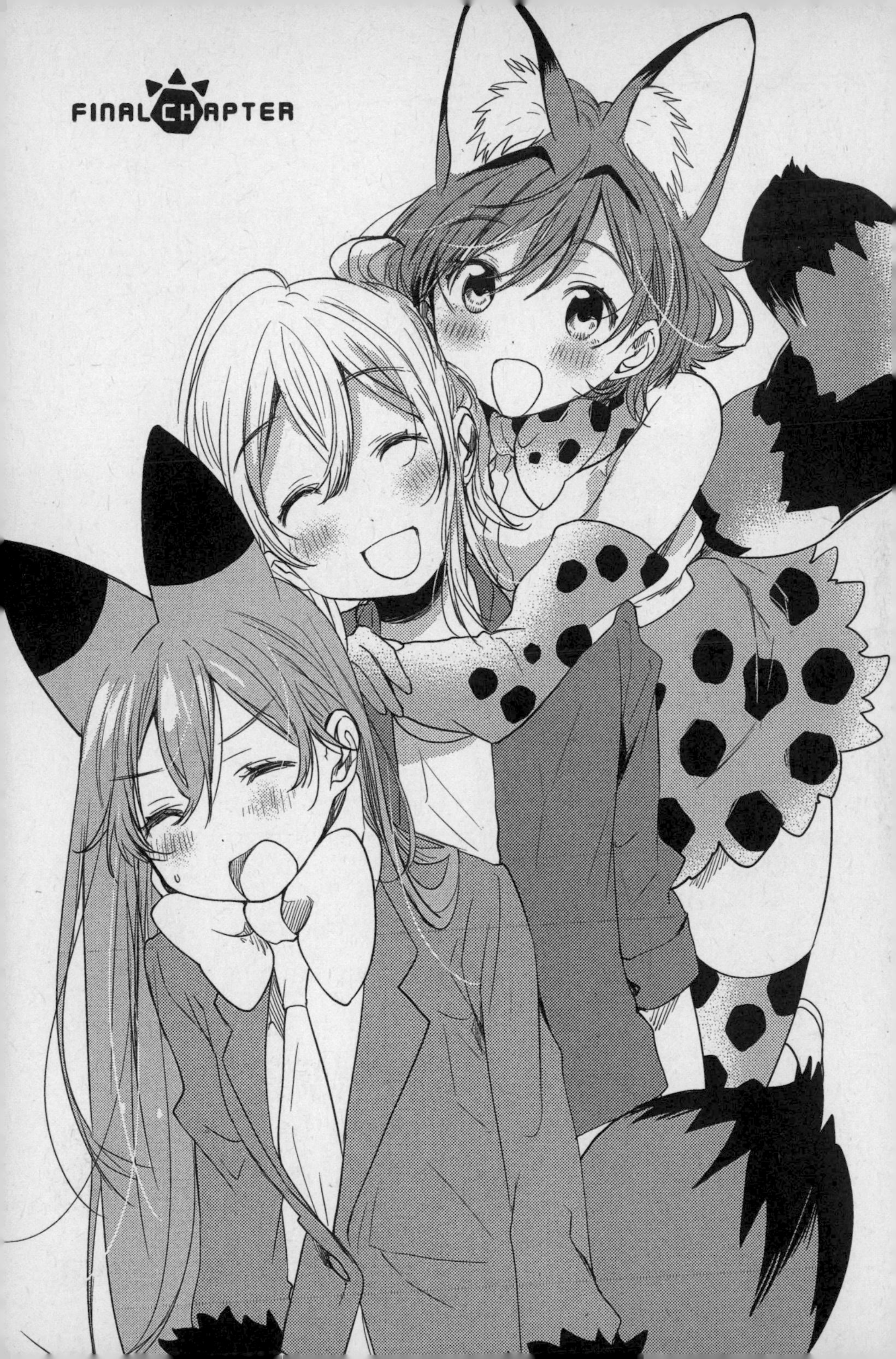
FINAL CHAPTER

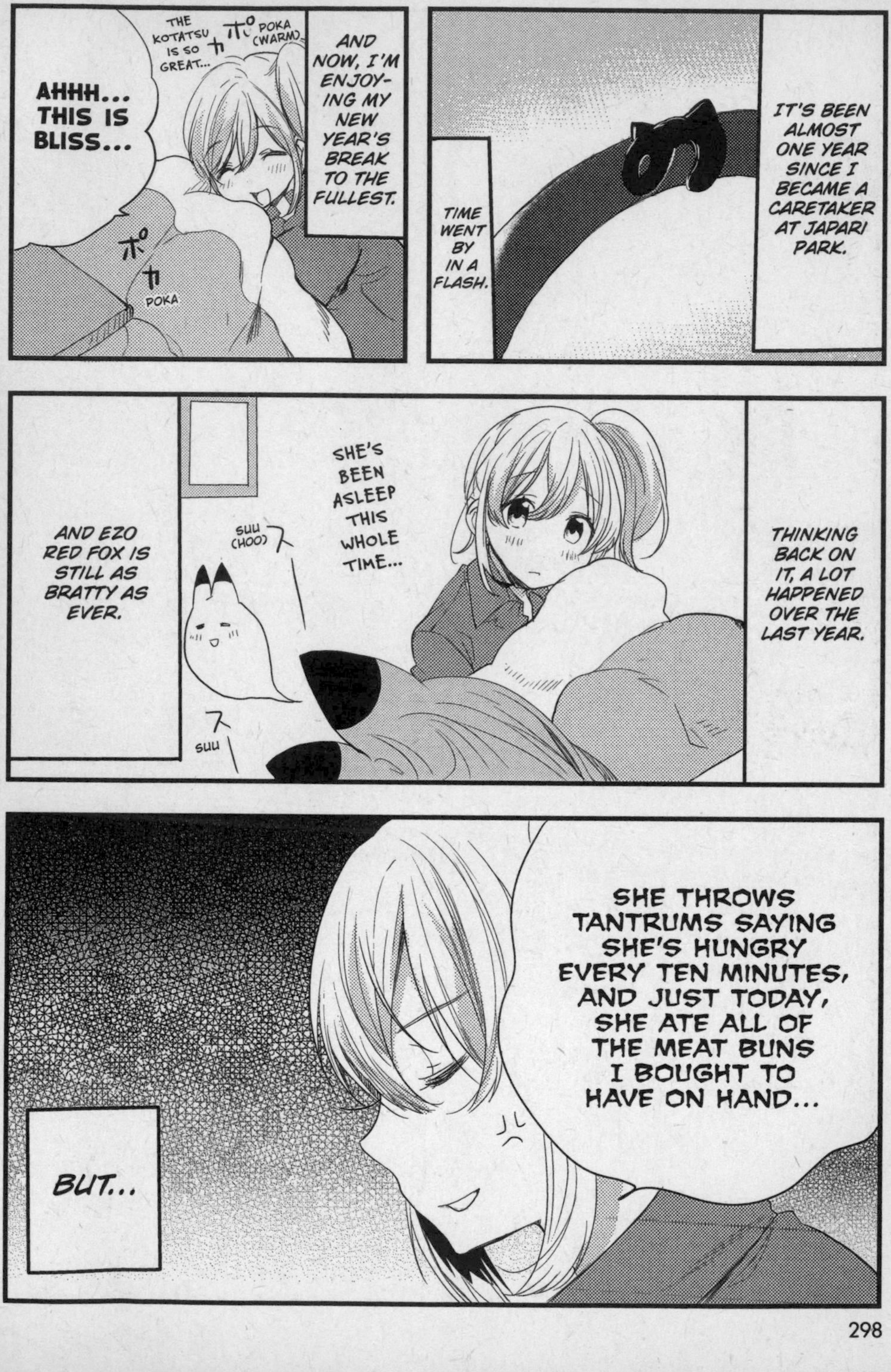
IT'S BEEN ALMOST ONE YEAR SINCE I BECAME A CARETAKER AT JAPARI PARK.
TIME WENT BY IN A FLASH.
AND NOW, I'M ENJOY-ING MY NEW YEAR'S BREAK TO THE FULLEST.
THE KOTATSU IS SO GREAT...
ポカ POKA (WARM)
AHHH... THIS IS BLISS...
ポカ POKA
THINKING BACK ON IT, A LOT HAPPENED OVER THE LAST YEAR.
SHE'S BEEN ASLEEP THIS WHOLE TIME...
ス SUU (HOO)
ス SUU
AND EZO RED FOX IS STILL AS BRATTY AS EVER.
SHE THROWS TANTRUMS SAYING SHE'S HUNGRY EVERY TEN MINUTES, AND JUST TODAY, SHE ATE ALL OF THE MEAT BUNS I BOUGHT TO HAVE ON HAND...
BUT...

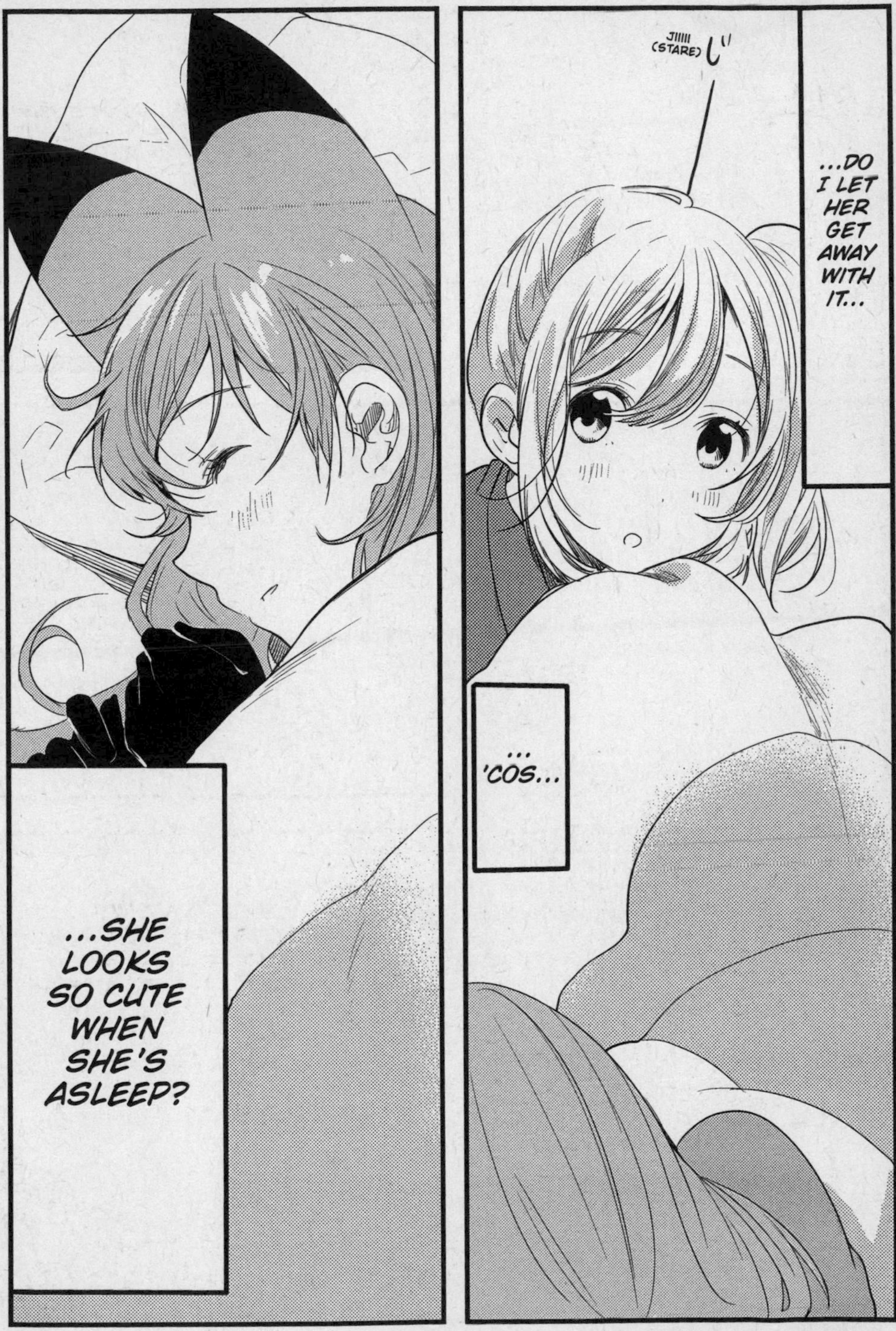
JIIIIII (STARE)
じ
...DO I LET HER GET AWAY WITH IT...
... 'COS...
...SHE LOOKS SO CUTE WHEN SHE'S ASLEEP?

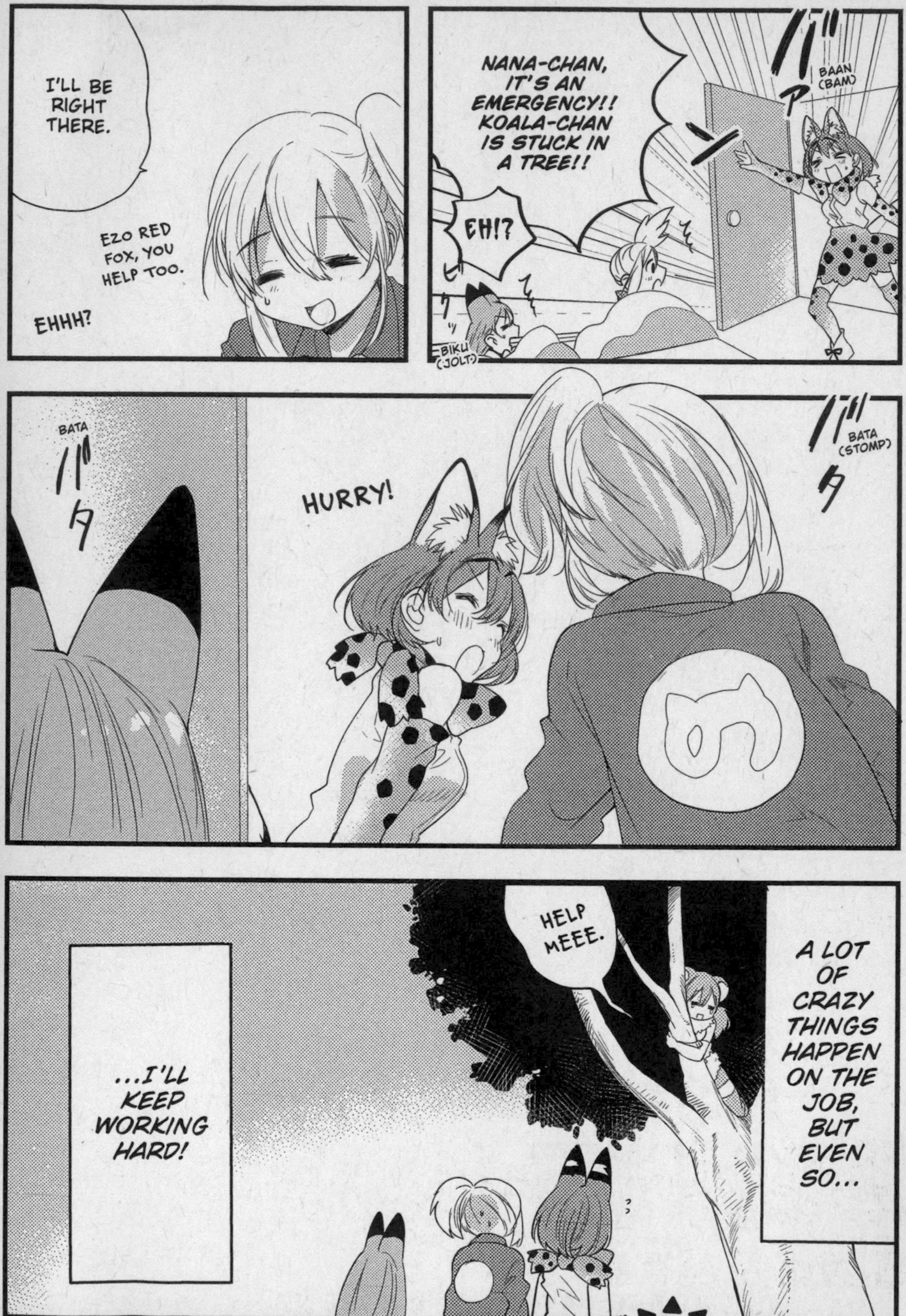
BAAN (BAM)
NANA-CHAN, IT'S AN EMERGENCY!! KOALA-CHAN IS STUCK IN A TREE!!
EH!?
BIKU (JOLT)
I'LL BE RIGHT THERE.
EZO RED FOX, YOU HELP TOO.
EHHH?
BATA (STOMP)
HURRY!
BATA
A LOT OF CRAZY THINGS HAPPEN ON THE JOB, BUT EVEN SO...
HELP MEEE.
...I'LL KEEP WORKING HARD!

FINAL CHAPTER: END

KEMONO FRIENDS

WELCOME TO JAPARI PARK!

AFTERWORD

Thank you for reading Kemono Friends: Welcome to Japari Park! Part 2 to the end! Since I have the space, here's a Serval-chan I drew before the manga serialization began.

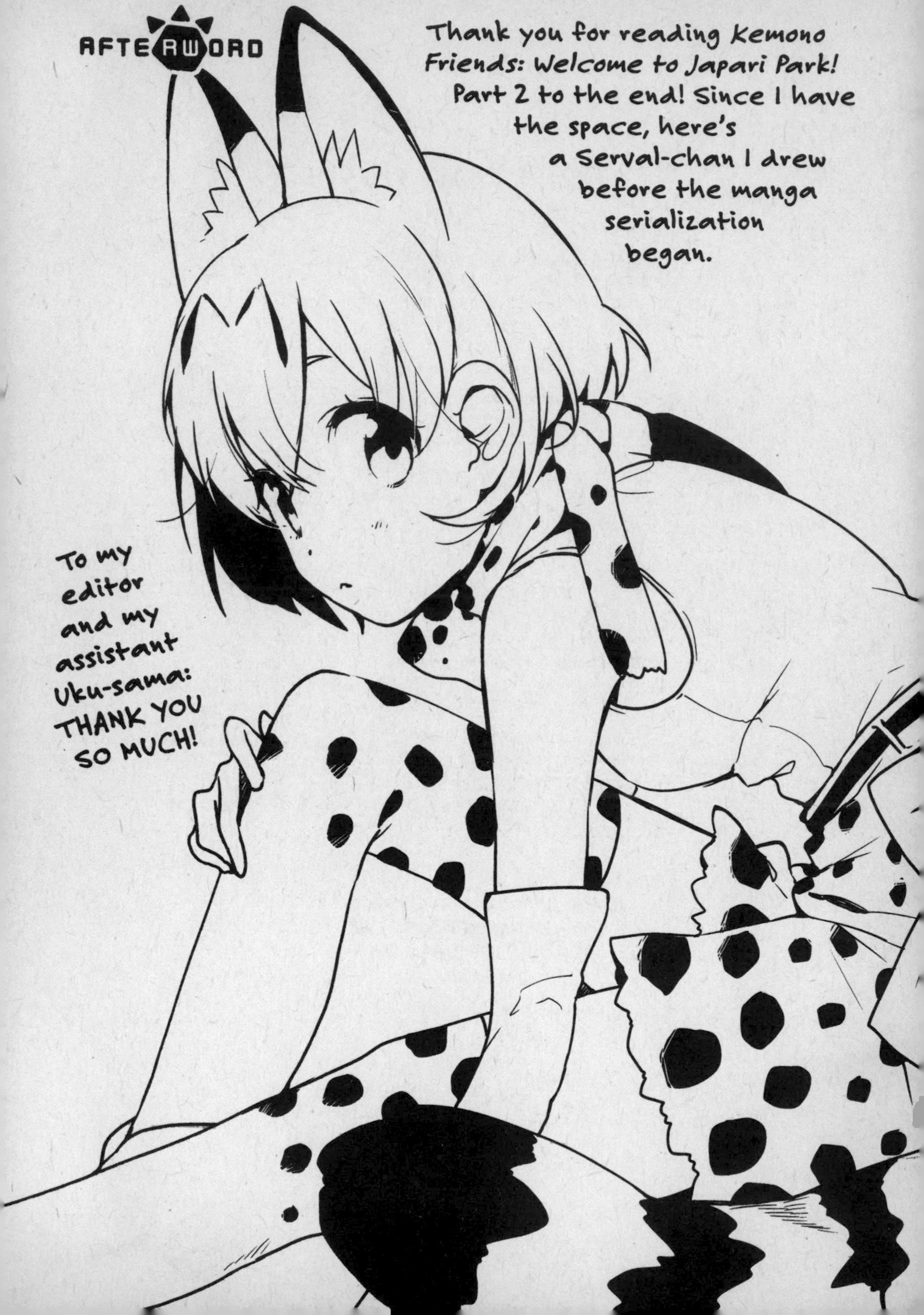

To my editor and my assistant Uku-sama: THANK YOU SO MUCH!

TRANSLATION NOTES

COMMON HONORIFICS

no honorific: Indicates familiarity or closeness; if used without permission or reason, addressing someone in this manner would constitute an insult.

-san: The Japanese equivalent of Mr./Mrs./Miss. If a situation calls for politeness, this is the fail-safe honorific.

-dono: Conveys an indication of respect for the addressee, but also implies an old-fashionedness on the speaker's part.

-sama: Conveys great respect; may also indicate that the social status of the speaker is lower than that of the addressee.

-kun: Used most often when referring to boys, this indicates affection or familiarity. Occasionally used by older men among their peers, but it may also be used by anyone referring to a person of lower standing.

-chan (also -tan): An affectionate honorific indicating familiarity used mostly in reference to girls; also used in reference to cute persons or animals of either gender.

-senpai: An honorific used to address upperclassmen or more experienced coworkers.

-sensei: A respectful honorific for teachers, artists, or high-level professionals.

100 yen is worth approximately $1 USD.

PAGE 15

In Japanese, **survival of the fittest** is written as *janiku kyoushoku*—"the weak become meat for the strong to eat." Ezo Red Fox is concerned with the "meat" part.

PAGE 50
Koala **pap** is a special type of liquid poop that koala mothers create to feed their babies. This pap allows the children to gain the gut bacteria needed to digest eucalyptus leaves—a highly toxic plant and the main diet of koalas. It indeed comes from the same place as the rest of the koala's feces.

PAGE 73
Tsuchinoko are creatures from Japanese folklore that resemble vipers but are wider in the middle.

PAGE 87
In the Japanese version, Crested Ibis's **do-re-mi** song goes: "Do is the do in *doriru* (drill). Re is the re in *reinboo* (rainbow). Mi is the mi in *midori* (green)."

PAGE 110
In the Japanese version, Reindeer's pun is based on the fact that the word for "stranded" (*sounan*) sounds like "yes we are" (*sou nanda*).

PAGE 132
38 degrees Celsius is 100.4 degrees.

PAGE 141
Hallo, Wien refers to the Vienna Boys' Choir, an Austrian choir consisting of all boy sopranos. *Wien* (pronounced ween) is the German/Austrian word for Vienna.

PAGE 154
Wish plaques, or *ema* (literally "picture-horse"), are from Shinto tradition. Visitors to Shinto shrines write their wishes onto these wooden plaques, and the gods are said to read them.

PAGE 161
Takoyaki are pan-fried balls of batter typically filled with chunks of octopus.

PAGE 176
Koala's Ma●ch is a reference to a Japanese brand of cream-filled cookies shaped like koalas.

PAGE 200
In the Japanese version, Reindeer says, "The sun hurts!" This is a pun based on the fact that the word for "sun" (*taiyou*) sounds like "it hurts" (*itaiyo*).

PAGE 227
Taiyaki are fish-shaped pastries filled most commonly with sweet red bean paste.

PAGE 288
Binary numbers in Japanese are called *nishinsuu*. This sounds similar to "herring and vinegar" (*nishin-suu*).

The **witch anime** mentioned is the *Little Witch Academia* TV series by Studio Trigger. In one episode, the characters visit Finland, where they eat *hapansilakka* pie—a baked item made with extremely pungent fermented canned herring. *Hapansilakka* is also known as *surströmming* in Swedish and has a notoriously powerful flavor.

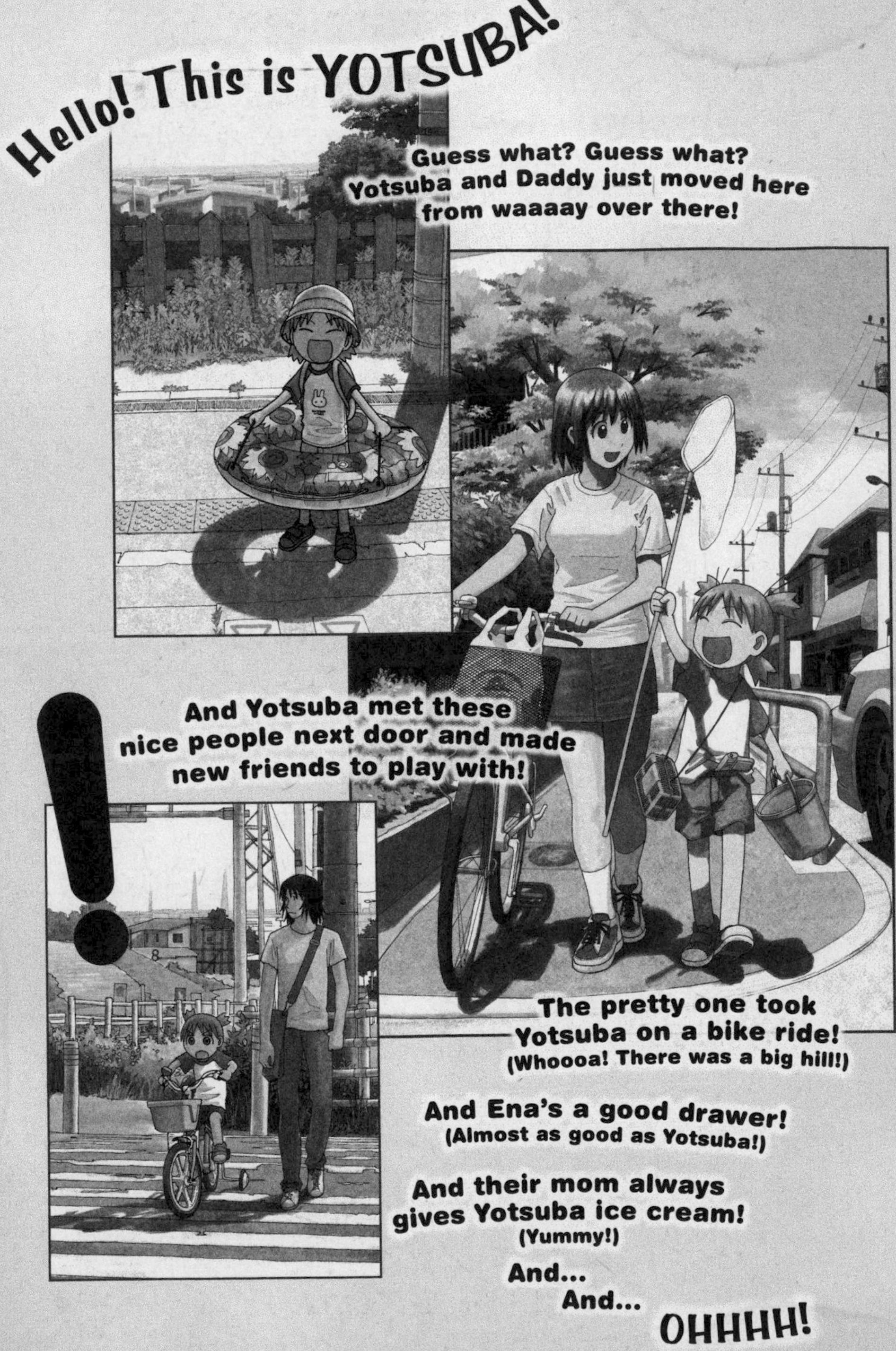
Hello! This is YOTSUBA!
Guess what? Guess what? Yotsuba and Daddy just moved here from waaaay over there!
!
And Yotsuba met these nice people next door and made new friends to play with!
The pretty one took Yotsuba on a bike ride!
(Whoooa! There was a big hill!)
And Ena's a good drawer!
(Almost as good as Yotsuba!)
And their mom always gives Yotsuba ice cream!
(Yummy!)
And...
And...
OHHHH!

Two girls, a new school, and the beginning of a beautiful friendship.

Volumes 1-4 available now

Kiss & White Lily for My Dearest Girl

In middle school, Ayaka Shiramine was the perfect student: hard-working, with excellent grades and a great personality to match. As Ayaka enters high school she expects to still be on top, but one thing she didn't account for is her new classmate, the lazy yet genuine genius Yurine Kurosawa. What's in store for Ayaka and Yurine as they go through high school...together?

Yen Press

PARK!

Art: Fly ♥ Created by: Kemono Friends Project

Translation: Amanda Haley ♥ Lettering: Rochelle Gancio

KEMONO FRIENDS -WELCOME TO JAPARIPARK- Volume 1–2
©Fly 2016–2017
©Kemono Friends Project
First published in Japan in 2016–2017 by KADOKAWA CORPORATION, Tokyo.
English translation rights arranged with KADOKAWA CORPORATION, Tokyo through TUTTLE-MORI AGENCY, INC.

English translation © 2018 by Yen Press, LLC

Yen Press
1290 Avenue of the Americas
New York, NY 10104

Visit us at yenpress.com
facebook.com/yenpress
yenpress.tumblr.com

twitter.com/yenpress
instagram.com/yenpress

First Yen Press Edition: January 2018

Yen Press is an imprint of Yen Press, LLC.
The Yen Press name and logo are trademarks of Yen Press, LLC.

The publisher is not responsible for websites (or their content) that are not owned by the publisher.

Library of Congress Control Number: 2017954704

ISBNs: 978-0-316-48061-1 (paperback)
       978-1-9753-2614-2 (ebook)

10 9 8 7 6 5 4 3 2 1

BVG

Printed in the United States of America